W9-BRV-972

REFERENCES TO HANDBOOK:

The numbered letter above the heading and the page number below it refer you to sections in the handbook.

SENTENCE STRUCTURE

S1	S2	S3	S4	S5	S6
Sentence Elements	Phrases & Clauses	Verbs & Verbals	Fragments (Period Fault)	Fused Sentences	Run-on Sentences
392	404	406	409	412	413
S7	S8	S9	S10	S11	
Comma Splice	Faulty Parallelism	Dangling Modifier	Shifts in Subject-Verb	Incomplete Construction	
414	416	418	421	424	

WORD ORDER

WO1	WO2	WO3	WO4
Normal Order	Ambiguous Order	Awkward Separation	Unemphatic Order
426	427	429	430

GRAMMATICAL FORMS

F1	F2	F3	F4	F5	F6
Wrong Principal Part	Tense Forms	Case	Agreement (Subject-Verb)	Agreement (Pronouns)	Vague Pronoun Reference
433	439	446	452	458	461
F7	F8				
Faulty Complement	Adjective Adverb				
462	465				

PUNCTUATION

P1	P2	P3	P4	P5	P6
Uses of Comma	Misuses of Comma	Uses of Semicolon	Misuses of Semicolon	Period	Question & Exclamation Marks
467	475	477	477	479	479
P7	P8	P9	P10	P11	P12
Colon	Quotation Marks	Punctuation with Quotation Marks	Apostrophe	Ellipsis & Dash	Parentheses & Brackets
480	481	482	484	485	486

MECHANICS

sp	abr	caps	hyph	ital	no
Spelling	Abbreviations	Capital Letters	Hyphenation	Italics	Numbers
491	502	503	506	508	509
gloss					
Glossary					
513					

A First Course in

College Composition

WRITING WITH

HOUGHTON

NEW YORK

A PURPOSE

THIRD EDITION

James M. McCrimmon
The University of Illinois

MIFFLIN COMPANY • BOSTON

ATLANTA   GENEVA, ILL.   DALLAS   PALO ALTO

Contents

PART ONE: *The Process of Composition*

PART TWO: *Special Assignments*

CONTENTS

PART THREE: *Handbook of Grammar and Usage*

Preface

Instructors who are familiar with the second edition of *Writing with a Purpose* may appreciate a brief summary of the changes that have been made in this third edition. Although every chapter has had some revision of text, illustrations, and exercises, the major changes are as follows:

Chapter 1: Expansion to provide an overview of the composition process and to illustrate the relation of purpose to each stage of the process. The intent is to encourage students to analyze assignments and to plan, develop, and revise their essays from the very beginning of the course. Because this expansion makes Chapters 3 and 5 of the second edition less necessary, these chapters have been dropped from the present edition.

Chapter 5: Substantial reorganization and rewriting to provide a more detailed treatment of the patterns of normal, parallel, and periodic sentences and to avoid duplication of the remedial emphasis of the handbook. The new emphasis in this chapter is on the recognition of major sentence patterns and on the shaping of material into these patterns, rather than on the revision of faulty sentences.

Chapter 11: A librarian's evaluation of reference sources in terms of their coverage, current usefulness, and general quality, and revision of the lists of sources and the chapter content in the light of that evaluation.

Chapter 12: Revision of the material on bibliography and documentation to make it more consistently follow the forms recommended in *The MLA Style Sheet* and Turabian's Manual, and the substitution of a new specimen research paper, including the notes from which it was written.

Chapter 13: The limitation of the treatment of persuasion to logical persuasion, a more complete presentation of deduction, a reorganization of the materials on fallacies, and greater emphasis on the evaluation of whole essays and articles.

Handbook: Reorganization and restatement of the sections dealing with parts of speech and sentence elements to eliminate or revise untenable definitions.

Reference Chart: Expanded to include parts of the text other than the Handbook.

These revisions do not alter the basic theme of purpose or the major emphases of the earlier editions. For the most part they are the result of suggestions made by instructors who have used the book in class and have pointed out where it could be strengthened to meet their students' needs. For detailed criticisms of the whole book and for extensive suggestions about revision, I am most indebted to Professors Frank M. Collins of the University of Wisconsin, Milwaukee; Patrick G. Hogan, Jr., of Mississippi State University; and George D. Stout of Washington University, St. Louis. I am also indebted for helpful criticism and suggestions about specific chapters to Professors Carter A. Daniel of Kent State University; Robert B. Holland of Mississippi State University; Ralph E. Howes of Somers, Connecticut; Kellogg W. Hunt of Florida State University; Lawrence J. Hynes of Miami University; Richard L. Jordan, F. P. Kroeger, and Eldon E. Shupe, Jr., all of Flint Junior College, Michigan; Fred K. Lingle of Southern Illinois University; Robert H. Moore of The George Washington University; Emanuel Mussman of State University Teachers College, Geneseo, New York; J. C. Nunan of Emory University; Joseph Rowan of Seton Hall University; Dorothy Rushing of Sam Houston State Teachers College; Redding Sugg of Georgia State College of Business Administration; and Allen M. Thomas of the University of Buffalo. To all these I wish to express my thanks for generous and constructive criticism.

To my wife, Barbara S. McCrimmon, I am indebted not only for her revision of the chapter on the library, but also for extensive assistance in planning, preparing, and proofreading copy and for aid in the selection of illustrative and exercise materials.

To Mrs. Elizabeth W. Schultz I owe thanks for her aid in typing the manuscript.

JAMES M. McCRIMMON

Urbana, Illinois

Bibliography

The following works, organized under subject headings, form a short, selective bibliography of writings on language. Since many of these works contain their own bibliographies, they may be used as starting points for any student who wishes to investigate the subject further. The critical comments following the citation attempt to describe briefly the contribution of the work.

General. Works in this section are not limited to any of the subjects of the remaining sections but include several or all of them.

Allen, Harold B., ed. *Readings in Applied English Linguistics.* New York: Appleton-Century-Crofts, 1958. An anthology of essays on linguistics and the application of linguistics to the teaching of composition and literature. A good introductory cross-section of the work being done in language by serious scholars. Some of the essays are a bit technical for undergraduates, but most are within the capacities of superior freshmen.

Bodmer, Frederick. *The Loom of Language,* edited by Lancelot Hogben. New York: Norton, 1944. A popular study of language, with special attention to the relation of English to other languages.

Carroll, John B. *The Study of Language.* Cambridge, Mass.: Harvard University Press, 1959. A comprehensive survey of the work in linguistics and related fields. Extensive bibliography.

Laird, Charlton. *The Miracle of Language.* Cleveland: World Publishing Company, 1953. Because of its imaginative organization and presentation, this is perhaps the best introduction to the study of language available to a freshman.

History of the English Language

Alexander, Henry. *The Story of Our Language.* Toronto: Nelson, 1940. A brief and very readable account of the evolution of English, with chapters on the major differences between British and American English.

Baugh, Albert C. *History of the English Language.* New York: Appleton-Century-Crofts, 1935. The standard history of the English language.

Jesperson, Otto. *The Growth and Structure of the English Language.* New York: Appleton-Century-Crofts, 1923. Also available in paperback form as a Doubleday Anchor Book. One of the major histories of the English language.

Robertson, Stuart. *The Development of Modern English,* revised by Frederic G. Cassidy. New York: Prentice-Hall, 1954. A series of studies in the historical backgrounds of modern English.

Grammar. At present two approaches to the study of grammar are available: "traditional" grammar, and an approach variously described as "structural," "linguistic," or "new." The basic difference between these two approaches is that the former analyzes the language in terms of traditional concepts (parts of speech, etc.) which have been inherited from the study of Latin, and the latter analyzes the language in terms of "structures" of sound, form, and order which were originally used to study primitive languages. The new grammar, although highly influential in the graduate schools and in the deliberations of the National Council of Teachers of English, has not yet reached the stage at which any one man or book may be said to represent the whole movement. The works of Francis and Fries, below, show different emphases but are probably the most widely known examples of the new grammar.

Curme, George O. *Syntax.* Boston: Heath, 1931. With *Parts of Speech and Accidence,* below, the most comprehensive grammar in this bibliography, and one of the best examples of the traditional approach. For most English teachers, this is the standard English grammar.

Curme, George O. *Parts of Speech and Accidence.* Boston: Heath, 1935. See *Syntax,* above.

Francis, Nelson W. *The Structure of American English.* New York: Ronald Press, 1958. An analysis of the means by which grammatical distinctions are made in English, with emphasis on sound structures. Written as a textbook for advanced undergraduates and graduates.

Fries, Charles C. *American English Grammar.* New York: Appleton-Century-Crofts, 1940. A description of the grammar of American English based on an analysis of more than 2000 letters written to a government agency. The result is both a helpful description of educated American language practices and an example of a scientific method applied to a description of grammar.

Fries, Charles C. *The Structure of English.* New York: Harcourt, Brace, 1952. A description of sentence structure based on an analysis of recorded conversations amounting to 250,000 words. Although the analysis has been criticized by other new grammarians on the grounds that it does not pay sufficient attention to sound, the book is one of the influential documents in the new grammar.

Sledd, James. *A Short Introduction to English Grammar*. Chicago: Scott, Foresman, 1959. The author himself calls his work a "transitional" grammar — that is, an attempt to provide a transition between traditional grammar and the new grammar. Because of this purpose and its refreshing modesty and fairness to traditional grammar, this little book is likely to be persuasive in urging a fresh look at English grammar.

Usage. Whereas grammar is concerned with describing the grammatical system, usage is concerned with discovering what language practices are acceptable among educated people.

Bryant, Margaret M. *Current American Usage*. New York: Funk & Wagnalls, 1962. The most recent and best documented of all the works in this section. Less comprehensive than Kennedy, below, but on matters on which it reports it may be said to be the standard reference.

Fowler, Henry W. *A Dictionary of Modern English Usage*. Oxford. Clarendon Press, 1926. An old favorite which has been the "bible" of many teachers, but its emphasis on British usage, its date, and its prescriptive tone make it less acceptable as an authority on contemporary American usage.

Horwill, H. W. *A Dictionary of Modern American Usage,* 2nd edition. Oxford: Clarendon Press, 1944. The American counterpart to Fowler, above, but less prescriptive in tone.

Kennedy, Arthur G. *Current English*. Boston: Ginn, 1935. A comprehensive survey of the knowledge of current English, containing a very useful bibliography.

Perrin, Porter G. *Writer's Guide and Index to English,* 3rd edition. Chicago: Scott, Foresman, 1959. Comprehensively applies the results of usage studies to the work in college composition.

Pooley, Robert C. *Teaching English Usage*. New York: Appleton-Century-Crofts, 1946. As the title suggests, this work is aimed primarily at teachers, but its discussion of common problems of usage is helpful generally. Good bibliography.

Semantics. Books in this section are concerned with the study of meaning, especially with the symbolic nature of language and the factors that influence response to words.

Hayakawa, S. I. *Language in Thought and Action*. New York: Harcourt, Brace, 1949. A revision of an earlier edition, entitled *Language in Action,* a popularization of Alfred Korzybski's *Science and Sanity,* and probably the most popular book ever written on the subject of semantics.

Lee, Irving J. *Language Habits in Human Affairs.* New York: Harper, 1941. Another popularization of Korzybski's work, unusually rich in illustrative material.

Ogden, C. K., and I. A. Richards. *The Meaning of Meaning,* 3rd edition. New York: Harcourt, Brace, 1930. Also available in paperback form as a Harvest Book. One of the earliest and most influential of the works on semantics, but rather heavy going.

Walpole, Hugh R. *Semantics: the Nature of Words and their Meanings.* New York: Norton, 1941. A popular work on the subject, influenced by the work of Ogden and Richards.

WRITING

WITH A

PURPOSE

Purpose: An Overview

Subjects into Theses

Outlining

THE PROCESS

OF COMPOSITION

Paragraphs: Compositions in Miniature

Effective Sentences

Right Words

1

Purpose: An Overview

A perceptive student once said, "The trouble with Freshman English is you're supposed to know everything about writing before you get a chance to study any of it." In one sense, at least, he was right. In mathematics, foreign languages, and the sciences, you begin with the rudiments, and successive lessons build on what has gone before. But in composition all the skills necessary at the end of the term are just as necessary at the beginning. Even in his first essay, a student must choose a subject, narrow it down to manageable size, select pertinent material, organize it logically, develop his ideas in detail, and express them in orderly paragraphs and clear sentences with due regard for the conventions of usage.

Chapters 2 to 6 in this book will take up these matters in turn, each at considerable length. But because from your very first essay you will be dealing with them all at once, this opening chapter will provide a quick overview of what you most need to know about writing. This advice will be based on the belief that your chances of doing a good job on any writing assignment will depend on how clearly you understand what you are trying to do. To put it another way, the theme of this book is that *effective college writing is controlled by the writer's purpose.*

Good writing is almost never accidental. It is a deliberate attempt by one person to communicate to others those ideas, facts, or impressions that will create the result *which the writer has intended to achieve.* He must therefore always begin with a clear sense of purpose. This means that before he starts to write he must think carefully about two related questions: "What *precisely* do I want to do?" and "How can I best do it?" Answering these questions clearly is the first step toward writing well.

These two questions are so closely related that a writer will sometimes know *what* he wants to do only when he has decided *how* he wants to do it. A simple analogy will illustrate. Imagine an expert golfer facing a twenty-foot putt on a rolling green. What is his purpose? To say that he wants to sink his putt is too general a description to be helpful. For him the important decision is *how* the shot should be played. Therefore he studies the contour of the green, observes the grain and texture of the grass, and plans the path he wants his ball to follow. Only when he has thought out his problem in this way can he be said to know what he wants to do. His precise purpose, then, is to stroke the ball in such a way that it will follow the contour of the green in a *predetermined* path to the cup.

In much the same way a writer must try to understand what is needed to make his writing do what he wants it to do. This means, first, that he must know precisely what his purpose is and, second, that he must realize how particular decisions about choice of material, organization, development, and style will help or hinder that purpose. Those requirements are neither simple nor easy. Sometimes they impose a discipline from which the writer has an understandable desire to escape. But taking the easy way out and running away from that discipline often exacts a heavy price, as some of the student essays printed later in this chapter will show.

Writing With and Without a Purpose

In this chapter we shall assume that your first essays will be written out of your own experience. For these essays you will first decide firmly what you want to do and then draw from your experience the materials you need to accomplish that purpose. Later in the course you will undoubtedly write papers which cannot be developed entirely from past experience but will draw their materials from your reading. In this latter kind of assignment you do not begin with a clear sense of purpose. You begin with a general subject, and as you study it and perhaps make notes, you learn what you want to do. Both kinds of assignments require purposeful writing; but in the first, you start with a purpose in mind; in the second, you arrive at a purpose as a result of your study, and that purpose is partly determined by the materials you have found.

With this distinction in mind, let us begin our study of purpose in writing by contrasting three essays on the same general subject — the experience of a freshman student during his first weeks in college. The first essay represents writing which is completely without purpose; the second shows an inadequate sense of purpose which fails to control the development of the essay; the third illustrates highly purposeful writing.

My First Impressions of the University

I knew this was one of the biggest universities in the country, but I never understood till I arrived on campus just how big it really is. When I first came here I was so scared that I felt like returning home, but then I convinced myself that I was being silly. After all, if thousands of other people could stand it, why couldn't I?

After looking around for a while I went to what would be my home for at least a semester. When I got to the door I saw a light seeping out from under it. I was scared again. I was going to meet my roommate. Cautiously I opened the door and looked in. He was lying in bed reading. It was now or never. I went in. We quickly became friends.

The next morning we got up and went to eat breakfast. After eating breakfast, we went off together to explore the campus.

Since Fred, my roommate, was especially interested in gymnastics, we went to the Old Gymnasium, where we worked out for a few minutes on the sidehorse. I tried to do some of the stunts he showed me, but I was no good at them. I like to watch gymnastic meets, but my sport is basketball. I am looking forward to the basketball season, and I hope I will be lucky enough to make the freshman squad.

When we got tired of walking around the campus we returned to our room. Fred turned out to be a swell companion. Getting to know him has helped me to overcome the loneliness that I first felt when I came to this huge campus.

There is no continuity in this essay. Each of its five paragraphs wanders off in a different direction. The first starts to explain how the size of the university made the student feel insignificant, lonely, and homesick. That general impression could have been developed into an effective essay, had the writer stayed with it and shown in detail how lonely and insecure he was. Instead, he changed direction in the second paragraph in order to report his first meeting with his roommate. That subject too could have been developed into a good essay; but again the writer stopped just as he was getting nicely started. He turned away from that first meeting, with all the evidence it could have provided of a new and satisfying companionship growing out of the loneliness of both boys, to record the unimportant detail that they had breakfast together before making a tour of the campus. Then the tour is interrupted, before it gets well started, by a digression on gymnastics and basketball. When that is over, so is the tour, without mention of any building except the Old Gymnasium. The total result is an essay which goes in no consistent direction and has no effect on a reader except to leave him wondering what the writer was trying to do.

The answer, of course, is that the writer did not know. He was just trying to get enough words on paper to satisfy an assignment. Because he had no clear sense of purpose, he had no control over what he wrote. As he thought of his first meeting with Fred, their breakfast together, and their workout in the Old Gymnasium, he wrote a little about each, without considering what relation these events had to the subject implied in his title. In all this meandering, no goal is quite reached. We never really feel the impact of the boy's loneliness; we get no clear picture of Fred's personality; we learn nothing about the campus except that it is big. What we get is a hodgepodge of material which has not been shaped into any unified structure. This is purposeless writing at its worst.

Now read the next essay carefully, paying special attention to the relation of the first paragraph to the rest.

ON YOUR OWN

Before I came to this campus I knew things would be rough. I had heard from friends ahead of me in high school how big the U was and that a new freshman was sure to feel lost and lonely for a time. I had also been told that the work would be much harder than I was used to and that students got less help from the teachers. All this advice got summed up in the phrase, "At the U you're on your own." Now after three weeks here I know what the older fellows meant.

During Freshman Week I didn't know whether I was coming or going. I never had so many different activities crowded into one week. The first thing I did when I arrived on campus was to go to the dormitory and get my room. There I met my roommate, whom I had written a couple of times to during the summer. He introduced me to some of the other fellows in the dorm, and we compared notes about what we had done in high school and what we wanted to do here. It was a nice beginning for college, for I got to know several students who have been my good friends ever since.

During the next three or four days we had something scheduled every minute. We took physical examinations and scholastic tests and I had to take an extra math test because I did not have enough math in high school. After the tests we went to see our advisers, who told us what subjects we should take and helped us plan our programs. I didn't have too much trouble because one of the older boys in the dorm had briefed me on the courses I'd have to take, although the adviser almost refused to OK my program because I had forgotten to bring the slip showing I had taken my physical.

Registration wasn't as bad as I had been told. I came early in the alphabet, so I was able to get all of the classes my adviser had approved, except that I had to switch hours for my PE section. Those who came later were less lucky. By then classes were pretty well filled up and some students practically had to tear up their programs and start over again.

My real troubles began when classes started. Where my most difficulty was was the assignments. I thought I understood the work as it was being taken up in class, but it was a different story when I tried to do the assignments. Worst of all, every one of my instructors seemed to have the idea that his class was the only one I was taking. I had more homework for each course than I had for all my courses together in high school. Fortunately several of us in the dorm studied together and were able to help each other out.

What is the purpose of this essay? What effect does the writer intend to achieve? The title and the opening paragraph suggest that he wants to make a reader understand what a hard time a new freshman has when beset by problems which he must solve without help. But, except for the last paragraph, the essay contains no evidence that the student had any serious difficulties. Nor does it show that he was "on his own." On the contrary, much of the essay suggests that this student made a rather easy and successful adjustment to college life, a suggestion which contradicts the title and the opening paragraph. The paper simply does not do what it presumably set out to do.

A careful rereading of this essay shows that the writer did not have his purpose clearly enough in mind to dominate his thinking; as a result, he lost control of his writing. After the opening paragraph he drifted into a mere summary of his activities and wrote down events in the order in which they occurred, without thinking what connection, if any, they had with his opening paragraph. His essay is not as bad as the first one; it does proceed in a constant direction; but the direction is not the one suggested in the title and the opening paragraph.

Now contrast both the preceding essays with this one:

THROUGH THE TREES TO THE FOREST

The old saying that we cannot see the forest for the trees represents a natural state of confusion. When we are learning to read we cannot see the sentence for the words, because each word is a new experience which has to be understood as a word before it can be understood as part of a sentence. When we are learning to dance we are so preoccupied with the mechanics of moving our feet properly that we have little sense of rhythmic motion. In such situations we respond to the parts before we respond to the whole: we see the trees before we discern the forest.

This is also true of the first few weeks in college. Then everything is so new that we are aware only of individual experiences, not of the pattern of these experiences. We move into a new home, live with strangers, try to find our way around an unfamiliar campus, make decisions we never had to make before, plan academic programs we do not understand, go through a registration process that baffles and frustrates us at every step, listen to lectures which seemed logical as they moved from one sentence to the next but defy reconstruction from our notes, or struggle with assignments which seemed clear when announced but grow increasingly vague as we work on them. In all these activities we lack a sense of relationship; we do not see how things fit together; so for a few days or a few weeks we live in a world of unrelated events to which we cannot give any cohesive shape.

The fact that most of us are away from home for the first time in our lives increases our sense of confusion. Our confidence in our own self-reliance disintegrates under the unrelieved pressure of readjustment. Home and parents offer a comforting retreat from too much responsibility thrust too suddenly upon us. At home we can take time out to assimilate one set of experiences before we encounter others. But during the first few weeks of college there is no time out. The whole new world of college life, with its demands and challenges, keeps crowding into our privacy. No wonder that some students yearn for the familiar ruts of home life. They write their parents that they are homesick. What they mean is that they long for an occasional break in their forced march into maturity.

But gradually a pattern begins to emerge. The campus itself takes on firmer contours, the strange roommate begins to display a consistent personality, lectures develop theme and direction, assignments make sense, instructors become less remote, and everywhere method becomes apparent. Most of all, habit takes over, and much of the business of daily living becomes routine. Then the sum of all our separate acts assumes a pattern. The forest becomes perceptible.

And, as all this happens, we begin to acquire a sense of identity with the college. Things which were apart from us become part of us, and we, in turn, become part of them. We become involved in the fortunes of the football team, in the issues and personalities of student elections, in the letters written to the college paper, and in the ideas that are presented in class. More and more, we respond to the people we meet in the classroom, on the sidewalks, and at the dining table. We feel the stimulus of their interests and their attitudes. We become members of a community, with a commitment to the concerns of that community. Almost without realizing it, we become an element in the pattern of college life. We become part of the forest.

In this essay the writer is in complete control of his material. Everything in the essay is there because it serves his purpose of showing the transition which was implied in the title, and nothing which detracts from that purpose is allowed to appear. Each paragraph has a particular and necessary job to do, and does it. The writer knows where he is going before he begins, and from the title to the concluding sentence he moves consistently in the direction he has chosen.

The contrast of these three essays illustrates the difference between purposeless and purposeful writing. That difference is control. A writer with an effective sense of purpose is like a man sailing by a compass: he can set his course at the beginning and check it as he goes. As a result, he arrives where he wanted to be. But a writer without a purpose is simply drifting. He may, like the writer of the first essay, drift every which way; or he may, like the writer of the second essay, drift steadily in the wrong direction. In either case, his chances of arriving at an intended destination are slight.

Purpose and the Whole Approach

In the essays we have been considering, each writer was free to treat the assignment as he pleased. Many assignments, however, do not allow the writer so much freedom. The wording of the directions or the situation in which the essay is to be written may limit his choice. For example, most essay-type examinations impose two conditions: they specify the subject (sometimes even the treatment of it), and they impose a time limit within which the answer must be written. No student who wishes to do well on an examination can ignore these conditions.

Often, therefore, the first step in a writing assignment is to analyze the situation. Sometimes the analysis requires little more than a careful reading of the directions and a decision about how to interpret the assignment. At other times, especially in persuasion, the analysis will require careful consideration of many factors, including the attitudes of the reader. For example, imagine yourself facing the following problem.

You have a sister, seventeen years old and about to begin her senior year in high school. She is very much in love with a boy of nineteen, a sophomore in college, who is about to be drafted and expects to be sent abroad. They want to get married now. His parents have given their consent; yours object to an immediate marriage because they feel that your sister is too young, that she ought to finish high school and delay the wedding until the boy gets out of service in about two years. Although your mother has explained her objections fully, your sister is not persuaded. Indeed, she is seriously thinking of eloping. But before doing so, she writes asking your advice. How will you reply?

Suppose you agree with your parents and want to persuade your sister to delay marriage until the boy has completed his military service. This supposition establishes the general purpose of the letter you will write, but there are elements in the situation that will affect both its content and its tone. Your first task, then, is to analyze the situation and discover these elements. Your analysis might go like this:

1. The fact that my sister is postponing elopement until she hears from me is a sign that she is still willing to listen to reason. She evidently considers elopement a last resort. My main effort, therefore, should be to persuade her not to elope, since elopement would end all consideration of her problem. The more I can get her to delay, the wiser her decision is likely to be and the less strain it will impose on both families.
2. My sister's appeal for advice suggests that she trusts me to be sympathetic with her problem. Nothing I say must destroy that confidence. Above all, I must not take a superior attitude or lecture her. The tone of my letter will be as important as my advice.
3. Obviously my sister believes (*a*) that she is mature enough to marry and (*b*) that her love for the boy is the real thing, not merely an adolescent infatuation. In her present disturbed state, contradicting her is sure to cause resentment and may hasten rather than delay an elopement. The question to be dealt with is *when* she should marry the boy, not *whether* she should marry him.
4. Since I have an obligation to my parents, too, I must not take sides with her against my mother, nor give the impression that I think mother entirely right and sister entirely wrong. My job is to lessen, not increase, family tension. If I can get sister to look objectively at mother's advice, she may be influenced by it more than she now seems to be.
5. Since sister probably knows all the stock arguments against hasty marriages, there is no point in my repeating them. The thing to do is to find the one argument that will best persuade her, and to concentrate on that.

This may seem like a great deal of analysis for a single letter, but the problem requires no less. Unless the writer is willing to think out his problem in some such way as this, *before he writes a single word,* he is not prepared to write. If he plunges into a hasty answer, he runs the danger of producing a letter as unfortunate as this one:

```
Dear Rhoda:

You are much too young to get married.  At seventeen
you simply haven't had enough experience with boys
to decide to tie your whole life to one of them.  So
the first question you should ask yourself is, "Am I
really in love with Ted or is it just a plain case
```

of infatuation?" If you married Ted what would you do when he was shipped abroad? Sit around night after night twiddling your thumbs while the other girls were having fun on dates? What would you do if you had a baby? If you married Ted now you would be leaving school, your parents, your friends, everything that you have always liked. Are you willing to give up all this just for a few extra months of married life? And then what?

To add to these, Rhoda, you know that doing something more or less behind your parents' back and without their consent would never leave you with a clear conscience. Mother and Dad have always done what was best for you, and it is really quite selfish of you to go against their wishes now. Even if their reasons seem a bit old-fashioned, you ought to recognize that they are older and wiser than you.

Rhoda, I am sure that if you read this carefully and think about it, you will make the right decision. I'm looking forward to having you as the maid of honor at my wedding next summer. You haven't forgotten that I was in the same predicament a few years ago. I listened to sensible advice, and the outcome has pleased everyone. Don't disappoint me with your decision.

Love,

Alice

In judging this letter, try to read it through Rhoda's eyes. How would you feel if the sister you had counted on to understand and sympathize with your problem had written you this reply? How would you react to her suggestions that you were being foolish, that your love was merely the infatuation of an inexperienced adolescent, and that your unwillingness to follow your parents' advice was selfish? What would you think of the tone of the letter? Would you be persuaded or repelled by the way Alice presents her advice and the smug example of her own conduct? Remember that the sole purpose of the letter is to persuade Rhoda. Whether or not the advice is generally good, whether the parents would agree with it, or even Rhoda herself in ten years — these considerations have no relevance. All that counts is the effect the letter has on Rhoda now.

It is most important to realize that all the faults of Alice's letter were committed *before she began to write.* Having failed to analyze the situation, especially the emotional state of her sister, Alice was not mentally prepared to write a persuasive letter. Analysis of the writing problem is the writer's method of discovering what is required of him, and any student who rushes into a difficult writing assignment without careful thought is inviting trouble. As you will see in Chapter 10, the tendency to begin writing before one is clear about what should be done is one of the chief causes of failure in essay-type examinations.

Purpose and Planning

In short essays, the plan of the paper is often determined by the act of deciding the purpose. Understanding what one wants to do brings understanding of how to do it. For example, suppose a student, early in his first term, is asked to write an essay on his impressions of college. On first approach he is not sure what he wants to do with the assignment, so he begins by jotting down a series of notes:

> First view of campus — Georgian architecture — crowds of students everywhere — traffic conditions dangerous — cyclists a nuisance — orientation meetings — many pretty girls, some not so pretty — not enough of them for the number of boys — faculty seems quite young — no gray beards — class procedure different from high school — being addressed as Mr. and Miss makes students feel mature — instructors, otherwise quite informal — some sit on desk while they lecture — registration sheer chaos — helpfulness of upperclassmen — some advisers very nice, others not — oh, the homework!

As he studies these notes, he sees that they have no purpose or direction. He can group some of them under headings such as *campus, students,* and *faculty,* but he can see no unity or theme. He would have only a series of paragraphs in no way related to each other except that they all dealt with some aspect of college life.

At this stage it occurs to him that he needs a point of view from which to look at his subject, so he puts his notes aside and begins to think about his dominant impression of college. And it occurs to him that college life is not what he had expected it to be. He recognizes that his previous ideas about college have been largely formed from the movies and occasional football games. He therefore decides to write an essay showing that college is not as Hollywood portrays it.

At this point he has determined his purpose. He now sees that he can use the division of material (campus-students-faculty) that had occurred to him earlier. But this time he can see how these groups fit into a unified essay. He has only to apply his purpose statement — *College is not what it is in the movies* — to each of these groups. He will have one paragraph contrasting the movie campus with this real one, and similar paragraphs for students and faculty. He can begin with a paragraph which introduces the basic idea and end with a paragraph which sums up the essay. The plan will look like this:

1. A paragraph describing what the movies had led him to expect, ending with the statement that this college does not fit the movie picture.
2. A paragraph developing the topic sentence that *this campus bears little resemblance to the kind of campus shown in the movies.* The material for this paragraph will be selected to build a contrast between the physical appearance of a movie campus and of this one.
3. A paragraph developing the topic sentence that *students here do not fit into the movie pattern.* The material will again be chosen to point up the contrast between real and movie students.
4. A paragraph developing the topic sentence that *this faculty is quite unlike the Hollywood stereotype of the college professor.* The material here will be chosen to show in what particular ways this faculty differs from the professors in the movies.
5. A final paragraph to round off the essay by restating the basic idea in the light of the evidence presented in paragraphs 2, 3, and 4.

You will notice several things about this plan. First, it was suggested by the purpose. Until the student had a dominant idea to develop, he saw no efficient way to organize his impressions. Once he knew what he wanted to do, it was easy to see how the material might be arranged. Second, the plan could be used for a much longer paper. The three middle paragraphs do not exhaust the subject; it would be possible to include paragraphs dealing with other aspects of college life — studies, social activities, athletics, dormitory or fraternity life, and so on. Finally, the decision on purpose required revision of the original notes. Once the student had committed himself to a purpose, he had to reject those notes which did not suit that purpose and bring in new material which did. The purpose, therefore, not only suggests the plan; it also suggests the kind of material needed to develop that plan. On a topic of this kind new material is not difficult to get, because once a writer has defined his purpose, he has so concentrated his thinking that the needed facts and illustrations come readily to mind. By clarifying his purpose he creates a channel through which his thoughts will flow easily, and he thus makes his thinking more efficient.

As an additional example of the relation between purpose and planning, let us plan an essay, the purpose of which is to make clear that the distinction between war and peace depends on whether one is considering them from a legal, a political, or a military point of view.

The structure of such an essay is implicit in the purpose statement. The essay must have three main units, one each for the legal, political, and military distinctions between war and peace. Suppose these distinctions are as follows:

1. Legally, a state of peace changes to a state of war at the moment war is formally declared. This is a clear-cut and precise distinction, but it may have little relation to the facts, since many people may have been killed before war is formally declared. Legally, therefore, the distinction between war and peace is deceptively clear.
2. Politically, nations may drift into a state of war. They may have been

engaged in politically hostile acts for years before they are officially at war. From a political point of view, then, there is no precise distinction between war and peace. The state of peace gradually degenerates into a state of war.

3. Militarily, troops may begin fighting battles, often at widely different places and times. At first these battles seem to be separate events or "incidents"; it is only later that they can be related into one war. The military distinction between war and peace is therefore best understood in retrospect.

Obviously, the simplest plan for such an essay is a three-unit structure, each unit of which deals with one of the points of view. Each unit may be developed in one paragraph or more, and the author may add an introductory paragraph stating the purpose of the essay and a concluding paragraph restating it in the light of the discussion in the main units. The completed essay would go something like this:

THE DISTINCTION BETWEEN WAR AND PEACE[1]

Purpose stated, with three units indicated

The definition of war and peace may be approached from three different points of view. The first is deceptively clear, the second is significantly vague, and the third becomes clear only in perspective.

First unit — the legal distinction

First, there is the legal aspect of the difference between war and peace. This is deceptively clear. In December 1941 Japan attacked the United States and declared war upon this country and Great Britain, and immediately thereafter Germany and Italy declared war upon the United States. In each case the United States reciprocated. The joint resolution declaring war upon Japan was adopted by Congress on the 8th of December and was signed by the President at 4:10 p.m. Eastern War Time. Under the Constitution of the United States, that was, for the American people, the legal change to war in place of peace. But by the time that signature became effective, every United States battleship based upon Pearl Harbor was already out of action. The legal inception of war did not correspond with the moment of war's physical impact, much less with its substantive reality. Yet that definite day, December 8, 1941, will be set down in all the books of history as the date for America's entry into the war. It corresponds with the legal status, but with no other; this is why, though it is clear, it is nonetheless deceptive. . . .

The legal distinction between war and peace is not

[1] From *Strategy of Peace* by Henry M. Wriston. Reprinted by permission of the World Peace Foundation.

without significance; property rights and many interests are modified by it. But relative to the total pattern of life as affected by war, this excessively precise legal distinction is vastly less important than the political aspect.

Second unit —
the political
distinction

By contrast, the political distinction between war and peace is significantly vague. People talk about the "white" war which preceded the "red" war. They refer to the economic war which preceded the battles. They speak of the "long armistice" between the Treaty of Versailles and the outbreak of this war, as though there never was an interval of genuine peace. Some regard the recent war as beginning in 1931 at the time of the Manchurian incident and the development of the Stimson Doctrine. Others say war began in 1934 when Japan denounced the Washington treaties. Still others think it started in 1935 when Italy attacked Ethiopia and defeated the concept of sanctions. Others would connect it with the German occupation of the Rhineland in 1936. Every person has his favorite time, some suggesting the civil war in Spain, others the *Anschluss,* yet others the Sudeten crisis. Each of those claims has a plausible basis. It is obvious that every act of aggression was part of a maturing crisis; the declaration of war is only a culminating step which completes the development.

Defining the state of war politically, therefore, is like inquiring when some functional disorder took on serious pathological qualities. It may start as some mild or benign affliction, but slowly or swiftly by unperceived degrees develop to a point where it menaces life itself. At what moment in that tragic sequence did the disease begin? . . .

Third unit — the
military distinction

The third distinction between war and peace is military; it is clear only in long perspective. This last was called a global war, and many insist it was one war. But common sense makes it obvious that so long as the Soviet Union was not at war with Japan or the United States with Finland, the statement that there was a single war was imprecise.

The same difficulty appears when the chronology of the war is examined. The use of force began with the Manchurian incident in 1931. The later phase of the war in China began in 1937. Fighting took place in Africa in 1935 with the conquest of Ethiopia, and on the continent of Europe with the occupation of Albania in the spring of 1939. In the period since the declaration of war by Great Britain against Germany on September 3, 1939, some thirty-five other nations have declared war and others have severed diplomatic rela-

14

tions with the Axis. Denmark and Norway, Belgium and the Netherlands, Italy, the Balkan States, the Soviet Union, Finland, Japan and the United States all became involved in the fighting at different times. . . .

Such military facts are characteristic of all war. The Hundred Years' War between France and Britain was by no means a period of uninterrupted fighting; the name could be applied to the era only in retrospect. Similarly, the Napoleonic wars were interrupted by truces, by reversal of alliances, and by treaties of peace which proved temporary. Yet in the long perspective the whole period had a certain unity; the successive phases of the lengthy series of struggles are now regarded as constituting one war. Those are illustrations of what is meant by the assertion that the military aspects of war and peace are comprehensible only in perspective.

Final restatement of purpose in light of discussion of all three units

War is a legal, political, and military fact; its appearance is different when observed from those various points of view. Since the distinction between peace and war is legally clear, politically vague, and militarily plain only in perspective, the effort to roll all three types of description into one has resulted in confusion of thought.

The plan here is much like the one for the essay contrasting a real college with the Hollywood version. First, the total subject is broken into units, so that structurally the essay will consist of an introductory paragraph, the development of each unit in turn, and a concluding paragraph. The basic idea of each unit can then be expressed as a topic sentence for one or more paragraphs. Finally, these topic sentences may serve as a *paragraph outline* or *topic sentence outline* of the essay. This simple kind of planning will probably be sufficient for most of the essays you will write early in the course. In Chapter 3 we shall consider more formal and more complex plans. The point to recognize now is that a sound plan, whether simple or complex, depends on the writer's understanding of what he is trying to do, and for whom.

Purpose and Development

Development is the working out of the purpose and the plan through the details of the essay. In "Through the Trees to the Forest" the purpose was developed by showing step by step the transition through which the new freshman becomes a functioning member of the college community. In "The Distinction Between War and Peace" the development consists of the explanatory details which make clear the differences between the legal, political, and military definitions of war.

Probably the most frequent criticism that English instructors make of student writing is its generality, its lack of specific detail. Many students fail to realize that a statement which is meaningful to them, because they know the specific experience behind it, may communicate almost nothing to a reader unless its meaning is spelled out in detail. This is true of all kinds of writing — of narration, description, exposition, argument — of impromptu essays, research papers, examination answers, even of social correspondence. It is probable that, next to a sense of purpose, the chief requirement of good writing is a concern for detailed development of general statements.

To appreciate the value of specific detail, consider a student writing an essay about a terrifying experience he has had. He and a friend had gone fishing one summer afternoon. Feeling tired, he had stretched out on the ground and fallen asleep. He was awakened by his friend's voice telling him not to move, that a rattler was crawling toward him, and that his best chance was to lie quite still until it had passed. Let us suppose that the student writer's attempt to tell what happened in the next few moments goes something like this:

> Soon I felt the snake's clammy body on my arm. I was terribly scared, but I had enough sense to remain motionless. I could feel the snake crawl slowly across my body, and once when I opened my eyes I could see him looking at me. Then, after what seemed ages, he moved on.
>
> I must have fainted, because the next thing I remember my friend was shaking me. He said I looked like a ghost, and the way I felt, he was probably right.

Not many students have such exciting material to work with, but this account does almost nothing to reproduce the terror that the student must have felt. It provides a minimum summary of the events; indeed, it would be difficult to do less with the material. Even though this summary may move a sympathetic reader, it moves him only because he is imaginative enough to recreate the situation for himself. If this version succeeds at all, it does so because the reader is doing the writing.

Now compare the flat summary given above with the version the student actually wrote.

> Suddenly I felt something on the biceps of my right arm — a queer light touch, clinging for an instant — and then the smooth glide of an oily body. I could feel the muscles of the snake's body slowly contract, then relax as it slid smoothly, oh, how smoothly across my naked arm. Again and again that body contracted, and again and again it relaxed. At last I saw a flat, V-shaped head, with two glistening, black protruding buttons. A thin, pointed, sickening yellow tongue slipped out, then in, accompanied by a sound like that of escaping steam. Slowly, slowly it advanced, the rounded spots on its back and sides drawing together and then stretching to their length as it moved slowly forward. When it was about in the middle of my chest, it paused, slowly turned its head toward me, and fixed its cold boring eyes in my direction. Now I could not have moved had I wished; I was

fascinated. So he remained, darting his tongue out and in. Finally he slowly, very slowly, turned his head, and again moved forward. Once more I had to see and feel the slow contraction, relaxation, contraction, relaxation. The body began to narrow, the spots grew smaller, the cracks on his revolting greenish-white stomach grew closer together and more minute. At last the slender, whipping tail appeared on my chest, and then so slowly slid along until . . .

My head felt so queer; up and down, up and down it went. Why, my face was all wet! I weakly shoved at the bronzed arm that shook me, and asked, "What's the matter?"

"God! and only a couple of minutes!" I heard a voice filter into my brain. "Wonderful! I don't think I could have let a rattler crawl across me. Lord! but you're clammy, and look at your muscles and veins. Your face looks like a dead man's."[2]

The difference between these two versions is the difference between writing and not writing. If the purpose of the writer was to share his experience with his readers, the first version fails, for it leaves out most of what happened. True, it tells you *something* about the experience, but the second version makes you live it. The second snake is no abstraction; it is as real as life. You can see its markings, feel the contraction of its muscles, see that thin tongue flash in and out. You can see the cracks on its greenish-white belly. And when the whipping tail finally slides off the boy's chest, you are almost as relieved as he was. The details of the second version are not artistic decoration. They are the materials that recreate the incident, and therefore are necessary to the author's purpose.

Now notice how a professional writer uses explanatory details to pound home his meaning. His purpose is to explain the time-lag between the onset of a rainstorm and the flooding of rivers. His readers, of course, know in a general way that the dry earth is capable of absorbing a great deal of water and that the rivers will not begin to flood until the earth is saturated. But the author is not satisfied with this general explanation. He wants his readers to understand the time-lag by seeing where the rain must go before it can reach the rivers. By spelling out in specific detail the total process of absorption, he makes his readers understand, as they probably never understood before, why it takes time for the rivers to flood.

By deep affinity, every grain of dust drew water to itself. The punky dryness of rotting logs grew slowly sodden. In the thickets of blackberry, and toyon, and poison oak, the dead leaves lay deep; beneath these rested the half rotted leaves and twigs of older years, and still deeper the mould of generations. This porous mass sucked moisture like a stiff sponge, and paradoxically the life-giving water even woke to new vigor the very processes of decay.

Still more, the living vegetation sucked in and held the rain. How many bucketfuls to change from black to green all the moss upon the rocks? How

[2] Joe Daly, "Too Close." From *The Green Caldron: A Magazine of Freshman Writing* (October, 1934), published at the University of Illinois, Urbana, Illinois. Reprinted by permission.

many tank-cars to wet all the pine-needles and all the oak leaves? How many trains of tank-cars to uncurl all the blades of grass upon all the hills? Leaves shrunken to conserve moisture expanded and grew heavy; drooping shoots stood up stiff and vigorous. The very cells expanded, and the protoplasm for its subtle chemistry absorbed to itself countless tons of water.

Even animal life drew in the water. Cattle and horses grew dark beneath the downpour. The fleeces of the sheep were heavy. Deer in the forest glades changed from dun to brown. Through the tunnels of ants and beetles the moisture seeped downward. The channels of earthworms were as millions of conduits. The myriad far-ranging burrows of gophers and ground-squirrels took the trickles deeper still. Then at last following the fissures of the earth itself the seeping moisture from the surface reached ground which was no longer dry, and began to join that great fluctuating reservoir of the waters which are beneath the earth.

Until all this should be fully achieved the river was low. As well expect water to stand in a sieve as streams to run high before the land itself was satisfied.[3]

A concern for detailed development will help the quantity as well as the quality of student writing. Many students have trouble writing 500 words on any subject, no matter how much they know about it. Often their trouble comes from lack of detailed development. They are dismissing in two or three sentences an idea or experience that needs a substantial paragraph, and after 150 words they find that they have nothing more to say. As a result, their essays are — like the first version of the snake incident — both short and shallow. If these students can discipline themselves to be dissatisfied with general treatments and to seek the details that give writing clarity and force, they will soon find that they have more to say and are saying it better.

Purpose and Style

Just as the way you dress depends on where you are going and what you intend to do, so a writer's style depends on his purpose, which, in turn, is influenced by his knowledge of his audience and the situation in which he is writing. In Chapter 6 we shall study the differences between formal and informal styles. At the moment we shall simply illustrate these differences by a contrast of two essays.

WHY WE NEED MORE WESTERNS ON TELEVISION[4]

The other night I saw a wonderful western on television. It had just about everything you'd want — fast horses, handsome men, beautiful women, mean outlaws, sneaky Indians, waving grass, rolling plains, covered wagons, smok-

[3] From *Storm* by George R. Stewart. Copyright, 1941, by George R. Stewart. Reprinted by permission of Random House, Inc.

[4] Mary Louise Borgman, "Why We Need More Westerns on Television." From *The Green Caldron: A Magazine of Freshman Writing* (October, 1960), published at the University of Illinois, Urbana, Illinois. Reprinted by permission.

ing pistols, hard liquor, torrid love, bitter tears, bloody death — just everything you could ask for, all packed together into one little hour, and early enough for the kids to see it, too. This program was really something and I think we need lots more just like it, because programs like that teach lots of things that everybody ought to know — things that help us in our everyday life, and at other times, too. I'll tell you what I mean.

Take making friends, for instance. Most people are pretty slow at this, but they don't have to be. This program showed that a person can make friends quickly if he really tries. There was a trail scout in this story and a Russian countess, and at the beginning, they didn't even know each other, but before the first commercial, which came about four minutes after they met, they were already lying in the grass and kissing, just as if they'd known each other for years. I think we should all take a lesson from this — it's sort of a symbol. A Russian and an American making love on the prairie under the sky. It has a lot of meaning to it.

Another thing about westerns is that they show the difference between good and bad people. After you watch a few westerns, it's pretty easy to tell which is which. The good men, for instance, seldom have beards or whiskers, and most of the bad men do. Also, the good man never shoots a person in the back — he waits until the person turns around to face him, which is the decent thing to do. On the other hand, bad men will shoot a man anywhere and will even shoot a woman or a dog sometimes. Speaking of women, there are good ones and bad ones, just like men. The good ones are usually married, while the bad ones usually aren't. The bad women usually wear real low-cut dresses or short ones, and the good women usually have on aprons; they might wear pretty tight dresses (the young good ones, that is; the old good women wear loose dresses), but they're hardly ever cut low. All these things are very helpful to people watching the program, because they know right away whose side to be on. And just like knowing how to make friends quickly, it's very helpful in life to know whose side to be on.

One of the best things westerns teach is our country's history. I'll bet people with television sets know lots more about history than people without television sets, because westerns on television are just crammed with history. They tell how we had to fight the pagan Indians every step of the way to get them to give us this land so that we could really make something out of it. (We let them go on living here, after we won the land fair and square, and we even gave them special areas called "reservations" to live on. They're real nice places — sort of like wild game preserves to keep animals from becoming what they call "extinct.")

When you start thinking about all the advantages of watching westerns, it's pretty plain to see that we ought to have more of them. There has been a lot of progress made toward getting more westerns on television, and you can see a good western almost any time except Sunday. Unfortunately, on Sunday afternoons there are things like symphony orchestras, documentary films, and panel discussions — real dull, long-hair stuff that most Americans wouldn't be interested in. The only good thing about Sunday is that before you know it, it's Monday again, and the beginning of a whole new week of interesting, educational, realistic, historical westerns. But friends, we've got to do something about Sunday afternoons.

You will notice that this essay contains many expressions that your high school English teachers may have objected to — contractions (*I'll, don't, aren't, they're*) and colloquial expressions (*kids, lots of, sort of, pretty slow, real low-cut, I'll bet*). In a formal style these constructions would be inappropriate, and they may have been out of place in the essays in which your teachers condemned them. But in this essay, and for this writer's purpose, these informal expressions are natural elements of the style which the writer is deliberately using. Any consistent attempt to change them would spoil the whole tone of the essay.

In contrast, such informal diction would be entirely out of place in the following essay.

COMMUNICATION EQUALS CIVILIZATION[5]

Good rhetoric is not in itself either a mystery or an occult art. It is the result of the conscientious and unified employment of several skills for the purpose of lucid communication. The subject to be communicated might be the result of student research, an account written home of daily events, or a job application. Practical uses of rhetoric confront us every day, and most students are aware of its importance in these applications. If this were all good writing meant, it could be said that most people are successful writers.

To say, however, that rhetoric is only useful on a practical level is to strip it of its most important dimension, to make of it another mechanical and brute accomplishment. Rhetoric does not begin with words on paper. It should begin somewhere within the human being, with whatever is essential and original about that being. Rhetorical skills like definition, logic, and organization of ideas help a man grasp and define his own uniqueness, as do poetic and artistic intuitions. The goal of knowledge, as it was expressed in *Dr. Zhivago,* is "to call everything in the universe by its right name." A rhetorical goal might be to call everything by its right name in terms of one's own uniqueness yet in terms accessible to as large an audience as possible. In short, the rhetorical goal is to say what no one else could ever have said in precisely the same way, yet to say it in a way that all can understand.

Experience is colorful and ever-varying for each individual. Suppose three people see a tree trunk with snow bending along it. One might describe the snow as seeming to rest calmly on the tree's gentle breast, another might say it was clinging there resisting the rudeness of the wind, and the third perhaps would imagine the snow strangling the tree with icy fingers. Each formula contributes in some way to the reader's picture of the actual sight, and each tells us something of the writer's personality or mood at the moment he saw it. To command word shadings, metaphors, rhythm, and diction successfully is to be able to reveal an original and human viewpoint.

Is this to say, then, that rhetoric serves only as a vehicle for the expression of individual self? For if so, it is not of very great help to man in society,

[5] Elizabeth C. Krohne, "Communication Equals Civilization." From *The Green Caldron: A Magazine of Freshman Writing* (March, 1961), published at the University of Illinois, Urbana, Illinois. Reprinted by permission.

although it certainly may gratify him in a selfish sense. No, for rhetoric should not stop at the revelation of individuality, but should perform an interpretive function as well. That original and valuable vision must be shared; and every sincere man is hungry to share it.

As rhetoric helps us define ourselves, then, it employs a medium which is universal — language and connotation. Because the medium is universal, the human, through communication, associates himself with humanity in general. This is the process of civilization in action, and it can be seen that communication and civilization are parts of, or words for, the same process, the relation of many parts within a harmonious whole.

There is no skill, no art whose development is more desperately important to the well-being of the world. Human beings seem less and less to be grasping and valuing their own uniqueness, and at the same time they have less and less to say to each other. The most profound human desires today are for economic security, peace, and the worth of the individual. But until we all are convinced of the universality of these desires, we cannot unite to secure them. For this reason, the development of skill in verbal and written communication ought to be a primary goal of every thoughtful person.

The style of this essay is much more formal than that of the previous one. It should be; for this author is dealing seriously with a subject she considers of great importance, and her style should suit her purpose. Informality in this essay would be just as wrong as a formal style in the essay about TV westerns.

Purpose and Revision

Revision is a necessary part of writing; it is not an extra touch to be added if one has time. To work out a significant idea through a well-organized, well-developed essay is more than most writers can do satisfactorily in a first draft. Nearly all professional writers have to revise their work into finished form. If this is true for them, how much more it is likely to be true for college freshmen!

But in an essay which has been carefully planned, the revision can usually be concentrated on particular paragraphs, sentences, and words. The basic structure of such an essay should be sound, but the writing will usually need careful editing before it is as good as the author can reasonably make it. For papers written early in the term, it may be wise to give special attention to four kinds of improvements: better paragraph development, reduction of wordiness, improved sentence structure and diction, and the correction of errors in spelling, punctuation, and grammar. Let us consider each of these briefly.

Paragraphs. In revising paragraphs, watch especially for two weaknesses: scanty development and awkward or confusing sequence of sentences. Look with extra care at short paragraphs. A paragraph is not necessarily bad because it is short. Transitional paragraphs — those intended merely to introduce a new unit or to provide a connection between two units — *should* be short. But, as we have seen, incomplete development is a common weakness of student writing, and incomplete paragraphs are nearly always conspicuously short. Check all short paragraphs to see if you could strengthen them by working in more detail or by giving evidence or examples.

Here is a paragraph taken from a student essay on Sophocles' play *King Oedipus.*

> The question arose in class as to whether or not Oedipus was predestined. In my opinion, he was not. The whole sequence of events is almost completely natural, so that one does not need to assume that predestination entered into Oedipus' actions.

After reading this paragraph the instructor wrote at the top of the page: "You say that the sequence of events is almost completely natural. What makes you think so? What is so natural about killing one's father and marrying one's mother? Rewrite this paragraph to show me what you have in mind." Here is the student's revised version.

> The question arose in class as to whether Oedipus' actions were predestined. In my opinion, they were not. When Laius tried to kill him, Oedipus struck back. What else would a man of spirit do? When he solved the riddle and was offered the kingship by the grateful Thebans, he married the dead king's widow. This was politically expedient. By marrying Jocasta, Oedipus, then a stranger with no known family and no political connections, allied himself with the royal family and so reduced the possibility that any other claimant, including Creon, would attempt to seize the throne. By insisting that Teiresias and the old shepherd tell what they knew, Oedipus was acting according to an accepted moral code. It was both his religious and civic duty to discover the murderer. Had he been a timid man, Oedipus might have retreated before Laius and taken the safe course of not pressing the witnesses when he sensed the drift of their testimony, but then he would not have been Oedipus. He did what his character required him to do. I am sure that he would have acted as he did even if there had been no prophecy.

Had the student handed in this paragraph originally, his grade would have been higher. As the revision shows, he had excellent reasons for his opinion, but it never occurred to him to give them until he was challenged to do so. Try to avoid his mistake. Learn to challenge your own general statements so that you can give them the support they need before you hand in your paper.

In a well-written paragraph, the main idea is developed in a clear and orderly sequence of sentences. To check on the order of your sentences, read the paragraph aloud, or have your roommate read it to you. If it sounds jerky or if there seems to be a gap in the thought between one sentence and the next, consider what can be done to remove the difficulty. Any sentence which interrupts the flow of thought will disturb a reader and keep him from thinking along with you. Therefore, if any sentence seems to digress or to repeat what has already been adequately said, cross it out. If there is a gap in the thought, see what you can do to bridge it. If the construction of paragraphs is a major problem in your writing, go directly to pages 69–101 and study the material there, particularly the sections on unity, pages 74–75, and coherence, pages 82–89.

Wordiness. Even in professional writing, first drafts tend to be wordy. At that stage the writer is chiefly concerned with working out his ideas, and he may at times be repetitious or use more words than he needs. As long as he intends to work over his first draft conscientiously, this wordiness is not serious, but if he lets it stand in the final draft it will weaken his writing and make reading difficult. Notice, as shown below, the wordiness in the first draft of two paragraphs from this chapter, and the means used to get rid of it:

The structural ~~plan~~ of such an essay is implicit

in the purpose statement. The essay must have three

main units, ~~the first unit discussing the distinction~~ *one each for the legal, political,*

and military distinctions between war and peace.

~~between war and peace from a legal point of view,~~ *Suppose these distinctions.*

~~the second considering the distinction from a polit-~~

~~ical point of view, and the third looking at the~~

~~distinction from a military point of view. More-~~

~~over, the purpose statement implies that the dis-~~

~~tinction between war and peace differs with each~~

~~point of view, so that each unit must be developed~~

~~to make these differences clear.~~

~~Let us suppose that the differences~~ are as

follows:

This revision cuts a 100-word paragraph to 40 words and still says all that was significant in the first draft. In this example the extra 60 words are waste. The author could not see that while he was writing, but the wordiness was obvious when he came to revise.

Here is another example:

Often, therefore, the first step in a writing

assignment is to analyze the situation. Sometimes

the analysis requires little more than a careful

reading of the directions and a decision about how
to interpret
∧the assignment. ~~is to be interpreted. But~~ at other
especially in persuasion,
times,∧the analysis will require careful considera-
attitudes
tion of many factors, including the,∧~~nature~~ of the

reader. ~~or audience. This kind of attention is~~

~~likely to be especially important in essays which~~

~~are designed to persuade someone to act or not to~~

~~act in a certain way.~~

The chief revision here is the substitution of a three-word phrase for a 28-word sentence. The extra 25 words do not do enough work to earn their keep.

You may at this point be bothered by what may seem like a contradiction in the last few pages. First you are told to expand your writing by adding details; then you are asked to condense it by reducing wordiness. There is no contradiction. Details add substance; empty words add nothing but take the same effort to read as if they did. The boy who revised his 42-word paragraph on Oedipus into a 195-word paragraph was not padding his paper; he was providing meaning which he had failed to give in his earlier version. You can test this difference. Go back over his revised paragraph and try to cut out unnecessary words. You will find that the revision cannot be significantly shortened without sacrificing useful evidence.

Sentences and Diction. Unless your purpose requires you to write dialogue, use full sentences and avoid fragments. Within each sentence try to revise anything that is not clear or is awkward, unemphatic, or wordy. The most common sentence errors are discussed on pages 112–123. If you make such errors, your instructor will probably refer you to these pages. Meanwhile, notice how revision of sentence structure and diction improves the following paragraph.

Why, then, did the brilliant, dashing Hedda
some answers
Gabler marry George Tesman? We get ~~a great deal of~~
chat
~~information~~ from Aunt Julia's ~~talk~~ with Berta.
Hedda had been very close to her father, a
~~Hedda's father was a famous general. They were~~
famous general, whom she idealized.
~~very close to each other and she evidently built~~
because,
~~him up into her ideal man.~~ She had many ~~lovers but~~

none of whom she could bring herself to accept.
~~she was reluctant to accept any of them. When she~~
When she finally married, she was 29.
~~was 29 she married Tesman.~~ One can be certain that
a belle and that her charms
she was no longer ~~so popular. Her attractions were~~
were fading. Meanwhile
~~probably past their peak. Also~~ her father had died
so
and she needed security; ~~That is why~~ she chose
a tedious plodding scholar, who wished to
~~George. He was tedious but scholarly and expected~~
marry her, whom she could dominate, and whose
~~to become a professor, which meant a certain amount~~
future career as a professor promised a measure of
~~of prestige. Also he wanted to marry her.~~ *prestige.*

Some of these revisions are substitutions of single words — "chat" for "talk," and "beaux" for "lovers," which has undesirable connotations. Other revisions consist in substituting a short phrase for a long one or combining two or more sentences for a more concise statement. There are also some changes in word order or in grammatical structure for emphasis. Thus "she was 29" is moved to the end of the sentence and made a main clause, because Hedda's age is the important information in the sentence and needs emphasizing. Still other changes introduce new information to explain more fully why Hedda married Tesman. At this stage it is less important for you to analyze each specific change than to recognize that the revised paragraph comes closer to realizing the writer's purpose than did the first draft. A writer should never feel that the first form his ideas take must be the final form.

Conventions of Usage. College students are expected to use grammatical forms, to spell, and to punctuate in accordance with the customs of educated people. These customs were not invented by English teachers, and they are not confined to English classes. Indeed, most English teachers tend to be somewhat more tolerant of occasional slips and lapses than are most businessmen. Both inside and outside the English classroom, carelessness in following the conventions of usage will discredit your work. It is therefore to your advantage to make sure that your grammar, spelling, and punctuation are as acceptable as you can make them. If you have difficulty with usage, you may find it helpful to do some of the remedial exercises in the handbook section of this text. For the most part, however, student errors in the conventions of usage can be detected and corrected by efficient proofreading.

Proofreading

Proofreading is the last step in writing. It must be done, and it should be done more than once, but only after you are thoroughly satisfied with your revision and have recopied your paper if necessary. *Then* the paper should be read aloud slowly, with attention focused on the forms of words rather than their meanings. If you are in doubt about the spelling of a word or the punctuation of a sentence, don't guess; consult your dictionary or your handbook (Part III of this text). As you get back graded papers which show errors you failed to catch, try to see a pattern in these errors. If you consistently overpunctuate, use commas where periods are needed, or make the same kind of spelling error, you will save time and improve your grades by checking the appropriate sections of the handbook and working intensively to understand and prevent these errors.

Exercises

A. Study the two essays that follow, and then compare them in terms of purpose, selection of material, development of the purpose, and over-all effectiveness.

A Fishing Trip

Even though my extent of travel is somewhat limited, I have had some very interesting and educational trips. My first venture from home took place a few years ago when some friends asked me to accompany them to Canada on a two weeks' fishing trip. I must admit that at the time I knew nothing about fishing but I had all the enthusiasm to learn.

It was a bright, sunny day when we left Columbus in a tightly packed car for Sparrow Lake, Canada. Along the way we stopped at Niagara Falls to see one of nature's beautiful creations, and then continued to drive what seemed to be an endless distance. At last we arrived in Orillia, Canada, bought a few necessary supplies, and drove several miles down a typical washboard road till we arrived at our destination.

As I think back, I can still see that huge old brick home standing on top of the hill — not a tree around. After unpacking our clothes and eating one of those delicious home cooked dinners, we sat around and talked to all the new people, and then prepared for a good night's sleep in preparation for the busy day ahead of us.

From that day on, most of our time was spent in the boat on the lake trying to catch muskies. Even though our luck was pretty good I just couldn't learn to like that rod and reel sport. Consequently I was bribed into steering the boat.

I found my pleasures in the evening, after dinner, in swimming and playing tennis. Many of us used to row boats into the deeper part of the lake, dive, swim around, climb into the boat and row back to shore. I met many new friends and I am still writing to them.

I fully understand that a good fisherman could not imagine such a story, but it is a true one nevertheless. I'm sure I'll not accept another invitation to go on a fishing trip.

A FISHING TRIP? NO THANKS!

Although I had never been on a fishing trip, I had seen how much pleasure Dad always got from his annual fishing vacation and I had imagined that fishing, especially for muskies, must be thrilling. Therefore, when some friends invited me to accompany them on a two weeks' fishing trip to Sparrow Lake, Canada, Lair of the Big Muskies, I jumped at the chance. I was so eager to fish that the necessary preparations and the long, tedious car trip were severe tests of my patience. When we finally reached our cabin, late at night, I had difficulty getting to sleep. Visions of successful catches chased each other through my head. Had I known what I know now, I would have slept soundly — and late.

From the first day at the lake, most of our time was spent in the boat trying to catch muskies. We would get up before daylight, slosh some cold water on our faces, and prepare breakfast on a capricious kerosene stove. By the time it was light enough to bait a hook we would be pushing off from the wharf. Usually we would fish until noon, take an hour out for lunch, and try again until evening. Once we took sandwiches and a thermos of coffee with us and ate lunch in the boat, after rinsing our fishy hands in the lake. Once was enough. After that, we girls insisted on being put ashore to prepare lunch.

The prerequisite for comfortable fishing, I found, is the right kind of anatomy. I didn't have it. Even three cushions, piled one on top of another, only partially modified the hardness of the boat seat. I am sure that if God had intended the human frame to be subjected to five or six continuous hours on a narrow, wooden plank, He would have designed it differently. The slimy business of baiting the hook and of unhooking a fish when I was unfortunate enough to catch one, I could usually delegate to the men. But I never found a way of getting somebody to sit for me.

I admit that muskie-fishing has its exciting moments — the sudden thrill of a hard strike, those delicious seconds when you wait for the muskie to turn the bait in his mouth before you set the hook, his final desperate dive as you bring him near the boat, the first gleam of his greenish-white body as you pull him close to the surface, and the pistol shot that finally dispatches him. But those moments are paid for by hours of boredom and discomfort, when you sit, cold and wet, with nothing to do but fend off the persistent horse fly that is enamored of your knuckles. Even the thrill of landing a big one soon descends to an anticlimax as you spend a frustrating fifteen minutes trying to pry or cut the hooks from his vicious mouth or fumbling with numbed fingers to untangle the line, now hopelessly snarled in the contents of the spilled tackle box.

And when all this dreary routine is over, and your line is paying out freely from the side of the boat, what is there to look forward to? At best, the same thing over again — and all this for a fish which is hardly fit to eat. Do you blame me for deciding that if I had to be involved in such foolishness I would confine my efforts to steering the boat? That way I could save my disposition and what was left of my fingernails.

B. Review the analysis of the situation on page 9 and write *your* letter to Rhoda.

C. Proofread the following copy carefully so as to detect and correct all errors in spelling, punctuation, diction, and grammar. Do not rewrite. Simply make specific corrections where required in the text.

The influence of context on meaning is so important, that even when a speaker says what he did not intend to say; his listeners may understand his intended meaning without difficulty. Thus, a proffessor lecturing on the economy of Japan remarked as how the Japanese lived on a "riot of dice." The class laughed, but it understood perfectly what he had meant to say. Again, a four-year-old boy had a slight skin erruption, which his mother treated with vaseline. Later the trouble returns, and the boy, holding out his arm, said, "Mama, put some gasoline on my itch." No sensible mother could have no doubt what "gasoline" meant in this context.

When words are reported out of context, the originil meaning may be badly distorted. What one whispers to their sweetheart in privacy can be made to sound ludicrous when reported next morning at the family breakfast, by an eavesdropping younger sister. Statements made in the intimicy of classroom discussion, can sound shocking or idiotic when paraphrased in the college paper. And few public officials escape the embarrassment of having their words torn out of context and being presented so that they seem to say much more or something differently from what was first intended, indeed, the trick of quoting words out of context might be said

to be a standard procedure for discrediting a

political opponent.

The peculiar effectiveness of this kind of

misrepresentation lie in the fact, that a convincing

rebuttal is difficult. The misrepresented speaker

cannot deny that these are his "exact words"; he

can only say that they are not all of his words.

And that they were not intended to mean what they

are now being used to mean. But before an unsophis-

ticated audiance, such a defense seems a very feeble

excuse. Until people become naturally suspicious

of quotations taken out of context; until they

develop the habit of asking, "What else did he say,

and under what conditions?" misrepresentation

through half-truths will remain a convenient device

for they who have no scruples about useing it.

D. Of the two passages that follow, the first is an excerpt from a student essay; the second is a revised version made after the instructor's criticism. Study both versions and decide what the criticisms were.

(*1*)

My response to the story itself was one of sympathy and anger. To me, the Greek concept of justice is unjustifiable. In basing their law solely on logic, the Greeks completely disregarded the fact that man is at least partially an emotional creature. In fact, there are times in every person's life when emotion is the dominating factor.

I felt extremely sorry for Oedipus. It is indeed tragic that such misfortune should befall so great a man while others, much more deserving of such a fate, are seemingly immune. Indeed, it seems to me that Oedipus was dealt an unjustly cruel fate, and, whether he was predestined or not, he was undeserving of what befell him.

(2)

My response to the story was one of sympathy for Oedipus and anger towards the Greek concept of justice. I felt exceedingly sorry for Oedipus.

His efforts to escape the fate prophesied for him showed that he was a man who despised evil and sought to avoid it. His insistence in uncovering the truth about the killing of Laius, even after that truth began to point to him as the killer, showed both obedience to the will of Apollo and moral courage of a high order. His willingness to impose upon himself a punishment exceeding that which he had decreed when he thought some other man was guilty showed great nobility. I saw in Oedipus a man who had first saved Thebes by his wisdom and then saved it again by sacrificing himself for the public good.

That such a sacrifice was necessary angered me. I felt myself in rebellion against the Greek concept of justice. This concept excused Laius for attacking Oedipus, but condemned Oedipus for defending himself. It tolerated a king's deliberate attempt to kill his baby son by piercing the infant's feet and abandoning it on a mountain, but later branded the son's unintentional killing of his father as murder. It held Oedipus responsible for his ignorance, but excused those, including Apollo, who contributed to that ignorance. This concept of justice held Oedipus to a standard of conduct that no one else was required to meet.

E. Study the following essay carefully, making notes on its strengths and its weaknesses; then come to class prepared to discuss any revisions you think desirable.

Somebody Does Care[6]

The tenderfoot hunters from the city followed amazed as their trusty guide directed them through the pathways and byways of the forest in search of game. By day and by night, his unerring sense of direction and location seemed infallible. This remarkable ability caused one of the hunters to inquire, "Say, have you ever been lost in your life?"

"Well, not exactly lost," came the reply, "but I was awfully confused for about a week once."

This little anecdote illustrates the quandary facing the average college freshman as he starts his college career. The degree of bewilderment will vary with the individual but the situation in itself is fairly universal. This condition is brought about by the abrupt transition from the humdrum of everyday life to the hurly-burly of the college campus during freshman week. All the roots of seventeen or eighteen years' growth are brutally yanked up and transported to an alien soil. Here the stripling must take root and become self-sustaining again. The job of thriving well in a new climate and environment is the crux of the problem. Unless the student can adjust favorably in a comparatively short time, he may find that the inability to do so will be a major deterrent to his progress in the classroom and elsewhere.

Certainly, it can be said that the first few weeks in school are hectic for the freshman. It cannot be otherwise when all the factors are considered.

[6] Ronald W. Sadewater, "Somebody Does Care." From *The Green Caldron: A Magazine of Freshman Writing* (October, 1957), published at the University of Illinois, Urbana, Illinois. Reprinted by permission.

Along with the acquisition of a new home, come new friends and neighbors. These friends and neighbors bring about adjustments in behavior and attitudes as the processes of "getting along" and "belonging" begin. All sorts of tests are taken, until the freshman wishes he had never heard of an IBM card or a placement examination. When the tests are finished, the freshman is plunged into the registration maelstrom and whirled around for a day or two. (If he is lucky, a weekend breather will follow this, before the beginning of classes and more woe.)

With the start of classes, the student must buckle down and apply himself immediately. Class schedules usually end up so arranged that the ten-minute break cannot be used in any manner except in running hither or yon. (Students who want morning classes attend in the afternoon; those desiring afternoon classes attend in the morning.) The first day in class finds homework being assigned, even though books have not yet been purchased. This is no problem, however, for the bookstores are seldom crowded or out of stock. The assignment itself is given in a low tone of voice as the instructor noisily stuffs his papers in a briefcase. Anyone who doesn't get the assignment is a rotten egg.

All of these things compounded together in the first few weeks make the university seem to be a cold and forbidding institution that has only one desire in mind, to discourage the meek and send them scurrying home disgusted, panicked, or dazed.

At this point the phrase, "nobody cares," suggests itself to the student. With this attitude in mind, the freshman plods along day by day in a zombie-like existence, little caring what happens. He goes here and there at a given time because that is what his schedule says to do. Classes somehow come and go with the student little realizing what is going on or why. If this state continues, another student will be gone before the term is very old.

Fortunately, however, at this point the transition usually begins to manifest itself. While sitting in a class one day, the words of the professor accidentally pierce the hard outer shell of the cranium and lodge in the soft core of the brain. One statement ignites a spark and causes the fledgling student to realize that the instructor knows his onions and, if this is true, that there might be something in college life after all. The neophyte begins to see things that were hidden for awhile under a cloak of homesickness or melancholy. He suddenly sees that people do care. His schoolmates care, although they are busy and have troubles of their own. They are not too busy, however, to lend a hand with a trig problem or a rhet theme that will not jell. Parents at home do care and didn't ship him off to be forgotten. By not running down to see their boy or girl every week, or not having them home, they are doing a great service to the student. They are removing a crutch that must be done without. Parents who assist their children too much perform a great disservice.

Teachers and faculty do care, also, although not in the overindulgent manner of their school cousins. In high school the teacher led the way while the student followed. If a student lagged, a teacher would help him forward. Balky students were even pushed through. Here in college the student must lead or lag on his own. Instructors will not chase a student and wipe his nose for him. A sincere student in difficulty, however, can find help close at hand.

31

A short session during a teacher's office hours has straightened out many a student. With a little effort on the student's part, college life can be profitable in both fun and education. The buildings that were cold and lonely become warm and friendly. Instructors that seemed to be of another breed turn out to be normal and understanding members of the human race. If the student is willing to carry his share, he need not fear. The way is hard, but the path has been blazed by thousands of others in the same situations. At times, the student may again become awfully confused, but at this point he should remember that people really do care.

2

Subjects into Theses

Much of the writing a student does in his Freshman English course is likely to be on subjects of his own choosing. The first thing he must do, then, is decide what he is going to write about. But choice of a subject is only a starting point. More important than the subject is how the writer views it, what he sees in it and has to say about it. The problem, in other words, is essentially one of arriving at a thesis, a controlling purpose or point of view. In this chapter we shall consider this whole process: choosing a subject, restricting it to a scope that can be treated with some thoroughness, selecting the material, and stating the purpose or dominant idea of the paper.

Choosing a Subject

When you are given a free choice of subject, do not spend too much time deciding between alternatives. A certain amount of cautious deliberation is wise, because you will almost certainly write with more confidence and authority if the subject is one with which you have had experience. Beyond that, the choice of a subject is less important than what you do with it. Recall how greatly the first three essays in Chapter 1 differed in grasp of purpose. The marked difference between "Through the Trees to the Forest" and the two others came not from the subject but from the writer's *thinking* about it.

To recognize that it is not the subject but what the writer does with it that counts, consider the following essay.

HONEST? OF COURSE I AM[1]

Last summer when I was being interviewed for a scholarship, the interviewer asked me if I considered myself to be an honest person. I replied,

[1] Anonymous, "Honest? Of Course I Am." From *The Green Caldron: A Magazine of Freshman Writing* (December, 1957), published at the University of Illinois, Urbana, Illinois. Reprinted by permission.

"Yes," and thought a little indignantly, of course I am. Does he suppose that I'm going to use the scholarship money for something besides college?

I was correct in saying that I was honest in respect to the scholarship money. I would have considered misusing it a crime. My definition of dishonesty included, among other things, any form of stealing. Actually, though, if I or one of my friends had taken a package of chewing gum or some other small insignificant item from the corner grocery, I probably would have made a joke of it.

It appears that I wouldn't have applied my standard of dishonesty to myself or to my friends. This would have been especially true if the dishonest act was committed on a dare or unthinkingly. That is, I wouldn't have applied it before I was caught in dishonesty myself.

I was employed last summer by a dairy company at the state fair. The employees where I worked received their lunches free by merely going through the kitchen and behind the counter to get the food. I had been eating in back of the kitchen with a friend who was working at another part of the fairgrounds. With the original intention of paying for it, I got his lunch at the same time I got mine, so that he wouldn't have to wait in the long lines. However when I couldn't get to the cashier, I didn't pay. The third time this incident occurred the manager called me aside, stated that he had seen me, and then fired me.

Of course my friends told me that everyone "stole" a milkshake now and then, and that I just happened to get caught. Probably it seems ridiculous to suffer a guilty conscience over a couple of pilfered milkshakes, but then most people haven't been caught stealing. They haven't had their inflated opinions of their honesty pricked, as I have.

When asked if they were honest, I wonder if these people could reply, "Honest? Of course I am." I couldn't.

This essay is more than a report of a stolen milkshake. It is a young man's evaluation of an experience which disturbed his own image of himself and forced him to explore the limits of his honesty. In the process he discovered something about himself. The reader not only shares that discovery but recognizes that it also applies to him, so that the trifling incident takes on wider significance and becomes a comment on people in general. The point to recognize is that this significance does not come from the subject but from what the writer has seen in the subject.

The poet Sir Philip Sidney once answered his own perplexity about suitable subjects by ending a sonnet with this advice to himself — "Fool, look in thy heart and write." It is good advice for most of us. The student who looks into his own experience and tries honestly to evaluate it is sure to have something fresh and interesting to say because his work will reflect the uniqueness of his own personality. Much freshman writing is dull and insipid because the writer does not involve himself in what he is writing. An essay which does reveal its author as a genuine personality rises conspicuously above run-of-the-mill performances. Test this observation against the following essay.

What I Am versus What I Want to Be[2]

Now I am a college coed. Now I go to winter formals and Coke exchanges. Now I go TGIF-ing* on Fridays. Now I cheer George Bonsalle, Ted Caiazza and the Fighting Illini on to victory. Now I study for hourlies and pray for "Aces."

I remember the hectic fun of freshman week. I remember the first date I had with a senior. I remember the thrilling excitement of the Michigan upset. I remember the carnival appearance of Homecoming. I remember that anxiously awaited Thanksgiving vacation and the first snowfall on campus.

All this I remember; all this I'm doing; all this I am.

To say that I've had fun is very true indeed. I've enjoyed being part of this campus. However, there's a voice within the soul of every man that keeps repeating, "What do I want to be?" Every man must answer it according to his conscience. Until a few short months ago I thought I had stifled the voice and answered the question. I had plans for a journalistic career. It seemed to be what I wanted more than anything else. But the voice didn't cease; the question wasn't answered.

A few short weeks ago amid the silent atmosphere of a church, I found the answer. At the end of the semester, I shall leave the bustle of campus life to enter the quietness of a convent. I shall leave the Illinois pennants and the dance bids; I shall leave the gold formal I bought especially for our house dance; I shall leave the Saturday night dates.

And what will I get in return? I will find the rarest thing on earth today — peace. I will find the opportunity to love and help. I will find a faith that is strengthened and a knowledge that is broadened. I will find new concepts and different ideals. But most of all I will find the answer to the question, the reply to the voice.

Do not assume, however, that I will forget the ways of college. I don't want to forget. College has been a part of my life, a part of my fondest memories. Who wishes to destroy a treasured memory? College has given me the ability to live among the people of this world, and I must understand if I am to help.

This is what I want to do.

Take time to consider your response to this essay. Ignore your agreement or disagreement with the girl's decision. Just consider the effect on you of what she wrote. Then try to state as clearly as you can what that effect was and what caused it.

Restricting the Subject

Often students overlook good topics because they fail to see that what they think of as one experience is really a series of experiences, any part

---

[2] Carrol Hinkle, "What I Am versus What I Want to Be." From *The Green Caldron: A Magazine of Freshman Writing* (April, 1957), published at the University of Illinois, Urbana, Illinois. Reprinted by permission.

* TGIF = Thank God it's Friday.

of which might make an effective paper. For example, see how a visit to New York may be broken into many separate topics.

>The New York skyline
>Driving in New York
>My first subway ride
>The view from the Empire State Building
>Rockefeller Center — A city within a city
>Chinatown
>Harlem
>Eating in an automat
>The waterfront
>The Stock Exchange in action
>Shopping in New York
>Greenwich Village restaurants
>New York cabbies — fact and legend
>A visit to the United Nations

When, as in the illustration above, we break a subject into subtopics, we are *restricting* it. Restriction not only reduces the subject to a scope that will permit thorough treatment; it also helps define the purpose of the essay and so guides the writer's thinking. For example, suppose you are interested in the Presidential election of 1960 as the subject of a long paper. You begin to read about that election and soon discover that it contains more subtopics than you can handle in one essay; so you restrict the subject by limiting it to the part that most interests you — let us say, the televised debates between the candidates.

Now you have a subject which, though still large, can be dealt with in one essay, and you also know what kind of material you need. You still do not have a clear purpose, but you have a much better chance of arriving at one than you had when you began. As you read more intensively on your restricted subject, you may come to a conclusion about the debates — that they were a great stimulus to public interest in the election, that they revealed no basic political issues between the candidates or their parties, that the method of conducting the debates deprived them of much of their potential usefulness, that agreeing to the debates was an error in Republican strategy, or some other. When you reach such a conclusion, you will have established your purpose.

Students are often tempted to restrict an autobiographical subject merely by cutting the time it covers — that is, by confining themselves to a single year of their lives or to a particular summer vacation. Such restriction is often more obvious than useful. The goal of restriction is to get a topic which can be completely developed in a single paper. Usually simple restriction in time does not achieve that goal. On the other hand, a paper may deal with several years of the writer's life and still be thoroughly restricted, as long as the author is selecting from these years only those experiences that have a clear connection with his main idea. Consider, for example, the following essay written by a University of Wisconsin student:

I Know the Value of Money[3]

My parents wanted me to grow up independent, capable of managing my possessions and my life. So when I was still a child, they began their training which has accomplished just the object they had in view.

On my twelfth birthday Mother and Daddy sat me down for a talk which I shall always remember. "It isn't just age that makes a person wise and capable," they told me. "Nor is it having lots of money and a fine social position. Knowing your own mind, your own affairs, and the value of money is one of the greatest things to which a person can aspire, and this is what we want to teach you."

So with $15 a month for my very own I began my life as a person within myself. With that money, $10 of which I got from Daddy the first of the month, and $5 from Mother on the fifteenth, I had to take care of all my expenses, clothes included. It was rather difficult at first, buying all my own things, but any important article I brought home and had Mother put on the final approval.

Fifteen dollars seemed enormous to me, but I soon discovered that I couldn't persist in eating sweets and ice creams to any great extent if I wanted to be dressed as well as the other girls and have my clothes in repair. Money just didn't go anywhere near that far. I was lucky to have a considerably well stocked wardrobe when I started out, for I didn't have to worry about needing such a thing as a coat, which would have been a little too expensive for me to know how to budget.

My parents took care of the expense of my school books, so I was relieved of that large burden. A typical monthly account for me from the ages of 12 to 14 was as follows:

Clothes	$10
Cleaning and repair	2
Spending	3
	$15

Through those years, my father was making a comparatively small salary, and I couldn't have had more even if it was merited. So when I was 14 years old and Daddy was given a raise, my allowance underwent a similar change.

As prices of wearing apparel went up considerably at that time, my family felt I needed a little more to make ends meet, so I was given $5 more, making my monthly allotment $20. I contrived to buy fewer clothes, thereby spending only slightly more for this item than I had in the previous two years.

I also learned to sew, and made four or five summer dresses each year, which carried me through the brunt of the season at a greatly reduced cost. By doing this I was able to have more during the winter, for I prodigiously saved whatever I could. From the time I was 14 until I reached 17, my expenses were:

[3] From "I Know the Value of Money" by Jean R. McDuffie, in *Parents' Magazine,* May, 1941. Reprinted by permission.

Clothes	$13
Cleaning and repair	2
Spending	5
	——
	$20

Daddy usually gave me a heavy coat at the beginning of the winter, and that was supposed to last clear through, but when I found I needed another for spring or fall, as a rule I bought one on the installment plan, paying $5 a month for it until the bill was paid. Only once did I have a charge account, and that was responsible for the only time I slipped up on my obligations.

There was a small all-purpose shop near where we lived, and there I did most of my shopping. For Christmas, I had many friends, aside from my family, to whom I wished to give presents.

Wanting to try my luck at a charge account some months before December, I opened one at the shop and proceeded to charge everything I bought. The end of the first month my pocketbook permitted the payment, but on the conclusion of the second month it was slightly in the reverse.

I wasn't a bit worried, for I figured I could stint through December and settle at the close of that month. There I didn't reckon with the Yuletide spirit, for when my bill came the second of January, I was $50 in debt. That was the only time I was forced to seek family aid. Daddy gave me $35 for a Christmas present and I added $15 to finish the charge account once and for all. . . .

When I was 17 . . . I began to want more substantial articles. I saw a beautiful radio one day for $65, and nothing would do but I should have it. Have it I did, on the installment plan, and I thought I would never finish paying for it. To bolster my depleted pocketbook, I undertook to teach ballroom dancing lessons in the recreation room of our home. . . .

Making my own decisions was wonderful. My parents never gave me any advice on any of them. When I asked their opinions they simply discussed the case from both sides, leaving the ultimate issue to my own discretion. . . . As a result, I have learned how and where to shop to get the most for the smallest sum. I know good quality from poor, and I am sure that when I marry, no matter how little money my husband may have, I will be able to get along on it and handle it efficiently.

My parents wanted me to grow up independent, capable of managing my possessions and my life. They have accomplished their purpose.

Here is an excellent example of purposeful restriction. The author knew exactly what she wanted to do — to show that she knew the value of money by telling in detail how she learned its value. That purpose required her to report her talk with her parents on her twelfth birthday. It also required her to show, through the years, her struggles to achieve financial responsibility: her temptations and mistakes, the need to supplement her income when she wanted things she could not afford, the determined way her parents forced her to make her own decisions. Her restricted purpose kept the paper unified. It acted as a safeguard against wandering into incidents which, however interesting, had no immediate connection with the title of her essay.

Selecting the Material

In general, your material will be drawn from memory, from direct observation, from reading, or from a combination of these sources. For essays like "I Know the Value of Money" and most of those printed in Chapter 1, selecting the material is not difficult. Most of it will come spontaneously to mind, because a sense of purpose stimulates the recall of pertinent information and blocks out what is irrelevant.

But for essays on subjects such as the 1960 election, information has to be deliberately sought in published sources and is usually recorded in notes. For such essays, material and purpose interact. You study your subject, make notes, and gradually begin to see what you can do with your material. This procedure involves some unnecessary note-taking, since some of the early notes will have to be discarded as your growing sense of purpose makes them no longer pertinent.

This interrelation between purpose and material makes it advisable to restrict your subject as much and as early as possible. Until you know what you want to do, you cannot tell what material you will use and therefore you cannot be sure what notes will be pertinent. Thus, a student working on the 1960 election is not ready to take useful notes until he has decided what aspect he is going to deal with — for example, the televised debates. The sooner he can reach that decision the more pertinent his note-taking will be.

If you wish to do successful work in college, you should develop the habit of checking the trustworthiness of your sources. Things are not necessarily so because they appear in print or because someone says they are so. In all areas, but especially in argument, you owe it to yourself, as well as to your reader, to challenge the reliability of the reports and judgments that you find in your sources. It is often difficult for a freshman to decide which of two conflicting reports or opinions or sets of statistics is the more reliable, but you can usually find out from a librarian or your instructor which of two magazines or newspapers is the more trustworthy, and you can check on the author of a book to learn whether he is a competent and unbiased authority. You are finally responsible for the sources you use, and you should be aware that any consistent use of unreliable material will discredit your work.

Stating the Purpose

A good title will often so restrict the topic that it implies the purpose of the paper. A title like "I Know the Value of Money" gives a reader a pretty good clue to the development of the essay. For short papers such a title may be sufficient to control the writer's and the reader's approach to the essay. But for most papers it will be wise to go one step further — to make a formal statement of the purpose which the title implies.

Purpose Statements: The Thesis

For many student essays the most useful — and the most exacting — kind of purpose statement is the *thesis*. A thesis is a single sentence, *preferably a simple sentence,* which expresses the basic idea the paper is to develop. The thesis is to the whole paper what the topic sentence or topic idea is to the paragraph. The following sentences might serve either as topic sentences for paragraphs or as theses for whole essays:

> The first requirement of a good speaker is a sense of confidence.
> Final examinations encourage cramming.
> All stories to the contrary, women drive as carefully as men.

A good thesis is *restricted, unified,* and *precise.* To be restricted, it must indicate which of several approaches to the subject the writer will take. It thus limits the scope of the paper to what can be properly discussed in the space available. For example, such a thesis as "There are serious objections to compulsory national health insurance" does not specify what objections the author is going to present. To discuss all the objections in detail would take several thousand words. The easy way is to state those that come readily to mind and discuss them superficially. In contrast, the following theses clearly say which particular objection the writer will discuss, and thus limit him to something he may do fairly thoroughly in 500 to 1000 words.

> Compulsory national health insurance would encourage hypochondriacs to monopolize a doctor's time.
> Compulsory national health insurance would destroy the friendly relationship that now exists between doctors and their patients.
> Compulsory national health insurance would reduce the doctor's incentive to keep abreast of new medical discoveries.
> Compulsory national health insurance would increase, rather than decrease, the number of man hours lost through sickness.
> Compulsory national health insurance has always cost much more than its supporters estimated it would cost.

All five of these theses, and several more, lay hidden under the general, unrestricted statement that "There are serious objections to compulsory national health insurance." The unrestricted thesis gives the reader no real clue to what the author plans to do, and often makes the writer think his purpose is clear when he has little more than a general subject and perhaps a title. An unrestricted thesis invites vague thinking, meandering organization, and superficial comment.

A good thesis is unified as well as restricted. To be unified, it must commit the writer to deal with only one dominant idea. Such a thesis as "The United Nations Organization has major weaknesses and cannot prevent a major war" requires the writer to do two things, not one. He must (1) demonstrate the weaknesses and (2) prove that the UN cannot prevent a major war. A paper with this double purpose will almost certainly fall into two parts having little connection with each other. If the writer believes that these two points are related — perhaps that one results from the other — he should show that relation in his thesis: "The organization of the UN makes it incapable of preventing a war between major powers." This thesis restricts the discussion to those features of organization which make the UN powerless to avert a major war and thus fuses the two parts into a unified purpose statement.

In the following theses the lack of unity at the left is removed in the revision at the right:

Printing has had a long and complex history, during which it has brought about social and cultural reforms.	The development of printing has brought about social and cultural reforms.
Fraternities have grown rapidly in this country and fulfill a social need.	Fraternities have grown rapidly in this country because they fulfill a social need.

In the first of these pairs, the thesis at the left requires the writer to do two things: first, to recount the history of printing — a big job in itself — and then to show the social and cultural reforms which have come from printing. The revision rules out much of the history and restricts the writer to the single task of showing how certain social and cultural improvements were made possible by advances in printing. Similarly, the first statement about fraternities would make two papers — one a history, the other a justification. The revision requires the writer to select evidence from the history to show that fraternities have flourished because they were useful. A paper with this thesis will be an argument which draws evidence from the social value which fraternities have demonstrated.

Note that the two revised statements express a logical relationship between two parts of a subject at first unrelated. In these examples the relationship is one of cause and effect. To find such a relationship is "to have an idea" — to perceive a truth or gain an understanding. This idea gives direction to your thinking and so shapes your writing.

Finally, a thesis should be precise. It should be phrased in words which permit only one interpretation. Especially it should avoid words and phrases which are so general that they convey no exact meaning. For example, such statements as

My home town is one of the most interesting towns in the state.
Winston Churchill has had a colorful career.

are useless as statements of purpose because the key words "interesting" and "colorful" could mean almost anything and hence exert no real control over what the writer does. A student who sets out to show that his home town is "interesting" is almost sure to end with an essay "about" his home town; one who intends to show that Churchill has had a colorful career is likely to write "about" Churchill's life. Any student who intends to write "about" a subject has not yet established his purpose. He has merely lulled himself into a false sense of achievement.

Avoid figures of speech in a thesis. Metaphors and similes can be vivid and expressive within a composition, or even in a title, but in a thesis they can easily hide a confusion that might be exposed in a more literal statement. Consider this: "Where instructors are concerned, all that glitters is not gold." Does the sentence mean that the most entertaining instructors are not always the most helpful, or that the most accomplished scholars are not always the best teachers? Or does it merely mean that instructors are not always what they seem to be? The statement does not communicate a clear purpose. It may seem apt or clever, but in a thesis clarity is more important than effect.

The unsatisfactory theses we have looked at all fail to define purposes clearly. We saw in Chapter 1 that a serious concern with purpose requires a discipline which a writer will often wish to escape. A student who escapes it by writing a statement of purpose which is unrestricted, not unified, or vague will fail to guide the development of his paper and will deceive only himself. He gains nothing by this self-deception. It is always wiser to thrash out the basic decision about purpose once and for all when writing the purpose statement.

✔ Can you identify the weaknesses of the following purpose statements and suggest how to improve them? Watch especially for figures of speech and vague words in key places.

1. Hockey is an exciting game.
2. Eisenhower was a greater President than Truman.
3. The U-2 incident was deplorable.
4. The atomic bomb is the most powerful instrument of destruction ever devised and there is no adequate defense against it.
5. During my senior year in high school I had some very interesting and educational trips.
6. This essay will deal with the advisability of working one's way through college.
7. The study of foreign languages is an excellent discipline.
8. The evils of professionalism in college athletics should be considered.
9. The forthcoming conference with Russia may pave the way to ending the cold war, but we better not count our chickens before they are hatched.
10. The life of Abraham Lincoln should be an inspiration to all of us.

Purpose Statements: Other Forms

A thesis is a statement of the basic *idea* of an essay. Many quite purposeful compositions, however, do not develop an idea, but present information or impressions. They may explain a process, give directions, or describe a person, place, or event. Such purposes require you to report what you see or know. They are concerned with facts rather than with ideas, and they do not require a thesis.

For example, if you want to explain the operation of a Diesel engine or to summarize the events leading to the Boston Tea Party, your paper will not have a dominant idea, although it will have a clear purpose. Any attempt to pretend it has a thesis by writing some such statement as "The operation of the Diesel engine is complex" or "The background of the Boston Tea Party is interesting" would waste time and distort your real intention. For you are concerned not with the complexity of the Diesel engine but with its mode of operation, and you have no intention of proving that the events leading up to the Boston Tea Party were "interesting" but only of showing what they were.

Although an essay may not have a dominant idea, it must have a purpose, and putting that purpose down on paper will be helpful. The following statements are not theses, but they make the purpose clear and help toward efficient development:

> In this paper I want to recreate the incident in which a rattler crawled over me. I don't just want to summarize the incident. I want to make the reader see what I saw and feel what I felt.
>
> I intend to illustrate the four most common kinds of changes in the meanings of words by tracing the evolution of *lady, gossip, boycott,* and *acorn.*
>
> This paper will explain how the New York Fair Employment Practices Commission works by reporting two case histories: one in which there was discrimination, and one in which there was not.

These statements not only record purpose but also suggest how the paper will be developed. Each is, in effect, a basic plan for the paper. A writer who states his purpose so explicitly has taken a long step in planning the development of his essay.

Summary

This chapter may be summarized briefly as five pieces of advice:

1. When you find yourself flitting from topic to topic, pick the likeliest one and concentrate on it until you see what to do with it. Remember that in the long run the subject is less important than your treatment of it.

2. If your subject is general (*A Trip to New York*), restrict it, either by breaking it into its parts or by adopting a point of view toward it (*Rockefeller Center — A City Within a City*). Restriction from a point of view will determine your purpose more quickly.

3. To develop your subject, you need material that is both adequate and pertinent. Frequently the material will be drawn from your own experience and will be suggested by your sense of purpose. If the material has to be selected from printed sources, be as sure as you can that these are reliable.

4. When you are satisfied that your topic is sufficiently restricted, establish your purpose by writing a thesis or other purpose statement. Make sure that this statement is restricted, unified, and precise.

5. If your paper is not going to develop a dominant idea, express its purpose in the form that best suggests its development.

Exercises

A. The following essays are representative of good freshman writing. Read them as preparation for Exercise B.

THE BULLFIGHT[4]

In Spain, the bullfight is more than a sport: it is a part of the country's culture. The crises, the exciting moments in American sports, seem trivial compared to the Spanish contest between man and beast. In every bullfight, the matador faces death, pits his skill, strength, and knowledge against that of a bull whose only desire is to kill him.

Every Spanish bullfight fan is an afficionado; he can tell a dangerous pass from one which simply looks dangerous, and a good kill from a cowardly one. Most of the fans know about bullfighting from having tried it in an amateur fight. In fact, almost all Spanish boys have the desire to be a matador; and a great many try, some succeeding, others becoming banderillos or picadors, but most settling for a seat at as many bullfights as they can possibly attend. Because of their knowledge of the sport, the spectators are extremely critical, and a poor performance is always marked by the boos of the crowd and a barrage of seat cushions, wine bottles, and shoes. However, it is the same knowledge which makes the sport an impromptu art, a communication of emotion between matador and crowd.

The bullfight fan is like the American jazz fan who goes to hear the same group night after night, waiting for that one electrifying moment of the creative artist at his best; most of the time the music is mediocre, but when it's at its best, nothing else matters. And when the great matador, reaching his peak with a brave, strong bull, stands poised over those horns, hoping (but not knowing) that they won't come up and dig his very guts out, hoping that the sword doesn't hit a bone and break off in his hand, plunges his sword down into the back of the bull's neck and punctures the bull's lungs (he hopes), and when every man who ever saw an amateur bullfight or faced a bull or ran from one, knowing what it means to lean over a bull's horns and expose one's groin, holds his breath and, not saying a word, watches the matador in the hot, bright sun, on the white sand prove for the whole world to see his courage and strength and skill, sees him become one with the proud, noble, strong bull — this is the moment of truth.

So the bullfight is not a sport at all, but an art — not comparable to

[4] George M. Highsmith, "The Bullfight." From *The Green Caldron: A Magazine of Freshman Writing* (April, 1960), published at the University of Illinois, Urbana, Illinois. Reprinted by permission.

American baseball or American anything — the art of the matador who fights one day in Madrid, then sleeps in the back seat of a car filled with costumes, capes, sword, and manager's cigar smoke as it bounces over dirt roads, and despite T.B. or syphilis, or probably both, gets out of the car in time to eat, dress, and enter the arena to face two specially bred bulls in one afternoon, hoping to kill those bulls honorably, knowing that if he does, he will be a hero, and if he doesn't, he will be insulted verbally and physically.

PUT THE MAN TOGETHER[5]

Dr. Ethel Alpenfels, the well-known anthropologist, spoke to a group of high school students recently on their role in society. After discussing the goals and the problems of her adolescent audience, Dr. Alpenfels related an anecdote which I consider to be invaluable to any teenager or adult who doesn't realize his individual worth and importance in our modern society.

On an especially humid and uncomfortable day, the doctor explained, a young child was annoying his weary father. "What can I do?" the youngster begged. "Give me something to play with, Daddy." The parent, wishing to be rid of the child, reached for a map of the world and cut it into varied shapes.

"Here," the lad's father said, "take this puzzle and see if you can put it back together."

Jumping at the unusual plaything, the child soon became engrossed in it, while his father relaxed and eagerly anticipated a few hours of peace.

In a few moments, however, the boy returned with the map, which was perfectly pieced together. His father was amazed. "How did you do this?" he demanded.

"Oh," his son replied, "there was a picture of a man on the other side of the map. So I just put the man together and the world came out all right!"

With this, Dr. Alpenfels concluded her speech, but each of us in the audience left remembering her important advice — "Just put the man together and the world comes out all right." It was a child's thought, and yet it is often difficult for the adults of today's society and those of us who will be adults of tomorrow's society to remember the importance of man in relation to the world. Men such as David Riesman, one of the authors of *The Lonely Crowd,* have emphasized the problem of conformity. *The Organization Man* also deals with this subject. For example, what are the citizens of our own country doing to create the feeling of individuality in American education and politics?

In our school systems too much importance is placed on being "a regular guy." Joe College and Betty Coed seem to have over-run the campuses of our country. Children are enrolled in our elementary schools at the age of five and usually progress upward on the educational ladder until they reach the end of their compulsory education. Group living and social studies are stressed in the child's elementary and high-school education, but is he taught to be an individual? I believe that there are too many cases in which he does

[5] Leah Meyer, "Put the Man Together." From *The Green Caldron: A Magazine of Freshman Writing* (December, 1957), published at the University of Illinois, Urbana, Illinois. Reprinted by permission.

not learn this important lesson. How much more satisfactory the process of learning would be if every student were allowed to progress at his own rate, feeling neither superior nor inferior to his group, but rather, feeling the importance of his individuality.

Our country's political affairs, too, stress the crowd rather than the human being. "Join the bandwagon and vote for our candidate!" is the campaign cheer, rather than "Think for yourself and vote wisely." Perhaps this too relates back to our educational system. Learning to reason and think for himself should be today's student's major lesson.

A better world, a hopeful future — these I believe could belong to posterity if only we would begin to realize the importance of "I" rather than "we." If our "indifference to being different" can be corrected, I believe we will have accomplished Dr. Alpenfels' dream. Like the young boy, we will have "put the man together" and the world will "come out all right!"

PLACES OF PLEASURE[6]

One night, because we had nothing better to do, my roommate and another girl and I hopped in the car and set off for a grand tour of the campus "joints." On my journey I found neither dens of iniquity nor glimpses of a promised land, but merely the mildly amusing sequence of scenes I had expected. I say amusing, for nothing is more a point of gentle laughter than a child; no one can help smiling when he sees a youngster mimicking the ludicrous actions of his elders in all seriousness; and at every place I went I saw children playing at being adults.

I saw children smoking in every way they had ever seen: in a nervous, endless chain; languidly as Cleopatra; in the fashion of underworld characters; or with a pseudo-sophisticated flick of the wrist.

I saw children talking in every tone imaginable: boisterously, pretentiously in earnest, in the manner of men and women of the world, or with an air of boredom.

I saw children drinking beer: they drank it from bottles, from glasses, from pitchers; they sipped it, they gulped it, they studied it; they adored it.

And all the time I felt I was in a land of Lilliputians with everything built to size: there were small rooms, cozy seats, tiny bottles, pint-sized ash trays, baby-faced proprietors, and little boy waiters. What could be more charming! And yet after a few moments of amusement I found myself becoming absolutely bored.

Not once did I see any one of these imitation cosmopolitans smoking for the sheer pleasure of it, talking because he had something to say, or drinking because he liked beer. Rather, they all gave me the impression that they had come, had sat, had smoked, had talked, had drunk, and were waiting for the enchanted words to be spoken and the magic dust sprinkled on their curly little heads and the wonderful miracle of "having a good time" to occur. I could see it running through their minds: "Adults can do what they want; this is what they do, so it must be fun."

[6] Jane Lewis, "Places of Pleasure." From *The Green Caldron: A Magazine of Freshman Writing* (December, 1961), published at the University of Illinois, Urbana, Illinois. Reprinted by permission.

My feeling of boredom melted to pity and I felt moved to cry out in a ringing voice with dramatic pauses — "Unhappy generation! You are right in your unhappiness. Your pleasures are not dictated to you. There is more joy to living than this. Rise up! Go forth!" — when suddenly it occurred to me that perhaps I was the odd personality, unable to enjoy standard entertainment. Maybe they were really having a good time.

In a cloud of uncertainty I followed my friends back to the dorm and got into the shower, the only place where my powers of reasoning function properly, and began to talk to myself.

"Jane," I said, "you have smoked L & M, Lucky Strike, Viceroy, Marlboro, Winston, Kentucky Brand, Camel, Chesterfield, and homemade cigarettes. You have talked to priests, psychiatrists, businessmen, teachers, teenagers, Chinese, Czechoslovakians, Japanese, Hawaiians, Germans, Hungarians, Swedish, English, and Americans about life, death, philosophy, sex, politics, morals, religion, and the future of America. You have drunk whiskey, vodka, rum, gin, vermouth, champagne, and your father's wine in bedrooms, barrooms, bathrooms, bowling alleys, basements, cocktail lounges, cars, and swimming pools. Have or have not all these things been fun?"

"Yes," I sighed, remembering.

"And have you or have you not enjoyed, along with smoking, jabbering, and drinking, the pleasures of reading, listening to music, watching plays, and praying on your knees to a hidden God?"

"I have," I replied, beginning to see the light.

"Then what right have you to laugh at, sneer at, pity, or judge the people you saw in the places you went to tonight?"

"No right at all," I whispered, scrubbing my ears.

But as I turned on the cold water all my confidence and defiance came back to me and "There was something sad and wrong in those places!" I cried to my departing self.

B. As an exercise in thinking out the purpose, plan, and content of an essay, select a specific subject from each of the general directions given below. Restrict that subject so as to deal with it from a particular point of view. Without writing an essay, think out what your purpose would be and how that purpose would affect your selection and arrangement of material. Carry the thinking out to the stage at which you could give your instructor or classmates a preview of the essay you have planned.

1. Using "The Bullfight" as a suggested procedure, choose a sport or other activity (Basketball, the Twist, the World Series, etc.), think of what it means to its enthusiasts, and plan an essay to communicate that meaning to others.

2. Using "Put the Man Together" as a suggested procedure, select some statement you have heard or read and use it as a text for an essay which is critical of some modern trend.

3. Using "Places of Pleasure" as a suggested procedure, select some phase of student conduct and evaluate it.

C. Select any one of the topics you have previewed in *B* above and develop it into an essay.

3

Outlining

Outlining is an intermediate stage between deciding the purpose and developing it. In short papers, especially narrative or descriptive ones, a student who knows what he is doing may safely write without an outline, though even for the simplest papers many students make "scratch outlines" — that is, they jot down the main topics they want to discuss. For essays like those in the first two chapters, the kind of *topic sentence* or *paragraph* outline illustrated in Chapter 1 is often sufficient. But for longer, more complex essays a more formal outline is usually needed.

Because making a sound outline is a rigorous exercise in logic, students sometimes try to escape it. Every instructor is familiar with the question, "Can't I write the outline *after* I write the paper? It's a lot easier that way." This is much like asking, "Can't I study the road map after I make the trip?" or "Can't I draw the plans after I build the house?" Such a request misinterprets the use of an outline, which is to work out a plan and a procedure. Once the paper has been successfully written, the plan is no longer needed. Certainly a writer may make changes in organization during the writing or revision if he feels they will improve his work. But if a paper requires careful planning, the planning should be done before the basic structure is obscured by illustrations and other details. A student who attempts to handle planning and development at the same time is trying to do two difficult jobs at once. The smart thing to do is to tackle them singly.

The Uses of an Outline

A formal outline has four uses: it helps a writer to clarify his purpose and organize his material to achieve that purpose; it offers a convenient way of testing a proposed organization; it occasionally serves as a complete communication in itself; and it may be used as an aid to efficient reading.

Outlining to Determine Purpose

In practice, most of us often begin to outline before we fully understand what we want to do. We use the outline as a tool to help us clarify our thoughts, somewhat as a housewife finds out how she wants the furniture arranged by moving it about the room. Like the housewife, we might save ourselves trouble if we could see, without all this experimenting, how our material should be arranged, but these preliminary outlines are often a necessary means of thinking out our purpose so that we can proceed to the final plan.

Suppose you are to write a long essay on the characteristics of superior college students. As you read and take notes, you will make tentative decisions about your plan. In fact, the plan will grow on you, and you may revise it frequently before you actually sit down to write a formal outline. But for the purposes of this illustration, let us suppose that you have collected a considerable body of pertinent information without making any decision about how to organize it. As you study your notes, you group similar kinds of information together and decide that superior college students show certain characteristics, which you list as follows:

1. They make a rapid survey before reading a chapter.
2. They associate what they learn in one course with work in another.
3. They study alone.
4. They tend to be nonsocial.
5. They are more introverted than other students.
6. They notice the headings in the textbooks.
7. They are more self-conscious than other students.
8. They are younger than most students.
9. They are relatively indifferent to the opposite sex.
10. They are less assertive, but more independent.
11. They take a slightly lighter schedule.
12. They are persistent.
13. They recite to themselves.
14. They clear up any point they do not understand before going on to another.
15. They spend a little more time than the average in study.
16. They are happy in college.
17. They participate in more extracurricular activities, but mostly in clubs in which the interest is intellectual rather than social.
18. They usually have abilities necessary for success in their chosen profession.[1]

As you study these characteristics you begin to see that some of them are related; so you begin to group them under what seem to be topic headings, which at first may look something like this:

> Study habits
> Age
> Personality traits
> Social characteristics

[1] For these characteristics I am indebted to Luella Cole's *The Background for College Teaching* (Copyright by Farrar & Rinehart, Inc., New York, 1940), p. 396. Reprinted by permission.

On reconsidering these headings you see that what you have to say about age could be dismissed in a sentence and that the two dominant topics seem to be study habits and personality traits. So you set these up as headings and group specific characteristics under them:

Personality Traits	*Study Habits*
nonsocial	spend more time on studies
introvertive	study alone
self-conscious	notice headings in textbooks
indifferent to opposite sex	make rapid survey before reading
persistent	recite to themselves
less assertive, more independent	clear up one point before moving on to another
(?) participate in more extracurricular activities, but of intellectual type	associate what they learn in one course with what they learn in another
	(?) take slightly lighter schedules

You put a question mark before some items because you feel that they do not fit very well under their headings, and you see that a pattern is beginning to emerge. Indeed, at this point you are tempted to draft as your thesis: "Superior college students have characteristic personality traits and study habits." But you recognize that if that is all you are going to show you might as well hand in your list of characteristics, since they show all that your thesis asserts.

As you study your material again, you begin to see a variety of possibilities. You could write a paper to show that the superiority of college students is determined by academic rather than by social success. But since that seems self-evident, you reject it. You try "Although superior students are happy in college, they are not socially successful." That looks better, but it puts too much emphasis on personality traits and not enough on study habits. Finally you decide that if you wrote an essay to show that superior students are better adjusted in their academic than in their social activities, you could get a unified paper in which you could use most of your material. So you begin to draft an outline which emerges like this:

Thesis: Superior college students are better adjusted to their academic than to their social environment.
  I. They are well adjusted to their academic environment.
    A. They have efficient study habits.
    B. They supplement their class work with intellectual extracurricular activities.
    C. They are happy in college.
  II. They are less well adjusted to their social environment.
    A. They are introverted and self-conscious.
    B. They are nonsocial.
    C. They are relatively indifferent to the opposite sex.

At this point, assuming that you have the material to develop these topic sentences, the basic organization of your paper is complete. You may still subdivide some of your headings. For example, the study habits might be subdivided, and different nonsocial attitudes might be recognized. But these are refinements.

Outlining to Test Organization

A badly organized paper will not be wholly successful, no matter how well it is written in other ways. Therefore, if there are flaws in your plan, it is wise to detect them before beginning the first draft. Since the outline serves as a sort of X-ray picture of the skeleton of a piece of writing, it offers a convenient and reliable test of organization and allows a change of plan before it is too late.

Examine the following outline made by an instructor from a student research paper which had been turned in without an outline. The purpose statement was taken from the opening paragraph which, as far as the instructor could judge, was intended to state the thesis. Successive paragraphs dealt with the topics shown in the reconstructed outline.

DEFENSE AGAINST NUCLEAR BOMBING

Purpose: To show how to defend against a nuclear attack.
  I. The history of the atomic bomb
     A. From the Chicago experiment to Nagasaki
     B. Since World War II
 II. The threat of nuclear warfare
     A. From Russia
     B. From China
III. The futility of disarmament proposals
 IV. The defense against the bomb
     A. Detecting an attack in time to act
     B. Intercepting attacking aircraft
     C. Reprisal as a deterrent
     D. Minimizing the effect of an explosion
        1. Shelters
        2. Education and civil defense
        3. Dispersal of industry and government buildings

A close look at this outline will show three major weaknesses. First, if the purpose statement is accurate, the first three units — I, II, and III — are irrelevant. They are certainly not main points in a defense against nuclear attack; at most they might make an introductory paragraph or two to emphasize the importance of defense. Second, unit IV of the outline and the purpose statement deal with the same topic, so that IV is not *part* of the purpose but the *whole* of it. This suggests that A, B, C, and D under IV should be made the main units of the outline. Third, if the purpose statement is *not* accurate, the outline has no other discoverable purpose, and is simply a collection of material "about" nuclear warfare.

The moral of this example is not merely that the organization of the essay is poor, but that its weaknesses show up clearly in the outline. Any time spent developing an essay from this outline will be time wasted. Had the student been able to see the organization of his essay as the outline reveals it, he might have saved the time and effort of writing a paper which was bound to fail. He might even have seen what he had to do to get a good essay out of his material.

Outlining as Complete Communication

Sometimes an outline serves as a communication in its own right. College assignments, including examination questions, may specify an outline as the final report. Sometimes an outline is required instead of a summary to show that the student has mastered the content of an essay or a lecture. Occasionally, as an exercise in organization, an instructor will ask his students to arrange material in logical outline form without developing the outline into an essay.

Outlining as a Reading Aid

Much of your college work will consist in digesting the contents of books and essays and explaining and evaluating what you have read. When material is complex — as it often is on such subjects as economics, history, literary criticism, philosophy, and political science — outlining has two advantages: it forces you to watch carefully what the author is doing and how he is doing it, and it gives you, in a form convenient for review, a digest of the basic content.

The following outline reduces a long article to a form which permits a quick review of the original. Even without reading the article you can tell from the outline what the author was saying. It is probable that on the evidence of the outline alone you could answer an examination question on the subject.

HEREDITY VS. ENVIRONMENT

Thesis: It is not possible to prove that either heredity or environment is more important than the other.

    I. In practice we are not able to define "heredity" or "environment" with precision.

        A. We are not able to define "heredity" except in terms of characteristics which may have been influenced by environment.

            1. Some inherited characteristics of fruit flies appear only when the environment encourages their appearance.

52

2. An acorn will never grow into anything but an oak tree, but whether it becomes an oak tree or not depends on soil, moisture, temperature, and other environmental conditions.

B. We are not able to define "environment" with precision.

1. The environment of individuals in a society is so complex that we cannot define it rigorously.

2. Except in very limited laboratory experiments, the word "environment" is so vague that it is useless for disciplined discourse.

II. We cannot reach any trustworthy conclusions about the relative influences of heredity and environment by studying the histories of famous or infamous people.

A. A study of Shakespeare, Newton, and Lincoln provides us no answer.

1. If their greatness was due to inheritance, why were other members of their families not distinguished?

2. If their greatness was due to environment, why did others in the same environment not achieve greatness?

B. A study of the notorious Jukes family provides no conclusive answer.

1. We know that the Jukes family had a bad inheritance and a record of delinquency, but we cannot be sure that the inheritance caused the delinquency.

2. The Jukes family members had each other as part of their environment, and it is probable that any child brought up in that environment would have become a delinquent.

III. We cannot experimentally study heredity or environment apart from each other.

A. We cannot do it by studying newborn babies.

1. They have had nine months of prenatal environment before they were born.

2. They may or may not later display characteristics which are assumed to be inherited.

B. We cannot do it by studying ordinary twins.

1. Such twins come from different eggs and have different inheritances.

2. Such twins may have quite different environments; for example, a boy twin has a different environment than a girl twin, even when brought up in the same family.

C. We cannot even do it by studying identical twins because, although they have the same inheritance, we cannot be sure about their environment.

Such an outline summarizes both the content and the structure of the original article. It is therefore useful whenever the material to be studied is difficult or important enough to warrant the time outlining takes. The following are the steps involved in preparing a reading outline:

1. Read the essay to form a general impression of its purpose and structure. Pay special attention to the opening paragraphs, which usually

state the intention or thesis, and to headings, which give clues to the units of organization.

2. Determine the writer's purpose by picking out his thesis. If none is explicitly stated, formulate the implied purpose.

3. Determine the main divisions of the article and mark them I, II, III, etc. Sometimes the author will have marked these for you. If the essay is well constructed, each part should constitute a major unit of the outline.

4. Express the purpose of each major unit as a topic heading. Test these headings to see whether they logically develop the main purpose statement.

5. After you have done all this, consider whether the headings established in 4 above should be subdivided. If they should, break each in turn into its parts and mark the parts A, B, C, etc. If still further subdivision is required, mark the new subdivisions 1, 2, 3, etc.

6. Check the completed outline against the article to see that it accurately reveals the structure and content.

This process may be simply illustrated by outlining the essay on the distinction between war and peace (pages 13–15). A first reading shows that the thesis is stated in the first paragraph and is then broken into three units. Each unit — the legal, the political, and the military distinction between peace and war — is then discussed in a major division of the essay. The outline, then, consists of the thesis and three units — I, II, and III, though subtopics can be added if more detail is desired.

Topic and Sentence Outlines

A *topic outline* is one in which the headings are single words or phrases, not complete sentences. The outline on nuclear defense on page 51 and the following example are topic outlines.

THE DIVISIONS OF FEDERAL AUTHORITY

Purpose: To show the main divisions of the federal government.

    I. The Executive
        A. The President
        B. The Cabinet
        C. Appointed authorities
    II. The Legislature
        A. The House of Representatives
        B. The Senate
   III. The Judiciary
        A. The Federal Courts
        B. The Supreme Court

The *sentence outline* has already been illustrated on page 50 and on pages 52–53. Each entry is a complete sentence.

Of the two forms, the topic outline is the more popular. Although it need not be less logical or precise than a sentence outline, most students find it easier to handle. In general, it is the more convenient form to use when the purpose of the outline cannot be expressed as a thesis — that is, when the outline does not develop one dominant idea. When the outline does contain a thesis, the sentence outline is usually the better form to use, since it provides a clearer and usually a fuller plan of development. Notice how the following sentence outline spells out the meaning of the thesis through three logical and related steps.

WHAT HYBRID SEED CORN HAS DONE FOR FARMERS

Thesis: The use of hybrid seed corn has raised the standard of living of the American farmer.
I. The use of hybrid seed corn has increased the production of corn.
 A. It has increased the yield per acre.
 B. It has decreased the loss due to disease and weather conditions.
II. The use of hybrid seed has brought about new markets for corn.
 A. The nature of the hybrid seed industry has encouraged successful exploration of new uses for corn.
 B. As a result of new industrial uses, the market for corn has been greatly expanded.
III. The combination of increased production and an expanded market has raised the farmer's standard of living.
 A. It has increased his annual net income.
 B. It has provided more leisure time by allowing the farmer to purchase time-saving machinery.
 C. The combination of more money and more free time has made the farmer eager and able to provide comforts and conveniences in his home.

Here the development of the thesis is carried beyond the mere blocking out of the material to be presented. The thesis is broken into its logical units, each of which, in turn, is subdivided. As a result, the whole outline is knit tightly together and there is little chance for the writer to stray from his purpose.

The Conventions of Outlining

A complete outline consists of three parts: the title, the purpose statement, and the body of the outline. The main divisions or units of the body are represented by Roman numerals; their divisions, in turn, are marked by capital letters. Successive subdivisions are indicated by Arabic numerals, small letters, Arabic numerals in parentheses, and small letters in parentheses. These symbols follow a progressive system of indention so that the relation and relative importance of topics may be seen at a glance.

TITLE

Purpose statement (or thesis) ....
  I. ....
    A. ....
      1. ....
        a. ....
          (1) ....
            (a) ....
            (b) ....
          (2) ....
        b. ....
        c. ....
      2. ....
      3. ....
    B. ....
      1. ....
      2. ....
  II. ....
    A. ....
    B. ....
    C. ....

There are two conventions that cannot be revealed by this model. First, different levels of division must not be confused. To represent main headings as subheadings or vice versa would misrepresent the logical division of the material and could mislead the student when he writes his paper. Contrast the two erroneous outlines that follow with the correct one on page 54.

I. The Executive
  A. The President
  B. The Supreme Court
II. The Legislature
  A. The House of Representatives
  B. The Senate

I. The Legislature
II. The Senate
III. The President
IV. The Judiciary

At the left, listing the Supreme Court as a division of the executive authority distorts the organization of the government into two divisions, not three. At the right, the failure to recognize the Senate as a division of the legislature has resulted in what looks like four main branches of government. A paper developed from either outline would probably be unsatisfactory, since it would inherit the confusion of the plan.

The second convention not illustrated in the abstract outline is the use of parallel structure. So far as possible the form of all entries in an outline should be consistent. Topic and sentence headings should not both be used in the same outline. In addition, parallel grammatical constructions throughout a topic outline make it easier to see whether the outline is actually logical. Notice below that the outline at the left obscures the equality of the topics by shifting from prepositional to infinitive phrases, while the one at the right is clearer because the entries are parallel.

Why I Came to College	*Why I Came to College*
I. For economic reasons	I. To improve my economic status
II. In order to improve myself socially	II. To develop social poise
III. To make myself a cultured person	III. To make myself a cultured person
IV. For fun	IV. To enjoy college activities

You may have noticed that neither the abstract outline on page 56 nor any of the outlines presented earlier includes entries for Introduction, Body, and Conclusion. These headings are common in high school outlines and have some usefulness, since most essays have an introduction and a conclusion. But these are not aspects of the purpose statement and need not appear in the outline. If a student wishes introductory and concluding paragraphs, he may write them when he writes the paper. Their content seldom appears in the outline.

Shaping and Testing the Outline

How easily you can shape your outline will depend on how clearly you have your purpose in mind. If you are still not sure what you want to do, you will probably have to experiment, much as we did on pages 48–50. You will probably have to list your information, as we listed the characteristics of superior students, group similar pieces of information together, organize these groups into major units, and finally determine what these units show. Until you have done these things you are not ready to begin the final outline, since you do not yet know to what end you are trying to organize your material.

Once you have a clear statement of purpose, it is best to lay out the main divisions of your outline before you worry about subdivisions. First establish all the Roman numerals, then break each Roman numeral into capital letters, and so on. This way you will keep better control of your outline: you will not be likely to distort the organization by developing some headings too much and others too little. Since any change in the main headings will probably require changes in the subheadings, too early attention to subheadings may be time wasted.

When a careful outline is required, keep the purpose statement and the main divisions in your mind and reconsider them at convenient moments before making a final commitment. Especially avoid trying to finish the outline at a single sitting. Second thoughts are often better than first, and since the outline is going to control the progression of ideas in the essay, you want to be satisfied with the structure of your ideas before you begin to develop them in detail. As a check on that structure, it is usually wise to test the outline by asking the following questions:

1. Is the purpose statement (thesis) satisfactory?
2. Is the relation among the parts clear and consistent?
3. Does the order of the parts (sequence) provide a logical progression from the purpose statement?
4. Is the outline complete?
5. Can each entry be developed in detail?

Is the Purpose Statement (Thesis) Satisfactory?

Since the purpose statement controls the whole outline, a faulty statement invites trouble all along the way. As we have seen, the statement of purpose should be restricted, unified, and precise. A poor one will probably lead to a badly organized or a pointless paper. A rigorous checking of the purpose statement is therefore the first and most important step in testing the usefulness of a tentative outline.

As an additional illustration of what may develop from an unsatisfactory statement, consider the following:

The purpose of this paper is to provide a better understanding of the American Indian by revealing a few facts about his everyday life and customs.

The author of this statement has not really clarified his purpose, and any paper he writes is likely to be superficial. Why does he think that "a few facts" about the everyday life and customs of the Indian will help us to understand him better? What kind of facts? What will be his criterion for using some facts and omitting others? When we look at his outline we see, as his purpose statement suggests, that he is going to write a pointless paper "about" the American Indian.

I. The Indian religion differs from the white man's.
   A. The Indian religion is complicated.
   B. His conception of the supernatural has a strong influence on his everyday life.
II. The Indian medicine man is one of the most important people in the tribe.
   A. The training of the medicine man begins at an early age.
III. Dancing is of great importance in the life of the Indian.
   A. There are many classes of dancing.
   B. The instruments used to accompany the dancers are of a wide variation.
IV. The education of the Indian was not very extensive.
   A. There were several Indian colleges built.
V. The government of the Indian was simple.
   A. There were four divisions in the government.

Do you see that the vagueness of the purpose statement encouraged the student to tack on anything that had any connection with his general subject? The only aim of this outline is to string together enough information to bring the paper up to the required length. This example is an unusually bad one, but it shows what can happen when a student bases an outline on a fuzzy, pointless statement of purpose.

Is the Relationship Among the Parts Clear and Consistent?

In a good outline one can see how each main unit brings out an important aspect of the purpose statement and how each subdivision helps to develop its main heading. If there is any doubt about the relation of any heading to the purpose statement, that heading is either poorly stated or is a potential trouble spot in the organization. Whatever the reason, the difficulty should be removed before beginning to write.

Notice how clear is the relation among all parts of the following outline. Each Roman numeral shows a clear relation to the thesis; each capital letter is a logical division of its Roman numeral. No entry in the outline fails to advance the purpose, and each introduces, at its proper place, a significant part of the argument. You can be confident that the paper written from this outline will be coherent and closely reasoned.

Thesis: The age at which a citizen may vote should be reduced to 18.
  I. The present age limit has no logical justification.
  A. It has no relation to physical maturity.
  B. It has no relation to intellectual maturity.
  C. It has no relation to economic maturity.
  II. Whatever justification the present age limit once had has been removed by changed conditions.
  A. In the last war we were forced to draft 18-year-olds because they made the best soldiers.
  B. The draft necessitates a change in the voting age if we are to respect the political maxim that the responsibilities of citizenship presuppose the privileges of citizenship.
  III. The objections against reducing the age limit, like the objections against female suffrage, are based on unsupported assertions.
  A. It was asserted that women would use the vote foolishly, but the facts have disproved that assertion.
  B. It is asserted that 18-year-olds neither care about voting nor will take the trouble to make themselves politically informed, but the facts do not support that assertion.
  IV. The argument that there has to be some minimum age begs the question, since reducing the age limit does not abolish it.
  V. Reducing the age limit would broaden the base of our democracy, a consequence which has been traditionally desirable.

A good way to test an outline is to ask yourself, for every entry, whether it "points back" to the one it is developing. Do the Roman-numeral entries point back to the thesis or purpose statement? Do those with capital letters point back to the main headings? Notice below how A, B, and C all point back to I, the contention that the present age limit for voting has no logical justification.

I. The present age limit has no logical justification.
   A. It has no relation to physical maturity.
   B. It has no relation to intellectual maturity.
   C. It has no relation to economic maturity.

Notice also that any inconsistency in the form of the entries or parts will make their relationship less clear.

I. The present age limit has no logical justification.
   A. It has no relation to physical maturity.
   B. Intellectual maturity varies with individuals.
   C. The law does not require people to be economically independent before they can vote.

In this version the subdivisions A, B, C are no longer parallel in structure, and it is now more difficult to see how they point back to I. If we use these entries as topic sentences for successive paragraphs of an essay, we may, unless we are careful, distort the structure of the whole argument and throw an unnecessary burden both on ourselves, as writers, and on our readers. Consistent form in topics of equal rank is not just a matter of style; it emphasizes the relation of A, B, and C to each other and to the Roman-numeral statement which they develop. Consistent form thus provides tighter control over what we write and makes for more efficient planning.

Does the Order of the Parts Provide a Logical Progression?

Just as the sentences within a paragraph must follow a logical order, so must the parts of an outline. If any of the parts are out of order, the disorder will be magnified in the essay, and a reader will be confused or irritated. In the following outlines, compare the faulty version at the right with the more logical one at the left.

Purpose: To show Elizabeth's contribution to the development of the English navy

I. Condition of navy prior to Elizabeth's reign
   A. Its size compared with first-rate navies
   B. Its lack of government support
   C. Its inefficient use

Purpose: To show Elizabeth's contribution to the development of the English navy

I. Condition of navy prior to Elizabeth's reign
   A. Navy relatively small in comparison with other first-rate powers
   B. Inadequate government attention to fleet

II. Elizabeth's support of the "Sea Dogs" — Drake, Frobisher, Howard, Raleigh, and Grenville
  A. Political and economic reasons for her support
  B. Nature and extent of her support
III. Results of Elizabeth's support of Sea Dogs
  A. Economic rivalry with Spain
  B. Defeat of Armada and new prestige of English navy
  C. Extensive shipbuilding program to forestall Spanish retaliation
  D. More efficient design for ships
  E. Improved theory of naval warfare
  F. Foundation of English naval tradition
IV. Summary of condition of navy at end of Elizabeth's reign in contrast to condition described in I above

II. Development of naval warfare during the period
  A. Importance of battle with Spanish Armada
    1. Types of warfare used by both sides
    2. Defeat of Armada a turning point in English naval history
  B. Brief description of offensive and defensive forces of English navy
    1. Classification of ships as to size and armament
    2. Location of forces
  C. Work of Elizabethan Sea Dogs
    1. Influence upon Elizabeth
    2. Sea Dog fighting tactics
      a. Work of Drake
      b. Treatment of Spanish ships
III. Comparison of formation and battle tactics of Elizabethan and modern navies
  A. Factors of formation and battle tactics
  B. Closing paragraph

The outline at the left follows a *before-during-after* order. Part I describes the condition in which Elizabeth found the fleet, part II shows her support of the new naval leaders, part III deals with the immediate results of that support, and part IV summarizes all the results in a contrast with part I. Within these main units there is a logical progression of ideas. Within II the order goes from why Elizabeth acted (A) to what she did (B). In III the order is a succession of related consequences of her actions, which builds up to the contrast between I and IV. Throughout the outline the emphasis is on Elizabeth's contribution, as the purpose requires.

The order in the outline at the right follows no evident logical progression from the purpose statement. Elizabeth is mentioned only once, late in the outline in a minor heading (II C 1), and then without suggesting her contribution. In the main units the order seems to be haphazard. Part II — the largest unit — is limited to naval warfare, and part III is a wholly irrelevant comparison between Elizabethan and modern navies. Within the big central part II the organization is puzzling. What is the relation between types of warfare used by both sides (A 1) and the importance of the battle with the Armada? Does B 2 overlap A 1? Why does C shift the emphasis from Elizabeth to the Sea Dogs, when she is the subject of the paper? And if C is concerned with the Sea Dogs, why is only Drake mentioned?

A careful comparison of these two outlines should suggest two conclusions. First, unless a writer seeks a logical progression, he can drift into a plan which does not organize, but merely ties material into bundles without regard to why things are put in one bundle rather than another, or even why the bundles were made up in the first place. Second, if the progression of ideas or materials is confused in the outline, it will be worse in the essay. The writer then simply passes his confusion along to the reader.

Is the Outline Complete?

This is really not one question but two: first, are all major units of the subject represented; second, is each major unit subdivided far enough to guide the development of the essay? In college essays, the second consideration is the more important. Obviously, if we are going to divide Gaul into three parts, we should deal with three parts. It is less obvious, but not less important, that if we are going to discuss the work of the Elizabethan Sea Dogs, we must not stop with Drake.

If you compare the two outlines we have just considered, you will see that part III of the left-hand outline provides a fuller subdivision of the material inadequately suggested in II C of the right-hand version. As a plan for a paper, the six headings under III at the left provide a fuller plan than the two headings under II C at the right. Of course, a writer may compensate for incomplete subdivision in the outline by complete development in the essay. But that requires him to do better planning while writing than he did when he was concerned only with planning. *In practice, students almost never correct the deficiencies of an outline during the composition of an essay.* Flaws in the outline are almost certain to be preserved.

Can Each Entry Be Developed in Detail?

Each entry in the outline should be fully developed when the essay is written. Every instructor has known students who construct outlines containing entries for which they have no material, so that all they have to say about these entries is what they have already said in the outline. *Every entry in an outline should be adequately developed, and no entry should appear unless the author has the material to develop it.* There can be no rigid rule about how much development each entry should receive. Sometimes a single entry will require two or three paragraphs in the essay; occasionally several minor entries may be dealt with in a single paragraph. For inexperienced writers, *a useful rule of thumb is that each entry will usually be developed into at least one paragraph.*

Summary

1. The ability to outline is useful: (*a*) as a tool for clarifying and developing purpose; (*b*) as a means of testing the proposed organization of a paper; (*c*) as a complete communication; (*d*) as a reading aid.

2. In a topic outline the entries are expressed in words or phrases; in a sentence outline each entry is a complete sentence. The topic outline is best for an essay which does not develop a dominant idea; for a paper that does develop an idea (thesis), the sentence outline is preferable. In practice, most sentence outlines evolve out of preliminary topic outlines.

3. The conventions of outlining require that all headings be given an appropriate symbol and be indented to show the degree of subdivision. They also require that the outline distinguish major and minor divisions and keep the grammatical structure of all headings parallel.

4. In preparing an outline, finish the major divisions before you touch minor ones. Do the Roman numerals before you begin the capital letters, and the capitals before the Arabic numerals. This will insure that you work out the outline in a series of stages.

5. When you think your outline is complete, test it by considering the following questions: (*a*) Is the purpose statement satisfactory? (*b*) Is there a clear and consistent relationship between the purpose statement and each main division, and between the main and minor entries? Do the Roman numerals point back to the thesis, and the capital letters to the Roman numerals? (*c*) Does the order of the parts provide a logical progression from the purpose statement? (*d*) Is the outline complete? Have all the major units been presented, and have the subdivisions been carried far enough to provide a reliable guide for the actual composition? (*e*) Can each entry be adequately developed in the final essay?

Exercises

A. Below are an original student outline and a revision made to satisfy an instructor's criticism. First decide which is the original and which the revision. Then decide what was the essence of the instructor's criticism. Finally, decide what would be the effect of the revision on the essay which the student was going to write.

Outline A	Outline B
Thesis: Many of the dissenting opinions of Supreme Court Justice Oliver Wendell Holmes, Jr., show his refusal to allow public pressure to affect his interpretation of the law.	*Thesis:* Supreme Court Justice Oliver Wendell Holmes, Jr., felt that the decisions of the Supreme Court should be made purely on legal considerations.

I. In general, Holmes' practice was to decide questions solely on legal grounds.
  A. He managed to remain apart from pressures which might influence his decision.
  B. As much as possible, he based his decisions on precedents which had been accepted as constitutional.
II. Some of his most important dissents illustrate this practice.
  A. His dissent in the Northern Securities case was contrary to strong public opinion but in accordance with legal precedents.
    1. The case involved a question of trusts and monopolies.
    2. Both the public and the President were opposed to monopolies.
    3. The majority decision agreed with public opinion.
    4. Holmes' dissent was based strictly on legal considerations.
  B. The case of *Meyers v. United States* also illustrates the emphasis that Holmes gave to legal considerations.
    1. The case involved a question of the powers of the President.
    2. The majority opinion granted the President theoretical powers.
    3. Holmes' dissent stressed constitutional considerations.
  C. The Milwaukee Social Democratic Publishing Company case further illustrates Holmes' refusal to allow public opinion to decide legal questions.
    1. The case involved the Espionage Act of 1917.

I. O. W. Holmes' ideas on the Constitution were not unusual, yet he was called "The Great Dissenter."
  A. His ideas on the Constitution were accepted as being sound.
  B. He managed to remain apart from the pressures which would tend to influence a justice's decision.
  C. He based his decisions, as much as possible, on laws and decisions that had already been accepted as constitutional.
II. Holmes' first major dissenting opinion was delivered in the Northern Securities Company case.
  A. Public opinion was very high at that time against big trusts and monopolies.
  B. The majority decision was important because of the President's role in it.
  C. Holmes' dissent contradicted the will of the President and the people.
III. The case of *Meyers v. United States* was important because it dealt with the powers of the President.
  A. The majority decision granted the President theoretical powers.
  B. Holmes' dissent showed his courage in opposing a popular decision.
IV. The Milwaukee Social Democratic Publishing Company case was one of the important cases involving the Espionage Act of 1917.
  A. This case was an example of the way a social panic could influence the decision on a case in the Supreme Court.
  B. Again Holmes dissented from the majority opinion.

64

2. The majority opinion revealed the extent to which a social pressure could affect Supreme Court decisions.
3. Holmes' dissent was based on legal implications of the Espionage Act.
D. The case of the *Toledo News-Bee* is a final illustration of Holmes' insistence that law alone should decide legal questions.
   1. The case involved a question of the freedom of the press.
   2. The majority opinion went outside the law to protect the lower court judge against public criticism of court decisions.
   3. Holmes defended the *News-Bee's* constitutional right to criticize judicial decisions.

V. The Toledo newspaper case had important ramifications.
A. The background of the case was unusual, but of basic importance.
B. Holmes' dissent was hardly needed to show that the decision of the majority was prejudiced.

B. Study the following list of words, and group like words together in accordance with some principle of spelling which they illustrate. Then state the principle or rule and group the illustrations with that statement.

Example:

a. brag-bragging
b. equip-equipped
c. equip-equipment
d. fat-fattest
e. fat-fatness
f. get-getting
g. ship-shipping
h. bear-bearing
i. tear-tearing

Rule: Words of one syllable double the final consonant before adding a suffix beginning with a vowel if (1) they end in a single consonant and (2) they contain a single vowel (as in examples a, b, d, f, g).

1. able-unable
2. absolute-absolutely
3. achieve-achievement
4. advance-advancement
5. ally-allies
6. baby-babies
7. bake-baking
8. believe
9. bore-boring
10. cargo-cargoes
11. ceiling
12. change-changing
13. chief
14. city-cities
15. county-counties
16. deceive
17. dine-dining
18. duke-dukedom

65

19. duty-duties
20. echo-echoes
21. entry-entries
22. experience
23. friend
24. grieve-grievance
25. grieve-grievous
26. hero-heroes
27. ice-icy
28. love-loving
29. mince-mincing
30. natural-unnatural
31. necessary-unnecessary
32. niece
33. noticed-unnoticed
34. opened-unopened
35. postpone-postponement
36. prince-princely
37. potato-potatoes
38. regard-disregard
39. relief
40. retrieve
41. ruby-rubies
42. service-disservice
43. similar-dissimilar
44. sincere-sincerely
45. spell-misspell
46. torpedo-torpedoes
47. time-timing
48. veto-vetoes
49. writhe-writhing

C. The following words may be grouped into four main divisions of a topic outline to show types of changes in meaning. For each word, the original and present meanings are given in parentheses, with the original meaning first. Group like changes together, supply a title, purpose statement, and topic headings, and, after each topic heading, place in parentheses the numbers of the words which develop that heading.

1. *acorn* (various kinds of nuts — the seed or nut of oak trees)
2. *bonfire* (a fire for burning bones or corpses — any large outdoor fire)
3. *boor* (a farmer — an ill-mannered person)
4. *boycott* (an Irish captain who was ostracized by his neighbors — refusal to associate with any person or group)
5. *cad* (a younger son of an aristocratic family — an ill-mannered fellow)
6. *cattle* (property or wealth — cows, bulls, and steers)
7. *champagne* (wine from a French district — any wine resembling French champagne)
8. *corn* (a hard particle — the seed of a particular cereal crop)
9. *cunning* (knowing or skillful — tricky or meanly clever)
10. *dean* (an officer in charge of ten people — a major college administrator)
11. *deer* (any small animal — a particular animal with antlers)
12. *discard* (reject a card — throw something away)
13. *ferry* (travel — travel by boat)
14. *gossip* (a godparent — a spreader of rumors)
15. *hussy* (a housewife — a woman of low morals)
16. *knave* (a boy — a villainous man)
17. *knight* (a young male servant — a titled person)
18. *lady* (a breadmaker — a woman of quality)
19. *martinet* (a French general who was a stickler for discipline — any rigid disciplinarian)
20. *minister* (a servant — a clergyman or statesman)
21. *pedagogue* (a slave — an educator)

22. *shibboleth* (a password used in the Bible — any word or phrase that identifies a particular group)
23. *shirt* (a loose outer garment worn by either sex — a garment worn by a man)
24. *skirt* (a loose outer garment worn by either sex — a garment worn by a woman)

D. Below are the thesis and the Roman-numeral statements of a student outline. Under them are statements which comprise the subdivisions (capital letters, Arabic numerals, small letters). From these reconstruct the outline. In order to avoid disagreements about which of two substatements should come first under a main statement, arrange statements of equal rank in order of their numbers — low numbers before higher numbers.

Thesis: As a law student Thomas Jefferson developed the scholarly habits of thorough study and independent thinking which were characteristic of his later writings.

I. As a law student Jefferson developed the habit of reading extensively and evaluating independently what he read.
II. Jefferson's later writings reflect the scholarly pattern which he developed as a law student.
   1. His *Summary View of the Rights of British America* shows extensive reading and independent thinking.
   2. His reading while studying law was unusually extensive.
   3. His entries in his notebooks reveal his independent evaluation of what he read in law school.
   4. The *Summary View* is based on a thorough knowledge of English history.
   5. His *Notes on Virginia* provides another example of his scholarly workmanship.
   6. Although not required to, he studied law for five years before seeking admission to the bar.
   7. The opinions he expressed about the rights of the colonies in *Summary View* were original, not a reflection of prevailing opinion.
   8. His reading in law school covered the whole history of legal literature.
   9. His *Life and Morals of Jesus of Nazareth* is an excellent illustration of Jefferson's scholarly procedures in writing.
   10. The accurate and detailed answers the *Notes* provided to a series of questions reflect the thoroughness with which he collected his data.
   11. While in college, he read widely and carefully outside the field of law.
   12. In the *Notes* his opinions are often at variance with those of his environment.
   13. The *Life of Jesus* was undertaken in a spirit of scholarly curiosity.
   14. Although a member of a slave-holding society, he opposed slavery in the *Notes*.
   15. The *Life of Jesus* was dominated by a concern for the facts as they were revealed through reason.

16. Although religious conformity was mandatory in his society, in the *Notes* he defended the right of individuals to believe what they pleased.

E. From your experience, jot down what seem to you to be the major differences between high school and college instruction. Study these differences, derive a thesis from them, then develop that thesis into a sentence outline which is itself a clear communication.

4

Paragraphs: Compositions in Miniature

A paragraph requires much the same process of composition as a whole essay, though in smaller scope. An essay must have a purpose; so must a paragraph. The purpose of an essay, if stated, is the *thesis;* that of a paragraph, if stated, is the *topic sentence.* An essay must have a clear structure and a reasonable progression of ideas; so must a paragraph. An essay must be developed in enough detail to make its general statements meaningful; so must a paragraph. In short, a paragraph is an essay in miniature.

Four Requirements of a Good Paragraph

A good paragraph does its job thoroughly. If its function is to develop a unit of an outline, every sentence in the paragraph should clearly relate to that unit, and the sum of the sentences should make the reader feel that the unit has been efficiently developed. To create this impression a paragraph should have four qualities: *completeness, unity, order,* and *coherence.*

Completeness

A paragraph is complete when it does all it was intended to do. Consider the following:

> Too cold to snow? It never gets too cold to snow, but it frequently gets too cold for snow to fall in flakes, because at subzero temperatures the air is too dry to produce snowflakes.

This brief paragraph poses a question and provides an answer. Is it complete? Whether it is or not depends on how thoroughly the reader understands why dry subzero air will keep snowflakes from forming. This you may decide for yourself. Could you, on the evidence of this paragraph alone, explain to your classmates why dry, cold air reduces the formation of snowflakes? If your answer is no, see if the following version is more helpful.

> Too cold to snow? It never gets too cold to snow, but it frequently gets too cold for snow to fall in flakes. *Flakes fall when the air through which*

they pass is 32° Fahrenheit or slightly lower. At this temperature the air usually holds enough moisture to allow the flakes to become fat and mat together, and the fall is likely to be heavy. As the temperature sinks lower, the air becomes drier, the snowfall lighter and more powdery. At temperatures below zero a heavy fall of snow is rare. The snow that does fall takes the form of ice spicules, ice needles, or fills the air with fine, glittering, diamond-like dust. The air at these subzero temperatures is usually too dry to produce flakes.[1]

Do you agree that this version gives a better explanation and that, by comparison, the first seems incomplete? The first answer is not detailed enough to meet the reader's needs; therefore it does not fully do what it was supposed to do. We saw in Chapter 1 that lack of detailed development often results in a statement which is too general to be fully meaningful. The explanatory details italicized in the revised paragraph are needed to bring out the meaning of the general answer in the first version.

Notice that the test of completeness is made by the reader. It is he, not the writer, who must be satisfied. The writer must, in effect, see his work as the reader will see it. He does so partly by being aware of his reader's needs — that is, by analyzing the situation — and partly by being eternally conscious that the reader gets the full meaning from detailed development, not from general statements alone. If you did not learn that lesson from Chapter 1, you would be wise to review pages 15–18, because you simply cannot do effective writing in college, or anywhere else, until you appreciate the importance of detailed development.

The most common devices for getting completeness in a paragraph are *supporting details, examples, comparison,* and *contrast.* We shall look briefly at each of these.

Supporting Details. Any details which tend to make general statements more specific may be said to *support* these statements. Such details may be explanatory, descriptive, narrative, or persuasive. The italicized details of the second snowflake paragraph are explanatory; they are chiefly concerned with clarifying a process. In the following paragraph, the details are descriptive and are used to make the reader visualize the scene at a particular moment in the sinking of the *Titanic.*

2:10 A.M. Below decks the steam is still holding, though the pressure is falling — rapidly. In the gymnasium on the boat deck the athletic instructor watches quietly as two gentlemen ride the bicycles and another swings casually at the punching bag. Mail clerks stagger up the boat-deck stairways, dragging soaked mail sacks. . . . The band still plays — but not ragtime:

> "Nearer my God to thee,
> Nearer to thee . . ."

A few men take up the refrain; others kneel on the slanting decks to pray. Many run and scramble aft, where hundreds are clinging above the silent

[1] From the *World Almanac*, 1945. Reprinted by permission.

screws on the great uptilted stern. . . . The hymn comes to its close. Band-master Hartley, Yorkshireman violinist, taps his bow against a bulkhead, calls for "Autumn" as the water curls about his feet, and the eight musicians brace themselves against the ship's slant. People are leaping from the decks into the nearby water — the icy water. A woman cries, "Oh, save me!" A man answers, "Good lady, save yourself. Only God can save you now." The band plays "Autumn":

> "God of Mercy and Compassion!
> Look with pity on my pain . . ."[2]

In the paragraph below, the supporting details serve to persuade a reader of the harm done to our natural resources through the erosion of irreplaceable topsoil.

The most obvious result of deforestation, overgrazing, and bad farming methods is soil erosion. American civilization, founded on nine inches of topsoil, has now lost one-third of this soil. Dr. Hugh H. Bennett, testifying before a Congressional committee in 1939, said, "In the short life of this country we have essentially destroyed 282,000,000 acres of land, crop and range-land. Erosion is destructively active on 775,000,000 additional acres. About 100,000,000 acres of cropland, much of it representing the best cropland we have, is finished in this country. We cannot restore it. It takes nature from 300 to 1000 years to bring back a single inch of topsoil and we sometimes lose that much topsoil as the result of a single rain, if it is an especially heavy torrential type of rain. . . ."[3]

The persuasion in this paragraph comes from the details, the facts and figures given by Dr. Bennett. Without their support, the argument would be too general to move a reader. If you drop out Dr. Bennett's testimony, you are left with nothing but an assertion that America has lost one-third of its topsoil through soil erosion. Such a statement will have no strong effect on a reader who is not an expert on that subject. He will feel that the situation is bad, but he will not understand how bad. But if you tell him that we have already lost 100,000,000 acres of our best cropland, he is likely to be disturbed; and if you add that it takes nature from 300 to 1000 years to replace a single inch of topsoil, he is likely to feel that something had better be done about the situation right away. That is the effect the paragraph is intended to achieve. The supporting details allow the writer to accomplish this purpose.

Examples. You know that when you have difficulty following an explanation, you often say, "Give me an example." The example completes the explanation by making it specific. Notice how the author of the following paragraph brings out the meaning of his first three sentences by providing three examples of the kind of conduct he is discussing.

[2] From "R.M.S. Titanic" by Hanson W. Baldwin, in *Harper's Magazine,* January, 1934. Copyright, Hanson W. Baldwin, 1934. Reprinted by permission of Willis Kingsley Wing.

[3] From *Road to Survival* by William Vogt. Copyright 1948 by William Sloane Associates, Inc. Reprinted by permission of the publishers.

The social dynamics of the adolescent peer-group are continuations of those of the juvenile era; there is no sudden shift or sharp break. But they become subtler and less crude. The group undertakes more complex activities; a wider variety of different kinds of competence proves to be useful; greater alertness in detecting and accepting them in otherwise unpromising individuals pays off. An odd and cranky boy who can nevertheless write an editorial for the school paper so skillfully that embarrassed authority can find no grounds for censorship is not now the butt of ridicule; he is a prize. It is worth a good deal of effort to keep him out of trouble; and it takes a good deal of skill. The ugly, rather taciturn girl who with fifty dollars can decorate the gymnasium for a school dance so skillfully that the Persian Room, by comparison, looks a little too Persian does not have to be able to attract partners when the dance takes place — does not have to want to; she is *in*. The pudgy boy who can actually cook finds that young couples are hungry after the dance is over; he is in, too.[4]

The topic idea of this paragraph is best expressed in the third sentence. That sentence alone would tell most readers almost nothing. If he wants to share his ideas with his readers, the writer must give a practical illustration of what he has in mind. The examples provide that illustration. When a reader sees the cranky boy, the ugly girl, and the pudgy boy being accepted by the group because of their special skills, he learns what the third sentence means.

Comparison (*Analogy*). Another common method of completing the thought of a paragraph is by the use of comparison or analogy. This method is especially helpful when the writer can liken a difficult subject to one which the reader already knows. Notice this use of analogy in the two paragraphs that follow.

(1)

Music has often been compared with language itself, and the comparison is quite legitimate. While it combines easily with actual language, it also speaks a language of its own, which it has become a platitude to call universal. To understand the significance of the organizing factors of rhythm, melody, harmony, tone color and form, the analogy of a familiar language is helpful. Music has its own alphabet, of only seven letters, as compared with the twenty-six of the English alphabet. Each of these letters represents a note, and just as certain letters are complete words in themselves, so certain notes may stand alone, with the force of a whole word. Generally, however, a note of music implies a certain harmony, and in most modern music the notes take the form of actual chords. So it may be said that a chord in music is analogous to a word in language. Several words form a phrase, and several phrases a complete sentence, and the same thing is true in music. Measured music corresponds to poetry, while the old unmeasured

[4] From *The Vanishing Adolescent* by Edgar Z. Friedenberg. Reprinted by permission of the Beacon Press, copyright © 1959 by Edgar Z. Friedenberg.

plain-song might be compared with prose. The relationship of modern music to free verse at once becomes apparent, and impressionism, expressionism, cubism and futurism can all be found in music as well as the other arts.[5]

(2)

In discussing the relative difficulties which the exact and inexact sciences face, let me begin with an analogy. Would you agree that swimmers are less skillful athletes than runners because swimmers do not move as fast as runners? You probably would not. You would quickly point out that water offers greater resistance to swimmers than the air and ground do to runners. Agreed, that is just the point. In seeking to solve their problems, the social scientists encounter greater resistance than the physical scientists. . . . The conditions under which the social scientists must work would drive a physical scientist frantic. Here are five of these conditions. He can make few experiments; he cannot measure the results accurately; he cannot control the conditions surrounding the experiments; he is often expected to get quick results with slow-acting economic forces; and he must work with people, not with inanimate objects.[6]

In each of these paragraphs the author introduces his subject by comparing it with a more familiar one. The first likens the structure of music to that of language; the second compares the difficulties of the social scientist's work to the resistance that a swimmer must overcome. The function of both analogies is to help the reader understand the more complex subject by appealing to his previous experience of the simpler one. This is especially true of the second paragraph, which wins the reader's quick acceptance of a distinction that will necessarily take time to develop.

Contrast. Like comparison, contrast may be an effective way of conveying an idea. In the following paragraph the italicized topic sentence is developed by contrasting details of death at sea and death on land.

Death is at all times solemn, but never so much so as at sea. A man dies on shore; his body remains with his friends, and "the mourners go about the streets"; but when a man falls overboard at sea and is lost, there is a suddenness in the event, and a difficulty in realizing it, which give to it an air of awful mystery. A man dies on shore — you follow his body to the grave, and a stone marks the spot. You are often prepared for the event. There is always something which helps you to realize it when it happens, and to recall it when it has passed. A man is shot down by your side in battle, and the mangled body remains an *object,* and a *real evidence;* but at sea, the man is near you — at your side — you hear his voice, and in an instant he is gone, and nothing but a *vacancy* shows his loss. Then, too, at sea — to use a homely but expressive phrase — you *miss* a man so much. A dozen men are

[5] From *The Art of Enjoying Music* by Sigmund Spaeth. Copyright 1933 by Sigmund Spaeth. Reprinted by permission of the McGraw-Hill Book Company.

[6] From "Are Social Scientists Backward?" by Donald L. Kemmerer, in the *American Association of University Professors Bulletin,* Autumn, 1948.

shut up together in a little bark, upon the wide, wide sea, and for months and months see no forms and hear no voices but their own, and one is taken suddenly from among them, and they miss him at every turn. It is like losing a limb. There are no new faces or new scenes to fill up the gap. There is always an empty berth in the forecastle, and one man wanting when the small night watch is mustered. There is one less to take the wheel, and one less to lay out with you upon the yard. You miss his form, and the sound of his voice, for habit had made them almost necessary to you, and each of your senses feels the loss.[7]

Notice two things about this paragraph: the wealth of specific details and the organization of these details. The paragraph proceeds by matching a detail of death on shore with a contrasting detail of death at sea. This contrast pattern not only spells out the meaning of the topic sentence but also binds the material into a tightly organized and balanced paragraph.

Whether in any given paragraph you use supporting details, examples, comparison, or contrast will depend on your subject and your purpose. No one method is suitable to all paragraphs, and there are still others. But these are a few good ways of bringing out a paragraph idea and making it complete, and if you do not find yourself using them naturally in the first draft, it may be useful to see where you can profitably introduce them in revision.

Unity

Since a paragraph develops a topic idea, stated or implied, there should be nothing in it which does not clearly serve that end. A unified paragraph makes clear reading. One which digresses or drifts away from the topic puts extra demands on the reader and sometimes thwarts him in his effort to follow the writer's line of thought.

A writer who sees clearly what he wants a paragraph to do is not likely to have much trouble with unity. Concentration on his purpose controls the sequence of his ideas, and he tends to grasp the paragraph idea and its development as a whole. He does not consciously plan the succession of sentences. He does not need to, because the sequence is part of his thought. It is when a writer is groping for ideas one sentence at a time that the unity of the paragraph is likely to suffer. A paragraph so written may reveal one of two flaws: (1) an obvious interruption in the sequence of ideas, caused by the introduction of irrelevant thoughts; (2) a gradual drift away from the stated purpose of the paragraph, as the author lets each succeeding sentence push him farther in the wrong direction. These flaws are illustrated in the following examples.

It is a good thing that we learn to speak as children. If the learning were postponed until we were adults most of us would be too discouraged by the difficulties to persevere in the task. Perhaps, *in that event, our political*

---

[7] From *Two Years Before the Mast* by Richard Henry Dana.

campaigns would be conducted in sign language and our radio broadcasters would be required to learn the Morse code. We take a child's learning to talk for granted, and not infrequently parents grow worried when their four-year-old stumbles over his consonants or becomes snarled in his syntax. Yet compared with the intellectual achievement of learning to talk, the discovery of the theory of relativity is a trifling accomplishment.

Clearly the author started with the idea that learning to speak is man's greatest intellectual achievement. But as he wrote he became interested in the possible consequences of our not learning to speak, and in an uncritical moment he introduced the italicized sentence. If he really wants to develop this idea — and it could be an entertaining one — he should save it for a new paragraph. But he should not let it intrude here, where it does not belong.

In order to bring about harmony in our economy, Congress must force unions to become more responsible. This is no reactionary proposal. It is made in the interests of labor itself. Organized labor is an asset to the economy of a nation. One has only to read of the conditions that prevailed in mills and mines and factories during the last century to understand what the lot of the workingman would be like if he were deprived of his right to unite with his fellow workers to force concessions from entrepreneurs whose short-sighted irresponsibility has been nourished on *laissez-faire.*

This writer drifts so steadily away from his topic sentence that he ends by saying the opposite of what he set out to say. If you study the paragraph carefully, you will see that he begins to go off the track in the second sentence. That sentence suggests to him that he must show that he is not a reactionary; so he begins to shift his point of view and to look at the labor movement historically. That viewpoint suggests the evils of management against which labor historically has fought. The reversal now becomes complete, and the writer ends by asserting the irresponsibility of management after starting out to assert the irresponsibility of labor.

The ability to see both sides of a question is valuable, but unless the topic sentence clearly implies that both sides are to be presented in the same paragraph, drifting from one side to the other frustrates the reader and produces a "broken-backed" paragraph. In revision this writer must go back to his topic sentence and develop the irresponsibility of unions throughout the whole paragraph. Then, if he wants to, he can point out in a second paragraph that he is sympathetic to unions and appreciates the role they have played in forcing management to be more responsible. There is nothing wrong with asserting that both unions and management should be responsible, but that assertion cannot be developed from the topic sentence with which this writer began.

Orderly Movement (Sequence of Sentences)

If the paragraph is to be an organic unit, its movement should follow some clear order. There are various ways in which the material of paragraphs may be arranged. But certainly some orders will be more effective than others.

Consider the following:

> (1) We all know that if we "burn" chalk the result is quick-lime. (2) There are a great many other ways of showing that chalk is essentially nothing but carbonic acid and quick-lime. (3) Chemists enunciate the result of all the experiments that prove this, by stating that chalk is almost wholly composed of "carbonate of lime." (4) By the procedure of burning we see the lime, but we do not see the carbonic acid. (5) If, on the other hand, you were to powder a little chalk and drop it into a good deal of strong vinegar, there would be a great bubbling and fizzing, and, finally, a clear liquid, in which no sign of chalk would appear. (6) Here you see the carbonic acid in the bubbles; the lime, dissolved in the vinegar, vanishes from sight. (7) Chalk, in fact, is a compound of carbonic acid gas, and lime, and when you make it very hot the carbonic acid flies away and the lime is left.

This paragraph is fully developed and unified. But a careful reader might notice a certain jerkiness in its development. Rereading, he would observe that the sequence of ideas in the paragraph is as follows:

1. A statement about a specific experiment — burning.
2. A statement about other experiments.
3. A conclusion drawn from all experiments.
4. A second statement about burning.
5. A statement about a specific experiment — dissolving.
6. A second statement about that experiment.
7. Another statement essentially about burning.

He would then understand what had bothered him on first reading: the author should have grouped the statements about burning in the first part of the paragraph, those about dissolving in the second part, and finally should have drawn the general conclusion about all such experiments. This is exactly what T. H. Huxley did in the paragraph from which our scrambled version was taken.

> We all know that if we "burn" chalk the result is quick-lime. Chalk, in fact, is a compound of carbonic acid gas, and lime, and when you make it very hot the carbonic acid flies away and the lime is left. By this method of procedure we see the lime, but we do not see the carbonic acid. If, on the other hand, you were to powder a little chalk and drop it into a good deal of strong vinegar, there would be a great bubbling and fizzing, and, finally, a clear liquid, in which no sign of chalk would appear. Here you see the carbonic acid in the bubbles; the lime, dissolved in the vinegar, vanishes from sight. There are a great many other ways of showing that chalk is essentially nothing but carbonic acid and quick-lime. Chemists enunciate the result of all the experiments that prove this, by stating that chalk is almost wholly composed of "carbonate of lime."[8]

Order in a paragraph is like organization in an essay, but because the

[8] From "A Piece of Chalk" by T. H. Huxley.

paragraph is smaller in scope, it may be simpler to consider paragraph order as *direction*. We shall therefore discuss it in terms of five directional patterns: (1) from one time to the next, (2) from one space to an adjoining space, (3) from particular statements to a general statement or conclusion, (4) from a general statement to particular statements, (5) from question to answer or from effect to cause.

Time. A time, or chronological, order is natural for narration and is commonly used in explaining the steps in a process. Events are recorded in the order in which they occur — first, second, next, and so on. Thus if you were telling a story or giving directions on how to reach a certain destination or how to bake a cake, the natural order would be a time order. Here is an illustration.

> While I jacked the fore end of the car up, and cleared away the snow from under it, Dan built a fire about a foot in front of the radiator to keep the car and us from freezing to death and to furnish light for the operation. The wheel correction was surprisingly easy; we were ready to leave again in a few minutes. Then we discovered that it would be more difficult to get out of the lane than it had been to get in. Because of the density of the timber there was no way of turning around without serious risk of getting stuck, and the whirling snow made the visibility poor everywhere except directly within the beams of the head lights. Dan therefore very carefully directed my backing; yet in spite of this I bumped several small pines which retaliated by dumping their burden of snow on top of the car. The Plymouth was little more than a snow drift on wheels by the time we reached the highway.[9]

Space. A space order is useful when the writer wishes to report what he sees. The movement of the paragraph thus follows the movement of his eyes. That movement must have some continuity which a reader can recognize and follow. It need not start at the far left and move steadily to the far right, or vice versa, since in any view an observer's gaze is likely to be drawn quickly to the most conspicuous object. But there should be some logical or natural progression from one descriptive detail to the next. It may be very confusing to flit haphazardly from left to right, to center, then to left again. Notice that the following paragraph begins with a front view, then moves right, down, and to the rear. This order reflects the relative conspicuousness of the objects described.

> I seated myself in the barber chair, which was only a rickety, straight-backed affair made of bamboo placed on a wooden box in the center of the room. Directly in front of this throne hung a dingy, blurred mirror, suspended by ropes from the roof. To my right stood a square table, upon which rested the barber's only tools — a pair of clippers, a dirty-looking

[9] Charles R. Goldman, "Luck and Wheels." From *The Green Caldron: A Magazine of Freshman Writing* (November, 1949), published at the University of Illinois, Urbana, Illinois. Copyright, 1949. Reprinted by permission.

comb, and a razor. As I cast my eyes downward, I was somewhat surprised to find that the floor was still in its natural state — dirt. It also showed evidence that hair had been cut here before. I noticed now for the first time an opening at the rear, over which a piece of gray material was draped. Evidently this archway led into the living quarters of the barber.[10]

Particular to General. A common order in expository paragraphs is from a succession of particular statements to the general statement or conclusion to which the particulars lead. Huxley used this order (page 76) when he began a paragraph by describing an experiment which shows that chalk contains lime, related a second experiment to show that chalk also contains carbonic acid, and finally stated the conclusion that chalk is composed of carbonate of lime. By this order the reader is led to the conclusion through details of evidence or illustration.

A paragraph so organized will have the topic sentence at or near the end. Notice how the author of the following paragraph leads up to his topic sentence, "Logic is fun."

If you enjoy working out the strategy of games, tit-tat-toe or poker or chess; if you are interested in the frog who jumped up three feet and fell back two in getting out of a well, or in the fly buzzing between the noses of two approaching cyclists, or in the farmer who left land to his three sons; if you have been captivated by codes and ciphers or are interested in crossword puzzles; if you like to fool around with numbers; if music appeals to you by the sense of form which it expresses — then you will enjoy logic. You ought to be warned, perhaps. Those who take up logic get glassy-eyed and absent-minded. They join a fanatical cult. But they have a good time. Theirs is one of the most durable, absorbing and inexpensive of pleasures. *Logic is fun.*[11]

General to Particular. The most popular order for expository paragraphs is just the reverse of the one above. It begins with a general statement, then moves to particulars which explain or illustrate, or persuade the reader to accept the generalization. In effect, the topic sentence at or near the beginning of the paragraph states the purpose, and the subsequent sentences develop it. In the paragraph that follows, the italicized topic sentence is developed by three sentences, each of which adds an illustration.

Beauty is the quality which makes to endure. In a house that I know, I have noticed a block of spermaceti lying about closets and mantelpieces, for twenty years together, simply because the tallow-man gave it the form of a rabbit; and I suppose it may continue to be lugged about unchanged for a century. Let an artist scrawl a few lines or figures on the back of a letter,

[10] James Hiser, "Filipino Barber Shop." From *The Green Caldron: A Magazine of Freshman Writing* (December, 1946), published at the University of Illinois, Urbana, Illinois. Copyright, 1946. Reprinted by permission.

[11] From *The Rhyme of Reason* by Roger W. Holmes. Reprinted by permission of Appleton-Century-Crofts, Inc., publishers.

and that scrap of paper is rescued from danger, is put in portfolio, is framed and glazed, and, in proportion to the beauty of the lines drawn, will be kept for centuries. Burns writes a copy of verses and sends them to a newspaper, and the human race take charge of them that they shall not perish.[12]

For the reader, this general-to-particular order has the great advantage that it announces the topic at the beginning and thus makes it easy to see the relation of each new sentence to the topic. For the writer, it has the advantage of holding his purpose clearly before him so that he is less likely to introduce irrelevant material or wander off on a digression.

Two variations of this general-to-particular order deserve special notice. The first is the paragraph that not only begins but also ends with a general statement. Until the last sentence, such a paragraph follows a general-to-particular order; then the topic idea is restated, usually in different words, as a concluding sentence.

Most disputes about whether or not men are stronger than women are meaningless because the disputants fail to consider that the word "stronger" may mean many things. Most men can surpass most women in lifting heavy weights, in striking an object (say a baseball or an opponent's jaw), in running, jumping, or doing heavy physical labor. But the statistics indicate that most women live longer than most men, that they have a better chance of resisting disease, that they can beat men at operations requiring finger-dexterity and the ability to work accurately under monotonous conditions. On this kind of evidence it would be legitimate to argue that women are stronger than men. The truth is that each sex can surpass the other in certain kinds of activities. *To say that one is stronger than the other is to indulge in an argument which would not arise if the word "stronger" were more sharply defined.*

A second variation is the paragraph which deliberately reverses its movement. It usually begins with a topic sentence that states or implies a qualification or a contrast. The first half of the paragraph develops one phase of the idea, and the second half qualifies what has been said. Usually the point of reversal is indicated by a transitional connective such as *but, on the other hand, nevertheless, still,* or *yet.* For example:

The statement that the German people were ultimately responsible for the war is a half-truth which encourages a convenient oversimplification. It is true that Hitler was the constitutionally appointed leader of the German nation and that, despite individual protests, his policies, as long as they were successful, had the approval, or at least the acquiescence, of the German voters. *But* in the world in which we live no man, no nation causes war. To fix any ultimate responsibility for World War II we must go beyond Hitler and the Nazi ideology; we must look before Munich and the invasion of Poland. And the farther we look the more clearly we will see that the roots of war were world-wide, and that no nation was guiltless of nourishing them.

[12] From "Beauty" by Ralph Waldo Emerson.

The italicized topic sentence suggests that (1) the German people were responsible for the war, (2) other people were also responsible. The next sentence supports the suggestion of German guilt. Then at the transitional *But* the paragraph reverses itself and moves toward the conclusion that all nations responsible for the war.

A word of caution is necessary about this kind of paragraph movement. In the hands of an inexperienced writer, a reversed paragraph may easily become disunified, and may end, like the one on page 75, by saying the opposite of what the author intended. To be successful, the reversal must be deliberate. The author must be aware at the outset that he intends to qualify his opening statement within the paragraph, and the topic sentence should be phrased to reveal that intention. Otherwise, it will often be safer to break the paragraph in two at the point of transition. For example:

> The statement that the German people were ultimately responsible for the war is a half-truth which encourages a convenient oversimplification. It is true that Hitler was the constitutionally appointed leader of the German nation and that, despite individual protests, his policies, as long as they were successful, had the approval, or at least the acquiescence, of the German voters.
>
> But in the world in which we live no man, no nation causes war. To fix any ultimate responsibility for World War II we must go beyond Hitler and the Nazi ideology; we must look before Munich and the invasion of Poland. And the farther we look the more clearly we will see that the roots of war were world-wide, and that no nation was guiltless of nourishing them.

Question to Answer, Effect to Cause. Less common than any of the orders we have considered so far is the paragraph that begins with a question and moves toward the answer, or begins with an effect and moves toward the cause. Such a paragraph may have no explicit topic sentence, since the answer to the question or the cause of the effect is explained by the paragraph as a whole. But the opening question, problem, or dilemma announces the purpose of the paragraph clearly if implicitly.

The following example moves from question to answer:

> *And when is water boiling?* It can be said, with few people to argue the point, that water boils at two hundred and twelve degrees Fahrenheit. Myself, I would say that when it bubbles with large energetic bubbles, and looks ready to hop from the kettle, and makes a rocky rather than a murmuring noise, and sends off a great deal of steam, it is boiling.[13]

The next paragraph first states a result, then gives the cause:

> *When Basil Rathbone was handed a scenario titled "The Monster," he gave it back to Paramount without reading it.* A wise man in the studio retitled it "Destiny" and sent the same script back to Rathbone. He read it,

---

[13] From *How to Cook a Wolf* by M. F. K. Fisher. Copyright 1942 by M. F. K. Fisher. Reprinted by permission of the publishers, Duell, Sloan and Pearce, Inc.

liked it, and assured me on the set that it is not a horror picture. "I'm through with horror and villainy," says Basil, "a man has only so many villains in him, and I've played all mine."[14]

The following table summarizes the types of paragraph movement we have been discussing:

Time order

(A chain of events recorded in the order in which they occurred. Paragraph begins with the first event and ends with the last one. Usually no topic sentence.)

Event 1
Event 2
Event 3, and so on.

Space order

(Sentences in paragraph move from one area to the next as these are viewed, in turn, by the writer. Movement may be in any direction but must be easy to follow. Usually no topic sentence.)

Left-right, front-rear, up-down, or any logical movement from one space to the next.

Particular to general

(From a series of explanatory or illustrative statements to the conclusion drawn from them. Topic sentence at or near end of paragraph.)

Details leading up to concluding topic sentence.

General to particular

(From general statement to supporting details which explain, illustrate, or prove it. Topic sentence at or near beginning of paragraph.)

Conclusion or general statement followed by details of explanation or proof.

(*Variation 1.* Topic sentence restated as conclusion at end of paragraph.)

Details

(*Variation 2.* Topic sentence implies qualification or contrast which requires paragraph to develop first one phase then the other of topic sentence. Point of reversal indicated by transitional connective: *but, yet, still, on the other hand.*)

point of reversal

[14] From Sheilah Graham's column, *Chicago Daily News*, March 6, 1940. Reprinted by permission of the *Chicago Daily News* and The Bell Syndicate, Inc.

Question-answer, Effect-cause

(Paragraph begins with question or effect, then answers the question or shows the cause. Usually no topic sentence.)

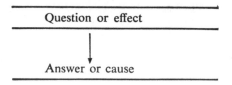

Coherence

Literally, the word *cohere* means to hold together. A paragraph is said to have coherence when its sentences are woven together or flow into each other. If a paragraph is coherent, the reader moves easily from one sentence to the next without feeling that there are gaps in the thought, puzzling jumps, or points not made. If a paragraph lacks coherence, the reader will feel that the sentence, not the paragraph, is the unit of writing, and that he is reading a collection of separate statements rather than an integrated discussion.

Coherence Within the Paragraph. A paragraph which lacks unity or orderly movement will not be coherent, since a reader cannot move easily from one sentence to the next if the second sentence has no clear relation to the first. But coherence is not simply a matter of unity and consistent order. Consider the following paragraph:

(1) I was accepted and started work. (2) My experience had been derived chiefly from books. (3) I was not prepared for the difficult period of adjustment. (4) I soon became discouraged with myself and so dissatisfied with my job that I was on the point of quitting. (5) My employer must have sensed this. (6) He called me into his office and talked to me about the duties of my position and the opportunities for advancement. (7) I realized that there was nothing wrong with me or the job and I decided to stay.

This paragraph is fairly well developed, it is unified, its development is orderly; yet it is a poor paragraph. The writer's ideas do not flow from one sentence to the next. Rather, they seem to come out in a series of jolts and jerks, because the connecting links between them are not expressed. The sentences are not knitted together, so the reader is forced to tackle each one separately, and in hunting the connections he loses the flow and continuity which a more carefully constructed paragraph would provide.

Now look at the same paragraph slightly altered:

I was accepted, and started work. *Until that time* my experience had been derived chiefly from books, *and unfortunately* those books had not prepared me for the difficult period of adjustment *that every inexperienced secretary must face in a new position. Consequently* I soon became *so* discouraged with myself and so dissatisfied with the job that I was on the point of quitting. *I think* my employer must have sensed this, *for* he called me into his office and talked to me about *both* the duties of my position and the opportunities *it offered* for advancement. *That talk helped me considerably. From then on,* I realized that there was nothing wrong with me or the job *that experience could not cure,* and I decided to stay.

The second version is distinctly better than the first, and if you read both aloud, the difference between them will be still more obvious. Why? The content is substantially the same, the diction is scarcely changed, and the second version is only slightly more fully developed than the first. The general answer is that the second paragraph is more coherent because the author has provided transitions — bridges — between the thoughts expressed in the original sentences. These transitions are created by two means: sometimes by filling a small gap in the thought, thus providing better continuity of statement; sometimes by the addition of connecting words and phrases which tie sentences together.

Transition Through Continuity of Thought. A writer who thinks of a paragraph as a unit developing a single topic, who consequently composes a whole paragraph at a time, is not likely to write paragraphs seriously lacking in coherence. Most incoherent passages are a result of thinking in single sentences rather than whole paragraphs. When a writer works that way, he is likely to write one sentence, stop, think a minute, write a second sentence, stop, and continue in a series of spurts and pauses. Paragraphs written this way are almost sure to be weak in coherence, for the writer is starting afresh at every new sentence. He loses the feeling of continuity with the last sentence before he begins the next one. Consequently, he is likely to omit significant links or details of thought and thus leave gaps in his writing.

For example, when the author of the incoherent paragraph stopped between sentences 1 and 2, she left out a small important detail of her thought. She was contrasting her previous experience with her new one and she needed somewhere to make the point that *now* her experience was changing. In the revised version the phrase "Until that time" supplies the necessary clue. Similarly, when she wrote that she was not prepared "for the difficult period of adjustment," she had in mind a particular adjustment, the kind that must be made "in a new position." But her original statement omitted that link in her thought. Again, she skipped a thought between sentences 6 and 7. She was helped by her talk with her employer. By failing to record that fact, she ran the talk and its result too closely together. In the revised paragraph the italicized sentence provides the missing detail and thus gives a fuller statement of what she meant. Finally, she omitted a necessary idea in her last sentence. There *was* something wrong with her, but nothing "that experience could not cure." The revision, by providing these omitted details, makes the paragraph most completely reflect all that was in the writer's mind.

Transition Through Related Sentence Patterns. A writer who thinks in sentences rather than in paragraphs often finds it hard to keep a con-sistent grammatical pattern running through a paragraph. In the first ver-sion of the example on page 82, the author herself is the subject of five sentences and her employer the subject of the other two. The following example is much less consistent:

> Although writing a research paper is a difficult assignment, many students make it more difficult than it need be because of inefficient work habits. The work on the paper is too often postponed until it is too late to do a decent job of it. Failure to find out at the beginning of the study whether sufficient material is available in the library often invites serious difficulty. Many students tackle the topic in detail before they have formed a general notion of the topic. It is unwise to begin reading the first book available and to plunge into fine points before the student has learned to understand the topic as a whole. The habit of taking notes too soon is inefficient. Students should postpone note-taking until they have decided what kind of information they need. It is also a mistake to quote a paragraph in its en-tirety. The notes should consist of the factual information taken from the paragraph.

Because this paragraph was obviously developed one sentence at a time, the writer failed to maintain any consistent point of view toward his material. He changes from active to passive voice, from a personal to an impersonal subject, and he uses seven different subjects for the nine sentences of his paragraph. As a result there is no grammatical consist-ency within the paragraph, and it reads as jerkily as it was composed.

Notice the improvement in this version:

> Although writing a research paper is a difficult assignment, many students make it more difficult than it need be because of inefficient working habits. Too often they postpone work on the paper until it is too late to do a re-spectable job of it. Often they invite avoidable difficulty by failure to find out at the beginning of their study whether sufficient material is available in the library. Instead of developing a general notion of the topic before tackling it in detail, they begin with the first convenient book and plunge into fine points before they see the topic as a whole. They take more notes than are necessary because they begin to take notes before they have decided what kind of information they need, and because they do not pick out the factual information in a paragraph but quote the paragraph in its entirety.

The biggest change here is that the noun *students* or its pronoun *they* has been made the subject of every sentence. This not only eliminates unnecessary and awkward shifting but allows the writer's purpose to develop easily and steadily through successive sentences.

It is of course not necessary that every sentence in a paragraph have the same subject. Changes of subject within a paragraph are often neces-sary or wise. But when arbitrary changes destroy coherence, revision to avoid these shifts will often greatly improve the paragraph.

Coherence Through Pronoun Reference. Since a pronoun refers to an antecedent, the use of a pronoun in one sentence to point back to an antecedent in the one before is a simple and natural connecting device. Notice how the alternating use of pronoun and antecedent provides effective transitions in the following sentences:

> In the history of the American film no other single personality has so endeared himself to the world as Charlie Chaplin. His presence is as much alive as ever in the thousands of 16 mm. revivals of his work. Every generation takes him to its heart anew. As with all great characters one sees in Chaplin what one brings to him.[15]

The use of pronouns often allows a writer to keep his subject running through the paragraph without falling into monotonous repetition. Notice how this is done in the following paragraph, in which nominative, possessive, and objective forms of the same pronoun bind the sentences together by inconspicuous repetition.

> He was a monster of conceit. Never for one moment did he look at the world or at people, except in relation to himself. He was not only the most important person in the world, to himself: in his own eyes he was the only person who existed. He believed himself to be one of the greatest dramatists in the world, one of the greatest thinkers, and one of the greatest composers. To hear him talk, he was Shakespeare, and Beethoven, and Plato rolled into one. . . .[16]

Transitional Markers. These are words or phrases placed at or near the beginning of a sentence or clause to signal the relationship between the new sentence and the one before it. The commonest markers are the simple connectives *and, or, nor, but, for,* which serve as bridges over which the reader may easily pass from one sentence or clause to the next. Others — sometimes called transitional connectives — indicate the direction which the new sentence is about to take and so prepare the reader for what is to follow. The commonest transitional connectives may be classified as follows:

1. To introduce an illustration: *thus, for example, for instance, to illustrate.*

2. To add another phase of the same idea: *secondly, in the second place, next, moreover, in addition, similarly, again, also, finally.*

3. To point a contrast or qualification: *on the other hand, nevertheless, despite this fact, on the contrary, still, however.*

4. To indicate a conclusion or result: *therefore, in conclusion, to sum up, consequently, as a result, accordingly, in other words.*

[15] From *The Rise of the American Film* by Lewis Jacobs. Copyright, 1939, by Lewis Jacobs. Reprinted by permission of Harcourt, Brace and Company.

[16] A description of Richard Wagner, from *Of Men and Music* by Deems Taylor. Copyright, 1937, by Deems Taylor. Reprinted by permission of Simon and Schuster, Publishers.

You have already seen a few of these transitional markers used in the revised versions of both faulty paragraphs discussed in the preceding pages. Here is another illustration.

> Such a controlling purpose, of course, limits the appeal of the book, and probably this work will have a greater attraction for the layman than for the professional historian. *Moreover,* it always runs the risk of producing a book which, because of its lack of any unifying theme, is merely another book about the subject with which it deals. There are, *indeed,* moments when one feels that the author has not sufficiently resisted the temptation to add another story merely because it is a good story, without concerning himself too much about the relationship of the story to the theme that he is developing. *Thus* the chapter dealing with Strang's kingdom on Beaver Island hardly escapes being an eight-page digression, since it has no other claim to being an integral part of the story of the development of the Great Lakes than the fact that Beaver Island happened to be located in Lake Michigan. The story, of course, is interesting, *but* like a cuckoo in a sea-gull's nest, it would be more at home in other quarters.

To see the value of the connectives in this paragraph, one need only read it again and omit them.

The following paragraph uses various transitional devices:

> The good educator is very serious but also very sensible. (And) somewhere in (his) soul there is a saving lightness. (He) understands, to begin with, the meaning of a recent remark: "Not everything can be learned." (Some things) are never taught; they are simply known. (Other things) cannot in the nature of things be known, either by student or by teacher. (And then) there is that endless series of knowable things only a few of which can be bestowed upon the student during the fragment of his life he spends in school.[17]

The transitional devices in this paragraph are the connectives *And* and *And then,* the pronouns *he* and *his* pointing back to the antecedent *educator,* and the connecting relationship between the words *everything, Some things,* and *Other things.* Still a subtler linking is achieved by the words *learned . . . taught . . . known . . . knowable.*

Here is another example:

	In a world in which the leaders of war democracies are the Daladiers and Chamberlains and Churchills, *we*
Deliberate	*have reason to be proud of* (Lincoln.) *We have reason to*
repetition	*be proud* that *with every opportunity* of setting up a dictatorship, (he) did not *succumb; with every opportunity*
Deliberate	of betraying democratic values under the guise of war
repetition	necessity, (he) did not *succumb. . . .* I have no intention of saying that Lincoln was wholly consistent in the strength of (his) humanism. . . . Yet there never was a

[17] From *Liberal Education* by Mark Van Doren. Copyright 1943 by Henry Holt and Company, publishers. Reprinted by permission.

Interconnection   time when it was more important for us than now to
of pronouns and   know the capacity of a democracy to turn up *greatness*
antecedents   of Lincoln's sort from its humblest sons — a *greatness*
                        that will survive the grime and savagery of war.[18]

All the transitional devices we have discussed are used in this paragraph. Lincoln, although his name is seldom the actual subject of a sentence, is referred to in almost every sentence and thus gives the paragraph a continuity of subject; the pronoun references help tie the paragraph together; the purposeful repetition of similar phrasing in the first half of the paragraph strengthens the coherence; and the transitional connective *Yet* links the last sentence with the one preceding it.

Coherence Between Paragraphs. We have been thinking of the single paragraph as a unit. But it is, of course, only one of several units in the larger scheme of the whole paper. Just as there should be coherence *within* the paragraph, so there should be coherence *between* paragraphs.

In a well-organized essay developing a thesis, the relationship between paragraphs will be clear, for the reader will be following the thesis, and, especially if the topic sentence appears at the beginning of each paragraph, he will have no trouble seeing the relationship of each new paragraph to what has gone before. For example, each topic sentence of the paragraph outline contrasting the real college with a movie version (page 12) related that paragraph to the thesis; each main unit of the outline on reducing the voting age (page 59) clearly referred to the thesis.

Relating each topic sentence to the thesis creates the effect of "signposting" each paragraph, of informing the reader in advance what each is going to do, what part of the thesis it is going to develop. Such signposts serve the double purpose of setting off each paragraph as a structural unit of the essay and of providing transitions between paragraphs. Notice the signposts in the next selection.

The politicians tell us, "You must educate the masses because they are going to be masters." The clergy join in the cry for education, for they affirm that the people are drifting away from church and chapel into the broadest infidelity. The manufacturers and the capitalists swell the chorus lustily. They declare that ignorance makes bad workmen. . . . And a few voices are lifted up in favor of the doctrine that the masses should be educated because they are men and women with unlimited capacities for being, doing, and suffering, and that it is as true now as ever it was that the people perish for lack of knowledge.

These members of the minority, with whom I confess I have a good deal of sympathy, . . . question if it be wise to tell people that you will do for them, out of fear of their power, what you have left undone, so long as your only motive was compassion for their weakness and their sorrows. And if ignorance of everything which it is needful a ruler should

[18] From Max Lerner's review of Carl Sandburg's *Abraham Lincoln: The War Years,* in *New Republic,* December 6, 1939. Reprinted by permission of *New Republic.*

know is likely to do so much harm in the governing classes of the future, why is it, they ask reasonably enough, that such ignorance in the governing classes of the past has not been viewed with equal horror? . . .

(Again,) (this sceptical minority) asks the clergy to think whether it is really want of education which keeps the masses away from their ministrations — whether the most completely educated men are not as open to reproach on this score as the workmen; and whether, perchance, this may not indicate that it is not education which lies at the bottom of this matter?

(Once more,) (these people,) whom there is no pleasing, venture to doubt whether the glory, which rests upon being able to undersell all the rest of the world, is a very safe kind of glory — whether we may not purchase it too dear; especially if we allow education, which ought to be directed to the making of men, to be diverted into a process of manufacturing human tools, wonderfully adroit in the exercise of some technical industry, but good for nothing else.

(And finally,) (these people) inquire whether it is the masses alone who need a reformed and improved education. . . . They seem to think that the noble foundations of our old universities are hardly fulfilling their functions. . . . And while as zealous for education as the rest, they affirm that if the education of the richer classes were such as to fit them to be the leaders and the governors of the poorer, and if the education of the poorer classes were such as to enable them to appreciate really wise guidance and good governance, the politicians need not fear mob-law, nor the clergy lament their want of flocks, nor the capitalists prognosticate the annihilation of the prosperity of the country.[19]

As the circled expressions show, Huxley uses two sets of transitional devices: the signposts *Again, Once more, Finally,* to mark the transition from one paragraph to the next; and the references *These members of the minority, this sceptical minority, these people,* to point back to the people holding the opinion described at the end of the first paragraph.

Transitional Paragraphs. Occasionally a whole short paragraph may serve as a transition. Such a paragraph always comes at a point where the author has finished one main unit of his composition and is about to start another. The transitional paragraph may be used in several ways. It may sum up what has been said before beginning the next unit. It may introduce one or more illustrations of a point already made. Or it may state what the writer intends to do next. The following paragraphs illustrate these uses.

To sum up before beginning the next unit:

Before we begin to analyze the merits of this proposal, let us review what we have already established. We have shown that the proposed program has several times been offered to the American people and has always been rejected. We have shown that its proponents have attempted

[19] From "A Liberal Education and Where to Find It" by T. H. Huxley.

to manufacture a need which does not exist. We have further shown that the program is being advocated by diverse groups which have nothing in common except a conviction that what is best for their special interests must also be best for the country.

To introduce a series of illustrations:

The point that I have been making is necessarily abstract. In order to make it more concrete, let me cite three illustrations, all of which are drawn from common experience.

To show what the writer intends to do next:

Now, you may admit all these things and yet inquire what can be done about them without sacrificing values that have become precious to us all. Since I realize that this question is a just one, I shall outline briefly the organization of the University of Utopia. It will be seen that not all the features of this university are new and original. At Wisconsin, Harvard, Swarthmore, and numerous other places, many phases of its plan have been tried and have succeeded. Much of the rest of the program has been under discussion at the University of Chicago and elsewhere for some years.[20]

These transitional paragraphs connect what has gone before with what is to follow. Each is a sort of aside to the reader in which the writer shows the relations between parts of his work. The transitional paragraph, then, links larger units as a transitional word or phrase connects sentences or paragraphs.

Assignments in Paragraphing

As a practical application of what we have been saying, let us take three assignments and work them out as finished paragraphs. For each we shall first state the problem, then analyze it, and finally present one possible solution.

Assignment A

A student is preparing a paper with the thesis that Thomas Jefferson's writings are characterized by habits of careful research and independent thinking. As one illustration of the thesis she wants to cite Jefferson's work, *The Life and Morals of Jesus of Nazareth*. Here is the material she has in her notes.

1. T. J. pasted Greek, Latin, French, and English texts of New Testament side by side.
2. T. J. thought the Bible should be read critically, like any other book.

[20] From "The University of Utopia" by R. M. Hutchins, in *The Yale Review*, March, 1931. Copyright 1931 by Yale University Press. Reprinted by permission.

3. T. J. accepted or rejected stories about Jesus on the basis of their agreement with natural laws. Thus the teachings of Jesus OK, but miracles out. Anything that had to be explained by revelation also out.
4. "I think that every Christian sect gives a great handle to atheism by their general dogma that, without revelation, there would not be sufficient proof of the being of God" — Letter to Adams
5. T. J. considered Christianity purest system of morality known.

If this student simply strings these notes together to look like a paragraph (as students sometimes do), this is the kind of product she will have:

Jefferson could read Greek, Latin, French, and English, so he pasted texts of the New Testament in these languages side by side. He thought that the Bible should be read critically, like any other book; so he accepted those stories about Jesus which agreed with natural laws, and rejected those that did not. He kept the teachings of Jesus but rejected the miracles. He also rejected anything that had to be explained by revelation. "I think," he wrote in a letter to Adams, "that every Christian sect gives a great handle to atheism by their general dogma that, without revelation, there would not be sufficient proof of the being of God." Jefferson considered Christianity the purest system of morality known.

Notice the weaknesses of this paragraph:

1. Although it discusses a book mentioned in a preceding paragraph, it does nothing to show a relation with that paragraph or any other. It needs some transitional sentence or phrase to tie it to what went before.
2. What is the purpose of the paragraph? We know from the description of the assignment that the writer wants to illustrate Jefferson's habits of careful research and independent thinking. The information does illustrate these habits, but its significance would be made clearer if stated in a topic sentence.
3. While the repetition of "He" provides some natural coherence within the paragraph, pronoun reference alone is not enough. The monotonous sentence structure and the lack of transition between the first two sentences and between the last two leave the paragraph merely a loose collection of sentences.
4. The last sentence seems to have no relation to the rest of the paragraph. If it is not a digression, its function should be indicated.

Now contrast the unsatisfactory paragraph with the one the student wrote:

The actual writing of the book was controlled by two disciplines: careful collection and comparison of the evidence, and the acceptance or rejection of it on the basis of reason rather than authority. To compare the evidence, Jefferson pasted texts from the New Testament in Greek, Latin, French, and English in columns side by side. As he was proficient in all four languages he felt that he could come closer to the true meanings of the words by reading them in this way. To ensure that reason rather than the authority of tradition would guide him, he followed his own advice that the Bible should be read critically, like any other book. Accordingly, he accepted those stories which revealed the teachings of Jesus, and rejected stories of miracles, which, he felt, had no real relation to these teachings. He also rejected those passages which had to be supported by revelation. "I think," he wrote in a letter to Adams, "that every Christian sect gives a great handle to atheism by their general dogma that, without revelation, there would not be sufficient proof of the being of God." The result was a work which emphasized what Jefferson considered the purest system of morality known and toned down or omitted incidents which required a supernatural explanation.

Notice:

1. The topic sentence, which states the purpose of the paragraph (and so gives point to all that follows) and also refers to the preceding paragraph by the phrase "The actual writing of the book."
2. The explanation of why Jefferson pasted the four different texts side by side. This explanation is necessary to illustrate the thoroughness of his working habits.
3. The clearer explanation of his selection and rejection of material ("To ensure that reason rather than authority . . ."). This explanation helps to bind together four sentences which, in the unsatisfactory version, were connected only by a common subject.
4. The concluding sentence, which not only shows the pertinence of what previously looked like a digression but also, by showing Jefferson's emphasis, sums up the content of the whole paragraph.
5. The more pleasing effect obtained by slight but significant variations in the basic sentence pattern.
6. Finally, the fact that in shaping her notes into a paragraph the writer was doing a creative piece of composition. She was making something from her material, giving form to the information she had acquired, not just presenting it unedited.

Assignment B

A student has been asked to write a paragraph on democracy. In thinking about that subject he recognizes certain advantages of democracy and certain difficulties, which he jots down in contrasting columns.

Advantages	*Difficulties*
1. freedom of speech	1. responsibility to be well informed about all pertinent matters
2. freedom to think as he pleases	
3. freedom to worship (or not to worship) as he pleases	2. responsibility to evaluate conflicting policies and sense their effects on the future
4. the right and opportunity to engage in whatever work he chooses	3. distinction between interests of special groups and general welfare
	4. conflict between rights of majority and rights of minority

He wants to organize this material into a unified, coherent, and well-developed paragraph. How should he proceed?

One way would be to begin with a topic sentence which states that democracy has both advantages and difficulties and then list first the advantages and then the difficulties. If he does that, the paragraph will not advance beyond the notes. It will simply present the notes in paragraph form.

Another way would be to tie each advantage to a disadvantage under a topic sentence which says that, for every advantage it offers, democracy imposes a corresponding difficulty. The pattern of development in this method would be similar to that of the contrast between death at sea and death on land in the paragraph given on pages 73–74. This method will not prove to be practical, because the advantages and the difficulties do not *correspond* — that is, there is no clear relation between any one advantage and any one difficulty, and so the contrast would seem arbitrary.

A third way is to recognize that the opposite of "difficult" is "easy," and to organize the material under a topic sentence which says that democracy is both the easiest and most difficult form of government, and then to present the material which makes democracy seem easy before the material which makes it seem difficult. The student tries this method and writes the following paragraph.

> Democracy is both the easiest and most difficult form of government for the citizen. It is the easiest because it allows people to speak and think and worship as they please and to engage in whatever occupations they think they are most fitted for. It is the most difficult because it requires them to be well informed about all political matters and to evaluate conflicting policies, not only for their immediate results but also for the effects they will produce in the future. It also requires people to be alert to the conflicts that arise between special interests and the general welfare and between the rights of the majority and the rights of the minority.

This paragraph is acceptable but not effective. Although it organizes the material of the notes in a straightforward manner, the result is not much better than what could have been achieved by the first method. But it will serve for a first draft. The student's problem now is to consider how it can be improved in revision. As he studies the paragraph, he makes the following notes to himself:

1. Change "people" to "the citizen" or "the individual" or "a man" so as to present the argument from the point of view of one person rather than of many and thus personalize the argument.
2. Get more contrast between the two parts of the paragraph by introducing the idea that the characteristics of democracy that make it easy for a man are not free; they have to be paid for by the difficulties.
3. Point up each half of the paragraph by a sentence that acts as a topic sentence for each half. This will tend to tie particular statements together.

4. Try to make more use of parallel structure in presenting particular difficulties. This will provide both greater coherence and greater emphasis.
5. The paragraph as now written is still pretty general. Try to provide more specific development in the revision, especially for the third sentence.

In accordance with his own directive to himself, he now revises the paragraph as follows:

> From the point of view of the ordinary citizen, democracy is both the easiest and most difficult form of government. It is the easiest because it permits each citizen a high degree of freedom. In a democracy, more than in any other form of government, he remains his own man — free to think, talk, and worship as he pleases, and, within wide limits, free to engage in whatever kind of profession or career he is fitted for. Yet these privileges are not purchased without a price. For a democracy makes heavy demands on each citizen. It places upon him the responsibility of being continually informed of the needs not only of his own country but of the whole world. It requires him to weigh and decide which of several conflicting policies will best meet these needs. It demands that he distinguish between the interests of special groups and the general welfare, and between immediate and long-range interests. It insists that he learn to observe the will of the majority without ignoring the rights of minorities. And it constantly requires of him the difficult task of seeing the implications of economic, political, and social theories and of sensing the effect that these implications will have in the lives of his grandchildren.

One way to describe the difference between the two versions of this paragraph is to say that the style of the second has been improved. Another way is to say that the second provokes a more complete response from the reader and so has more meaning for him. For our purposes, the important thing to recognize is that the writer's job was not finished with the first draft. That draft was still an unfinished product, as most first drafts are.

Assignment C

In the play *Antigone,* Polynices, the brother of Antigone and Ismene, is killed while leading a rebellion against the state. Creon, the king, decrees that the corpse shall be denied the burial which the practices of religion require. Ismene accepts this decree but Antigone defies it and buries her brother at the cost of her own life. After reading the play, a student writes an essay containing the following paragraph.

> It is not surprising that Antigone and Ismene react quite differently to Creon's ban on the burial of their brother. Antigone has spent much of her life with death, misfortune, and hardship. It wasn't an easy task, I'm sure, for her to look after her blind father, Oedipus, during the wanderings of his exile, no matter how much she loved him, but during these years she learned a sense of responsibility to one's family which Ismene was not required to

learn. Oedipus was constantly talking about the will of the gods and the importance of putting religious duties first. He talked frequently, too, about death as a release from pain. He had a temper that would fly up suddenly and cause him to act impulsively and rashly, without thinking about his own safety. And he despised Creon and his concern with only political considerations. It is only natural that some of this temperament would rub off on Antigone — like father, like daughter — and cause her to defy Creon's order. Ismene has been less influenced by Oedipus. She has been brought up by Creon and taught to obey him.

In a conference the instructor tells him:

The point you are making is a good one, but this paragraph does not make it as clearly as it might, partly because the paragraph needs tightening up and partly because the structure of the contrast is blurred through making Oedipus the subject of four sentences in the middle of the paragraph. I suggest the following procedure for revision:

1. Before you begin to write, make two lists, one containing the attitudes or values that Antigone learned from Oedipus, the other containing the attitudes that Ismene learned from Creon. Use these lists as the basic material of your paragraph.

2. Explain Antigone's background in less space than you now use, without leaving out anything that helps develop your topic sentence. Keep Oedipus in the background. You want to focus on the Antigone-Ismene contrast, and the more attention you give to Oedipus, the more you blur that basic contrast.

3. Then develop the Ismene side of the contrast; her background can stand more detailed treatment.

4. It might be wise to work into your topic sentence the idea that the two girls had quite different backgrounds. That is the important point. It is only because their backgrounds were different that their different reactions are not surprising.

5. Mark the transitional point in the contrast by some transitional device — *But, Yet, On the other hand,* etc.

6. Clinch the idea of the paragraph by restating the topic sentence in new form as a conclusion.

The student studies these directions and rewrites the paragraph as follows:

It is not surprising that Antigone and Ismene react quite differently to Creon's ban on the burial of their brother. The two sisters are products of different experiences. As the constant companion of Oedipus, Antigone has acquired from her father a strong sense of religious and family obligation and a conviction that divine laws take precedence over human laws. She has also learned to subordinate personal considerations of security and happiness to her religious duties. Perhaps she has also acquired something of her father's contempt for Creon as a person and for the narrow political values which he represents. It is natural, therefore, for her to reject Creon's authority when it clashes with her conviction that her brother must be given a burial service. Ismene, by contrast, has been little influenced by her father's religious values. She has grown up safely and securely in Thebes as a member of Creon's household. In her environment the values were political rather than religious, and the emphasis was on unquestioning obedience to political authority, to Creon as the ruler of the state and the ruler of the household. In accepting Creon's decree she merely did what she had been brought up to do. It is not necessary to assume that she loved Polynices less than Antigone did. Given their different backgrounds, it was as natural for Ismene to obey Creon as it was for Antigone to defy him.

Contrast the original and revised versions and decide: (1) whether you agree with the instructor's criticism of the original, (2) whether the student satisfied that criticism in his revision, (3) whether the revised version shows enough improvement to justify the efforts of both the instructor and the student.

Exercises

A. Study the structure of the following paragraphs carefully. Notice, especially, what the purpose of each paragraph is, how that purpose is expressed, what kinds of material are used to develop the purpose, what order the sentences follow, and what means the writer uses to obtain coherence. Then select two or three paragraphs, make notes on their contents and, without further reference to these paragraphs, recompose them from your notes. Finally, compare your reconstructed version with the original and make any needed revisions in content and style.

(1)

The major artist, the tragic realist who wishes to present the world common to all rather than a dream world, must temper his insight with detachment. Once he has created a fictional personage with a definite character or moral bent — a Romeo, a Hamlet, an Othello, a Captain Ahab — that character or moral bent becomes an antecedent from which certain consequences inevitably follow. The tragic realist cannot save his hero from the consequences of character, nor does he attempt to do so. He cannot rescue his hero from the universal tragic predicament of human beings, nor does he attempt to do so. The best he can do for his hero is to grant him (and us as spectators or readers) a flash of insight into the meaning of human destiny, an insight which reconciles him to his fate. At the end Captain Ahab must die, but he accepts his fate, content to be what he is. And we, as we view with insight the full unfolding of the inevitable consequences of individual character and of universal human nature, are content to be what we are, human beings who share a common fate which is both terrible and glorious.[21]

[21] From "Literature, Science, and Democracy" by Henry Myers, in *Pacific Spectator,* Vol. VIII, No. 4, Autumn, 1954. Reprinted by permission.

(2)

In the year 1830 a French customs official unearthed, in the valley of the Somme, strange implements of flint now recognized by the learned as the weapons with which the men of the Old Stone Age made war. These stones are called *coups de poing,* or "blows of the fist," for one end was rounded to be grasped in the hand, while the other end was pointed for persuasion. With these modest tools of death, it seems, Neanderthal men from what is now Germany, and Cro-Magnon men from what is now France, fought fifty thousand years ago for the mastery of the continent, and, after a day of lusty battle, left perhaps a score of dead on the field. Twenty years ago, modern Germans and modern Frenchmen fought again, in that same valley, for that same prize, with magnificent tools of death that killed ten thousand men in a day. One art alone has made indisputable progress in history and that is the art of war.[22]

(3)

In the United States life, liberty, and the pursuit of happiness are constitutionally guaranteed. But if life hardly seems worth living, if liberty is used for subhuman purposes, if the pursuers of happiness know nothing about the nature of their quarry or the elementary techniques of hunting, these constitutional rights will not be very meaningful. An education in that wise passiveness recommended by the saints and the poets, by all who have lived fully and worked creatively, might help us to transform the paper promises of a democratic constitution into concrete contemporary fact.[23]

(4)

An examination of a bit of skin under a high-powered microscope indicates that the matter [the assumption that each spot on the skin has a specialized sensory ending which produces sensations of cold, heat, pain, or touch] is not so simple. The deep layers of the skin contain a large number of sensory fibers of various sizes. Each fiber branches like a tree, and its branches interweave with the branches of many neighboring fibers. At the end of each branch is a sensory receptor characteristic of that particular fiber. These receptors range in complexity from highly organized structures of considerable size to "bare" undifferentiated fibrils with no more than a tiny knob at the tip. The intermingling of the fiber branches and the great number of different endings at any one skin spot suggest how difficult it would be to stimulate one ending or one fiber selectively. An ordinary stimulus, whether a pinprick, a light touch or pressure, invariably activates a large number of different sensory fibers. The evidence is inescapable that the sensations we describe as "touch" and "pain" must be derived from the concurrent activation of many different sensory fibers of various sizes and distribution.[24]

[22] From "Why Men Fight" by Will Durant, in *The Saturday Evening Post,* July 10, 1937. Reprinted by permission of the author and the Curtis Publishing Company.

[23] From "Education on the Nonverbal Level" by Aldous Huxley, in *Daedalus* (the Journal of the American Academy of Arts and Sciences), Vol. 91, No. 2, Spring, 1962. Reprinted by permission of publisher and author.

[24] From "What Is Pain?" by W. K. Livingston, in the *Scientific American Reader* (New York: 1953). Reprinted by permission of the original publisher, *Scientific American.*

(5)

Below them lay a little semicircular green cove. At its deepest indentation a full brook splashed into the lake. The curving, shining channel led back up to a large white frame house shaped like an L with the long side facing the wide water. It stood in dazzling brightness and its reflecting white sides gave it so clean and luminous a quality that sight of it seemed almost unbearable in the intense clarity. The effect was the stronger for the softness of the atmosphere that lay upon the lake. Out there was blueness and a misty blending of light and air. Here the sun seemed to have sent a straight shaft down to illumine the objects within a sharply defined circle. In the center stood the tall white house, and on the edges but still within the light squatted weathered gray log cabins. Beyond the circle other cabins, many of them, were indistinct in the blurred distance. Where the upward slope of the shore ended on a high plateau a grove of towering hickories dispelled the light and seemed to keep it from spilling outside the circle.[25]

(6)

Conversely, it may be doubted whether things do in fact change as much as they sometimes seem to. The evidence for the stability of human affairs is just as easily at hand. Even where the change is most dramatic, there is always an undertow. The tide looks as though it will engulf everything, as science at one time looked as though it might engulf religion, but there is always the ebb. In social affairs, one might even propound a weaker version of the second law of thermodynamics: To every action there is a *nearly* equal and usually opposite reaction. Political traditions, for example, do not easily change simply because men wish it so. Whether we see the stability or the flux depends, to a large extent, on us.[26]

(7)

What we know of prenatal development makes all this [attempts to mould the unborn child's character by the conduct of the mother during pregnancy] seem utterly impossible. How could such extremely complex influences pass from the mother to the child? There is no connection between their nervous systems. Even the blood vessels of mother and child do not join directly. They lie side by side and the chemicals are interchanged through the walls by a process that we call osmosis. An emotional shock to the mother will affect her child, because it changes the activity of her glands and so the chemistry of her blood. Any chemical change in the mother's blood will affect the child — for better or worse. But we cannot see how a liking for mathematics or poetic genius can be dissolved in the blood and produce a similar liking or genius in the child.[27]

[25] From *Genesee Fever* by Carl Carmer. Copyright 1941 by Carl Carmer. Reprinted by permission of the author.
[26] From "A Fable of Time and Class" by K. R. Minogue, in *The American Scholar*, Vol. 30, No. 2, Spring, 1961. Copyright © 1961 by the United Chapters of Phi Beta Kappa. Reprinted by permission of the publishers.
[27] From *Psychology You Can Use,* by William H. Roberts. Copyright 1943 by Harcourt, Brace & World, Inc. Reprinted by permission of the publishers.

SUSTAINED EXAMPLE *(8)*

The merely *eventful* men in history [as contrasted with the *event-making* men] play a role that may be compared to that of the little Dutch boy who kept his finger in the hole in the dike and saved the town. Without meaning to strip the legend of its glamour, we can point out that almost anybody in the situation could have done it. All that was required was a boy, a finger, and the lucky chance of passing by. The event itself in the life of the community was of tremendous significance. It saved the town just as a little Dutch boy at Pearl Harbor might have saved the fleet if his alarm had been acted upon in time. But the qualities required to cope with the situation were of a fairly common distribution. Here, so to speak, one stumbles upon greatness just as one might stumble on a treasure that will ransom a town. Greatness, however, is something that must involve extraordinary talent of some kind and not merely the compounded luck of being born and of being present at the right place at a happy moment.[28]

(9)

To see fallout radiation in proper perspective it should be compared not only with other kinds of radiation but also with other dangers to health. Some estimates are, for example, that being 10% overweight seems to reduce a person's life expectancy by 1.5 years, that the life-long habit of smoking one package of cigarets a day cuts it by seven years, that living in the city instead of in the country reduces life expectancy by five years, and so on. On this statistical scale the reduction in life expectancy from worldwide fallout at present levels totals less than two days. Or, to put it another way, the worldwide fallout is as dangerous to human health as being one ounce overweight, or smoking one cigaret every two months.[29]

(10)

I think, too, that the way in which boys and girls differ is not what the masculine and feminine stereotypes have led us to expect. Boys, for example, seem to me usually more concerned with their appearance than girls and also to have more idea what they actually look like and how other people will respond to the way they look. Our image of a beautiful girl is so rigidly defined and constantly reiterated by every medium of communication that it has become in a sense highly impersonal. Not every girl can be beautiful; but even a girl who is gets less credit for it than she deserves. It is always a little like seeing the Riviera; however breathtaking the effect, one's very first response is that it looks exactly the way it is supposed to, and that one has seen it before. Girls, therefore, are likely to approach beauty as if it were an effect to be achieved — not an *artificial* effect but still an *external* one — the invocation of a social norm which exists altogether independently of themselves. And their attitude toward the result is likely to be quite detached. A vain young woman is, in my experience, rare.

[28] From Sidney Hook, *The Hero in History,* published by The John Day Company. Copyright, 1943, by Sidney Hook. Reprinted by permission of the author.
[29] From *Our Nuclear Future* by Edward Teller and Albert L. Latter (New York: 1958). Copyright 1958 by Criterion Books, Inc. Reprinted by permission of the publishers.

Boys, in contrast, are often very vain; and their vanity is very personal; if they are handsome, they think of their handsomeness as peculiarly their own. They dress for it specifically, not according to social norms; a well-built, sun-bronzed boy will fight like a tiger to keep his mother from getting him out of his torn T-shirt and Ivy League pants with the useful buckle in the back, and into a conservative suit designed to conceal his fearful symmetry. Boys seem to get a different kind of satisfaction than girls from response to their physical attractiveness. Girls, I believe, are likely to find admiration for their beauty stimulating — not in the erotic sense, but as an awareness that physical attraction may open avenues to a variety of interesting relationships and experiences; they become more alert. Boys seem to become less alert; they bask in physical regard like alligators on a log. Provided there is no seductive purpose behind the response they arouse — and this they are very quick to sense and resent — it seems to reassure them, and they get sleepy.[30]

B. Study the following selection, with particular reference to: (1) the purpose, (2) the function of each paragraph with respect to the purpose, (3) the means by which each paragraph is developed, (4) the means by which the various paragraphs are connected into a coherent whole. After you have studied the structure of the selection, outline it, make notes on its content, and, without referring to the original, reconstruct the essay in your own words from your notes and outline.

Death is the great scandal in the experience of man; for death — as the destruction of the human person after a finite span of time — is the very negation of all man experiences as specifically human in his existence: the consciousness of himself and of his world, the remembrance of things past and the anticipation of things to come, a creativeness in thought and action which aspires to, and approximates, the eternal. Thus man has been compelled, for the sake of his existence as man, to bridge the gap between death and his specifically human attributes by transcending death. He has done so in three different ways: by making himself, within narrow limits, the master of death; by denying the reality of death through the belief in the immortality of his person; by conquering the reality of death through the immortality of the world he leaves behind.

Man can make himself the master of death by putting an end to his biological existence whenever he wishes. While he cannot live as long as he wants to, he can stop living whenever he wants to. While he cannot choose life over death when his life has reached its biological limits, he can choose death over life regardless of these limits. He can commit suicide; or he can commit what Nietzsche has called "suicide with a good conscience" by seeking out death, especially at the hand of someone else. He is capable of sacrificial death. In his self-chosen death for a cause in particular, on the battlefield or elsewhere, man triumphs over death, however incompletely. He triumphs because he does not wait until his body is ready to die, but he offers his life to death when his chosen purpose demands it. Yet that triumph is incomplete because it cannot overcome the inevitability of death but only controls its coming.

[30] From *The Vanishing Adolescent* by Edgar Z. Friedenberg. Reprinted by permission of the Beacon Press, copyright © 1959 by Edgar Z. Friedenberg.

Man also denies the reality of death by believing in the immortality of his person. This belief can take two different forms. It may take the form of the assumption that the finiteness of man's biological existence is but apparent and that his body will live on in another world. It can also take the form of the assumption that what is specifically human in man will survive the destruction of his body and that man's soul will live on forever, either separated from any body or reincarnated in someone else's. This belief in personal immortality, in defiance of the empirical evidence of the finiteness of man's biological existence, is of course peculiar to the religious realm. It presupposes the existence of a world which is not only inaccessible to the senses but also superior to the world of the senses in that what is truly human in man is there preserved forever.

It is a distinctive characteristic of our secular age that it has replaced the belief in the immortality of the human person with the attempt to assure the immortality of the world he leaves behind. Man can transcend the finiteness of his biological existence either in his consciousness or in objective reality by adding to that existence four different dimensions which are in one way or another independent of that finiteness. They are different dimensions of immortality. He can extend his consciousness into the past by remembering it. He can extend his consciousness into the future by anticipating it. As *homo faber,* he embeds his biological existence within technological and social artifacts which survive that existence. His imagination creates new worlds of religion, art, and reason that live after their creator.

By thus bestowing immortality upon the past, man assures himself of immortality to be granted by future generations who will remember him. As the past lives on in his historic recollection, so will he continue to live in the memory of his successors. The continuity of history gives the individual at least a chance to survive himself in the collective memory of mankind. Those who are eminent, or believe themselves to be so, aspire to posthumous fame which will enable them to live on, perhaps forever.

The ability to remember and the aspiration to be remembered call for deliberate action to assure that remembrance. The assurance of his life after death becomes one of man's main concerns here and now. Man on all levels of civilization is moved to create monuments which testify to his existence and will live after him. He founds a family and lives on in his sons, who bear his name as he bears his father's. He leaves an inheritance of visible things not to be consumed but to be preserved as tangible mementos of past generations. Over his grave he causes a monument of stone to be erected whose durability, as it were, compensates for the impermanence of what lies beneath. Or he may even refuse to accept that impermanence altogether and have his body preserved in the likeness of life. At the very least, he will have pictures made of himself to perpetuate his physical likeness.

This concern with immortality in this world manifests itself on the highest level of consciousness in the preparation of man's fame. He lives in such a way as to make sure that his fame will survive him. All of us, from the peasant and handicraft man to the founders of churches, the architects of empires, the builders of cities, the tamers of the forces of nature, seek to leave behind the works of our wills and hands to testify to our existence. "*Roma eterna,*" "the Reich of a thousand years" are but the most ambitious attempts to perpetuate man in his deeds. The tree that he has planted, the house that he has built, have been given a life likely to last longer than his own. At best, he as a person will live on in his works; at worst, he has the satisfaction of living on anonymously in what he has created.

It is, however, in the works of his imagination that man conquers the mortality of his body in the most specifically human way. The artists and poets, the philosophers and the writers, can point with different degrees of assurance to their work and say with Horace: "I have finished a monument more lasting than bronze and loftier than the Pyramids' royal pile, one that no wasting rain, no furious north wind can destroy, or the countless chain of years and the ages' flight. I shall not altogether die. . . ." In the works of his mind it is not just his physical existence, the bare fact that he once lived, that is remembered. Rather, what is remembered is the creative quality that sets him apart from all other creatures, that is peculiar to him as a man. What is remembered is not only the specifically human quality, but also and most importantly the quality in which he lives on as a unique individual, the like of whom has never existed before or since. In the works of his mind, man, the creator, survives.

Yet why are those works a "monument more lasting than bronze," and why can their creator be confident that "on and on shall I grow, ever fresh with the glory of after time"? Because the man endowed with a creative mind knows himself to be a member in an unbroken chain emerging from the past and reaching into the future, which is made of the same stuff his mind is made of and, hence, is capable of participating in, and perpetuating, his mind's creation. He may be mortal, but humanity is not, and so he will be immortal in his works. This is the triumphant message of Horace.

Our life, then, receives one of its meanings from the meaning we give to death. What we make of life is shaped by what we make of death; for we live in the presence of the inevitability of death and we dedicate our lives to the proof of the proposition that death is not what it seems to be: the irrevocable end of our existence. We search for immortality, and the kind of immortality we seek determines the kind of life we lead.[31]

C. Select any three of the following statements. Use each of them as the topic sentence of a substantial paragraph. Develop the paragraph so that it is complete, unified, and coherent.

1. The transition from high school to college life is a difficult one.
2. Essentially, college is a place in which students learn from each other.
3. Student activities belong to the students.
4. The educational value of fraternity bull sessions is greatly overrated.
5. There is a significant distinction between self-confidence and conceit.
6. Much adolescent shyness is sheer egotism.
7. What is college spirit?
8. There never yet was a self-made man.
9. It is easier to confess our sins than our weaknesses.

[31] From "Death in the Nuclear Age" by Hans J. Morgenthau, in *Commentary,* September, 1961. Reprinted by permission of author and publisher.

5

Effective Sentences

In good writing, the sentences should be so constructed that, taken individually and together, they succeed fully in conveying to the reader what the writer has in mind. The handbook section of this text (pages 385 ff.) is concerned with *usage* in the construction of sentences, that is, with conventional forms. In this chapter we shall consider the *effectiveness* of sentences—a rhetorical quality which goes beyond the arrangement of sentence elements and has to do with the best ways of expressing ideas.

Types of Sentences

Approaching sentences from the rhetorical point of view, we may begin by classifying them as *normal, parallel,* and *periodic.* These classifications are not mutually exclusive. A normal sentence often has parallel or periodic elements. But for the purpose of our discussion here it will be useful to recognize these three different types.

Normal Sentences

A normal sentence is the kind you most frequently write and read. It is the kind you find on this page — a sentence of moderate length, usually following a subject-verb-object order, and consisting of at least a main clause but often of a combination of main and subordinate clauses. We can best get at the characteristics of a normal sentence by considering its basic patterns.

Basic Patterns. Most normal sentences are constructed by expanding half a dozen basic patterns. The fundamental pattern of an English sentence is subject followed by predicate. The subject may be a noun or a pronoun, a combination of nouns and pronouns, or anything that can be substituted for a noun or a pronoun in the subject position. Thus we can substitute for "(The) man" in *The man fell* any of the following subjects: *she and I, Bill and his father, all but one of the pins, all the king's horses and all the king's men.*

Predicates are of four types:

1. Verbs without objects (intransitive verbs) — The child *cried.*
2. Verbs with objects (transitive verbs) — The instructor *dismissed the class.*
3. Verbs with complements (linking verbs) — Tom *is a doctor.*
4. Verbs with completing modifiers (linking verbs) — Dad *was angry;* Mother *looked tired.*

The combination of any one of these predicates with a subject gives us four basic types of sentences:

1. S-V (subject + intransitive verb)
2. S-V-O (subject + transitive verb + object)
3. S-v-C (subject + linking verb + complement)
4. S-v-M (subject + linking verb + modifiers)

In addition, English has two other common sentence patterns: the *passive* and the *expletive.* In the passive pattern the positions of the subject and object of a Type 2 sentence are interchanged so that the object now becomes the subject — *The class was dismissed by the instructor.* In the expletive pattern the sentence begins with "There," and the verb, or part of it, comes before the real subject — *There is someone at the door. There have been no tickets sold yet.*

Any two or more of these basic patterns may be combined in a single sentence. If we use numbers for the first four types and *P* and *E* for passive and expletive respectively, we can identify the combinations in the following sentences:

$$\overset{1}{\text{The child cried}} \quad \text{and} \quad \overset{2}{\text{stamped her feet.}}$$

$$\overset{2}{\text{The instructor dismissed the class}} \quad \text{and} \quad \overset{4}{\text{seemed ill.}}$$

$$\overset{3}{\text{He is a doctor}} \quad \text{and} \quad \overset{2}{\text{will help you.}}$$

$$\overset{1}{\text{She blushed}} \quad \text{and} \quad \overset{4}{\text{looked angry}} \quad \text{but} \quad \overset{2}{\text{said nothing.}}$$

$$\overset{P}{\text{The house had been sold}} \quad \text{but} \quad \overset{2}{\text{I did not know that.}}$$

$$\overset{E}{\text{There is a man at the door}} \quad \text{and} \quad \overset{2}{\text{he wants you.}}$$

In each of these sentences two or more types have been combined by joining them with a simple conjunction and sometimes using the same subject for both parts of the sentence.

Phrases and Clauses. Phrases and subordinate clauses are groups of words which act as single elements in a sentence. Thus, in the sentences

$$\underline{\text{Writing}} \quad \text{is difficult}$$
$$\underline{\text{To do that}} \quad \text{is difficult}$$
$$\underline{\text{What you are asking}} \quad \text{is difficult}$$

103

the underlined words act in each instance as a single element — here, the subject. Both the second and third examples are groups of words, but they differ in that the third has a subject (*you*) and a verb (*are asking*) of its own. We call the second subject a *phrase* and the third a *subordinate clause*.

A phrase may be substituted for any basic element in a sentence, even the verb — "She *has been having* trouble." A subordinate clause can serve as subject, object, or complement, or as a modifier of any of these elements, but it is not an independent or main clause — that is, it cannot serve as a sentence by itself. It can serve only as an element in a sentence. Thus, *The child cried* is an independent statement, but *The child who had lost her mother* is not.

Expansion of Basic Patterns. The relatively simple patterns we have considered so far may be expanded by one or more of three rhetorical devices — *coordination, modification, subordination.* Let us examine these in turn.

Coordination. The word "coordinate" means "of equal rank." Ideas are coordinate when they are of equal importance; structures are coordinate when they have similar grammatical forms. Thus in *Yesterday was hot and muggy,* "hot" and "muggy" are equally important and have the same form (adjectives). Whenever such coordinate elements are used in a sentence, they are either joined by a coordinating conjunction (*and, or, nor, but, yet*), as in the example above, or are arranged in series — *a hot, muggy, unpleasant day.*

The device of coordination allows us to compound the elements of our six basic patterns or to combine different types within the same sentence, as we saw earlier. More important, it allows us to combine several ideas in a single sentence. For example, we can join a series of main clauses into one sentence — *John provided the transportation, Mary brought the food, and Jean and I did the cooking.* Or we can precede or follow a main clause with a series of subordinate clauses or phrases:

> If John will provide the transportation and [if] Mary will bring the food, Jean and I will do the cooking.

> My instructions are *to make a thorough study of the subject, to present the essential information in a brief report,* and *to recommend the two most promising courses of action.*

We shall see later that the construction of parallel and periodic sentences depends on this kind of coordination.

Modification. The basic sentence patterns may also be expanded by modifying any of the elements. When we modify, we make the reference more specific by adding limiting or descriptive words to the *headword* — that is, to the word we are modifying. For example, in *The woman had an accident,* we can specify a particular woman and a particular kind of accident — *That pleasant little old woman who delivers fresh eggs in our neighborhood every Monday caught her fingers in the car door.* We can modify objects and complements in the same way, and we can modify verbs by stating when, where, how, why, or under what conditions the action suggested by the verb took place.

Subordination. Subordinate is the opposite of coordinate, and means "of lesser rank." Ideas are subordinate when they are of less importance than other ideas in the same sentence; structures are subordinate when they form phrases or subordinate clauses in contrast to main clauses. Thus in *Her father, who is a reporter, has just won a Pulitzer prize,* the important idea is that her father won a Pulitzer prize. The fact that he is a reporter, instead of a poet, a biographer, or a novelist, is less important in this sentence, and so is reduced to a subordinate clause.

Subordination allows us to expand the basic sentence patterns by incorporating material without simply coupling it to other information or arranging it in series. Through subordination, we are able to express a great deal of information in an economical way and still emphasize what is most important. For example, we could combine the following pieces of information in one sentence by coordination:

1. Our regular physician is Dr. Meyers. 2. He is on vacation. 3. We called Dr. Johnson. 4. He shares an office with Dr. Meyers.

But coordination would merely allow us to string the pieces together. If, instead, we select the third item as the most important, and subordinate the other items to it, we can get the sentence:

Because our regular physician, Dr. Meyers, is on vacation, we called his office mate, Dr. Johnson.

The economy of this combination is obvious. By subordinating three items to the fourth we are able to express all the information in a single sentence, in fewer words, and with more fitting emphasis than we could possibly do by coordination alone.

Word Order. In English the word order of the basic patterns is so securely fixed that, except for questions and the expletive pattern, we assume that what precedes the verb is the subject and that what follows it is likely to be object or complement. This word order is so dominant in our thinking that a change in the order of the parts will automatically cause a change in our interpretation of the sentence. Thus *The Yankees beat the Tigers* and *The Tigers beat the Yankees* will be interpreted as having two quite different meanings, even though the words are exactly alike. Even if the words are meaningless, we impose a subject-verb-object order on them, so that *The X's elled the Y's* will be interpreted as a statement about something the X's did to the Y's, a subject-verb-object statement.

Beyond the basic patterns, word order is only relatively stable. Single word modifiers of subjects or objects nearly always precede their head-words (a *clever* answer), although some exceptions are possible (the body *beautiful*). Modifying phrases, other than a series of single words, usually follow their headwords (the girl *in the red dress*). Subordinate clauses modifying subjects, objects, or complements also follow their headwords (*The man* **who did it** *has been arrested. They caught the man* **who did it.** *I am the man* **who did it.**) The chief exception to this regularity is the modifiers of verbs. Adverbs are conspicuously flexible. For example, *quickly* can occupy any position in the sentence, *He went away quickly*. For this reason, adverbial clauses are just as likely to precede as to follow their main clauses.

But when we are building material into complex sentences, we have a considerable choice of orders. Suppose we have four pieces of information to express as a sentence:

1. A railroad signal was faulty.
2. An express plunged into the rear of a freight train.
3. Five people were killed and 47 injured.
4. This accident happened last night.

If you are mathematically inclined, you will recognize that there are 24 possible orders in which these four items can be arranged. Even if some of these arrangements would sound strange as English sentences, we have still a great variety of ways of arranging the items. We can begin with any one of the four:

Last night an express train . . .
Five people were killed . . .
An express train plunged into the rear of a freight train . . .
A faulty signal caused . . .

And with each of these starts we have various ways of arranging the other items. How we will actually order the items is determined less by what orders are possible than by what order best suits our purpose.

Constructing Normal Sentences. When we compose material into normal sentences, we use all the tools we have so far recognized. We start with our sense of the basic patterns and we manipulate these by coordination, subordination, modification, and word order. Let us illustrate the procedure by taking a collection of material and working it into a sentence. Here is the material:

1. The man is tall. 2. He has gray hair. 3. He is wearing a raincoat. 4. He is standing by the information booth. 5. He looks disconsolate. 6. He has missed a bus. 7. The bus was going to Onargo. 8. It was the last bus. 9. He had been having a snack in the restaurant. 10. The jukebox in the restaurant was playing loudly. 11. The departure of the bus was announced. 12. The man did not hear the announcement.

The composition problem is how to combine all this information in a single sentence. There is, of course, more than one way, and the best way will depend on our chief interest in the material. We could begin with the jukebox and write a sentence to the effect that the jukebox in the restaurant was playing so loudly that it drowned out the announcer's voice and caused a certain man to lose the last bus to Onargo. If we were chiefly interested in the man, we would make him the subject of the sentence. That decision would require us to make *missed the bus* the predicate. We would then have a basic sentence pattern of the S-V-O type: *The man missed the bus.* Assuming that we want this pattern, we then select the information that modifies "man" and relate it to that headword to expand the subject. By subordination we reduce the first two sentences to a phrase — *The tall gray-haired man.* We cannot say *a raincoat man* or *a standing-by-the-information-booth man,* because these are not English word orders, but we can put "raincoat" in a modifying phrase after the subject and we can reduce the fourth sentence to a subordinate clause and the fifth to a phrase, and thus get the complete subject of the sentence. Then we can subordinate sentences 7 and 8 to the object "bus" and sentences 9–12 to "missed" as the reason for missing the bus. If we do this, our sentence takes the following form:

> The tall gray-haired man in the raincoat who is standing by the information booth looking so disconsolate missed the last bus to Onargo because he was having a snack in the restaurant and could not hear the announcement of the bus's departure over the din made by the jukebox.

The complexity of such a sentence makes it hard to recognize the basic pattern, but it is still a sentence about a man missing a bus and is an expansion of the S-V-O pattern. The expansion may be diagramed as follows:

> (Subject modifiers) **S** (Subject modifiers) **V** (object modifier) **O** (object modifier) (verb modifiers)

We could change this order around somewhat. We could transfer the verb modifiers to the beginning of the sentence to read: *Because he was having a snack . . . the man . . . missed the . . . bus . . .* But the sentence as it is shown in the diagram is the standard pattern for a normal sentence.

The Parallel (Balanced) Sentence

A parallel sentence is one which emphasizes coordinate structures. We have already seen that coordination is a common device in normal sentences. Technically, any sentence in which elements are joined by coordinating conjunctions contains an example of parallelism. But, as the term is used here, a parallel sentence is one in which the coordinate elements are so pronounced that rhetorically the effect of the sentence is very different from that of a normal sentence.

A common pattern of the parallel sentence is the *series.* In this construction three or more elements of the same grammatical pattern are linked together, as illustrated by the following example:

We become involved
- in the fortunes of the football team,
- in the issues and personalities of student elections,
- in the letters written to the college paper, and
- in the ideas that are presented in class.

The parallel elements may, as in this example, be phrases; they may be subordinate clauses, or main clauses, or single words, such as a series of adjectives. The idea being presented in each element of the series is logically related to the ideas in the other elements. For example, each element in the series given above identifies a particular kind of involvement. In a parallel sentence, then, all the coordinate elements are logically and grammatically consistent.

When a parallel sentence consists of two contrasting major elements, often main clauses, we say that it is balanced. In such sentences the contrasted clauses are usually joined by a coordinating conjunction which serves as a fulcrum on which the two structures are balanced. Notice how the contrast in the following passage is developed in a series of balanced compound predicates.

I felt myself in rebellion against the Greek concept of justice. That concept excused Laius for attacking Oedipus, but condemned Oedipus for defending himself. It tolerated a king's deliberate attempt to kill his baby son by piercing the infant's feet and abandoning it on a mountain, but later branded the son's unintentional killing of his father as murder. It held Oedipus responsible for his ignorance, but excused those, including Apollo, who contributed to that ignorance.

The structure of this paragraph can literally be diagramed as a scale, with the contrasted parts balanced on the fulcrum of the repeated conjunction *but*.

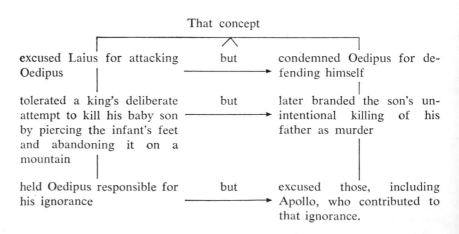

Such a balanced structure points up the contrast in the thought so that the rhetorical pattern reflects and supports the logical pattern. Moreover, the regular rhythm of the matching clauses is itself attractive to a reader. But notice it is the *repeated* contrast in the example that gives the sense of balance. If, instead of following the arrows across the scale, you read down the left side before reading the right, much of the balanced effect is lost. This experiment should suggest to you that when you are contrasting two things you will get better parallelism by contrasting them a part at a time. This was the technique used on pages 73–74 in the balanced contrast between death at sea and death on land.

Intricately balanced sentences can be tremendously effective, but continuous use of them would seem excessive, affected, and mannered. Bacon's essays are classics of balanced sentences, but if they were offered by a modern writer in, say, *Harper's Magazine,* most readers would think them self-consciously arty. Judge for yourself. Here are the opening lines of his essay, "Of Parents and Children."

> The joys of parents are secret; and so are their griefs and fears. They cannot utter the one; nor they will not utter the other. Children sweeten labours; but they make misfortunes more bitter. They increase the cares of life; but they mitigate the remembrance of death.

If this balanced repetition of the contrast continued for a page or two you might well become tired of it. Nevertheless, as an exercise in developing a sense of both the structure and the rhythm of a balanced sentence, you could do worse than to imitate the style of this selection.

The Periodic Sentence

A periodic sentence is one in which the main idea is withheld until the end *for rhetorical effect.* For the purpose of the following discussion, the italicized phrase is important. Any sentence which consists of a subordinate clause preceding a main clause withholds the main idea to the end, but it does not necessarily do so for rhetorical effect. In *If you are going to the store, bring me a pack of cigarettes,* the main idea comes at the end but is not withheld for rhetorical effect. For our purposes here, we would prefer to consider that a normal sentence. What we mean by a periodic sentence is one like the following, in which the main clause is quite deliberately held till last.

> To this queer mixture of cultured and uneducated, of lowly and exalted, of those who came for love of drama and those who came to show their superiority, *the Elizabethan drama was shaped.*

Such a periodic sentence builds up to the main clause, usually through a series of phrases or subordinate clauses, and the longer the sentence is, the greater the build-up. In a really sustained periodic sentence, there is a real effect of rising to a climax, which can be very effective.

Because of the complexity of its structure, a sustained periodic sentence requires considerable skill, since the writer must clearly foresee the whole pattern before he begins to write. In a normal sentence, he has much more freedom to continue or to stop. He can connect several main clauses or begin a succession of sentences with conjunctions. But the basic pattern, at least, of a periodic sentence has to be shaped in advance. For example, the writer of the following sentence is moving toward his main clause through a series of "if" clauses which successively deal with life, liberty, and the pursuit of happiness, and what he has to say about each of these subjects must be chosen for its contribution to the idea of the main clause. It would be easy for an inexperienced writer to get lost or to fail to do what must be done at every part if the final product is to come out as planned.

> But if life hardly seems worth living, if liberty is used for subhuman purposes, if the pursuers of happiness know nothing about the nature of their quarry or the elementary techniques of hunting, *these constitutional rights will not be very meaningful.*

The longer the sentence is, the more complex its pattern may become. The following example, taken from a student paper we saw on page 44, is incredibly complex.

> And when the great matador, reaching his peak with a brave strong bull, stands poised over those horns, hoping (but not knowing) that they won't come up and dig his very guts out, hoping that the sword doesn't hit a bone and break off in his hand, plunges his sword down into the back of the bull's neck, and punctures the bull's lungs (he hopes), and when every man who ever saw an amateur bullfight or faced a bull or ran from one, knowing what it means to lean over a bull's horns and expose one's groin, holds his breath and, not saying a word, watches the matador in the hot, bright sun, on the white sand prove for the whole world to see his courage and strength and skill, and sees him become one with the proud, noble, strong bull — *this is the moment of truth.*

This sentence is so involved, contains so many ideas within ideas, that it defies clear diagraming. We can, however, simplify it somewhat by omitting some of the material and reducing the sentence to its basic design.

> And when the great matador . . . stands poised over those horns . . . and
>   plunges his sword down into the bull's neck . . . and
>   punctures the bull's lungs . . .
> and when every man . . .
>   holds his breath and . . .
>   watches the matador . . . and
>   sees him become one with the . . . bull —
> *this is the moment of truth.*

A student needs to be very sure of himself to start out on a sentence like that. Most would be well advised not to try. But if the writer can handle it, such a sentence is impressive. In addition to its cumulative effect, it gets a great deal said in its 150 words and is therefore, despite its length, an economical statement. If you think not, if you think it is wordy because it is long, try to present every idea and image it contains in your own words.

You may be able to cut out a few adjectives, but you will have difficulty saying as much in the same space. This is a point to remember when we come later to talk of economy as the relation of the number of words to the meaning they convey.

The basic pattern of the periodic sentences we have looked at consists of two elements: a set of parallel structures followed by a main clause. The elements in parallel structure could be single words, though they are usually phrases or subordinate clauses. If we use P for phrase, C for subordinate clause, and M for main clause, we will have a convenient way of diagraming periodic sentences. After the following examples the diagrams are given in brackets. When a series consists of phrases within a clause, the phrases are placed in parentheses.

> If we could retain the curiosity of our childhood and the idealism of our youth, and if we could combine both of these with the disciplined judgment of maturity, what men we might become! [C C M]

> But when there is no hope of success, when every new effort is foreseen as another failure, and when each succeeding failure serves only to make frustration deeper and more acute, then surely no useful purpose is served by exhorting the poor fellow to try, try again. [C C C M]

> If stories of sinking ships and burning towns, of killing cold and windlashed waves, of reckless men engaged in dangerous pursuits make up the warp of *The Long Ships Passing,* the woof is formed by the pressure of an expanding economy in an era becoming increasingly mechanized. [C (P P P) M]

> > To die, to sleep; to sleep, perchance to dream;
> > Aye, there's the rub . . . — *Hamlet* [P P P P M]

The habit of analyzing the structure of sentences is worth cultivating both for the knowledge it yields about rhetorical patterns and for the pleasure of recognizing and appreciating a writer's technique. You are not likely to have either the need or the desire to write in a freshman essay such a sentence as Lincoln's magnificent conclusion to his Second Inaugural Address, but just as you get pleasure from recognizing the design of a dress, a car, or a building, so you may get pleasure from seeing how the sentence is designed.

> With malice toward none, with charity for all, with firmness in the right, as God gives us to see the right, let us strive on to finish the work we are in — to bind up the nation's wounds, to care for him who shall have borne the battle and for his widow and his orphan, to do all which may achieve and cherish a just and lasting peace among ourselves, and with all nations.

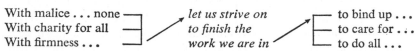

The diagram reveals the basic structure of the sentence: a series of three phrases preceding and three following the main clause. The opening phrases build up the periodic effect; but unlike the normal periodic pattern, the sentence does not end with the main clause. Instead it proceeds to a new climax as Lincoln uses the final series to define "the work we are in."

Characteristics of Effective Sentences

An effective sentence is one that does for a reader what the writer meant it to do. Usually its purpose is to advance the development of the topic sentence of a paragraph. Except in a grammatical sense, it is not an independent unit of composition, and, at least in the first draft, a student's wisest course is to let his understanding of the purpose of the paragraph determine what he does in individual sentences. Revision is another matter. Then he can consider the internal structure of his sentences and do whatever can be done to improve their efficiency.

Effective sentences have four qualities: *unity, economy, emphasis,* and *variety.* These are by no means independent of each other. Unified sentences are often economical and emphatic, and emphatic sentences are always unified and usually economical. But, despite some overlapping, it will be convenient in this chapter to deal separately with these four characteristics.

Unity

When we say that a sentence has unity we mean that everything in it has a logical relation to the purpose of the sentence as a whole and that nothing is omitted which is necessary to that purpose. For example, the sentence "If you like skiing, you will like Oregon" expresses a complete idea. If we try to express that idea in one of the following ways we destroy the unity of the sentence.

1. *If you like skiing.* (This is only part of the idea, a fragment)

2. *If you like skiing, you will like Oregon, with its magnificent trout streams.* (What relevance have the trout streams in a sentence about the winter attractions of Oregon?)

3. *You like skiing. You like Oregon.* (The two ideas here are not joined into one as they were in the original statement)

These examples illustrate the chief causes of lack of unity. The first omits a necessary part of the thought, so that the sentence is logically as well as grammatically incomplete. So obvious an omission is usually a sign of carelessness, or even faulty proofreading, though it could reflect an almost complete ignorance of English sentence structure. If the latter is the explanation, the student needs remedial work; he must now learn what he should have learned in grade school — the mechanics of a written English sentence.

The second error is more common and more forgivable. As was pointed out in Chapters 1 and 4, unless a sense of purpose controls everything we do, we are in constant danger of letting irrelevant ideas creep into what we write. Even experienced writers have this trouble and often have to remove its effects in revision. Inexperienced writers, especially when feeling their way through a sentence, are often led away from their original purpose by new thoughts or associations which arise in their minds as they write. This tendency leads them to drift into confusion, as in the following sentence.

> His mother, who has been living in Kansas, where she has been keeping house for her nephew who lost his wife in a car accident three years ago and needed help in bringing up his three small children, having been in poor health since her husband died, because she suffered from chronic asthma, had to move to Colorado.

This sentence got out of control because the writer allowed all sorts of associations to get imbedded in it. The usual advice for his ailment is to write shorter sentences and be sure each deals with only one idea. And this is usually good advice, though in this instance little improvement would come from chopping the material into a series of short sentences — "His mother has been living in Kansas. She has been keeping house for her nephew. He lost his wife in a car accident, etc. . . ." What this writer needs is to get clear in his own mind what one idea he is trying to express, hold fast to it, and be sure in revision to delete all departures from it.

The third example (*You like skiing. You like Oregon.*) illustrates an error best taken care of in revision. The two ideas are no doubt related in the writer's mind, but not in his sentences. The problem is to subordinate one idea (and one part of the statement) to the other. The writer has first to see that the skiing is one reason why he likes Oregon; and second, that evidence for a conclusion, though important, is subordinate to the conclusion itself.

Economy

Economy, the second main quality of effective sentences, is a relation between the number of words used and the amount of meaning conveyed. A sentence is not economical just because it is short, or wordy just because it is long. The test is not the number of words but the amount of work they do for the reader. Such classics of condensation as "Sighted sub, sank same," and "I came, I saw, I conquered" owe some of their effect to parallelism and alliteration and are probably a little too clever to be good models for freshman writing; but they do show that a person with a knack for concise statement can often say a great deal in very few words.

The opposite of economy is wordiness, and again the test is qualitative, not quantitative. The long periodic sentence from "The Bullfight" (page 110) contains about 150 words, but it is not wordy. In contrast, the sentence at the left in the following example is wordy; it says no more in 54 words than is said in 16 words at the right.

Wordy	*Economical*
Although I cannot truthfully say that I was acclaimed during my high school career as a prodigy, being what is generally known as an average student, I was able to survive the rigors of four years of academic pursuits and to achieve graduation without ever having received a single failing grade in any subject.	Although I was only an average student in high school, I graduated without failing a course.

Wordiness is one of the worst weaknesses in writing. For the reader, it can often be worse than bad grammar, misspellings, and other lapses from educated usage. Bad grammar may irritate, but it will only occasionally confuse. But sustained wordiness obscures meaning and may baffle the reader completely.

In student writing the chief causes of wordiness are (1) misguided attempts at a literary style and (2) failure to eliminate useless words in revision.

Pretentious Diction. Good writing is first of all clear. "Literary" flourishes that make the reader's task harder are worse than useless; they are harmful. Consider this:

> It was fortunate, or unfortunate, depending on the circumstances and the evaluation thereof, that I had no formulated or precise conceptions when I left high school and commenced work as a telegraphist in the Public Service. While on duty one evening, a colleague, who was interested in weight-lifting, allowed me to peruse a book on the subject entitled *Big Arms,* by Bob Hoffman. Not yet having realized my latent interest in athletic endeavors, I was surprised at the manner in which the book held my interest. This I only realized after a while. It was that book which stimulated me to make a purchase of a weight-lifting set, and despite the inhibiting influences of long work hours, little sleep and irregular meals, to exercise in my free moments.

It would be hard to imagine a less successful paragraph, yet the student who wrote it has something to say: that his interest in weight-lifting stemmed from a book which a fellow worker in the telegraph office once lent him. That is not a difficult idea to express. Yet the student's inability — or unwillingness — to put it down in simple language traps him into a pretentious style and smothers his thought with words, many of them inappropriate and most of them unnecessary. The revision that follows has no special literary merit, except the greatest merit of all — it expresses a simple observation in suitable and concise language.

> I became interested in weight-lifting while I was working as a telegraphist. One of my office mates who was enthusiastic about the sport lent me a book

called *Big Arms,* by Bob Hoffman. That book so stimulated me that I bought a weight-lifting set and began to exercise in every spare moment.

The second version has less than half as many words as the first; yet it includes everything that bears on the writer's purpose. It contains no distinguished diction, but none is required. The big words of the original version ("evaluation thereof," "formulated or precise conceptions," "commenced," "colleague," and "latent interest in athletic endeavors") are liabilities in such a paragraph. The second version is not only more concise; it is much more effective.

A student who feels that "lofty" diction helps to create a literary style should read successful modern writers. Many of our best plays, poems, short stories, articles, and essays are simply and informally written. Indeed, to write simply is a better test of literary ability than most students realize, for it is easy to use pretentious diction, but quite hard to present a complex idea or a moving experience in simple, natural language. There is a great deal of truth in the playwright Sheridan's comment that "easy writing's curst hard reading" — and it is equally true that hard writing makes for easy reading. Readability is one good test of writing, and good, readable prose is often the fruit of careful revision.

The following contrasted sentences further illustrate how a "pretentious" style obscures meaning. In so far as they can be translated, the student sentences at the left have been revised into the more natural statements at the right.

Pretentious and Obscure	*Clearer*
As I grew older I became more interested in the different fields of occupation and what they had to offer me as far as choosing a life's occupation was concerned.	As I grew older I began to examine more carefully the relative advantages of different occupations.
Our educational system is not lacking in any way as to its purpose of helping one to prepare oneself for the requirements of a future career.	Education succeeds in preparing us for our future careers.
Trusting that I have imparted the fact that I, too, have dreamed the same dreams that girls always do, I deem it best to conclude this version of my innermost fancies.	I end this description of my reveries with the hope that they reveal me as a normal girl.
I found myself stepping from the rather casual high school life into a world of serious, studious adults. The three months' interlude between classes was hardly enough to adapt oneself to the new environment. The transitory extent of those ninety-six days was astonishing, and soon those of us who chose a higher degree of education found ourselves among unfamiliar gray walls.	The summer vacation was all too short to prepare me to bridge the gap between the adolescent level of high school and the adult level of college.

Useless Words. If you have ever composed a telegram you have had a valuable lesson in cutting out unnecessary words. Such ruthless pruning is neither necessary nor advisable in most college writing. But often a single word will do the work of two or three, and a short phrase may replace a long clause without hurting style or meaning.

The three most common means of reducing wordiness are excision, substitution, and direct statement.

Excision means pruning out useless words. Here are two examples.

1. Cutting out a purposeless introductory phrase:

> ~~With reference to the relationship between the laws of today and the laws of ancient times,~~ I think that the author is wrong in stating that the laws of today are based on ancient laws.

2. Cutting out deadwood[1] within the body of the sentence:

> I ~~only~~ hope I get as much ~~benefit~~ out of ~~my years of~~ college ~~work and study~~ as I got from ~~the four years I spent in~~ high school.

Substitution is the replacing of a wordy expression by an economical one.

1. Substituting one word for a phrase:

> I took an academic *course.* ~~line of subjects.~~

2. Substituting a phrase for a clause:

> She is the girl *in blue.* ~~who is wearing a blue dress.~~

3. Substituting a simple sentence for a compound or complex sentence:

> ~~He married~~ The former Jane Smith / ~~she~~ is his third wife.
>
> They live in Eau Claire, ~~which is in~~ Wisconsin.

Direct statement is explicit statement. It says, rather than implies, what the author means, and it avoids *circumlocutions* — words or phrases which shy away from clear statement through timidity, false modesty, or literary affectation. Contrast the original and revised versions of the following.

> I was so sick that I *vomited.* ~~released the contents of my stomach.~~

---

[1] Professor Perrin, from whom I have borrowed this term, defines *deadwood* as "a lazy word or phrase that adds nothing to the meaning of the sentence." *Writer's Guide and Index to English,* 3rd edition, p. 186.

He was ~~, shall we say?—in an inebriated condition.~~ drunk.

I ~~find myself~~ do not ~~in~~ complete~~ly~~ ~~agreement~~ with Dr. Jones.

In the following contrasts, the sentences at the right are not just shorter but are clearer and more precise. At the left, important ideas, such as logical subjects, are often put into modifying phrases, so that the structure of the sentence does not reflect the structure of the thought. At the right this does not happen.

Wordy	*Economical*
I was born in the city of Bangor. It is located in the state of Maine.	I was born in Bangor, Maine.
All persons should strive to develop a usage of good English.	Everyone should try to use good English.
In the way of college mathematics, I have had College Algebra, Trigonometry, and Analytical Geometry.	I have had College Algebra, Trigonometry, and Analytical Geometry.
I believe, to some extent, about the same as the author in his attitude toward crime and criminal tendencies.	I agree with the author's attitude toward crime and criminal tendencies.
Dealing with the idea about the use of property in ancient times and the use of property today, I think it is about the same.	The uses of property have not changed during the centuries.
In regard to specific influences on my speech and writing, I might say that there has been nothing outstanding to influence either. It has been gradual all the way along. In other words, I've had nothing to overcome, such as impediments in speech, accent, or influence of foreign tongue being used in the family. The latter being rather impossible since the fact exists that my ancestors came over in the Mayflower.	There have been no significant influences on my use of English. I have had no speech impediments, and, as a descendant of an old American family, I have not been exposed to a foreign language at home.

Notice that these sentences do not all yield to the same treatment. The first needs simple pruning; the others require more radical rephrasing and reconstruction, because the wordiness is often the result of fuzzy thinking that leads to faulty structure.

Emphasis

Emphasis — the third main quality of effective sentences — is a relation between purpose and the form of expression. Almost any idea can be

117

expressed in more ways than one. The thoughtful writer chooses the way that best achieves the effect he has in mind. For example, compare these two statements:

> Don't shoot till they come close enough.
> Don't shoot till you see the whites of their eyes.

Both express the same command, but the second does it in a more emphatic and memorable way and so is far more likely to have the desired effect.

This illustration shows the effect gained by choosing the right diction. We shall be concerned with that kind of emphasis more fully in the next chapter. At present we are chiefly interested in changes which can be made in the structure of a sentence to gain greater emphasis. In general, these are changes in *word order, rank,* and *voice.*

Emphatic Word Order. In an English sentence the positions of greatest emphasis are the end and the beginning. It is usually wise, therefore, to put the most important material in these positions on the principle that rhetorical emphasis should reflect logical emphasis. If unimportant details pile up at the end of a sentence they may get emphasis they do not deserve, while important points may be buried in unemphatic positions. When this happens, a sentence tends to trail away weakly. Notice the difference between the following:

Unemphatic Order	*Emphatic Order*
He was accused of cheating and was expelled from college by the Discipline Committee yesterday afternoon at a meeting.	He was accused of cheating and, at a meeting of the Disciplinary Committee yesterday afternoon, he was expelled from college.

The sentence at the left is anticlimactic. The reader loses interest after the dramatic event, the expulsion, is announced. If the agent and time of expulsion are important enough to be included in the sentence, they should be placed in the middle, as they are in the version at the right.

Climactic order presents the material of the sentence so as to build up to a major idea. We have seen that the force of periodic sentences derives from this order, but climax may also be used in normal sentences when items can be arranged in order of importance. The following examples give anticlimactic order (left) versus climactic order (right). Study these contrasts and explain what changes were made in revision, and why.

Anticlimactic Order	*Climactic Order*
In a magnificent stretch run the favorite overtook six horses and won by a nose, thrilling the crowd.	The favorite thrilled the crowd by a magnificent stretch run in which he overtook six horses and won by a nose.

Anticlimactic Order	Climactic Order
The prosecution asked in its summing up that the jury bring in a verdict of guilty, which was the only possible verdict considering the violence of the crime and the lack of provocation.	In summing up, the prosecution asked the jury to consider the lack of provocation and the violence of the crime and then bring in the only possible verdict — guilty.
He said that the U.N. had failed in its chief function, to preserve the peace of the world, although it had done much of which it could be proud and was still performing valuable services in many areas.	He said that, though the U.N. had done much of which it could be proud and was still performing valuable services in many areas, it had failed in its chief function, to preserve the peace of the world.

Emphatic Rank. We have already used the terms "coordination" and "subordination" to mean equal and lesser rank respectively. This distinction is most important to emphasis. If we reduce the rank of one of two statements we make it grammatically less important than the other and thus tend to give it less emphasis — for example:

Coordinate	Explanation	Subordinate
He was discouraged by his grades and was homesick and confused and he withdrew from school.	At the left, the student's discouragement, homesickness, confusion, and withdrawal are given equal emphasis. The right-hand version subordinates the reasons for withdrawing and so emphasizes the withdrawal.	Discouraged by his grades, homesick and confused, he withdrew from school.
Rider attended Oxford and there he met young Sebastian Flyte and the two boys became friends. Sebastian was the youngest son of the Marquis of Marchmain.	The main idea here is that the two boys became friends. The version at the right emphasizes that idea by subordinating everything else to it. Notice the economy achieved by this subordination.	At Oxford Rider became friendly with Sebastian Flyte, the youngest son of the Marquis of Marchmain.

Whether any given element in a sentence should be made coordinate or subordinate depends on the writer's purpose. Does he want to give elements equal emphasis, or to emphasize some at the expense of others? Many students use too much coordination and could make their sentences more effective by judicious use of subordination. But it can be just as wrong to subordinate an important idea as not to subordinate a minor one.

Illogical Subordination	Explanation	Logical Subordination
The workman stepped on a live wire when he was electrocuted.	The important fact is the electrocution, not the cause of it. The subordination at the left is backwards.	The workman was electrocuted when he stepped on a live wire.

Illogical Subordination	*Explanation*	*Logical Subordination*
There was a great deal of excitement in the neighborhood caused by the attempts to capture the escaped bull.	This sentence puts relatively unimportant material in the main clause and reduces the most important phrase — "attempts to capture the escaped bull" — to an object of a preposition. The revision makes that phrase the subject of the sentence.	The attempts to capture the escaped bull caused a great deal of excitement in the neighborhood.

One way of describing the difference between the parallel and the periodic sentence is to say that the parallel sentence emphasizes the equal importance of ideas by keeping them in coordinate forms, while the periodic sentence builds up to a climax by subordinating preliminary ideas to the final one. As types of sentences, neither is better than the other; in a given situation, that kind is better which better achieves the writer's purpose.

Emphatic Voice. It is common in composition courses to urge students to use verbs in the active rather than the passive voice. This advice is generally sound, because the active voice is usually more natural and the so-called "weak passive" sometimes leads to wordiness and to awkward shifts in structure.

Weak Passive	*More Emphatic Active*
A final examination was failed by both starting halfbacks.	Both starting halfbacks failed a final examination.
The instructor said that the papers would be graded by him in two or three days.	The instructor said he would grade the papers in two or three days.
He was not prepared for the test and so only half of the questions were answered.	Because he was not prepared for the test he answered only half of the questions.

But there are times when the passive is the more natural and the more emphatic form. In general, the subject gets more emphasis than the object. Therefore the object of a verb in the active voice may be given stress if it is made the subject of a passive verb. Whenever the subject of an active statement is obvious, or is unknown, or is less important than the object, a more fitting emphasis may be achieved by using the passive voice.

Active	*Explanation*	*Passive*
They elected Kennedy.	"Kennedy" is the important word, not "They."	Kennedy was elected.
The legislature founded the University ninety years ago.	Unless the context deals with the work of the legislature ninety years ago, the most important word is "University." The passive form makes it the subject.	The University was founded ninety years ago.

Active	Explanation	Passive
A man drove us around Old Quebec in an open carriage.	The driver here is not important and receives unnecessary emphasis in the subject position.	We were driven around Old Quebec in an open carriage.

We see a fine illustration of what can be gained by such a shift if we contrast a common misquotation of Churchill's famous tribute to the Royal Air Force with the correct version. Churchill wished to express three ideas: (1) the greatness of the service performed by the RAF; (2) the small number of men who performed it; and (3) the large numbers who benefited by it. If you keep in mind that the sentence is about the wonderful work of the RAF, you will agree that the greatness of the service and the few men who provided it are more important than the number who benefited. Yet the misquotation puts the least important idea in the important subject position:

"Never . . . have so many owed so much to so few."

In his actual words Churchill put the verb in the passive voice and thus made grammar more precisely show the emphasis he wanted:

"Never . . . was so much owed by so many to so few."

Deliberate Repetition. We saw on page 86 that deliberate repetition can strengthen the coherence of a paragraph. It can also be used within a sentence to emphasize key words. Notice the force gained by the intentional repetitions in the following sentences:

It was an act of senseless *brutality, brutally* planned and *brutally* executed, serving no purpose except to indulge a *brute* passion.

The beatnik motivation is negative; they are *against* things — *against* the present and *against* the past, *against* materialism and *against* mysticism, *against* whatever has been considered valuable in literature, art, music, and philosophy, *against* anything associated with middle-class morality, and *against* all conventions but their own. With apologies to St. Paul: whatsoever things are of good repute, the beatnik is *against* them.

Variety

Logically, a discussion of variety in sentence structure belongs in a chapter on paragraphs. Variety is not a characteristic of a single sentence but of a succession of sentences. We consider it in this chapter simply because it is convenient to discuss variety *after* we have considered parallel and periodic sentences, word order, and subordination.

Consider the following paragraph:

Shakespeare's chronicle history of *Henry the Fifth* is a drama of kinghood and war. It is essentially a play about a young king's coming of age. Henry V had been an irresponsible young prince before his accession to the throne.

121

He had to prove his worthiness as king by leading his army in war. He invaded France and captured Harfleur, and then tried to withdraw his troops to Calais. He and his men were confronted by a numerically superior French army at Agincourt. In a famous passage in Shakespeare's play, Henry urges his soldiers on to an incredible victory. The superior mobility and firepower of the English proved too much for the heavily armored French.

As you have probably noticed, all the sentences in this paragraph are similar in length and pattern. The number of words is respectively 14, 12, 14, 14, 15, 14, 16, 16; and, with one exception, the word order is subject, verb, and object or complement.

This much similarity may not become monotonous in a single paragraph, but a 500-word essay in this style could be quite tedious. A writer, like a baseball pitcher, is more effective with a change of pace, and varied sentences are more effective than those that plod along in constant lengths and patterns.

But a word of caution: *too much variety may be as bad as none at all.* The subject-verb-object pattern is the favorite order of English sentences, and a student who strives too hard to avoid it may end up with an affected and unnatural style or he may fall into the kind of inconsistencies that we considered earlier in this chapter. If you keep this caution in mind, the following discussion of ways to obtain variety will be helpful.

The best way to get variety of sentence structure is to be conscious of the need of it. Nothing that follows in this section will help a student unless he at least senses that his sentences are monotonous. Once he sees that they are too much alike in length and pattern, he can easily make specific revisions to break up monotony. Even one or two changes in a paragraph may produce a marked improvement.

Variation may be achieved by three methods: by inverting normal word order, by subordination, and by occasional use of periodic sentences. Usually these methods are used together. For example, when we revise the following passage at the left into the form at the right, we combine inversion, subordination, and periodic structure.

I had only a single paddle and I was not used to handling a canoe in rough water. I could not hold its nose into the waves. The canoe tacked from side to side. I expected every moment to capsize.	Unaccustomed to handling a canoe in rough water with a single paddle, I could not hold its nose into the waves. As the canoe tacked from side to side, I expected every moment to capsize.

Here the first sentence of the original has been reduced to a phrase preceding the main clause in a short periodic sentence. The third sentence has been reduced to a subordinate clause preceding the main clause of another periodic sentence. The two subordinations and two inversions of the revised paragraph not only get rid of the monotony of the original but also achieve better emphasis by giving greater grammatical importance to the two main ideas in the passage — *I could not hold its nose into the waves,* and *I expected every moment to capsize.*

Here is another illustration. For ease of reference, the sentences at the left are numbered.

1. John Stuart Mill was born in 1806 and died in 1873. 2. He was famous as a child prodigy. 3. His fame continued through his life. 4. He was a logician and a political economist and a man of letters. 5. He was one of the most influential thinkers of the nineteenth century.	John Stuart Mill (1806–1873) was a child prodigy whose fame did not cease at maturity. As a logician, political economist, and man of letters, he was one of the most influential thinkers of the nineteenth century.

In this example sentences 1–3 have been combined by reducing the dates to a parenthesis and making sentence 3 a subordinate clause. Sentence 4 has been reduced to a phrase and placed before the main clause (5) to form a periodic sentence.

As a final illustration, study the contrasted paragraphs below. First read both to get the general effect of the revision; then compare the two versions sentence by sentence. Be prepared to discuss the changes made or to suggest others that you think might be more effective.

Original	*Revised*
The Levenford of Dr. Cronin's book is really the town of Dumbarton. It is one of the oldest towns in Scotland. It was the most important town north of the Tweed at the time of the Anglo-Saxon invasion, and was called Alcluyd. The Pict chieftains gathered there when they were preparing to swoop down into England in search of plunder; and they always returned there to divide the spoils of victory. The town stands at the gateway to the highlands and has been the field of many battles. Its great island rock has served successively as a fortress for Picts, Romans, Northmen, Jacobites, and Royalists. It has often served as a refuge for the townspeople whenever they were attacked by superior forces. They would retreat to the rock, as the Athenians retreated to their ships, until an opportunity presented itself for overthrowing the invaders.	Dumbarton, the Levenford of Dr. Cronin's book, is one of the oldest towns in Scotland. At the time of the Saxon invasion, Alcluyd, as it was then called, was the only town of any importance north of the Tweed. It was there that the Pict chieftains gathered before swooping down into England in search of plunder, and there that they returned to divide the spoils of victory. Standing as it does at the gateway of the highlands, the town has been the field of many battles, and the great island rock of Dumbarton has served successively as the fortress of Picts, Romans, Northmen, Jacobites, and Royalists. When attacked by superior forces, the townspeople, like the Athenians deserting their city for the ships, would seek refuge in this great rock and bide their time until an opportunity for overthrowing the invaders should arise.

Exercises

A. Check the following words, or any ten of your own choice, in your dictionary: *ambivalent, blatant, contrite, enigmatic, furbish, garrulous, jargon, myopic, punctilious, sanctuary*. For each word make brief notes on its source, original meaning, one present meaning, and an illustration of its use in that sense. Work all this information into a single sentence, as illustrated in the following example:

> *Synchronize*, from the Greek words for "together" and "time," originally meant "contemporaneous," but now means "to cause to move at the same time," as in "The sound track was synchronized with the film."

B. Each of the following numbered collections of material is a note for a two-paragraph paper on Jefferson's *Summary View of the Rights of British America*. First, work all the information in each note into a single sentence; then combine the sentences into two paragraphs. An illustration of a sentence derived from a note is given. It would, of course, be reasonable for different students to produce different sentences from the same material.

Example:

1774 — Jefferson elected county delegate to convention — Convention held at Williamsburg — two purposes: to consider state of colony, to elect Virginia representatives to First Continental Congress — J. then member of House of Burgesses

In 1774 Jefferson, then a member of the House of Burgesses, was elected a delegate for his county to a convention at Williamsburg to consider the state of the colony and elect the Virginia representatives to the First Continental Congress.

1. J. wrote *Summary View* — This was pamphlet — J. wrote it in preparation for convention — Because of it J. established as writer and revolutionary leader — Later selected to frame Declaration of Independence — His selection influenced by pamphlet

2. In *Summary View* J. drew analogy — Settling of American colonies by British likened to settling of England by German and Scandinavian adventurers — This happened fifth to tenth centuries — J. argued British claims to authority over colonies no more valid than would be German or Scandinavian claims to authority over modern Britain — This was his thesis

3. J. read extensively in history of colonizing — Anglo-Saxon migrations in particular — Sought legal precedents for establishing ownership of property during early English history — All this to develop thesis

4. *Summary View* revolutionary document — very thorough job — respected by British lawyers and liberal statesmen — Burke read it — Burke trying to force Lord North into conciliation with Americans — He made some alteration in *Summary View* and published it to support his purpose against North

5. *Summary View* far in advance of times — considered radical — denied British any real control over colonies — Most Americans would not go so

far — Most protested British taxation but acknowledged Britain's right to control

C. Following the method illustrated on page 124, reduce each of the following passages to a single efficient sentence:

1. A leader is a man who is leading a people to a preconceived goal. He can see the goal. They cannot. Washington, Lincoln, and Franklin Roosevelt were such leaders.

2. The crucial test of excellence in a President is not simply to *represent* the voters in the narrow sense. He must move ahead of them. He must ignore their more transient and petty interests. In a sense he must *misrepresent* them.

3. Biology allows us to follow the Greek injunction to know thyself. Biology should be a required course. It should emphasize the complex interrelations of living things and their environment. It should also emphasize the growing power of man to destroy the age-old balance.

4. Men are unequal in every respect. They are unequal in size, shape, color, strength, wealth and social position. They are also unequal in intelligence and virtue. If our measurements were precise enough, what would we find? Two individuals equal in any single respect? Unlikely. Two men equal in all measurable respects? Inconceivable.

5. The responsibility for increasing the significance of literature in our culture rests chiefly with the interpreters of literature. These men are critics, scholars, and teachers. They should devote less time to technical and aesthetic problems. They should be more concerned with the insights which literature provides. This is the heart of literature.

6. In teaching poetry it is a mistake to insist that poetry is art. Teachers who do that run into several difficulties. They cannot help students to understand the meaning of a poem. Students cannot see the idea of a poem. They cannot perceive what a poem has to tell them about man and the world and life and death. These are the things that make a poem important.

7. The search for understanding will never be finished. The historical situation changes continuously. New sciences will arise; old ones will progress. New technological discoveries will continue to be made. These discoveries will have a profound influence on human life. Look at the changes that radio, television, airplanes, and automation have made in our lives during this century.

D. The following student essays get little said, partly because of wordiness. Revise them for greater economy. Do not summarize the essays, but, using the method illustrated on page 116, cut out the deadwood and substitute more economical diction.

More Homework

There is a great deal of homework given to a student in college, more than in high school.

The first week I was down here, I noticed what a great change I would have to adapt myself to. I realized that the teachers at the University gave out a lot of homework compared to my teachers at high school. This didn't bother me too much for I enjoy doing homework as long as I learn something. After a few weeks quickly passed by, and my courses seemed to get a little bit harder, it seemed as if all I had to do was homework. Now, I began to wonder about all this homework I had been assigned to do, so I talked to my adviser. He told me that a student was on his own out here, and if he wanted to receive good grades he had to do everything assigned to him. He also told me that a freshman was used to getting away with a lot of things in high school, but it was much different in college.

The importance of homework in college aids the student in his learning. It wasn't so important in high school, but it means the difference between an A and an E in college.

You Are the Company You Keep

Do you judge a person by his personality, scholastic ability, attractiveness, or do you judge a person by the company he keeps? Most of the people in this modern era judge people by the company they keep.

For instance, if a person sees a group of boys who are from the slums and are known as hoodlums, talking to a lone girl, that person will immediately come to the conclusion that the girl is a pickup or a lewd girl.

Another example is the situation involving people who dress and look like beatniks. Because of the great difference in the attitudes of people to beatniks, an individual who is seen at a play, opera, movie, or meeting with a bearded young man in a not-too-clean sweatshirt will be considered a beatnik. These two examples are ways of judging a person by the characteristics of the company he keeps.

There is still another way in which to judge a person by the company he keeps. A Dr. Smith from the University is talking to a distinguished group of men who are also doctors. You do not know that Dr. Smith is a doctor, but after a few minutes you will conclude that he is a doctor also. This illustration shows that a man is judged by the company he keeps.

Are you judging people by the company they keep or by the characteristics I mentioned earlier in this essay?

E. Study the basic structure of each of the following sentences, set up the structure as a pattern, then follow that pattern exactly in expressing an idea of your own. An illustration of the procedure is provided in the first sentence.

1. Just as faith cannot be conferred but has to be experienced, just as character cannot be taught but has to be developed, so, too, respect cannot be commanded but has to be won.

[Pattern]   Just as . . . cannot be . . . but has to be. . . .
              Just as . . . cannot be . . . but has to be. . . .
              so, too, . . . cannot be . . . but has to be. . . .

Example: Just as knowledge cannot be granted but has to be sought,
           just as wisdom cannot be purchased but has to be earned,
           so, too, peace cannot be declared but has to be achieved.

2. A soft answer turneth away wrath; but grievous words stir up anger.

3. With the exception of those who graduated from high school by courtesy of the faculty, any high school graduate can earn a degree in some accredited college, if he really cares.

4. To say, however, that rhetoric is useful only on a practical level is to strip it of its most important dimensions, to make of it another mechanical and brute accomplishment.

5. But gradually a pattern begins to emerge: the campus itself takes on firmer contours, the strange roommate begins to display a consistent personality, lectures develop theme and direction, assignments make sense, instructors become less remote, and everywhere method becomes apparent.

6. For words, like people, are born and die, are changed and weathered by the seasons, and, passing, do not altogether disappear, but leave their imprint in the language.

7. Without words, no scientist could learn of the discoveries of his colleagues, no doctor could remove an appendix, no religious or moral beliefs would be possible; without words, each man would literally be an island unto himself, for there would be no human relations, except the crudest, and no society worthy of the name.

8. When a boy earns his whole way through college, when he graduates with honors, and when he does both of these things and still has time for normal extracurricular and social activities, I think you will agree he is quite a boy.

9. A man dies on shore; his body remains with his friends, and the "mourners go about the streets"; but when a man falls overboard at sea and is lost, there is a suddenness in the event, and a difficulty in realizing it, which gives to it an air of awful mystery.

10. In the thickets of blackberry, and toyon, and poison oak, the dead leaves lay deep; beneath these rested the half-rotted leaves and twigs of older years, and still deeper the mould of generations.

6

Right Words

The English writer Jonathan Swift defined good writing as the art of putting "proper words in proper places." Although this definition tremendously oversimplifies, it does stress the fact that words are the units with which a writer works. Words are the medium of communication, even of communication to oneself. We think with words just as we write with them, and neither thinking nor writing can be efficient unless the words are accurate. A concern about right words, therefore, is not just a matter of style. It is a matter of ordering experience, evaluating it, and communicating the results.

How Words Work

Symbols and Referents. Words are symbols for experience. They represent what we see, hear, feel, smell, taste, and do, and the attitudes and thoughts we derive from these experiences. The word is not the experience itself. We cannot drink the word "water," ride in the word "car," or refresh our bodies with the word "sleep." But we can use words to "stand for" these experiences. Therefore we say that the word is a *symbol* for the experience. Whatever the word refers to — water, car, sleep — is called the *referent*.

The relationship between a word and its referent is a mental one. The word makes us "think of" the referent, and this "thinking of" gives the word its meaning. In the sentence "The President will speak on television tonight," a number of connected symbols make us think of a number of related referents. We think of a particular person who will perform a definite action through a certain medium at a specified time. By means of this thinking we are able to anticipate an event that will take place in the future and at a considerable distance. Similarly, the statement "Christ was crucified" makes us think of an event in a far country nearly two thousand years ago. By words we are able to draw on the experience of people in all ages and in all places and to use it to understand the present and to plan for the future. In a sense, then, words give us a degree of control over time, space, and action by giving us a means of thinking about events in other times and places.

Context. Since the relation between a word and its referent is a mental one, we can think of different referents for the same word. Thus a *spring* may be a season, a source of drinking water, or a metal bar or coil. This multiple use of the same word allows us to describe a limitless number of experiences with a limited number of words. The people to whom we are speaking or writing can usually tell which meaning we have in mind by noticing the whole statement or situation in which we use a word — "I'll be glad when spring comes"; "Fill this bottle at the spring"; "The car has a broken spring." The whole statement or situation in which a word is used is called its *context.*

In practice we learn the meanings of words by their contexts. When we are learning our language we do not meet the word "run" by itself; we always meet it in some situation — a man running for a bus, a child running a temperature, a quarterback running a team, and so on. We learn the meanings of "run" by repeatedly experiencing it in context. This is exactly how the writers of dictionaries get their definitions. They gather sample contexts and write the definitions to describe the meanings these convey, so that when a dictionary lists different meanings for the word "spring," it is recording the contexts in which "spring" most frequently occurs.

✔ To illustrate the relationship between context and meaning, suppose you were editing a dictionary and had found for "man" and "make up" the following contexts recurring in your samples. For each of the two terms, write as many definitions as your samples require. Then check your dictionary to see if it records your definitions. If it does not, consider whether your definitions or the dictionary's are deficient.

Man:

1. Man was made to mourn.
2. He was her man, but he done her wrong.
3. Man the boats!
4. He is his own man; he takes orders from nobody.
5. Man, but I'm tired!
6. A man has a deeper voice than a woman.
7. Come on, be a man!

Make up:

1. I'll be with you as soon as I make up my face.
2. You must make up the test that you missed.
3. Make up your mind!
4. You make up the beds while I do the dishes.
5. This is a serious quarrel; I'm afraid they won't make up.

The Principle of Usage. We can sum up this discussion by saying that: (1) the only meanings a word has are those that exist in the minds of people who use it; (2) a word is always used in some situation or context; (3) the context shows how a word is being used, or what it means. These three conditions comprise the *principle of usage:* that the meanings of a word are determined by the ways in which speakers and writers *generally* use it. This principle could be applied to uneducated as well as to educated usage and to local as well as national uses, but we are concerned here only with the meanings generally given a word by educated people throughout the United States. The study of uneducated usage, or of the dialects of particular regions, lies outside the scope of this book. For our purposes, the principle of usage explains how the dictionary meanings of words are established.

The principle of usage has two important corollaries. First, a word has no *intrinsic* meaning, that is, no meaning of its own apart from those which people give it. Second, current meanings of a word will change if users accept the changes. As a consequence of these corollaries, the vocabulary of our language is ceaselessly changing, as old words die out or are given new meanings, and as new words are adopted.

Many words have quite different meanings from those they once had. "Wench" once meant a child and had no unpleasant associations; "buxom" was once complimentary, so much so that a fifteenth-century writer could use it to refer to the Virgin Mary; "manufacture" meant "to make by hand," but when goods came to be machine-made we retained the old name for the new process; "lingerie," when imported from France, meant "linen goods," but its most popular use today has nothing to do with linen; "quarantine" has long since lost its original Italian meaning of "forty days."

In addition, the language is steadily adding new words for new discoveries or events. Quite apart from slang, which comes and goes with the seasons, what would Abraham Lincoln make of such words as *airport, auto, basketball, blitz, carburetor, dentifrice, gyroscope, motel, movie star, nuclear fission, radar, television, world series, astronaut, launching pad, space shot,* and thousands of others? Yet these additions and changes are normal signs of growth. There is nothing static about the meanings of words in a living language. LATIN IS A DEAD LANGUAGE ←

Denotation and Connotation

The many meanings which a word may have may be generalized into two main types. Consider these two sentences:

> Who is that *girl* with Bill?
> Who is that *wench* with Bill?

Both italicized words point to the same referent — a relatively young human female. But, in addition, "wench" suggests unpleasant associations; it not only points to a person but also expresses the speaker's attitude toward that person. We contrast these two uses by saying that here the meaning of "girl" is a *denotation* — the physical referent which the word denotes — and that the meaning of "wench" is a *connotation* — a compound of physical referent and an attitude of the speaker or writer toward it.

The distinction, then, between denotation and connotation is that the latter reveals attitudes about an object or event but the former does not. These attitudes may be favorable or unfavorable. In "That is a cute hat" and "That is an absurd hat," the word "hat" is used denotatively in both sentences, but "cute" has favorable and "absurd" unfavorable connotations. Some words, such as *cute, brave, efficient, fame, glory, hope,* and *valuable* usually have only favorable connotations. Others, such as *absurd, callous, hate, idiotic, lust,* *treason* and *vicious* usually have only unfavorable connotations. Still others have favorable connotations in some contexts but unfavorable ones in others. Compare, for example, *free enterprise* and *free speech* with *free thinker* and *free love,* or a *fat check* with a *fat girl.*   FREE TUITION?

The following verses aptly contrast favorable and unfavorable connotations:

> Call a woman a kitten, but never a cat;
> You can call her a mouse, cannot call her a rat;
> Call a woman a chicken, but never a hen;
> Or you surely will not be her caller again.
>
> You can call her a duck, cannot call her a goose;
> You can call her a deer, but never a moose;
> You can call her a lamb, but never a sheep;
> Economic she likes, but you can't call her cheap.
>
> You can say she's a vision, can't say she's a sight;
> And no woman is skinny, she's slender and slight;
> If she should burn you up, say she sets you afire,
> And you'll always be welcome, you tricky old liar.[1]

The denotative and connotative uses of words are sometimes referred to as *scientific* and *poetic* uses. These descriptions remind us that a writer's purpose determines his diction. A writer interested only in providing information will tend to use words at a denotative level. Since clear pointing to specific facts is his main aim, he cannot afford to let his readers make all sorts of private interpretations; therefore he tries to restrict interpretation by choosing words and contexts which are relatively free from connotations.

The following paragraph is a good example of scientific writing at a popular level. Notice that the words point to things, not to attitudes, and that the diction makes no attempt to create either favorable or unfavorable responses in the mind of the reader.

[1] "Semantics" by John E. Donovan, in *The Saturday Evening Post,* July 13, 1946. Reprinted by permission of Mrs. Gertrude D. Crane and *The Saturday Evening Post.*

When a beam of sunlight enters a darkened room with dust in it, one can see the beam of light clearly defined as the light is scattered from the dust particles. The more dust particles in the room, the more the light is scattered; and if there is a real cloud of dust, the light is scattered so much that one can hardly see beyond it. The same thing happens to the beams from the headlights of a car in a fog. The small particles of water making up the fog in the air scatter the light that shines on them. The denser the fog, the more the light is scattered, the less of it gets through the fog, and the less one can see through a fog with even the most powerful beam of light. By measuring the fraction of the incident light that goes straight through the fog and the fraction that is scattered by the fog particles, one can estimate the number of water droplets in the fog — or the number of dust particles in the air. This method is accurate for determining the number of fine particles in a cloudy suspension in air or in water and is used frequently in analytical chemistry.[2]

The poet, in contrast with the scientist, is more concerned with creating emotional responses than with conveying information. His poetry may contain facts, may even be highly informative. But since his chief desire is to stimulate the imagination, he makes greater use of figurative language and of connotations which invite emotional responses. As the following passage illustrates, a poet who failed to do this would be most disappointing:

> The use of emotionally toned words is not, of course, always to be condemned. They are always harmful when we are trying to think clearly on a disputable point of fact. In poetry, on the other hand, they have a perfectly proper place, because in poetry (as in some kinds of prose) the arousing of suitable emotions is an important part of the purpose for which the words are used.
>
> In "The Eve of St. Agnes," Keats has written:
>
> > Full on this casement shone the wintry moon,
> > And threw warm gules on Madeline's fair breast.

These are beautiful lines. Let us notice how much of their beauty follows from the proper choice of emotionally colored words and how completely it is lost if these words are replaced by neutral ones. The words with strikingly emotional meanings are *casement, gules, Madeline, fair,* and *breast. Casement* means simply a kind of window with emotional and romantic associations. *Gules* is the heraldic name for red, with the suggestion of romance which accompanies all heraldry. *Madeline* is simply a girl's name, but one calling out favorable emotions absent from a relatively plain and straightforward name. *Fair* simply means, in objective fact, that her skin was white or uncolored — a necessary condition for the colors of the window to show — but also *fair* implies warm emotional preference for an uncolored skin rather than one which is yellow, purple, black, or any of the other colors which skin might be. *Breast* has also similar emotional meanings, and the aim of scientific description might have been equally well obtained if it had been replaced by such a neutral word as *chest.*

[2] From *Explaining the Atom* by Selig Hecht. Copyright 1947 by Selig Hecht. Reprinted by permission of The Viking Press, Inc., publishers.

Let us now try the experiment of keeping these two lines in a metrical form, but replacing all the emotionally colored words by neutral ones, while making as few other changes as possible. We may write:

> Full on this window shone the wintry moon,
> Making red marks on Jane's uncolored chest.

No one will doubt that all of its poetic value has been knocked out of the passage by these changes. Yet the lines still mean the same in external fact; they still have the same objective meaning. It is only the emotional meaning which has been destroyed.[3]

✔ Decide from the context whether the italicized words in the following sentences are being used denotatively or connotatively. If connotatively, are the connotations favorable or unfavorable?

1. The *baby* is *asleep*.
2. I wish you would not *baby* her so much.
3. The *shortstop* was *asleep* on that play.
4. She was wearing a *red* dress.
5. He talks like a *red*.
6. Such *slander* makes me see *red*.
7. I thought the room was *colorful*, but my wife said it was *gaudy*.
8. My girl is always *cold* to me when I have a *cold*.
9. He *used* the money to buy a car and he *used* his friends to keep up the payments.
10. The *critics* disagreed about his acting in that *scene*. Some said he gave a *sophisticated performance;* others said he *catered to vulgarity*.
11. Even her worst *critics* were embarrassed by the *scene* she made on that occasion.
12. It was a *dark* night, and a night for *dark* deeds.
13. The surgeon cut the damaged *nerve*. It takes *nerve* to make that first parachute jump. What a *nerve* that woman has!
14. He said he was a man of *firm purpose,* but his wife said he was just *selfishly stubborn*.
15. The difference between *a boyish prank* and *an act of vandalism* depends on whether it is your children or the neighbors' who do the mischief.
16. He is a *wolf* and his wife is a *cat*.
17. I am *portly*, my wife is *chubby;* but Bill and his wife are *obese*.
18. Mary said he was *shy;* I thought he was *sullen*.

The Accurate Word

Words are not right or wrong in themselves but as they succeed or fail to do what a writer wants them to do in a particular situation. But in any context the right word has certain characteristics: it must be *accurate;* it must be *appropriate;* it should be as *specific* as possible; it may be *figura-*

---

[3] Reprinted from *How to Think Straight,* by Robert H. Thouless. Copyright, 1939, by Simon and Schuster, Inc. Canadian copyright, Hodder and Stoughton, Ltd., publishers.

tive; and it should be _unspoiled_. The rest of this chapter will deal with each of these qualities in turn.

If a word is to say what it was intended to say, it must have the right denotation and the right connotation. It must refer the reader accurately to the things and ideas which the writer wishes to communicate, and it must express only those attitudes which he intends to express.

Choosing the right denotation is usually easier than choosing the right connotation. Most student errors in denotation come from three sources: confusion of words with similar forms (_affect-effect, respectful-respective, stationary-stationery_); confusion of antonyms — words with opposite meanings (_antagonist-protagonist, port-starboard, urban-rural_); and the student's failure to be clear about what reference he wants made. The first of these mistakes is often considered an error in spelling. The second is usually a temporary confusion which will disappear as the student gets experience with the terms that cause trouble. The third error is the most difficult. More attention to specific diction will often help (page 147), but the only sure cure is to develop the habit of concern for accurate statement. There is no formula for developing that habit, but reading over your first draft slowly and challenging your diction is a constructive approach.

Most choices of diction are choices of connotations. When a word has obviously wrong connotations, as "skinny" for "slender" in a complimentary context, the fault is easy to spot and correct. Less obvious are the distinctions between words which are near synonyms (have similar meanings), but may have important differences in particular contexts. For example, "dawdle," "procrastinate," and "vacillate" all have the general meaning of not getting on with the job at hand, but they suggest different kinds of inaction. Hamlet vacillates, and his vacillation leads to procrastination, but he does not dawdle.

✔ In the following list, all the words in each line have roughly the same general meaning as the italicized word at the left; yet they cannot always be used interchangeably. Can you distinguish their differences by showing how they would affect the meaning of the phrase if they were substituted for the italicized word?

> To _adore_ a girl: be infatuated with, dote upon, idolize
> An _angry_ remark: annoyed, belligerent, indignant, irritable
> A _careful_ answer: cautious, circumspect, deliberate, painstaking
> A _dirty_ house: disorderly, filthy, messy, untidy
> An _embarrassed_ speaker: abashed, chagrined, flustered
> An _odd_ costume: bizarre, unmatched, ridiculous, unconventional, quaint
> To _plead_ for a favor: beg, coax, wheedle
> To _reprimand_ an offender: admonish, rebuke, scold, castigate
> A _sharp_ answer: clever, discriminating, quick, unfriendly
> A _tired_ man: exhausted, sleepy, weary

The Appropriate Word
(*Levels of Usage*)

Social Levels: Standard and Nonstandard English

Words not only point to things and to attitudes; they also reflect the social level of the person using them. Thus, "I have no money" and "I ain't got no money" refer to the same financial condition. One is just as clear as the other; but the connotations of the second statement invite the judgment that the speaker is not very well educated. We distinguish between these two uses by saying that the first is *standard English* and the second is *nonstandard English*.

Standard English is a class dialect. It may be defined as the speech of those who enjoy a favored economic and social status in our society, and since this class may be roughly described as the educated class, we may say that standard English is the way that educated people speak and write. It is, therefore, the kind of English written and spoken by business executives, lawyers, doctors, ministers, teachers, writers, editors, artists, engineers, and other professional people, and, of course, by their wives. All these comprise a small minority of those who use the language.

Nonstandard English is the language of the farm, the factory, the mine, the lumber camp, the railroad, and, in general, of those occupations which do not require what we call "higher education." It is essentially a spoken rather than a written language, but it is often imitated in writing by novelists, dramatists, and short-story writers when they are representing characters who would be expected to use nonstandard English. It is occasionally used by educated people for humorous effects.

Standard English is more expressive than nonstandard. The latter serves well enough the purposes for which it is commonly used, but it has a limited vocabulary, especially for terms referring to ideas, and its grammar is simple. So it can express many complex thoughts poorly if at all. Yet the strongest objection to it is social. Indeed, the use of nonstandard expressions is usually taken as a sure sign of inferior social background, and the unlucky speaker is handicapped in his struggle for economic and social advancement. This is one reason why teachers try so hard to weed nonstandard expressions out of student speech and writing. Colleges are preparing students to take their places on the economic and social levels at which standard English is spoken and written. Therefore college students are committed to study and use it, and to avoid expressions which are nonstandard. Save in special assignments (chiefly fiction) in which the writer must represent uneducated speech, *nonstandard English has no place in college writing*.

Stylistic Levels: Formal, Informal, Colloquial

Standard English may be *formal, informal,* or *colloquial*. Each of these levels is appropriate to particular purposes, and when it is appropriate, it is correct. The differences between the levels are essentially stylistic. Just as different social occasions call for different styles of clothing, so different writing purposes require different styles of writing. The writer's obligation is to select the style appropriate to his particular purpose.

Before we can profitably discuss these styles, it will be necessary to consider five classes of words into which the vocabularies of educated people can be divided. These are *popular words, learned words, idiomatic diction, colloquialisms,* and *slang.*

Popular and Learned Words. In English, as in other languages, a great part of the total vocabulary consists of words which are common to the speech of educated and uneducated speakers alike. These words are the basic elements of our language. They are indispensable for everyday communication, and by means of them people from widely different social levels are able to speak a common language. These are called *popular words;* they belong to the whole populace.

Contrasted with these are words which we read more often than we hear, and write more often than we speak — words more widely used by educated than by uneducated people, and more likely to be used on formal than on informal occasions. These we call *learned words.* The distinction can be illustrated by contrasting some pairs which have roughly the same meaning.

Popular	Learned	Popular	Learned
agree	concur	lying	mendacious
beggar	mendicant	make easy	facilitate
behead	decapitate	near (in time)	imminent
break	fracture	prove	verify
clear	lucid	queer	eccentric
end	terminate	secret	cryptic, esoteric
fat	corpulent	surrender	capitulate
hair-do	coiffure	truth	veracity

Learned words are usually imported by educated people from a foreign language and, at first, retain their foreign pronunciations, meanings, and grammatical forms. If they become so useful that they pass into the vocabulary of all classes, they lose their foreign characteristics and become Anglicized or naturalized — that is, treated as native words. They lose their foreign pronunciations (*cottage, garage, lieutenant*), give up their foreign grammatical features (*gymnasia* and *indices* become *gymnasiums* and *indexes*), and acquire new meanings (*curfew, lingerie, quarantine*). In the process of being naturalized they usually pass through a transitional stage when both the foreign and the naturalized uses are common (*data are* — *data is; detoúr* — *détour; flair* meaning "capacity to detect" and also "having a knack for"). When the new uses begin to be popular they are often denounced as "mistakes," but when the process of naturalization is complete, the learned words, in their new uses, become part of the popular vocabulary.

Idiomatic Diction. Every language contains many expressions which are not subject to logical analysis but are so characteristic that until one has learned to use them naturally he has not mastered the language. These are called idioms. Unless one has learned the language as a native, they are often difficult to use. For example, a foreigner who has learned what *hard* and *up* mean in English will still be puzzled by the phrase *hard up*. A Frenchman to whom the greeting "How do you carry yourself?" seems the most natural kind of expression will be puzzled by "How do you do?" Yet the only real difference between these two salutations is that one is the French way of talking and the other is the English way. Each is natural to the people who use it. Each is an idiomatic expression.

Because idioms are traditional rather than logical, they can be learned only by experience, not by rule. There is, for example, no rule that will tell us in advance what verbs will govern what prepositions. We say aim *at,* abide *by,* account *for,* arise *from,* and adhere *to.* The meaning of a verb may be no clue to its meaning in an idiomatic verb-adverb combination. A dictionary definition of *get* will be of little use in such phrases as *get ahead, get by, get over.* It is this arbitrary nature of idioms that causes trouble.

The following list illustrates common English idioms.

all in all	fight shy of	meddle with
at any rate	get a move on	mull over
be taken in	get away with	nice and cold
by and large	get behind	off and on
call off	get off	pull through
call up	get on	put up with
catch fire	hard and fast	right away
come in handy	in any event	set about
do away with	keep up	set up
do up	kill off	strike a bargain
down and out	look down on	take heed
drink up	look over	tear down
eat away	look up to	tear out
eat up	make no bones about	tear up
every now and then	make out	watch out

You will notice that these idioms are mostly made up of popular words. They are used by all classes of people and are common to both standard and nonstandard speech. Often a particular idiom may be replaced by a more learned word. Thus "periodically" may be used for "every now and then" and "eradicate" for "root out." As we shall see later, whether such substitution is advisable will depend on the formality of the style.

Colloquialisms. The word *colloquial* is defined by the *American College Dictionary* as "characteristic of or appropriate to ordinary or familiar conversation rather than formal speech or writing." It does not mean here, as it is sometimes taken to mean, "incorrect," "slovenly," or "undesirable." Its closest synonym is "conversational." A colloquialism, therefore, is any word or expression which might appropriately be used in conversation among educated people.

This definition of *colloquial* makes it a broader term than *popular words* or *idiom.* Colloquialisms include popular words and idiomatic constructions; they also include learned words with popular meanings (the use of *alibi* to mean *excuse,* for example), and constructions which are not strictly idioms, especially abbreviated or clipped forms of more formal words, such as *ad* for *advertisement.* The following are illustrations:

aggravate (annoy)	fix (predicament)	out loud (aloud)
anyway (at any rate)	folks	outside of (aside from)
auto	heap (a great deal)	over with (completed)
awfully (very)	it's me	party (person)
back of (behind)	kind (sort) of	peeve (annoy)
bank on (rely on)	like (as though)	phone
bust (failure)	locate (settle)	plenty (adv.)
cute	lot(s) of	reason is because
enthuse	mad (angry)	show (movie)
exam	math	show (chance)
expect (suppose)	mean (nasty)	sure (certainly)
fellow	mighty (very)	terribly

Slang. The *Oxford Dictionary* defines slang as "language of a highly colloquial type." Notice that the adjective is *colloquial,* not *vulgar, incorrect,* or *nonstandard.* There may be specific slang words which are confined to standard or to nonstandard speakers, but slang is used at all social levels. Its use is less frequent and more discriminating among educated speakers, but, though a college president would usually avoid slang in a public address, he might well use it in many informal speech situations.

Slang has its origin in a desire to be vivid and original. People, especially young people, are constantly experimenting with language, using old words in unconventional ways and, very rarely, coining new words. Many slang expressions are borrowed from the specialized vocabularies of particular occupations or recreations and put into general use — *brass* (army), *ham* (theater), *on the beam* (radio), *southpaw* (baseball), *behind the eight ball* (pool), *raise the ante* (poker). Most of them are figurative uses of expressions in the general vocabulary with literal meanings — *no sweat, flipped, cool.*

If these adaptations serve a useful purpose, they may survive and, in time, be accepted as established usage. For example, the words *bus, cab, canter, hoax,* and *mob* were once slang terms but are now acceptable even in formal English; the clipped forms *auto, phone, taxi,* and the words *enthuse, mad* (angry), and *show* (movie) were once slang but are now classified as colloquial; and such current slang as *sick* (disgusted), *swell* (good), *kickback,* and *windbag* are so common that their recognition as colloquialisms seems certain.

The great majority of slang terms, however, soon depreciate in value. The freshness that made them effective at first is soon worn off by overuse, and what was once creative becomes lazy borrowing. This is the chief reason why instructors often object to slang in college writing. If the slang words were carefully chosen and if they were appropriate to the purpose and style of the paper, they might be effective. But if slang were so chosen, there would be much less of it in student compositions.

Let us now return to the formal, informal, and colloquial styles; but because an informal style has some of the characteristics of the other two, let us treat it last.

Formal Style

Formal English is primarily a written style, though it is occasionally used in public speeches of a serious or ceremonial nature. Its chief characteristics are (1) relatively long and involved sentences, with frequent rhetorical devices such as parallel and periodic sentences (see pages 107–112); (2) an extensive vocabulary which makes a liberal use of learned words and avoids abbreviations, contractions, colloquialisms, and slang; (3) conservative grammatical usage which tends to observe distinctions often ignored at a less formal level; (4) an impersonal tone; and (5) a serious and dignified attitude toward the subject and the reader.

The following paragraph is moderately formal:

There are, indeed, other objects of desire that if attained leave nothing but restlessness and dissatisfaction behind them. These are the objects pursued by fools. That such objects ever attract us is a proof of the disorganization of our nature, which drives us in contrary directions and is at war with itself. If we had attained anything like steadiness of thought or fixity of character, if we knew ourselves, we should know also our inalienable satisfactions. To say that all goods become worthless in possession is either a piece of superficial satire that intentionally denies the normal in order to make the abnormal seem more shocking, or else it is a confession of frivolity, a confession that, as an idiot never learns to distinguish reality amid the phantasms of his brain, so we have never learned to distinguish true goods amid our extravagances of whim and passion. That true goods exist is nevertheless a fact of moral experience. "A thing of beauty is a joy forever"; a great affection, a clear thought, a profound and well-tried faith are eternal possessions. And this is not merely a fact, to be asserted upon the authority of those who know it by experience. It is a psychological necessity. While we retain the same senses, we must get the same impressions from the same objects; while we keep our instincts and passions, we must pursue the same goods; while we have the same powers of imagination, we must experience the same delight in their exercise. Age brings about, of course, variation in all these particulars, and the susceptibility of two individuals is never exactly similar. But the eventual decay of our personal energies does not destroy the natural value of objects, so long as the same will embodies itself in other minds, and human nature subsists in the world. The sun is not now unreal because each one of us, in succession, and all of us in the end, must close our eyes upon it; and yet the sun exists for us only because we perceive it. The ideal has the same conditions of being, but has this advantage over the sun, that we cannot know if its light is ever destined to fail us.[4]

Notice the style of this passage. The tone is serious and dignified. The diction (*objects of desire, disorganization of our nature, inalienable satisfactions,* etc.) tends to be learned. The sentence structure is frequently inverted, and there are many long sentences. The whole mode of expression, as the following contrasted excerpts show, is far removed from the style in which the same ideas would be expressed in conversation or in informal writing.

Formal	*Informal*
There are, indeed, other objects of desire that if attained leave nothing but restlessness and dissatisfaction behind them. These are the objects pursued by fools. That such objects ever attract us is a proof of the disorganization of our nature, which drives us in contrary directions and is at war with itself. If we had attained anything like steadiness of thought or fixity of character, if we knew ourselves, we should know also our inalienable satisfactions.	We all have foolish desires. We want things which do not satisfy us when we get them. The fact that we want these things is evidence of our inconsistent nature. We are subject to conflicting desires and want to go in opposite directions at the same time. If we had a clearer understanding of our own needs and purposes, we would know what course was best for us.

The contrast between these two passages need not imply that a formal style is necessarily superior to an informal one. In skilled hands each style has merits that the other lacks. Ideally, the style should fit the purpose, and the purpose should take into account the audience to whom the writing is addressed. For some audiences in some situations much is gained by the eloquence and dignity of a formal style. But for other audiences in other situations, ease and clarity may be what is most needed. On pages 18–21 we saw good examples of both styles. Surely no sensible critic would want the author of "Why We Need More Westerns on Television" to write that piece more formally, or the author of "Communication Equals Civilization" to write less formally.

Colloquial Style

A colloquial style is fundamentally the style used by educated people when speaking informally to their social equals. It is basically a spoken style, and its characteristics are (1) relatively short simple sentences, often grammatically incomplete, with few rhetorical devices; (2) a generous use

[4] From *The Sense of Beauty*, by George Santayana, copyright, 1896, 1936, by Charles Scribner's Sons. Reprinted by permission of Charles Scribner's Sons.

of contractions (*I'll, we've, didn't, can't*), clipped words (*cab, exams, phone*), and the omission of relative pronouns (*who, which, that*) which would be retained in a formal style; (3) a vocabulary marked by general avoidance of learned words and by inclusion of some less objectionable slang terms; (4) a simplified grammatical structure which leans heavily on idiomatic constructions and sometimes ignores the fine distinctions of formal grammar; and (5) a personal or familiar tone which tries to create the impression of speaking intimately to the reader.

Here is an example:

> You're going to paint that picturesque old barn. All right. One vertical line (better use charcoal) will place the corner of the barn, another line the base. A couple of lines for the trunk of the tree, and maybe a branch or two. Then a line to indicate the horizon — whatever divides the sky from whatever meets it (tree, barn, hill). That's all! No leaves, door-knobs, cats, mice, or daffodils. It's the painting that's fun, and any time wasted in getting into a mess of details is to be deplored. As we start to paint, anything resembling a real drawing on our canvas is purely accidental. . . .
>
> Now squeeze out little blobs of color on your palette, and a big blob of white. And take a look at that sky. It is, let's say, cloudless. And it really is blue. Still not as blue as Uncle Ed's shirt. Take a half of a butter ball of white on your palette knife and plaster it on the front of your palette. Careful now! Just a pinch of blue and mix with the white until there are no streaks. Not blue enough? All right, just a tiny bit more — but easy! Satisfied? Dip your brush in the turpentine, then in the paint and slap it on! Boldly — never mind if you slop over the barn a bit.[5]

Notice, first, the sentence structure. The twenty-two sentences average only ten words in length and half of them are fragments, a kind of structure that almost never occurs in formal writing and only rarely in informal writing. Notice also the simplicity of the diction and the frequent use of contractions. Finally, notice the intimate tone. It is as though the writer were looking over the reader's shoulder and telling him what to do. The whole effort in these paragraphs is to talk simply, directly, and familiarly to the reader. These are the characteristics of a colloquial style.

Informal Style

The informal style tries to follow the broad middle way between formal and colloquial styles. Its sentence patterns are less involved than those of formal English without being as loose or fragmentary as colloquial patterns. It avoids the nice requirements of formal grammar without being dominated by conversational usages. It may use learned words, but it prefers idiomatic expressions and words which are easy rather than im-

[5] From "Get in There and Paint" by Joseph Alger, in *Recreation,* November, 1944. Reprinted by permission of the National Recreation Association.

pressive. Its tone may have the seriousness of the formal style without its dignity, and the informality of the colloquial style without its easygoing familiarity. The following paragraphs illustrate an informal style.

> A man in whom I have complete trust once looked me in the eye and told me he had seen a snake, when alarmed, open its mouth and allow its six young to crawl down its throat out of sight, and when danger was past, permit them to reappear. Now cannibal snakes which subsist wholly on their fellows (once or twice removed) are not rare. A nearsighted parent black snake might conceivably, tempted by the pangs of hunger, devour one of its own offspring, but I cannot believe in the willful use by an infant serpent of its mother's acid-filled tummy as a shelter.
>
> A strange thing about nature fakes is that they are almost always gone one better by actual truths. The snake-swallowing sanctuary idea becomes a minor stunt when compared with certain common tropical fish, which look like little perch. If you want to see sheer magic, tap on the glass of an aquarium which holds a mother, father, and one hundred (count them) tiny young. The moment after an alarm, there will be only two fish visible; every youngster being snugly hidden within the mouth of a parent. When danger is over, the whole mob is gently spewed forth, rolling head over tail to form a dense, orderly cloud around and behind their parents.[6]

This passage compromises the differences between the formal and the colloquial. The sentences are longer and more complex than those in our colloquial example, but shorter and simpler than those in the formal one. There are no sentence fragments, although an occasional one may be found in informal writing. With the possible exception of "subsist" and "devour," there are no learned words, and no colloquialisms except "fakes," "tummy," and "stunt." Nearly all the diction is drawn from the popular vocabulary. In one sentence the reader is addressed directly as "you," but the author makes no attempt to establish the kind of over-the-shoulder intimacy we noticed in the painting instructions.

Since the informal style is really a range between formal and colloquial, some samples will be more formal and some more colloquial than others. This broad range makes it the most useful all-purpose style. In the informal range come much narration and description, many reports of events, most nontechnical exposition, and critical and argumentative papers addressed to general readers. Most modern novels, essays, stories, and magazine and newspaper articles are informal. Most of the lectures and speeches you listen to and many of the textbooks you study — including this one — are informal. The following selections illustrate the wide uses of this style.

Light Verse

Jenny kissed me when we met,
Jumping from the chair she sat in;
Time, you thief, who love to get

[6] From "Nature in False Face," by William Beebe in *Collier's,* January 29, 1944. Reprinted by permission of author and publishers.

Sweets into your list, put that in:
Say I'm weary, say I'm sad,
Say that health and wealth have missed me,
Say I'm growing old, but add,
Jenny kissed me![7]

Serious Poetry

When I, the People, learn to remember, when I, the people,
use the lessons of yesterday and no longer forget
who robbed me last year, who played me for a fool —
then there will be no speaker in all the world say
the name: "The People," with any fleck of a sneer in
his voice or any far-off smile of derision.[8]

Political Statement

Suppose my neighbor's house catches fire and I have a length of garden hose four or five hundred feet away. If he can take this garden hose and connect it up with his hydrant, I may help him to put out the fire. Now what do I do? I don't say to him before that operation, "Neighbor, my garden hose cost me fifteen dollars; you have to pay me fifteen dollars for it." No! What is the transaction that goes on? I don't want fifteen dollars — I want my garden hose back after the fire is over.[9]

Scientific Statement

Prior to Einstein the universe was commonly pictured as an island of matter afloat in the center of an infinite sea of space. There were several reasons for this concept. The universe, most scientists agreed, had to be infinite; because just as soon as they conceded that space might come to an end somewhere, they were faced with the embarrassing question: "And what lies beyond that?" Yet Newtonian law prohibited an infinite universe containing a uniform distribution of matter, for then the total gravitational force of all the masses of matter stretching away to infinity would be infinite, and the heavens would be ablaze with infinite light. To man's feeble eyes, moreover, it appeared that beyond the rim of our milky way the lamps of space became sparser and sparser, diffusing gradually in attenuated outposts like lonely lighthouses on the frontiers of the fathomless void. But the island universe presented difficulties too. The amount of matter it held was so small by contrast with an infinity of space that inevitably the dynamic laws governing the movements of the galaxies would cause them to disperse like the droplets of a cloud and the universe would become entirely empty.[10]

[7] Leigh Hunt.

[8] From "I Am the People, the Mob" by Carl Sandburg. Copyright, 1916, by Henry Holt and Company, Inc. Copyright, 1943, by Carl Sandburg. Reprinted by permission.

[9] Franklin D. Roosevelt introducing the Lend-Lease program at a press conference on December 17, 1940.

[10] From *The Universe and Dr. Einstein* by Lincoln Barnett. Copyright 1948 by Harper & Brothers; Copyright 1948 by Lincoln Barnett; Copyright 1950, 1957 by Lincoln Barnett. Reprinted by permission of the publishers, William Sloane Associates.

THE PROCESS OF COMPOSITION

Editorial

Do you know that hobbyhorses are now hard to come by? I don't mean the sort that you and I ride but the old-fashioned kind which has a head at one end of a stick and is very suitable for use either in the nursery or the back yard.

Perhaps the fact is not very important in itself. But the reason why the toy shops no longer stock the horses is. That reason — as given by S. H., *The New Yorker's* shopper who keeps an eye out for the little amenities of life — is simply this: the playschool consultants have decided that a hobbyhorse "does not develop the group spirit." . . .

Here is a straw in the wind if there ever was one, and the warm winds (sometimes called hot air) which blow lustily around the child psychologists are full of straws. . . . Nowadays even "self-expression" is routinized. My young friend tells me that if you don't want to fingerpaint when the others do, that is just too bad. "Do what you want" is the rule. But you jolly well better want what you ought to want and what you ought to want is what others "at your age level" are supposed to want.[11]

Literary Criticism

I had to learn American just like a foreign language. To learn it I had to study and analyze it. As a result, when I use slang, colloquialisms, snide talk or any kind of off-beat language I do it deliberately. The literary use of slang is a study in itself. I've found that there are only two kinds that are any good: slang that has established itself in the language, and slang that you make up yourself. Everything else is apt to be passé before it gets into print . . .[12]

Correspondence

Dear Ike:

Now that we have all signed in Berlin I suppose we shall soon begin to run our own affairs. I would like, before this happens, to say what a privilege and an honor it has been to serve under you. I owe much to your wise guidance and kindly forbearance. I know my own faults very well and I do not suppose I am an easy subordinate; I like to go my own way.

But you have kept me on the rails in difficult and stormy times, and have taught me much.

For all this I am very grateful. And I thank you for all you have done for me.

Your very devoted friend,
Monty[13]

[11] From "Little Man on a Horse" by Joseph Wood Krutch, in *The Saturday Review,* July 24, 1954. Copyright 1954 by *The Saturday Review*. Reprinted by permission of author and publishers.

[12] From *Raymond Chandler Speaking,* edited by Dorothy Gardiner and Kathrine Sorley Walker (Boston: Houghton Mifflin Company, 1962), p. 80. Copyright © 1962 by the Helga Greene Literary Agency. Reprinted by permission.

[13] From *Crusade in Europe,* by Dwight D. Eisenhower. Copyright, 1948, by Doubleday & Company, Inc. Reprinted by permission of the publishers.

Few, if any, of your college assignments will require any other than an informal style. Once you understand this, you will be more likely to avoid those twin plagues of college composition: the pretentious writing that we saw illustrated in Chapter 5 and the over-colloquial writing which sacrifices the conventions of sentence structure and diction to a striving for conversational usages in assignments which do not call for them.

The table on page 146 summarizes this discussion of formal, informal, and colloquial styles.

Confusion of Stylistic Levels

A writer should choose the stylistic level most appropriate to his purpose, and he should stay with it. Words which are too formal or too colloquial for their context are discordant, or even ludicrous, and betray a lack of sureness. Notice the misfit diction in the following passage from an essay in which a student is relating how his service in the Marines helped to free him from the domination of his twin brother.

> I was never allowed to fight my own battles, for he was at my side and would step in and pound the hell out of my diabolical enemies. This, too, contributed to my shyness.
> During the terminating days of my high-school career I came to the conclusion that life in the Marine Corps would cure me of this bad attribute. I quickly told my brother. His eyes seemed to be glaring like a dragon's. He then told me, "I am going to join the army and you shall do such also."

The lapses here are clear enough. Except in some kinds of dialogue, profanity is almost never justifiable in college writing. If it is used at all, the whole style of the paper must be so obviously colloquial that the profanity does not call attention to itself. Yet here is profanity followed immediately by learned words like *diabolical, terminating,* and *attribute.* These two levels of usage, however justifiable either might be alone, are impossibly inconsistent in the same paper. Other choices of diction are just as bad. The description of the brother's eyes "glaring like a dragon's" is a trite and far-fetched metaphor, and his words "you shall do such also" are comically unidiomatic. What the brother would probably say is, "I'm going to join the army, and so are you."

Incongruous diction is most conspicuous in writing which is clearly formal or clearly colloquial, as may be shown by substituting inappropriate diction in a passage quoted earlier.

> There are, indeed, other objects of desire that if *got* leave nothing but restlessness and *griping* behind them. These are the objects pursued by fools. That such objects ever attract us is a proof of the *cussedness* of our nature, which drives us in contrary directions and is at war with itself. If we had attained anything like steadiness of thought or fixity of character, if

145

LEVELS OF STANDARD ENGLISH USAGE*

STYLISTIC LEVELS	LINGUISTIC CHARACTERISTICS	REPRESENTATIVE USES
Formal (more often written than spoken)	1. Relatively long sentences, complex in structure, employing many rhetorical devices. 2. Extensive vocabulary, numerous "learned" words. 3. General avoidance of abbreviations, contractions, omitted relative pronouns, and other colloquial shortcuts. 4. Conservative grammatical usage which observes distinctions generally ignored in popular speech. 5. Impersonal tone and dignified attitude towards subject and reader.	1. Books and articles on scholarly or technical subjects, written for experts in the field. 2. "Belles-lettres": novels, essays, stories, poems, written for highly educated readers. 3. Prepared serious or ceremonial addresses to restricted audiences.
Informal (both written and spoken, the general level of educated writing and of educated, deliberate speech)	Overlaps formal and colloquial styles, but avoids the extremes of both.	1. Books and articles on important subjects, but for general readers. 2. Most novels, essays, poems, magazine and newspaper articles and editorials. 3. Most college writing. 4. Most speeches to general audiences; the deliberate conversation of educated speakers in formal speech situations.
Colloquial or Conversational (more often spoken than written)	1. Short sentences, simple in structure, usually in subject-verb-object order, few rhetorical devices. 2. Many contractions, abbreviations, clipped words; tendency to omit relative pronouns and other constructions not necessary to meaning. 3. Few "learned" words, many idiomatic expressions, the use of less objectionable slang.	1. Light, chatty writing for general readers. 2. Dialogue in fiction, and any writing which attempts to catch the rhythms of conversation. 3. The letters of educated people to intimate friends. 4. Almost all the conversation of educated people when they are at ease.

* This table is indebted to a similar table in Porter G. Perrin's *Writer's Guide and Index to English*. The differences between Professor Perrin's table and this one arise out of differences of classification.

we knew ourselves, we should know also *what's good for us.* To say that all goods become worthless in possession is either a piece of *half-baked bunk* that intentionally denies the normal in order to make the abnormal seem more shocking, or else it is a confession of frivolity, a confession that, as an idiot never learns *what the score is,* so we have never learned to distinguish true goods amid our extravagances of whim and passion. That true goods exist is nevertheless a fact of moral experience. "A thing of beauty is a joy forever"; a great *yen,* a *bright idea,* a profound and well-tried faith, are eternal possessions. And this is not merely a fact, to be asserted upon the *say-so* of those who know it by experience. It is a psychological necessity.

There are contexts in which *got, griping, cussedness, what's good for us, half-baked, bunk, what the score is, yen, bright idea,* and *say-so* could be appropriate, but this is not one of them. These colloquial and slang expressions are as much out of place in a formal style as a ukulele in a symphony orchestra.

Conversely, the italicized learned words in the following colloquial selection are hopelessly out of tone.

Have you ever tried to quit smoking? It's quite simple. I know. I have *achieved abstinence* thousands of times already. In fact, I quit every day. I awaken in the morning — my nose and throat dry and parched. Then, I decide to *renounce all further association with the weed.* But it's a terrible vice over which I no longer have any control. I've got to have a smoke. Just one. Then I'll *refrain from further indulgence* the rest of the day. Just one to take care of my terrible longing. I can go without food, without drink. But I must have a cigarette. Just one.

So I smoke one before going to school. Only that one. I promise myself, I'm not going to smoke any more today. I'll leave my cigarettes home today. Yeh, that's what I'll do. And since I have no cigarettes, I *shall be unable to make even a momentary concession to appetite.*

The Specific Word

"Specific" is the opposite of "general." A specific word points to a particular referent — a particular person, object, or event; a general word points to a group or class of referents. Thus "Arnold Palmer," "Mickey Mantle," "the present heavyweight champion," "the apple tree beside my garage," and "last night's rain" indicate particular referents. But "golfer," "baseball player," "pugilist," "tree," and "rain" indicate group referents. The general term, therefore, includes a number of specific terms, as "red" includes carmine, coral, crimson, maroon, rose, scarlet, vermilion, and so on, and as "Midwest" includes Michigan, Minnesota, Illinois, Indiana, Iowa, and several other states.

Actually the contrast between "specific" and "general" is relative. A term may be specific in contrast to one word, but general in contrast to another. We can show this relativity by the following table.

Very General	Less General	More Specific	Quite Specific
athlete	baseball player	Yankee outfielder	Mickey Mantle
college student	freshman	member of Dr. Jones's composition section	Bill Mason
vegetation	tree	apple tree	the apple tree beside my garage
criminal	thief	pickpocket	the man who stole my wallet

As you see, the words in the middle columns are more specific than those at the left but more general than those at the right.

The more general words are, the harder it will be for a reader to see precisely what a writer intends them to mean. For example, "The man was making preparations for a journey" is such a general statement that we get almost no idea of what the man was actually doing. He may have been making hotel reservations, buying a railroad ticket, having his car tuned up, arranging for someone to handle his business affairs, or packing a suitcase.

Notice below how the specific diction at the right communicates meaning which is not conveyed by the general diction at the left.

General	Specific
He is an accomplished athlete.	He is a top-flight golfer.
He drives an old car.	He drives a 1957 Buick.
The boy has a serious disease.	The boy has diphtheria.
I have been reading a Shakespearean play.	I have been reading *Macbeth*.
Her grades at midsemester were unsatisfactory.	She received two failing grades and a D at midsemester.
After the strenuous activities of the day, I did not feel like dancing.	After playing 36 holes of golf, I did not feel like dancing.
In the past, girls in rural communities had no facilities for bathing except those offered by some neighboring stream. In such circumstances a bathing suit was not always a necessity, but if one was worn it was likely to consist of nothing more than some discarded article of clothing tailored to fit the occasion. Women in urban areas seldom owned their own costumes. Only those who moved in the more wealthy and sophisticated social circles had private bathing suits.	Twenty years ago if the farmer's daughter went swimming she swam in the crick below the pasture, and if she wore a bathing suit, which was not as customary as you may think, it was likely to be a pair of her brother's outgrown overalls trimmed with scissors as her discretion might suggest. Her cousin in such a town as Great Bend (Kansas) rented a shapeless gray cotton suit at an amusement park. Only the Banker's daughter, who had been to a finish-

148

The usual practice was to wear a rented one. This distinction no longer exists. Now the modern country girl owns a bathing suit similar to those worn at fashionable beaches in the East. ing school, had a bathing suit of her own. There are no such distinctions now; all women have bathing suits, and they are exactly like those worn at Hyannis, Southampton, and Narragansett Pier.[14]

The last example shows you that the more specific diction is, the more pictorial it is likely to be. "A pair of her brother's outgrown overalls trimmed with scissors" makes a clearer picture than "some discarded article of clothing tailored to fit the occasion." "The crick below the pasture" is easier to visualize than "some neighboring stream." "Her cousin in . . . Great Bend (Kansas)" instead of "Women in urban areas" and "the Banker's daughter" in place of "those who moved in the more wealthy and sophisticated social circles" provide sharper identification.

To find the most telling specific word or phrase takes thought, and too many students are willing to take the easy way out and use "utility words" instead. Of these words, Professor A. G. Kennedy says, "Any long-used and well-developed language accumulates ultimately a supply of general utility words which have such broad meaning and general application that they can be utilized in a great many different ways with no special change of meaning."[15] These, as their name implies, are useful words. In conversation, their general meaning is often sharpened by tone of voice, facial expression, or gesture. Their discreet use in writing needs no defense, but when a writer uses them to excess, his work is likely to be colorless and inexact, as the following sentences show.

1. It gave me a *funny feeling* to hear him say that another war was inevitable. (Precisely what is a "funny feeling" in this context — a feeling of despair, of panic, of hopelessness, of shock, of disgust, of revulsion?)

2. His wife is always a *classy dresser.* Today she wore a *lovely outfit.* It was a *nice shade of blue.* She also wore a *cute* little hat with a matching blue ribbon. ("Classy" in what sense — chic, tasteful, glamorous? What was the "outfit" — a suit, a blouse and skirt, a sweater and skirt, a one-piece dress? Precisely what shade of blue was it? Can you imagine a fashion reporter describing a woman's costume as "an outfit in a nice shade of blue"? Does "cute" give you a clear picture of the hat?)

3. That kind of publicity is always *bad business* for *an organization,* and the boys in our chapter house felt *pretty bad* about it. (What is meant by "bad business" here? Does it cause the fraternity to lose prestige on campus? Does it make it more difficult to get dates? Does it hurt pledging? Does it invite administrative interference in fraternity management? If the organization is a fraternity, why not say so? When the boys feel "pretty bad," how do they feel? Angry? Ashamed? Disgusted? Embarrassed? Resentful? Indignant?)

[14] From "Main Street Twenty Years After" by Bernard DeVoto, in *Harper's Magazine,* November, 1940. Reprinted by permission of *Harper's Magazine.*
[15] *Current English* (Ginn and Company), p. 552.

The italicized words in these sentences are so vague, could mean so many different things, that the sentences fail to communicate any precise meaning. They reveal either fuzzy or lazy thinking and should never be allowed to get beyond the first draft. The way to revise them is, first, to sharpen the idea to be expressed and, second, to choose words specific enough to express it exactly.

Sensory Words. A number of specific words refer to sensory experiences, to what we see, hear, touch, taste, and smell. Because these words call up sensory images, they are particularly effective in description. In the following list, some words could fit into more than one sensory category.

Touch: chill, clammy, cold, corrugated, grainy, gritty, harsh, jarring, knobby, moist, nubby, numb, plushy, rough, satiny, slimy, slithering, smooth, sting, tingle, tickly, velvety.

Taste: bland, biting, bitter, brackish, briny, metallic, minty, nutty, peppery, salty, sour, spicy, sweet, tainted, vinegary, yeasty.

Smell: acrid, fetid, greasy, mouldy, musky, musty, pungent, putrid, rancid, rank, reek, stench, sulphurous, woodsy.

Sound: bellow, blare, buzz, chatter, chime, clang, clatter, clink, crackle, crash, creak, gurgle, hiss, hum, murmur, pop, purr, rattle, rustle, screech, snap, splash, squeak, swish, tinkle, whine, whisper.

Sight: blaze, bleary, bloody, burnished, chalky, dappled, ebony, flame, flash, flicker, florid, foggy, gaudy, glare, glitter, glossy, glow, golden, grimy, haze, inky, leaden, lurid, muddy, roiled, sallow, shadow, smudged, spark, streak, tawny, turbid.

Sensory words help the reader feel the experience that the writer is recording. If you reread the two versions of the rattlesnake incident on pages 16–17 you will see that much of the detail in the second version is expressed in words that appeal to the senses and so make it easy for the reader to re-live the incident in his imagination. Notice how the following description makes the reader feel, hear, see, and smell the details of ploughing.

The ploughing, now in full swing, enveloped him in a vague, slow-moving whirl of things. Underneath him was the jarring, jolting, trembling machine; not a clod was turned, not an obstacle encountered, that he did not receive the swift impression of it through all his body; the very friction of the damp soil, sliding incessantly from the shiny surface of the shears, seemed to reproduce itself in his finger-tips and along the back of his head. He heard the horse-hoofs by the myriads crushing down easily, deeply, into the loam, the prolonged clinking of trace-chains, the working of the smooth brown flanks in the harness, the clatter of wooden hames, the champing of bits, the click of iron shoes against pebbles, the brittle stubble of the surface ground crackling and snapping as the furrows turned, the sonorous, steady breaths wrenched from the deep, laboring chests, strap-bound, shining with sweat, and all along the line the voices of the men talking to the horses.

Everywhere there were visions of glossy brown backs, straining, heaving, swollen with muscle; harness streaked with specks of froth, broad, cup-shaped hoofs, heavy with brown loam; men's faces red with tan, blue overalls spotted with axle-grease; muscled hands, the knuckles whitened in their grip on the reins, and through it all the ammoniacal smell of the horses, the bitter reek of perspiration of beasts and men, the aroma of warm leather, the scent of dead stubble — and stronger and more penetrating than everything else, the heavy, enervating odor of the upturned, living earth.[16]

Now notice what happens to the paragraph when most of the sensory words are removed.

He abandoned himself to his ploughing to such an extent that he became a part of the total process and identified himself with the machine beneath him. He could detect the resistance of the damp soil to the impact of the plough, and whenever an obstacle of any sort was encountered, he felt the repercussion in his own body. He was conscious too of the noises that the team and the harness produced as the work continued, and of the appearance of the horses and their immediate environment. All around him was a confusion of sensory impressions, the strongest of which was the odor of the horses and the characteristic smell of upturned earth.

Do you agree that the rewritten paragraph is merely a flat and lifeless summary of the original?

Our stress on the value of specific words should not imply that general diction is never desirable. For example, when you are asked to summarize a 5000-word essay in 500 words, your purpose is to state the central thought of the essay, not its illustrative detail, and your summary has to be more general than the original. Moreover, a writer will not always intend to be specific. His statement may depend not on a set of particular facts but on a broad or universal truth. Whether a subject should be treated generally or specifically is part of the decision about purpose. An excellent illustration is the writing of the Declaration of Independence.

The committee appointed to write the Declaration had a double duty to perform. It had, in the same document, to make a general statement of the relationship between free people and their governors and a particular statement of the abuses which George III had committed against the Colonies. The first part of the Declaration is necessarily, and wisely, general:

We hold these truths to be self-evident, that all men are created equal, that they are endowed by their Creator with certain unalienable rights. . . . That to secure these rights, Governments are instituted among Men, deriving their just powers from the consent of the governed. . . .

These remarks could apply to any nation, and have been interpreted by other nations as applying to them. The second part is more specific:

[16] From *The Octopus* by Frank Norris.

For quartering large bodies of troops among us. . . .
For cutting off our Trade with all parts of the world:
For imposing taxes on us without our Consent:
For depriving us in many cases of the benefit of Trial by Jury. . . .

These charges refer to particular acts of a particular monarch. This part of the Declaration is less valuable as a universal inspiration but more informative as a statement of why the Colonies renounced their allegiance to George III.

The contrast between the two parts of the Declaration shows that there is a time to be general and a time to be specific. Your own analysis of the assignment should guide your choice, but you should know that college instructors emphasize specific diction mainly because much college writing is more general than it need be.

Figurative Language

Figurative language communicates by analogy. One thing is likened to another, usually familiar, and the comparison invites the imagination to visualize the similarity. For example, a scientist wishes to describe the structure of an atom for lay readers. Knowing that they will be familiar with the pattern of the solar system — the elliptical rotation of planets round the sun — he can give a quick, easily visualized description of the atom:

> An atom is a submicroscopic solar system in which electrons, like tiny planets, swing in their orbits around a central nucleus.

An atomic system is not a solar system, and electrons are not planets, but the structural similarity is close enough so that the comparison is informative and vivid.

The commonest figures of speech are metaphors, similes, allusions, and personification.

Metaphors and Similes

Both metaphor and simile compare two things, but the former says they are the same, whereas the latter, usually by inserting *as* or *like,* merely says they are similar. Metaphor says the atom *is* a submicroscopic solar system; simile says it is *like* one. Here are other examples:

Metaphors	*Similes*
The sky was a vast black blanket riddled with tiny star holes.	The star-dotted sky was like a vast black blanket riddled with tiny holes.
The moon was a ghostly galleon tossed upon cloudy seas.	As fresh he was as is the month of May.

Metaphors	*Similes*
Marriage had modified his conception of her. Once she had been his lovely wild rose; now she was the thorn in his flesh.	Like summer tempest came her tears.
Mussolini's attack on France was not only a stab in the back. It was a stab with a pocket-knife by a small boy who was taking advantage of the fact that his victim's arms had already been securely tied.	The judge's head oscillated from one side of the net to the other, for all the world like the pendulum of a grandfather clock.
	Her death destroyed all that was meaningful in his existence. Thereafter his life was like a building which had been gutted by fire.

The effectiveness of metaphors and similes lies in their power to suggest ideas too difficult to communicate in literal terms. They picture vividly in a few words what would be less effectively described in many. Consider how the following figure of speech describes abstract and complex phenomena in terms which a reader will at least think he understands:

> Life's but a walking shadow, a poor player
> That struts and frets his hour upon the stage
> And then is heard no more. It is a tale
> Told by an idiot, full of sound and fury,
> Signifying nothing.

One might write a long essay on life's insignificance without driving the point home as thoroughly as Shakespeare did in this triple metaphor in which Macbeth sees his own life as unsubstantial as a shadow, as unreal as a poor play, and as meaningless as a madman's babbling.

Many words and phrases no longer thought of as figures of speech were originally metaphors and similes. Thus *foil* and *parry* derived from the sport of fencing; *checkmate* was a metaphor from chess; *rosy red* and *sapphire blue* were similes, as were *dirt cheap* and *silver hair*. *At bay* once described a hunted animal when it finally turned to face the baying hounds; a *crestfallen* cock was one which had been injured in a fight; and an *alarm* was a call to arms. Many other expressions retain their metaphorical appearances, but are so common that we no longer think of them as figures of speech — expressions such as the mouth of a river, the face of a clock, the front (originally "forehead") of a house, the brow of a hill, the top of the morning.

Allusions

Allusions are figures of speech which suggest a similarity between people, places, or events, real or imaginary, as in "the Babe Ruth of bowling," "the Athens of the Midwest," "a dog-in-the-manger attitude."

Like metaphors and similes, allusions are vivid and memorable short cuts. Instead of trying to describe the bewilderment of a football crowd watching a strong team beaten by a weak one, a writer may suggest their stunned surprise by saying, "The crowd couldn't have been more shocked if the Christians had started to eat the lions." Or he may sum up a story of world suffering as "the Gethsemane of our age."

Allusions must be used with care. When successful, they not only communicate effectively but also give the reader the pleasure of recognition. But if the reader does not recognize an allusion, it will mean nothing to him and may annoy him. Rather than blame his own ignorance, he will then label the allusion "pedantic" — that is, so erudite that no "normal" reader should be expected to understand it. For this reason, a writer should always be reasonably sure that his allusions will be familiar to the audience he is writing for.

Personification

Personification is the device of endowing animals, inanimate objects, abstractions, and events with human qualities and abilities:

> The eagle, perched on his mountain throne, surveyed the far reaches of his kingdom.
> Truth, crushed to earth, will rise again.
> The flames ate hungrily at the wooden foundations.
> The once proud trees bent meekly before the storm.
> All around, the forest united in a conspiracy against them.
> Her clothes not only invited attention, they commanded it.

Personification, like metaphor, simile, and allusion, implies and pictures a similarity. But whereas metaphor may compare any two things, one of the elements of a personification must be a human characteristic. The subject must be described in terms of human actions, attitudes, feelings, or responses.

Inappropriate Figures

The power of figures of speech to call up vivid images in our minds sometimes leads an uncritical writer into trouble. For if the figures are inappropriate, they may call up images which are ludicrous or incredible. The student who described his brother's eyes as "glaring like a dragon's" (page 145) was writing without thinking. If he had asked himself, "Is this really the way he looked?" he might have realized that his simile was neither fresh nor appropriate. Obviously he did not "see" what he was saying. The habit of using figurative language without visualizing its probable effect often results in confused imagery like this:

> When spring comes, the face of old Mother Earth is arrayed in garments of breath-taking beauty.
> Efforts to help the veterans were sidetracked by a bog of red tape.

The President's ill-advised action has thrown the ship of state into low gear, and unless congressmen wipe out party lines and carry the ball as a team, it may take the country months to get back on an even keel.

The beauty of spring has often been compared to that of a woman's face, or to a woman's clothes; but telescoping the two images suggests a face wearing clothes, and is merely funny. Sidetracked effort is a common enough metaphor, but to mix this railroad image with that of a bog, and then with red tape, shows that the writer was not visualizing. The third sentence, more chaotic still, mixes images of a ship, a car, some lines that can be erased (chalk or pencil lines?), a football team, and a ship again — all in one blurred comparison! Mixed images, like shifts in sentence structure (pages 418–422), show what comes of changing purpose halfway through a sentence. They also show what comes of using words because they "sound good," not because of what a reader will get from them.

Similes, too, may go wrong if images are mixed inappropriately.

He felt as uncomfortable and out of place in the room full of ladies as a wolf in a sheepfold.

The huge rock went crashing down the hill like a lover rushing to meet his beloved.

Far-fetched similes like these invite the reader to see unlikely similarities which are difficult to imagine. It is hard, for instance, to think of a wolf being uncomfortable in a sheepfold, or to picture a rock crashing downhill in the same mood and manner as a lover going to meet his lass. A reader is more likely to laugh at such a comparison than to take it seriously.

✔ Identify the following figures of speech. If you consider any of them inappropriate, explain why.

1. The grades that a student makes are not the only yardstick for his academic success.
2. I saw Eternity the other night
   Like a great ring of pure and endless light.
3. The great liner acknowledged the acclaim of the passing tugs with dignified blasts of her horn.
4. We expected Bill to win the debate in his rebuttal, but, like Casey at the bat, he fumbled every chance.
5. All afternoon this pigskin Proteus consistently eluded his All-American opponent.
6. Life like a dome of many colored glass
   Stains the white radiance of eternity.
7. Drivers who drink keep Charon working overtime.
8. Into this great forest the hand of man had never set foot.
9. His words fanned the flame of her indignation and caused it to boil over.

10. Along the river bank the willows were whispering in the wind.

11. I cannot praise a fugitive and cloistered virtue . . . that never sallies out and sees her adversary, but slinks out of the race, where that immortal garland is to be run for, not without dust and heat.

12. Like the foolish virgins in the Bible the politicians have been asleep at the switch and have allowed a glorious opportunity to go down the drain.

13. The trouble with arguing with your wife is that, even if you win, it's a Pyrrhic victory.

14. Can Honour's voice provoke the silent dust,
Or Flattery soothe the dull cold ear of death?

15. For anyone who has slept in one of those hammocks the bed of Procrustes would have no terrors.

The Unspoiled Word

The terms *trite, hackneyed, shopworn, threadbare* are used to describe expressions which have been spoiled by overuse. Just as cloth may lose its luster and fruit its texture by excessive and careless handling, so words may lose their value by being used too much. Trite words, like most slang, were once fresh and crisp. Such phrases as "a calculated risk," "a near miss," "a moral victory," and such figures of speech as "blind as a bat," "busy as a bee," "close as a clam," "safe as the bank" were once forceful expressions, but they have lost the freshness which once made them effective and are now little more than conspicuous utility words, common in casual conversation, but undesirable in any writing in which the choice of diction is important.

The worst thing about trite diction is the way it blocks thought. A writer who uses a ready-made phrase instead of fashioning his own thought into words soon has no thought beyond the stereotyped comment which his trite diction suggests. Consequently his ideas and observations follow set patterns: any change in personnel becomes a "shakeup"; all hopes become "fond," "foolish," or "forlorn"; standard procedure for making a suggestion is to "drop a hint"; defeats are "crushing"; changes in the existing system are "noble experiments" or "dangerous departures"; unexpected occurrences are "bolts from the blue"; and people who "sow wild oats" always have to "pay the piper" even though they are "as poor as churchmice." The result is a kind of automat-thinking in which the writer puts in a trite phrase and pulls out a platitude.

Triteness can be cut out in revision, and should be. But the best way to keep it out of your writing is to keep your diction specific. As long as you are thinking about what you want your writing to do, you are likely to use clear, fresh words to convey your meaning. Any considerable use of trite words is usually a sign that the writer stopped thinking. Notice how the writer of the following essay fails to provide the illustrative detail and specific diction necessary to make her thoughts clear, and resorts instead to trite statements which serve as escapes from thinking. Underline every trite expression you detect in the paper.

To be taken out of a little world, high school, and placed on a large university campus was a big step in my life. From the first day I arrived at the University, I changed. I could no longer be "mother's little girl" and run to her for advice on what to do about this and how to do that. I had to change.

I am, from all outward appearances, the same person I was when I left home in September and yet, I'm not. Being with people who are more mature has helped me grow up. I've developed a more grown-up idea of life. I've had to make decisions and judgments I've never before been faced with. I've had to give my own opinions and as the old saying goes, "fend for myself." Life isn't a bower of roses, and I've learned it. I've learned to think more seriously of why I'm at school and what I'm deriving from it. Am I doing my best down here? If not, I'd better get busy. People depend on me and I've had to shoulder responsibility. I've grown up a lot. I'm on my own. I have to be able to prove to myself and my parents I can take my place in the world.

Money doesn't grow on trees and how well I've learned that. What a rude awakening, when I finally realized all the odd change I used to ask for at home wasn't with me at school. I had thought my allowance was an enormous amount and, before I knew it, it was gone. College has taught me "a penny saved is a penny earned." I've learned to live within my allowance and have some left to store in my bank for a rainy day.

College has helped me to become a more mature person who has the ability to make decisions for herself. It's not all in the books, what you learn at college. It's your everyday existence with different people and situations that gives you something more, perhaps helps you grow up a little. It's made me a better person and more able to cope with any situation which is to come.

Exercises

A. Study the diction of the following story from the point of view of its appropriateness to the characters, then write a short report explaining and illustrating your findings.

Interruptions, Interruptions[17]

"This seat taken?" Mr. Stacey asked hurriedly, glancing back at the crowd struggling down the aisle.

The man with the book glanced up briefly. "No."

Mr. Stacey stretched his stubby figure, shoved his bag into the overhead rack, and sank into the vacant seat. "Boy, was I lucky!" he observed.

"Yes," responded the other, abstractedly.

Mr. Stacey permitted himself a slight chortle. "Yes, sir, guess I was the early bird, all right, all right. Like to read?"

"Yes," said the other.

"Me, too," Mr. Stacey said, gratified at their kindred tastes. "Only I

[17] By Edgar Brooke, in *Collier's,* February, 1948. Reprinted by permission of *Collier's* and Ann Watkins, Inc.

don't get much time for it. Always interruptions, interruptions. That way with you?"

The other glanced up while turning a page. "Yes," he said and turned back to his book.

"Yes, sir," Mr. Stacey continued musingly, "don't guess I've read a whole book for several years. Just can't get the time." He reached into his pocket. "Have a smoke?"

"No."

"Mind if I do?" Mr. Stacey asked considerately.

"No," said the other, his eyes going back to the beginning of a paragraph.

"Remember once," Mr. Stacey said, "feller gave me a Mexican cigarette. Boy, was that something! I don't see how anybody can smoke 'em. Just cigar scrapings and chocolate; what a taste! Yes, sir, give me an American cigarette every time. Sure you won't have one?"

"Yes."

"That's America for you," Mr. Stacey declared, holding up his cigarette. "Best cigarette, best everything. Greatest country in the world. We've got our problems, all right, but we'll lick 'em. Won the war, now we'll win the peace. Yes, sir, I'm a one-hundred-per-cent believer in America."

The man lowered his book and considered for a moment. "Which America?" he asked.

"Beg pardon?" Mr. Stacey said.

"I asked," the other repeated, "which America?"

"I don't get you," Mr. Stacey said. "You mean North America? The United States?"

"Weren't you referring to the United States?"

"Yes — that's right," Mr. Stacey said with relief.

"Well, which United States?"

Mr. Stacey's mystification was complete. For a wild moment he glanced around to assure himself that he was in his right mind, on the right train.

"Look," he said uncertainly, "we aren't connecting. I don't know what you're talking about."

"Why," said the other quietly, "I'm simply asking you to which United States you were referring."

The pale, soft hands of confusion fumbled over Mr. Stacey's brain. His eyes took on a hunted look.

"Listen," he exclaimed, "there isn't but *one* United States. It's all around us. We're in it right now."

"Ah," said the other, "but are there not many United States — or, if you prefer, many Americas?"

"Look," Mr. Stacey said, "imagine we are in a plane flying over the Mississippi, halfway between Chicago and Miami. High, you see, so high that we can see from Canada to Mexico, from Maine to California. That's America. That's the United States. That's what I'm talking about."

"Very clear," said the other, and Mr. Stacey sighed. "But, there is a difficulty. By the time our plane reached the ground again, the America which we viewed from the air would be a different America."

"How's that?" Mr. Stacey was startled.

"By the same reasoning," the other continued evenly, "America is not the same as it was when this train departed from New York. The change, in all likelihood, has been slight, but still, unquestionably, change has occurred. So, that America of the recent past and the one of this precise instant are not the same."

"What's happened to it?" Mr. Stacey asked dully. He involuntarily glanced out of the window at the landscape passing at blurring speed.

"Happened to it?" said the man. "If all the human beings in the world were to undertake together the problem of measuring all the minute changes — psychological, physical, human, social, cultural, economic — which have occurred in America since we left New York, they would fail ignominiously."

"That so?" said Mr. Stacey.

"Again," the man proceeded remorselessly, "America may be viewed as the embodiment of a political concept, framed by the Declaration of Independence and the Constitution, and evolving through the years under such influences as the activities of political parties, Supreme Court decisions, governmental changes effected by vested interests operating through lobbies, and so forth, with the result that 'America' as a political concept is seen to be an ever-changing one. Then, there is the historical America, by which we mean the land and the people, and the story of all that has happened here since our forefathers landed on these shores — the opening of the West, the Civil War, the growth of cities, and so on. There is yet another America — the member-state of an anarchic world community, in which we see our country playing a role analogous to that of one of the original thirteen colonies before the Union was formed, attempting to act as if complete independence of all other countries were possible in a world community which has already inextricably bound our interests, responsibilities and destinies together. There are, of course, still other Americas, as you are doubtless fully aware. So," and he turned full upon Mr. Stacey, "I ask: Which America?"

"What America?" Mr. Stacey replied blankly.

"Precisely," said the other, "which America — or, if you prefer, *what* America do you have in mind?"

"If you don't mind," said Mr. Stacey feebly, "let's skip it."

"Skip it?" said the man. "Very well, but which?"

"Which what?" Mr. Stacey mumbled thickly.

"America," the other replied, lifting his eyebrows in surprise.

A dizziness passed over Mr. Stacey. He wiped his face with his hand. He began to climb lumberingly to his feet. "Very interesting, but if you don't mind," he said heavily, "think I'll go and have a beer. You understand. Some other time, maybe."

"Not at all," said the other. "Perhaps we can take it up again."

In the diner, the steward ushered Mr. Stacey to a chair beside a sharp-faced woman eating a salad. He ordered a beer and methodically reviewed the puzzling conversation. It began to make sense now. This fellow had simply given him the brush-off. Mr. Stacey was nettled. But — it must be admitted that the guy did a fancy job. In fact, a superduper job. Not only that, the guy was a really deep thinker. Possibly a college professor. Well, he was not the one to harbor a grudge. Mr. Stacey smiled wryly. Yes, sir, that was one for the books. He took a long satisfying draw on his beer. As he lowered the glass, he glanced at the woman beside him and found her looking with distaste and disapproval at the beer bottle.

159

"Hope you don't mind my having this beer," Mr. Stacey said politely. "Like with smoking, I like to consider the other fellow."

"Well," the woman said with a cold semblance of a smile. "I shan't pretend that I approve of drinking in any form. But you are within your legal rights, of course." She paused and added primly, "Not that I approve of those either. I sometimes wonder where America is headed."

With great deliberation, Mr. Stacey poured the rest of the beer into his glass, lighted a cigarette, turned slightly toward her and said, "Which America?"

B. Write as many specific words as you think of for each of the following italicized general words. You may interpret the general word in any way you please or in more than one way. For example, for "call" you might specify the calls of different animals — "bark," "bellow," "bleat," etc. — or human calls — "cry," "roar," "yell," etc. What is important is not how you interpret the general term but how many specific terms you can draw from it. To get you started, three specific words are suggested in each example.

1. *Clever:* artful, bright, cunning . . .
2. *collection:* armada, band, bevy . . .
3. *concise:* brief, compact, terse . . .
4. *dog:* cur, hound, mongrel . . .
5. *dress:* costume, gown, robe . . .
6. *eat:* devour, gorge, nibble . . .
7. *falsehood:* deception, fraud, sham . . .
8. *happy:* gay, glad, jovial . . .
9. *inflexible:* firm, stubborn, unyielding . . .
10. *noise:* clang, din, hubbub . . .
11. *quick:* agile, brisk, nimble . . .
12. *refuge:* asylum, haven, retreat . . .
13. *road:* boulevard, path, street . . .
14. *shameless:* barefaced, brazen, wanton . . .
15. *slight:* flimsy, slender, trivial . . .
16. *small:* petite, short, tiny . . .
17. *stupid:* dull, obtuse, moronic . . .
18. *talkative:* chatty, garrulous, loquacious . . .
19. *walk:* limp, march, saunter . . .
20. *wet:* drenched, moist, saturated . . .

C. Some of the following figures of speech are effective; some are not. Study them; then write a brief report in which you identify each figure and explain why you judge it effective or ineffective.

1. Once the "phony war" was over and the German invasion of the Lowlands had begun, Hitler had committed himself irrevocably. In a very real sense he had crossed his Rubicon.

2. Physically they were as alike as two peas in a pod, but intellectually they were as different as day and night.

3. The facts were presented in all their stark nakedness and their implications hit us like a bolt from the blue.

4. She was as cute as a bug's ear and he looked like something the cat had dragged in. They made a strange pair: a lily of the valley and a disheveled dockweed.

5. The hydrogen bomb may yet prove to be another Frankenstein.

6. He had hoped to live until his granddaughter graduated from college, but the Grim Reaper mowed him down.

7. You shall not press down upon the brow of labor this crown of thorns. You shall not crucify mankind upon a cross of gold.

8. Even as a young man, this colossus of industry, this Napoleon of finance, was recognized as a budding business genius.

9. Such appears to me, king, this present life of man on earth in comparison with the time which is unknown to us, as though you were sitting at the banquet with your leaders and thanes in winter and the fire was lighted and the hall warmed, and it rained and snowed and stormed outside; and there would come a sparrow and quickly fly through the house, come in through one door and go out through the other. Now in the time that he is inside he is not touched by the storm of winter; but that is only the twinkling of an eye and the least interval, and at once he comes from winter back to winter again. So this life of man appears save for but a little while; what goes before or what follows after we do not know.

10. But at my back I always hear
   Time's winged chariot hurrying near.

D. As an exercise in illustrating triteness, write a short speech to be read to the class. Try to work into it every trite expression that will fit the context.

E. As a review of all that we have been concerned with in this chapter, study the following selections and, for each, write a report on the diction.

(1)

Facing a big-league pitcher with a bat on your shoulder and trying to hit his delivery is another vital experience in gaining an understanding of the game about which you are trying to write vividly. It is one thing to sit in the stands and scream at a batsman, "Oh, you bum!" for striking out in a pitch, and another to stand twenty yards from that big pitcher and try to make up your mind in a hundredth of a second whether to hit at the offering or not, where to swing and when, not to mention worrying about protecting yourself from the consequences of being struck by the ball that seems to be heading straight for your skull at an appalling rate of speed. Because, if you are a big-league player, you cannot very well afford to be gun-shy and duck away in panic from a ball that swerves in the last moment and breaks perfectly over the plate, while the umpire calls: "Strike!" and the fans jeer. Nor can you afford to take a crack on the temple from the ball. Men have died from that. It calls for undreamed-of niceties of nerve and judgment, but you don't find that out until you have stepped to the plate cold a few times during batting practice or in training quarters, with nothing at stake but the acquisition of experience, and have seen what a fine case of the jumping jitters you get. Later on, when you are writing your story, your imagination, backed by the experience, will be able to supply a picture of what the batter is going through as he stands at the plate in the closing innings of an important game, with two or three men on base, two out, and his team behind in the scoring, and fifty thousand people screaming at him.[18]

(2)

And the watch by night. "Half past twelve o'clock and a fine, clear morning." "One o'clock and a severe snowstorm." Boston was not so much quieter then than now, but its noises were different. From hundreds of shipyards and shops, from sunup to sundown, came the tapping of hammers, the creak of wooden machinery. The hooves of horses on cobbles and the rattle of carts may have been louder than the meshing of gears and swishing of tires. But one still heard the crying of gulls and the beat of the sea upon headlands, or the croak of frogs along Frog Lane (now Boylston Street). At night the stars were close and wonderful as they still seem to us on dark, country roads. Paul Revere would be well up in his thirties before he served on the first committee to consider street lamps for Boston.[19]

(3)

Frontier towns burned like tinder. The board streets and sidewalks, the open frame buildings, the lack of water pressure and of fire-fighting apparatus made them terribly vulnerable. Nearly every American city has had a great fire in its brief history. Often the lumber towns had a series of them. The very ground they rested on, built up of sawdust, slabs and refuse from the mills, was inflammable. The drying yards, with lumber stacked and open to the air, could quickly roar into acres of flame. There were always sparks from the big consumers and the straining boilers of the steam engines to start the disaster. Sawdust towns lived violently, with the rumble of logging, the snarl and scream of the buzz saw, and the tumult of the loading wharfs. And mostly they died violently. A sawmill town could not expect a peaceful end.[20]

(4)

Suppose it were perfectly certain that the life and fortune of every one of us would, one day or another, depend upon his winning or losing a game at chess. Don't you think that we should all consider it to be a primary duty to learn at least the names and the moves of the pieces; to have a notion of a gambit, and a keen eye for all the means of giving and getting out of check? Do you not think that we should look with a disapprobation amounting to scorn, upon the father who allowed his son, or the state which allowed its members, to grow up without knowing a pawn from a knight? Yet it is a very plain and elementary truth that the life, the fortune, and

[18] From *Farewell to Sport* by Paul Gallico. Copyright 1937, 1938 by Paul Gallico. Reprinted by permission of the author and Alfred A. Knopf, Inc., publishers.
[19] From *Paul Revere and the World He Lived In* by Esther Forbes. Reprinted by permission of the publishers, Houghton Mifflin Company.
[20] From *The Long Ships Passing* by Walter Havighurst. Reprinted by permission of The Macmillan Company, publishers.

the happiness of every one of us, and, more or less, of those who are con-nected with us, do depend upon our knowing something of the rules of a game infinitely more difficult and complicated than chess. It is a game which has been played for untold ages, every man and woman of us being one of the two players in a game of his or her own. The chessboard is the world, the pieces are the phenomena of the universe, the rules of the game are what we call the laws of nature. The player on the other side is hidden from us. We know that his play is always fair, just, and patient. But also we know, to our cost, that he never overlooks a mistake, or makes the smallest allow-ance for ignorance. To the man who plays well, the highest stakes are paid, with that sort of overflowing generosity with which the strong shows delight in strength. And one who plays ill is checkmated — without haste, but with-out remorse.[21]

(5)

From those high storied shelves of dense rich bindings the great voices of eternity, the tongues of mighty poets dead and gone, now seemed to speak to him out of the living and animate silence of the room. But in that living silence, in the vast and quiet spirit of sleep which filled the great house, amid the grand and overwhelming stillness of that proud power of wealth and the impregnable security of its position, even the voices of those mighty poets dead and gone now seemed somehow lonely, small, lost and pitiful. Each in his little niche of shelf securely stored — all of the genius, richness, and whole compacted treasure of a poet's life within a foot of space, within the limits of six small dense richly-garnished volumes — all of the great poets of the earth were there, unread, unopened, and forgotten, and were somehow, terribly, the mute small symbols of a rich man's power, of the power of wealth to own everything, to take everything, to triumph over everything — even over the power and genius of the mightiest poet — to keep him there upon his little foot of shelf, unopened and forgotten, but possessed.[22]

(6)

What always gets me about these scholarly excursions into the language of the underworld, so to speak, is how they smell of the dictionary. The so-called experts in this line have their ear to the library, very seldom to the ground. They do not realize what a large proportion of these cant terms (using cant a bit too broadly) is of literary origin, how many of them crooks and cops use *after* writers have invented them. It is very difficult for the literary man to distinguish between a genuine crook term and an invented one. How do you tell a man to go away in hard language? Scram, beat it, take off, take the air, on your way, dangle, hit the road, and so forth. All good enough. But give me the classic expression actually used by Spike O'Donnell (of the O'Donnell brothers of Chicago, the only small outfit to tell the Capone mob to go to hell and live). What he said was: "Be miss-ing." The restraint of it is deadly.

Throughout his play *The Iceman Cometh,* O'Neill used "the big sleep" as

[21] From "A Liberal Education and Where to Find It" by T. H. Huxley.
[22] From *Of Time and the River,* by Thomas Wolfe. Reprinted by permission of Charles Scribner's Sons, publishers.

a synonym for death. He used it, so far as one can judge from the context, as a matter of course, apparently in the belief that it was an accepted underworld expression. If so, I'd like to see whence it comes, because I invented the expression. It is quite possible that I reinvented it, but I never saw it in print before I used it, and until I get the evidence I shall continue to believe that O'Neill took it from me, directly or indirectly, and thought I was using a standard term.

Those who investigate cant, underworld or sports jargon etc. at the source are always surprised by how little of the picturesque lingo is used by the very people who are supposed to use nothing else . . . Some invented slang, not all, becomes current among the people it is invented for. If you are sensitive to this sort of thing, I believe you could often, not always, distinguish between the colored-up lingo that writers produce, and the hard simplicity of the terms that originate in the circle where they are actually used. I don't think any writer could think up an expression like "mainliner" for a narcotic addict who shoots the stuff into a vein. It's too exact, too *pure*.[23]

[23] From *Raymond Chandler Speaking,* edited by Dorothy Gardiner and Kathrine Sorley Walker (Boston: Houghton Mifflin Company, 1962), pp. 88–89. Copyright © 1962 by the Helga Greene Literary Agency. Reprinted by permission.

Using a Dictionary

Improving Vocabulary

Synopses and Summaries

The Essay-Type Examination

SPECIAL

ASSIGNMENTS

Using the Library

The Research Paper

Argument and Persuasion

The Critical Review

The Business Letter

7

Using a Dictionary

To make the best use of your dictionary, you should understand both its scope and its limitations. A good dictionary is much more than a guide to spelling, pronunciation, and meanings. It is also less than the absolute and infallible authority some people think it is. To understand the real value of a dictionary you must know what it is intended to do and how it does that.

What Dictionaries Are, and Are Not

Kinds of Dictionaries. Dictionaries are of two main kinds, general and specialized. A general dictionary, which is the type usually thought of as "the dictionary," records information about words in general use among educated speakers and writers. It does not limit its vocabulary to any special field, but neither does it include highly technical, scientific, or professional terms. Specialized dictionaries are confined to restricted fields or purposes — law, medicine, philosophy, pronunciation, dialects, slang, and so on. Some of the commonest specialized dictionaries are cited in Chapter 11 on "Using the Library."

General dictionaries come in unabridged, desk, and pocket sizes. Unabridged dictionaries, because of their completeness, are the best sources of information about words in the general vocabulary. But because they are too big and expensive for most students, they are primarily library reference works. You should, however, become acquainted with them as supplements to your personal dictionary. The best known (in alphabetical order) are:

A Dictionary of American English, 4 vols., University of Chicago Press, Chicago.

New Standard Dictionary of the English Language, Funk and Wagnalls, New York.

The Oxford English Dictionary, 12 vols. and supplement, Clarendon Press, Oxford. (A corrected reissue, in 1933, of *A New English Dictionary on Historical Principles,* 10 vols. and supplement, 1888–1928, Clarendon Press, Oxford.)

Webster's New International Dictionary of the English Language, Second Edition, G. & C. Merriam Co., Springfield, Mass.

Webster's Third New International Dictionary of the English Language, G. & C. Merriam Co., Springfield, Mass.[1]

Pocket dictionaries are useful because they can be carried in one's pocket and be used as an ever-present reference to the spelling, pronunciation, and meanings of words. But the information they contain is so limited that they are not satisfactory as the only dictionary a student owns.

For the college student, the best all-purpose dictionary is a desk dictionary. Although the best of these contain less than a quarter of the entries in an unabridged dictionary, they are so well edited that they provide nearly all the information one is likely to need about words. Consequently, when instructors require a "college-level" dictionary, they mean a desk dictionary.

The best-known desk dictionaries (in alphabetical order) are:

The American College Dictionary, Random House, New York.

College Standard Dictionary, Funk and Wagnalls, New York.

The Concise Oxford Dictionary (one volume) and *The Shorter Oxford English Dictionary* (two volumes), Clarendon Press, Oxford.

The Thorndike-Barnhart Comprehensive Desk Dictionary, Doubleday & Co., New York.

Webster's New Collegiate Dictionary, G. & C. Merriam Co., Springfield, Mass.

Webster's New World Dictionary, The World Publishing Company, Cleveland.

Winston's Simplified Dictionary, John C. Winston Company, Chicago.

(Three of these dictionaries are so popular that we will often refer to them in this chapter by their initials: *ACD* for *The American College Dictionary, NCD* for *Webster's New Collegiate Dictionary,* and *NWD* for *Webster's New World Dictionary.*)

The Date of a Dictionary. The date of a dictionary is more important than many of its users realize. Since English is a living language, continuously adding new words, dropping others, and suffering changes in meanings and pronunciations, an old dictionary may be as outmoded a description of current usage as a ten-year-old photograph is of your appearance today. It is false economy, therefore, to try to save a few dollars by using an old dictionary that somebody else no longer wants or uses.

Moreover, there may be little relationship between the date on the title page and the date at which the work on the dictionary was done. Not all "new editions" are new throughout. They may be merely reissues of older dictionaries or reprints with minor revisions. Usually your instructor will recommend one or a number of satisfactory dictionaries. If you are given a completely free choice, a good policy is to select the latest edition of one of the popular desk dictionaries already identified.

[1] Both the second and third editions of the *New International* are cited here because, at present, both are in general use.

The Authority of the Dictionary. A dictionary is a record of established, educated usage. It shows, among other things, the spellings, pronunciations, and meanings which educated people have given to words. It is an indispensable guide for words with which we have had little personal experience. It is a most reliable guide to the usage of the past. When it is used to settle controversies about today's usage, it has two limitations: it is necessarily incomplete; and it is necessarily somewhat behind the pace of an ever-changing language.

The incompleteness of a dictionary is intentional. Even the most extensive unabridged dictionary is deliberately restricted. Not only does it make no attempt to cover all special fields, but its definitions cannot indicate all the finely shaded meanings which a word may be given in different contexts. For reasons of space, a dictionary must restrict itself to those meanings which most frequently occur.

The Contents of Desk Dictionaries

The quickest way to become acquainted with the contents of your dictionary is to study its table of contents. When you do, you may be surprised to learn that the book contains useful information about a variety of subjects: biographical data about famous persons, the population of cities, the location and size of American colleges and universities, the forms used in addressing public officials, proofreader's marks, standard signs and symbols, tables of weights and measures, and many other kinds of information.

In general, the contents fall into three parts: the front matter, the dictionary proper, and the supplements or appendixes. The front matter contains much important introductory and explanatory material. You should at least skim over this material, paying special attention to the "Guide to Pronunciation" and to any parts that may help you to use the dictionary efficiently. The supplementary material can usually be identified from the table of contents, but the *ACD* and the *NWD* record information about people and places in alphabetical order within the dictionary proper, not in an appendix.

✔ Check the table of contents of your dictionary and answer the following questions:

1. What sections of the front matter may help you to use your dictionary more effectively?
2. What is the standard of pronunciation and what is the editors' attitude toward less formal pronunciations?
3. In what order are the definitions arranged?
4. How does your dictionary indicate that a particular entry is still considered a foreign word?

5. What kinds of information are provided in the supplements or appendixes?

6. If biographical and geographical data are not contained in an appendix, are they provided within the dictionary proper? If in doubt, look up *Hangchow, Indonesia,* and *Mussolini.*

Our main concern, however, is with the dictionary proper — 1000 to 1700 pages of information about words. The kinds of information it provides can best be seen by studying a representative entry:[2]

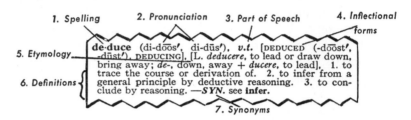

1. Spelling. The centered period between the syllables shows how the word may be divided, if necessary. If the word is usually capitalized (*Negro*) or hyphenated (*self-centered*) or if two words are written with a space between them (*cross section*) or solid (*setback*), the vocabulary entry provides that information. If more than one spelling is acceptable (*sextet, sextette*), the variant spelling is indicated, usually in the same entry but sometimes separately. When two spellings are listed, the first is said to be "preferred." But different dictionaries sometimes prefer different spellings, and the preference means only that in the samples studied by the editors one spelling occurred more frequently than the other. Do not conclude that the spelling which is not preferred is in any way less acceptable. If one is the American spelling and the other the British, that fact is usually noted.

2. Pronunciation. The pronunciation given in a general dictionary is the sound the word is given when pronounced by itself, as in a spelling test, or in careful platform delivery. In their introductory explanations most reliable dictionary editors point out that less formal pronunciations are accepted in the conversation of educated people. A general dictionary, therefore, is useful for pronunciation when a reader wishes to know the pronunciation of a word with which he is not familiar. A strongly stressed syllable is marked with a heavy accent mark ('), a weaker stress with a lighter accent ('). Because the symbols used to represent pronunciation are likely to seem a bit strange at first, you should, until you are familiar with them, check their values in the "Guide to Pronunciation." Both the *ACD* and the *NWD* make this task easier by providing a brief key at the

[2] Copyright © 1957, 1958, 1959, 1960 by The World Publishing Company.

bottom of each right-hand page. The *NCD* has a simplified pronunciation key on the inside covers.

3. Part of Speech. Since a word may be used in several parts of speech, the labeling of each entry as a noun (*n*), transitive verb (*v.t.*), intransitive verb (*v.i.*), and so on, is helpful in avoiding confusion among different grammatical functions of a word.

4. Inflectional Forms. Only those inflectional forms that are considered "irregular" are cited in a dictionary. Thus the *-s* plural form of a noun is not usually given, nor are the past tense and present participle forms ending in *-ed* and *-ing*. Irregular inflectional forms are listed after the part of speech. Thus in *deduce,* the past tense is formed by adding only *-d,* not *-ed,* and the final *-e* is dropped before the *-ing* of the present participle.

5. Etymology. Etymologies — the sources of words — are recorded in square brackets, either (as in the *NCD* and the *NWD*) immediately after the part of speech, or (as in the *ACD*) after the definitions. Thus *deduce* was borrowed directly from the Latin combination *de + ducere.* When a word is borrowed from one language through the agency of another, as when a Latin word comes through French, that fact is shown. For example, the *NCD* lists the etymology of *pardon* as follows:

OF. *pardoner,* fr. LL. *perdonare,* fr. L. *per* through, thoroughly + *donare* to give.

This means that our word *pardon* was borrowed from the Old French *pardoner,* which, in turn, came from the Low (or Late) Latin *perdonare,* which originally came from the Latin combination *per donare.* The abbreviations for the various languages will be less troublesome than they seem here, partly because they can quickly be identified in the "List of Abbreviations" given in the front matter, and partly because the more common abbreviations occur so frequently that you will soon become familiar with them. The most common are L. (Latin), Gr. (Greek), F. (French), G. (German), N. (Norse), O. (Old, as in Old English — OE., Old French — OF., Old Norse — ON.), LL. (Late or Low Latin), and ME. (Middle English). When no etymology is given, the word is usually derived from an earlier entry, where the etymology has already been given. Thus the etymology of *cockerel* is the same as that of *cock,* and the etymology of *deathbed* has already been explained under *bed* and *death.*

6. Definitions. Since different dictionaries record their definitions in different orders, it is important that you learn from the front matter what order your dictionary uses. The *ACD* lists definitions in order of frequency, with the most-used meaning first. The *NCD* uses a historical order, with the oldest meaning first. Except for definitions accompanied by a usage label (see next paragraph), the *NWD* also uses a historical order.

The order of meanings should never be taken to imply that some meanings are preferred to others. All recorded meanings should be interpreted as conventional uses of a word unless the definition is accompanied by a usage label which limits that meaning to a particular area, group, or situation. Thus the label *U.S.* or *Brit.* shows that a usage is American or British, not common to both. *Colloq.* (or *Colloquial*) shows that a definition is acceptable only in conversation or informal writing. Labels such as *Chem., Law, Mil.* (chemistry, law, or military affairs) indicate technical usage. If any label is not self-explanatory, its meaning may be checked in the "List of Abbreviations."

7. *Synonyms and Antonyms.* A synonym is a word having the same general meaning as the vocabulary entry. An antonym is a word having the opposite meaning. In a desk dictionary, only some entries show synonyms and antonyms. For fuller treatment, consult a specialized dictionary such as *Webster's Dictionary of Synonyms.*

8. *Foreign Words.* Different dictionaries use different means to indicate that a word or phrase (*Gestalt, bon voyage*) is still classified as a foreign expression in English. Since it is conventional in print to italicize (and in writing to underline) such words, this information is sometimes useful. The *ACD* gives the nationality of words in italics immediately after the part of speech. The *NCD* and the *NWD* place a special symbol before the vocabulary entry — ‖ in the *NCD* and ‡ in the *NWD*.

It will be useful to spell out the information given in a simple entry from each of the leading desk dictionaries.

From the *ACD*:[3]

lyre (līr), *n.* **1.** a musical instrument of ancient Greece, consisting of a sound box (usually a turtle shell), with two curving arms carrying a cross bar (yoke) from which strings are stretched to the body, used to accompany the voice in singing and recitation. **2.** (*cap.*) *Astron.* Lyra. [ME *lire*, t. OF, t. L: m. *lyra*, t. Gk.]

Woman playing an ancient Greek lyre

The noun *lyre,* pronounced to rhyme with *fire,* as the key at the bottom of the next dictionary page shows, is used in two ways: when spelled with a small letter it is the name of an ancient Greek musical instrument; when spelled with a capital, it is used in astronomy as a variant spelling of the

[3] Reprinted by courtesy of the publishers from *The American College Dictionary,* Copyright 1947–1956, © 1957–1962 by Random House, Inc.

constellation Lyra. The word came into Middle English with the spelling *lire* from an Old French form which had been taken from a modification of the Latin *lyra,* which the Romans had originally borrowed from the Greek. Thus the word came from the Greek through Latin and Old French into English.

From the *NCD:*[4]

fi·du′cial (fĭ·dū′shăl), *adj.* [L. *fiducia* trust, confidence.] **1.** Founded on faith or trust, esp. religious beliefs. **2.** Having the nature of a trust; fiduciary. **3.** *Physics, etc.* Taken as a standard of reference; as, a *fiducial* line, point, etc. — **fi·du′cial·ly,** *adv.*

The adjective *fiducial* is a three-syllable word with the accent on the second syllable. As we learn from the pronunciation key on the inside cover (also from the more comprehensive "Guide to Pronunciation" in the front matter), the first *i* is pronounced like the *i* of *ill* or *habit; u* is long as in *cube;* and the last syllable rhymes with the second syllable of *martial.* The word came into English directly from the Latin *fiducia,* meaning *trust* or *confidence.* Of the two general meanings shown in definitions 1 and 2, definition 1 was the earlier. Definition 3, as the usage label shows, is confined to the sciences. The adverbial form, except for the *-ly* ending, has the same spelling and pronunciation.

From the *NWD:*[5]

‡**ka·mi·ka·ze** (kä′mi-kä′zi), *n.* [Japan., lit., divine wind < *kami*, (Shinto) god or goddess + *kaze*, the wind], **1.** a suicide attack by a Japanese airplane pilot in World War II. **2.** the airplane or pilot in such an attack.

The noun *kamikaze* is a four-syllable word with the main stress on the third syllable and a secondary stress on the first. The key to pronunciation at the bottom of the dictionary page shows that the first and third vowels are pronounced like the *a* in *car* and the second and fourth vowels like the *i* in *is.* The symbol before the entry shows that the word is considered foreign, and the etymology tells us it is Japanese. In Japan its literal meaning (divine wind) is a compound of the word for divinity in the Shinto religion and the Japanese word for wind. It was first used in English to denote the kind of attack explained in definition 1 and was later extended to include the agent of the attack, the plane or the pilot.

✔ For each of the following words write out all the information provided by the entry in your dictionary:

autocrat	divan	harridan
bawl	esprit de corps	illiterate
cherub	fluster	non sequitur

[4] By permission. From *Webster's New Collegiate Dictionary,* copyright 1949, 1951, 1953, © 1956, 1958, 1959, 1960, 1961 by G. & C. Merriam Co.
[5] Copyright © 1957, 1958, 1959, 1960 by The World Publishing Company.

Dictionary of Synonyms

A dictionary of synonyms groups together words essentially similar in meaning and distinguishes the particular differences in their uses. Thus *Webster's Dictionary of Synonyms* lists after the first meaning of *nice* the synonyms: *dainty, fastidious, finical, particular, fussy, squeamish, per-nickety,* and then goes on to distinguish among the connotations of these words. Then comes a series of analogous words ("near synonyms"), then a series of contrasted words ("near antonyms"), and finally a series of antonyms, words with meanings the very opposite of *nice.*

A dictionary of synonyms is the best reference source when you wish an answer to either of two questions: How do two or more words of the same general meaning differ in denotation or connotation in actual use? What other words might be substituted for a particular word? The following entry illustrates:[6]

dwarf, *n.* **1** Dwarf, pygmy, midget, manikin (*or* manni-kin), homunculus (*or* homuncle, homuncule), runt come into comparison when they mean a person of diminutive size. **Dwarf** is the general term not only for a human be-ing but for any animal or plant that is far below the normal size of the species: often, but not necessarily, the term suggests stunted development. "His [the fool's] value was trebled by the fact of his being also a *dwarf* and a cripple" (*Poe*). **Pygmy,** in earliest use, was applied to one of a race (or races) of fabled dwarfs mentioned by Homer and others, and now is applied especially to one of a dwarf people found in central Africa. The term carries a stronger connotation of diminutiveness and a weaker suggestion of arrested development than *dwarf;* when used generally in refer-ence to a person, it often implies tininess (often relative tininess), sometimes in body but more often in intellect. "To him all the men I ever knew were *pygmies.* He was an intellectual giant" (*Byron*). **Midget** stresses abnormal diminutiveness but, unlike *dwarf,* carries little suggestion of malformation or deformity, the term is applied usually to a tiny but otherwise shapely person exhibited in a circus or employed in place of a child in theatrical per-formances; as, P. T. Barnum's famous *midget,* Tom Thumb. **Manikin** is often applied contemptuously not only to a dwarf but to any human being who for one reason or another seems despicably small or weak. "Can it be fancied that Diety ever vindictively Made in his image a *mannikin* merely to madden it?" (*Poe*). **Homun-culus** usually suggests even greater diminutiveness and often greater perfection in form than *midget:* it is the specific term for an exceedingly small artificial human being such as was supposedly developed by Paracelsus, a famous Renaissance alchemist; it is also applied, as a technical term, to the human fetus. **Runt,** usually a contemptuous designation, applies to a dwarf or under-sized person, especially to one who is conspicuously puny or undeveloped or, occasionally, to one who is thick as well as short. "I always did admire a good, sizable, stout man. I hate a *runt*" (*McClure's Mag.*). The term is also applied to an animal, especially a domestic animal, small of its kind; and, dialectically in the United States, it is applied specifically to the undersized one of a litter, as of pigs.

[6] By permission. From *Webster's Dictionary of Synonyms,* copyright 1942, 1951 by G. & C. Merriam Co.

Thesaurus

A *thesaurus* is a special kind of word book which records under a single entry all words expressing the general notion of that entry. The most popular of such works is *Roget's* (pronounced Rozhay's) *Thesaurus,* published in a number of editions. The simplest way to use this work is to look up the general word in the index, note the section number under which it is entered, and consult that section in the main part of the book. Thus if you want to find words referring to the ideas of *obedience* and *disobedience,* you look in the index for the section numbers (764–765 in this case), turn to these sections, and this is what you find:[7]

764. OBEDIENCE

NOUNS 1. obedience or obediency, compliance, acquiescence; submission 763; dutifulness, duteousness; observance, attentiveness; law-abidingness.

VERBS 2. obey, mind, heed, keep, observe, regard, listen to; comply, yield obedience; do what one is told, do as one says, do the will of, do one's bidding, come at one's call, lie down and roll over [slang]; take orders, attend to orders, do suit and service, follow the lead of; answer the helm; submit 763.6.

ADJS. 3. obedient, compliant, complying, acquiescent; submissive 763.12; dutiful, duteous; loyal, faithful, devoted; lawabiding.

4. at one's command, at one's pleasure, at one's disposal, at one's nod, at one's call, at one's beck and call.

5. henpecked, tied to one's apron strings, on a string, on a leash, in leading strings.

ADVS. 6. obediently, compliantly, acquiescently; submissively 763.17; dutifully, duteously; loyally, faithfully, devotedly; in obedience to, in compliance with.

7. obediently yours, at your service, ∼ command or orders, as you please.

765. DISOBEDIENCE

NOUNS 1. disobedience, nonobedience; undutifulness, unduteousness; insubordination, unsubmissiveness, indocility, noncompliance, unresignedness; lawlessness, waywardness, frowardness; intractability 624.4.

2. refractoriness, recalcitrance, contumacy, contumaciousness, obstreperousness, unruliness, restiveness, fractiousness, orneriness [coll. or dial.]; breachiness.

3. rebelliousness, mutinousness, riotousness; insurrectionism, insurgentism; seditiousness.

4. revolt, rebellion; mutiny, mutineering; insurrection, insurgence, riot, *Putsch* [Ger.], *emeute* [F.]; uprising, rising, outbreak; general uprising, *levée en masse* [F.]; *Jacquerie* [F., peasant revolt]; sedition; revolution 147; strike 787.7.

5. rebel, revolter; insurgent, insurrectionist; mutineer; rioter, brawler; malcontent, *frondeur* [F.]; agitator 646.11; revolutionist 147.3; insubordinate.

VERBS 6. disobey, not mind, not heed, not keep or observe, not listen to, pay no attention to, ignore, disregard, defy, fly in the face of, go counter to, set at naught.

7. violate, transgress 767.4.

8. revolt, rebel, kick over the traces; rise up, rise, arise, rise up in arms; mutiny, mutineer; insurrect [coll.]; riot, run riot; revolutionize 147.4; strike 787.9.

ADJS. 9. disobedient, transgressive, violative, lawless, wayward, froward; undutiful, unduteous.

10. insubordinate, unsubmissive, indocile, uncompliant, uncomplying, unresigned; intractable 624.12.

11. refractory, recalcitrant, contumacious, obstreperous, unruly, restive, resty [dial.], fractious, ornery [coll. or dial.]; breachy.

12. rebellious, rebel, rebelly [coll.]; mutinous, mutineering; insurgent, insurrectionary, insurrectional, riotous; seditious, seditionary; revolutionary 147.5

ADVS. 13. disobediently, insubordinately, unsubmissively, indocilely, uncompliantly, unresignedly; intractably 624.17; obstreperously, contumaciously, restively, fractiously; rebelliously, mutinously.

---

[7] From *Roget's International Thesaurus,* Third Edition. Copyright © 1962, by Thomas Y. Crowell Company, New York, publishers. Reprinted by permission.

Exercises

A. From what languages are the following words derived and what did they mean originally?

1. alcohol	9. devil	17. nice
2. algebra	10. dollar	18. opera
3. automobile	11. flannel	19. pajamas
4. bantam	12. husband	20. quixotic
5. boor	13. inertia	21. shampoo
6. candy	14. lemon	22. skipper
7. caravan	15. loot	23. slogan
8. chorus	16. mosquito	24. tobacco

B. Which of the following expressions should be italicized? What do they mean and how are they pronounced? Use each of them in a sentence.

1. anno Domini	6. en rapport	11. fiasco
2. belle	7. enfant terrible	12. in absentia
3. belles lettres	8. ensemble	13. matériel
4. debutante	9. faux pas	14. nom de guerre
5. décolleté	10. fiancé	15. nom de plume

C. Pronounce the following words aloud, making a guess at the pronunciation of those not in your spoken vocabulary. Then check against a dictionary and use each word correctly in a spoken sentence.

1. abdomen	13. inquiry	25. robot
2. acclimate	14. joust	26. sagacious
3. alias	15. massage	27. schism
4. banal	16. nascent	28. secretive
5. clandestine	17. niche	29. status
6. data	18. nuance	30. technics
7. ennui	19. obesity	31. vagary
8. fugue	20. penalize	32. vestigial
9. hazard	21. precedence	33. victuals
10. heinous	22. query	34. Wagnerian
11. impious	23. quixotic	35. zealot
12. impotent	24. rancid	36. zenith

D. Choose any five of the following words for which your dictionary gives synonyms and distinguish the differences in meanings among the synonyms by using each correctly in a written sentence.

1. ambition	7. emergency	13. juncture
2. apt	8. examination	14. luster
3. bad	9. excuse	15. melancholy
4. contention	10. fiendish	16. restive
5. deface	11. haste	17. voracious
6. discover	12. ideal	18. wild

E. Choose any half-dozen words you wish, go to the library and check the treatment of these words in each of the following unabridged dictionaries, make notes on what you discover, and write a short paper contrasting the three dictionaries:

Webster's New International Dictionary, Second Edition
Webster's Third New International Dictionary
The Oxford English Dictionary

8

Improving Vocabulary

Most students know how important it is to have an adequate vocabulary. They know that diagnostic vocabulary tests are often used to predict the ability to do well in college studies. They quickly see that college lectures and textbooks will require them to learn many new words. They also know that there is a relationship between vocabulary and success in business or professional life. For these reasons serious students have already answered the question whether increasing vocabulary is desirable. Instead, they are concerned with the question of method — *how* to improve vocabulary. It is with that question that this chapter deals.

Improving Your Recognition Vocabulary

It is useful to distinguish two kinds of vocabulary: *recognition* and *active*. The recognition vocabulary is the total stock of words that a person knows well enough to understand them when he meets them in context. He may not be able to define all these words, and there are many of them that he will never use in his speech or writing, but if he can interpret them correctly when he meets them in context, they are part of his recognition vocabulary. The active vocabulary, on the other hand, is the stock of words that a person actually uses in his own speech or writing. It is, of course, a much smaller stock — perhaps only a third or a quarter the size of the recognition vocabulary.

Not all attempts to increase one's recognition vocabulary are equally profitable. Many ambitious students confuse vocabulary building with the learning of big words rarely met and seldom used, either by the student or by anyone else. Uncritical memorizing of learned words is pretty much a waste of time. So, too, is that old favorite method of learning a new word every day. Even if the daily word is carefully chosen for its usefulness, rather than for its impressiveness, a student following only this method will improve his vocabulary not more than one per cent in a year. Such an improvement is trifling. A college student of average ability should increase his recognition vocabulary by at least ten per cent during his freshman year *by doing nothing more than becoming familiar with the words he encounters in his studies.* If, in addition, he deliberately and consistently attempts to cultivate a useful vocabulary, his improvement will be significantly larger.

The one prerequisite for increasing vocabulary is a desire to learn — not just a desire to learn words, but a desire to know more about any subject that comes one's way. Consider how your knowledge of mechanical terms increased as you progressed from kiddie cars to bicycles to automobiles. You did not discover *rim, spoke, tire, battery, carburetor,* and *piston* in a dictionary. You learned these words because you were interested in bicycles and cars and simply had to have the words to think about and operate your machines. If you have a similar interest in the subjects you study in college, each of them will make its contribution to your vocabulary, even if you do not consciously do anything about vocabulary building. If you do not have that interest or cannot cultivate it, no techniques for vocabulary building will do you much good. A person's vocabulary is a product of his intellectual growth. It cannot be artificially constructed apart from that growth.

For most of us, the great source of new words is the printed page. Therefore anyone who wishes to increase his recognition vocabulary must do a good deal of reading. Your college assignments in all courses will probably require you to read more extensively and more critically than you have done before, but if you wish to make significant increases in your vocabulary you should supplement required reading by a program of voluntary reading. Probably the best way to begin is to develop the habit of reading carefully a daily newspaper and such newsmagazines as *Newsweek* and *Time,* and gradually add some of the excellent inexpensive paper-backed books on social and scientific subjects, as well as fiction or poetry to your taste. This reading should follow your personal interests and needs. It should be regarded as pleasure, not a chore, because what is required is to develop a liking for reading. A student who likes to read will find the things that are most valuable for him, and as his reading experience widens, his taste in books will grow.

Once a student has the desire to learn through reading, he will discover the techniques of increasing his vocabulary — perhaps even without recognizing that they are techniques — in his efforts to understand what he is studying. Let us try to illustrate this point by watching an intellectually curious student at work. Suppose that, as an outside reading assignment in sociology, he is reading the following passage dealing with the Bantu, a primitive tribe living in the forests of the Congo, and that he is meeting for the first time the words in italics.

> What seems to be most relevant [in a study of the relation of the personality and culture of the Bantu] can be stated in more general terms, in terms which also apply to hundreds of small tribes in many parts of the world. . . . We may point out certain aspects of these cultures in a series of words hyphenated with the prefix "pre-," meaning "before," or "not yet." Therefore we can say that they are *preliterate, prescientific, preindustrial,* and *preindividualistic.*
>
> The *Phoenician* alphabet traveled west and north but did not penetrate these isolated regions [the Bantu homeland]. They are preliterate, not

because they cannot learn to read and write but because they have had no opportunity. Now when *scribes* make and preserve books, a profound change comes upon a society and the whole character of their culture undergoes *momentous* alterations. Preliterate peoples have not added that *increment*. And until they do have it, there are certain important ways in which they differ from those who have letters.[1]

Even though there are eight words in the passage that the student has never seen or heard before, there are only three of them that he will have to look up in his dictionary. He can tell directly from the text what *preliterate* means, because the author explains the prefix *pre-*, and the second paragraph makes it clear that a preliterate people is one that has not yet reached the stage of having an alphabet and therefore has had no opportunity of learning to write or read. Thus, although he has never met the word before, the student will understand it quite clearly from the context. And once he understands *preliterate,* he will not only recognize the meaning of *prescientific, preindustrial,* and *preindividualistic,* but, more important, the principle of putting *pre-* before other words to form new compounds. Thus he will be prepared to interpret correctly *preatomic, precancel, predate, prehistoric, prenatal,* and so on when he first encounters them.

Phoenician and *increment,* however, cannot be interpreted from the context. Since the student has no clue to their meaning, he must consult his dictionary. When he does so, he will find that the Phoenicians, an ancient people who lived in what is now Syria, are credited with being the inventors of the alphabet from which all Indo-European alphabets are descended. He will find that *increment* has the same ancestry as *increase* and means an "addition" or "growth" — in this passage an advantage that preliterate peoples have not received. *Momentous alterations* may be recognized as a repetition of the idea expressed in *profound change,* or from the fairly well-known phrase *matters of great moment.* If these associations do not serve as clues, the student will have to consult his dictionary. There he will find that *momentous,* like *momentum,* a word he may have learned in physics, comes from the same root as *moving* and means in this context "very important."

Since the context of the second paragraph shows that a scribe is one who makes and preserves books, the student may get the meaning of that word directly from its context. Or his familiarity with the related word *scribble* may suggest to him that a scribe is one who writes. Or, if he knows a little Latin, he may recognize *scribe* as a derivative of *scribere,* "to write." In other words, he may recognize the meaning in either of two ways: through the context or through the similarity of the unknown word to other words which he does know. If neither of these methods works, he will have to consult his dictionary.

[1] From "Culture and Personality Among the Forest Bantu" by Ellsworth Faris, in *American Journal of Sociology,* May, 1934.

Here, then, are the three principal techniques for recognizing the meanings of new words: recognition by context, discovery by dictionary reference, and recognition by word analysis. In our illustration the student used these techniques successfully without being conscious that he was using them. His main concern was not to improve his vocabulary but simply to understand what the sociologist was telling him. Let us consider these techniques as procedures which can be used intentionally.

Recognition by Context. For a number of reasons, the best way to improve your recognition vocabulary is by watching context. First, it is the method you must use in understanding spoken communications, since you cannot usually stop a speaker to look up his words in a dictionary. Second, it is the method used by lexicographers (makers of dictionaries), and far from being a "lazy" or "guessing" method, it is the only way to become sensitive to educated usage. Third, it is the method you have been using for the last sixteen or seventeen years and by it you have learned nearly all the words now in your recognition vocabulary.

As you acquire skill and confidence in interpreting words from context, you will learn to spot the ways in which a speaker or writer helps to make clear the meanings of unusual words. Sometimes he will actually define the new word, as we did with *lexicographers* above and as the sociologist did with *pre-*. Sometimes he will explain the word by showing it in operation, as when we are told that a scribe makes and preserves books. Sometimes he will repeat the meaning in other words of similar meaning, as when the sociologist coupled *profound change* and *momentous alterations.* Sometimes he will use a practical illustration to make the meaning clear, like our imaginary student reader. By learning to look for such aids you will not only become a better reader and listener, but you will begin to use these explanatory techniques yourself and so become a better speaker and writer.

✔ Each of the following passages contains an italicized word, the meaning of which may be obtained from the context. Can you tell without consulting a dictionary what each of these words must mean?

> The lawyer said that such newspaper stories were *prejudicial* because they encouraged the public to judge the defendant guilty before he had been tried.

> The *pediatrician* examined the baby carefully and recommended a change in formula.

> There was an obvious *disparity* in their ages; he looked old enough to be her father.

> An Englishman who says that he finds American women homely may not be *disparaging* them. He may just mean they make him feel at home.

> We are often uncertain what punishment to inflict for such offenses. If we are too harsh, we may seem to be seeking vengeance rather than justice; if we show too much *clemency,* we may give the impression that we do not consider the offense a serious one.

Discovery by Dictionary Reference. When you look up a word in your dictionary you should try to find out as much as you can about it. You know that when you are introduced to someone your chances of remembering his name or even recognizing him again are influenced by the extent of your first experience with him. If all you learn is his name, you may forget that quickly; but if you talk with him and find out what he does for a living, where he comes from, what his background is, and what his chief interests and hobbies are, you may remember him well months or even years later. The same thing is true of your introduction to new words. The more you find out about them from your dictionary, the better you will remember them; and the better you remember them, the more likely you are to transfer them to your active vocabulary.

The things you most need to know about a new word are its pronunciation, etymology, and meanings. The pronunciation not only helps you to pronounce it conventionally in reading aloud or in speech, but also helps you fix the word in your memory. Since the appearance of a word is often no safe clue to its sound, we have all had the embarrassing experience of making a very obvious mispronunciation when called upon to read an unfamiliar word aloud. Even such fairly common words as *abyss, blatant, caprice, decade, echelon, façade, gauge, impious, impotent,* and *ribald* can be troublesome for a person who has met them only in his reading and has never heard them spoken. The habit of checking pronunciation as you look up a new word greatly reduces the chances of mispronunciation.

The etymology of a word gives you its family history and thus makes your knowledge of it more complete. When you know, for example, that *crucial* comes from the Latin word for *cross,* you can see that in a crucial decision we figuratively stand at a crossroads and decide which way we will go, and you may discover a hitherto unsuspected relationship among *crucial, crucify, crusade,* and *crux.* Similarly, when you learn that *critical* comes from a Greek phrase meaning "able to discern" and was originally used for one who was able to discern the implications of a work or a policy and thus to judge it, you will better understand how the word can be used today in such different senses as: "It is an excellent critical discussion of the problem," "He is a critical user of the dictionary," and "His condition is now critical."

Apart from its usefulness in making you a more discerning or more critical user of words, the study of etymology can be a pleasant hobby. It may not make the study of the *calculus* any easier to know that its name came from the Latin word for a pebble and goes back to the days when the Romans used pebbles to help them with their arithmetic; but it is interesting to be reminded from what primitive origins modern calculating machines have come. It is a testimony to human intolerance that *sinister* originally meant *left-handed* and a *barbarian* was once a *stranger.* And it is amusing to discover that our slang phrase *in the coop* perpetuates the original meaning of *jail*, a cage or coop. It is not surprising that some people find it as much fun to collect etymologies as to collect stamps, and much less expensive.

Recognition by Word Analysis. Looking up an etymology inevitably leads to word analysis, the breaking down of a word into its parts and the recognition of the original meaning of each part. Thus we are analyzing *preliterate* when we recognize that it is a compound of the prefix *pre-* and the root *litera*, "a letter"; and we are analyzing *docile* when we see that it is made up of the root *docere*, "to teach," and the suffix *-ile*, "capable of," so that a docile person is literally one who is capable of being taught.

Because so many Latin and Greek words have been borrowed and assimilated by English, a knowledge of the most common Latin and Greek prefixes and roots (the suffixes are less important for our purposes) helps us to recognize, at least in a general way, the meanings of many words. For example, the ability to recognize *-cede* (*-ceed*) and *-cess* as forms of the Latin *cedere*, "to yield" or "go," gives us a partial clue to the meanings of the English words *cede, cessation, cession, accede, access, accession, accessory, antecedent, ancestor, concede, concession, concessionaire, exceed, excess, incessant, intercede, intercessor, precede, precedence, predecessor, procedure, proceed, process, procession, recede, recess, recessive, secede, succeed, succession*, and their inflectional forms. One writer has estimated that a knowledge of fourteen Latin and Greek roots will help us to recognize over 14,000 words.[2]

Common Latin prefixes and roots, their original meanings, and illustrative English words derived from them are given in the following list:

ab (away from, down): abase, abate, abdicate, abduct, abhor, abject, abnormal, abort

ad (to, toward): adapt, addict, adduce, adequate, adhere, adjacent, admit, adolescent

ante (before): ante-bellum, antecedent, antedate, antemeridian, anterior, anteroom

bellum (war): bellicose, belligerent, rebel, rebellion

bene (well): benediction, benefactor, beneficent, benefit, benevolent, benign

bi (two): biannual, biaxial, biceps, bicuspid, bifocal, bigamist, bilabial

cap, cept (take): capable, captivate, capture, concept, deception, intercept, precept

cide, cis (cut, kill): decide, matricide, suicide, concise, incision

circum (around): circumference, circumlocution, circumnavigate, circumspect

cogni (know): cognition, cognizance, connoisseur, incognito, recognize

com (with): command, commence, commend, commission, compact, compare, compass, compeer

contra (against): contraband, contradict, contrapuntal, contrary, contrast

---

[2] James I. Brown in *Efficient Reading* (D. C. Heath and Company, 1952), p. 117.

cor (heart): cardiac, core, cordial, courage, discord, encourage, record
cult (care for): cult, cultivate, culture, agriculture, horticulture
curr, curs (run): currency, current, curriculum, courier, course, excursion
de (off, down, wholly): debase, decapitate, decay, deceive, decline, deduce
dent (tooth): dental, dentifrice, dentoid, denture, indent, trident
dict (say): dictate, diction, edict, indicate, indict, predict, verdict
duc, duct (lead): conduct, deduce, duct, duke, educate, induct, product
ex (beyond, from, out): examine, exceed, excel, except, excite, extend
extra (outside): extracurricular, extradite, extraneous, extrapolate
fac, fect (make): facile, fact, factory, faculty, manufacture, affect, effect
fin (end): confine, define, final, finale, finish, infinite, refine
in (on, in, toward): inaugurate, incarcerate, incipient, incline, include
in (not): inactive, inane, inarticulate, incest, infamous, insensible
inter (among, between): interaction, intercede, intercept, interfere
ject (throw): abject, dejected, eject, interject, projectile, reject, trajectory
loqui, locut (talk): colloquial, eloquent, loquacious, ventriloquist, elocution
luc (light): elucidate, illustrate, lucid, pellucid, translucent
mal (bad): malady, malcontent, malefactor, malice, malignant, malpractice
mit, miss (send): admit, commit, intermittent, remit, transmit, missile
mor (dead): morbid, moribund, mortal, mortify, mortuary
ped (foot): biped, impediment, pedal, pedestrian, pedicure, pedometer
pel, puls (drive): compel, dispel, expel, propel, repel, impulse, pulse
pon, posit (place): component, exponent, postpone, preposition, transpose
port (carry): deport, export, import, portable, report, support, transport
post (after): postdate, posterity, postgraduate, posthumous, postmortem
pre (before): preamble, precaution, precede, predict, preface, prefer
pro (forward): proceed, procession, produce, profane, profess, proficient
re (again, back): react, rearm, reassure, recall, recede, recreate, return
rupt (break): abrupt, bankrupt, disrupt, erupt, interrupt, rupture
scrib, script (write): circumscribe, inscribe, script, scripture, transcription
spect (look): aspect, inspect, perspective, retrospect, spectator, spectrum
sub (under): subaltern, subconscious, subject, submerge, subside
super (above): superb, supercilious, superfluous, superior, supersede
tain, ten (hold): abstain, contain, detain, retain, tenable, tenacious, tenet
tang, tact (touch): tangent, tangible, contact, tact, tactical, tactual
trans (across, over): transcend, transcribe, transfer, transfuse, transgress
uni (one): unicorn, uniform, unify, unilateral, union, Unitarian, unity
vene, vent (come): convene, intervene, revenue, adventure, invent
vers, vert (turn): verse, version, avert, convert, extrovert, invert, vertical
vid, vis (see): evident, provident, revise, supervise, vision, visor, vista
voc (call): advocate, avocation, convocation, evoke, provoke, vocabulary

Common Greek forms and their derivatives are shown below:

anthropo (man): anthropoid, anthropology, misanthrope, philanthropy
auto (self): autobiography, autocracy, autogamy, automobile, autotoxin
bio (life): biochemistry, biogenesis, biography, biology, biometry, biotic
chrono (time): anachronism, chronic, chronicle, chronological, synchronize

gen (birth, race): eugenics, genealogy, genesis, genetics, homogeneous
gram, graph (write): diagram, epigram, telegram, graphic, phonograph
homo (same): homocentric, homogenize, homograph, homonym
hydr (water): hydrant, hydraulic, hydrogen, hydrophobia, hydroplane
log (science, speech): biology, cosmology, etymology, epilogue, eulogy
micro (small): microbe, microfilm, micrometer, microphone, microscope
mono (one): monocle, monogamy, monograph, monolith, monologue
morph (form): amorphous, anthropomorphic, metamorphosis, morphology
pan (all): panacea, Pan-American, pancreas, pandemonium, panorama
phil (friend): Anglophile, bibliophile, Philadelphia, philharmonic
phon (sound): euphony, gramophone, phoneme, phonetic, symphony
poly (many): polyandry, polychromatic, polygamy, polyglot, polysyllabic
syn (together): synonym, syntax, synthesis, sympathy, symposium
tele (far): telegraph, telepathic, telephone, telescope, television

Improving Your Active Vocabulary

Although your active vocabulary is the stock of words you actually use in speaking and writing, we have considered the recognition vocabulary first because we almost always recognize words others use before we begin to use them ourselves. The active vocabulary is expanded chiefly by converting words from the recognition vocabulary. Usually this conversion takes place naturally as we become more and more familiar with a word. For example, some of the words you have met in this book have probably passed over into your active vocabulary — such as *analogy, antonym, coherence, colloquial, context, etymology, idiom, inflection, learned words, standard English, synonym, thesis,* and *transition.* And if you were to write down all the words you have begun to use as a result of your experience in college, you would surely have a long list.

This natural conversion can be extended and accelerated by practice. A student can practice using a word as he looks it up in his dictionary. When he revises his writing he can consider what other words he knows that might fit the context of a particular sentence. He can make a note of words he is quite familiar with but never uses, and begin deliberately to introduce them into his writing and speaking.

The techniques of conversion are less important than the will to do something about it; but of the methods that may be used, four are most worth recommending. The first of these is to explore your recognition vocabulary deliberately for words that might be used for a particular subject. For example, what words can you recall that deal with government? If you start to prepare a list, you will be surprised how rapidly it grows, as you begin to think of all the ramifications of government — *franchise, ballot, election, electorate, nominate, nominee, candidate, canvass, vote, plurality, majority, primary, campaign, issue, returns, caucus, adjournment, recess, amend, veto, repeal, sustain, filibuster, cloture, frank, immunity,* and so on. Probably all or most of these words are in your recognition vocabulary, but how many of them do you use? Recalling them or writing them in a list reminds you that you do know them and can therefore use them if you wish.

The second method is to sharpen your understanding of certain words by distinguishing their meanings from those of similar words — for example, to distinguish among *quick, prompt, ready, apt* — so that you may confidently use them in context. To differentiate clearly among such words, you should consult a dictionary of synonyms, either your own or a library copy. But even if no dictionary of synonyms is handy, you can still do much with a general dictionary. This kind of exercise not only makes you aware of shades of meaning but at the same time helps to convert the words into your active vocabulary.

The third method is a combination of the first two. First, consult a thesaurus for all the words that may be used to express a general idea; next, select from that list all words which are part of your recognition vocabulary only; then look up these words in a dictionary of synonyms or a general dictionary to be quite sure that you know how to use them; finally, use each word in a phrase or sentence that clearly reveals its meaning.

The fourth method — and the best as far as your writing is concerned — is to discipline yourself to seek specific words whenever anything you have written is unnecessarily general. The effort to find the specific word will require you to think of various terms that might be used in place of the general one. Since the new words must come from your recognition vocabulary, you will repeatedly be reviewing part of that vocabulary with a view to conversion. For example, in trying to specify "lacking order," you may think of many words referring to some kind of disorder — *bedraggled, chaotic, confused, dislocated, disoriented, entangled, irregular, jumbled, lawless, muddled, mussed, scrambled, shapeless, slovenly, unsystematic, untidy*. As you turn these words over in your mind, looking for the one that best conveys your thought, you are bringing all of them, not just the one you finally choose, into your active vocabulary.

Two words of caution are necessary before we leave this discussion of conversion. First, new words must be chosen for their usefulness, not for their impressiveness. The real purpose of increasing your vocabulary is to increase your ability to communicate, and communication is not improved by calling a daily newspaper "a diurnal publication" or a sick friend "an incapacitated colleague." Second, the new words must fit the contexts in which they are to be used. Although *glib* means *smooth* in such phrases as *a glib speaker* and *a glib argument,* we cannot talk about *a glib surface* or *a glib texture.* It is better not to use the word at all than to use it in the wrong context. For this reason, it is usually safer to introduce new words in writing rather than in impromptu speech, since the written word may be more easily checked and revised. If these two cautions are observed, deliberate conversion from the recognition to the active vocabulary can be a profitable exercise.

Exercises

A. 1. In the following words both the prefixes and the roots are derived from Latin forms. Can you analyze each word and give the literal meaning of its parts? Do not consult your dictionary until you have at least made a considered guess about each word.

abduct	eject	postpone
abstain	except	produce
adjacent	excursive	propel
antecedent	expect	recede
beneficiary	expedite	recognize
bilateral	facsimile	subdue
circumstance	induce	subscript
contact	inspect	subvene
contain	interpose	supersede
decide	intervene	transcribe
describe	malefactor	transmit
effect	postmortem	unilateral

2. Both the prefixes and the roots of the following words are derived from Greek forms. Analyze each word and give the meaning of its parts.

autobiography	monologue	polymorph
bibliophile	morphology	symphony
genealogy	philanthropy	synchronize
homogeneous	phonology	telegram
monograph	polygamist	telephone

3. Without consulting the list on pages 183–184, give the meaning of the following Latin prefixes. Then check your answers against the list.

ante-	extra-	post-
bene-	inter-	sub-
circum-	mal-	super-
contra-	pre-	trans-

4. Without consulting the list on pages 184–185, give the meaning of the following Greek forms. Then check your answers against the list.

auto-	homo	morph
bio-	log	poly-
chrono-	micro-	sym-
graph	mono-	tele-

5. Choose five Latin and five Greek forms from questions 3 and 4 above and for each choice write as many English words as you can recall containing the Latin or Greek form.

B. Using the example of "government" on page 185 as a model, write as many words as you can recall which have some clear relation to each of the following subjects:

agriculture	crime	mathematics
architecture	doctors	philosophy
art	education	poetry
astronomy	engineering	real estate
biology	factory	scientists
chemistry	geology	sea
church	law	war

C. Differentiate the meanings of the following sets of synonyms. Use whatever reference works you wish.

1. autocratic, despotic, arbitrary, tyrannical
2. conform, adjust, reconcile
3. bedeck, decorate, embellish, garnish
4. artist, artificer, artisan
5. mean, median, average, norm
6. pithy, terse, succinct, concise
7. perennial, perpetual, constant, incessant
8. balky, restive, perverse, wayward
9. mock, mimic, copy, ape
10. weep, wail, whimper, blubber
11. gnarled, warped, contorted
12. assimilate, embody, incorporate
13. idle, inert, supine, passive
14. damage, harm, hurt, mischief
15. grudge, spite, malice
16. apprentice, probationer, novice
17. ardor, fervor, zeal
18. buff, burnish, polish
19. ascend, soar, surge
20. maudlin, mushy, sentimental

D. The following five columns of fifty words each were selected from a book of freshman readings. Check off and ignore those words which are already in your active vocabulary. For those which are in your recognition vocabulary only, prepare a sentence which clearly reveals a correct use of the word. For those which are entirely new to you consult your dictionary. Come to class prepared to demonstrate that you know how to use each word.

abyss	affluent	acrid	adroit	abortive
accost	agnostic	amplify	apocryphal	abstruse
admonish	anonymous	analogous	appraise	affix
affront	arrogant	annul	ascertain	amenable
alleviate	authentic	bestial	aural	apt
amend	bland	chronic	bogus	benign
basic	blatant	collaborate	brash	bracing
biased	boisterous	colloquial	bullish	brazen
boon	caricature	conducive	carping	brusque
capitulate	complacent	corroborate	castigate	callous
caption	consensus	derive	caustic	cede
component	contemporary	discordant	competent	condone
concept	covetous	enervating	confront	deficit
congenial	cynical	entomology	cursory	delete
congested	dextrous	etymology	deluded	deviate
context	dialect	fastidious	denuded	ecstasy
conversely	diminutive	flippant	dormant	elated
corollary	dogmatic	gilded	empirical	elicit
decade	dynamic	incentive	espouse	elongate
deprive	echelon	inherent	exquisite	eminent
diagnosis	enigmatic	insular	feign	felicitate
dilate	extol	inter	frugal	fictitious
dupe	fabulous	intermittent	fugue	fortify
epitaph	fealty	lucrative	gaunt	glib
epithet	futile	miniature	haphazard	harried
equilibrium	garrulous	mulch	innate	hoary
facile	germinal	nullify	intrinsic	illegible
fluent	guise	ostracize	invective	indelibly
gist	hapless	panacea	jargon	indolent
habitually	hierarchy	philology	jubilant	interminable
heresy	humble	pungent	keystone	inveterate
hybrid	implicit	regime	kiln	ironic
illiterate	impostor	reticent	liaison	laconic
illusion	inarticulate	secular	mandatory	linguistic
ingenious	integrity	smirk	millennium	odious
ingenuous	interlude	tantalize	naïve	opaque
initiate	interpolate	tenacious	nebulous	optical
layman	intransigent	tumult	obsolete	pliant
lax	irksome	usurp	omnipotent	putrid
mediocre	maudlin	usury	pariah	rampant
morose	nucleus	valid	pecuniary	recalcitrant
obscure	pediatrician	vandal	replica	ribald
periodic	Pollyanna	venomous	rupture	spontaneous
pompous	rubble	vicarious	status quo	spurious
prosaic	rudimentary	virile	stipulate	staid
rebuff	semantics	virtuosity	suppliant	tawdry
regress	specious	waspish	terrestrial	toxic
specific	tenure	wayward	vapid	trite
tangible	thesis	welt	vestigial	wanton
ultimate	ubiquitous	writhe	watt	whorl

E. In each line of words select and write out the word closest in meaning to the italicized word. The closest meaning may not be synonymous.

adamant: gracious, amenable, unyielding, courageous, stupid, wealthy
adhere: ruin, stick to, break off, overhear, wipe out, betray, upset
anecdote: poison, cure, malady, rumor, story, lover, opponent, praise
bedlam: restaurant, hotel, station, madhouse, garage, resort, store
bigotry: narrow-mindedness, patriotism, miserliness, immoral love
clemency: conviction, payment, proof, weakness, falsehood, mercy, fate
cogent: dull, tricky, mean, facetious, wise, empty, flabby, late
contrite: gay, optimistic, careful, sorry, overworked, worn out, greedy
dearth: debt, scarcity, soil, abundance, mistake, honor, redemption
doctrine: literature, paintings, teachings, medicine, refuse, sediment
dolt: an old woman, a racehorse, a trained animal, a stupid person, a thief
edict: lie, promise, platitude, celebration, proclamation, song, boycott
excerpt: rebuttal, addition, exception, law, receipt, fragment, letter
facet: error, attitude, water tap, drain, value, surface, cost, labor
fallacy: truth, error, virtue, vanity, stimulant, lunacy, fracture
fiscal: legal, governmental, new, political, monetary, corrupt, ethical
gregarious: fond of company, sulky, merry, confident, not willing, tired
hackneyed: incapable, tragic, trite, tawdry, unkempt, swollen, hired
heinous: unfinished, out of date, absurd, sharp, heavy, happy, hateful
impeccable: hard, metallic, self-righteous, flawless, faint, calm, lazy
impunity: without hope, not sullied, not infected, without harm, obsolete
indigenous: not edible, sick, salty, robust, nice, native, indiscreet
inert: tired, slow, lifeless, weighing nothing, trivial, wet, extra
inference: thought, gain, excuse, burden, lament, interlude, clothing
jeopardize: endanger, make light of, suppress, buy off, discount, omit
jibe: swear, smile, sing, taste, taunt, trip, salute, make friends with
mitigate: impress, scorn, esteem, make milder, add to, repair, try again
mores: additions, customs, natives, crimes, foods, servants, friends
mutilate: ponder, rescue, upbraid, tease, tickle, mix, maim, migrate
myriad: a rare volume, a forged document, a large number, a tiny specimen
nominal: not known, in name only, not yet elected, subdued, part, regretful
novice: artist, artisan, old-timer, commanding officer, beginner, culprit
noxious: too sweet, difficult to do, pleasant, poisonous, expensive, anxious
obtuse: irregular, belligerent, dull, attractive, well padded, innocent
officious: authorized, incompetent, official, severe, meddlesome, well done
opiate: allowance, quarrel, recitation, decoy, drug, greeting, invitation
palatable: sticky, pure, tasty, revolting, cloying, dear, unsupervised
petulant: prickly, peevish, prudish, irate, agreeable, modest
prodigious: precocious, proud, tardy, wary, clear, enormous, everlasting
rectify: receive, return, denounce, cajole, correct, explain, undermine
restive: tranquil, impatient, sleepy, angry, tired, frigid, restful
servile: cheap, irritable, efficient, eager, slavish, delightful, mad

sordid: heavy, dull, gluttonous, dirty, bright, novel, silly, wasteful
synopsis: bold attack, happy thought, brief version, clever pun
tentative: provisional, fixed, untrustworthy, hasty, inaccurate, partly right
torpid: inflammable, exotic, incandescent, slight, cold, sluggish, hot
ultimate: unknown, expected, initial, final, revised, brilliant, long
unique: old, valuable, broken, queer, salable, singular, lost, redundant
verbatim: genuine, word for word, at long last, without fail, vocal, trivial
zealot: criminal, scholar, manager, apprentice, grouch, enthusiast, fraud

9

Synopses and Summaries

Probably the skill most necessary to success in college is the ability to read effectively. College success is largely determined by examinations, and examinations are necessarily concerned with finding out how well the student understands what he has read. The ability, therefore, to restate in one's own words the ideas and information contained in books, articles, and essays is one of the main tests by which academic success is measured. This is true even when an examination is deliberately designed to test a student's evaluation of his reading or what he thinks about it, since he must understand what he reads before he is in a position to evaluate and discuss it.

Any device which helps a student to read more effectively is therefore worthy of his serious attention. You are already familiar with one such device — the outline, which was discussed as a reading aid on pages 52–54. In this chapter we shall consider two other reading aids — the *synopsis* and the *summary*.

The Synopsis

In your literature courses you will be asked to read novels, plays, and stories, on which you will later be examined. Every student knows that after reading a number of plays or stories, it is often difficult to keep the details of each plot clearly in mind and to keep the separate characters distinct. While the pre-examination review helps, there is never time to reread all the original material. What is needed for review is some record of the document short enough to read quickly but detailed enough to give the essentials. For such purposes the synopsis is most useful.

A synopsis is a summary of a plot. When you return from a movie and are asked what it was about, your answer is a synopsis. You identify the main characters and tell what happened to them. By so doing, you review the whole movie in a small fraction of the time required to see it.

The following is a synopsis of a play that you may have read or are likely to read in college. In order to be clear, even to a student who has not read the play, the synopsis has been made fuller than would be required for purposes of one's own review.

IBSEN, "A DOLL'S HOUSE," 3 ACTS

Characters: Torvald Helmer; Nora, his wife; Dr. Rank; Nils Krogstad; Mrs. Linde.

Act I. The play opens with a picture of the domestic happiness of the Helmer household. Nora is represented as a pretty, helpless woman, dependent on her husband in all worldly concerns. Torvald is the strong, wise husband who paternally guides his wife's life. *From the man's point of view,* he is the ideal husband, and she the ideal wife. Their home is a doll's house, with Nora the doll.

From Mrs. Linde, a woman who has earned her way in the world, we learn that the tranquillity of the doll's house rests on a deception. At a time when her father was dying and her husband was seriously ill Nora had borrowed from Krogstad enough money to finance a trip to Italy, ostensibly a pleasure trip for her but really a journey to save her husband's life. Rather than worry her dying father, who would have given her the money, Nora forged his name to the security she gave Krogstad. Since then she has been paying the interest by practicing all sorts of domestic economies. Her husband, who knows nothing about the transaction, is always teasing her about her domestic extravagance.

At the moment the play opens the finances of the Helmers are about to improve, for Torvald has been appointed manager of the bank and Nora hopes soon to retire the debt. But the dramatic turn from happiness to disaster is occasioned by Torvald's giving Mrs. Linde the job at the bank now held by Krogstad. Krogstad threatens to reveal Nora's forgery unless she persuades her husband to retain him in his position. Nora tries to do this but fails.

Act II. Nora determines to borrow the money to pay Krogstad from Dr. Rank, a good friend of the family. Knowing that he is about to die, Rank visits her and confesses his love for her. Under the circumstances she feels she cannot ask for the loan, although there is no question that she would get it. Krogstad brings pressure on Nora, but she refuses to interfere with her husband's decision, and in her refusal indicates that she is thinking of committing suicide or of leaving her family in order to spare her husband's name. Krogstad leaves a letter for Torvald, explaining the whole transaction. Nora, who wants to postpone the showdown until after the Christmas party, delays her husband's reading of the letter.

Act III. While the Helmers are at the party, Krogstad and Mrs. Linde decide to get married. Krogstad says that he will ask Torvald for the letter unread, but Mrs. Linde, who understands that Nora is not happy in her role of doll, tells him it would be better if Torvald read the letter.

The Helmers return from the party, and are visited by Rank, who leaves a marked card which Nora understands as a notice that he is about to die. Torvald later reads Krogstad's letter and bitterly accuses Nora as an immoral woman, unworthy to be the mother of his children. His conduct opens her eyes and she prepares to leave the house. At this time, a second letter arrives from Krogstad, in which he returns Nora's bond and thus frees her from the consequences of her forgery. Torvald is overjoyed and announces his forgiveness of Nora. But the experience has made a serious woman out of her. She reviews for her husband their relationship together and denounces the doll-like status in which she has been kept by both him and her father. They talk it over quietly, with Torvald getting the worst of it. Nora decides to leave him. There is a suggestion that their marriage may be resumed after they prove themselves. Then the door slams as Nora leaves.

The next synopsis will have less meaning for a student who has not read the play, but it would probably be adequate to recall the whole action to a student who had read *Candida* several months earlier.

G. B. Shaw, "Candida," 3 Acts

Characters: Rev. James Morell; Candida, his wife; Eugene Marchbanks, a young poet; James Burgess, Candida's father; Proserpine, Morell's secretary; Mill, Morell's assistant.

Act I. The main job of this act is to portray the characters of Morell, Candida, and Marchbanks. Morell is drawn by showing: (*a*) the attitudes of Proserpine and Mill toward him; (*b*) the attitude of Burgess toward him; (*c*) his activities in affairs of the church and of socialism; (*d*) the attitude of Marchbanks toward him; and (*e*) his own attitude toward Marchbanks and Burgess. Marchbanks' character is revealed by his own actions and by the attitudes of Morell and Candida toward him. The action of the play during this act sets up the triangle of Morell, Candida, and Marchbanks and develops the theme far enough so that Morell's final defeat is indicated. At the beginning of the act Morell is almost a symbol of the confident and competent master of every situation, while Marchbanks is a symbol of naïve incompetence. During the act Marchbanks succeeds in reversing this judgment.

Act II. This act carries on the conflict to the point at which Morell decides to leave Marchbanks and Candida alone while he goes to a meeting. His decision is a desperate attempt to force the issue and find where he stands in Candida's affections.

Act III. Marchbanks makes poetic love to Candida while Morell is gone. Morell returns and forces Candida to make a decision between the two men. Marchbanks is horrified at his crudeness. In the auction scene Candida chooses her husband as the weaker of the two men and therefore the one who needs her most. Marchbanks, who had anticipated her decision, leaves after receiving Candida's final advice.

Although this second synopsis will seem less satisfactory to a student who has not read the play, it is actually more useful to one who has, since it not only identifies the characters and reviews the plot, but also shows the relationship of the separate acts to each other and to the whole drama. A synopsis need not do this, but since the relation of a particular act to the play as a whole may well be asked about on a final examination, this kind of synopsis has an additional merit.

It takes from fifteen to thirty minutes to write an adequate synopsis. A student who feels that he has the details of a play or a novel clearly in mind when he has just finished reading it may see no reason for spending additional time on the assignment. But one test of his reading is not how clearly he knows the work then but how clearly he knows it at the end of the semester. For most students the discipline of making a synopsis as a part of the total reading assignment is rewarded by easier and more accurate recall and hence by better examination grades.

The Summary

The synopsis is useful only for novels, plays, and stories. For all other reading the summary is used. A summary is a condensation of the original. In its simplest form it is nothing more than purposeful note-taking. The student boils down the original passage to the bare facts or ideas which it contains, as illustrated by the following examples:

Original	*Summary*
The sun is a fiery, flaming star well toward a million miles in diameter and nearly a hundred million miles from us. Surrounding it is a very deep atmosphere at temperatures running up to 10,000 degrees Fahrenheit, composed of gases and vapors all of which are common on the earth.	Diameter of sun, one million miles. Distance from earth, 100 million miles. Highest atmosphere temperature, 10,000° F.
When comparing the financial success of two business firms of the same kind, we do not simply say that the firm making the greater profit is the more successful. What we compare is not profits alone, but profits relative to total investment. That is, if p and i represent profit and investment, respectively, the value of the quotient p/i (that is, the percentage of profit) serves to measure relative financial success.[1]	Comparative financial success of two firms not measured by profits alone, but by formula p/i, when $p =$ profit, and $i =$ investment.

For many purposes the notes at the right offer the most useful kind of summary. We shall see in Chapter 12 that the use of such notes is recommended in carrying out investigations for a research paper, because this habit of gleaning the facts from a passage encourages alert reading and avoids the possibility of unintentional plagiarism.

However, the kind of summary with which we are principally concerned

[1] From *Introduction to Mathematics,* by Cooley, Gans, Kline, and Wahlert. Copyright, 1949, by Hollis R. Cooley, David Gans, Morris Kline, and Howard E. Wahlert. Reprinted by permission of Houghton Mifflin Company.

in this chapter is the *paragraph summary,* in which the reader condenses the content of the whole paragraph into a few sentences. He reads the paragraph, determines what it says, and expresses its essential meaning in short and simplified form. He thus achieves two results: he proves that he understands the paragraph by translating it into his own words, and he reduces it to a more convenient form for review. The following examples illustrate:

Original

I often wish that this phrase, "applied science," had never been invented. For it suggests that there is a sort of scientific knowledge of direct practical use, which can be studied apart from another sort of scientific knowledge, which is of no practical utility, and which is termed "pure science." But there is no more complete fallacy than this. What people call applied science is nothing but the application of pure science to particular classes of problems. It consists of deductions from those general principles, established by reasoning and observation, which constitute pure science. No one can safely make these deductions until he has a firm grasp of the principles; and he can obtain that grasp only by personal experience of the operations of observation and of reasoning on which they were founded.[2]

Summary

The attempt to differentiate "pure" and "applied" science misleadingly suggests that "pure" science is not useful. It is useful in two ways: it provides the scientific principles to be applied, and it provides the method which makes application possible.

Explanation

The first sentence of the summary expresses in 16 words the idea stated in 50 words in the first two sentences of the original. The second sentence of the summary restates in 23 words the content of the last four sentences of the original (83 words). The summary, therefore, conveys the basic meaning of the original in less than one-third of the space.

Original

Economists write of the "agricultural revolution," of greater productivity per farm worker, of the advantages of farm mechanization and the ability of the farmer to feed more people than he did prior to the nineteenth century. What most of them completely fail to recognize is that production-per-farmer is utterly meaningless divorced from production-per-acre. For a few decades the Western world was able to get along on this

Summary

The belief that improved agricultural techniques will increase the productivity of land is an illusion. Mechanization will allow one man to farm more acres and, hence, get a bigger crop, but it will not produce a greater yield per acre, except in rare instances. On the contrary, by exploiting the natural resources of the soil it may in time decrease the yield per acre.

[2] From "Science and Culture" by T. H. Huxley.

assumption — while it still had new lands to open up and while it produced by mining its topsoil. But modern agriculture has not raised the earth's biotic potential; except in very limited areas, it has not reduced environmental resistances. Over most of the earth it has enormously increased them, to the point of destroying hundreds of millions of productive acres. Discussion of the agricultural revolution in terms of increased production-per-farmer — or even in terms of pure agriculture, leaving aside the problem of water tables, forests, nonagricultural lands, fauna and noncrop plants, etc. — expresses a most fallacious and dangerous form of thinking. One man, under an improved technology, might be able to farm a full section; this would not bring into being more sections of agricultural land — nor raise or even maintain productivity on other acres.[3]

Explanation

The summary reduces the 209-word original to 64 words by picking out the two main reasons why the "agricultural revolution" will not increase the biotic potential of the earth and ignoring the details by which these reasons are explained. In other words, the summary confines the argument to a statement of the thesis and the two factors into which that thesis is broken.

Original

The object of this Essay is to assert one very simple principle, as entitled to govern absolutely the dealings of society with the individual in the way of compulsion and control, whether the means used be physical force in the form of legal penalties, or the moral coercion of public opinion. That principle is, that the sole end for which mankind are warranted, individually or collectively, in interfering with the liberty of action of any of their number, is self-protection. That the only purpose for which power can be rightfully exercised over any member of a civilized community, against his will, is to prevent harm to others. His own good, either physical or moral, is not a sufficient warrant. He cannot rightfully be compelled to do

Summary

The thesis of Mill's essay *On Liberty* is that society has no right to interfere with the liberty of an individual in matters which concern only himself. He cannot be restrained by penalties or social pressure so long as his conduct does not harm others. The belief that it would be better for him to change may justify persuasion, but not compulsion.

[3] From *Road to Survival* by William Vogt. Copyright 1948 by William Sloane Associates, Inc. Reprinted by permission of the publishers.

or forbear because it will be better for him to do so, because it will make him happier, because, in the opinions of others, to do so would be wise, or even right. These are good reasons for remonstrating with him, or reasoning with him, or persuading him, or entreating him, but not for compelling him, or visiting him with any evil in case he do otherwise. To justify that, the conduct from which it is desired to deter him, must be calculated to produce evil to some one else. The only part of the conduct of any one, for which he is amenable to society, is that which concerns others. In the part which merely concerns himself, his independence is, of right, absolute. Over himself, over his own body and mind, the individual is sovereign.[4]

Explanation

The original paragraph takes 80 words to state the thesis and then explains that thesis by seven restatements through 180 words. By stating the thesis in 27 words and restating it only twice in 35 words, the summary boils down the 260-word original to 62 words. Of course, the summary leaves much that has to be inferred, but for a student who had read the original, it would probably be adequate to allow him to restate Mill's position in an essay-type examination.

The preparation of such digests is more a matter of reading than of writing, and the reading is made easier by an understanding of paragraph construction. As we saw in Chapter 4, most paragraphs develop a single idea by explanation or illustration. The first task in writing a digest is to find the topic idea of the paragraph. If that idea is not explicitly stated, it must be distilled out of the sentences which come closest to stating it. In the selection from *On Liberty,* the introductory phrase, "That principle is," has almost the effect of turning a spotlight on the main idea of the paragraph. The topic ideas of the other two examples are less obvious, since neither is explicitly stated in a single sentence. Both paragraphs have to be read completely before we can be sure of their purpose but, once read, the central thought of each becomes clear.

The second step in preparing a paragraph summary is to eliminate whatever is not essential to a clear understanding of the topic. For ordinary readers a writer must explain his topic sentence to be sure that its implications will not be missed, but a person preparing a summary of a paragraph is not an ordinary reader. He is unusually alert, and so he can dispense with the explanation and illustration which might otherwise be necessary. Therefore, he concentrates on just those sentences which are necessary to explain the topic idea, and ignores the rest. As he does so, he makes up his mind exactly what the paragraph is saying.

The third step is to write the summary. The safest way to do this is to

4 From "On Liberty" by John Stuart Mill.

put the original aside and rewrite the paragraph out of the knowledge already obtained. A student who cannot do that has not read the paragraph carefully enough. If he follows it as he writes his digest, he may be tempted to pick out a few sentences in their original form and string them together. If he does this, he is quoting from the paragraph, not summarizing it, and what he produces may distort the meaning of the original. The real value of the summary as a reading device is that it requires the student to master the paragraph and make it his own. This he cannot do by copying selected sentences.

The final step is to compare the digest with the original for accuracy and to make whatever revisions this comparison suggests. Even for students who have had considerable experience writing paragraph summaries this final step often results in further condensation and simplification of the summary.

To summarize:

1. Read the paragraph to determine its basic idea.

2. Read it again to pick out the essentials, summarizing mentally as you read. If necessary, make notes.

3. Without consulting the paragraph, express its content in your own words. If you get stuck, stop writing and repeat step two.

4. Compare your summary with the original and make any necessary revisions.

The technique of the paragraph summary may be applied to a series of paragraphs or to a whole article. In summarizing a selection of many paragraphs, remember that not all paragraphs are equally significant. Some introduce or restate main points; others are transitional; still others give illustrations of a point already made. Since the summary requires you to restate the content, not the paragraphing, you need not summarize each paragraph separately. The best procedure is first to determine the purpose of the selection, then outline the main topics, and finally summarize each of these without being unduly influenced by the original paragraphing. For example, "The Distinction Between War and Peace" (pages 13–15) contains nine paragraphs, yet structurally it consists of three parts — the *legal, political,* and *military* distinctions between war and peace. These three parts would be the real units of the summary, and the essay would be summarized as though it contained three paragraphs instead of nine.

In the illustration that follows, the organization of the article is shown by the outline symbols at the left; the main points are underlined in the text; and the significance of the material is indicated in the notes at the right. In its present form, therefore, the illustration represents the first two steps in preparing a summary of a long article.

LANGUAGE PLANNING FOR A NEW ORDER[5]

OUTLINE SYMBOLS

NOTES

I.

As far as we can see into the future, there will always be a multiplicity of regional languages for everyday use. Those who advocate the introduction of an international medium do not dispute this. What they do assert is the need for a second language as a common medium for people who speak mutually unintelligible tongues. They envisage a world, of at least federa-

This paragraph says, in effect, that the proposal of a second language is not impractical.

A. 1.
tions of what were once sovereign states, where people of different speech communities would be bilingual. Everyone would still grow up to speak one or other of existing national languages, but everyone would also acquire a single auxiliary for supranational communication. This prospect is not

2.
incompatible with the mental capacities of ordinary human beings; nor does it involve a total break with existing practice. Bilingualism exists already in Wales, Belgium, South Africa, and many other parts. Throughout the English-speaking world all secondary-school children study at least one foreign language, that is, French, Spanish, or German; and in some countries pupils who leave school with a smattering of a foreign language are in the majority.

Evidence for IA2.

In Britain they are not. Most of the children enter the labor market with a knowledge of no language other than their own. Consequently millions of adult workers are excluded from direct communication with their Continental comrades. Postponement of the school-leaving age will provide an opportunity for bringing the curriculum for elementary instruction in Britain into line with that of many other countries. Thus the adoption of an international auxiliary implies no more than regularization of existing educational practice, i.e., universal instruction in a second

This exception to IA2 does not affect author's thesis and may be omitted in summary.

Restatement of IA2.

[5] Reprinted from *The Loom of Language,* by Frederick Bodmer, by permission of W. W. Norton and Company, Inc. Copyright, 1944, by W. W. Norton and Company, Inc., New York. Permission to reprint in Canada by courtesy of George Allen & Unwin, Ltd., publishers.

OUTLINE
SYMBOLS

language and agreement to use one and the same second language everywhere. Creation of conditions for uniformity of educational practice by international agreement, as a prelude to universal bilingualism, as defined above, is not a language problem. It is a political problem.

B.

1. Many well-informed people still doubt whether the social need for a single universal second language will prove strong enough to override human laziness. At first sight the plight of modern language teaching in Great Britain and elsewhere lends some support to pessimism. Hitherto our schools have produced poor results. After years of travail the British public-school product may have mastered enough French to get in Paris what Paris is only too willing to sell without French. This need not make us hopeless. Any society ripe for adopting an interlanguage will be faced with a new set of problems. Pupils who now take French or German as school subjects rarely have a clear-cut idea of the purpose for which they are learning them and, more rarely still, the chance of using what knowledge they acquire. The future is likely to

2. provide incentives and opportunities hitherto unknown. Fantastic delays, misunderstandings and waste due to the absence of a single common language for international co-operation will impress even those who are not knowingly affected by it at present.

This support for IBI may be omitted in summary.

A hundred years ago Europe witnessed perhaps less than a dozen international congresses in the course of a whole decade. Delegates were invariably drawn from the upper class. So communication was easy enough. Deliberations were in French. When international congresses became more numerous, they assumed a more gaudy linguistic character. Consequently procedure had often to be conducted in two or more "official" languages. One could choose delegates who were able to compete with the polyglot attendant of an international sleeping car, but the delegate

This paragraph is an illustration of the difference between the past and the future and may be ignored in the summary.

201

with the best linguistic equipment would rarely be one with the best understanding of relevant issues. This obstacle to international communication becomes more formidable as time goes on. People of new strata and more diverse speech habits discover community of interest, and no single language enjoys the prestige of French during the eighteenth century.

In short, the prospects for language planning depend on the extent to which the impulse to international co-operation keeps step with the new potential of prosperity for all. Socialist planning, that is, planning for the common needs of peoples belonging to different nations or cultural units, will bring about incessant contact between medical officers of health, town-planning experts, electrical engineers, social statisticians, and trade-union representatives. Increased leisure combined with improved traveling facilities will give to a large floating section of the population opportunities to establish new social contacts through the medium of an interlanguage; and its adoption would find a ready ally in the radio. Even those who stay at home perpetually would be tempted to avail themselves of opportunities to learn more of large-scale social enterprise in neighboring communities of the supranational state.

This paragraph develops IB2. Most of these details may be omitted in the summary.

II.

The choice for those of us who cherish this hope lies between a constructed language and an already established medium, either in its existing shape or in some simplified form, such as Basic English. The second involves nothing more than an agreement between educational authorities expressing the will of the people. On account of its grammatical simplicity, its hybrid vocabulary, its vast literature, and, above all, its wide distribution over the

A.

planet, the claims of Anglo-American would undoubtedly exclude those of any other current language which could conceivably have a large body of promoters in the near future; but political objections

Two kinds of international languages, each of which is to be considered.

English is the logical choice if a national language is chosen, but political considerations will rule it out.

to such a choice are formidable. <u>It is most
unlikely that a socialist Continent would</u>

B. <u>decide for Anglo-American as its interlanguage if Britain remained hostile to the
new order.</u> The chances might improve if
a Britain free of its imperial incubus entered into close co-operation with its neighbors next door to build up a world without
class, war, and want. Even so there is
much to say for the adoption of a neutral
medium cleansed from the all too evident
defects of existing natural languages.

III. A.   <u>Some linguists meet the plea for a constructed auxiliary with the assertion that
language is a product of growth.</u> It is less
easy to detect the relevance than to recognize the truth of this assertion. Admittedly it is beyond human ingenuity to construct a live skylark, but the airplane has
advantages which no flying animal possesses. Apple trees and gooseberry bushes
are also products of growth, and no reasonable man or woman advances this trite
reflection as sufficient reason for preventing
geneticists from producing new varieties of
fruit by combining inherited merits of different strains or allied species. The work
accomplished by pioneers of the science of
synthetic linguistics shows that it is also
possible to produce new language varieties
combining the inherent merits of different
forms of natural speech. In the light of
their achievements and shortcomings we
can now prescribe the essential features of
a constructed language which would be
free from the conspicuous defects of any
natural, or of any previously constructed,
language.

B.   Professional linguists who do not dispute the possibility of constructing a language to meet the requirements of international communication, sometimes raise
another objection. They say that the <u>adventure would be short-lived, if ever attempted; that no auxiliary could remain
intact for long.</u> Even if confined to the
territory of Europe itself, it would split

First of two objections against constructed language.

Answer to objection. All this may be reduced to statement that creation of a fully-developed synthetic language is quite possible.

Second objection.

into dialects. Each speech community would locally impose its own phonetic habits and its own system of stress; and the Tower of Babel would come crashing down on the builders. Only a perpetual succession of international congresses could thus prevent a new disaster. Such is the gloomy view which Professor Wyld of Oxford takes. There are three sufficient reasons

C. why it need not intimidate us.

1. To begin with there is nothing inherently absurd in a suggestion for setting up a permanent interlinguistic commission to check the process of disintegration. For three centuries the forty immortals of the Académie Française have tried, not without success, to keep literary French in a strait jacket; and Norway has changed its spelling and grammar by three Acts of Parliament in less than forty years. If national governments can control the growth of national languages, an international authority could also maintain an accepted standard for its own medium of communication. Though international committees to supervise scientific terminology, e.g. the International Commission on Zoological Nomenclature, are already in existence, our universities cling to the conviction that intelligent language planning on a world-wide scale is out of the question.

By the nature of their training academic linguists are unduly preoccupied with times when few people could travel beyond a day's journey on horseback or by cart, when reading and writing, like stenography today, were crafts confined to a few, when there were no mechanical means for distributing news or information. It is true that languages have broken up time and again in the past, because of dispersion over a wide area, geographical isolation, absence of a written standard, and other disintegrating agencies. Those who enter-

2. tain the hope of international communication by an auxiliary envisage a future in

First answer to that objection.

All this may be reduced to statement that the experience of France, Norway, and the Commission on Zoological Nomenclature shows that prevention of disintegration is possible.

Transition to IIIC2. May be ignored in summary.

Second answer to same objection.

which these agencies will no longer operate. Indeed, we have experience to sustain a more hopeful view than is customary in academic quarters. During the centuries which have followed the introduction of printing, the gradual dissolution of illiteracy, and revolutionary changes in our means of communication, English has established itself as the language of North America and of Australasia. It is not true

3. to say that the three main Continental varieties of the common Anglo-American language are drifting further apart. It is probably more true to say that universal schooling, the film, and the radio are bringing them closer together. In any case, experience shows that geographical isolation during several centuries has not made the speech of New England unintelligible to the people of Old England, or vice versa. Experience should therefore encourage, rather than discourage, us in pressing for an international auxiliary.

Third answer to same objection.

This article presents an argument in favor of creating a synthetic language as an international auxiliary language. The argument is in three parts: that an auxiliary language is feasible, that a synthetic language would be more acceptable than any existing natural language, and that the old objections against synthetic languages no longer hold good. It would be logical to summarize each part in a single paragraph, but since the third part deals with two different objections, it might be better to devote a paragraph to each of them and to write the summary as follows:

The hope of a universal auxiliary language, by which people who speak different national languages may have a medium of international communication, is not an impractical one. In many countries people now use two languages, and the practice of teaching some foreign language in secondary schools is generally established. It is true that the level of student achievement in mastering these secondary languages is low, but this lack of success can be explained by the fact that students of foreign languages have little motivation for learning them and little opportunity to use them after they have been learned. Those who advocate the adoption of a universal auxiliary foresee a world in which the needs and opportunities of international cooperation will both demand a universal second language and provide the incentive to make its study efficient.

Whatever auxiliary is chosen must come either from some existing national language or from a constructed language. Of all existing languages, English, because of its grammatical simplicity, its hybrid vocabulary, its vast literature, and its wide distribution, would seem to have the strongest claim to become the world language. But political considerations might make it unacceptable to many nations. A constructed language would not be subject to political objections and would be free of defects which all national languages now show.

There are two common objections to a constructed language. One is that since language is a product of growth there is no chance of constructing a living language. This objection is hardly significant. The work already done on synthetic languages proves that the creation of a successful constructed language presents no linguistic impossibilities.

The second objection is that, while a constructed language could be made, it would not remain a universal language but would break up into mutually unintelligible dialects. While such disintegration has been common in the past, there are three reasons why we need not fear it: (1) as the experience of France, Norway, and the International Commission on Zoological Nomenclature shows, the tendency towards disintegration can be held in check by an authoritative commission; (2) the agencies of disintegration are less likely to operate in the interdependent world for which the auxiliary language is to be designed; (3) the fact that the common language of Britain, America, Australia, and New Zealand has not broken up into mutually unintelligible dialects proves that the agencies of disintegration can be offset by such integrating influences as universal education and improved means of communication.

If a shorter summary is required, the whole argument may be condensed to little more than its thesis:

> The advocates of an international auxiliary language think it possible to make people bilingual and that the needs of the future will make the task easier. They think Basic English would be the best natural auxiliary but that political and linguistic considerations favor a constructed language. The chief objections to a constructed language are that (1) languages cannot be constructed, but must grow; and (2) a constructed language would soon disintegrate. The proponents of a constructed language reply (1) it is now possible to construct a satisfactory synthetic language, and (2) experience shows that, under modern conditions, disintegration need not occur.

This version reduces a 1700-word article to about 100 words. Whether such drastic condensation is wise will depend on the purpose of the summary. If the shorter version gives the content in sufficient detail so that it can be recalled later, it is adequate.

Exercises

A. As an exercise in efficient notetaking make a note on a 3 × 5 inch card for each of the following paragraphs. Each note should be as short

and as accurate as possible and en
examples on page 195 as a model. H
who may return one of them to you
paragraph.

(1)

and as accurate as possible and entirely in your own words. Use the examples on page 195 as a model. Hand your notes in to your instructor, who may return one of them to you and ask you to develop it into a paragraph.

(1)

The history of the English language is divided into three periods. The first period begins with the invasion of Britain by Germanic tribes during the fifth and sixth centuries, but since we have almost no literary records before 700, this latter date is usually given for the beginning of the Old English or Anglo-Saxon period. The beginning date of Middle English, the second period, is about 1100, shortly after the Norman Conquest. Its closing date is about 1500, or 100 years after the death of Chaucer. The period since then is known as Modern English. Roughly, then, the history of the English language falls into three periods of 400 years each.

(2)

We do not know what language or languages the first settlers of Britain spoke. The first natives for whom we have historical references, the Britons, spoke Celtic, a non-Germanic language which has had comparatively little influence in the development of English but is the ancestor of Scottish and Irish Gaelic. During the four hundred years the Romans occupied Britain (43–410), some Latin words passed into popular speech and have come down to us — words like *castra* for *camp,* which came down as *caster* and *chester* in place names (Lancaster, Manchester), and common nouns like *street* and *wine.*

(3)

Before Chaucer's time, the greatest influences on the English vocabulary were Scandinavian and French. From the Viking raiders who attacked the coast during the ninth and tenth centuries and finally took over the northern part of England, we got many of our words starting with *sk* (*sky, skill, skin, skirt,* etc.) and a considerable number of common terms, like *happy, husband, ill, egg, ugly,* and the pronouns that begin with *th.* The French influence, beginning with the Norman Conquest in 1066 and continuing for about three hundred years, was much greater, and for a time it seemed that French would become the national language of England. Next to Latin, French has had the greatest influence on English vocabulary, and it is estimated that nearly half of all the French borrowings now in Modern English came in during this period.

B. For each of the following paragraphs, write the shortest possible summary which will still communicate the author's meaning fairly.

(1)

We do not believe that the objectives of science study in general education are best met by survey courses covering a large area in a limited time. These are too likely to be courses about science rather than courses in science.

They are apt to be dogmatic rather than inherently convincing. The student is likely to be taught a great many dramatic contemporary results of science rather than underlying principles and fundamental facts. If a survey course is to be completely outmoded in a few years by new advances, one cannot blame the student for failure to appreciate the basic fundamental truths; science is indeed to him a casual, ephemeral thing. This is not to imply that no advantage should be taken of new applications of science or recent discoveries to stimulate interest and secure motivation; however the cake should not be all frosting. It is usually less confusing and far more satisfying actually to learn and understand the principles behind a group of phenomena and how they bring these phenomena into being than to learn and attempt to remember a large number of superficial facts about the phenomena.[6]

(2)

It is not possible to depend entirely upon what each nation says of its own habits of thought and action. Writers in every nation have tried to give an account of themselves. But it is not easy. The lenses through which any nation looks at life are not the ones another nation uses. It is hard to be conscious of the eyes through which one looks. Any country takes them for granted, and the tricks of focusing and of perspective which give to any people its national view of life seem to that people the god-given arrangement of the landscape. In any matter of spectacles, we do not expect the man who wears them to know the formula for the lenses, and neither can we expect nations to analyze their own outlook upon the world. When we want to know about spectacles, we train an oculist and expect him to be able to write out the formula for any lenses we bring him. Some day no doubt we shall recognize that it is the job of the social scientist to do this for the nations of the contemporary world.[7]

(3)

We should know that all the money in the world could not have built an atomic bomb in 1936. Atomic energy was known, and many of its properties were understood. It had been released in small quantities in laboratories, and its release in large quantities in the sun and the stars had been studied. But the critical information and the critical direction to follow for releasing it in large amounts on earth were lacking in 1936, and no one could have used two billion dollars for making an atomic bomb at that time. It is this that is important in understanding the relation of science to industry, to medicine, and to the public. There has to be knowledge before it can be applied. At a certain stage of scientific development, theoretically critical knowledge becomes available. Before that moment — which no one can guarantee in advance — the knowledge cannot be applied. After that moment application is reasonably certain and only the special technics for its utilization need be worked out.[8]

[6] From *Toward General Education* by Earl J. McGrath and others. Copyright, 1948, by The Macmillan Company and used with their permission.
[7] From *The Chrysanthemum and the Sword* by Ruth Benedict. Copyright, 1946, by Ruth Benedict. Reprinted by permission of the publishers, Houghton Mifflin Company.
[8] From *Explaining the Atom* by Selig Hecht. Copyright 1947 by Selig Hecht. Reprinted by permission of The Viking Press, Inc., publishers.

(4)

. . . Take the matter of clothes as a simple touchstone of individuality. Every American woman who goes to London is either shocked, interested, or amused by the variety of women's dress there. Most of it, except sport clothes, is I admit, extremely bad, but the point is that a woman dresses just as she pleases. Little girls may have long black stockings or legs bare to their full length; older women may have skirts that display the knee or drag the ground; hats of the latest mode from Paris, or from Regent Street when Victoria was a girl. Watching the passing crowd on the Broad Walk is like turning the pages of *Punch* for half a century. A man may wear any headgear from a golf cap to a pearl satin "topper." Compare this, for example, with New York and the mass antics of the Stock Exchange where if a man wears a straw hat beyond the day appointed by his fellows they smash it down over his eyes, and where he is not safe from similar moronic hoodlumism even in the streets. . . . One has to fight to be oneself in America as in no other country I know. Not only are most Americans anxious to conform to the standards of the majority, but that majority, and the advertisers, insist that they shall.[9]

(5)

Often it is impossible to say whether what appears to us a bit of racy slang (sometimes because it duplicates a current locution) had anything like the same association a century or several centuries ago. We are surely right, in general, in feeling that in Chaucer, for example, the conversation of Pandarus is as utterly natural as it is partly by reason of the colloquialisms and the slang it contains. But has Chaucer's use of *the bones* (for "dice") in the *Pardoner's Tale,* directly anticipating a bit of contemporary slang, exactly the same flavor as the word now has? "Slang phrases from Shakespeare" are sometimes compiled: for example, these: "beat it," "done me wrong," "she falls for it," "not in it," "not so hot," "if he falls in, good night," and "let me tell the world." What seems to us slang, however, is by no means necessarily slang to Shakespeare, who sometimes means literally what we take metaphorically, and sometimes, through sheer coincidence, hits upon what has become, in another context, twentieth-century slang. Chaucer and Shakespeare certainly use slang enough, as must any poet who realistically echoes the conversational speech of his day; but their slang is almost never ours.[10]

(6)

The child's experience with words should teach us two things about class names. First, as our knowledge of individuals grows it is necessary to group them into classes. The child can do without class names only so long as his experience is confined to a few individuals. As his world grows, he must begin to see resemblances between individuals and to invent or learn class names for these resemblances. Second, the child's experience should remind us of something we too easily forget, that individuals existed as individuals

[9] From *Our Business Civilization* by James Truslow Adams. Reprinted by permission of Albert & Charles Boni, Inc.
[10] From *The Development of Modern English,* Second Edition, by Stuart Robertson and Frederic G. Cassidy. © 1954. Prentice-Hall, Inc. Reprinted by permission.

before they were grouped into a class, and that the class names do not point to all the characteristics of an individual but only to those he has in common with other individuals. Thus the word *man* is useful to name what Bill Mason, Fred Jones, and Tom Smith have in common. It is not useful as a name for any of these particular men, because it does not indicate the individual characteristics which distinguish them from each other.

(7)

The flag flying over the building to signify "a play is on" brought, indeed, a strange audience: a pit crowd of apprentices playing "hookey," town idlers, a few shameless women, travellers intent on seeing the sights, fighters off duty, seafarers ashore, etc.; and above in the balconies students and poets and a few shrewd burghers or minor court hangers-on (perhaps with ladies, who dared come only under masculine protection); and on the stage itself the fops and beaux and noblemen, as anxious to be seen as to see, interrupting the action if they willed, smoking and talking and displaying their figures and their finery. To this queer mixture of cultured and uneducated, of lowly and exalted, of those who came for love of drama and those who came to show their superiority, the Elizabethan drama was shaped. No doubt about its vociferous reaction if the lines or the action became too slow or too tame. Coarseness went down agreeably, but literary fineness might kill comedy or tragedy. If anything on the stage bored, the audience took to the dice or cards; and always there was much drinking of ale and widespread eating of fruits and sweets.[11]

C. Read or review the three methods of improving recognition vocabulary (pages 181–183). Summarize each method in a short paragraph; then condense your three paragraphs into one short one.

D. The following selection is a unit of a longer essay. Read it carefully with a view to purpose and organization. On a 4 × 6 inch note card summarize the first paragraph as the thesis of the selection. Then reduce each of the numbered sections to a single note-card summary. Finally, use your six note cards to write a one-paragraph summary of the selection.

ARE SOCIAL SCIENTISTS BACKWARD?[12]

In discussing the relative difficulties of analysis which the exact and inexact sciences face, let me begin with an analogy. Would you agree that swimmers are less skillful athletes than runners because swimmers do not move as fast as runners? You probably would not. You would quickly point out that water offers greater resistance to swimmers than the air and ground do to runners. Agreed, that is just the point. In seeking to solve their problems, the social scientists encounter greater resistance than the physical scientists. By that I do not mean to belittle the great accomplishments of physical

[11] From *The Theatre* by Sheldon Cheney. Reprinted by permission of Longmans, Green and Co., publishers.

[12] From "Are Social Scientists Backward?" by Donald L. Kemmerer, in the *American Association of University Professors Bulletin*, Autumn, 1948.

scientists who have been able, for example, to determine the structure of the atom without seeing it. That is a tremendous achievement; yet in many ways it is not so difficult as what the social scientists are expected to do. The conditions under which the social scientists must work would drive a physical scientist frantic. Here are five of those conditions. He can make few experiments; he cannot measure the results accurately; he cannot control the conditions surrounding the experiments; he is often expected to get quick results with slow-acting economic forces; and he must work with people, not with inanimate objects. Let us look at these conditions more closely.

1. Before a physical scientist will admit that his experiment has proved successful, he generally repeats it in his laboratory a great many times, sometimes hundreds of times. The economist, or the political scientist, however, has no laboratory other than the world before him, and its history. An economist who wants to find the effect of war on national income in the postwar period in major nations in modern times can uncover perhaps a score of usable examples. The business-cycle analyst knows that business cycles are a product of only the past century and a half, and that the major business cycles in leading industrial nations are comparatively few in number.

2. Chemists and physicists can weigh and otherwise measure solids, liquids, and gases fairly accurately, but the economist has less effective means of measurement. True, statisticians have devised many ways of correlating figures, determining and eliminating margins of error, and so forth, to the nth decimal point. Unfortunately, this exact mathematics is all too often used to measure units of differing quality or figures collected under uncontrolled conditions. Being able to measure to the nth decimal place has less meaning under such circumstances.

One or two examples will illustrate the point. For the past generation Americans have attached increasing importance to wholesale price indexes and cost-of-living indexes. As you know, in calculating these, a so-called normal year like 1896, 1913, 1926, or 1939 is selected as a base, and prices of several hundred representative goods and services are collected for that year and allotted their proper importance or weight in figuring the index. The prices of these same goods and services are again collected and similarly weighted for each subsequent year. This is done every month now. These indexes have proved extremely useful to social scientists, and I do not want to underestimate their importance. They do have their limitations, however.

According to Bureau of Labor Statistics figures, the cost of living in December, 1947, was 136 per cent higher than it was in 1913. The comparison cannot be so accurate as that. For example, the quality of many of the manufactured goods involved in the 1913 index has improved greatly. Automobile tires cost about the same but will run five times as many miles before wearing out; also gasoline will carry the car farther; and, of course, the cars themselves are greatly improved. Transportation by car or train is faster, thereby saving valuable time; medical knowledge is better so that the average doctor's advice is worth more; fuel for heating homes is cleaner; and so on.

To take a more modern example of difficulties in using indexes, some of you may recall the Battle of the Indexes that raged in 1944. The government maintained that the cost of living had risen only about 23.1 per cent since January, 1941, and did not justify further wage increases, but the AFL and the CIO contended that 43.5 per cent was a more accurate measurement.

That was a sizable difference of opinion. The labor statisticians emphasized that some important goods in the index were simply not available at OPA prices and could be obtained only on the black market. All of us had some experience with the poorer quality of numerous wartime goods and learned firsthand that items like white shirts or rented houses were virtually unobtainable at the ceiling prices on which the indexes were based. Under the circumstances, price indexes should be regarded as valuable trend indicators but should not be accepted as highly accurate measuring devices. When someone starts analyzing a price index to explain why it has risen, say 0.45 of 1 per cent, skepticism is in order. Yet it is by such accurate measurements that physical scientists reach significant conclusions.

3. The physical scientist can generally control the conditions surrounding his experiments, whereas the social scientist cannot. As my colleague, Professor Ralph Blodgett, has neatly described the situation, "The student of chemistry, for example, can place a quantity of iron filings in a test tube, cover them with a certain amount of hydrochloric acid under controlled conditions, and be fairly confident of being able to observe and measure the results accurately. The economist cannot place the consumer in a test tube, pour a solution of lowered prices over him, and measure the results. Instead, he must rely on his observations of the consumer in the ordinary business of life where he will react to lowered prices in some way or other, amid a welter of other influences."

Let us take the example of a specific economic experiment. In 1933–34 the government, on advice of certain economists, devalued the gold dollar by 41 per cent. It was expected by the authors of this scheme that it would shortly raise the price level by 69 per cent and thereby restore prices to the so-called normal level of 1926. The purpose was to lighten the debt burden of farmers and others. But the wholesale price level rose only about 21 per cent in the next two years, much less than the experimenters anticipated. Even this disappointing rise could not be definitely ascribed to any single cause. There was good reason for believing some of it was owing to severe droughts, some to the AAA program, some to price increases due to rising wage and other costs under the NRA, and some to normal recovery from the depths of the depression. How much of the price rise was due to each of these? Who can do more than make a rough guess?

4. At this point some thoughtful person may interject, "Ah, but you are asking too much to expect the full results of that experiment to be apparent in so short a time as two years." The objection is well taken. In fact, the matter of time is the fourth difficulty which the social scientist must attempt to solve and yet cannot solve very well. The longer time he allows for his experiment to work out, the more extraneous factors are likely to creep in; and the shorter the time he allows, the more open he is to the accusation that his experiment is incomplete. Yet as the country and the world become more populous and more industrialized, the longer it takes economic and other forces to make themselves felt. At the same time, if the experimenting social scientist is, say, a government economist trying out some plan he has sold the administration, he must be able to show results quickly, convincingly, and on the first try. Otherwise, his theory is tagged as a failure. Would the physical scientists like to make experiments under such conditions?

5. Another reason a government economist's experiment may fail is that people are necessarily the subject of the experiment; they know they are the subject, and they may want the experiment to succeed or to fail. In wartime, by economizing and working harder than usual to help win the war and combat inflation, they may successfully delay the operation of inflationary forces. Or people may sabotage an experiment because they dislike the political and economic philosophy behind it — many persons found the intricate regulations of NRA and OPA distasteful — or because the experiment hurts their pocketbook or the prestige they enjoy in their business, or both. The nature and purpose of any experiment cannot long be kept secret in a democracy. Increased pump-priming by the government in the latter 1930's seems to have made businessmen more distrustful. It slowed down the turnover of currency and the investment of risk capital and partially neutralized just what pump-priming was intended to achieve. As late as 1940 we still had considerable depression left if a figure of ten million unemployed means anything. Professor Joseph Schumpeter of Harvard went so far as to say about that time that recovery from depression had been slowest where the greatest efforts had been made by governments to promote it — in France and in the United States.

Let us take another example. There has been a fairly serious depression in every major nation after every long war in modern times. We have been expecting one almost daily since V-J day in August of 1945. Government economists were especially sure in 1945 that widespread unemployment would follow the war and urged the administration to lay its plans accordingly and the public to prepare for the worst. But the depression has not come yet. It is frequently said that when a depression does come, it will be the best advertised one in history. This may be one important reason that it does not come, or at least that it has been so long delayed. To sum up the situation: the physical scientist does not have to contend with iron filings that resist being dissolved or whose character may change because they expect to be dissolved.

Once you understand the social scientist's difficulties, you will have more patience with him. You will recognize that he can make few experiments, that even history offers him few clear-cut, documentable examples, and that he therefore has to supplement his findings with logic and intangible common sense. That is admittedly to depart from the realm of science and to invade that of judgment. It is at this point that the social scientist is most apt to make mistakes and that disagreements are most likely to arise. You should therefore be most skeptical when he relies on logic alone; yet at the same time you have to admit the necessity for his doing so.

In the past two generations few new principles have been established in the social sciences. This is contrary to the layman's beliefs, but it is true. If you doubt it, name some. True, many interesting theories have been advanced, but most of them have not been widely accepted. The reasons, it may be surmised, lie in the five difficulties just described, namely, fewness of experiments, uncontrolled conditions, difficulties of measuring results, concluding experiments at the right time, and resistance by the subject of the experiment. Even if the social scientists eventually accept some of the new theories as principles, it will take many more years before the public and its leaders do likewise.

10

The Essay-Type Examination

The essay-type examination is one of the most practical of all composition assignments. By requiring a student to compose in one or more paragraphs an answer to a specific problem, it calls forth most of the skills which the composition course tries to develop. It tests the student's ability to read accurately and to write purposefully within a rigid time limit. It is thus as much a test of thinking and writing ability as of knowledge.

Failure to recognize this fact usually leads to unsatisfactory answers and poor grades. Instructors frequently complain that the worst student writing is done on essay-type examinations. Of course the pressure under which examinations are written is not conducive to stylistic finish. But the chief weaknesses of examination answers are not that they are ungrammatical or awkward but that they are not *composed* at all. The student does not first plan what he wants to say and then develop his intention into an adequate answer; too often he begins to write without any clear purpose and assumes that as long as he is writing he is answering the question. The result is frequently an answer which is irrelevant, inadequate, unclear, and even self-contradictory.

The purpose of this chapter is to help students get better grades on essay-type examinations by sketching the procedure of taking such a test and by analyzing good and bad answers. This chapter, of course, cannot teach the content of examination answers. A student who does not know his subject will not learn here how to conceal his ignorance. But many of the serious errors in examination papers are caused by careless thinking and writing rather than by ignorance. It is with these faults that this chapter is concerned.

Recommended Procedure

Listed below are ten recommendations for taking an essay-type examination. There is one other that may be considered a prerequisite for these ten: that is, that a satisfactory answer must first of all be legible. Anything that seriously interferes with ease of reading — careless or crowded handwriting, excessive scoring-out, failure to indicate which question is being answered, or penciled writing which is too faint to read — is bound to affect an instructor's evaluation of the answer. College instructors do not grade on neatness. An occasional erasure or revision between the lines is not objectionable. But an instructor who has difficulty deciphering your answer certainly cannot have a high opinion of it. Therefore, you owe it to yourself and your instructor to see that your paper is reasonably easy to read.

1. Come prepared. The best preparation for an essay-type examination is conscientious attention to the daily assignments followed by a general review before the examination. This review should focus on the major emphases in the course. An essay-type examination is not suited to testing knowledge of a large number of details. Essentially it tests the student's ability to grasp main ideas, form generalizations of his own from the facts, and select and relate details to develop the generalization. It tests thinking, not simply memory. For this reason, a grasp of the major points is more useful than memorizing a host of isolated facts. Indeed, a student who attempts to prepare himself by cramming his mind with detailed information is likely to find himself in the state traditionally described as being unable to see the forest for the trees.

2. Come relaxed. The essay-type examination requires more sustained concentration than does an objective test. A three-hour essay examination is a strenuous intellectual exercise. All things being equal, a student who is fresh and relaxed will do better work than one who is tired and tense; yet the practice of going short on sleep the night before a final examination in order to allow the time for a final review is still a traditional means of preparation. Such a practice is sometimes worse than useless, especially for a student who has a reasonable grasp of the course content. The final preparation for an essay-type examination should be eight hours of sleep.

3. Before beginning to answer any part of the examination, read it through, paying special attention to the directions. If it serves no other purpose, this act will at least encourage a more deliberate attitude toward the examination. In their eagerness to start writing, some students ignore important directions or confuse the number of questions they are to answer. It is a wise discipline to survey any task before beginning it, and this habit is especially useful when some questions are marked as counting more toward the total grade than others.

4. If you are given a choice of questions, make your choice carefully but quickly, and then stick to it. Procrastination steals confidence as well as time. A student who shifts from one choice to another as soon as he strikes a snag is likely to have just as much trouble with his second choice. If any one of a choice of questions is definitely easier, that advantage should be obvious on first inspection.

5. Determine how much time is available for each question. This advice is often more necessary for good students than for poor ones. The student who knows the subject well and is eager to demonstrate his knowledge sometimes cannot resist the temptation to let himself go on the first question and to write four pages where only one was expected. Such a student should remember that examination questions are not opportunities to write all that can be said on the topic; they are invitations to write the best answer possible within the time limit. Usually each question receives a prescribed number of points so that no more can be given no matter how thorough or brilliant the answer. Therefore it is not possible to pile up on some questions extra credit to be used on others. If you feel that you want to say more on a question than time permits, leave a space at the end of your answer. Then, if you have time to spare after finishing all questions, you can make additional comment.

6. Read each question carefully before starting to answer it. Unwillingness to heed this advice is probably the greatest single cause of failure. We shall see later in this chapter examples of answers that failed because their authors began to write before they had learned what the question required. You should recognize that if you misinterpret the question your whole answer may be off the point. For that reason it is wise to ask before you begin to write: "What does this question require me to do?" Notice, especially, whether the question asks you to *explain, summarize, evaluate,* or *compare.* These are often key words in an essay-type question and each of them requires a different approach to the answer. Failure to recognize the implications of such key words could cause you to misinterpret the question.

7. Think out your general answer before you begin to develop it. Since there is almost no opportunity for rewriting in an essay examination, your answer must be satisfactory as it is put on paper. If a student has the purpose or topic sentence of his answer clearly in mind, explanatory and illustrative details will suggest themselves as he writes. But a student who has not determined what he wants to say before he begins may fall into either of two errors: he may unconsciously veer away from the question or he may write a series of unrelated sentences which do not add up to a unified answer. On some questions, it may be advisable to jot down on the back of the blue book or the mimeographed examination sheet the information you want to work into your answer; on others, framing the topic sentence will be preparation enough.

8. Remember that nothing so annoys a grader as a series of unsupported, unexplained generalizations. Next to irrelevance, vagueness is the chief sin of examination answers, and an answer which is too general is sure to be vague. So far as time permits, give the details which support your generalizations and, if possible, cite or suggest the textual sources for your observations. You will see this procedure repeatedly illustrated in the examination answers presented later.

9. When you have finished your answer, read it over critically to see if you have done what you intended to do. Even though extensive revision is impracticable, this rereading may suggest specific changes or a comment or illustration which you can insert between the lines or in the margin. It will also give you a chance to correct any obvious errors in grammar, spelling, or punctuation.

10. Above all, remember that an essay-type question requires an essay-type answer. If your instructor wanted an answer that could be given in a single sentence, he could have saved himself both time and effort by setting up the question as a completion-type or short-answer question.

Basic Errors

Given below are contrasted answers to a question on selected poems of Wordsworth and Byron in a sophomore examination in English literature. The students had one hour in which to develop a paragraph for each of the five parts of the question. The answers given on the left are those which the instructor hoped to receive; those on the right are unsatisfactory ones, taken from actual papers. Here is the question:

How do Wordsworth and Byron compare with respect to
A. Their choice of subjects
B. Their attitudes toward their subjects
C. Their appreciation of nature
D. Their attitudes toward the culture of their times
E. Their attitudes toward the French Revolution and Napoleon?

Here are the answers:

A

Choice of subjects. Wordsworth chose as the subjects of his poetry incidents and experiences drawn from rustic life, whether they occurred to himself (*Prelude*) or to others (*Michael*). In general these incidents are undramatic but owe their interest to the poet's treatment of them. Byron preferred dramatic events — legends of ill-fated lovers (*Bride of Abydos*), the exploits of amorous adventurers (*Don Juan*), or accounts of the travels and reflections of his autobiographical hero, Childe Harold.

Wordsworth chose incidents and situations from common, rustic life. Byron wrote descriptions of nature, and of his ridicule of sham and his keen insight into the hearts of men. He often wrote of one man and of his many escapades and trials.

COMMENT: The answer lacks specific illustration. It does not identify a single poem by either poet, and the contrast is too general to provide a clear answer to the question. As a result, the student seems to have only a hazy knowledge of the poetry; yet on an objective quiz over the poems mentioned at the left he showed that he was familiar with them.

217

B

Attitudes toward their subjects. In general Wordsworth adopted a serious, sympathetic, and dignified attitude toward his subjects. He tended to idealize his rustic heroes (*Michael, The Leechgatherer, The Solitary Reaper*) and to see poetic and universal implications in common incidents and people (*My Heart Leaps Up, The Ode*). Byron's attitude varies with his subject. He is sympathetic with the victims of oppression (*The Prisoner of Chillon*), satirical with contemporary writers (*English Bards*) and with social mores (*Don Juan*), and in *Don Juan* he is serious, indignant, satirical, and flippant in different parts of the poem.

Wordsworth generally dealt with humble rustic people because he felt that the character and language of such people were suited to poetry. Byron seldom wrote of humble people. He usually dealt with romantic episodes in the life of one individual. A great deal of his poetry is about himself.

COMMENT: This answer was written by the same student who answered A above. Clearly, he is still answering the previous question. His failure to distinguish between related but separate questions causes him to repeat. He simply has not read the question intelligently.

C

Their appreciation of nature. Both men appreciated nature, but Wordsworth's reactions were more intense. Byron was interested chiefly in impressive or dramatic scenery — the ocean and the mountains. For him the beauty of such scenes was an antidote for world-weariness (*Childe Harold*) or a contrast between the insignificance of man and the power of nature ("Roll on thou deep and dark blue ocean"). For Wordsworth, nature is the embodiment of the mystic power which pervades all living things. It not only pleases and refreshes him; it dominates him and becomes his intellectual and moral guide (*Tintern Abbey, The Tables Turned*). His reactions are essentially religious rather than esthetic.

Wordsworth says that you will learn more from nature than from all the teachers and books. This was stated in *The Tables Turned*. In *Lines Written in Early Spring* he states that nature has made everything beautiful and in *The Prelude* he tells of his love of nature. Byron's appreciation was less sensitive. He presented nature as he saw it, usually with pictorial realism.

COMMENT: The answer on Wordsworth is not general enough. It cites two pieces of evidence but draws no conclusion. The answer on Byron is too general and vague. The examiner will have to guess what the last sentence means. The whole answer shows a paragraph being written one sentence at a time without concern for the relation between sentences. The student has not thought out his answer before beginning to write. So he fails to present a clear-cut contrast.

D

Their attitudes toward the culture of their times. Both condemn their culture, but for different reasons. Wordsworth condemns the material- ism and lack of mystery (*The World Is Too Much With Us*); he regrets the indifference to cultural values (Cambridge in *The Prelude*); and he misses the free, dignified, and dis- ciplined spirit which he thought existed in Milton's time. Byron con- demns the hypocrisy of social life, the smug and dull standard of virtue represented by Southey, polite edu- cation (as represented by the educa- tion of Don Juan), and the political autocracy which he found dominant in Britain, France, and Greece (*Childe Harold*).

Wordsworth regarded the culture of his time as superficial. His atti- tude was that the literature of his time placed too much emphasis on sensational incidents and situations and thus encouraged an artificial cul- ture. Byron regarded the other liter- ary products of his time as being far below the level of his own works. He illustrates this by his denunciation of the work of contemporary poets.

COMMENT: This student has inter- preted the question too narrowly. His answer would be much more satis- factory if the question had been con- fined to literature, but it was not. His answer is incomplete.

E

Their attitudes toward the French Revolution and Napoleon. Both men at first welcomed the French Revolu- tion and the rise of Napoleon; both later turned against them. Words- worth changed first. He was ready at one time to throw in his lot with the revolutionists (*Prelude*), but their excesses and a conservative inclina- tion made him increasingly unsym- pathetic. Byron seems to have been less shocked by the terror of the rev- olution and more shocked by the apostasy of Napoleon. His attack on Napoleon in *Childe Harold* is bitter, all the more bitter because of Byron's appreciation of what Napoleon might have done for Europe.

Wordsworth was opposed to the French Revolution and to Napoleon's tyranny; Byron first admired Napo- leon but later denounced him.

COMMENT: While this answer is correct, it is inadequate because the student fails to develop it. It is merely the topic sentence of a satis- factory answer. What the examiner still wants to know is why Words- worth was opposed, and where he recorded his opposition; and why Byron admired Napoleon and where he denounced him. Since the student had more than ten minutes in which to develop his answer, a single sen- tence is not enough.

Now here is an important point to notice about all the answers at the right. The students who wrote them were not ignorant of the subject. Most of them, under questioning, could show in class discussion that they knew the poems. They did poorly on the examination because their procedures were bad. Two of the five answers were unsatisfactory because their authors failed to read the question carefully to see what it required. The other three answers were so general that they failed to develop clearly or convincingly the contrast which the question required. In other words, the answers were poor because they were badly composed.

By contrast, the answers at the left are pertinent, adequate, and well illustrated. They do the job required and avoid digressions or irrelevant details. They develop the general answer in enough detail to point the contrast so that it will be clear to a reader. And they illustrate their points by naming particular poems.

A subtler error, one that often separates an average answer from a superior one, is failure to bring the answer to a focus. The student discusses the question but does not quite answer it. He provides a substantial body of factual material, but his facts are not exactly pertinent. Consider, for example, the following contrasted answers to the question: "Illustrate the differences between early and late Renaissance painting by contrasting Fra Filippo Lippi's *Madonna and Child* with Raphael's *Sistine Madonna*."

C Answer

Filippo's picture is simply designed, and the figures are naturalistic. The Madonna is sweet, gracious, and human, dressed in the mode of the times. The Bambino is a natural, playful child. He is being lifted up by two older boys — undoubtedly Fra Filippo's family posed for the picture. The background is a stylized landscape of rocks and streams, bounded by a frame. The Madonna is seated in a chair with an elaborately carved arm which stands out in the foreground.

Raphael designed the Sistine Madonna in a pyramid with the Madonna herself at the apex. She carries the curly-haired Child, and although she is standing still, her garments swirl as in a strong wind. One's eye is first caught by the figure of Pope Sixtus at the lower left, and through the folds of his garment and his uplifted eyes, drawn toward the central figure of the Virgin. Her garments, billowing to the right, draw the eye downward again to the figure of St. Barbara, kneeling on a cloud. Her eyes are

A Answer

Fra Filippo's picture is a good example of early Renaissance naturalism. The Madonna — his own wife — is wearing a stylish gown, which is painted in faithful detail. Her hair is dressed in the mode of the time. She is seated — as though in her own home — on an elaborately carved chair, with a framed painting of a landscape serving as the background. Her pose and expression are calm, perhaps devout, but neither exalted nor humble. She is an ordinary worldly mother with a chubby baby, who is being lifted to her rather ungracefully by a saucy angel. The entire scene is intimate, personal, and joyous, but hardly reverent. Filippo, pleased with the new-found technical mastery of his age, is content to paint what he sees.

Raphael was able to get above his technique and make it expressive of lofty emotion. The figures in the *Sistine Madonna* are monumental and stand out against a subdued background. The Madonna, her feet resting weightlessly on a cloud, wears an

cast down, and the glance follows hers to discover two jaunty cherubs leaning on the lower frame. They look upward, thus deflecting the eyes of the beholder up again, completing the movement of the design. This painting is one of the high points of the development of Renaissance art.

expression of sublime dignity. She holds with graceful ease the Child, whose sober eyes reveal the portent of His future. The figures wear classic robes, whose flowing lines give a wonderful, circling movement to the painting. A cloud of tiny cherubs' heads, peeping through the effulgence surrounding the Virgin, completes the heavenly setting. Where Filippo's work is mere copying, Raphael's is imaginative and spiritual. This loftiness of conception combined with grace of design and beauty of execution is the flower of the High Renaissance.

What is the difference between these two answers? Why did one receive an average and the other an excellent grade? Both are roughly the same length; both are well written; both show an intimate knowledge of the pictures they are contrasting. The difference is essentially one of the selection of details. The answer at the left is unsatisfactory because it drifted away from the question. What the student actually wrote was a description of the *Madonna and Child* and another description of the *Sistine Madonna*. The details she presents describe the pictures effectively, but they do not contrast the differences between early and late Renaissance painting. Therefore her answer does not satisfy the question. The answer at the right selects those details which illustrate the differences between the two periods, and thus gives purpose to the contrast between the pictures. The author is not merely describing two pictures; she is describing the characteristics which make them represent their periods. That is what the question required.

All the errors we have been considering are of three general kinds: (1) failure to read the question carefully enough to see what it required; (2) failure to provide the detailed treatment necessary for an adequate answer; (3) failure to point up the significance of factual information. The first error is a failure to analyze the assignment and is therefore a basic error in determining its purpose, not unlike the purposeless essay we saw on pages 4–5. The other two are errors in composition, failures to see how the writer must go about the task which the assignment requires of him.

Exercises

A. Read the following imaginary case history and write an analysis of John's errors.

John Doe wanted to do a good job in his examination on English literature. He just had to get a C in the course or he would be ineligible for initiation into his fraternity. True, his grade at midsemester had been D, and most of the semester he had known that he had been slighting his work. But he had really studied hard the last two weeks. When he went to bed at two o'clock on the morning of the examination, he was, as he told his roommate, all set for anything old Jonesy could throw at him. But, just to be safe, he set the alarm an hour early and got in a good hour's cramming before examination time. Indeed, he studied longer than he meant to, and though he ran all the way to class, he arrived, out of breath, after the test had begun. He sat down, puffing, sticky, and a little embarrassed.

As soon as he received his copy of the examination he read the first question hastily and began to write. After a few minutes he had an uncomfortable feeling that his answer was getting off the track; so he crossed it out and began over again. His new answer started out confidently, but after three sentences he felt he had said all he had to say on the question. But this was an essay-type test. The directions said "Write at least a paragraph." John restated in different words what he had already said and was relieved to find that his answer now looked like a normal paragraph.

The second question was a pure gift. It dealt with the one part of the course that John knew thoroughly. He had been hoping this question would be asked, and here it was. What a break! He wrote with unusual intensity. From the very first sentence he knew he was writing well. No need to worry about stretching this answer into a paragraph. Of its own accord it grew into a page, then two pages. Midway on the third page John finished, tired but glowing. He reread his answer with scarcely-decreased enthusiasm. He changed a couple of words and added a clinching sentence which suddenly occurred to him. That made it just about perfect.

He began the third question with a new sense of confidence, but his pen ran dry. He looked around anxiously and finally observed a student three rows away with a bottle of ink on his desk. He was embarrassed at having to disturb several people to fill his pen, and when he returned to his seat his confident mood had disappeared. In an attempt to recapture it he reread the last page of his second answer, but that did not help, except to catch a couple of misspellings. Mechanically he ground out an answer to question three, hoping the instructor would see what he had in mind.

The fourth question was a difficult one. John started a tentative answer and stopped. The directions said he was to write on six of the eight questions. He would skip four and do five. Unfortunately, the fifth question was as bad as the fourth. After a few preliminary passes at it, John scored out his answer and moved to number six. As he did so, the instructor announced that only ten minutes remained.

For a moment the announcement threw John into a panic. Ten minutes in which to do three questions! He read the remaining questions hurriedly, looking for an easy one; then he went back to question four and wrote whatever came into his head. There was no time now to worry whether the answer was completely satisfactory. The thing to do was to get an answer of any kind. He was perspiring when he moved to question six, but his resolution to put down some kind of answer helped him through. He wrote a fair-sized paragraph before the bell rang. Then, while the papers were being collected, he managed a one-sentence stab at question seven.

John left the examination room somewhat shaken in his assurance of getting a C. But the memory of his answer to the second question revived him. And, after all, he had answered all six questions. Even if his last answer was short he would get partial credit for it. On the way to the fraternity house he was enjoying the probability of a B.

B. Below are given an examination question and three answers. Read the question carefully; then study each of the answers and write a short report in which you select the best answer and show why it is superior to the others.

Question: Just before he dies, Laertes says to Hamlet, "Mine and my father's death come not on thee, nor thine on me." Discuss specifically the relation of this statement to the facts.

Answer 1: Laertes returns from France and learns that his father has been killed by Hamlet. He is almost mad with grief and rage and in a stormy scene with the king he demands revenge. He and the king conspire to arrange a duel between Laertes and Hamlet in which Laertes will use a poisoned sword. The duel takes place after Ophelia's funeral, and Laertes cuts Hamlet with the poisoned sword. Then, in a scuffle, their swords are knocked from their hands and Hamlet picks up Laertes' sword and wounds him. Meanwhile the king has put poison in a goblet of wine he intended for Hamlet, but the queen drinks it instead. When Hamlet sees she is dying he kills the king; then both Hamlet and Laertes die.

Answer 2: Laertes' statement fits some of the facts but not all of them and is best understood as a rationalization or as a request to let bygones be bygones. True, Hamlet is not responsible for Laertes' death, because Hamlet thought he was engaging in a friendly bout with blunted swords. When he picked up Laertes' sword in the mix-up he did not know it was poisoned. Since Laertes deliberately put the poison there, he was responsible for both Hamlet's death and his own. Hamlet killed Polonius by mistake, thinking that the person behind the curtain was the king. To that extent it was an accidental killing, but a killing nevertheless. I think Laertes' statement is not intended as a literal description of the facts but as a reconciliation speech. I interpret the statement as meaning: "We have both been the victims of the king's treachery. Forgive me for your death, as I forgive you for mine and my father's."

Answer 3: The statement is not true. Hamlet did kill Polonius, and Laertes did kill Hamlet. As for Laertes' death, that was his own fault.

C. Select any four of the following topics. Without consulting the textbook, for each topic write a short paragraph that explains the topic accurately. Then check your answer against the appropriate pages in the textbook and make any revisions you think necessary.

1. The relation between purpose and planning in an essay
2. The meaning of "development" in an essay
3. The characteristics of a good thesis
4. The relationship between symbol and referent
5. The difference between connotation and denotation
6. The difference between formal and colloquial style

D. For any course you are now taking write a series of essay-type questions which seem to you to constitute a fair examination. Word the questions carefully so that a good answer will show both a knowledge of the facts and an ability to draw valid conclusions from them. Discuss your questions with friends or classmates and plan satisfactory answers. Then develop your plan into a set of finished answers which may be filed as review material for the course.

11

Using the Library

The library is an indispensable part of higher education because it provides the literature of all areas of study and research. As you progress through college, your courses will require more and more use of an ever-wider variety of library materials. It will be to your advantage to learn, as early as possible, the titles and location in your library of the chief works of general reference and also the standard "specialized" sources in your chosen field of study. Although this chapter will give you an introduction to these, you may want to acquire for your personal book collection Jean Key Gates's *Guide to the Use of Books and Libraries*,[1] available in a paperbound edition, which gives more extensive and detailed information.

The Card Catalog

A card catalog is a register of all the materials held by a library. It consists of cases of trays in which 3 × 5 inch cards, marked with information, are filed alphabetically. A single tray of cards looks like this:

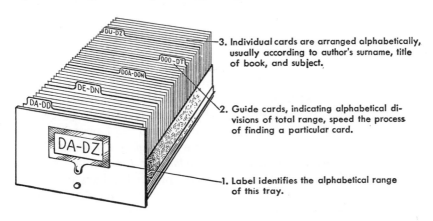

3. Individual cards are arranged alphabetically, usually according to author's surname, title of book, and subject.

2. Guide cards, indicating alphabetical divisions of total range, speed the process of finding a particular card.

1. Label identifies the alphabetical range of this tray.

In most libraries today the card catalog has several kinds of cards filed together according to the first *significant* word on the topmost line of the card. An "author card" has the author's surname first on the top line, a "title card" has the title on the top line, and a "subject card" has a subject

[1] New York: McGraw-Hill Book Company, 1962.

heading at the top. There should be at least one of each kind of card for every book.

Here is a typical author card:

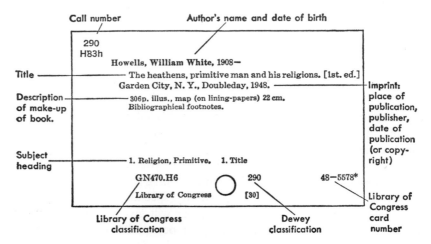

Call number   Author's name and date of birth

290
H83h

Howells, William White, 1908—

Title ———— The heathens, primitive man and his religions. [1st. ed.]
Garden City, N. Y., Doubleday, 1948. ————

Description ———— 306p. illus., map (on lining-papers) 22 cm.
of make-up   Bibliographical footnotes.
of book.

Subject ———— 1. Religion, Primitive.   1. Title
heading

GN470.H6   290   48—5578*
Library of Congress   [30]

Imprint:
place of
publication,
publisher,
date of
publication
(or copy-
right)

Library of
Congress
card
number

Library of Congress   Dewey
classification   classification

This is a facsimile (reduced) of an author card manufactured by the Library of Congress for use in all libraries. It contains the basic and authentic information about the book. The call number (see page 227) is added by the individual library. A duplicate of this card becomes a title card when *The heathens* is typed above the author's name. Another duplicate becomes a subject card when *Religion, Primitive* is typed across the top, in capitals or in red ink. There will then be three cards in the catalog for this book, each filed in its alphabetical place — two in H-trays and one in an R-tray.

In this subject heading, *religion* is the dominant word, so the normal word order is inverted. In the heading *Religious education,* however, the word *education* is not considered dominant, and so comes last. Subject headings can be confusing to the student until he has become familiar with library terminology. Remember that subject headings are made as specific as possible, and that you will save time by looking *first* for the precise topic you have in mind. For example, if you want to read about St. Paul's Cathedral in London, you would look for *St. Paul's Cathedral,* not for *Churches — England* or *Cathedrals — England* or *London — Churches.*

The card catalog will help you to find the proper headings by means of "cross-reference cards." A "see" reference gives a heading that is not used and tells which related term can be found in the catalog:

Farming.   Humor.
See   *See*
Agriculture.   Wit and humor.

"See also" cards refer to headings under which similar materials are placed, and come at the end of the filing sequence:

Cocoa.
See also
Chocolate.

Pessimism.
See also
Optimism.

Classification Systems

Most academic libraries use either the Dewey Decimal System or the Library of Congress System for identifying and arranging materials on the shelves. Printed editions of these systems will be found at the main desk of the library, and brief versions may be posted in certain places. The Dewey Decimal System will be used as an example here.

The main divisions of the Dewey subject classification are as follows:

000–099	General Works	600–699	Applied Sciences
100–199	Philosophy and Psychology	700–799	Fine Arts and Recreation
200–299	Religion	800–899	Literature
300–399	Social Sciences	F	Fiction in English
400–499	Languages	900–999	History, Travel, Collected Biography
500–599	Pure Sciences	B	Individual Biography

Each piece of material is given a Dewey number and, in addition, a "book number" consisting of the initial of the author's surname followed by digits, as *H83*. Sometimes a small letter may be added to indicate the first word of the title, as *H83h*. The book number is written below the Dewey number, and together they comprise the "call number," which will be typed in the upper left-hand corner of each catalog card used for the book. There may also be added below these the year of a new edition of a work, or the volume number of a multivolume work. Because the *complete* call number is the most accurate designation of an individual book in a library collection, it must be copied *exactly* on a withdrawal slip in order to get the book referred to by the card.

Filing Rules

The following are widely accepted rules or conventions practiced by libraries in filing cards alphabetically, and a knowledge of them will help you make thorough and efficient use of the card catalog.

1. Filing is done word-by-word, or short-before-long, rather than letter-by-letter.

> North America
> North Sea
> Northanger Abbey
> Northern Ireland
> Northern Rhodesia
> The Northerners

2. Abbreviations and numbers are filed as though they were spelled out — *Dr. Faustus* will be found under *doctor*, *St. Lawrence* under *saint*, *U.S. News* under *United States*, *19th Century Authors* under *nineteenth*.

3. In personal names *Mac, Mc,* and *M'* are filed as though they were all *Mac*. The foreign prefixes *de, van,* and *von* are ignored — *Hindenburg, Paul von.*

4. Cards for books *by* an author are filed before those *about* him, and in between will be books of which he is a "joint author," that is, one whose name does not appear first on the title page.

5. For the same word or name, the filing order is person, place, title.

> Hudson, William Henry
> Hudson, N. J.
> The Hudson and its Moods

6. Titles are filed according to the first significant word, ignoring *a, an,* and *the* and their foreign equivalents.

7. Subjects are usually subdivided in alphabetical order, but history is divided chronologically.

Printing — Exhibitions	Italy — History — To 1559
Printing — Specimens	Italy — History — 1559–1789
Printing — Style manuals	Italy — History — 1789–1815

The Shelf List

In addition to the main alphabetical card catalog, every library maintains a "shelf list," or catalog of the books in the order in which they stand on the shelves. The shelf list consists of one 3 × 5 inch card for each item in the library collection, the cards being arranged in trays in the order of the call numbers. This is the subject catalog of the library, where you can find in one compact group of cards a list of the books the library has on any subject. You may not use the shelf list often, but you should know that it is possible by this means to check the library holdings in your special field of interest. In some instances, too, you may be referred to the shelf list to learn what issues of a periodical the library has, or in what location on campus a certain work can be found.

The Reference Collection

When you need to get information for your themes and research papers, you will go first to the reference room. There you will find dictionaries, encyclopedias, indexes, directories, handbooks, yearbooks, guides, and atlases covering almost every area of human knowledge. You should know what kinds of reference works are available and should become acquainted with the most important works of each kind.

Printed Catalogs

Catalogs in book form are often useful supplements to the card catalog of the library. The card catalog is a list only of books in the library, not of all books available.

Most academic libraries have the two great printed library catalogs, those of the British Museum and the Library of Congress. The former is a reliable source for older authors and titles, the latter for recent ones. Both are used more by scholars and librarians than by undergraduates.

Current publication lists are more generally useful, the main ones for the United States being these:

Cumulative Book Index. A monthly list of books published in the English language, except government documents. It is "cumulated" periodically, that is, several issues are combined into one volume.

Publishers' Trade List Annual. A collection of American and Canadian publishers' catalogs bound together.

Books in Print. The annual author-title index to the *Publishers' Trade List Annual.*

Subject Guide to Books in Print. Also published annually.

The main lists of periodicals and newspapers are the following:

Union List of Serials in Libraries of the United States and Canada. This is the most comprehensive single-volume guide, but it was last published in 1949.

New Serial Titles. A monthly supplement to the *Union List,* published since 1950 by the Library of Congress.

N. W. Ayer & Son's Directory of Newspapers and Periodicals. This is the best source of information about newspapers of the United States and its possessions.

Ulrich's Periodicals Directory. The broad coverage of foreign as well as domestic periodicals makes this volume important.

Indexes to Periodical Literature

Periodicals are publications, other than newspapers, which appear at regular intervals — weekly, monthly, quarterly, and so on. Since much of your writing will be based on periodical articles, and since these articles are not included in the card catalog, you will need to make use of periodical indexes. A "specialized index" includes only articles from periodicals in the field to which it is confined, as education or law. A "general index" is not restricted in subject matter.

The great general index of periodicals is the *Readers' Guide to Periodical Literature,* which indexes a selected list of American periodicals of a nontechnical nature. It is published semimonthly and cumulated biennially. At the front of each issue and each bound volume is a list of the more than 100 periodicals indexed, the abbreviations used for their titles, and a key to other abbreviations used, such as *por* for portrait. Although mainly a subject index, *Readers' Guide* lists some authors and titles, such as those of poems, plays, and operas. Here are some sample entries:[2]

ADAPTATION (biology)
   Animals in the snow. W. O. Pruitt, jr. il Sci Am 202:60–8 bibliog (p 188) Ja '60

Subject entry for an illustrated article in volume 202 of *Scientific American,* pages 60 through 68, with a bibliography on page 188, of the issue for January, 1960.

   Pool on Frenchman's bay. A. B. Adams. il Audubon Mag 62: 280–2+ N '60
      See also
Acclimatization
Evolution

The + means that this article is continued on other pages not immediately following page 282.

Cross reference to related subjects.

ADAPTATION (botany)
   Chemical basis for adaptation in plants. E. B. Kurtz, jr; reply. A. W. Galston. Science 129:357 F 13 '59

A second subdivision of the larger subject *adaptation.* Galston's reply to an earlier article by Kurtz appears on page 357 of the issue for February 13, 1959.

ADAPTATION, *Social.* See Adjustment, Social.

Cross reference from a heading not used to the one used.

ADCOCK, Irma Fitz
   Royal cloth of China; drama. Plays 20:49–55 F '61

Author entry.

ADD a dash of pity; story. See Ustinov, P.

Title entry referring reader to author entry.

When you find a reference to an article you wish to read, copy the entire entry and check your copy once before you move on. You will need to use all the parts of the entry: the *full title,* volume, number, and date of the periodical, to get the proper issue; the page numbers, to find the article; and all this information for your bibliography. Be sure to write down everything the first time, completely and accurately, so you will have to do it only once. This is the efficient way to work in the library.

For research on a technical or highly specialized topic you will need to consult a specialized periodical index, of which the most widely used are:

Agricultural Index
Applied Science and Technology Index
Art Index
Bibliographic Index

Biography Index
Biological Abstracts
Book Review Digest
Business Periodicals Index

[2] *Readers' Guide to Periodical Literature,* March 1959–February 1961 (New York: H. W. Wilson Company, 1961), p. 7.

Chemical Abstracts
Economic Abstracts
Education Index
Engineering Index
Essay and General Literature Index
Index Medicus
Index to Legal Periodicals
International Index
Nuclear Science Abstracts

Psychological Abstracts
Public Affairs Information Service Bulletin
Science Abstracts: A. Physics; B. Electrical Engineering
Social Science Abstracts
United Nations Documents Index
Zoological Record

Most of these titles are self-explanatory, but you should know that the *International Index* specializes in the humanities and the social sciences, giving references to a selected list of foreign and American periodicals. The *Public Affairs Information Service Bulletin* is an index to American social science publications, including books and pamphlets. The *Bibliographic Index* cites bibliographies published separately as well as those appended to foreign and American periodical articles. Some Indexes and all Abstracts give brief summaries of the contents of the materials listed.

The standard newspaper index for the United States is the *New York Times Index*. Published semimonthly and cumulated annually, this index will help you find the date of an event, so that you can consult the *Times,* or another newspaper of that date, for the comments of the press.

For quick reference and brief accounts of important news, the weekly world news digest, *Facts on File,* is useful. Published since 1940, it is indexed annually and every five years.

Government Documents

The bulk of government documents are neither cataloged nor indexed in periodical indexes; but two lists of documents are published by the United States government, and these lists are bound and kept in libraries — the *Monthly Catalog of United States Government Publications* and the *Monthly Checklist of State Publications.*

General Encyclopedias

The chief general encyclopedias for the college level are the *Encyclopaedia Britannica* and the *Encyclopedia Americana*. The *Britannica* is no longer published in England, but the influence of its distinguished British contributors since its beginning, in 1771, remains. If you are interested in the humanities, you should know that among scholars the eleventh edition of the *Britannica* enjoys the highest repute for the quality of its articles in that area. The *Americana,* the second oldest of the general encyclopedias, is also scholarly in approach.

The *Columbia Encyclopedia* is a good one-volume work which is being added to by supplements.

Yearbooks

Yearbooks are devoted to the chief occurrences of the preceding year and are published as quickly as possible after its close. Each of the major encyclopedias publishes an annual supplement as a means of keeping its material up to date, and these you will find shelved with the parent sets.

Two general yearbooks published in paper covers, either of which would make a good addition to a student's personal library, are:

Information Please Almanac, Atlas and Yearbook. Named for a once-popular radio program, this is a handy collection of events, records, and statistics for the year, with some pictures and maps. The tables contain historical material.

World Almanac and Book of Facts. The older and more conservative almanac. Material is taken mostly from newspapers.

There are many yearbooks in specialized fields. Some, such as the *Social Work Year Book,* are published every two or three years. Some, such as the *Yearbook of Agriculture* and the *Yearbook of the National Society for the Study of Education,* provide thorough coverage of one topic each year.

For information on governmental matters, there are several valuable publications. All but the first of these are annuals:

Book of States. A biennial publication giving data on state governments.

Congressional Directory. Gives detailed information about Congress.

Statesman's Year-book. A British publication covering the nations of the world. Gives political and economic data.

Statistical Abstract of the United States. Published by the Bureau of the Census. Gives data on political, economic, and social institutions.

United States Government Organization Manual. Describes the departments of government and prints the Constitution of the United States.

Yearbook of the United Nations. Has résumés of the sessions of the General Assembly, and reports on the other activities of the U.N.

Specialized Sources

The following list identifies the best reference works for undergraduates in several large areas of specialization. The arrangement is alphabetical by title. For complete bibliographic details, omitted here to save space, you may consult the standard source, *Winchell's Guide to Reference Books.*[3]

Biography

Chambers's Biographical Dictionary. A general work with commentaries on people and events, and with an unusually useful subject index.

Current Biography; Who's News and Why. An annual publication of sketches about contemporary celebrities, with photographs.

[3] Constance M. Winchell, *Guide to Reference Books,* 7th ed. (Chicago: American Library Association, 1951). *Supplements, 1950–1952, 1953–1955, 1956–1958.*

Dictionary of American Biography. A multivolume set containing scholarly articles about important Americans no longer living.

Dictionary of National Biography. The British equivalent of the above. These two are the classic biographical works.

National Cyclopaedia of American Biography. More than fifty volumes to date, containing a broad coverage of American historical biography.

New Century Cyclopedia of Names. Includes literary characters, names from myths and legends, places, and events, in one volume.

Webster's Biographical Dictionary. One volume of brief factual data and pronunciation of names of famous persons of history.

Who's Who. An annual listing of prominent living British persons, with abbreviated biographical data. *Who Was Who* is a separate list of the biographees now deceased, with date of death.

Who's Who in America. A biennial equivalent of the British work, with the companion volume *Who Was Who in America.*

Who's Who in ——. Besides those of other countries, there are many specialized publications using this general title, such as *Who's Who in Atoms* and *Who's Who in New England.* There is an *International Who's Who* and an *American Catholic Who's Who.* Other comparable lists of living persons can be found under different titles, such as *American Men of Science, Directory of American Scholars, Standard American-Jewish Directory,* and *Leaders in Education.*

Education

American Junior Colleges. Published by the American Council on Education. Gives detailed basic information on each institution.

American Universities and Colleges. A companion publication to the above.

Dictionary of Education. Gives definitions of educational and related terms.

Education Directory. Published by the U.S. Office of Education in four sections, listing institutions, educational officers, and education associations. All levels, from city to federal.

Education for the Professions. By the U.S. Office of Education. Gives the over-all picture of higher education in the United States for each profession.

Encyclopedia of Educational Research. The most important source in the field. Published about every ten years, contains articles by educational leaders on developments in various aspects of education.

The Foundation Directory. Lists foundations supporting educational research and programs.

Mental Measurements Yearbook. Appears every four or five years. Reviews tests, and refers to reviews published elsewhere.

Scholarships, Fellowships, and Loans. Three volumes through 1955.

Study Abroad. An annual publication of UNESCO.

World of Learning. An annual list of educational, scientific, and cultural organizations of the world.

World Survey of Education. A three-volume publication of UNESCO. The first volume deals with education in general, the second with primary education, the third with secondary education; by countries.

Fine Arts

Adeline's Art Dictionary. An old but classic source for definitions of art terms.

American Art Directory. Source for names and information of museums, art schools, art associations, and art publications.

Ballet Annual. A yearbook of events in ballet, published in England.

Dance Encyclopedia. All forms of dance are discussed in articles by specialists.

Dictionary of Architecture and Building. Although old, the standard dictionary in this field in English.

Encyclopedia of Jazz. One volume with definitions, history, biography, discography.

Encyclopedia of Painting. Covers the world from prehistoric times; includes appraisals of paintings.

Encyclopedia of World Art. An exhaustive treatment of the subject in a projected fifteen-volume set, six volumes of which are in print to date.

Focal Encyclopedia of Photography. One volume on a newly recognized art form.

Grove's Dictionary of Music and Musicians. A classic multivolume British work, kept up to date by supplements.

Harvard Dictionary of Music. A reputable one-volume work.

History of American Sculpture. Edited by Lorado Taft.

History of Architecture. By Sir Banister Fletcher. A standard work with a new edition in 1961.

International Cyclopedia of Music and Musicians. A one-volume compilation of broad scope.

New Oxford History of Music. A complete replacement for a classic English work, three volumes having been produced from 1954 to 1962.

Oxford Companion to the Theatre. Includes history of the popular theater.

Theater and Allied Arts. A guide to the literature of the theater.

History

Cambridge Histories: Ancient, Medieval, and *Modern.* The greatest multivolume histories, published by the Cambridge University Press. The oldest of these, the *Cambridge Modern History,* is presently being replaced by an entirely new publication based on recent scholarship, called the *New Cambridge Modern History.* Six volumes have been published from 1957 to 1962.

Dictionary of American History. A multivolume work edited by James Truslow Adams, with short articles. A companion volume is the *Atlas of American History.*

Dictionary of Dates. A chronology of historical events.

Encyclopedia of American History. A one-volume compendium of events, facts, and biographies.

Encyclopedia of World History. Similar to the above, chronologically arranged.

Guide to Historical Literature. A valuable bibliography of selected works in history.

Guide to the Study of the United States of America. A source book of the literature, published by the Library of Congress.

Harvard Guide to American History. Compiled and published at Harvard University, this is a selective book of information on resources.

Oxford History of England. One of several Oxford histories, all representative of excellent scholarship.

Shepherd's *Historical Atlas.* First published in 1911, and in its eighth edition in 1956, this book of maps on historical principles covers world history from ancient to modern times, with emphasis on European history.

Literature

Allibone's Dictionary of Authors. An older standard work.

American Authors 1600–1900, British Authors Before 1800, British Authors of the Nineteenth Century, Junior Book of Authors, Twentieth Century Authors. A series edited by Stanley Kunitz and Howard Haycraft.

Bartlett's *Familiar Quotations.* Commonly called by the name of its original compiler, the best-known of several books of quotations from prose and poetry, identifying authors and works.

Cambridge Bibliography of English Literature. A major work in four volumes and one supplement, covering books published to the mid-1950's.

Cambridge History of American Literature. Dated 1921, but still a classic.

Cambridge History of English Literature. A fifteen-volume standard set covering literature to 1927.

Columbia Dictionary of Modern European Literature. Begins just before the turn of the century, gives critical comment.

Granger's Index to Poetry. An index of collections of poetry.

Index to Children's Poetry. Similar to the above.

Index to Fairy Tales, Myths, and Legends. A literary guide.

A Literary History of England. A useful one-volume work, edited by Albert C. Baugh and published in 1948.

Literary History of the United States. Sometimes identified by the name of one of its editors, R. E. Spiller, this is an evaluative three-volume work, published in 1948, the third volume a bibliography. A supplementary volume brings the bibliography up to 1958.

Oxford Companions to: American Literature, English Literature, Classical Literature, French Literature. Useful volumes for quick reference.

Oxford History of English Literature. A new compilation begun in 1947, with twelve volumes projected.

Play Index. One volume, annotated.

Short Story Index. Published in 1953, with supplements through 1958.

Mythology and Classics

Atlas of the Classical World. An English publication of 1959.

Dictionary of Greek and Roman Biography and Mythology. Sir William Smith, editor. Although originally published in 1880, this three-volume work is still useful.

Dictionary of Non-Classical Mythology. Source for material not easily found elsewhere.

Gayley's *Classic Myths in English Literature and in Art.* An old multi-volume work, known by its editor's name. Also in a one-volume edition.

The Golden Bough. By Sir James Fraser. A great exhaustive study of mythology, in twelve volumes, also condensed into one volume.

Harper's Dictionary of Classical Literature and Antiquities. An older work useful for general reference.

Larousse Encyclopedia of Mythology. One of a new series of translations of great French reference works. One volume.

Mythology of All Races. The standard multivolume set in the field.

New Century Classical Handbook. A recent compilation for handy reference.

Oxford Classical Dictionary. Scholarly articles.

Natural Sciences and Technology

Because currency of information is of overriding importance in science, dates are given for the works listed below.

Bibliography of North American Geology. Annual publication of the U.S. Geological Survey.

Chambers's Technical Dictionary. 1958.

Chemical Publications. 1958.

Dictionary of Atomic Terminology. 1959.

Dictionary of Scientific Terms. 7th edition, 1960.

Electronics and Nucleonics Dictionary. 1960.

Encyclopedic Dictionary of Physics. A new set, of which three volumes have been published to date.

Encyclopedia of Chemistry. 1957 and one supplement, 1958.

Encyclopedia of the Biological Sciences. 1961.

Gray's *Anatomy of the Human Body.* Known by the name of its editor, a classic, in its 25th edition in 1949.

Guide to the Literature of Chemistry. 1957.

Guide to the Literature of Mathematics and Physics; Including Related Works on Engineering Science. Second edition, 1958.

Guide to the Space Age. Space terminology. 1960.

Harper Encyclopedia of Science. A new four-volume work. 1962.

International Dictionary of Applied Mathematics. 1960.

International Dictionary of Physics and Electronics. Second edition, 1961.

Larousse Encyclopedia of Astronomy. A one-volume compendium; 1959, revised 1962.

Larousse Encyclopedia of Geography. 1961.

Larousse Encyclopedia of the Earth. 1961. Concerned with the origins of the earth and the early development of man.

Mathematics Dictionary. 1959.

McGraw-Hill Encyclopedia of Science and Technology. 1960. In fifteen volumes.

Stedman's Medical Dictionary. 1957. One of several good medical dictionaries.

Introduction to the History of Science. By George Sarton. 1948. A classic work, excellent for background material.

Scientific, Medical, and Technical Books Published in the United States of

America. R. R. Hawkins, editor. Second edition, 1958. A standard bibliography of selected works.

Survey of Biological Progress. 1949–1962. Articles and bibliographies covering recent developments.

Van Nostrand's Scientific Encyclopedia. Third edition, 1958. A useful one-volume reference on science in general.

Philosophy and Psychology

Annual Survey of Psychoanalysis. A source for recent developments.

Comprehensive Dictionary of Psychological and Psychoanalytical Terms; A Guide to Usage. Published in 1958.

Dictionary of Philosophy and Psychology. Edited by J. M. Baldwin. Although dated 1925, this three-volume work has never been replaced, and is still a classic.

Dictionary of Psychology. One volume, which includes foreign terms; edited by Howard C. Warren, and published in 1934.

Harvard List of Books in Psychology. A compilation by psychology professors at Harvard; with its supplements, covers publications to 1958.

History of American Philosophy. By Herbert W. Schneider. Because of a dearth of reference books in philosophy, histories will be valuable sources for general information.

History of Psychology in Autobiography. A four-volume compilation of "intellectual histories" written by great psychologists about themselves.

History of Western Philosophy. By Bertrand Russell.

Psychiatric Dictionary. An Oxford University Press publication, in its third edition in 1960.

Thales to Dewey; A History of Philosophy. By Gordon H. Clark.

Religion

Atlas of the Bible. A recent British publication.

Atlas of the Early Christian World. Similar to the above.

Catholic Encyclopaedic Dictionary. Explains terms, gives biographies of saints.

Catholic Encyclopedia. A new edition of this broadly useful seventeen-volume work is in progress.

Dictionary of the Bible. Edited by James Hastings. In five-volume and one-volume editions.

Dictionary of Religion and Ethics. Definitions of terms and some biographies.

Encyclopaedia of Religion and Ethics. Edited by James Hastings. A multi-volume standard work.

Jewish Encyclopedia. An older multivolume work.

New Schaff-Herzog Encyclopedia of Religious Knowledge. A standard work that has recently been re-edited.

Oxford Dictionary of the Christian Church. Gives history and doctrine as well as definitions.

Standard Jewish Encyclopedia. A recent one-volume work.

Treasure House of the Living Religions; Selections from their Scriptures. A classified anthology of quotations.

Social Sciences

Commercial Atlas and Marketing Guide. One of Rand McNally's most important contributions to geographical publishing.

Dictionary of Economics. Definitions, and digests of statutes.

Dictionary of Social Science. A broader scope than the above.

Dictionary of Social Welfare. Defines terms, from technical to slang.

Encyclopaedia of the Social Sciences. In fifteen volumes, the main comprehensive reference work in the field.

Europe's Needs and Resources. A present-day estimate and projections into the future.

Index of Economic Journals. The years 1886–1954 are covered in four volumes.

International Bibliography of Economics. Annual, published by UNESCO.

International Bibliography of Sociology. Similar to the above.

London Bibliography of the Social Sciences. Lists holdings of nine London libraries. The most extensive bibliography in the field, published serially.

McGraw-Hill Encyclopedia of Russia and the Soviet Union. History, geography, resources, culture, and biography, with many illustrations.

New Dictionary of American Politics. A companion volume to the *Dictionary of Economics,* above.

Palgrave's Dictionary of Political Economy. In three volumes, a classic older work.

Political Handbook of the World. An annual publication of the Council on Foreign Relations.

Worldmark Encyclopedia of the Nations. A very useful one-volume publication of 1960.

Exercises

A. Suppose that you are going to write a paper on one of the following subjects. Write down the titles of *all* the sources named in this chapter that you would consult for general preliminary information, and the indexes you would search for periodical articles on the subject.

Remedial reading	Liberia
The iron ore industry	Mental aberrations
Socialism	Chartres Cathedral
Medieval music	Jacksonian democracy
Chemical research	Your congressman
The concept of sin	The Apostles
Wordsworth's poetry	A major recent news event

B. Choose a famous author and look him up in all the likely biographical reference works, noting which gives the most information about him.

Make a list of his works and find out how many of them your library has.

Note the number of books in your library of which your author is the *subject.* See if there are any cross references from the name of your author, or of one of his works.

12

The Research Paper

The research paper is a standard assignment in college classes. It goes under various names, but whether it is called a "research paper," a "documented paper," a "library paper," a "term paper," or a "reading report," it is one written to present the results of a student's reading on a subject. The student selects a topic, reads about it in books and periodicals, takes notes, and writes a long paper based on the information he has uncovered.

There are four reasons for the prevalence of this assignment. First, because it combines reading, note-taking, organization, and development at a mature level, it provides the student with a worthwhile experience in using many of the skills cultivated in the English course. Second, it gives him a practical introduction to his college library and helps him to use it efficiently thereafter. Third, it makes him familiar with research procedures and conventions that he will use increasingly in college. Fourth, it gives a conscientious student the intellectual satisfaction of becoming, at least by freshman standards, something of an expert on a particular subject. It is for this reason that good students finish their research papers with a sense of achievement. They have been given a chance to show what they can do on their own, and they have the satisfaction of knowing that they have proved themselves.

But if the research paper is to have the educational value it is intended to have, it must be an honest job. Any student who perverts the assignment by deliberately plagiarizing the paper not only convicts himself of dishonesty but raises the question whether the money and effort being expended for his education are justified.[1] Few college students will deliberately plagiarize, but some drift into unintentional plagiarism because of careless habits of note-taking which may have been tolerated in high school. For this reason, no student should assume from his high school experience that he knows how to write a college research paper. Before he begins work on the assignment, he should make a careful study of what it requires of him. It is the purpose of this chapter to make these requirements clear.

[1] Plagiarism is the presentation of another's writing as one's own. Legally, socially, and academically it is considered a form of theft, and is usually punished in college by automatic failure in the course or by expulsion.

In general, undergraduate research papers are of two kinds: *reports* and *theses*. The chief difference between these types is one of purpose. The writer of a report wishes to find out the facts of his subject and present them in a clear, orderly, and detailed account. The writer of a thesis research paper is studying the facts to draw a conclusion from them; this conclusion becomes the thesis of his essay; and he selects and organizes his material to develop his thesis. Because it usually presents a more difficult problem, the thesis paper will be emphasized in this chapter, but the kind of paper you write will be determined by your instructor's directions for the assignment. Most of the advice in this chapter applies to both types of papers.

Preview of Research Procedure

Before we consider the separate steps in preparing a research paper, let us preview the whole procedure. Suppose you have been asked to choose a topic, study it, and write a 2000-word thesis paper. You have five weeks for the assignment. At the end of that time you are to hand in a paper complete with sentence outline, footnotes, and bibliography.

Because you have recently become interested in photography, you choose that as your general subject. You know you will have to restrict that topic, but at present you do not know enough about it to limit it intelligently. You decide that for this subject the first thing to do is to make a preliminary survey of the books listed in the card catalog. As you notice the titles and descriptions of contents, you see how the general subject is broken down into subtopics. You find chapters, even whole books, devoted to the history of photography, the chemistry of photography, celestial photography, commercial photography, color photography, miniature photography, and to studies of developers, lenses, and photographing techniques.

You realize almost at once that each of these limited topics would be enough for a 2000-word paper and that the first step in restricting your topic is to select one of them. You recognize that some topics require more chemistry or mathematics than you can handle and that others would result in highly technical papers. Miniature photography seems both interesting and possible. With the aid of the card catalog, the *Readers' Guide to Periodical Literature,* and the *Photo-Lab Index,* you draw out the most promising publications, scan them to form a judgment of their usefulness, and begin to prepare a preliminary bibliography of the most useful sources.

Since you know very little about miniature photography, you wisely decide to begin with some introductory reading — books and articles which will give you a general background for more detailed reading later. Accordingly, you begin with the most general and popular works on the subject — perhaps the *Leica Manual,* an elementary textbook on visual aids, and a promising magazine article. Because these works are designed merely to give you an introduction to your subject, you skim them quickly. You have already recognized that even miniature photography is a large topic, and you decide that you had better postpone careful reading and note-taking until you have decided what *precisely* you intend to do with your subject.

At the end of the first week you have a general knowledge of your subject — its history, its popularity, its wide range of uses. You know its advantages and limitations as contrasted with other types of photography, and you see that the topic is still too big for a 2000-word paper. Already certain specific phases of the subject have begun to suggest themselves as suitable for intensive study. You are particularly impressed by references to the ways microphotography has revolutionized techniques in a wide variety of professions, and you think you would like to write a paper on these developments.

You now discard from your preliminary bibliography all titles which seem to have no relation to your restricted subject. When you see how much has to be discarded, you are glad you did not waste time taking notes on your general subject. But now it is time to take notes; so, as you begin to read intensively on the uses of microphotography, you copy significant evidence on note cards, making sure that the source of the material, including page number, is shown on *each* card. You use a separate card for each note so that you will be able to organize your notes according to whatever scheme you later decide is best.

At the end of the second week you have a respectable pile of note cards, and you have become something of an expert on the application of microphotography to industrial and professional uses. Indeed, you know so much about the subject that you are beginning to be worried about discussing all these uses in a 2000-word paper. You begin to think it might be wise to limit your topic still further. As you review your notes with this thought in mind, you see that you could turn your research project into any one of several more specialized studies. With more work, you could show what miniature photography has done for visual aid programs; you could show its uses in banking; you could show how it has revolutionized the techniques of scholarly research; and you could sketch its possibilities in a half-dozen uses which are beginning to emerge. Your material, however, is best suited for a paper on banking or one on scholarly research. After some thought, you decide to show what the miniature camera has done for academic research.

You now discard those notes which no longer have value for your restricted subject, and you spread out your remaining notes to see what kind of pattern they suggest. You will probably experiment with running outlines, as we did on page 50, in an effort to see to what purpose your material lends itself. You find that most of your cards may be grouped under four headings: the quantity of work that photography makes possible, the saving in time, the greater accuracy that exact copies provide, and the saving in total costs to the scholar. After several tries you write as your thesis: "By the use of microphotography, scholars are able to do more work, more accurately, in less time, and at less cost." You even think of a title for your paper — *Streamlined Scholarship.*

It has taken you almost three weeks to see exactly what you wanted to do. Until now, you have been groping toward a decision, but now that your purpose is precise, the rest of your work will move forward rapidly and economically. As you begin to work out trial outlines, you recognize that there are still some gaps in your material. You need more evidence about the development of microfilm libraries in universities. You require estimates of the comparative cost of photostating and microfilming. You need more information than you have about the different types of reading machines. But, at least, you know exactly what you are looking for, and probably you know where to find it. If in the next two weeks you can organize and present your material to develop your final purpose, you will have a superior paper.

The imaginary assignment which we have been considering illustrates the recommended procedure preparatory to writing a research paper. That procedure may be summarized as follows:

1. Make a survey of the material available on your general subject and prepare a preliminary bibliography.

2. Become familiar with the general subject through introductory sources, but postpone note-taking.

3. Restrict the general subject as quickly as you can. Remember that your reading does not become fully pertinent until you have decided the question you wish to answer or the specific phase of the subject that you wish to develop.

4. When you feel that your subject is becoming specialized, begin to take notes.

5. Continue to restrict your subject as soon as the results of your specialized reading suggest further restriction.

6. When you feel that restriction of the subject is complete, begin to consider what precisely you intend to do with that subject. Remember that when you decided to show how microphotography had streamlined scholarship, you had a thesis as well as a subject.

7. Begin the preliminary outlining of the paper. You have probably already begun to plan the organization in your head or by means of scratch outlines, but you are now ready for more formal outlines.

8. Fill in by additional investigation the blank spots that remain.

9. When the research is complete, make a final outline and write the first draft of your paper.

Most of the steps summarized above are preparatory. The total process would be considerably shortened if you knew at the beginning what you know by the time you have reached step 6. The more quickly you arrive at step 6, therefore, the more profitable will be your investigations and the less time they will require. Under favorable conditions you may be able to skip some of the preliminary stages, but even if you cannot, a clear realization that you are looking for a phase of the subject that may be dealt with completely within the limits of your paper will help you to speed up the first steps.

We may now profitably consider the separate stages of carrying out the research assignment.

Choosing a Subject

The choice of a subject for research depends partly on the purpose of the assignment and partly on your preference. The purpose of the assignment is fourfold: to teach you to use the library efficiently; to help you develop habits of purposeful reading and note-taking; to give you practice in organizing information drawn from a variety of sources and in developing it into a unified essay; and to make you familiar with the conventions of bibliography and footnoting. Since a successful research paper must satisfy all these purposes, the following kinds of topics should be avoided for the reasons noted below:

1. *Topics which would be developed largely from personal experience.* Since such topics do not require library research, they would ignore at least three of the four purposes stated above.

2. *Topics which could be satisfactorily developed from a single source.* Such subjects as "How Plastics Are Made" and "Producing Synthetic Rubber" are undesirable for three reasons: first, all the information necessary could be obtained from a single book or article, thus eliminating the need for consulting various sources; second, since the organization of the paper would inevitably follow that of the source, the paper would offer no real problem in composition; third, the whole assignment could be adequately treated with a few hours' work, and would therefore not be suited to the amount of time usually allowed for it. For freshman research papers, then, these objections rule out many highly technical topics which are basically descriptions of processes. They also eliminate straight biographies — that is, narrative accounts of a man's life.

3. *Topics for which satisfactory evidence is not available.* Such questions as "Are Women More Honest Than Men?" "Do Extroverts Make Good Husbands?" "Who Was the Greater Poet — Chaucer or Milton?" are likely to be answered by the writer's preference. They depend too much on subjective, personal judgments and values to serve as questions which can be answered by the techniques of research. It would be difficult, for example, to get generally accepted criteria of what constitutes a "good" husband or a "great" poet. Lacking such criteria, a writer would be reduced to selecting evidence which supported his own bias or opinion.

4. *Unrestricted topics which could be treated only superficially within*

the scope of the assignment. All that was said about restriction in Chapter 2 applies with added emphasis to the research paper. An unrestricted topic offers almost no problem in either research or composition. Since *the most common cause of failure in undergraduate research papers is lack of restriction,* review pages 35–38 carefully before choosing a subject.

5. *Highly controversial subjects, especially those advocating the adoption or rejection of a proposal that calls for action.* Such subjects are objectionable for two reasons: (1) they are too comprehensive to be dealt with thoroughly in a paper of 2000–3000 words, and (2) giving reasons for or against a proposal, without careful consideration of all the evidence on both sides of the question, often results in irresponsible and undisciplined argument. For example, such a proposal as "Congress Should Provide Federal Aid to Education" not only includes many issues, each of which has been argued at length, but also requires a sophisticated understanding of types of reasoning and of the nature of acceptable authoritative testimony. It is therefore hard to avoid a superficial argument which does little more than present unweighed evidence to support the writer's preference. The line between argument and the exposition of a thesis is sometimes a thin one, but a student should consult his instructor before beginning to work on a subject with the intention of persuading his reader that something should or should not be done.

If these five kinds of topics are avoided, almost any subject can yield a satisfactory research paper. Probably your wisest course is to look on the research project as an opportunity to investigate a field which seems to you worth looking into. If, through your work in other courses, you have become interested in history, social science, physics, chemistry, or the fine arts, select from one of these fields a particular topic that you would like to investigate. Sometimes the topic will occur to you as a quite specific question — "What was behind the abdication of Edward VIII?" "Why is English spelling so illogical?" "What are modern painters trying to do?" "Which is the more important — environment or heredity?" "What can be done to help slow readers?" "How does the British Parliament differ from our Congress?" If you would like an answer to any such question, you not only have a subject worth investigating, but, since the answer to the question will give you your thesis, you may be able to skip some of the preliminary steps summarized on page 242. Even if you do not have a specific question to answer, an awareness that the research project provides you with an opportunity to learn more about some phase of a subject that interests you may get you off to a better start and make the whole assignment a rewarding experience.

Above all, do not choose a subject for trivial reasons. Some students elect to write on a particular subject because they wrote on it in high school and they naïvely assume that they can re-use most of what they have already done. Usually these are sad papers for both instructor and student, because by the time the student realizes that his instructor is not going to accept a warmed-over high school paper he has lost so much time that failure is almost inevitable. Other students choose a subject because they have two or three books on it in their personal libraries and they mistakenly believe that these will give them all or most of the information they will need. If a student commits himself to an extensive research project for no better reasons than these, he is not likely to have the curiosity that justifies the time and labor that research involves. Without the drive provided by a real desire to learn the answer to a problem, research can be pretty tedious; with that drive, it can be an intellectually exciting experience.

Preparing a Bibliography

In the sense in which you will be using the term in your college work a *bibliography* is a list of books, articles, and other publications. A *preliminary* bibliography lists the works you expect to use for a paper. A *final* bibliography lists the works you actually did use. A preliminary bibliography is made on 3 × 5 inch cards, with each title on a separate card. A final bibliography is typed or handwritten as a solid list. Both contain the same basic information for each item included — author's name, title of work, and facts of publication (place, publisher, and date).

The Preliminary Bibliography

In preparing a bibliography, as in other tasks, a few minutes' careful consideration of the problem may save hours of needless work and result in a better product. Many students rush uncritically to the card catalog. Before you begin your actual search for titles, ask yourself two questions: What kind of material do I want? What are the most likely places to find it?

It is wise to ask these questions, because different subjects require different approaches to the preparation of a bibliography. If you are dealing with a subject recently developed, the card catalog will be of little use to you. It records only books, and the very latest material in a book is usually at least a year old. For a current topic you must get most of your information from newspapers and recent magazine articles. On the other hand, many subjects — the development of the alphabet, for example — have been thoroughly treated in books, and little of significance will be found about them in current periodicals. The best general sources of information are the card catalog and the *Readers' Guide to Periodical Literature*. For some subjects the best approach will be through an index to technical publications; for others, *The New York Times Index* may yield the required information most readily. Before beginning the bibliography, you should check the appropriate lists of reference works in Chapter 11.

Once you have started to prepare your bibliography, the following advice may be helpful:

1. Try to make your bibliography selective as you prepare it. There is no point in listing three titles which contain the same information, or books which have little to say on your subject. Develop the habit of guessing intelligently whether a book will be useful to you. In some subjects — atomic energy, for example — an old book is likely to be outdated. Usually the best way to guess at a book's usefulness is to draw it out of the library and look at it quickly. Read the preface, or part of it; check the table of contents; see how much space it gives to your subject. With a little practice you will usually be able to tell within three minutes whether the book will be of use to you.

2. Watch for critical bibliographies, which evaluate the works they list and thus tell you what sources are best and for what topics. Many serious studies contain such bibliographies, at the ends of chapters or the end of the whole work, and so give you valuable leads to other sources.

3. Study the indexes of books on related subjects. A book on physics may contain a pertinent discussion of atomic energy. But do not begin to read it through merely in the hope that it *may* contain such information. Instead, turn to the index and see how many references are given under *atomic energy* or related headings. Sample the most likely of these references. Similarly, if your study is biographical, check the indexes of memoirs and letters by people acquainted with your subject.

All this advice may be summed up in two words: *act purposefully*. You will save much time, and work with more confidence and enjoyment, if you feel that you are not just drifting around in a library hoping to pick up useful information but are following a calculated plan for discovering it.

The Form of the Bibliography

Each bibliographical card should contain three essential pieces of information: (*1*) *the name of the author,* (*2*) *the title of the work,* (*3*) *the facts of publication.* In addition, a card may contain, for the convenience of the student, the library call number and a note concerning the contents of the work. The following card is typical for a book.

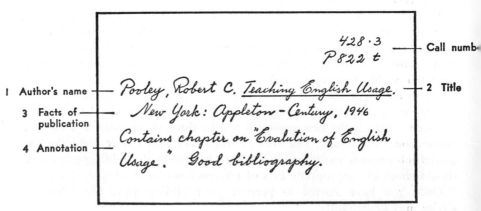

The form of the entry varies with the kind of publication being cited, and the major variations are illustrated in the sample bibliographical entries shown below.

1. A Book by a Single Author or Agency

Gulley, Halbert E. Essentials of Discussion and
    Debate. New York: Henry Holt and Company,
    1955.

a. The author's surname comes before his given name or initials for ease in alphabetizing.
b. If the book is the work of an agency, committee, organization, or department, rather than of an individual, the name of the agency takes the place of the author's name.
c. If no author is given, the citation begins with the title.
d. The title of the book is italicized (represented in manuscript by underlining each word separately).
e. The facts of publication are the place of publication, the publisher, and the date of publication, in that order.
f. If more than one place is given on the title page, use only the first.
g. If no date of publication is given, use the last copyright date, usually found on the reverse of the title page.
h. The punctuation in the sample above is the preferred form.

2. A Book by Two Authors

Wellek, René, and Austin Warren. Theory of Lit-
    erature. New York: Harcourt, Brace and Com-
    pany, 1949.

a. The name of the second author is not inverted; otherwise the form is the same as that of Example 1.
b. The order of the authors' names is the same as that on the title page; hence Wellek comes first, even though Warren would be alphabetically earlier.

3. A Book by Several Authors

Murray, Elwood, and others. Integrative Speech.
    New York: The Dryden Press, 1953.

a. The Latin abbreviation *et al.* is a common variation of "and others" and may be used if preferred.

b. When there are three authors, but not more than three, it is a common practice to give all three names. Thus the first part of the entry shown above could have been listed:

> Murray, Elwood, Raymond H. Barnard, and J. V. Garland.

4. *An Edition Other Than the First*

> Bailey, Sydney D. British Parliamentary Democracy. 2nd ed. Boston: Houghton Mifflin Company, 1962.

a. If the work is a revised or later edition, the appropriate abbreviated designation (Rev. ed., 2nd ed., 3rd ed., 7th ed.) is placed immediately after the title and separated from it by a period.

b. Only the date of the edition being cited is given.

5. *A Work of More Than One Volume*

> Johnson, Edgar. Charles Dickens: His Tragedy and Triumph. 2 vols. New York: Simon and Schuster, 1952.

a. The number of volumes follows the title, is separated from it by a period, and is always abbreviated as shown.

b. If the volumes of a multivolume work were published over a period of years, the inclusive dates are given, as shown in the next entry.

6. *An Edition of an Author's Work*

> Haight, Gordon S., ed. The George Eliot Letters. 7 vols. New Haven: Yale University Press, 1954–55.

a. If the edition is by more than one person, the names of the editors are arranged as in Example 2 or 3, whichever form is appropriate.

b. In *A Manual of Style* (University of Chicago Press) the abbreviation for "editor" or "editors" is enclosed in parentheses — (ed.) or (eds.). The form used above is preferred by *The MLA Style Sheet*.

7. *An Edited Collection or Anthology*

> Thomas, Wright, and Stuart Gerry Brown, eds. Reading Prose. New York: Oxford University Press, 1952.

8. A Translation

Gouzenko, Igor. The Fall of a Titan, trans.
Mervyn Black. New York: W. W. Norton & Company, 1954.

9. A Pamphlet

Because there is considerable variation in the bibliographical information given in pamphlets, they are sometimes difficult to cite. Whenever possible, treat them like books, with or without an author (Example 1). If the bibliographical information is so incomplete that you cannot confidently describe the pamphlet, show it to your instructor and get his advice. Following are three variant forms:

Chafee, Zechariah, Jr. Freedom of Speech and
   Press. New York: Carrie Chapman Catt Memorial
   Fund, 1955.

Bureau of the Budget. The Federal Budget in
   Brief: Fiscal Year 1954. Washington, D.C.:
   U.S. Government Printing Office, 1953.

Your Library: A Guide for Undergraduate Students,
   University of Illinois [n.d.].

a. The last example is intended to show a difficult pamphlet, since the only bibliographical information given is the title.
b. The symbol [n.d.], meaning "no date," is used to show that no date of publication or copyright is given and that the omission is not an oversight. If your typewriter does not have brackets, put them in by hand.

10. An Essay in an Edited Collection

Highet, Gilbert. "The American Student as I See
   Him," Patterns in Writing, ed. Robert B. Dore-
   mus and others. New York: William Sloane
   Associates, 1950.

a. This entry requires two titles and both an author and an editor.
b. The title of the essay (or story or poem) is in quotation marks, and the title of the book is italicized.
c. The comma separating the two titles comes *inside* the final quotation marks.

11. An Article in an Encyclopedia

Macaulay, Thomas Babington. "Samuel Johnson,"
Encyclopaedia Britannica, 11th ed., XV, 463-471.

"Navigation Acts," The Columbia Encyclopedia,
1950, pp. 1367-68.

a. Some encyclopedia articles are initialed, and the authors are identified in a list at the beginning of the volume. The article on Johnson is signed *M*, Macaulay's initial.

b. The British spelling *Encyclopaedia* is often bothersome to American students. Copy the title exactly as it is given on the title page.

c. Either the edition number *or* the date of publication may be used. Thus "1911" could have been used instead of "11th ed." in the first example, and "2nd ed." instead of "1950" in the second.

12. A Magazine Article

McCall, Raymond G. "H. L. Mencken and the Glass
of Satire," College English, XXIII (May, 1962),
633-636.

Hammond, E. Cuyler. "The Effects of Smoking,"
Scientific American, 207:39-51 (July, 1962).

Hacker, Andrew. "The Boy Who Doesn't Go to College," The New York Times Magazine, June 24,
1962, pp. 11, 14-18.

a. Two titles are separated and differentiated, as in Example 9.

b. No place of publication or publisher is given, but volume, date, and page numbers are shown. The first entry shows the preferred form in nonscientific fields, with Roman numerals for volume and Arabic numerals for pages and a parenthetical date between the two number systems. The second entry shows the preferred form in scientific fields, with the volume number preceding the colon and the page numbers following it. The third entry shows the form for magazines included as newspaper supplements.

c. The words "volume" and "page" (or their abbreviations "vol." and "p.") are not used when, as in the first two entries above, both volume and page numbers are given.

13. A Newspaper Article

Reston, James. "Washington: A Trial Balance Sheet
at the Mid-Year," The New York Times, June 29,
1962, p. 26.

Editorial, The [Champaign-Urbana] News-Gazette, June 14, 1962, p. 12.

"Dublin ReJoyces," Newsweek, July 2, 1962, p. 80.

a. The examples successively illustrate a signed article, an untitled editorial, and a titled but unsigned story.
b. The name of the city is italicized if it appears on the newspaper as part of the title. If not, as in Example 2, it is inserted without italics in square brackets. The definite article is italicized only if it is part of the title.
c. News magazines, such as *Newsweek* and *Time,* are treated as newspapers rather than as magazines.

✔ In order to get practice as quickly as possible with the various forms illustrated in this discussion, convert the following information into conventional bibliographical form. Since the number of each item corresponds to the number of a preceding illustration, you can check your answer against the appropriate illustration.

1. A book by John R. Reinhard called Medieval Pageant, copyrighted in 1939 and published by Harcourt, Brace and Company in New York.
2. A book called The Reader Over Your Shoulder, written by Robert Graves and Alan Hodge, and published in New York by The Macmillan Company in 1944.
3. A book published by the University of Illinois Press at Urbana, Illinois, in 1952. The book was written by Gordon N. Ray, Carl J. Weber, and John Carter and is called Nineteenth Century English Books.
4. The second edition of a book entitled A Browning Handbook, written by William Clyde DeVane and published by Appleton-Century-Crofts of New York. This second edition was published in 1955.
5. A two-volume edition of Selected Works of Stephen Vincent Benét, prepared by the author and published by Farrar and Rinehart of New York in 1942.
6. John M. Manley's edition of Chaucer's Canterbury Tales, copyrighted in 1928 and published in New York by Henry Holt and Company.
7. Masters of American Literature, a two-volume work edited by Leon Edel, Thomas H. Johnson, Sherman Paul, and Claude Simpson, and published in Boston by Houghton Mifflin Company in 1959.
8. A translation by Dorothy Bussy of a novel by André Gide. The translation, called Lafcadio's Adventures, was published by Alfred A. Knopf, Inc. of New York in 1928.
9. A pamphlet entitled Memo: The Citizen and International Trade prepared by the League of Women Voters and printed in Washington, D.C. in 1952.
10. Charles Lamb's essay on Old China, reprinted in Literary Masters of England, which was edited by Nelson S. Bushnell, Paul M. Fulcher, and Warner Taylor and was published in 1950 by Rinehart & Company, New York, as a revised edition.

11. An article by M. S. Fisher on pages 573–576 of volume XI of the Encyclopedia of the Social Sciences. The article is entitled Parent Education.

12. An article entitled, Present Status of Advanced Composition and Rhetoric, on pages 177–179 of volume 16 of College English. The article was written by Tyrus Hillway and appeared in December, 1954.

13. A newspaper story headed Spanish Students Opposed to Franco in the St. Louis Post-Dispatch. The story was written by Camille M. Cianfarra and appeared on page 13A of the issue for January 5, 1956.

The Final Bibliography

The final bibliography will be typed from the bibliographical cards and will follow the forms already discussed. It should contain a citation for each work mentioned in the footnotes. It may also contain a few works which you found to be useful background references, even though you neither cited nor quoted them in your paper. But padding a bibliography to make it look imposing is more likely to annoy than to impress an instructor. If your instructor prefers, your bibliography may be annotated — that is, it may contain a brief statement explaining the significance of each item or of selected items.

In typing or writing your bibliography, observe the following conventions unless your instructor recommends modifications.

1. If the bibliography is long, group the publications according to type: books, magazine articles, newspaper articles, etc. When the bibliography consists of a single page, this grouping is less necessary. If in doubt whether grouping is desirable, consult your instructor.

2. Within each group list items alphabetically by author's surname or, if the author is not given, by the first letter of the title (not counting "A," "An," or "The").

3. If more than one book by the same author is being listed, you may substitute a 7-space line for the author's name after you have once given it:

```
Baldwin, T. W.  William Shakespeare's Five-Act
  Structure. . . .

--------.  William Shakespeare's Petty School. . . .
```

4. Single-space each item and double-space between items.

5. In each item, indent two spaces for all lines after the first.

The bibliography of the sample research paper on pages 312–313 illustrates some of these conventions.

Introductory Reading

For most research studies the reading may be divided into three stages — introductory, intensive, and supplementary. The introductory reading gives the background needed in order to begin the investigation intelligently. The intensive reading provides the bulk of the information from which the paper will be written. The supplementary reading fills in gaps and provides added information needed to make your paper complete.

Thus, in our imaginary assignment on pages 240–243, all reading done before the decision to restrict photography to the uses of microphotography in industry and the professions was introductory. All reading done after the final decision to write on "Streamlined Scholarship" was supplementary. That in between was intensive. Of course, it would have been more economical if no introductory or supplementary reading had been required, if you had known from the beginning that you were going to write on "Streamlined Scholarship." But few research papers actually develop that way. Even so, a careful concern with purpose can greatly reduce the introductory and supplementary reading.

Once the function of the introductory reading is understood, it will be clear that note-taking at this stage is not profitable. The information obtained from this reading is probably not going to appear in your paper, or if it does, it will probably be so general that notes are not needed. This reading should therefore be done quickly. Indeed, the early accumulation of miscellaneous notes may actually be confusing, since a student who has notes on every aspect of his subject is likely to have a harder time deciding which phase of it to concentrate on. Again, as in the preliminary bibliography, the test is usefulness, not quantity. And it is therefore wise to take no notes until you are reasonably sure you will use them.

Usually the best sources for introductory reading are general works — articles in encyclopedias, chapters in elementary textbooks, histories, biographical references, and specialized dictionaries. For example, a student setting out to answer the question, "How Did English Spelling Become So Illogical?" might profitably begin with the article on the English Language in a good unabridged dictionary, the *Encyclopaedia Britannica,* or such textbooks as Baugh's *History of the English Language* or Jesperson's *Growth and Structure of the English Language.* These works would not only refer him to more specialized studies but would also provide him with the background necessary to profit from such studies.

Note-Taking

Once you begin intensive reading, it will be necessary to take notes. The results of your preliminary reading may be carried in your head, but you are now beginning to collect the actual evidence from which your paper will be written, and it is important to the success of all the rest of your work that both the form and the content of your notes be satisfactory.

The Form of the Notes

All notes should be written on cards[2] and should contain two kinds of

[2] Some instructors prefer 4 × 6 inch cards in contrast with the 3 × 5 inch bibliographical cards.

information: (1) the fact or opinion being noted, and (2) the exact source from which you took it. This second item is absolutely necessary, since you will be required to identify the sources of your material in the footnotes to your paper. Usually that means you must identify the author, title, and page of the book or article from which the note was taken. Here is a typical note made from a book:

> *Morison, Samuel E.*
> <u>*Admiral of the Ocean Sea*</u>, *p. 7*
>
>   *Columbus born in Genoa, 1451, between Aug. 25 and October, of family of woolen weavers who had lived in Genoese Republic for at least 3 generations.*

If you are making a number of notes from the same source, the complete identification given above may be abbreviated. Thus, if you are using no other work by this author, "Morison, p. 7" would be enough, since your bibliographical card would provide the full title. Or you may give each of your bibliography cards a separate identification symbol and use that symbol and the page number on every note card made from that work. But no matter what system is used, each card must be accurately identified. To avoid any possibility of a slip, *always write the identification before you begin the note.*

The practice of using note cards instead of notebooks has grown out of the experience of thousands of research workers. To be really useful your notes must be so flexible that you can shuffle them to suit whatever order you finally decide upon and can discard useless notes easily. Notes written solid in a notebook cannot conveniently be rearranged or edited. They are fixed in the order they had in the source from which they were taken, whereas the order which suits your final purpose may be entirely different. Recording information in a notebook is therefore inefficient, no matter how easy it may seem at first glance.

Only one note should be placed on a card. Two notes on one card are inseparably bound together. Since you must be free to shuffle your notes, to discard useless ones and add supplementary ones, the only satisfactory method is to use a separate card for each.

It is wise to leave enough space at the top of each card so that you may write in a subject heading when you group your cards and develop your outline, thus:

Learned Superstitions

Danzig, p. 40

Pythagoreans identified numbers with human qualities. Odd numbers male, even numbers female.

1 = reason   2 = opinion

3 = justice   4 = marriage

Because these subject headings may be changed as your organization develops, it is wise to enter them in pencil.

The Content of Notes

Your notes may contain statements of fact or of opinion, in your own words or in the words of the author from whose work they came. The cards shown below contrast a quoted opinion and the same opinion stated

zero

Danzig, p. 35

"In the history of culture the discovery of zero will always stand as one of the greatest single achievements of the human race."

zero

Danzig, p. 35

Discovery of zero one of greatest cultural accomplishments.

in the student's words. *If the wording as well as the content is taken from a source, be extremely careful to use quotation marks, both on your note card and, later, in your paper.* Failure to use quotation marks on the note card may later lead you to think that the information is expressed in your own words and thus may trap you into unintentional plagiarism.

Whenever possible your notes should be summaries of the source material, not direct quotations. Too many quotations result in wordiness and give the impression that the student has merely strung together statements made by others without digesting these statements or doing any thinking about them. The technique of summarizing is discussed in Chapter 9 and it might be wise to read over that chapter before you begin intensive reading for the research assignment.

If the information you are noting is factual, confine yourself to a bare statement of fact; do not copy out the whole paragraph in which the facts are embedded. Most students need practice in this discipline, for it takes less thought to copy a paragraph verbatim than to thresh out the significant facts. But the threshing has to be done some time before the paper is written, and it might as well be done as the notes are taken. Even if the job seems at times like extracting a needle from a haystack, remember that taking home the whole haystack does not help at all.

> *Phony estimates*
>
> Morison, pp. 190-191
>
> According to Morison, Columbus overestimated distance sailed by about 9%. Intentional underestimate of "phony" reckonings designed to allay fears of crew actually more accurate, therefore, than secret reckonings which he believed true.

> *Number sense*
>
> Danzig, pp. 1-3
>
> Says number sense not to be confused with counting. Counting confined to humans, but some animals, birds, insects have remarkable sense of number. Illustrations:
>
> Crows and "Solitary Wasps"

Long statements of opinion or of fact and opinion combined should nearly always be summarized. Nothing is more irritating to an instructor or more detrimental to the purpose of the research assignment than the habit of padding the paper with several long quotations, each of which could have been summarized in two or three sentences. The accompanying cards (opposite page) show economical but effective summaries of extensive passages. The first note is a digest of a three-paragraph passage containing about 480 words; the second condenses the material of five paragraphs totaling about 500 words. Notice that these cards are identified just as carefully as if they contained direct quotations. The material was taken from the work of another and must be acknowledged in footnotes.

In making notes, the student must be careful that what he writes is consistent with the meaning of the whole source. If what is put on the note card is qualified by something said in a preceding sentence or paragraph, the student should record that qualification. All notes must honestly and accurately reflect the content of their sources.

What we have said about note-taking may be summarized as follows.

1. Put notes on cards, not in notebooks, with one note to a card.

2. On each card identify the exact source of the note, including the page number. Abbreviations may be used only if there is no danger of ambiguity.

3. The actual words of an author must be placed in quotation marks, regardless of whether the notes are statements of fact or opinion.

4. Summarize extensive quotations if possible, but still identify the source.

5. Digest factual information out of a long passage before making the note.

6. Be careful that your notes — whether direct quotations or digests — do not distort the meaning when taken out of the original context.

7. Finally, remember that these conventions governing note-taking are designed to teach you good research habits as well as to protect you from beginners' mistakes. Follow the conventions at all times, even when a home-made system might seem more convenient.[3]

✔ Suppose you were writing a research paper to show that social scientists work under more difficult conditions than do physical scientists and one of your sources was Kemmerer's "Are Social Scientists Backward?" (pages 210–213). From that source make whatever notes you think you might use and hand them in for your instructor's inspection.

Stating and Outlining the Thesis

Before you formulate your thesis, be sure to review pages 33–44. The following observations supplement that discussion and are confined to four kinds of difficulties that students encounter at the thesis-writing stage.

[3] It might be wise at this point to study the set of student notes provided with the research paper on pages 273–313.

The most serious difficulties have their origin in faults which occurred long before the writing of the thesis. If a student has chosen a subject about which no thesis can be formulated, or if he has failed to restrict his general subject and so has gathered only a miscellany of information, he cannot write a satisfactory thesis, and there is nothing at this late date that his instructor can do to help him. The only solution is to start over from the beginning, and there is not time for that. The student simply has to accept the consequences of his failure to understand the assignment and to work purposefully toward carrying it out.

Many students create trouble for themselves by trying to avoid the discipline that writing a thesis normally imposes. Faced with the task of expressing a controlling idea in a single sentence, they take one of two escapes: they write a thesis which is so general that it exerts no control over the development of the paper, or they write one which looks good but has no relation to the material in their notes and therefore does not represent the idea they intend to develop. Faulty theses are usually exposed if there is time to discuss them in class, through the collective criticism of twenty students exploring the meaning of a sentence on the blackboard.

Since the research paper is usually one of the longest and most complex papers written by college students, it nearly always requires a careful outline. Indeed, many instructors make the writing of a detailed outline a critical stage in the preparation of the paper and do not allow students to begin actual composition until the outline is approved.

The best preparation for outlining your research paper is a careful review of Chapter 3, with special attention to pages 57–62, which discuss shaping and testing the organization. Most good students begin to develop the outline mentally while they are doing their intensive reading. From time to time they spread their notes on a table and study ways of grouping them. When they find them falling into logical groups, they begin to write the subject label on each card in the group. Students who work this way actually tackle outlining in three stages: (1) classifying information by subject groups while the information is still in the notes, with periodic attempts to work the groups into a running outline; (2) preliminary outlining to discover a thesis or to test one which is beginning to take shape in the mind; (3) final outlining, in which the structural pattern which has been developing through the two earlier stages is given its finished form.

The final outline, then, is merely a refinement of the organization already suggested by the study of your notes. But observe that the notes will suggest a pattern only if they have been efficiently made — that is, if each note is on a separate card, if useless cards are discarded with each restriction of the subject, if the content of the note cards is economically stated so that you can see at a glance what information each card contains. If the notes have not been efficiently taken — if they are long, undigested excerpts crowded together on both sides of the pages of a notebook — they will suggest neither a thesis nor an outline. The student who makes such notes must expect to have a hard time with his outline.

✔ Each of the following numbered excerpts contains the thesis and the main statements of a student outline. To be satisfactory, an excerpt should give you at least a clear hint of what the student proposes to do in his paper and how he proposes to do it. In each excerpt, study the thesis and the relation of the main statements to that thesis. If the excerpt is satisfactory in both respects, mark it O.K. If it is not satisfactory, explain why.

1. Quaker education is essentially a religious education.
    I. Family life is oriented to the belief that parents must set a moral example for the children.
    II. The school program, in its curriculum, conduct, choice of teachers, and texts, emphasizes religious instruction.
    III. The Meeting, to which children are admitted at an early age, establishes a pattern of silent worship.

2. Adolf Hitler's rejection as an artist led him to develop psychological complexes which resulted in the destruction of his beloved Germany.
    I. As a boy Hitler rebelled against his father's wish to make him a civil servant.
    II. Hitler's failure to graduate from high school kept him from being admitted to art school in Vienna.
    III. During his Vienna years, opera was Hitler's chief passion.
    IV. While in Vienna, Hitler first conceived of himself as a political leader.

3. The potentialities of many gifted children are left undeveloped because of certain social pressures.
    I. The parents create strong pressure to force the child to be "normal."
    II. Teachers often are unaware of, neglect, or overemphasize the child's potentialities.
    III. Other children put tremendous pressure on a gifted child to conform to the practices and preferences of his age group.

4. The best way to achieve a perfect life on earth is through the perfect contemplation of the Trappist monks.
    I. Perfect contemplation is the giving over completely of one's life to God, thus giving Him the worship He most desires.
    II. The life of a monk is kept as simple as possible so that he may keep his mind on God and his duty.
    III. Justification of monasticism may be found in its ability to survive and flourish in spite of constant persecution.

5. A better knowledge of the facts of the disease is bringing new hope to lepers and a new understanding of leprosy to others.
    I. Down through history all cultures have had erroneous beliefs about leprosy.
    II. This fear can be driven out of men's minds only by a knowledge of the facts concerning leprosy.

6. The popular conception of a schizophrenic as a person with a "split personality" is inaccurate.

I. The "split personality," as popularly conceived, is a symptom of amnesia, not schizophrenia.
II. The split which actually is present in schizophrenia is the separation of a person from his social and physical environment.

Composing the Paper

All that has been said about composition in Part One of this book applies to the research paper. But in addition the research assignment has its special problem — the relationship between borrowed material and the use that is made of it. The research paper is admittedly and necessarily written from information derived from printed sources. But that information has to be woven into an essay which is essentially the student's own work. A student who has worked purposefully will not have too much difficulty reconciling these two conditions, for he will have selected his material with a view to using it in support of a purpose he has been forming as he reads. In a sense he is like a man who is building a house with bricks obtained from others. The bricks are not his, but the design and construction of the house are. *Writing a research paper, then, is not just stringing together statements from books and magazines. It is a complete reorganization and reworking of the source material into an original composition.*

Failure to recognize this sometimes results in a paper which is merely a transcription of the information in the note cards. The following excerpt from a student research paper reveals this weakness:

Article 123 of the Mexican Constitution has the sole purpose of solving the labor problem. It is looked upon as the declaration of the rights of the workmen.[10]

The workers' hours have a maximum limit of eight hours for a day's work. At least one day's rest for every six days' work is to be enjoyed by everyone.[11]

Children over twelve and under sixteen years of age can work only six hours a day, and children under twelve are not permitted to be made the subject of a contract.[12]

The minimum wage that can be received by a workman should be considered sufficient according to the conditions of life prevailing in the workman's particular region of the country. This same com-

pensation is to be paid without regard to the sex of
the worker.[13]

Wages are required to be paid in legal currency
rather than by any other representative token with
which it is sought to substitute money.[14]

---

[10]Tannenbaum, p. 529
[11]Ibid.
[12]Ibid.
[13]Ibid.
[14]Ibid., p. 530.

Obviously, all this student is doing is setting down the contents of five
note cards, all from the same source and four from the same page. He has
not organized his material to develop any judgment of his own. The noticeable inequalities of style suggest to a reader that he has occasionally copied
the actual wording of his source without using quotation marks. At any
rate, there is nothing in the excerpt to suggest any contribution of the
student's own. The same facts built into a paragraph which the student has
actually created himself might come out like this:

Article 123 of the Mexican Constitution attempts to standardize labor conditions by setting
up basic principles governing hours and salaries.
It provides a maximum work-week of six eight-hour
days, prohibits the contractual hiring of children
under twelve years of age, and limits the employment
of children between twelve and sixteen to six hours
a day. It requires that all wages be paid in legal
currency, thus eliminating company scrip and other
cash substitutes. It provides for a minimum wage
scale which takes into account differences in the
standard and cost of living in various parts of the
country. It abolishes discrimination against women
by making the wage rate the same for both sexes. In
general, therefore, it seeks to establish a uni-

form code which will provide the general pattern of labor-management relations throughout the country.[10]

---

[10] Tannenbaum, pp. 529-530.

The first of these two versions is a series of raw notes; the second is a unified paragraph created by the student. Both contain exactly the same facts, but the revised version rearranges and rewords the facts to make them develop the idea stated in the opening sentence. It also avoids the over-documentation of the first version by acknowledging the two pages of Tannenbaum's book as the source for all the information in the paragraph. If an instructor were to compare the second version with the notes from which it was written, he would clearly see that the writer had mastered the information he was using and had shaped it to suit his own purpose. This point has already been illustrated by an assignment in paragraphing on pages 89–91. It is further illustrated by the comparison of notes and text of the sample research paper on pages 273–313.

Because of the importance of the research paper, the composition should usually be done in three stages: writing the rough draft, preparing the final revision, and proofreading the finished paper. No two of these stages should be completed at a single sitting; indeed, it is best to allow at least a day between the completion of one and the beginning of the next.

How a student should compose the rough draft will depend partly on his work habits and partly on the nature of his material. For the average student the best advice is to break the total job into the main units of the outline and to tackle these units in order. The first draft of a paper so developed is likely to be a bit stiff, to proceed rather mechanically from one step to the next, and to lack the qualities that make for an interesting or effective style. But these are not serious weaknesses if careful revision is to follow.

Footnotes and any graphic illustration being used should be written into the rough draft so as to avoid difficulties with spacing in the final version. Even though footnotes are finally placed at the foot of the page, some students find it convenient in the first draft to insert them between ruled lines within the text immediately after the line containing the footnote marker. Not all research papers need or are suited to graphic illustrations — tables, graphs, charts — but since these aids present complex or cumbersome data compactly and thus make the reader's task easier, they should be used when they are appropriate.

The revision should turn the rough draft into a finished essay. It should provide smooth transitions between units — a more difficult task in a long composition than in a short one. It should polish the diction and sentence structure and remove any awkward constructions. It should check the relationship of detailed information to the topic idea. It should make sure that direct quotations are clearly marked and that indirect quotations and summaries actually serve the purpose of a paragraph and are not merely strung together without any purpose other than to get *something* written.

When the paper has been revised, the final bibliography should be added. This will be a list of the sources actually used in preparing the paper. It should include all sources cited in the footnotes and may contain one or two works which were valuable as background material even though not actually cited in the paper. The form of this bibliography was discussed on page 252.

Finally, the paper should be proofread at least twice to detect any errors which survived the revision. These readings should be mainly concerned with mechanical matters — doubtful spellings, punctuation, usage, and typographical errors. The proofreadings should include both the footnotes and the bibliography, and it is wise at this stage to check these against the recommended forms. Proofreading should be done slowly — more slowly than reading for content. Some students find it helpful to read the paper aloud slowly so as to concentrate on the appearance of each word.

Documenting the Evidence

As we have said, all information taken from a specific source must be identified in a footnote.[4] That is, the evidence must be *documented*. The purpose of this convention is twofold: (1) to avoid the appearance of representing somebody else's work as yours; (2) to let the interested reader consult your sources and so check the accuracy of your investigation or carry on his own. This convention is so important in research writing that inaccurate documentation — or none at all — is regarded as a serious offense. For the research writer it is both good manners and good morals to acknowledge sources fairly and accurately.

When to Footnote

Inexperienced research writers often have difficulty in deciding what statements require documenting. The general principle is that you should cite the source of any statement for which you are indebted to the work of another. For most student research this general principle can be broken down into six conditions. You should provide a footnote whenever:

1. You use a direct quotation.
2. You copy a table, chart, or other diagram.

[4] The kind of footnote discussed here is called a "reference footnote." Footnotes may also qualify, explain, or comment on statements made in the text when it would be awkward to include such matters in the main discussion. Such footnotes may be called "explanatory footnotes." This footnote is explanatory. It provides an explanation which, though necessary, would be awkward to include in the body of the text.

3. You summarize a discussion in your own words.

4. You construct a diagram from data provided by others.

5. You paraphrase an opinion which you have read rather than reached independently.

6. You present specific evidence which cannot reasonably be considered common knowledge.

The first four of these conditions are sufficiently definite to require no discussion. Difficulties, if any, will come from the last two, and these difficulties are better resolved by experience than by definition. By the time you have got well into any research project, you will have reached conclusions you did not have when you began your study. Unless these conclusions came specifically from one of your sources, they need not be documented. They are products of your total reading, not borrowings from any specific source.

Similarly, as you become familiar with a subject, you will find that facts of which you at first were ignorant are so well known that they must be considered common knowledge. For example, you probably do not now know the dates of Matthew Arnold's life. But if you were writing a research paper on Arnold you would find them common knowledge to all the writers you were reading. It would be unnecessary, and a little naïve, to footnote these dates. This does not mean that no factual information need be footnoted. If you were recording the number of fatalities at Gettysburg, the tonnage and dimensions of the *Santa Maria,* or the population of London in 1450, you would be expected to cite your source in a footnote. The question of what can legitimately be considered common knowledge is difficult to answer in the abstract, except by the general advice, *When in doubt, footnote it.* Since one function of the freshman research paper is to give experience in using footnotes, your instructor will probably prefer too many rather than too few.

How to Footnote

A footnote consists of two parts: the footnote marker, a number placed in the text at the end of the statement to be documented and slightly above the level of the typed or handwritten line; and the footnote proper, which usually comes at the foot of the page and is numbered to correspond with the marker. Footnotes are separated from the text by a triple space and from each other by a double space. The first line of a footnote is indented, and footnote numbers do not start afresh on each page but run consecutively throughout the paper. These conventions are illustrated in the sample paper on pages 273–313.

The purpose of the footnote is to identify as precisely as possible the source to which the statement in the text is indebted. Although no one form is universally preferred, the minimum information required is a clear reference to the author, title, and page. The first reference to a source needs to give fuller information than do subsequent references to that source.

In general, a footnote reference is similar in form to a bibliographical citation, *but there are noteworthy differences.* The following summary presents the most important conventions of footnoting.

1. Author

a. In a footnote the author's name is given in its normal order — John Smith — not inverted as in a bibliography.

b. When more than one author is to be named, the form is the same as that used in a bibliography (page 247) except that the first author's name is not inverted.

c. In a reference to an edited work, the editor's name, in normal order, goes in place of the author's name and is followed by "ed." — with or without parentheses as in the bibliographical form.

d. After the first reference to a work in a footnote, the author's or editor's name is usually shortened to surname only, in subsequent footnotes.

e. If there is no author's or editor's name, the footnote begins with the title.

2. Title

All titles follow the forms used in bibliography, but after the first footnote reference, the author's surname and the page number are enough — for example: Gulley, p. 11 — provided that only one author is being cited by that name and only one book by that author. Unless both these conditions are true, a short form of the title is commonly used — Gulley, *Essentials,* p. 11. After the first reference to a magazine or newspaper article, the title of the magazine or the newspaper may be used without the title of the article — *Life,* p. 17, or *The New York Times,* p. 23. Obviously these short forms cannot be used if more than one issue is being cited. For the use of "ibid." and "op. cit.," see pages 266–268.

3. Facts of Publication

a. The place and date of publication are given in the first reference to a book. After that they are omitted. When given, both are enclosed in parentheses and separated by a comma — (Boston, 1957). The name of the publisher, which is also a fact of publication, is often omitted in the first footnote reference, particularly if there is a bibliography which gives this information. If the publisher is given in the first footnote reference, the style is as follows — (Boston: Houghton Mifflin Company, 1957).

b. The facts of publication for a magazine article do not include place and publisher, but do include the volume and page numbers (see heading 4 below), and the date of issue — month (not abbreviated), day (if the magazine is published oftener than once a month), and year. The date is enclosed in parentheses.

c. The facts of publication of a newspaper article consist of the month, day, and year, *not in parentheses,* and the page.

4. Volume and Page Numbers

a. In references to a one-volume work, the abbreviation "p." is used for *page* and "pp." for *pages.*

b. When the reference is to a work of more than one volume, both the volume number and the page number must be given.

c. When both volume and page numbers are given, the abbreviations "vol." and "p." (or "pp.") are *not* used. Instead, use Roman numerals for the volume number for both books and magazines — X, 48. One major exception to this form is the practice in scientific studies of using Arabic numerals for both volume and page in citing magazines. In this form the volume number comes first and is separated from the page number by a colon — 10:58.

5. Use of "Ibid." and "Op. cit."

As noted above (see under heading 2, page 265), a short form is commonly used for a footnote reference after the first, which is given in full. There are, however, two other ways of making subsequent references: by the use of "ibid." or "op. cit."

Use of "Ibid." "Ibid." (an abbreviation for *ibidem,* "in the same place") is used to refer to a work cited in the *immediately preceding* footnote. If the second reference is to the same volume and page of the work, "ibid." alone is sufficient. If the second reference is to a different volume or page of the work, then "ibid." must be followed by a comma and the new volume and page numbers.

"Ibid." cannot be used to refer to a preceding footnote if a reference to another source intervenes. The following examples illustrate correct and incorrect uses of "ibid."

Correct Uses of "Ibid."

[1]Edgar Johnson, <u>Charles Dickens</u>: <u>His Tragedy and Triumph</u> (New York, 1952), I, 24.

[2]<u>Ibid</u>. (This is a reference to the same volume and page as the preceding.)

[3]<u>Ibid</u>., p. 27. (Still referring to Volume I, but to a different page.)

[4]<u>Ibid</u>., II, 95.

[5]<u>Ibid</u>., I, 28.

Incorrect Uses of "Ibid."

[1]Edgar Johnson, <u>Charles</u> <u>Dickens</u>: <u>His</u> <u>Tragedy</u> <u>and</u>
<u>Triumph</u> (New York, 1952), I, 24.

[2]Ibid., I, 24. (Omit I, 24.)

[3]Ibid., II. (Page number required.)

[4]George Orwell, <u>Dickens</u>, <u>Dali</u>, <u>and</u> <u>Others</u> (New
York, 1946), p. 68.

[5]Ibid., p. 26. (This is correct if it refers to
Orwell's work, but not if it refers to Johnson's,
because of the intervening reference to Orwell.)

Notice that "ibid." is followed by a period. It is capitalized when it begins a footnote. Since usage varies with respect to italicizing "ibid.," follow your instructor's preference.

Those who prefer the short form of subsequent footnote reference consider that "ibid." is most acceptably used as a later reference on a page which already has the footnote in full or short form, so that the reader can see immediately, without turning back one or more pages, to what work the "ibid." refers.

Use of "Op. cit." "Op. cit." (an abbreviation for *opere citato,* "in the work cited") may be used to refer to a work which has already been cited but not in the *immediately* preceding footnote. It serves as a substitute for the title only, and must be preceded by the author's name and followed by the volume and page numbers. If more than one work by the same author is being cited, "op. cit." cannot be used, since a reader could not tell which work by that author was being cited; in such a case, a short form of the title must be used instead of "op. cit." The following footnotes show the correct use of "op. cit."

[1]Edgar Johnson, <u>Charles</u> <u>Dickens</u>: <u>His</u> <u>Tragedy</u> <u>and</u>
<u>Triumph</u> (New York, 1952), I, 24.

[2]George Orwell, <u>Dickens</u>, <u>Dali</u>, <u>and</u> <u>Others</u> (New
York, 1946), p. 68.

[3]Johnson, <u>op</u>. <u>cit</u>., I, 26.

[4]Orwell, <u>op</u>. <u>cit</u>., p. 88.

As with "ibid.," usage is divided on italics for "op. cit." Consult your instructor's preference.

Notice that "op. cit." is not used in a paper which is also using the author's surname and the page number as a short form. You have a choice, therefore, whether to use

Johnson, *op. cit.,* I, 26
or Johnson, I, 26

Because the second form is simpler, there is a growing tendency to prefer it to the "op. cit." form.

6. Punctuation

The punctuation of the footnote need present no problem, since, except for periods after abbreviations and at the end, commas may be used throughout. Even the period at the end is optional, though its use or omission should be consistent.

The following footnotes illustrate the preceding discussion and may be used as models against which to check your own footnotes.

First Reference to a Book

[1]René Wellek and Austin Warren, Theory of Literature (New York, 1949), p. 5.

> SUBSEQUENT REFERENCE: *Ibid.,* p. 22; OR, Wellek and Warren, p. 22; whichever is applicable.

Reference to an Essay in an Anthology

[2]George Santayana, "Lovers of Illusion," Reading Prose, ed. Wright Thomas and Stuart Gerry Brown (New York, 1952), p. 486.

> SUBSEQUENT REFERENCE: *Ibid.,* p. 489; OR Santayana, p. 489; whichever is applicable.

Reference to a Magazine Article

[3]Hugh L. Dryden, "The International Geophysical Year," The National Geographic Magazine, CIX (February, 1956), 289. OR 109:289 (February, 1956).

> SUBSEQUENT REFERENCE: *Ibid.;* OR Dryden, p. 289; whichever is applicable.

Reference to an Article in an Encyclopedia

[4]"Mississippi Scheme," The Columbia Encyclopedia, 2nd ed., p. 1294.

Reference to a Newspaper Article

[5]Dudley McAllister, "Heating Bill Up? Company Explains Why," Champaign-Urbana Courier, January 27, 1956, p. 2.

[6]"Salt Treatment of Trees Described," St. Louis Post-Dispatch, January 5, 1956, p. 4C.

Miscellaneous Abbreviations

In addition to those already used, the following abbreviations are in common use in footnotes:

cf., "compare."

chap(s)., "chapter(s)."

f., ff., "and the following page(s)." (pp. 17 f.: "page 17 and the following page"; pp. 17 ff.: "page 17 and the following pages")

l., "line." (l. 10).

ll., "lines." (ll. 6–12).

loc. cit., "in the place or passage cited." Not a synonym for *op. cit.,* but used to refer to a source already cited, regardless of whether another footnote intervenes. Commonly used to refer to collections of material, often unpublished collections. Seldom used in undergraduate papers.

passim, "in various places in the text." Used to indicate a number of scattered references to a subject.

sic, "thus." Used in brackets to indicate that an apparent error is not a miscopying but appeared thus in the source.

Presenting the Finished Assignment

The assignment has not been fully met until the paper has been presented to the instructor in the form which he has stipulated. A typical student research paper consists of the following parts:

1. A title page containing at least the title of the paper and the student's name and section number.

2. A detailed sentence outline of the paper.

3. The body of the paper, typed if possible, each page numbered and adequately footnoted. Only one side of the page is used, of course. If the paper is typed, the text should be double-spaced. Quotations of five or more lines should be indented and single-spaced without quotation marks.

4. Conventional footnotes with corresponding footnote markers at appropriate points in the text.

5. A bibliography of works used in preparing the paper.

6. The note cards used in writing the paper, arranged in the order in which they were used, labeled with outline symbols to show their relation to the outline, and tied together or sealed in an envelope. The purpose of

handing in the notes is to allow the instructor to trace the development of your paper from outline and notes to finished composition.

If your instructor wishes to modify these requirements, he will notify you. Make sure that you understand clearly what is wanted. If you are uncertain, consult your instructor well in advance of the deadline.

Exercises

A. For any subject of your choice:

1. Explain briefly what procedure you would follow in preparing a preliminary bibliography for it.

2. Following the procedure you have explained, prepare a bibliography of ten sources for the subject you have chosen. Do not include any source until you have examined it briefly, and indicate on each bibliographical card the features for which you selected that work. Do not spend more than two hours on this part of the assignment, but try to get the best sources available in your library.

B. As preparation for a short paper to be entitled "Colloquial Usage: What It Is and Is Not," study both the pertinent introductory material and the dictionary entry "Colloquial" in the sources that follow. Make notes on your reading on 3 × 5 or 4 × 6 inch cards, whichever your instructor prefers. Following the model shown on page 50, organize your notes as a first step towards an outline; then write a sentence outline and label each card with the outline symbol which it would develop. Hand in both the outline and the cards.

> *The American College Dictionary.*
> Kennedy, Arthur G. *Current English* (check index for page references).
> Kenyon and Knott. *A Pronouncing Dictionary of American English.*
> *The Oxford English Dictionary.*
> *Webster's New International Dictionary, Second Edition.*
> *Webster's New World Dictionary.*

C. Assume that the following footnotes appeared in this order in a student paper. If you think the footnote is acceptable, mark it O.K. If you think it needs revision, revise it.

[1]Morris L. Ernst and David Loth, Report on the American Communist (New York, 1952), p. 28.

[2]Ernst and Loth, ibid., p. 28.

[3]Morris, R., and Angell, E., "Should Congress Investigate?" Sat. Review, vol. 38, pg. 9, Feb. 26, 1955.

[4]Morris and Angell, _op_. _cit_., p. 10.

[5]_Ibid_., pg. 10.

[6]Eugene Lyons, "Red Decade," American Mercury, 38 (April 29, 1955), 66.

[7]_Ibid_., 67.

[8]Ernst and Loth, _ibid_., p. 29.

D. The following student research paper, complete with outline, notes, text, footnotes, and bibliography, is presented as an exhibit for detailed study. It is not offered here as a perfect paper but as a fair sample of what a superior freshman student will do with a research project. If you analyze it according to the following directions, you will have a useful review of the process of writing a research paper.

First, study the outline, paying particular attention to the relationships among the sentences. Do the Roman numeral statements show a clear relation to the thesis? Do the subordinate parts clearly relate to the main units? Challenge every statement to test its relation to the idea it is being used to develop.

Second, study the text for structure alone. Is there a clear relation between successive parts of the paper and the outline? Does every paragraph play a part in advancing the purpose of the thesis, or are there any irrelevant paragraphs? Is there adequate transition between the paragraphs? Check the relation of text and outline by inserting the outline symbols in the margin opposite appropriate units of the text. If you find paragraphs which do not relate directly to the outline headings, consider whether they are legitimate transitions or are mistakes. Comment on the opening paragraph, and especially the first sentence, as an introduction to the paper and as a statement of purpose; can you suggest how this introductory paragraph might be improved?

Third, study the notes as notes, to see what kind of material they contain. Is each note accurately identified as to source? Is the content of the note pertinent to the student's purpose? Is the student digesting material as he makes the notes, or is he mostly copying material without digesting it?

Fourth, study the relation of notes and text. Are the paragraphs merely strings of notes in the same form they had in the note cards or is the author *composing* from the notes? If the author is more successful sometimes than others, notice where he is successful and why. If there are paragraphs which contain information not in the notes, try to determine whether such information would normally be part of the background a student would build during such a study. If there are notes that were not used, should they have been used, or was the author wise in omitting them? Try to see the development of the paper from the notes so that you will be better prepared to handle this problem when you come to it in your own paper.

Fifth, check the footnotes and bibliography. Do the forms used in this paper agree with your understanding of the conventions?

Finally, evaluate the whole paper in terms of: (1) the purposefulness of the author's procedure as it is revealed in notes, outline, and text, (2) the thoroughness of the development of the paper within the limits of a 2000-word assignment, (3) the success of the author in communicating to you, as a reader, the results of his study.

The following student research paper is printed by permission of the author, Charles Derber.

Not all instructors require a title page, but if one is required, the form shown here may be used as a model.

The format, or physical appearance, of this paper illustrates general principles of good usage. The text is double-spaced. Footnotes are single-spaced, but a blank line between footnotes allows for raising the footnote number. As shown here, following the MLA Style Sheet *recommendations for Masters' and Doctors' theses, the first footnote on each page is separated from the last line of text by triple-spacing (that is, two blank lines), not by a typewritten or hand-ruled line. A ruled line of separation is entirely permissible, however, and the instructor's preference in this respect should be followed. Each footnote begins on a new line (with regular paragraph indention). Two very short notes are sometimes placed on the same line, for appearance' sake.*

White typewriter paper of standard size (8½ × 11 inches) should be used, on one side only. Pages should be numbered, and margins should be generous.

WINGATE'S RAIDERS: THE NUCLEUS OF A NATIONAL ARMY

by

Charles Derber

English 111, Section C

Mr. Draperson

May 25, 1962

273

Wingate's Raiders: The Nucleus of a National Army

Thesis: The Jewish concept and conduct of defense against Arab guerrilla warfare were modified significantly by Orde Wingate's military innovations.

I. Before Wingate's military operations in 1938, the concept and conduct of Jewish defense proved favorable to the Arabs in their peculiar guerrilla offensive.
   A. The organization and tactics of the Arab guerrilla fighters enabled them to wage a devastating hit-and-run warfare from 1936 to 1938.
   B. The Jewish defensive strategy did not meet the military challenges of Arab warfare.

II. Wingate's study of the warfare in Palestine from 1936 to 1938 convinced him that basic changes in the Jewish defense were necessary.
   A. His experience in Jewish settlements convinced him that Haganah's strategy of limited defense was suicidal.
      1. He believed that it was militarily unsound to defend against Arab attacks from the inside of the settlements.
      2. He believed it necessary to track the movement of Arab gangs and supplies by penetration of small patrols into Arab territory at night.
   B. His study convinced him that the Jewish fighting force must reorganize into a national army and adopt the discipline and duty procedure of a regular army.

III. By carrying through his plans in the establish-
ment and operation of the Special Night Squads,
Wingate implemented his theories of defense.
   A. His Special Night Squads adopted the strategy
   that a defense must be offensive.
      1. The S.N.S. operated at night in small
      patrols outside of the settlements in
      defense of the Haifa pipeline.
      2. They perfected the use of the surprise
      attack to destroy Arab gangs and supplies
      whose movements they had charted.
   B. The Special Night Squads became the core of a
   national army and adopted a severe discipline
   and duty procedure.
      1. In his training courses, drill exercises,
      and military operations, Wingate inflicted
      the discipline of a regular army on his
      men.
      2. In the duty procedure that he enforced,
      Wingate imbued his men with the regularity
      of standard army routine.

On the pages opposite the text are shown the notes from which this paper was written. No notes were required for the introductory first paragraph, or for the transitional paragraph on page 10. As the paper was developed, some notes were combined; others were not used; still others were used in the first draft but deleted in revision. These notes do not include background material which the author collected before he decided on his thesis. Note cards containing information actually footnoted are identified here by a number corresponding to the footnote.

WINGATE'S RAIDERS:

THE NUCLEUS OF A NATIONAL ARMY

This paper deals with the contribution that
Captain Orde Wingate made to the Jewish defense
against Arab attacks during the years 1936-1939.
When Wingate arrived in Palestine as a British intelligence officer, the Jews were meeting these attacks
with strictly defensive measures inherited from the
Haganah, an underground resistance organization.
When he left three years later, the Jews had learned
to defend by preventive guerrilla attack. In bringing about this change Wingate provided a pattern for
the creation of a unified Jewish national army.

The historical background of the Arab-Jewish
conflicts with which this study is concerned may be
summarized briefly. After World War I Palestine
became the scene of a conflict between the Jewish
drive for a national home and the Arab opposition
to that drive. The conflict began with the Balfour
Declaration of 1917 in which the British government

1

Jewish immigration

Enc. Brit., p. 134
Jewish immigration 1920-38

1920-24... 42,784
1925-29... 57,022
1930-34... 91,258
1935.........61,854
1936.......29,727
1937......10,536
1938.......12,868

Arab objectives

Wells, p. 25
In 1930's Arabs fighting for:
1. Stop Jewish immigration
2. Arab nat'l govt. in Pal.
3. Br. withdrawal of Balf. Decl.
4. End Br. mandate
5. Stop sale of land to Jews
6. Treaty with Brit. recognizing Arab sov'ty in Pal.

Start of Arab revolt

3

Royal Inst., p. 76
April 15, 1936 - First sign of revolt when Arabs held up Jews, killed 1, on road from Nablus to Tulham. False report of this affair led to several conflicts betw. Arabs + Jews.

Arab terrorism - org.

4

Viton, p. 321
Arab terrorists in countryside well organized in bands of 80-150 under some experienced leaders - replaced local govts. in places they controlled, even taxed the people.

5

Arab arms

Royal Inst., p. 76
Prohibition of sale of arms did not affect Arabs because they had rifles from pre-war and war years, also smuggled arms from Trans-Jordan.

Haj Amin el Husseini

Collins, p. 175
Prominent Arab trouble maker, Haj Amin el Husseini, the Grand Mufti, religious head of the Sunni Sect of Moslem faith in Pal. Had power to inflame local Arabs and initiate indirectly most Arab attacks on Brit. and Jews. Was allied with Hitler.

supported the Zionist movement; it increased in intensity as Arabs rioted against the immigration of 100,000 Jews in the 1920's and another 150,000 between 1930 and 1935.[1] In 1935 the Arabs demanded that Britain end its mandate over Palestine and recognize Arab sovereignty in that area.[2] When this demand was refused, the Arabs, in 1936, began a series of attacks on the Jews which were to last four years and be known as the Arab Revolt.[3]

The Revolt quickly expanded into a guerrilla war. Organized into bands of 80 to 150 men,[4] well armed with rifles left over from World War I or smuggled from Trans-Jordan,[5] and led by men experi-

[1] Encyclopaedia Britannica, 1959, XVII, 134.

[2] Linton Wells, "Holy Terror in Palestine," Current History, XLIX (December, 1938), 25.

[3] Royal Institute of International Affairs, Great Britain and Palestine, 1915-1939 (London, 1939), p. 76.

[4] Albert Viton, "It's War in Palestine," Nation, CXLVII (October 1, 1938), 321.

[5] Royal Institute, p. 76.

Arab leader - Kaukji

Royal Inst., p. 80
 Sept. 3, 1936 - Fawzi Kaukji - famous
Syrian revolutionary transferred his activities
to Pal. and became head of guerrilla offensive

Arab terrorism

Royal. Inst., p. 77
 By June - July, 1936, revolt raging.
Typical action: acts of violence against
Jews; destruction of crops + property; cutting
of telegraph lines; blowing up railway tracks
bridges; ambushing of trains + car convoys

Arab terrorism

Brit. Reports (1937), p. 6
 Terrorist campaign in 1937: isolated
murder; armed attacks on military, police,
and civilian road transport; attacks on
Jewish settlements and Arab and Jewish
private property

Arab terrorism

N.Y. Times, Mar. 15, 1937, p. 12
 3 Jews slain by Arabs hiding in ditch -
1 Jew stabbed by Arab - 2 Jews injured by
Arab bombs - numerous shootings of Jews by Arabs

1937 terrorism - statistics

Brit. Reports (1937) pp. 11-12
1937 Statistical Terrorist Record

(p.11) Bomb + firearm attacks against:		(p.12) Total Casualties	Killed	Wounded
Police	109	Police		
Jewish Settlements	143	British	4	2
Jewish transports	38	Arab	10	4
Arab transports	23	Jewish	2	2
British houses	2	Officials		
Arab houses	109	Civil	2	—
Shepherds	11	Mil.	5	5
Ploughmen	3	Civilians		
		Arabs	44	53
		Jews	32	83

8

Mosley, p. 40
 Arabs led by guerrilla fighter named Kaukji
from Syria - purely hit + run tactics - waged a
running campaign almost impossible to counter
by normal military methods. Thus British efforts
fairly unsuccessful.

enced in guerrilla tactics, the Arabs destroyed
crops and property, cut telegraph lines, dynamited
railway tracks and bridges, and ambushed trains
and convoys.[6] In 1937 alone they made 143 attacks
on Jewish settlements, killing 32 civilians and
wounding 83.[7] In conducting this guerrilla war
the Arabs had two great advantages. First, they
were mobile and hence could wage a hit-and-run
campaign extremely difficult to oppose with ordinary military procedures.[8] Second, the bands
could dissolve quickly when seriously threatened
and mix with the civilian Arab population, who
would hide them and their weapons. The members
of the guerrilla bands were thus personally protected and their arms and supplies were easily

[6]Royal Institute, p. 77.

[7]League of Nations Mandates. British Reports
on Palestine and Trans-Jordan, 1937-1938, Report
for 1937 (London, 1939), p. 12.

[8]Leonard Mosley, Gideon Goes to War (New York,
1955), p. 40.

9

Arab terrorist tactics

Royal Inst., p. 104

Rebels mixed with sympathetic population which wouldn't expose them or their weapons. Thus difficult to capture.

Haganah - origin

Koestler, p. 67

Origin of Haganah in "Watchmen" - defended selves and families before World War I - romantic figures - rode horseback, wore Arab headgear, spoke Arabic fluently, knew Arab customs.

10

Haganah

Koestler, pp. 69-71

After W. W. I, Watchmen disappeared, replaced by Haganah - illegal, semi-underground group which rose to meet Arab terrorism in 1929.

10

concealed.[9]

In attempting to defend themselves against Arab attacks, the Jews were limited both in organization and in strategy. They were not permitted by the British to have any organized fighting force or even to possess firearms. The nucleus of their defense was a semi-underground organization called the Haganah, which in Hebrew means "defense." The Haganah had its origin in pre-war Jewish settlers known as "watchmen," who protected themselves from Arab attack by patrolling their lands on horseback. After the Balfour Declaration, in response to the increasing Arab hostility, these watchmen were unofficially replaced by the Haganah, which operated relatively independently in each Jewish settlement.[10] Its function was to defend the settlement against attack. To do this it smuggled in weapons and supplies, but its policy was limited to defense; it did not engage in

[9]Royal Institute, p. 104.

[10]Arthur Koestler, Promise and Fulfilment (New York, 1949), pp. 67-71.

Haganah - Havlagah

Syrkin, p. 314

1936-39. Haganah adopted principle of Havlagah, meaning self-restraint. Arab acts of terrorism not met by similar acts, but arms and supplies smuggled in for defense of individual settlements.

Supernumeraries

N.Y. Times, Sept. 12, 1938, p. 4

British could not handle Arab terrorism and thus forced to give Jews some measure of self-defense, so created supernumeraries.

Supernumeraries

Koestler, p. 73

Certain number of Haganah men made into supernumerary police force. First time some aspect of Haganah organization became legal.

Supernumeraries

Brit Reports (1937), p. 13

Training of Jewish supernumeraries:
1. recruits given course in weapon training under military instructors - given rank of lance corporal and sent back to settlements.
2. supernumeraries trained other supers in each settlement
3. supers armed with rifles + Greener guns

counter or preventive attacks. Its own description of its policy was "Havlagah" or self-restraint.[11]

Because the British were unable to protect Jewish settlements and because they respected the policy of Havlagah, they established a Jewish Supernumerary Police Force.[12] Haganah sent certain of its members to be trained as supernumeraries. These recruits were given military instruction, rifles, and Greener guns, and sent back to train other supernumerary police.[13] This police force was the only legal part of the Haganah. It strengthened the Haganah, but it did not change its basic organization or concept of operation.

In September of 1936, while the Revolt was in full force, Orde Wingate, a new intelligence officer of the British Headquarters, arrived in Palestine.

[11]Marie Syrkin, Blessed Is the Match (Philadelphia, 1947), p. 314.

[12]The New York Times, September 12, 1938, p. 4.

[13]British Reports, Report for 1937, p. 13.

Wingate - to Pal.

Mosley, p. 34

Sept. 1936 - Wingate and wife sailed for Pal. - Appointment as Intelligence Officer on staff of H. Q. British Forces, Jerusalem - worked first in Haifa under Brigadier Evetts

14

Wingate - background

Dict. of Nat. Biog., p. 962

Wingate born in India - Feb. 26, 1903 - Military ancestry, both father and grandfather were well known military men - brought up in strict Puritan atmosphere.

Wingate - char.

Weizmann, II, 398

Wingate's two passions - military science and Bible - an amazing combination of student and man of action

16

Wingate - Zionist

Sykes: pp. 109-10

Wingate arrived in Pal. sympathetic with Arabs. In less than month, he became extreme Zionist. This caused by seeing reality of land situation, seeing determination and restraint of Jews, and influence of Bible.

Wingate's thinking and action were to have a profound influence on the conduct of the Jewish defense
during the next three years. Born in India in 1903,
he had been brought up in a stern Puritan atmosphere
which deeply affected his perspective on affairs in
Palestine.[14] He was described by his friend, Chaim
Weizmann, as having two passions--the Bible and
military science.[15] His knowledge of the Bible convinced him that the Jewish drive for a homeland in
Palestine was divinely sanctioned, and within a
month of his arrival he was converted to Zionism.[16]
His passion for military science led him to make a
thorough study of the warfare in Palestine and convinced him that basic changes in the Jewish defense
were necessary.

[14]Dictionary of National Biography, 1941-1950,
p. 962.

[15]Chaim Weizmann, Trial and Error, The Autobiography of Chaim Weizmann (Philadelphia, 1949), II,
398.

[16]Christopher Sykes, Orde Wingate (Cleveland,
1959), pp. 109-110.

17

Wingate in Jerusalem

Sykes, p. 127
    1937 – Wingate in Jerusalem – spent time
in study of land and on reports of all recent
military activity – familiarized self with Hebrew
and met more Jews in Haganah and Jewish
political leaders.

During the next two years Wingate devoted his
time to a study of the geography of the land and the
military activities of the Jews and Arabs.[17] He
conducted this study by personally making long ex-
ploratory journeys throughout Palestine and certain
neighboring countries where rebels were based. He
observed the defense activities of many Jewish settlements, studying in detail the settlements at
Afikim, Hanita, and Tirat Tsevi.

The major conclusion that Wingate drew from his
observations was that Haganah's concept of limited
defense was suicidal. The Jews must not wait for
Arab attacks and meet them within the settlements
but must meet the enemy near the Arab villages and
adopt their guerrilla tactics. He first reached this
conclusion at Afikim and developed it more fully
during his stay at Hanita. One night, after several
weeks at Hanita, he called the settlers together and
told them, "You Jews of the settlements have been

[17]Sykes, p. 127.

Wingate on tactics.

Mosley, p. 53

Wingate tells Hanita settlers that new tactics must be adopted. "You Jews of the settlements have been fighting a defensive war against the Arabs for too long. It will not save your lives or your settlements .... We must try a new kind of war."

19

Wingate on tactics

Sykes, p. 145

Wingate arrived at Hanita where 40 supernumeraries were stationed - observed defense was from inside of settlement - Argued that Jews must defend from the outside and organize patrols to operate outside

Wingate on tactics

Sugrue, p. 70

Wingate's proposition to Haganah staff of what the S.N.S. would involve: operate on the basis of reliable info; strike at night; hit the bands in their hide-outs or at villages where they are quartered

fighting a defensive war against the Arabs for too long. It will not save your lives or your settlements. . . . We must try a new kind of war."[18] He told the forty supernumeraries stationed at Hanita that they must organize patrols to defend the settlement from the outside rather than the interior.[19]

Wingate's concept of the use of these patrols soon changed from defensive to offensive. He proposed to the Haganah General Staff the formation of Special Night Squads which would penetrate enemy territory, spy out the location of supply depots and routes, and observe concentrations of guerrillas.[20] With this information the patrols could better defend their settlements by launching preventive attacks and thus destroying Arab potential for new raids. Wingate himself demonstrated both the operation and the value of this policy. From Hanita he took small groups of men across the Syrian border

[18]Mosley, p. 53.   [19]Sykes, p. 145.

[20]Thomas Sugrue, Watch for the Morning (New York, 1950), p. 70.

22

Wingate preparation

Mosley, p. 51

At Hanita, Wingate would make long trips at night into Arab territory. Discovered routes and depots and planned attacks.

Wingate preparations

Sykes, p. 140

Wingate first put his months of study to use at Tirat Tsevi - worked out paths of entry for arms smuggling and organized supernumeraries into small patrols which guarded these paths and discovered many of the Arab supply routes

Wingate on offensive policy

Sykes, p. 113

Wingate meets Wilenski: At first meeting tells him that policy of selfrestraint was out of date - situation now required an offensive on part of Jews. "The need was for the formation of an army, and he declared in all seriousness that it was his ambition to lead a Jewish army into battle."

under cover of night and showed them Arab supply
bases and how to attack them.[21]   At Tirat Tsevi he
organized the supernumeraries into small patrols
which scouted supply routes and then guarded the
paths by which the Arabs were smuggling their
weapons.[22]

The changes that Wingate believed necessary in
the Jewish defense were not confined to military
strategy. From the beginning of his stay in Palestine he was convinced that the Haganah had to be
replaced by a Jewish national army, and that he was
the man to develop that army and lead it. After
only a month in the country, he insisted to Emanuel
Wilenski, chief intelligence officer of the Haganah,
that a Jewish army must be formed.[23]   During a long
discussion with Wilenski, on whom he made a deep and
lasting impression, he said, "There will be no free
Palestine for the Jews unless you fight and win.

[21]Mosley, p. 51.   [22]Sykes, p. 140.
[23]Ibid., p. 113.

Wingate on Jewish fighting

Mosley, p. 36

. In conversation with Wilenski - Chief Intell. Offic. of Haganah - Wingate declared Jews would have to fight to win independence. Said "There will be no free Palestine for the Jews unless you fight and win. And you will not win, my friend, unless I teach you how to fight and lead you into battle."

25

Wingate on mil. sit,

Sykes, pp. 120-24

After 4 months in Pal. Wingate wrote letter to cousin with following observations about military situation : military strength of Arabs is negligible; potential strength of Jews equivalent to two Brit. Army Corps; in case of war, essential to have Jewish trained fighting force. He concluded that he wants to raise Jewish brigade in Pal.

Wingate to Weizmann

Sykes, pp. 130-1

Wingate in late 1937 wrote letter to Weizmann saying :

1. Weizmann must obtain for Jews right of self-defense

2. Jews must be permitted to raise "Jewish Palestine Defense Force"

3. Wingate offers services to assist in formation of this force

10

And you will not win, my friend, unless I teach you how to fight and lead you into battle."[24] Three months later, he wrote to his cousin analyzing the potential strength of a Jewish brigade and expressing his desire to stay in Palestine and organize such a force.[25] In 1937 he wrote to Weizmann, then in England negotiating with British officials, urging him to persuade the British to permit the organization of a Jewish Palestine Defense Force, which Wingate offered to train.[26]

By the end of 1937 Wingate had thus reached certain definite conclusions about necessary changes in Jewish military strategy and organization. His establishment and operation of the Special Night Squads in his remaining years in Palestine brought about many of these changes and significantly modified the Jewish defensive efforts.

Early in 1938 Wingate requested permission to

[24]Mosley, p. 36.   [25]Sykes, pp. 120-124.
[26]Ibid., pp. 130-131.

27

Sykes, p. 141

In Haifa, Wingate asked permission to form SNS from Jewish supers and Brit. soldiers — said these patrols working at night were only way to counter Arab terrorist activities

28

Mosley, p. 61

Wingate sent to patrol pipeline to Haifa. Officially was Intell. Offic. in Nazareth, but let second in command do work and established self in Ein-Harod where Haganah sent him their best men to be trained for SNS.

29

Sykes, p. 149

Original S.N.S. organization: two platoons at each of four settlements including Ein-Harod — working originally with 39 Br. soldiers and 80 Haganah men — eventually more supers so that he formed nine patrols.

organize from Jewish supernumeraries and British
volunteers small patrols which could effectively
stop the night raids and arms-smuggling of the
Arabs.[27]   At this time Arab gangs were making repeated night attacks on the main oil pipeline which
extended from Trans-Jordan across the northern half
of Palestine to Haifa. Wingate was given permission
to organize Special Night Squads to protect the
pipeline. He was officially given the new position
of intelligence officer of Nazareth, but he ordered
his second-in-command to take full charge in Nazareth, while he established himself in the small
community of Ein Harod, where he spent all his time
constructing the Special Night Squads, the S.N.S.[28]

As organized by Wingate, the S.N.S. consisted
of eight small patrols--two stationed at each of
four settlements including Ein Harod.[29] These
patrols operated exclusively at night, and their

[27]Sykes, p. 141.   [28]Mosley, p. 61.
[29]Sykes, p. 149.

SNS—1st operation

Sykes, p. 150

June 3, 1938 – first operation of SNS.
Wingate with 7 others went out and successfully
defeated gang of saboteurs: adventure outside
settlement, at night, offensive and successful.

SNS tactics

Mosley, pp. 62-3

Wingate taught deception in transportation
men start in mil trucks and jump off
sides into ditches and hide - Arab spies follow
trucks while men reassembled and began raids

30

SNS—1st big operation

Sykes, p. 151

First real battle for SNS - June 11 - 2
patrols left in civilian cars in eve. - dropped off
at intervals so spies couldn't track them -
patrols led by 2 outposts 20 yds. apart with
grenades, then 2 scouts 20 yds. apart, then main
body of patrol in single file - moved in wide
arcs across pipeline - met raiders at Danna
whom outposts with grenades chased into the
village - patrols surrounded gang and captured
men + weapons.

function was twofold: to protect the pipeline and
to wipe out in surprise raids supply bases and gang
hideouts which had been located by reconnaissance.
The procedure of carrying out the first function is
illustrated by the first major S.N.S. attack on
June 11, 1938. That night two squads left the settlement in civilian cars and were dropped off at
intervals, so that Arab tracking of their movements
would be extremely difficult. Reassembled, the
patrols organized in the strict formation Wingate
had taught them--two outposts in front, armed with
grenades and marching twenty yards apart, followed
by two scouts also twenty yards apart, followed by
the main body marching single file. In this fashion
the patrol crisscrossed the pipeline area in large
sweeping arcs and came across a gang of saboteurs
near the village of Danna. Under cover of the rest
of the squad, the outposts, using their grenades,
chased the gang into Danna, where the entire patrol
surrounded and captured it.[30] This type of opera-

[30]Sykes, p. 151.

31

SNS effectiveness

<u>Brit. Reports</u> (1938), p. 11

July 1938 - pipeline damaged only once due to intensive defensive patrolling. In previous months damaged 10, 7, and 18 times.

An SNS operation

Sykes, p. 176

Most successful venture of SNS - perfect use of surprise - surrounded at night large gang of raiders planning to sabotage pipeline - 5 SNS surrounded Khirbet Beit Lidd - attack totally successful, all men & weapons captured

tion in defense of the pipeline proved so efficient that in July of 1938 the Arabs were able to damage the pipeline only once, as contrasted with an average of twelve successful attacks during each of the three preceding months.[31]

The second function of the S.N.S.--surprise attacks on gang and supply locations previously charted by reconnaissance squads--is illustrated by the raid on Khirbet Beit Lidd, in which Wingate with several squads surrounded the village and then launched an attack which totally destroyed a large gang and all its supplies.[32] In attacks of this kind, Wingate's long study of the Arab routes of supply and infiltration enabled him to find his way to Arab hideouts over the most difficult terrain late at night and to surprise the rebels. On one such venture he led a small patrol for many miles over rough countryside to a smugglers' hideout. The

[31]British Reports, Report for 1938, p. 11.
[32]Sykes, p. 176.

33

An SNS operation

Sykes, p. 168

Wingate leads SNS across miles of difficult land to surprise gang of smugglers — perfect timing and marching lead them to hideout at 3 AM as planned — 11 smugglers killed and 4 wounded — SNS confiscated arms & drugs.

Wingate: SNS→ Jewish A

Sugrue, p. 72

Wingate tells Hag. Gen. Staff after they accepted his plan for SNS that this was beginn of a Jewish Army.

34

Wingate: SNS→ Jewish Army

Sykes, p. 175

Wingate made clear to corpsmen he considered them to be the core of a Jewish army — his opening address in training courses was: "Our purpose here is to found the Jewish Army".

Wingate's SNS training cou

Mosley, p. 69

At SNS along with courses in discipline & strategy were rigorous exercises in marching drilling and frequent operations against Ara gangs.

surprise was complete when the patrol reached its destination at 3 A.M. as planned. Eleven smugglers were killed and needed supplies and arms were confiscated by the patrol.[33]

During his work with the S.N.S. Wingate was dominated by the thought that he was building the core of a Jewish national army. His opening words to his Haganah recruits were, "Our purpose here is to found the Jewish Army," and he and his men then worked with a mutual appreciation of this purpose.[34] There were three phases of training: first, rigorous courses in discipline and strategy; second, exacting exercises in marching and drilling; third, experience in actual night raids.[35] In all of these phases Wingate inflicted the discipline of a regular army on his men.

The basic training course, entitled "A Course for Jewish Sergeants," has become a part of the

[33]Sykes, p. 168.   [34]Ibid., p. 175.
[35]Mosley, p. 69.

36

Wingate's training course

Mosley, pp. 66-7

Wingate taught course at training scho[ol]
entitled "A Course for Jewish Sergeants" - now
part of training handbook for Israeli Arm[y]

37

Wingate's training course

Sykes, p. 174
Notes on 8 lectures have survived:
1. Nature of war; 2. infantry platoon in
battle; 3. infantry in defense; 4. infantry in
attack; 5. leadership and military vices;
6. tasks of different forces; 7. field artillery in
support of field infantry; 8. tasks of engineers
and cavalry.

"Soldiers' 10 Commandment[s]"

Mosley, p. 67
"Soldiers' Ten Commandments" -
1. Know + love what you fight for; 2. Carry out
every proper order of your commander; 3. Use your
equipment sparingly and only for your duty; 4. Abst[ain]
from brutality and cruelty; 5. Keep body and equip. i[n]
good condition; 6. Be able to endure physical
hardships; 7. Place welfare of comrades before you[r]
own; 8. Increase technical ability whenever possibl[e]
9. Carry out entrusted tasks speedily; 10. Submit
complaints to commander thru proper channels.

39

Wingate's training course

Mosley, p. 69
Wingate taught Jews to avoid worst
vices of soldier: "quarrelsomeness, laziness,
indulgence." It is the bad soldier who loses
self control under arduous physical strain.

training handbook for the modern Israeli Army.[36]
Notes from eight of the lectures in this course are
extant. The subjects of these lectures are the
functions of various army units in war, particularly
those of the infantry, and the duties and conduct of
the soldier.[37] Wingate was especially concerned
with the latter topic and delivered long lectures on
proper soldierly conduct and the virtues of leadership. He wrote a code, labeled "The Soldiers' Ten
Commandments," which enumerated the obligations and
values of the virtuous soldier.[38] He taught his men
that the worst vices of the soldier are quarrelsomeness, laziness, and indulgence, and that the best
soldier is the one who can keep his restraint and
control under any physical or mental strain.[39]

During the operations of the S.N.S., Wingate
carried out the discipline that he preached in his
training courses. Numerous examples can be cited of

[36]Mosley, pp. 66-67.   [37]Sykes, p. 174.
[38]Mosley, p. 67.   [39]Ibid., p. 69.

Wingate's discipline

Mosley, pp. 58-9

On first raid - Wingate teaches discipline. Makes a Jewish soldier shoot an Arab who refused to identify location of supply base - this taught soldiers necessity of obedience and coldness in war. Strikes a soldier who accidentally made noise by kicking stone when silence was imperative.

Wingate's discipline

Sugrue, pp. 72-3

Jewish soldier on night march had new boots which squeaked - Wingate told him to keep them quiet but it was impossible although he tried - Wingate struck him with butt of pistol - boy took boots off and walked barefoot.

his ruthlessness towards men who refused or failed to execute orders during operations. On his first raid, he forced a young Jewish soldier to shoot in cold blood an Arab who refused to give information on the location of Arab armaments. Later when returning from that same raid, Wingate struck a soldier who accidentally disturbed a stone which made a slight noise when Wingate had ordered complete silence.[40] Another example of Wingate's severity occurred during a night march when a Jewish soldier who was wearing new boots found that he could not keep them from squeaking. Wingate ordered him to stop the noise, and when the squeaking continued despite the desperate efforts of the soldier, Wingate struck him with the butt of his pistol. The boy then took off his boots and walked barefoot over the rough terrain, only in this fashion being able to appease Wingate.[41]

In addition to teaching army discipline, Win-

[40]Mosley, pp. 58-59.   [41]Sugrue, pp. 72-73.

42

SNS schedule

Sykes, pp. 151-2
   SNS schedule of duty: (1) few days of
day instruction, then beginning of service
with regular SNS at night. (2) duty for
fortnight - patrol on 9 or 10 nights - week's
leave. (3) 2 wks. duty. After 3 wks. recruit
was veteran soldier.

gate accustomed his men to the regularity of standard army procedure through the duty routine that he
enforced. The regular schedule of operation for a
new Haganah recruit was several days of instruction
followed by the beginning of service with the squads
at night. They were on active duty for two weeks,
nine or ten nights of which they engaged in night
patrol. They were then given a week's leave, after
which they returned for another two weeks of duty.
It was generally acknowledged that after three weeks
of this kind of training, the green recruit with no
previous military experience became a veteran soldier.[42] When the S.N.S. expanded with the arrival
of an additional 100 men, Wingate revised his former
schedule into an eleven-day cycle, but maintained
the regularity of the procedure. The men thus
became accustomed to a routine characteristic of an
organized army.

Thus, in organization, strategy, and tactics,

[42]Sykes, pp. 151-152.

43

Wingate's contribution

Dict. Nat. Biog., p. 963

Wingate in his SNS taught that reprisals to Arab terrorism should and could be better done by Jews from the settlements than organized British soldiers.

Wingate's contribution

Koestler, p. 74

Wingate taught Jews to counter Arab hit & run raids - in particular to move and fight at night.

Wingate's contribution

Sugrue, p. 74

Wingate taught Jews that Jews could win in Arab-Jew war, that intelligence, equipment and skill, not numbers, count, and that Arab disturbances could be quelled at initial stage of rioting.

SNS → Jewish Army

Sykes, p. 155

Thru leadership of Wingate, SNS became "beginnings of Jewish army." He gave them confidence in their fighting ability and instilled in them a unity and an esprit de corps which provides the core for an army

Wingate achieved definite modifications in the concept and conduct of Jewish defense. Although the S.N.S. was dissolved by command of the British in 1939, and Wingate left Palestine in that same year, the successes of his S.N.S. had proved certain things to the Jews that permanently altered their perspective. They had learned that Jewish soldiers operating in small groups from the settlements were more capable of carrying out reprisals to Arab acts of terrorism than were the British soldiers.[43] More generally, they had learned that they could preserve their own security and were not dependent on the British. They had learned that, despite their inferiority in numbers, they were capable of winning a full-scale war with the Arabs.[44] Perhaps most important, they had acquired a sense of unity which provided a basis for the creation of a unified Jewish National Army.[45]

[43]Dictionary of National Biography, p. 963.
[44]Sugrue, p. 74.   [45]Sykes, p. 155.

Bibliography

Collins, R. J. Lord Wavell: A Military Biography.
London: Hodder and Stoughton, 1948.

Koestler, Arthur. Promise and Fulfilment. New York:
The Macmillan Company, 1949.

League of Nations Mandates. British Reports on Palestine and Trans-Jordan, 1937-1938. London: H. M.
Stationery Office, 1939.

Mosley, Leonard. Gideon Goes to War. New York:
Charles Scribner's Sons, 1955.

The New York Times, March 15, 1937, p. 12.

The New York Times, September 12, 1938, p. 4.

"Palestine," Encyclopaedia Britannica, 1959, XVII,
133-135.

Royal Institute of International Affairs. Great
Britain and Palestine, 1915-1939. London: Oxford
University Press, 1939.

Sugrue, Thomas. Watch for the Morning. New York:
Harper and Brothers, 1950.

Sykes, Christopher. Orde Wingate. Cleveland: The
World Publishing Company, 1959.

Syrkin, Marie. Blessed Is the Match. Philadelphia:
The Jewish Publication Society of America, 1947.

Viton, Albert. "It's War in Palestine," Nation,
CXLVII (October 1, 1938), 320-323.

Weizmann, Chaim. Trial and Error, The Autobiography
of Chaim Weizmann. 2 vols. Philadelphia: The
Jewish Publication Society of America, 1949.

Wells, Linton. "Holy Terror in Palestine," Current
History, XLIX (December, 1938), 24-26.

"Wingate, Orde Charles," Dictionary of National Biography, 1941-1950. London: Oxford University Press,
1959.

13

Argument: Logical Persuasion

We are likely to think of argument as a means of persuading others to accept our opinions, but it is first of all a method by which we ourselves arrive at these opinions. We examine evidence and reach a conclusion from it, and the relation between the evidence and the conclusion is our argument. In this sense, argument is a form of thinking.

Persuasion is a broader term. We can persuade people by the logic of an argument, in which case we are using *logical* persuasion. Or we can persuade them by an appeal to their emotions, in which case we are using *psychological* persuasion. Or we can use both appeals at once. Although emotional appeals are often abused, they need not be unethical or cheap. Indeed, our greatest teachers, preachers, and statesmen have always joined logical and psychological persuasion in their attempts to influence human conduct. But in this chapter, as the title suggests, we are limiting ourselves to the kind of persuasion that comes from the logic of the argument.

The Structure of Argument

In its simplest form an argument consists of two statements, one of which is a conclusion drawn from the other. Thus

> *He is a careless driver.* He has been involved in four automobile collisions within the past year.

is an argument in which the italicized conclusion is drawn from the other statement, which we call a *premise. Whenever we have two statements so related that one is inferred as a conclusion from the other, we have an argument.*

Since this premise-conclusion relationship is the basic unit of argument, let us fix it in mind by contrasting statements which are related as premise and conclusion (P-C) with statements which are not so related. Below, each pair of statements at the left consists of a premise and an italicized conclusion drawn from it, and is therefore an argument. In contrast, the statements of the pairs at the right are not related as premise and conclusion and are therefore not arguments.

P–C Relationship	*No P–C Relationship*
Steam is coming from the kettle. *The water must be boiling.*	Will you have some tea? The water is boiling.
He has a weakness for blondes. Every girl he has dated has been a blonde.	He has a weakness for blondes. He also likes brunettes and redheads.
Final examinations cause unnecessary hardships for both students and instructors. *Final examinations should be abolished.*	Final examinations cause unnecessary hardships for both students and instructors. Final examinations encourage cramming.
Bill Smith is sure to make the All-Conference team; he is the leading scorer in the conference.	Bill Smith is the leading scorer in the conference. He is only a junior.
Judges are college graduates with much legal experience; therefore *a board of judges would be better qualified than a jury to decide lawsuits.*	Judges are college graduates with much legal experience. Many judges are elected to office.

The arguments at the left are not necessarily convincing. Not everybody will accept them. Some may deny that the premises are true; others may object that the conclusions do not necessarily follow from the premises; still others may want additional premises or "proof." But whether acceptable or not, the paired statements at the left are related as premise and conclusion, while those at the right are not.

So far we have been considering arguments of the simplest structure — a single premise and a single conclusion. Most arguments are more complex. They may consist of several premises from which a single conclusion is inferred — for example: Final examinations should be abolished because (1) they are detrimental to student health, (2) they place undue emphasis on memorizing facts, (3) they encourage last-minute cramming instead of daily preparation, (4) they penalize the nervous student. Or a conclusion from one or more premises may become a premise for another conclusion, as one unit of argument is built on another. In the following series the parenthetical comment identifies the P–C relations among the statements:

1. The adoption of the 13-month calendar would create serious disadvantages. (Conclusion from all other statements.)
2. It would require large-scale conversions to the new system. (Premise for 1; conclusion from 3 and 4.)
3. All dates in existing books would have to be changed. (Premise for 2.)
4. Existing contracts and leases would have to be redated. (Premise for 2.)

5. It would be expensive. (Premise for 1; conclusion from 6, 7, and 8.)

6. The cost of redating documents would be expensive. (Premise for 5.)

7. The cost of operating a business would increase. (Premise for 5; conclusion from 8.)

8. Monthly statements and payrolls would have to be prepared thirteen times a year instead of twelve times. (Premise for 7.)

If we set up these statements in outline form, the outline symbols help us to see the structure of the argument, which is also indicated by the P–C symbols at the left:

C	*Conclusion:*	The adoption of the 13-month calendar would create serious disadvantages.
P–C	I.	It would require large-scale conversions to the new system.
P	A.	All dates in existing books would have to be changed.
P	B.	All contracts and leases would have to be redated.
P–C	II.	It would be expensive.
P	A.	The cost of redating documents would be expensive.
P–C	B.	The cost of operating a business would increase.
P	1.	Monthly statements and payrolls would have to be prepared thirteen times a year instead of twelve times.

An outline of an argument, then, is a P–C outline. It is an arrangement of premises and conclusions into a structure which reflects the author's thinking. Traditionally, such an outline begins with the conclusion and moves down to the premises, though the direction of the author's thinking is usually from the premises to the conclusion.

Assumptions. Literally, an assumption is something taken for granted. If we are planning to buy an expensive article — say an air conditioner — and a friend tells us that he can get us the model we want at a 20 per cent discount, he does not usually ask if we would like to save 20 per cent of the normal price; he assumes or takes for granted that we would.

Whenever we go from a premise to a conclusion, some kind of assumption is implied in our inference. When a student concludes that his answer to a problem in algebra is correct because it is the same as the answer in the textbook, he is assuming that the textbook answer is correct. We might structure his reasoning this way:

Premise: My answer agrees with the one in the textbook.

↓

Assumption: The textbook answer is correct.

↓

Conclusion: My answer is correct.

Usually the assumption is not stated as part of the argument. The student may not even be conscious that he is making an assumption. Yet the assumption is implied in his inference, since it would not be logical to believe that an answer that agrees with the textbook is correct unless one first believed that the textbook is correct.

Recognition of the assumptions in an argument is necessary in any evaluation of the argument. The following additional illustrations should give you enough experience with assumptions so that you can detect those that are implied in later exercises.

Argument	*Assumption*
Better pass that car; the driver is a woman.	It is dangerous to follow a woman driver.
A careful study at thirty widely scattered colleges shows that the heights and weights of entering freshmen are greater than they were thirty years ago. This indicates that young men and women are both taller and heavier than they were a generation ago.	A conclusion derived from these thirty colleges will hold true for the country as a whole.
Just as a citizen cannot take the law into his own hands but must settle his differences with others through the courts, so must a nation be required to renounce war as a means of settling international disputes.	With respect to settling their differences, nations are like individuals, and a procedure that works well among individuals will work well among nations.
The fact that so many young men failed the army physical tests when called in the draft shows that the general health of the nation is poor.	The tests provide a reasonable measurement of general health and the draftees are a fair sample of the whole population.

✔ The following exercises are designed to increase your familiarity with the premise-conclusion relationship so that you can better perceive the structure of arguments. Since all we are concerned with now is the relationship between premise and conclusion, do **not** bother about the truth or soundness of the conclusions.

A. In each pair of statements, one is a conclusion inferred from the other. For each pair write the letter (*a* or *b*) which labels the conclusion and state the assumption implied in each inference.

1. *a.* A board of judges would be better than the jury system.
   b. Judges can distinguish between emotional appeals and facts.
2. *a.* Judges would be better qualified than a jury to decide complex questions.
   b. Judges are college graduates with much legal experience.

3. *a.* Judge Knott says, "Because of the inefficiency of the jury system, the United States is the safest place in the world in which to commit murder."

   b. The jury protects the criminal.

4. *a.* The average juror ignores the facts in arriving at a decision.

   b. Questions put to the jurors by a correspondent of the *New York World* after the Sinclair-Doheny trial revealed the jury's ignorance of the fundamental facts of the case.

B. In each set of three statements, one is the conclusion, one is the premise, and the remaining one has no P–C relation with the other two. We can call it an irrelevant statement. Mark the conclusion C, the premise P, and the irrelevant statement X.

1. Final examinations foster bad study habits.
Final examinations encourage cramming as a substitute for daily preparation.
Final examinations penalize the nervous student.

2. Final examinations are all crowded within a two-week period.
Final examinations do not provide a fair test of what a student knows.
Final examinations cannot cover all the work of the course.

3. Final examinations create student-faculty antagonism.
Final examinations force students to compete with each other.
Final examinations force students to compete with the faculty.

4. Students seldom get enough sleep during final examinations.
College students generally do not get enough physical exercise.
Final examinations are detrimental to student health.

C. In each set of three statements one is a conclusion from both the others, one is a conclusion from one statement and a premise for the other, and one is a premise only. Mark the conclusion C, the combined premise and conclusion P–C, and the premise P.

1. We should adopt Federal Aid to Education to provide uniform educational standards in all states.
The amount spent on education by different states is unequal.
New York spends much more on each child's education than does Mississippi.

2. Federal support for Land Grant colleges has resulted in compulsory ROTC.
Federal Aid to Education would bring federal control over the curriculum.
The University of Illinois, a Land Grant college, is required to have an ROTC program.

3. Federal Aid to Education is necessary to raise teachers' salaries.
Compared with doctors and lawyers, teachers have less real income now than they had in 1940.
Teachers' salaries have failed to adjust to the increased cost of living to anywhere near the extent that salaries in other professions have increased.

4. Arkansas pays a higher percentage of its income for education than does Ohio.

The Southern states especially need Federal Aid to Education.

The Southern states are making a greater effort to improve their educational systems than are the Northern states.

D. In each set of four statements, any statement may be: (1) a conclusion only, (2) a premise only, (3) a combined premise-conclusion, or (4) an irrelevant statement. Mark each statement in the set P, C, P–C, or X to identify its relation to the others in the set. Do not assume that there must be an X or a P–C in each set.

1. The office of the Presidency is made more exacting than is necessary.

The President has many obligations that could easily be discharged by an assistant.

The President must sign every commission in the armed services.

The annual tour dates of the marine band must be approved by the President.

2. Most European countries compress their highly intensified pre-college activities into 10 years compared to 12 years in the United States.

School children in Europe work harder and play less than those in the United States.

Technical training in European schools is based on the needs of individual countries.

For the European student extracurricular activities are rare.

3. Joining the Common Market would seriously damage our trade with Latin America.

We can compete successfully with the Common Market.

The United States should not join the Common Market.

Since the Common Market was formed, our sales to European countries have increased.

4. A $6 increase in the price of a ton of steel would have increased the cost of armaments by more than a billion dollars.

An increase in the cost of steel would have placed the United States at a disadvantage in the competition for foreign trade.

The President was justified in condemning the announced increase in steel prices.

An increase in steel prices would have greatly increased the cost of national security.

5. Red China is a nation of more than 600 million people.

Red China does not meet the "peace-loving" requirement of the U.N. charter.

Red China should not be admitted to the U.N.

Some countries in the U.N. have a population less than that of Chicago.

Types of Premises

The most common types of premises are statements of fact, judgments, and expert testimony. *Statements of fact* may be verified by checking them against the facts which they report. If the statement corresponds to the facts, it is "true"; if it does not, it is "false." Since the facts lie outside the mind of the person making the statements and are presumably the same for all people, the truth or falsity of a factual statement does not depend on anyone's opinion.

Statements of fact make the most reliable premises. Among intelligent people the authority of facts is decisive; hence the common saying, "The facts speak for themselves." This saying is something of an exaggeration, since different conclusions can sometimes be inferred from the same factual premise, but controversies tend to dissolve when they are reduced to questions of fact. For this reason, the best preparation for argument is a diligent search for the facts.

Judgments are conclusions inferred from the facts. The inference may be so obvious that the judgment hardly differs from a statement of fact, or the judgment may go so far beyond the facts that we have trouble seeing what the facts were. For example, consider these judgments:

> The cost of a new car in 1962 is more than double what it was in 1942.
> All things considered, a new car in 1962 is a better buy for the money than a new car was in 1942.

The first statement is a conclusion from a contrast of the prices, but the inference involves nothing more than a simple computation. The inference of the second statement includes a consideration of the relative purchasing power of the dollar in 1942 and 1962, a consideration of the improvements available in modern cars, and a decision that the increase in value of the 1962 car more than offsets the increase in cost. This kind of value judgment depends as much on an *evaluation* of the facts as on the facts themselves, and since evaluation may differ with different people, such a judgment will often be less reliable than a statement of fact.

Expert testimony is a statement by a person presumed to be an authority on the subject. His statement may be factual, as when a doctor describes the conditions revealed by an autopsy; or it may be a judgment, as when a psychiatrist testifies that in his opinion a defendant is insane. Since expert testimony is always a statement of fact or a judgment, it could be dealt with under those two categories. It is here considered separately (1) because factual statements by an expert are often extremely difficult for a nonexpert to verify (for example, ordinary citizens cannot usually check the facts to determine whether a swimmer's death was caused by heart failure or by drowning); and (2) because the qualifications of the expert require special consideration.

Expert testimony is often abused. It is too easy to assume that the testimony of any prominent person is reliable, though most of us — if we stop to think — realize that a man may be distinguished in one field but not in another, or may be expert in one phase of a subject and still know little about another phase of it. To be reliable, expert testimony must meet two requirements: the expert must be an authority on the particular point at issue, and there must be no reasonable probability that he is biased. Thus the testimony of a college president might be more reliable on the organization of his college than on the needs of the public schools or on the wisdom of deferring college students from the draft. For he might not be expert on public school matters, and his position might prejudice him toward keeping young men in college.

✔ In the following arguments,[1] identify the premises as statements of fact, judgments or expert testimony. If the premise is testimony, consider its reliability.

1. "If English speaking people will streamline their spelling . . . they will soon save enough money to pay the entire cost of World War II. George Bernard Shaw repeatedly states this opinion in letters to the London *Times*."

2. "Our attempts to make a foreign alphabet of twenty-six letters do the work of forty-two are pitiable. We write the same vowel twice to give it a different sound . . . or make two consonants represent simple sounds for which the alphabet does not provide."

3. "As a result of these discrepancies between alphabet and pronunciation, most letters represent different sounds. The Merriam-Webster dictionary, for example, lists eight different pronunciations for the letter *a* and illustrates them by the following words: *ale, chaotic, care, add, account, arm, ask*, and *sofa*. (The *a* in *ale* is accented, that in *chaotic* unaccented.)"

4. When we realize that fifty per cent of all words in English are not spelled as they are sounded, we see what a mess English is.

5. "On this side of the Atlantic, too, the demand for reform in spelling is strong. For example, in the *Journal of the National Education Association,* Dr. Frank C. Laubach, who has developed at Columbia University a new system known as 'Basic Spelling,' declared, . . . 'I have asked several hundred audiences how many favored reformed spelling and three-fourths of them have raised their hands.' "

6. The confusion of English spelling has been encouraged by misguided attempts to "correct" what seems like faulty spelling. Caxton's Dutch type-setters put the *h* in *ghost* to make it conform to Dutch spelling, although there never was an *h* in the Old English *gast* from which our *ghost* is descended. Then Dr. Johnson, the great eighteenth-century lexicographer, inserted the *h* in *ghastly* and *aghast*.

7. There is a tremendous lack of agreement between sound and spelling in English. "A single one of the eight *a* sounds is represented by at least fourteen different symbols: *a* in *ale, ae* in *maelstrom, ai* in *bait, ao* in *gaol* (pronounced jail), *au* in *gauge, ay* in *day, aye* in *aye* (meaning always), both *e* and *ee* in *melee, ea* in *break, eh* in *eh, ey* in *prey, et* in *beret*, and *eigh* in *weigh*."

8. English is full of silent letters. "Of the 604,000 words in the Merriam-Webster unabridged dictionary, over 400,000 have at least one silent letter; and many, of course, have more than one."

[1] Adapted from "Should Spelling Be Streamlined?" by Falk Johnson in *The American Mercury* for September, 1948. Reprinted by special permission of *The American Mercury* and the author.

9. The spelling of college students is worse today than it ever was. According to an editorial in the local newspaper, two out of every five college graduates consistently misspell such common words as *Britain, committee, duly, niece, professor, tragedy,* and *weird.*

10. English spelling is sadly in need of revision. It is not a system, but a jumble of historical accidents overlaid with well-intentioned but erroneous "corrections."

Types of Inferences

Inferences are traditionally classified as of two main types: *inductive* and *deductive,* and the processes as *induction* and *deduction.* In induction we start with specific information and try to see some pattern in it. In deduction we start with a general statement and try to discover more specific implications or particular instances of it. For example, if we polled a number of Iowa voters and inferred from their answers that Iowa will vote Republican in the next election, we would be making an inductive inference — reasoning from facts to a general conclusion. But if we began with the knowledge that farm states usually vote Republican and reasoned that since Iowa is a farm state it will vote Republican, we would be making a deductive inference — reasoning from a general statement to a particular implication of it. Although induction and deduction are often combined in our reasoning, it will be convenient to separate them here.

Induction

Induction may be divided into three subtypes: *generalization, causal relation,* and *analogy.*

Generalization. A generalization is a conclusion about a whole class or group based on a study of some of its members. Thus if we measured 2000 American soldiers and 2000 British soldiers and found that the average height of the Americans was greater, we might infer that American soldiers as a group are taller than British soldiers. We would be studying a sample of each group and, on the basis of the sample, drawing a conclusion about the whole class of American soldiers as contrasted with the whole class of British soldiers.

Obviously, a generalization based on a few samples, all things else being equal, is riskier than one based on many samples. The measurements of twenty American and twenty British soldiers would be too few to warrant any conclusion. But the mere size of a sample is not by itself a trustworthy test of generalization. If we measured 10,000 British soldiers, all members of crack regiments with minimum height requirements of six feet, we could draw no reliable conclusions about the average height of all British soldiers, since we would have no reason to assume that the sample was representative — indeed, we might conclude that it was not. The members of the crack regiments are not *typical* in height.

It is important to understand this distinction, because hasty assumption that samples are typical is the chief cause of unsound generalization. It is often very difficult — sometimes impossible — to be sure a sample is typical, and much useful reasoning is based on samples which can only be presumed so. But for any serious generalization, all possible care should be taken to see that the samples probably are typical. Any sample which tends to be "loaded" — that is, more likely true for part of a class than for all of it — should be rejected. The following samples are all loaded.

A study of college hospital records to determine how many days a semester a student is likely to be sick. (The sample will exaggerate because it ignores the healthiest part of the student population — those who did not need hospitalization.)

A contrast of unemployment figures in Michigan in June and January to determine whether unemployment is increasing. (A comparison between two Junes would be safer, since the January figures may be increased by "seasonal unemployment.")

An analysis of all automobile accidents reported in a state during a year to determine whether men or women are the safer drivers. (If there are more men drivers than women drivers, or if men drive more frequently for longer distances or under adverse conditions, one would expect more men to be involved in accidents. The sample is likely to be loaded.)

The commonest safeguard against "loading" is to choose samples at random. A random sample is one in which the items are selected entirely by chance, as in a lottery, or by some other procedure so arbitrary that it is almost the same as a chance selection — for example, choosing the first word on every twentieth page of a dictionary. The assumption behind random selection is that any inference made from a sample so selected would be equally valid for any other sample selected at random.

Causal Relation. Probably the most common kind of inductive reasoning is that which relates two events and concludes that one is the cause of the other. Such a conclusion reflects an underlying assumption called the *principle of causation.* According to this principle, every event has a cause, so that whenever we discover that event B must follow event A, we may say that A is the cause of B and B the effect of A.

Causal reasoning may go from cause to effect or from effect to cause. Either way, we reason from what we know to what we are trying to determine. Sometimes we reason from an effect to a cause and then on to another effect. Thus, if we reason that because the lights have gone out the refrigerator won't work, we first relate the effect (lights out) to the cause (power off) and then relate that cause to another effect (refrigerator not working). This kind of reasoning is called, for short, *effect to effect.* It is quite common to reason through an extensive chain of causal relations. For example, if when the lights go out we take the milk out of the refrigerator, we reason in the following causal chain: lights out — power off — refrigerator not working — temperature will rise — milk will sour. In other words, we diagnose a succession of effects from the power failure, each becoming the cause of the next.

Causes are classified as necessary, sufficient, or contributory. A *necessary cause* is one which must be present for the effect to occur, as the presence of a spark is necessary for combustion in a gasoline engine. A *sufficient cause* is one which can produce an effect unaided, as a dead battery is enough to keep a car from starting. A *contributory cause* is one which helps to produce an effect but cannot do so by itself, as running through a red light may help cause an accident, though other factors — the presence of pedestrians or other cars in the intersection — must also be present.

Most of our concern with causal relations arises from a need to discover causes. Something happens, and immediately we ask "Why?" In attempting to answer that question — to find the cause — we usually go through one or more of the following stages in our thinking:

1. *Whatever the cause is, it must exist in the situation and it must be sufficient to produce the effect.* This assumption requires us: (1) to check the situation carefully in order to identify possible causes, and (2) to consider which of the possible causes is sufficient to produce the effect. In making this analysis we are influenced by our past experience with similar situations. If we have repeatedly observed that event B follows event A, we incline to infer that A is the cause of B. But we should remember that, although a cause always precedes an effect, one event can regularly precede another without being its cause. Eight o'clock classes always come before nine o'clock classes, but the first do not cause the second.

2. *If a sufficient cause is eliminated from the situation, the effect will be eliminated, unless other causes are also operating.* At this stage in our reasoning we are ready to test the possible causes to see if there is any connection between them and the effect. If the effect ceases when we remove a possible cause, this possible cause is the actual one. If we suspect that a light failure is caused by a faulty bulb, we can substitute a new bulb and see whether the effect (no light) is removed. If it is, we need look no further for the cause. But if the new bulb does not give light, we cannot infer that the original bulb was all right, since the effect could have been produced by any of several sufficient causes or a combination of them — for example, a defect in the bulb, the wiring, the outlet, or in more than one of these.

3. *If the cause is introduced into a similar situation it will produce a similar effect.* This is an additional way to test possible causes. If we suspect that a light failure is due to a faulty bulb, we can predict that the bulb will not light when placed in a socket where another bulb has been burning. If the bulb does light, we must reject the hypothesis that it was faulty and caused the light failure. If the bulb does not light, we have additional support for our belief that it is the cause we are seeking.

Whether we go through all three of these stages to discover a cause will probably depend on how important finding the cause is to us. To find our faulty bulb we need not go beyond the second stage, once we find that changing bulbs removes the difficulty; but a laboratory scientist attempting to establish the cause of a disease would perform every experiment he could think of before reaching a final conclusion.

Causal Generalization. The kind of causal analysis we have been considering works best when we are dealing with events in which all possible causes can be isolated and tested independently of each other. But many problems do not permit such a procedure. We cannot, for instance, test the hypothesis that fluorides prevent tooth decay by eliminating all other possible factors affecting tooth decay — hereditary factors, prenatal environment, diet, etc. All we can do is to contrast the amount of tooth decay in people who use fluoridated tooth paste or drink fluoridated water with the amount in people who do neither, and draw a conclusion from the contrast. Basically, we are generalizing from contrasted samples and making a causal-relation inference from the generalization. We are thus combining two types of inductive reasoning in what is called a *causal generalization.*

Causal generalizations are useful for suggesting causes that cannot otherwise be identified, but we should be careful to recognize that, like all generalizations, what they establish is a *probability*. How reliable that probability is will depend on how reliable the reasoning is. If the generalization is sound — if enough typical samples have been examined — and if care is taken to ensure that other possible causes have not been ignored or underestimated, the probability revealed by the causal generalization may be sufficient for practical purposes. Thus the causal generalization that doctors can reduce infection in surgery cases by scrubbing their hands and sterilizing their instruments before operating has yielded great practical benefits. But if the generalization is a hasty one and if the alleged cause is not sufficient to produce the effect, a causal generalization may lead to nothing more than a superstition, such as the belief that breaking a mirror brings seven years of bad luck.

The following extract from a long article illustrates a causal generalization. Test it both as a generalization and as a causal relation and decide whether it is logically persuasive.

> After designing and pretesting a questionnaire in the fall of 1951, we trained more than 22,000 American Cancer Society volunteers as researchers for the study. Between January 1 and May 31 of 1952 they enrolled subjects in 394 counties in nine states. The subjects, all men between the ages of 50 and 69, answered a simple confidential questionnaire on their smoking habits, both past and present. A total of 187,783 men were enrolled, filled out usable questionnaires and were successfully kept track of for the next 44 months. Death certificates were obtained for all who died, and additional medical information was gathered for those who were reported to have died of cancer. All together 11,870 deaths were reported, of which 2,249 were attributed to cancer.
>
> The most important finding was that the total death rate (from all causes of death combined) is far higher among men with a history of regular ciga-

rette smoking than among men who never smoked, but only slightly higher among pipe and cigar smokers than among men who never smoked.

Men who had smoked cigarettes regularly and exclusively were classified according to their cigarette consumption at the time they were enrolled in the study. It was found that death rates rose progressively with increasing number of cigarettes smoked per day. The death rate of those who smoked two or more packs of cigarettes a day was approximately two and a quarter times higher than the death rate of men who never smoked. . . .

During the course of the study 7,316 deaths occurred among subjects with a history of regular cigarette smoking (some of whom smoked pipes and/or cigars as well as cigarettes). We divided these deaths according to primary cause as reported on death certificates. Only 4,651 of these cigarette smokers would have died during the course of the study if their death rates had exactly matched those of men of the same age who had never smoked. The difference of 2,665 deaths (7,316 minus 4,651) can be considered the "Excess deaths" associated with a history of regular cigarette smoking. Of these excess deaths 52.1 per cent were attributed to coronary artery disease of the heart, 13.5 per cent to lung cancer and the remainder to other diseases. From this it is apparent that as a cause of death coronary artery disease is by far the most important disease associated with cigarette smoking. . . .

All together 127 deaths were attributed to cancer of other tissues (mouth, tongue, lip, larynx, pharynx and esophagus) that are directly exposed to tobacco smoke and material condensed from tobacco smoke. In 114 of these cases the diagnosis was confirmed by microscopic examination. Of these 114 men, 110 were smokers and only four had never smoked. The figures suggest that pipe and cigar smoking may be more important than cigarette smoking in relation to cancer of one or more sites included in this group, but the number of cases was not sufficient for a reliable evaluation of this point. Nevertheless, these cancers were the only causes of death for which the death rate of pipe and cigar smokers was found to be far higher than the death rate of nonsmokers.

Other reported causes of death showing a fairly high degree of association with cigarette smoking were gastric and duodenal ulcers, certain diseases of the arteries, pulmonary diseases (including pneumonia and influenza), cancer of the bladder and cirrhosis of the liver. Many other diseases appeared to be somewhat associated with cigarette smoking. . . .

After reviewing the evidence, the mildest statement I can make is that, in my opinion, the inhalation of tobacco smoke produces a number of very harmful effects and shortens the life span of human beings. The simplest way to avoid these possible consequences is not to smoke at all. But one can avoid the most serious of them by smoking cigars or a pipe instead of cigarettes, provided that one does not inhale the smoke. An individual who chooses to smoke cigarettes can minimize the risks by restricting his consumption and by not inhaling.[2]

Analogy. Analogy is the type of reasoning in which we infer that if two things are alike in several important respects they will also be alike in

[2] From "The Effects of Smoking" by E. Cuyler Hammond, in *Scientific American,* July, 1962. Reprinted by permission.

certain other respects. The following selection shows how this inference develops.

> We often wonder whether or not Mars is inhabited. . . . Did you ever ask yourself why it is *Mars* that interests us so much in this connection? It is because Mars is so similar to the earth in major respects. It has a similar history, a comparable temperature, an atmosphere, is subject to similar solar seasons; it revolves around the sun, it gets light from the sun, it is subject to the law of gravitation, etc. May it not also be similar in respect to harboring life? If Mars were without water, like the moon, or experienced great extremes of temperature, like Mercury, we should not be so much interested in it. But we entertain the idea because Mars is so similar in many respects to the earth *and life has evolved on the earth!*[3]

In Chapter 4 we saw the use of analogy to provide explanatory detail. In exposition and description analogy can often make abstract ideas concrete or explain the unfamiliar by likening it to the familiar. In argument, however, analogy can be both useful and misleading. It is helpful in suggesting hypotheses for further investigation. For example, if we have found that the best protection against one virus disease is to isolate the virus and prepare an immunizing serum from it, we can predict that the same method will work with another virus disease. If the prediction proves true, the analogy has helped to solve our problem. If the prediction proves false, the suggested solution will be quickly rejected and no great harm will have been done.

Analogy is also useful when we have no other means of reaching a conclusion. For example, we cannot descend to the bottom of the ocean and collect evidence about the kinds of life, if any, existing there, but we can infer by analogy that the characteristics we observe in the depths we can penetrate will hold true in those we cannot reach. But such inferences are, at best, tentative, and we replace them by more reliable evidence where possible.

When analogy is used as the sole proof of a conclusion it is even less reliable. It may be more persuasive than it should be and lead us to a conclusion which is not valid. For a single difference can render a whole analogy false. The test of an analogy is the question, *Are the two things analogous for the purpose for which the analogy is being used?* They may have many differences which are unimportant to the inference based on the analogy. But they must not be different in any detail essential to that inference. Thus the analogy that a motherless baby ape could be reared by feeding it as if it were a human baby would be sound because, despite many differences, young apes and human babies have similar digestive systems. But to reason that because mushrooms and toadstools look much alike, toadstools will be good to eat, is to indulge in a false analogy, since the fact

[3] From *The Rhyme of Reason* by Roger W. Holmes. Reprinted by permission of Appleton-Century-Crofts, Inc., publishers.

that toadstools are poisonous is a crucial difference — in this case a fatal one.

In the following analogy the famous eighteenth-century philosopher David Hume compares the universe to a machine and uses that comparison to infer the existence of a Divine Intelligence. Comment on the structure and persuasiveness of the argument.

Look round the world, contemplate the whole and every part of it: you will find it to be nothing but one great machine, subdivided into an infinite number of lesser machines, which again admit of subdivisions to a degree beyond what human senses and faculties can trace and explain. All these various machines, and even their most minute parts, are adjusted to each other with an accuracy which ravishes into admiration all men who have ever contemplated them. The curious adapting of means to ends, throughout all nature, resembles exactly, though it much exceeds, the productions of human contrivance — of human design, thought, wisdom, and intelligence. Since therefore the effects resemble each other, we are led to infer, by all the rules of analogy, that the causes also resemble, and that the Author of nature is somewhat similar to the mind of man, though possessed of much larger faculties, proportioned to the grandeur of the work which he has executed. By this argument . . . do we prove at once the existence of a Deity and his similarity to human mind and intelligence.

✔ As a review of the types of inductive inferences, identify the kind of reasoning used in each of the following examples. If more than one type is used in an example, identify them all.

1. An income-tax clerk checks every tenth return coming into his office and concludes that the average citizen is weak in arithmetic.

2. A doctor notes a patient's symptoms, takes a blood test, and concludes that the patient needs his appendix removed.

3. A government official tells newspaper reporters that a proposed policy will be a good one because it has worked well in large business corporations.

4. A famous statistician of the twenties was fond of comparing the average salary of college graduates with that of high school graduates who never went to college and concluding that a college education soon repaid its cost.

5. A study of the educational background of people whose names were included in *Who's Who in America* led the investigator to conclude that the sons of ministers had the best chance of being successful.

6. In preparing his annual budget a college president finds through a statistical study that (*a*) a steadily increasing number of students transfer to his college in the junior year, and (*b*) the cost of instruction in junior and senior classes is markedly higher than in freshman and sophomore classes. The president decides that, even if there is no increase in total enrollment, he will need more money to run the college.

7. Although your car has been driven only 7000 miles, the engine has developed a disturbing knock. You consult a mechanic. He listens to the engine and says, "Either you need a new ring job or the elevators are stick-

ing. If the rings are bad I'll have to take the engine apart and the cost will be about $150. If the trouble is with the elevators it can often be fixed by using a special kind of oil." You have him the change the oil and the knock ceases.

Deduction

Deduction is the kind of reasoning in which we start from given statements and draw a conclusion which is implied in the statements. The classical form of deduction is the syllogism, which is an argument consisting of a *major premise,* a *minor premise,* and a *conclusion.* Although there are different types of syllogisms, they all reveal an underlying pattern of thought: *that if two things are known from the premises, a third thing can be concluded, because the conclusion is another way of stating the information already given in the premises.* To use an obvious illustration, if we know that all members of the Varsity are seniors and that Tom is a member of the Varsity, we know that Tom is a senior, because the statement that all Varsity members are seniors implies the statement that any particular member of the Varsity is a senior.

If a syllogism is as elementary as this illustration suggests, why do we bother with it? There are two reasons. First, although any single syllogism may seem to make only a trifling contribution to knowledge, the kind of intellectual discipline involved in reasoning deductively has led to most of our discoveries in mathematics and physics, and to much of our knowledge in other areas. Second, just as an outline allows us to check the organization of an essay by presenting that organization in its simplest form, so a syllogism reveals the structure of a deductive argument in the form best suited for testing, and thus allows us to check the validity of the argument.

Before we look at different types of syllogisms in detail, we should understand what the term "validity" means when applied to a syllogism. A syllogism is said to be "valid" when the conclusion follows logically from the premises — that is, when the conclusion accurately states what is implied in the premises. Since validity refers to the soundness of the inference, a syllogism may be valid even though one or both of the premises from which the conclusion is drawn are false. For example, *All college professors wear glasses; Mickey Mantle is a college professor; therefore Mickey Mantle wears glasses,* is a syllogism containing two untrue premises; yet the syllogism is valid, because the conclusion necessarily follows from the stated premises. If we are given in the premises that Mickey belongs to a class of people, all of whom wear glasses, we must conclude that Mickey wears glasses. The fault of this syllogism does not lie in the reasoning, but in the information from which the reasoning proceeds. To be *reliable,* a syllogism must be both true and valid — that is, the information provided in the premises must accord with the facts, and the conclusion must necessarily follow from the premises.

After this general introduction to the syllogism let us look at the four major types. For each type we shall provide a general description, a model, and an example, and then consider what kinds of conclusions can validly be drawn in that type. Since we shall be primarily concerned with validity, we shall ignore consideration of the truth of the premises.

Type 1: The Categorical Syllogism

In this type each statement consists of two terms connected by a verb. There are three terms in all, each used twice. In the following example the terms have been underlined and lettered to make the example more clearly reveal the structure of the model. (To save space we shall abbreviate major premise, minor premise, and conclusion to *MP, mp,* and *c* respectively.)

Model	*Example*
MP. All A are B.	All college students are high school graduates.
mp. C is A.	Joe Smith is a college student.
c. C is B.	Joe Smith is a high school graduate.

Notice that, except for the necessary change from plural to singular in A and B, each term has precisely the same meaning each time it is used. This is important, because a term used in two meanings is actually two terms, and we therefore have more than three terms. As the model shows, this syllogism cannot have more nor less than three terms. The following example illustrates a violation of this rule.

> *MP.* All superior students receive better than average grades.
> *mp.* Three-letter men are superior students.
> *c.* Three-letter men receive better than average grades.

In the major premise the term "superior student" is used to mean "academically superior"; in the minor premise the term means "athletically superior." There are therefore four terms, not three, and the argument is not a syllogism but only looks like one.

Now let us get some experience with validity in a categorical syllogism by taking a series of premises and seeing what conclusions may validly be derived from them. Remember that we are chiefly concerned with seeing what the premises imply. We cannot draw any conclusion which is not necessarily implied in the premises.

> *MP.* All college professors are absent-minded.
> *mp.* Father is absent-minded.

We can draw no valid conclusion from these premises. The major premise is a statement about college professors, not about absent-minded people; therefore we cannot infer that father is a college professor. But if the major premise read, "Only college professors are absent-minded," we could infer that father is a college professor. Or if the minor premise said, "Father is a college professor," we could conclude that he is absent-minded.

> *MP.* All college professors are absent-minded.
> *mp.* Father is not absent-minded.

We can conclude that father is not a college professor. If he is not absent-minded he does not qualify as a college professor according to the major premise. In this syllogism, saying that father is not absent-minded is another way of saying that he is not a college professor.

> *MP.* No college professor is absent-minded.
> *mp.* Father is absent-minded.

We conclude that father is not a college professor, since his absent-mindedness rules him out of the class according to the major premise. Notice that although this major premise does not start with "All," it is still a statement about all college professors, since to say that none of them has a certain characteristic is the same as to say that all of them lack that characteristic.

> *MP.* No college professor is absent-minded.
> *mp.* Father is not absent-minded.

We can draw no valid conclusion. The major premise does not say that *only* college professors are free of absent-mindedness. If it did, we could conclude that father is a college professor. But, as stated, the major premise does not imply that freedom from absent-mindedness is a sure sign of being a college professor.

Quite frequently we find the categorical syllogism expressed in a shortened form:

> Father is a college professor; therefore he is absent-minded.
> Father must be absent-minded, because he is a college professor.
> Since all college professors are absent-minded, father must be absent-minded.

From the examples already studied you will recognize that the first two of these omit the major premise, and the last one omits the minor premise. This short-cut form does not affect the validity of the syllogism. It still has three terms, and the omitted premise is implied or understood. But in testing the validity of the shortened form, it would be wise first to rewrite the syllogism in its full form.

Type 2: The Conditional or Hypothetical Syllogism

This type poses a condition or a supposition and predicts what will happen if the condition is satisfied or if the supposition proves true.

Model	*Example*
MP. If A, then B.	If Jones gets an A in history he will go off probation.
mp. A.	He gets an A in history.
c. B.	He goes off probation.

Notice that the model does not record a *Not A* minor premise. Can we conclude that if Jones does not get an A in history he will not get off probation? We cannot. The major premise predicts only what will happen if the condition is met. It does not rule out the possibility of Jones's getting off probation by other means — say, by earning a B in history and A's in all his other subjects, though such a possibility would be excluded if the premise said, *"Only* if Jones gets an A in history. . . ." For the same reason, we cannot infer that if Jones goes off probation he must have got an A in history. But if we learn that he is still on probation we can validly infer that he did not get an A in history, since that A would have guaranteed his being off probation according to the major premise.

Type 3: The Alternative Syllogism

This type pairs two statements and says that if one is not true, the other is.

Model	*Example*
MP. Either A or B.	Either the power is off or the tubes are defective.
mp. Not A (*or* Not B).	The power is not off.
c. B (*or* A).	The tubes are defective.

The model shows that we can draw a valid inference only if the minor premise is negative. If either of the two statements in the major premise is false, the other one must be true. But what can we infer if the minor premise is affirmative: if the power is off or if the tubes are defective? We can make no valid inference from an affirmative minor premise because, although the major premise asserts that one of the two statements must be true, it does not exclude the possibility that both are true. Therefore if the power is off we can conclude nothing about the tubes: they may or may not be defective. And if we know that the tubes are defective, it does not necessarily follow that the power is on.

This kind of syllogism bothers students who interpret "either A or B" as meaning "only one." That interpretation would be justified if the major premise read, "Either A or B, but not both at the same time." Without such a qualification, the major premise must be interpreted as meaning "at least one of the two." For example, when a college course has as a prerequisite "either algebra or physics," that prerequisite does not exclude the student who has had both algebra and physics. The prerequisite requires at least one of the two; so does the alternative syllogism. *In an alternative syllogism "either . . . or" does not imply that the alternatives are mutually exclusive.*

Type 4: The Disjunctive Syllogism

This type sets up two mutually exclusive statements and says that if one is true, the other must be false.

Model	*Example*
MP. Not both A and B.	She cannot love me and tell lies about me.
mp. A (*or* B).	She does tell lies about me.
c. Not B (*or* Not A).	She cannot love me.

In the example the mutually exclusive statements are "love me" and "tell lies about me." The major premise tells us that if she does either, she cannot do the other; so we could deduce the conclusion "She does not tell lies about me" if the minor premise were "She loves me." But what conclusion could we draw from a minor premise "She does not love me" or from "She does not tell lies about me"? We could draw no valid conclusion from either of these premises. The syllogism implies that if one statement is true, the other must be false; but it does not rule out the possibility that neither is true — that the girl neither loves the man nor tells lies about him. This distinction you know from experience. You know that a statement in the college catalog that "Students cannot take physics and chemistry in the same year" does not imply that a student who does not take physics must take chemistry. He may take neither. *The disjunctive syllogism permits a valid conclusion only when one of the two statements is affirmed in the minor premise.*

✔ As a test of your own ability to determine the validity of syllogisms, decide which, if any, conclusion would be a valid inference from each of the following sets of premises.

1. MP All independent voters voted for X.
   mp Mr. B voted for X.
   c

2. MP All independent voters voted for X.
   mp Mr. C did not vote for X.
   c

3. MP If you are an independent voter you will vote for X.
   mp You are not an independent voter.
   c

4. MP Either you vote for Y or you are an independent voter.
   mp You do not vote for Y.
   c

5. MP Either you vote for Y or you are an independent voter.
   mp You vote for Y.
   c

6. MP You cannot vote for Z and be an independent voter.
   mp You vote for Z.
   c

7. *MP*   You cannot vote for Z and be an independent voter.
   mp   You are not an independent voter.
   c

8. Which of the following lettered statements would be valid deductions from the data given in the table?

Car Speed miles per hour	Reaction distance feet	Braking distance feet	Car Speed miles per hour	Gasoline miles per gallon
30	33	40	30	24
40	44	70	40	21.6
50	55	109	50	19
60	66	156	60	16
70	77	240	70	12.5

a. Reaction distance varies with individuals.
b. Doubling the speed doubles the reaction distance.
c. Doubling the speed doubles the braking distance.
d. Increasing the speed decreases the life of the tires.
e. To avoid hitting a roadblock, a driver traveling 60 mph must see it more than 200 feet away.
f. The legal speed limit should not exceed 60 mph.
g. The greater the speed, the less control the driver has over the car.
h. The total distance required to bring a car to a stop is almost three times as great at 70 mph as it is at 40 mph.
i. Doubling the speed doubles the gas consumption.

Fallacies

A fallacy is an error which makes the argument unreliable. It may be an untrue or incomplete premise, an invalid inference from the premises, an unacceptable assumption, a confusion brought about by ambiguous terms, or some other weakness which impairs the logical persuasion of the argument. In the process of reaching conclusions about difficult and complex problems (for some of which the necessary information is not fully available) and communicating our reasons to others, we are constantly subject to error. If we realize this, we are likely to be cautious and to recheck the facts and the inferences we make from them. The most obvious fallacies usually appear when we are overconfident and are so sure of our arguments that we fail to test them rigidly.

The preceding pages of this chapter have given you the tests for reliable induction and deduction. You know that the soundness of a generalization will depend on the number and nature of the samples, that a satisfactory causal explanation must show that the cause is present and is sufficient to produce the effect and that no other sufficient cause is present, that an analogy must show an *essential* similarity, not just a number of similarities, that a deduction must start from true premises and then draw only those conclusions implied in the premises, and that failure to observe these requirements will result in fallacious reasoning. In the discussion that follows we shall group fallacies into two general classes: those that result in irrelevant argument, and those that produce oversimplified arguments.

Fallacies of Irrelevance

These are arguments which, intentionally or unintentionally, fail to deal with the question at issue. We say that they "ignore" or "beg" the question.

Ignoring the Question. To ignore the question is to digress into an irrelevant argument. The digression may be a result of inability to keep the issues clearly in mind and to distinguish what is and is not pertinent, or it may be a deliberate attempt to distract attention from the real issues. The best rebuttal is to point out the digression, refuse to follow it, and insist that the discussion return to the real issues. The following examples illustrate various means of ignoring the question:

Examples	*Analysis*
My opponent asks me to tell him what is wrong with this proposal of compulsory medical insurance. I'll tell him what is wrong with it. It is a half-baked plan cooked up by him and other Fellow-Travelers who are more interested in socializing a great profession than they are in providing better medical care. These men will sacrifice everything to their bigoted faith in a system of regimentation that is abhorrent to the American people. They want to begin by socializing medicine; they will not rest until they have made over the whole American economy into the image of the dictatorship to which their secret allegiance is pledged.	*This argument attempts to refute a plan by attacking the character of the people who support it. It is an argument against the man, not against the plan, and is called either* **name calling** *or* **argumentum ad hominem.** *It is legitimate to attack the trustworthiness of an opponent when his argument rests largely on his own testimony or on experts of his choosing, but such an attack should supplement, not replace, criticism of the plan itself. In this argument the plan is completely ignored.*
The professor says that two negatives do not make an affirmative in English. Well, professors, like other people, are entitled to their opinions, no matter how eccentric they may be. But in this case the facts are against the professor. Any high school freshman could tell him that two negatives do make an affirmative. When you multiply minus *a* by minus *b*, the re-	*This is an example of ignoring the question by shifting to another question. The point at issue is whether two negatives make an affirmative in English usage. There is no dispute about what happens in mathematics. This fallacy is sometimes called the device of the* **straw man.** *Instead of tackling one's real opponent, one sets up an easy substitute and puts on an*

sult is a plus or positive quantity. That is not just the freshman's opinion, or my opinion, or the opinion of educated people everywhere. It is a mathematical law. And it holds true whether it is written in English, Latin, Greek, or Hindustani.

effective demonstration of tearing it to pieces.

Closely related to the "straw man" is the device of **extension,** *in which an argument is extended beyond its author's intention and attacked in its extended form, as when the statement that spanking a child sometimes does as much harm as good is represented as being an argument that children should never be spanked.*

Begging the Question. A question is "begged" when one or more of the premises by which it should be proved are assumed to be true without proof. The best defense against this fallacy is to show how the begging takes place. The following examples illustrate such arguments:

Examples	*Analysis*
Dad, you don't need to worry about lending me the money for this business. Just as soon as the profits come in I can pay you back with interest.	*This argument assumes that the profits will be sufficient to pay off the debt. That, however, is a major part of dad's doubt, and needs to be proved.*
Much of this talk about spending millions for slum clearance is based on the fallacy that if we provide fine homes for people who live in the slums they will suddenly become responsible and productive citizens. This argument puts the cart before the horse. The basic trouble is with the people who live in the slums. These people are thoroughly shiftless and irresponsible. The conditions under which they live prove this. If they had any initiative or industry they would not be living under slum conditions.	*This is an* **argument in a circle.** *The thesis that slum-dwellers are responsible for slum conditions is supported by asserting that if they were not responsible they would not be living in slums. The writer assumes that what he has to prove is true, and his argument goes round in the following circle: Slums are caused by shiftless tenants; this is true because shiftless tenants cause slums.*
Resolved: That the farce of the Honor System be abolished.	*This assumes the truth of the affirmative position in the resolution. The affirmative must prove that the Honor System is a farce.*
"There is bound to be life on other planets." "Can you prove it?" "Well, can you prove there isn't?"	*This example* **shifts the burden of proof.** *In arguments both inside and outside law courts, "He who asserts must prove." We cannot prove an assertion by defying the opposition to disprove it.*

All these fallacies — *name calling (argumentum ad hominem), straw man, extension, circular argument, shifting the burden of proof* — ignore or beg the question and thus lead attention away from the main issue.

Fallacies of Oversimplification

Any argument that allows us to reach a conclusion without considering all pertinent factors tends to oversimplify the problem. The most common of these are *hasty generalizations, stereotypes, inadequate causal relationships, either-or fallacies,* and *trivial analogies.*

Hasty Generalization. A hasty generalization jumps to a conclusion from insufficient evidence. Unless the samples are clearly typical, a small number proves nothing, or at least much less than is claimed. Here is a representative example.

Example	Analysis
Girls just aren't any good at logic. Although there are twelve girls to ten men in our logic section, the four highest scores on the final exam were made by men and the four lowest by girls.	*In the first place, what would make us believe that what is true of twelve girls in one class will be true of all girls? In the second, are the top four and bottom four scores typical of the scores in the class? Even as a comparison for this class alone, the sample is faulty. It would be better to take the median score of the girls and compare it with the median score of the men. If the comparison favored the men, it would justify the conclusion that girls in this class do less well than men in this class on an examination in logic. That is a less impressive conclusion than the one offered in the original argument.*

Stereotype. The fallacy of stereotyping is the mistake of paying too much attention to characteristics or traits which members of a group are supposed to have in common and not enough attention to individual differences within the group. We begin with a number of individuals who have at least one thing in common (let us say that they all have married children); we group them into a class (mothers-in-law); we develop an attitude towards that class (mothers-in-law are interfering) based on a hasty generalization; then we apply that attitude to individual mothers-in-law without waiting to see whether or not they are interfering. The reasoning behind the stereotype can be set up as a syllogism: *All mothers-in-law are interfering; she is a mother-in-law; she is interfering.* This syllogism is unreliable because the major premise is not universally true.

To help us avoid this fallacy some students of language advise us to use index numbers after the class names to remind us that each member of a group has his own personal characteristics — that German$_1$ is not German$_2$ that college professor$_A$ is not college professor$_B$, that freshman$_{1962}$ is not freshman$_{1942}$. Whether we actually write these index numbers or merely think them, they are useful reminders that it is unintelligent to assume that individuals with a common class name will be alike in all respects.

Inadequate Causal Relation. As superstitions illustrate, it is easy to find a cause, even for very complex events, if we just pick a convenient factor and call it the cause. Such a procedure, however, does not advance our understanding of the event. Two ways to oversimplify a causal relation are to accept a contributory cause as a sufficient cause and to accept another effect as the cause. An example of each type of oversimplification follows.

Example	*Analysis*
I know my spelling is terrible. All the members of my family are poor spellers.	*Family environment may contribute to poor spelling, but it is not the sole cause. The student has oversimplified by failing to consider other causes, about which he could do something.*
I failed the course because the instructor had a prejudice against me.	*Even if we assume that the prejudice existed, it must be the effect of some cause. This reasoning mistakes a possible effect for a cause. A more probable reason is that the student's conduct caused both the alleged prejudice and the failure.*

The Either-Or Fallacy. In deciding a course of action we often make a choice between alternatives. Sometimes there are only two alternatives, but if there are several, we oversimplify the choice by limiting it to two possibilities.

Example	*Analysis*
On the question whether the husband should be the boss in the household, there are only two alternatives: either the man will be the boss or the woman will. Any man who lets himself be dictated to by a woman is a sorry specimen and probably deserves what he will get. But most of us will not make that mistake. We will make it known at the start, gently but firmly, that we intend to be masters in our own homes. The sooner the little lady gets that idea through her head, the better for everybody.	*There are three possible positions to take on this question: the husband should be boss; the wife should be boss; nobody should be boss. This argument overlooks the third possibility; therefore it is not true that if the husband does not dominate, the wife will. Essentially the example oversimplifies the question by unnecessarily limiting the alternatives.*

Trivial Analogies. Although an analogy is always suspect when it is not supported by other kinds of reasoning, a carefully planned analogy is often persuasive. But, except possibly for hasty generalizations, there is no more common fallacy in college arguments than the use of impromptu, ill-considered, and trivial analogies. Often these are mere clichés — *You can't teach an old dog new tricks.* But even when they are not clichés, they may still be based on a superficial resemblance between two events or conditions. In any controversy analogies come easily — usually too easily — to mind. It would be wise not to accept them until they have been carefully examined to see if there is a significant difference between the things being compared.

Example	*Analysis*
A French Minister of Education is reported to have told a visitor that at that moment every fourth-grade pupil in all France was studying exactly the same lesson. In France the national government controls education. If we adopt the proposed federal aid to education bill, we will bring about federal control of our schools and get the same kind of regimentation that exists in France.	*A student using this analogy should first satisfy himself that there are no essential differences in the governmental structures of the two countries. When he tries to do so he will discover that France does not have a federal form of government and that the educational control in France more nearly resembles our state control. That discovery would make the student question the worth of the analogy in a question primarily concerned with federal control. If he still wants to use the analogy he will at least feel an obligation to show in detail that, despite this difference, the two countries are analogous where education is concerned.*

All these fallacies — *hasty generalizations, stereotypes, inadequate causal relations, either-or fallacies,* and *trivial analogies* — oversimplify the problem by allowing us to reach conclusions more easily and more quickly than would be possible in disciplined deliberation.

✔ Examine the following arguments for reliability. If they are fallacious, show what makes them so.

1. Dad, I think you will be making a mistake if you take out a big insurance policy now. The mortality tables show that you have a life-expectancy of 69, and you are only 44 now. That means that you have a reasonable expectation of living 25 more years. In four years both Joe and I will be through college and will be self-supporting. If you postpone the insurance until then, we won't have to skimp to pay the premiums.

2. Add together two facts — that there are as many men as there are women, and that movie actresses get married as often as they please — and you see that the only reason some girls don't get married is that they don't make themselves attractive to men.

3. The papers say that Senator Blank won by a landslide. There is something fishy about that. I have checked with my friends and neighbors and have found only two who voted for Blank.

4. We would not have all these wars, strikes, riots, and crimes if people would only return to religion.

5. The argument that football is a dangerous sport is disproved very simply by showing that the death rate — not total deaths, but deaths per thousand — among high school, college, and professional players combined is much less than the death rate of the total population.

6. It is a waste of public funds to send a girl to a state university. All a girl wants from college is a husband. A good matrimonial agency would meet her needs at less cost to the taxpayers.

7. In giving a blood transfusion doctors must be sure that the patient and donor are of the same race; otherwise the patient may acquire the racial characteristics of the donor.

8. College students, at least American college students, are different from all other people on this planet; they are the only people who try to get as little as possible for their money. They will spend the most valuable years of their lives, thousands of dollars of their parents' money and some of their own, if they can get any, in trying to derive as little as possible out of their college courses, provided only that they will receive their coveted diplomas at the end of four years of such effort.

9. I hear their first-string quarterback has an A average. Can you imagine that?

10. Habitual drunkards lack will power; that is why they are habitual drunkards.

11. The fact that no national fair employment law has been passed is proof that the people will not accept such laws. If people would accept them, these laws would have been passed long ago.

12. I was quite surprised when I met my professors for the first time. Some of them were young and none of them was bald.

13. If the University allows men to live in unsupervised houses and keep what hours they please, it should extend the same privileges to coeds.

14. Statistics show that the average age of college students at the time of graduation is 21. They also show that superior students graduate before the average age and less capable students graduate after the average age. Since Jones was almost thirty when he graduated, we must conclude that he is not very bright.

15. Careful research shows that the most successful men have the largest vocabularies. This proves that the development of an extensive vocabulary is a cause of success.

Evaluating Controversy

So far we have been concerned with understanding the structure of argument, recognizing assumptions, distinguishing different types of premises and inferences, and detecting fallacies. We are now ready to combine all these considerations in an evaluation of controversy.

When we evaluate a controversy we are trying to determine how well each party to the dispute does what he is trying to do. Our main concerns are with the pertinence and persuasiveness of arguments, but we can best proceed by asking three questions: (1) What are the issues in the controversy? (2) What are the arguments used to resolve them? (3) How persuasive are these arguments? Let us apply these questions to the following debate.

SHOULD COMMUNISM BE STUDIED IN OUR SCHOOLS?

YES[4]

I assume that the word "Communism" means Russian Communism, and not the philosophical Communism which has been the subject of theoretical speculation since ancient times. I assume that the word "studied" means careful, comprehensive, systematic, and critical examination of facts for the purpose of achieving understanding, and not the inculcation of political doctrines. I assume that the word "schools" means secondary schools, colleges and universities, and not kindergartens and elementary schools.

The answer to the question, as thus interpreted, is in my judgment an emphatic "yes." In fact, failure to provide for the serious study of Russian Communism at the upper levels of our educational system would be enough to convict the older generation of either stupidity or violation of trust. In the world as it is today, any person who does not have at least an elementary knowledge of Russian Communism — its controlling ideas, its institutions and practices, its impact on the world, its powerful outward thrust, and its challenge to our democracy — must be regarded as politically illiterate. The Russian revolution of 1917 and the development of the Soviet state together constitute perhaps the outstanding political event of this century. It can no more be ignored with safety than the atomic bomb.

To those who think that the young can be shielded from the ideas of Russian Communism by prohibiting their study in the schools, the answer is they do not understand American society. Our youth hear about Communism daily in the discussions of their elders, on the platform, and over the radio. They read about it in newspapers and magazines. Moreover, they are sure to encounter it in any study of recent history, of world geography, of comparative governments and social systems, and even in any honest and complete study of our American society. Indeed, they encounter it in their own organizations and their informal relations with one another. Only by abandoning our political liberties and by establishing a system of thought control on the pattern of Russian Communism itself, or any other totalitarian state, could we hope to keep the young in complete ignorance on this question. Certainly, few Americans would want to follow this course and thus insure without a struggle the triumph of totalitarianism in the United States.

It is my conviction that knowledge — accurate and balanced — is the

[4] George S. Counts in *Talks*, October, 1947. Copyright, 1947, by Columbia Broadcasting System, Inc. Reprinted by permission of CBS and the author.

only secure foundation of human liberty. Therefore, instead of leaving the young to the mercies of the organized and unorganized propaganda of the home, the street, the marketplace, the radio, and the movie, we should do everything possible to acquaint them, through scholarly study under the guidance of well-trained teachers, with Russian Communism in all of its aspects. By pursuing such a course, we shall prepare our youth to discharge intelligently the responsibilities of citizenship and defend the cause of freedom in the difficult period ahead. If informed men and women are faced with the choice between democracy and dictatorship, they will, I am confident, choose democracy. To deny this is to repudiate the faith that sustains and inspires our system of government.

The study of Russian Communism should be projected on a background of understanding of and loyalty to the principles of democracy. From the earliest years of formal education, children should be reared by both precept and practice in those principles. There is needed here a profound reorganization of our entire school system from the bottom to the top. At no time in our history have we faced squarely the task of developing an educational program carefully and imaginatively designed to cultivate in the young the loyalties, the knowledges, and the understandings essential to the guarding and the strengthening of the great tradition of American liberty. If we undertake this task successfully, we shall not have to worry about shielding our youth from the doctrines of any totalitarian system. We shall equip them, also, to correct all weaknesses and deficiencies in our democracy and thus add greatly to its strength and guarantee its indefinite perpetuation.

No[5]

"Know the enemy" is the first law of self-preservation. Communism is the self-styled enemy of the American way of life. Therefore, in the interest of national survival, every American adult should study the aims of Communism and the methods by which it proposes to achieve these aims.

But today's discussion is limited to whether or not young people should be taught Communism in our schools. I believe not, for what is wise for adults is often unwise for young people. Whether they fancy themselves to be fully grown or not, there are certain qualitative differences between maturity and immaturity. These are primarily differences in judgment, and the law itself recognizes them by denying minors certain privileges and protecting minors from certain responsibilities. The law should provide similar safeguards in the field of ideas. Therefore, Communism should *not* be studied until intellectual and emotional maturity is reached and the individual is competent to take it or leave it on the basis of experience with human nature and knowledge of history.

There are three major counts against teaching Communism in our schools.

First, adolescence ranges in age roughly from 14 to 21, the seven crucial school years. One of the by-products of adolescence is emotional instability and a tendency toward sentimentality. Whenever youth sees poverty and delinquency its natural sentiment is to try to remedy these tragedies. But youth lacks the experience of age which tempers impulse with judgment.

[5] Ruth Alexander in *Talks,* October, 1947. Copyright, 1947, by Columbia Broadcasting System, Inc. Reprinted by permission of CBS and the author.

Youth observes the effects of poverty and delinquency, but is unable or unwilling to see clearly the causes. Communism cunningly proclaims the cause to be purely social. It willfully ignores or covers up the historic fact that the predominant cause lies in the ancient universal and durable evils of human nature. And it vigorously denies the historic fact that the American system of civil liberty, voluntary enterprise, and private property has humanized human nature and evolved a finer, higher scale of living than any society known to mankind.

Second, whenever Communism is taught in our schools, it is seldom taught objectively, although there are exceptions, of course. Instruction too often degenerates into indoctrination. It does not confine itself to a rational portrayal of Marxist doctrine, but seeks rather to convert the young student to the Marxist point of view. Masquerading under the cover of academic freedom, many teachers propagandize Communism which, if adopted, would suppress not only academic freedom, but all other freedoms as well. It does not make sense.

Frankly, there is considerable reason for widespread academic sympathy toward Communism. Teachers are notoriously underpaid in view of long and costly preparation for their noble profession. But the remedy is not Communism. The remedy is to pay our teachers the highest wage of all civil servants. Until that fortunate day, a study of Communism in our schools would put the young pupil at the mercy of those whose viewpoint is warped by poverty and discontent and who favor any system that promises a phony utopia. Many teachers are innocent of intent to further Communism. Others in high places who teach teachers what and how to teach youth, boldly proclaim a Soviet challenge to America and dare the schools to build a new social order, behind the smoke screen of academic freedom.

Third, Communism is a dangerous dose for youth because it is more than a politico-economic doctrine. Its explosive emotional content amounts to religious fanaticism. It despises and represses orthodox religions as the so-called "opiate of the people." At the same time it substitutes itself as both an opiate and a stimulant. Communists seduce the minds and souls of youth by the prospect of a perfectly functioning "planned economy" wholly at variance with the inescapable laws of economics. They cunningly neglect to mention that their self-styled welfare state is a slave state, achieved and maintained by the firing squad and the concentration camp.

It would sound ridiculous to ask, "Should robbery be studied in our schools?" Yet, if academic freedom is the sole issue rather than national survival, such a question is consistent and in order. If carpentry, why not burglary? Both are ways and means of getting a living. But carpentry is socially constructive and robbery is socially destructive. Communism is likewise socially destructive, for its methods frankly include robbery, murder, arson, lying, and incitement to violence. These it defends and advocates on the basis of its working slogan that the "ends justify the means."

We protect our young people from harmful epidemic diseases of a physical nature such as smallpox, by quarantining them. We expose our young people to harmful epidemic diseases of an ideological nature, such as Communism, by a false suicidal interpretation of academic freedom. What youth does when it reaches maturity is something else again. At that time, in the interest of national survival, adults should study Communism to be able to recognize it and fight it for dear life whenever and under whatever disguise it rears its hideous head.

In order to evaluate this debate, let us first reduce it to its essentials in a summary. In doing this we must take special care not to distort either argument. If our summary is a faithful one, both speakers should agree that they have not been misrepresented. Since each of them has three major reasons for his conclusion, we can set them up in parallel columns, thus:

Counts	*Alexander*
1. Russian Communism is such an important political factor that it would be political illiteracy to ignore it.	1. Young people between the ages of 14 and 21 are not mature enough to withstand the sentimental appeal of Communism.
2. In a democracy it is not possible to withhold information; so young people will learn about Communism anyway.	2. Teachers would be sympathetic to Communism and would not teach it objectively. NOT NECESSARILY, BUT...
3. An informed electorate offers the best defense of democracy; so a scholarly study of Communism would prepare young people to combat it.	3. The emotional content of Communism makes it a dangerous subject for young people to study.

These two speakers differ on two main questions: whether high school and college students are mature enough to study Communism, and whether teachers would conduct the study objectively. These are the main issues in the debate. To each of these questions Mr. Counts would answer "Yes" and Miss Alexander "No."

What is the reasoning by which each speaker reaches his conclusions and how persuasive are the arguments? On the first issue — the maturity of adolescents — neither speaker offers a sustained argument. Mr. Counts *assumes* that they are mature enough; Miss Alexander *asserts* that they are not. In the absence of specific evidence, the audience will have to fall back on its previous experience with adolescents on similar questions. The persuasion, then, will depend less on what the speakers say than on what the audience feels.

On the second issue, Mr. Counts assumes that the teaching will be done objectively. In defining his terms he assumes that "studied" means "a careful, comprehensive, and critical examination of the facts for the purpose of achieving understanding, and not the inculcation of political doctrines." Miss Alexander generalizes that the teaching of Communism in the schools is seldom done objectively. She offers no evidence for that generalization; so her statement is an assertion rather than an argument. She does give an explanation of *why* teachers are sympathetic to Communism, but that explanation assumes that they are sympathetic. On this issue also persuasion will depend less on what the speakers say than on what the audience feels, or has experienced in the past.

To supplement her main arguments, Miss Alexander uses two analogies: one comparing Communism to robbery, the other comparing it to a disease like smallpox. Of the two, the second is likely to seem more pertinent, but the persuasiveness of that analogy will depend on whether the audience sees a similarity between exposure to germs and exposure to ideas.

In this debate there is on both sides an obvious lack of evidence, partly because each speaker had only about ten minutes in which to make his position clear. But a person who comes to the debate without previous convictions is likely to feel that he needs more information before he can reach a decision. He needs to know what evidence is available about how adolescents respond to subjects like Communism, and he needs to know whether teachers generally are sympathetic to Communism. Unless he knows these things, he will feel that he cannot logically answer the questions. Recognizing such a need is often a useful result of analysis. On important questions it is often wise to delay decision until the best available information has been obtained.

Exercises

The materials that follow will give you an opportunity to put to use much of what has been said about logical persuasion in this chapter. For each selection decide what issues are being dealt with, what kinds of arguments are being used, how persuasive they are and why, at what points additional information is needed; then give your total judgment of the controversy. In considering the arguments distinguish between premises and conclusions and comment on both.

A. The following selection consists of excerpts from a 5000-word paper written by a high school senior who took the Abominable Snowman question as the subject for a special research project. His conclusion was that the Snowman (or Yeti) is either an advanced ape or a primitive man, and that all arguments which deny that thesis are logically unsatisfactory. Here he is considering the evidence of footprints and scalps and is especially concerned with refuting the evidence presented by Sir Edmund Hillary, the conqueror of Everest, in *Life* magazine. The illustrative drawings which accompanied the student paper are not reproduced here, but the source references are given in footnotes (identified here by letters, instead of numbers, to separate them from our chapter footnotes).

THE ABOMINABLE SNOWMAN[6]

The Abominable Snowman prints are too well authenticated to be just stories. Many people have seen them; many have taken photographs of

[6] By Charles Johnson. Printed by permission of the author.

them. The classic example of a snowman's print is a photograph taken by Eric Shipton, a naturalist on the Hunt expedition to Everest. For the sceptics, I bring in here a partial list of the names of people, explorers mostly, who have seen the tracks and given details that fit the Shipton photograph: Colonel Howard Bury, Major L. A. Waddell, N. A. Tombozi, J. R. P. Gent, Ronald Kaulbach, H. W. Tilman, W. H. Murry, and Ralph Izzard.[a] . . .

One of the popular arguments against the existence of the snowman is that his supposed tracks could be made by a small quadruped and through melting of the snow by the sun these tracks became large and distorted enough to resemble human footprints. Sir Edmund Hillary recently reported that he found snowman tracks which, upon entering the shade of a large rock, changed immediately into tracks of a smaller animal — a snow-wolf, he thought.[b] . . . But Hillary gives only one photograph of the print he found and that shows the print as an undistinguishable mark in the snow. He gives no photograph of the surrounding area. . . . To make matters worse, he gives no description of the prints — their length, width, depth, or shape. He gives no details of the entire print pattern — distance between prints, which way they were pointing, how great the angle of the print with a medial line of the whole set of prints. He gives no description of the scene except that one kind of track changed into another. Were there other tracks in or near this area? What happened to the tracks *after* they left the shade, if they did leave it? These questions go unanswered. . . .

It is quite possible for a small quadruped, *if* both its hind and fore feet have the same size and shape and if it is running, to leave tracks like those of a biped. . . . But this answer is unsatisfactory for two reasons: first, *both* fresh and distorted tracks have been seen; and second, if a small animal did make the tracks, the prints would be very close together. Concerning the first point, Eric Shipton remarks in his book that although some of the prints were obviously distorted by the melting snow, others were well preserved and the details of the foot could be seen.[c] The biologist Robert Enders, writing in *Science* in 1953 about his findings in the Himalayas, observed that both fresh and old tracks were seen; the fresh were "large — four to six inches wide and ten to fourteen inches long."[d] The second point is, it seems to me, completely obvious. A small animal, even when it runs, leaves tracks which are close together, the distance between each print being from three to eight inches depending on the size of the animal (for example, a thirty pound dog leaves prints about three inches apart). The snowman prints are eighteen inches apart,[e] about the length of a medium-sized man's stride. Tilman speaks my feelings: "A little thought should have made it obvious that if a small animal's footprints were enlarged by the snow melting, the length of its stride would appear to decrease; the prints might even merge."[f]

One last point about the small animal tracks — it would be quite a co-

---

[a] Willy Ley, *Exotic Biology* (New York, 1959), pp. 75–89.
[b] "Epitaph to the Elusive Abominable Snowman," *Life,* 50:71 (January 13, 1961).
[c] Eric Shipton, *The Mount Everest Reconnaissance Expedition* (New York, 1952), p. 127.
[d] "The Abominable Snowman," *Science,* 126:858 (October 25, 1957).
[e] Shipton, p. 127.   [f] Tilman, pp. 142–143.

incidence for the shape of the print to change every time from a four-digit paw with claw marks to a five-digit human-like foot with toes. . . .

Snowman relics are kept in the Himalayan monastery of Thyangboche and the most important single item among them is a set of scalps claimed as snowmen's.

Hillary mentions that supposed antique scalps were investigated by scientists in Chicago, Paris, and London and that their conclusions were the same — molded out of the hide of another animal, probably from one of the rare goat-antelope family.[g] . . . But he fails to give the names of the experts, what they really said, and why they said it. . . . The all-round scientist Willy Ley says that the hairs taken from a scalp were thought by experts to be from the shoulder hide of a large mammal.[h]

The scalp is huge, having a circumference of about twenty-two inches at its widest point (base), and a height of about eight inches.[i] It is slightly flattened laterally, rises to a peak from a rounded base, and has yellow-brown hair. If it is truly a scalp, it has two unique qualities: if it was cut from immediately above the ear, then the height — eight inches — is much taller than any other scalp we know of; and along its sagittal plane (along a line down the middle of the "forehead" and the back of the head) is a thick ridge of skin covered with hair as is the entire scalp. Of course, in the "genuine" scalp, there are no seams or stitches; it is made of material of which every scalp is made — skin and hair.

Hillary very proudly announced that he was able to mold a snowman-shaped scalp out of the hide of another animal, and that therefore, in all probability, snowman scalps were similarly fabricated. But a French zoologist, Heuvelmans, who is an expert on "queer" beings, tried the very same thing, came up with the very same results, yet concluded differently — the scalp could *not* be made from another animal's hide. In none, he says, do the hair tracts even closely resemble the tracts on the snowman's head.[j] The hair on the back of any animal flows along a direct path towards the hind quarters, along what is called "the primitive cranio-caudal stream." Even though there might be a whorl on the shoulder of the animal, the general direction of the hair would be the same. The snowman's scalp, however, has a completely different hair pattern. From the base of the forehead the hair flows in a straight line towards the top of the head. Before reaching the peak, the hair branches off in two directions — a stream to the left and a stream to the right towards the expected attachment of the ears (such as is the case with man). Across the top of the head, *the hair does not point towards the back of the scalp,* but points towards the sides of the head. At the crown (approximately where it is in humans) the hair streams out in a finger-like fashion to all points on the back of the scalp. Of course the molding of a hide would alter the hair tract pattern somewhat, but not nearly so much as to resemble the hair tracts of the snowman scalp. As Heuvelmans says, "it would be utterly impossible. . . . I challenge those who have said that these scalps are fakes to concoct one out of the shoulder of

[g] Hillary, p. 72.   [h] Ley, p. 81.
[i] Bernard Heuvelmans, *On the Track of Unknown Animals* (New York, 1959), p. 170.
[j] *Ibid.,* p. 171.

some hooved animal or indeed from the skin of any animal they choose. The result may well be an attractive fur cap, but I am certain that not even the most shortsighted of experts would ever mistake it for a relic of the snow-man."[k]

B. The three letters that follow are taken from a controversy in *The Saturday Review*. Here the first two are paired as pro and con in a debate.

PSEUDONYM, SHAKESPEARE[7]

Sir:

In the review of G. B. Harrison's "Shakespeare: 23 Plays and the Sonnets" (SRL June 5) there is a misstatement so gross as to vitiate any claims to scholarship. Mr. Redman speaks of "those who hold fuzzily to the notion that 'we know nothing about him' (Shakespeare) instead of realizing that we know more about him than about 'any other Elizabethan dramatist.' "

The most meager knowledge of the Shakespeare mystery recognizes the fact that all we know of the Stratford Shakespeare, Shacksper, or Shaksper, could easily be printed on a half column of this page. It consists of perhaps a score of often sordid facts — baptisms, marriage, real estate deals, law-suits, fines, etc. Not one of these records indicates in the slightest way that the Stratfordian was a writer. Nor do the few recorded items regarding the actor Shakespeare (who may or may not have been the Stratfordian) give any such evidence.

While there were many laudatory references to the *author* "Shakespeare" by his contemporaries, not one of them identifies him as the man of Strat-ford. The name was as much a pseudonym as Mark Twain or O. Henry, and it was a common practice in Elizabethan times to use stooges, often ignorant, whose names were put on title pages, even by the clergy. The anonymity of several important Elizabethan works has never been pierced.

What Mr. Harrison and Mr. Redman "know" about Shakespeare is a fictitious biography based on hearsay, conjecture, and old wives' tales col-lected by the actor Betterton seventy years after the Stratfordian's death, and, in Mr. Harrison's case, inflated by inferential interpretations of topical subjects in the "Plays and Sonnets." The assertion that Shakespeare of Stratford was the author was not asserted in print until many years after his death.

On the other hand, what we know about "other Elizabethan dramatists" is considerable. Of such writers as Edmund Spenser, Marlowe, Ben Jonson, Nash, Lyly, Peele, and others we have a good picture of their education, the books they owned, and their artistic interests which qualified them as writers.

While many of the best-known and most influential scholars in England — such men as the Dean of St. Paul's Cathedral in London, the Canon of Chelmsford Cathedral, principal of Victoria College, University of Liverpool, head master of the Charterhouse School, the professor of English at the Royal Naval Academy, etc. — have publicly attested to their belief that the true author was Edward De Vere, seventeenth Earl of Oxford, hardly a

[k] *Ibid.,* pp. 171–172.

[7] By Gelett Burgess. From "Letters to the Editor," in *Saturday Review of Litera-ture,* October 2, 1948. Reprinted by permission.

single important professor of English literature in the United States has been willing even to consider the new historical evidence that has changed the whole Elizabethan picture. They rest content, like the *Encyclopaedia Britannica,* with historical data derived from sources no later than 1897. Many of the college faculties have been invited to refute, if possible, the new evidence that has accumulated since then. All have refused.

It is true what Mr. Redman says, that we know more about Shakespeare than about any other Elizabethan writer — but the "Shakespeare" is not the Shakespeare of Stratford. He was the brightest star in the firmament of talent in that splendid era. A royal ward, brought up at Court, he was familiar with its usages. Highly educated, with degrees from both Oxford and Cambridge, familiar with the Greek and Latin classics, he could give the plays their sophisticated touch. A student at Gray's Inn for three years, his references to the intricacies of law are easily accounted for. Traveled in Italy, a champion in the tournament, an aristocrat *pur sang,* an expert falconer, a musician, a poet praised as the best, and excellent in comedy, and above all, as Lord Great Chamberlain in charge for years of the company of players who performed Shakespeare's dramas, he had every possible qualification for authorship, while the dummy of Stratford had not one.

A Reply to Mr. Burgess[8]

Sir:

The present Oxford theorist affirms that Oxford wrote the plays, but assumed the name of Shakespeare; and the Stratford Shakespeare whom he calls the "Dummy of Stratford" hadn't the qualifications to produce them.

1. If Shakespeare was only a country bumpkin, and without any education, why was he buried in the Stratford church, and a carved stone bust of him placed on the chancel wall? This stone bust represents Shakespeare with one hand resting on a scroll, and a pen in his other hand. So the bust is a memorial to a writer.

2. At the age of about nineteen Shakespeare went to London. He had a brother, an actor, there. Richard Burbidge, a famous London actor who subsequently played leading roles in Shakespeare's great dramas, was a Stratford man. There is no doubt that these two Stratford men read specimens of Shakespeare's work, and induced him to go to London, the Mecca for talented youth.

3. In London Shakespeare had his poem "Venus and Adonis" published. He wrote this in Stratford. The very man who published his poem was a printer who also went from Stratford to London a few years before Shakespeare. Shakespeare had known this printer in Stratford. His name was Richard Field, and his father was a tanner in the town. Shakespeare dedicated "Venus and Adonis" to the Earl of Southampton, and called the poem: "The first heir of my invention." Here we have evidence that the Stratford Shakespeare states that he is a writer.

4. In Shakespeare's plays you will find names of people he knew in Stratford. In the Induction to "The Taming of the Shrew," Sly the tinker is the chief character. There was a tinker in Stratford by the name of Sly. In the

[8] By Hoy Cranston. From "Letters to the Editor," in *Saturday Review of Literature,* November 6, 1948. Reprinted by permission.

same comedy Sly refers to a woman who kept a public house in the village of Wincot, a village near Stratford. Sly says: "Ask Marian Hacket the fat ale-wife of Wincot." Sly states that he is the son of old Sly of Burton Heath, a village near Stratford.

5. Two associates of Shakespeare's in London, and men who were also actors in his plays, collected Mss. of all Shakespeare's plays and published them seven years after his death. There are documents extant that also prove that Shakespeare was a Stratford man, for Shakespeare's youngest daughter, Judith, took from Stratford a bundle of Mss. to her own home, soon after her father died.

6. Shakespeare's will proves that he was a Stratford man, that he frequently went there from London, that he died and was buried in Stratford. His will also proves that he was the same Shakespeare who wrote plays and produced them in London. In his will, which was made and signed in Stratford, he left legacies to relatives and friends living in Stratford. He bequeathed his Stratford home to his daughter Susanna. All this proves that Shakespeare was a Stratford man. The will also proves that the same Shakespeare produced plays of his own in London theatres. We find in the will the following: "And to my Fellows (all actors with shares in London theatres) John Hemmynges, Henry Cundell, Richard Burbidge XXVi^s Viij^d apiece to buy them rings." Burbidge was leading tragedian in Shakespeare's great tragedies. The other two men were Shakespeare's associates and fellow actors in London. "Fellows" means associates. Hemmynges and Cundell were the first to publish all Shakespeare's plays in one volume, which is called "The 1623 Folio." Shakespeare's will alone furnishes absolute proof that the Shakespeare who produced the plays was a Stratford man, and not a Stratford "dummy." We know that Shakespeare was also an actor, and speeches in his tragedies prove it, for he knew the art of making points.

Many years ago Mr. William Winter, the greatest dramatic critic in America, took me with him to see Edwin Booth as Othello. After the wonderful performance Mr. Winter said: "Shakespeare did not make those great speeches of Othello's sitting down alone in a room. I'm sure he dictated them, while standing, and when roused to 'the top of his bent.'" Shakespeare the actor-dramatist knew how to fit an actor with a "role to tear a cat in," the kind Bottom the weaver required to properly demonstrate his histrionic ability.

C. This third letter represents a different kind of argument from those presented in the letters of Exercise B. What method of reasoning is used here? Write a short critique of the argument, analyzing it in terms of its structure and persuasiveness.

A Reply to Mr. Burgess[9]

Sir:

Mr. Gelett Burgess's discovery that there are ignoramuses who, after all the evidence presented to the contrary, still believe the plays attributed to Shakespeare were actually written by that unlettered lout of a horseholder, has alarmed me. I am now convinced that any further delay in arousing the

[9] By Clark Kinnaird. From "Letters to the Editor," in *Saturday Review of Literature,* November 6, 1948. Reprinted by permission.

reading public's attention regarding certain facts about George Bernard Shaw, as he is called, may make it more difficult to establish the true authorship of the plays bearing his name.

It will be seen from the evidence I am presenting that it is just as unlikely that the real Shaw wrote the plays attributed to him as that Shakespeare wrote the plays of Edward De Vere.

Let us consider that the facts about Shaw's life are no better established than that "perhaps score of sordid facts," as Mr. Burgess puts it, we have about Shakespeare. We are dependent upon birth and marriage records, reports in the notoriously unreliable press, and biographies which disagree throughout, and which are questionable on other grounds. For example, we know that the so-called biography of Shaw by one who supposedly knew him, Frank Harris, was written by one Frank Scully, who never saw Shaw and therefore could not prove Shaw ever lived! In other cases, Shaw, as he is called, when mysteriously given access to the Ms., changed the original text of the author to suit his purpose. (We shall show what the purpose was!)

From the small body of uncontestable fact about Shaw, it is certain that he was not of royal blood, or even lordly lineage. His father was no more than a corn merchant. George Bernard Shaw, as he is called, never had any formal schooling after the age of fourteen. Indeed, it is questionable whether he had much schooling earlier, because of his apparent inability to spell or punctuate correctly. Any who have seen his letters know them to be studded with "thru," "dont" (without the apostrophe), etc.

How could one who never went to college or even high school have possibly written such a masterpiece as "Candida"?

There is no evidence whatever that the real Shaw even tried to write anything in his youth. He was certainly content to work for five years in, of all places, a real estate office. It's simply incredible that the author of "Pygmalion" could have existed five years in such a stultifying atmosphere. However, we do not have to believe our senses; for staring us in the face is indisputable evidence of the man Shaw's ineptitude as a writer when he did try to make his living with a pen. In nine years after he left the real estate office (under circumstances which we can conjecture), he earned exactly £6. Four novels, as they were called, were rejected one after the other by publishers. One was about prize-fighting, which is only further evidence of what low tastes he had. Try to couple that with the authorship of "Saint Joan"!

His family had to struggle for existence. "I did not throw myself into it, I threw my mother into it," Shaw said. That sufficiently characterizes the man who some persons believe, oddly, wrote "Mrs. Warren's Profession."

The real Shaw did, it seems, work in the lowest type of literary endeavor, criticism, but drifted from publication to publication — *Pall Mall Gazette, The Star, The Saturday Review,* apparently unable to keep a job. It is well known that any person capable of creating first-rate plays (such as "The Apple Cart," "On the Rocks," etc.) devotes himself to creative work and does not resort to making a living as scavenger among other men's ideas; the critic at best is one who knows how but cannot do it himself.

Realization of this might have made him disposed to allow his name to be used on another man's work. He practiced such deceit himself, as those aware of the relationship of Shaw and Corno di Bassetto know. But that is another story.

And now for a conjecture.

The other man with great plays in his mind and heart was in a position that required deceit, as De Vere was. He was an aristocrat, son of a lord and grandson of a duke. He had the education, background, and ability for his chosen profession of playwright, such as De Vere had. But playwriting was no occupation for one of his social position. Persons of the theater were not acceptable in his set. Also, the kind of plays he was determined to write would, he realized, inevitably compromise the political career for which he was destined by his family and its traditions — if presented in his own name.

The circumstances demanded that the plays bear another's name. A nom-de-plume would be more easily penetrated. So a deal was made, I conjecture. How wise the playwright must have regarded his decision when he rose to high office — the highest office! How embarrassing it might have been for him then if Backbenchers had quoted lines he put in John Tanner's mouth in "Man and Superman." Or for him to have had to receive an ambassador from Bulgaria who was aware the prime minister was the author of "Arms and the Man."

That reference gives you a hint as to the true identity of the author of George Bernard Shaw's plays. You will find stronger hints in a comparison of the literary styles of a recent autobiographical work of an exalted personage in Great Britain. But I now present, for the first time, plainer evidence of the true author of Shaw's plays. His name is concealed in the titles of the plays! Look:

*"**W**idowers' Houses"*
*"Sa**i**nt Joan"*
*"Ma**n** and Superman"*
*"Ar**m**s and the Man"*
*"**T**he Philanderer"*
"Too Good to Be True"
*"A**n**drocles and the Lion"*

*"M**r**s. Warren's Profession"*
*"**P**ygmalion"*
*"Ov**e**rruled"*
*"**O**n the Rocks"*
*"**B**ack to Methuselah"*
*"Ge**t**ting Married"*
*"G**r**eat Catherine"*

*"The Do**c**tor's Dilemma"*
*"**H**eartbreak House"*
*"Y**o**u Never Can Tell"*
*"Majo**r** Barbara"*
*"**C**aesar and Cleopatra"*
*"**T**he Man of Destiny"*
*"Cand**i**da"*
*"Misa**l**liance"*
*"John Bu**l**l's Other Island"*

14

The Critical Review

As the term is used in an English class, a critical review is an essay in which the author appraises his subject. The subject may be almost anything — a philosophy, a social trend, an exhibition of paintings, a concert, a movie, a television program, or a piece of literature. In English classes the emphasis is on books, and it is with the critical review of a book that this chapter is chiefly concerned.

The Requirements of the Review

A good critical review communicates to a reader the critic's evaluation of a work in such a way that the reader can then make his own estimate of it. To do this the critic must meet three requirements: he must report what the book does; he must judge how well it does it; and he must provide enough evidence from the book itself to support or illustrate his judgment.

Each of these obligations is important. To the extent that the reviewer slights any of them, the usefulness of his review decreases. If his report of what the book does is inadequate for a reader who does not know the book, that reader will have difficulty following the critic's analysis. If, on the other hand, the reviewer tells only what the book does, and not how well it does it, he is writing a synopsis, not a critical review. Finally, if he fails to support or illustrate his judgments from the book itself, he gives the reader no opportunity of forming his own judgment. No reviewer has the right to assume that his unsupported opinions will be accepted as facts. If he says the book is badly organized, that its style is turgid, or that it is full of inaccuracies, he should present evidence for these assertions.

A fourth obligation is taken for granted, that the reviewer will be fair to the work he is judging. He must not allow his prejudices on a subject to influence his appraisal unduly. He has no right, for instance, to condemn a history of capitalism or trade-unionism simply because he dislikes capital or labor. He must not allow his own preferences to blind him to the merits or demerits of the work he is reviewing.

Observe how the following student review meets these requirements.

The Secret Life of Walter Mitty[1]

"The Secret Life of Walter Mitty" is a delightfully clever satire that ridicules one of the most common human idiosyncrasies, imagination. To illustrate the wonders of imagination, Thurber creates Walter Mitty, a timid, mouselike little man, who is forever being victimized by a nagging wife and an arrogant, "know it all" society. With the entire world against him, the only escape left for poor Walter Mitty is his imagination, which he uses to the utmost of his ability.

What makes "The Secret Life of Walter Mitty" more than just another amusing short story is Thurber's unique and effective use of contrasts. Consider, for example, the first three paragraphs. Here the Walter Mitty of imagination is placed side by side with the Walter Mitty of reality. The contrast between the iron-hearted Naval Commander, bravely giving orders to his men, and the chicken-hearted Walter Mitty, timidly taking orders from his wife, is quite apparent. But the use of contrasts is by no means restricted to the beginning of the story. On the contrary, it is employed all the way through to the very last word. Compare the quick-thinking Doctor Mitty, famous surgeon, to the Walter Mitty who cannot park his car, remove his tire chains, nor readily remember to buy a box of puppy biscuits. Compare also the "greatest shot in the world" or the daring Captain Mitty, or the "erect and motionless, proud and disdainful, Walter Mitty the Undefeated" with the Walter Mitty who seeks the quiet refuge of a big leather chair in a hotel lobby. Contrasts are effective tools for any writer, but the straightforward manner in which Thurber employs them enhances their effectiveness considerably.

After briefly skimming through the collection of contrasts that makes up "The Secret Life of Walter Mitty," one might feel that there is little connection between the paragraphs describing the imagined Walter Mitty and the Mitty of reality. However, closer observation reveals that Thurber does, by the use of suggestive words and phrases, cleverly establish links between the Mitty of fact and the Mitty of fancy. Examine the following lines taken from the end of paragraph one and the beginning of paragraph two of "The Secret Life of Walter Mitty":

". . . The Old Man'll get us through," they said to one another. "The Old Man ain't afraid of Hell!" . . .

"Not so fast! You're driving too fast!" said Mrs. Mitty. "What are you driving so fast for?"

We shudder to think that there might be a connection between Hell and life with Mrs. Mitty, but, unfortunately, such could be the case. Consider how Mrs. Mitty's mention of Doctor Renshaw and the event of driving by a hospital lead to a daydream in which Walter Mitty, a distinguished surgeon, assists Doctor Renshaw in a difficult operation. Take note also of how a newsboy's shout about the Waterbury trial initiates the trial of Walter Mitty in the following paragraph. Such skillful employment of transitions, by

[1] Philip G. Plotica, "The Secret Life of Walter Mitty." From *The Green Caldron: A Magazine of Freshman Writing* (December, 1960), published at the University of Illinois, Urbana, Illinois. Reprinted by permission.

which an event in reality triggers an event in the imagination, is sound not only from the literary standpoint, but also from the psychological point of view.

"The Secret Life of Walter Mitty" affects the reader in a variety of ways. The purposeful use of excessively dramatic, imaginative heroes, the repetition of the sound "pocketa-pocketa," the use of meaningless pseudo-medical terms such as "obstreosis of the ductal tract" — all these make us want to laugh. The plight of Walter Mitty, at the mercy of his domineering wife, arouses our sympathy. However, we neither laugh at nor sympathize with Walter Mitty. Thurber has created Mitty not as an individual, but as a representative of human beings in general. He has made us realize how similar our imaginative worlds are to those of his character. We cannot laugh at Mitty without laughing at ourselves. We cannot sympathize with him without feeling sorry for ourselves. The strength and heart of the satire lie in the reader's perception of the similarity of his own daydreams and those of Mitty.

To see what is happening in this review, let us make a paragraph analysis.

Paragraph 1 begins with a general judgment of the work and continues with a brief description of what Thurber is doing in the story. This paragraph serves a double function: it both introduces the subject and announces the thesis of the review.

Paragraph 2 selects what the reviewer feels is the most effective device in the story and presents enough illustration of that device to make it clear to the reader. In addition, the paragraph ties into the last two sentences of the first paragraph, so that the review moves from the general, introductory comment to the specific implications of that comment.

Paragraph 3 moves on to a still more specific device, the use of transitions between both parts of the contrasts. Again the device is illustrated, and again the paragraph ties into what has gone before. It refers directly to the contrasts discussed in the second paragraph and echoes the theme of escape through imagination which was identified in the first paragraph.

Paragraph 4 begins by borrowing the words "Hell" and "Mrs. Mitty" from the preceding paragraph and combining them in a new meaning. This is a very clever transition to a paragraph showing that Mitty's dreams are an escape from his wife's nagging, an idea that relates directly to the thesis. Unfortunately the student does not follow up that idea but returns to further illustration of the transitions which he discussed in paragraph 3. For the first time the movement of the essay falters and the paragraph, good as it is, makes less of a contribution to the total effectiveness of the essay than any of those which preceded it.

The final paragraph opens by identifying a series of incidents that add to the humor of the story; then this movement is checked as the reviewer realizes that we cannot laugh at or be sorry for Mitty without laughing at or feeling sorry for ourselves. The final sentence sums up the interpretation.

of the story by returning to the thesis that the secret life of Walter Mitty is the secret life of all of us, and that Thurber's story is a gentle satire on human nature.

This student essay does everything a good review need do. It gives us all the information about the plot and purpose that we need without at any time drifting into mere synopsis. It shows us how the author goes about his job by discussing the techniques he uses. It tells us clearly the reviewer's interpretation of the work and his judgment of it. And it provides concrete illustration of every point the reviewer makes. A reader comes away from this review with a feeling of confidence that the reviewer has appraised his subject fairly and thoroughly.

With the next review a reader may be less confident.

AGE OF THUNDER[2]

Frederic Prokosch's *Age of Thunder* is ample evidence that beautiful writing is not enough. Few living writers can handle the English language with more distinction than this poet turned novelist. Even Thomas Mann has paid tribute to the Prokosch prose. But, I think Prokosch's isolated talent of turning exquisite sentences or fashioning fabulously beautiful passages (sometimes several pages in length) actually destroys his chances of achieving greatness. His character development, plot construction, and even intellectual honesty tend to disappear in a purple mist of liquid syllables.

Prokosch's novel pictures the life and death struggles of the maquis in the Haute-Savoie during the years of French underground resistance. Jean-Nicolas, a loyal parachutist spy, dropped for vague reasons of collecting information, dreams his way toward the Swiss border on a magic carpet of Prokosch philosophizing. Later, Jean-Nicolas is betrayed to a German officer by a shadowy caricature named Robinson. That this Robinson or the German commandant would entertain and edify this obvious spy with long and rather juvenile philosophical essays sounded unreal to me.

I do not believe that three mountain gangsters who waylay Allied sympathizers would talk like three versions of Prokosch while planning the murder of Jean-Nicolas. And I do not believe that Susanna, the convenient virgin who tosses the conventions aside like the "winter garment of repentance" upon meeting Jean-Nicolas, would talk or act as she did. In fact, the whole novel is Prokosch any way you cut it.

Incidentally, logical readers who have an eye for detail will want to know why the Swiss border was always a line of hills as these poetic escapists approached it, and how it suddenly became a river when they reached it. But Prokosch, in his illogically slap-happy approach to the problem, undoubtedly thinks such matters are beneath his attention. Personally, I think Prokosch had better stick to poetry.

The only good points I can see about the whole book are the beautifully

[2] Miriam Graham, "Age of Thunder." From *The Green Caldron: A Magazine of Freshman Writing* (November, 1945), published at the University of Illinois, Urbana, Illinois. Reprinted by permission.

written passages and the romantic backdrops. However, the reader wants to know how the maquis operated, how the Germans and the collaborationists countered their efforts, and what men would do, think, and say under such circumstances. It is here that Prokosch evades the issue and covers it up with his philosophizing.

As freshman work, this review has many good qualities. It describes the book, makes a clear judgment, and supports it with some evidence. But there are some things in the review that may bother a reader. First, judgments about style usually need illustration. A few sentences, even a phrase or two, showing Prokosch's style would lend meaning to the reviewer's judgment. Second, a little more restraint would make the review more convincing, for such expressions as "even intellectual honesty tends to disappear," "illogically slap-happy approach," "the whole novel is Prokosch any way you cut it," and "Prokosch had better stick to poetry" may strike a reader as intemperate condemnation, if not arrogance. Third, a reader may reasonably ask why it is illogical to describe a boundary from a distance as a line of hills and later define it from close up as a river — lines of hills are visible from a distance; rivers are less visible. Finally, in a context of such unsympathetic comment, a reader may wonder if, in condemning Prokosch's work for its lack of realism and its failure to explain how the resistance movement actually operated, the reviewer has not missed the author's purpose. As these doubts become cumulative, a reader is likely to lose confidence in the reviewer.

Reading for the Review

The preparation of a good review requires careful reading as well as careful writing. Lazy or uncritical reading will nearly always result in a poor review; therefore, you should begin to read the book *with the intention of reviewing it*. An awareness of this intention will help to point your reading, just as the intention of outlining or summarizing an essay helps you to read it more purposefully. This does not mean that one should make up his mind about a book in the first thirty pages and then skim the rest merely to find additional evidence to support a hasty judgment. Except in rare cases, an honest reviewer will not make a final judgment until he has read the whole book. But if he reads alertly, he will begin to formulate tentative judgments as he goes along.

In beginning to read, always pay special attention to the introductory or prefatory material. The opening paragraphs of an essay usually reveal the purpose and may even summarize the organization. The preface of a book is often the clearest statement of what its author proposes to do. It may also contain explanations which will affect your review. For example, if the author of a biography of Franklin Delano Roosevelt states in his preface that he has limited himself to a study of Roosevelt's political life, it would be embarrassing to miss that statement and condemn the book on the ground that it failed to present an adequate picture of Roosevelt's personal life. A reviewer has a right to point out, even regret, the limitations the author has imposed on himself. But he does not have the right to condemn a writer for not doing what he never intended to do.

For most books it will be wise to take notes as you read. These notes should contain at least a clear statement of the purpose of the book, some hints about its organization, and references to pages and passages which illustrate the author's style or which deserve special mention in the review. These notes will serve a double purpose: they will help to keep your reading alert and so give you a keener insight into the success or failure of the work, and they will reduce or eliminate the time required to go back and find what you remember as good evidence to support your observations.

Writing the Review

The writing of a critical review presents no special problems of composition. As long as you satisfy the three requirements discussed earlier, you are free to organize and present your material in whatever way best suits your purpose. The writing of a critical review, therefore, is merely the application to a particular assignment of the principles of composition which were discussed in Part One of this book.

As always, the first step is a concern with purpose. Before you begin to write, you must be clear about two things: your obligations to your readers and your over-all judgment of the book. If you are sure of these things, the organization of your paper should present no unusual difficulty. But if you begin without understanding what is expected of you or what you want to do, your review may be hard to write and even harder to read. Therefore, if you have no clear opinion of the work when you finish reading it, you should review your notes and analyze your impressions in order to form a judgment.

For most students the most difficult part of the review is the opening paragraph. It is quite reasonable, of course, to plunge at once into your final judgment of the book and then devote succeeding paragraphs to the reasons for that judgment. But if you feel that this is too abrupt — and it often is — there are various other ways of beginning, such as:

1. With an introduction of the author, telling the reader who he is, what other books he has written, or how he came to write this one.
2. With a summary of the problem which the author is discussing. Thus, a review of a book on juvenile delinquency might begin with a brief report on the growth of juvenile delinquency and the attempts being made to curb it.
3. With an anecdote or an illustration, either to suggest the mood of the review or to introduce the author's attitude toward his subject.
4. With a quotation that sums up the purpose of the book.

5. With a description of the book in general terms in order to give the reader a brief, comprehensive picture of it.

6. With a classification of the book to show how it resembles or differs from others of the same kind.

7. With a combination of two or more of these openings.

As you develop your review be on guard against these common weaknesses:

1. Taking up a disproportionate space to explain the action or content of the book so that the review is essentially a digest instead of a criticism.

2. Picking out parts for review instead of reviewing the book as a whole. It is justifiable to criticize particular parts in relation to the whole, but a student who concentrates on particular sections is likely to produce a distorted picture of the whole book.

3. Drifting into digressions which better illustrate the reviewer's philosophy than the merits or demerits of the book.

4. Allowing the style of the review to dominate the reviewer's purpose, thus creating an exaggerated or biased treatment.

5. Keeping the review at too general a level by failing to provide specific illustration of general statements.

The first four of these weaknesses result from failing to keep the purpose of the review clearly in mind. The last comes from a failure to remember that the reader cannot see into the reviewer's mind and hence can never be quite clear about what these general judgments mean unless he is shown. In the critical review, as in all writing except summaries, the writer must elaborate his general observations in order to make them convincing.

Reviewing Nonverbal Works. A review of a movie, a television program, a concert, or a painting does not differ basically from a review of a book. Differences in the media of communication require different techniques, and therefore the critics must write about the work in different terms. But he still stands between the work and the reader and interprets the work as he sees it. He is still concerned with the basic questions: What is being done here? How is it being done? What is its significance?

The Short Review

Critical reviews range in length from a few sentences to a long article, even to a volume. Those we have considered are close to 500 words, a conventional length in English assignments. But a shorter review is often desirable when the assignment calls for a contrast of two or more works on the same subject, or for a survey of a series of works. Such assignments usually require that the review of each work be confined to a single paragraph.

The major problem in a one-paragraph review is how to do a thorough job in such small space. Obviously there is not room for the kind of detailed analysis we saw in the Walter Mitty review. Yet if the short review is too general, it may be of no help to the reader, who must know not only what the reviewer thinks of the work but why he thinks so. To satisfy these needs in a single paragraph is sometimes a challenging assignment.

The following paragraph is one of a series of seven short reviews which evaluate recordings of *Julius Caesar* in order to advise high school English teachers on the best recordings for class use. Preceding the review are certain facts of publication useful for identifying and ordering the records.

William Shakespeare. *Julius Caesar*. A Dublin Gate Theatre production, with Michael MacLiammoir as Antony and Hilton Edwards as Brutus. Directed by Hilton Edwards. Spoken Arts Record 809. Spoken Arts, Inc., 95 Valley Road, New Rochelle, N.Y. $5.95.

Of all the recordings, this is the finest. In a playing-time of less than one hour, it succeeds in presenting every important scene and passage without conveying an impression of haste. That the omitted passages contribute little or nothing to the integrity of the play is demonstrated in the recording as the action moves inexorably to its tragic end. The superb acting company has produced a masterpiece of timing; every speech is given its due weight in the whole. The music of a symphony orchestra, tastefully used as background, is impressive without becoming intrusive. Parts of the orchestra are cleverly used to represent the presence of the ghost of Caesar at Philippi as Cassius and Brutus kill themselves. Of all the abridged versions of this play, this is the most satisfying. To those who will tolerate abridgement, this recording will be most acceptable. It should inspire all but the dullest students, and it deserves wide use.[3]

For an English teacher who wants advice on choosing a recording, this is a most helpful review. Go over it sentence by sentence and see what each sentence contributes to the whole. Especially notice how much detailed information the reviewer is able to provide in a paragraph of about 150 words. Notice also how much less information the teacher would receive if the review were confined to the general judgment of the last three sentences.

Exercises

A. Using the analysis on page 355 as your model, study the following review and make a paragraph analysis of it. Then write a one-paragraph review of the essay.

[3] From "A Study Guide to the Recordings of William Shakespeare's *Julius Caesar*" by John T. Muri, in *Studies in the Mass Media,* November, 1961. Reprinted by permission of the National Council of Teachers of English.

The Seesaw Log

On January 16, 1958, a play by William Gibson called "Two for the See-saw" began a long and highly successful run at the Booth Theater on Broadway. *The Seesaw Log* is the story of that play from its conception early in 1953 through more than three years of writing, a year of hunting a producer and the two actors who would constitute the total cast, four months of rehearsals and out-of-town performances to its successful opening in New York.

The publisher's blurb on the jacket of the *Log* calls it "a day-by-day account of the making of a smash hit and a vivid portrait of the contemporary theater at work." If the book were no more than that, it would have considerable value; for the chronicle of events gives a reader a view of the theater that he seldom gets in so sharp detail. The problems of getting a manuscript accepted by a producer, of financing a play, of selecting the right director, the right designer, and — of paramount importance — the right actors, of shaping a script into good theater, and of the complexities and intricacies of a Theater Guild contract are all clearly presented. As a contribution to our knowledge of the mechanics of big-time, commercial drama, *The Seesaw Log* is both significant and interesting.

But to provide this contribution is not the main function of the *Log*. Mr. Gibson was only incidentally concerned with the mechanics of the theater. His reason for writing the book was essentially to record in detail the tribulations of a stubborn and sensitive author who finds himself trapped in a conflict between loyalty to his art, as he understands it, and loyalty to the demands of the commercial theater, as the actors and director understand it. It is this conflict that provides the real drama of the *Log,* and to this reviewer the drama of the *Log* is more moving than that of the play itself, the text of which is included in the book.

The protagonist and antagonist are William Gibson, the author, and Henry Fonda, the star. Gibson is motivated by a conviction of the integrity of his characters. If his hero, Jerry, is a confused character, then Jerry's confusion must become explicit in the play, even though that confusion may, in turn, confuse the audience. If Gittel, his heroine, is a profane, promiscuous, but endearing little Brooklyn gamin, she has to be profane and promiscuous in the play, even at the risk of alienating the audience. Fonda is motivated by a sense of what an audience will accept, of what constitutes good theater. He wants the characters to be "likable"; therefore he wants potentially objectionable traits toned down. But there is an ironic twist to the conflict between these two points of view. Gibson and Fonda cannot simply slug it out to decide whose play is to be produced. They are committed to a two-million-dollar business enterprise, the success of which demands their complete cooperation.

Given the personalities of the two men, this cooperation cannot be achieved without considerable wear and tear on their nervous systems, even though both are honest, competent, and conscious of the importance of subordinating their personal preferences to the common good. Because Mr. Gibson has written the *Log* we know what he suffered: the constant frustration of seeing his play misunderstood by the one man without whom it could not be produced; the incessant demands for revision of the dialogue at every stage of production; the hours spent rewriting speeches which satisfied the star but were rejected by the director or which satisfied the director but were rejected by the star; the desperate decision to let Fonda improvise in rehearsals and copy his words verbatim, only to have the new version rejected by both star and director when it was written down; the physical and psychological exhaustion from working endlessly to satisfy demands that, to the author, were both unclear and artistically repugnant — in short, the soul-sapping despair of being caught in an unbearable yet inescapable situation. We do not know what Fonda suffered. There is no suggestion in the book that he is less sensitive than the author or less conscientious or less concerned about building a successful play. We do know, because Gibson tells us, that much of the time Fonda was morose and unhappy, that he wanted to escape from his contract as soon as he could honorably do so, and that he finally gave orders that Mr. Gibson was not to be admitted to his dressing room. From these facts we may infer that the actor, as well as the author, paid a price for his compromises.

The Log of the Seesaw is Mr. Gibson's apologia for his play. Those of us who have no commitment either to art or to Broadway may feel that no apology was necessary, that the strains and tensions Mr. Gibson records are inherent in the production of a play. We may even think that the author is sometimes too proud of his integrity and that at least some of the revisions seem to have been justified by the success of the production. Yet we will leave the reading of the book with respect and sympathy for both the author and the actor and with a clear insight into the problems that have to be resolved in producing a smash hit.

B. Make a paragraph analysis of the following review and see what it reveals about the relative proportions of the introduction and the body of the review. If you are familiar with *The Catcher in the Rye,* do you agree that "Mr. Salinger's main purpose is to expose the shocking 'phoniness' that exists in our society and to demonstrate the disastrous effect that such 'phoniness' can wreak in the delicate, formative years of adolescence"? Whether or not you know the novel, judge this review according to how well it satisfies the criteria discussed in the chapter.

Psychologists use a very interesting type of test in studying the human mind. I believe they call it a "word association" test. As the psychologist reads a certain word, the patient answers with whatever word he first thinks of. This immediate response indicates to the psychologist the feeling or meaning which the first word evokes in the patient's mind. After many tests of this type, psychologists have learned that many people respond with exactly the same word to the first mention of a given word; whenever "Civil War" is mentioned, the majority of patients respond with "Gettysburg" or "Gettysburg Address."

Selecting a word to cover and explain so varied and controversial a book as J. D. Salinger's *The Catcher in the Rye* is a very difficult task, if not an impossible one. But if *The Catcher in the Rye* were given as the first word in a word association test, I feel that the majority of the people who had read the book would respond with either "phony" or "phoniness." By "phoniness" is meant a conscious or unconscious attempt to make the observed appearance seem different from the actual reality. A simple, concrete example would be the wearing of old, ragged underwear beneath a good-looking, new suit of clothes. A "phony" then would be any person who attempts to perpetrate "phoniness" — anything which is insincere, hypocritical, or counterfeit. In the light of these definitions, I think that *The Catcher in the Rye* is primarily a study of "phonies" and "phoniness." I think that Mr. Salinger's main purpose in writing this book was to expose the shocking "phoniness" that exists in our society and to demonstrate the disastrous effect that such "phoniness" can wreak in the delicate, formative years of adolescence.

Mr. Salinger attempts to accomplish his difficult, yet extremely worthwhile purpose by presenting a succession of "phonies" for us to consider, and by showing their continued effect upon a single person, Holden Caulfield. The adjective which best describes Holden is "confused." He is confused and puzzled about life and its essential purposes, about morals, religion, education, and — not least of all — about "phoniness." It is the concern about "phoniness" which aggravates Holden's confusion and eventually causes him to become self-destructive. As Holden comes in contact with more and more "phonies," each exhibiting subtler and subtler types of "phoniness," the trend becomes unmistakable. Holden becomes more suspicious and distrustful of people, and he becomes "phony" himself in his confusion. Eventually he becomes completely unbalanced and cannot be sure whether "phoniness" really does exist, or whether his distorted mind is producing "phoniness" where none really does exist. This end is, indeed not "pretty," but I think it does accomplish the purpose which Mr. Salinger intended.[4]

C. Write a one-paragraph critical review of this student review.

King of Pontus; the life of Mithradates Eupator

Alfred Duggan's *King of Pontus* is a tale of valor in a hopeless cause, the valor of one Asian king who struggled against the might of Rome for fifty years, impeding the course of empire by refusing to stay defeated. When he finally came over to the Romans, he came in a coffin sent across the Euxine Sea by his treasonous son as a tribute. Pompey the Great, who had chased this renegade king all over Asia Minor, looked long and carefully at the corpse to make sure the old man was really dead. Then with a magnanimity born of respect, Pompey had Mithradates buried in the ancestral tomb of the kings of Pontus, a 250-year-old dynasty claiming descent from Darius and Xerxes. It was the end of a proud royal line, but not an ignominious end. Mithradates had been a name to be reckoned with in the first century B.C.

He was the sixth Mithradates, and he chose the adjective Eupator (Good Father) as a distinguishing mark. It proved to be a curious appellation, for although he had many children, he killed three of his sons, and the one he spared out of affection was the one who caused his death. That he also had

---

[4] David M. Klingel, "Phonies and Phoniness." From *The Green Caldron: A Magazine of Freshman Writing* (April, 1957), published at the University of Illinois, Urbana, Illinois. Reprinted by permission.

put to death his wife, who happened to be his sister, two more sisters, a brother, a brother-in-law and a nephew was accepted without question by the society in which he lived. That he did not kill his mother, but merely had her imprisoned, was a matter of credit to him.

The story by which his name is almost entirely known today, through a poem by A. E. Housman, is the one about his immunizing himself to poison by taking small daily doses. Duggan accepts this as true and as a highly intelligent precaution. (What he really took was an antidote, but he had a bit of poison afterward to make sure he was safe.) He was so afraid of his mother's plots, after she had his father assassinated and assumed the throne, that he left home at the age of fourteen and remained away for seven years, living like a Robin Hood in the forests. Then he returned to take over the kingdom in a palace coup.

He was tall, strong, skilful, intelligent, and handsome, as all heroes should be. He began his conquests by luxuriating in his palace like a true Asian king while his generals invaded neighboring lands. Surprisingly soon he ruled most of Asia Minor and part of Greece; but he overplayed his hand when he ordered the massacre of ten thousand Italian civilians in an attempt to be rid of the foreigners forever. Then the Romans came after him — first Sulla, who drove him back into his own kingdom; next Lucullus, who spent seven years keeping him there; and finally Pompey, from whom he fled to the Crimean side of the Euxine, defiantly plotting an invasion of Italy itself. The Roman victory had been far from easy, for in the meantime Mithradates had become a seasoned fighter, administrator, and leader of men.

His development in character and ability is one of the most interesting aspects of the story. He retained his heroic qualities to the end, and the use he made of them became more admirable as he matured. The limitations of the Asian royal mind made him a tragic hero, but he rose above them in his fierce independence, in his adherence to a personal code of honor, and in his dauntless courage. Reading of his final days, we almost wish Mithradates would slay his upstart son so that we could watch the rugged old campaigner march on Rome with the wild Goths he meant to add to his army on the way through their homeland. We have no doubt that he would do it.

Most of the book is concerned with war, since fighting Rome was Mithradates' total preoccupation, and fighting Mithradates became a slippery means to a Triumph for the great Roman generals who pursued him. The battles are enjoyable to read about because by twentieth-century standards they seem like ridiculous and haphazard games. Despite the vaunted superiority of the Roman troops, the close calls they had at the hand of Mithradates are astonishing. It was a supremely fantastic series of comic-opera incidents that spelled successive doom to the great armies he raised. But he never gave up. Betrayed and bereft, he would retire only to gather more legions and make more plans, a classic underdog who would not stay under.

Duggan's style is informal and full of humor, and he brings these distant events into lively reality in modern terms. He tells the story as straight as possible, without imaginative padding. Even in its bare outlines the life of Mithradates is exciting and eventful. As here presented it gives an unusual view of the Roman conquest through Asiatic eyes. Mithradates did not feel like a terrier nipping at the feet of an elephant; he felt like a king and he behaved like a king.

There is only one thing more to say about this book: read it.

D. With one exception, the reviews printed in this chapter have been favorable. The following one is unfavorable. The author watched a television program and was disappointed in it. When a work is a poor one, a reviewer may ignore it as not worth reviewing. But if, as in this case, the work was extensively advertised and created a great deal of interest in advance of its release, the reviewer may feel that he owes it to the public to point out the weaknesses of the production. If we know the work, we can compare our own judgments with those of the critic; otherwise we can only consider whether the critic gives us adequate evidence for his judgment and whether that evidence would lead an impartial reader to a similar conclusion. With this consideration in mind, write a short review of this criticism.

Noah and the Flood[5]

The CBS television network presented Thursday night an hour-long program entitled "Noah and the Flood." The event was preceded by great waves of publicity that proclaimed the coming of art to television.

This was to be the world premier of the first work Igor Stravinsky had consented to compose for television, and it was to bring together some of the world's greatest talents to insure the finest possible introduction of the work. Nothing was to be spared in this mighty cultural venture.

Nothing was. Not even consideration for the artistic reputation of Stravinsky, George Balanchine, Jacques d'Amboise, Edward Villella, and other conscientious artists who took part in the production. Nor, so it seemed, was much thought given to the intelligence of the millions of viewers that might really be seeking a cultural experience on the video screen.

The program did include the promised premier, and it turned out to be a work of something less than 25 minutes in length. It was introduced with an arty essay on "creation" myths that had been written by Jack Richardson and was read as pompously as possible by Lawrence Harvey. There were also warm-up speeches by John H. Breck, head of the sponsoring commercial concern, and Stravinsky.

Following the advertised work came a grab-bag summary of the composer's career that included photographs, costume sketches, snatches of ballet scores, films of orchestra and ballet rehearsals conducted by Stravinsky and George Balanchine, and goodness knows what else.

In this viewer's opinion, the hour as a whole was enough to retard the progress of the arts in this country by a great deal. Literature, music, art objects, dance, and by implication their creators, were made to seem insufferably pretentious, disorganized and dull.

[5] By Allen Hughes, in *The New York Times,* June 17, 1962. Copyright by The New York Times. Reprinted by permission.

The faults were clearly not those of the truly creative individuals involved in the program, but of the production individuals, or committee perhaps, who jumbled them together.

The score Stravinsky composed for "Noah and the Flood" will surely not rank as one of his greatest achievements, but it is a serviceable and thoroughly listenable work. Most of the music is in the style Stravinsky has pursued since he became attracted to Anton Webern's 12-tone compositions nearly a decade ago.

The "Flood" score, like the text Robert Craft has assembled from the book of Genesis and York and Chester miracle plays, is in fact a collection of bits and pieces. But these bits and pieces could be the bones of a cohesive work in a production consciously conceived to unite them.

The production on television may have been conceived to provide unity, but by the time it got taped it was too spotty, scrappy and nervous to prove useful.

On the basis of this production, it is impossible to know just what the theatrical potentialities of this latest Stravinsky work may be. The pity is that all the money, time and effort expended on this introduction of it should not have provided an answer to that question.

15

The Business Letter

The writing of a business letter as a college assignment serves a double purpose: it makes students familiar with the conventional forms of business correspondence and it provides a practical application of the principles of effective composition. Of the two purposes, the latter is the more important. The conventions of business correspondence should be understood and followed, but it should also be understood that a good business letter is primarily a good composition. Indeed, the writing of a convincing letter of application is often a more exacting test of a student's ability to select, organize, and present pertinent information than many of the more usual composition assignments.

The Form of a Business Letter

All business letters follow a relatively standardized form which is illustrated by the example given below. For convenience, the various parts of the letter have been numbered.

```
                                    115 Ohio Street          1
                                    Galesburg, Illinois
                                    December 28, 1962         2


        Fisher Paint Company
3       212 West Madison Street
        Chicago 7, Illinois


4       Gentlemen:


        In your advertisement of Colopake in recent
        issues of Time you say that the superiority
        of Colopake over other paint products is
        achieved by reducing the size of the pigment
5       particles.  Since I am making a comparative
        study of various paints I should like to have
        more information on this point.  Would it be
```

possible for me to obtain a copy of the comparative data which were the basis of your advertis-
ing statement?

6

Yours truly,

John A. Baker

7

John A. Baker

As our illustration shows, a business letter consists of at least seven parts:

1. The Return Address. This part will be omitted, of course, if stationery containing a printed letterhead is used, since the letterhead itself is the return address. The form used in our example is called a *block* heading with *open* punctuation. In a block heading the lines are not indented; each line begins flush with the one preceding. In open punctuation no marks are used at the ends of lines, but elements within the lines are separated in accordance with the usual conventions. Alternative forms — *indented* headings and *closed* punctuation — are common and accepted but not preferred. In indented headings each line is indented a few spaces to the right of the line preceding. In closed punctuation a comma is used after the street and the state. Addresses should be written in full, though figures are generally used for numbered streets, and *North, South, East* and *West* are often abbreviated — *42nd Street, 15th Avenue, 212 W. Madison Street;* but *300 Fifth Avenue.*

2. The Date Line. The date line is written as part of the first heading and takes the same form as the return address — flush or indented, with open or closed punctuation, the latter requiring a period after the date.

3. The Inside Address. This heading consists of three or more lines and follows the form established in the first heading. Abbreviations such as *Co.* and *Inc.* are used only if these terms are abbreviated in the letterheads of the companies being addressed. When the title of the addressee is given, it is usually placed after his name on the first line; but if this practice would result in an awkwardly long line, the title may be given as a separate line.

Dr. David D. Henry, President
University of Illinois
Urbana, Illinois

```
Dr. Robert B. Downs
Director of the Library School
University of Illinois
Urbana, Illinois
```

Names which would be awkward or impossible in a single line are written in two lines:

```
North Carolina State College
of Agriculture and Engineering
University of North Carolina
Raleigh, North Carolina
```

4. *The Salutation.* When an individual is being addressed, the salutation usually takes one of the following forms: *Dear Mr.* (or *Mrs.*) *Blank, Dear Sir* (or *Madam*). Such an informal salutation as *Dear Bob* is acceptable only in writing to a personal friend. The form, *My dear Mr.* (or *Mrs.*) *Blank* may be used in distinctly formal letters. When the letter is addressed to a company, rather than to an individual, the accepted salutation is *Gentlemen;* the form *Dear Sirs* is seldom used in modern business letters. If the company is known to consist of women, the salutation may be either *Mesdames* or *Ladies.* A colon follows the salutation.

5. *The Body.* The body of the letter usually consists of one or more paragraphs of single-spaced text, with double spacing between paragraphs. There is a marked preference for starting all paragraphs in a business letter at the left margin, with no indention to mark the opening of a paragraph. However, the older style of starting the first paragraph under the colon of the salutation and thereafter indenting the first line of each paragraph seven spaces from the margin is still common. The opening lines of paragraphs may be indented even when no indention is used in the headings.

6. *The Complimentary Close.* The most common endings are *Yours truly, Yours very truly, Very truly yours, Yours sincerely,* or *Sincerely yours.* Such closes as *Cordially,* or *Cordially yours,* are used only when the writer is on familiar terms with his addressee. *Respectfully* is a formal close used chiefly in submitting a formal report to a superior. A comma is used at the end of the complimentary close.

7. *The Signature.* The signature consists of two parts: the written signature, and below this the writer's name and official position, if any, typed in. Both parts are necessary. The written signature is the legal identification of the writer; the typed name is a safeguard against misreading of the signature. Since it is conventional in business to address a woman as

Miss unless she signifies that she is married, married women enclose *Mrs.* in parentheses before their typed signatures.

Helen White or *Helen White*
(Mrs.) Helen White   (Mrs. John White)

When an individual writes a letter in the name of his company, it is frequent practice to place the company name before his written signature, thus:

> Very truly yours,
> Main Motor Sales Company
>
> *W. R. Smith*
>
> W. R. Smith, Secretary

When a letter is typed by someone other than the author, the typist puts first the author's initials, then her own (with a colon between them) flush with the left margin and below the author's signature:

WRS:HW

The Appearance of the Letter

The appearance of a business letter is extremely important. As much as possible the letter must be centered on the page and framed by adequate margins. The various parts of the letter should be separated from each other by extra spacing — usually a minimum of two spaces between the first and second headings, and double-spacing (one blank line) between the inside address and the salutation, between the salutation and the body, and between the body and the complimentary close. Single-spacing is used within the headings. Within reasonable limits, the margins may be adjusted to get a long letter on a single page or to keep a short letter in the center of a page. A letter, of course, may consist of more than one page, but the spacing should be so contrived that the second page does not consist of only two or three lines. It goes without saying that the typing must be neat and accurate.

The Letter of Application

The rest of this chapter will be devoted to the letter applying for a position. This is the kind of business letter which students are most likely to write, and of all business letters it probably presents the problem of composition at its most difficult level. A student who can write an effective letter of application has had a useful introduction to the art of business correspondence.

Although some variation is possible, letters of application generally follow a standardized organization. The body of the letter usually consists of five parts: the lead, the record of education and experience, the references, the request for further communication (usually an interview), and the data sheet. These parts are illustrated by the following letter.

56 Shrewsbury Place
Worcester, Massachusetts
March 1, 1962

The Director of Personnel
Westerly Electric Corporation
Schenectady, New York

Dear Sir:

Lead

From Mr. A. J. Burns, director of the placement bureau at Massachusetts Technological College, I learn that you have openings for junior engineers and that you are interviewing men who are about to graduate in industrial engineering. I should like to apply for such a position with Westerly.

Education

I am a senior at Massachusetts Technological College and will be graduated from the four-year course next June, with the degree of Bachelor of Science in Engineering. I have specialized in industrial engineering, taking both required and elective courses in that field. These courses include Production Planning, Work Control, Materials Handling, Production Design, Safety Engineering, Methods Analysis, and Plant Design. I have also had basic courses in Electrical Engineering, Mechanical Engineering, Computer Programming Techniques, Engineering Graphics, Industrial Accounting, and Industrial Psychology.

Experience

During the past two summers I have been employed as a draftsman by the Milvania Electrical Products Corporation (Applied Research Division), doing a large amount of quality industrial drawing--about 25 plates a month. This year, for my senior field problem, the Clinton Press kindly permitted me to make a full-scale survey of its plant and operations as the basis for a report on production control. Though this was only a student exercise, several of the recommendations are being put into effect.

The enclosed data sheet summarizes my record and gives other relevant information,
References including the names of four men who have known me as student or employee and have consented to be my references.

If my qualifications warrant, I would be happy to come to Schenectady for an inter-
Request for view. I would prefer a Friday or Saturday,
Interview because of my class schedule, but could, if necessary, make arrangements for another day at your convenience. May I look forward to hearing from you?

Sincerely yours,

Alan M. Field

Alan M. Field

Separate Enclosure

Data Sheet
Qualifications of Alan M. Field
56 Shrewsbury Place, Worcester, Massachusetts
(Applicant for position as Junior Engineer)

Personal Information

Age - 21
Place of birth -
  Manchester, N.H.
Weight - 165
Height - 5'11"
Marital status - single

Physical condition -
  excellent health; no
  physical defects
Leisure interests - water
  sports, skiing,
  mountain climbing

Education

Manchester Central High School, Manchester,
  New Hampshire - graduated in 1958

Massachusetts Technological College, Worcester,
  Massachusetts - 1958-62. Will graduate in
  June 1962, B.S. in Engineering

Partial List of College Courses
Courses in industrial engineering:
  Principles of Industrial Engineering
  Industrial Organization and Management
  Production Planning
  Work Control
  Materials Handling
  Production Design
  Safety Engineering
  Methods Analysis
  Plant Design
Allied courses:
  Electrical Engineering
  Mechanical Engineering
  Computer Programming Techniques
  Engineering Graphics
  Industrial Accounting
  Industrial Psychology

Significant Facts in College Record
  Member, Alpha Pi Mu (national honor society)
  Member, student chapter of American Institute of
    Industrial Engineers
  Secretary-Treasurer, Outing Club, 1960-62

Experience

Draftsman, Milvania Electrical Products Corporation,
  Waltham, Mass.
  (Applied Research Division) - Summer, 1960, 1961
Mechanic, Roche's Garage and Service Station,
  Manchester, N.H. - Summer, 1959
Student project: Production analyst, Clinton Press,
  Clinton, Mass. - 1961-62

References

Mr. William A. Harlow
Director, Engineering Research
Milvania Electrical Products Corp.
Waltham, Mass.

Mr. George O. Spaulding
Professor of Industrial Engineering
Massachusetts Technological College
Worcester, Mass.

Mr. Mark F. Trainor, President
The Clinton Press
Clinton, Mass.

Mr. Victor Roche
Roche's Garage and Service Station
Merrimack Street
Manchester, N.H.

Each of the five parts has its own special role in developing the total purpose of the letter. These functions may be stated briefly.

1. The Lead. The lead is an introductory statement in which the applicant establishes contact with the potential employer and declares himself a candidate for a position. The source of the lead is usually an advertisement, the recommendation of a friend or an employee of the company, or, as in our sample, the college placement service. If the writer is applying for a specific job and knows the requirements, he usually indicates his knowledge in the lead — for example:

> Mr. Bruce Benedict, Senior Accountant in
> your office, tells me that you intend to
> hire an additional secretary at the begin-
> ning of the year. I understand that the
> position requires someone who has had both
> bookkeeping and secretarial experience.
> Since I am qualified in both fields I should
> like to be considered as a candidate.

When the writer is making an unsolicited application the lead might take such form as this:

> I wonder if, within the next few weeks, you
> intend to add an additional typist to your
> staff. I find that in order to finance my
> college education it will be necessary for
> me to seek a part-time position and, since I
> live on the campus, I should particularly
> like to work for the University.

2. Education and Experience. This section is the main part of the letter, since candidates are selected for interviews chiefly on the strength of their education and experience. If either of these is slight, the other should compensate for it. The writer of our sample letter has had only limited experience, so he wisely detailed the nature of his training. A man with considerable experience would give a much briefer account of his education, but he would not pass hurriedly over *both* his education and his experience. As we shall see in the next section, one of the most serious weaknesses of student letters is that they do not adequately develop this important part of the application.

3. References. The references are the names and addresses of people who can do for the applicant what he cannot, with any modesty, do for himself — testify to his abilities, accomplishments, and desirable characteristics. It is both wise and courteous to obtain permission to use names as references before writing the letter.

4. Request for Further Communication. The conventional ending of a letter of application is a request for an interview. This request should be neither obsequious nor demanding but should be stated something like this:

> I should appreciate a personal interview at
> our mutual convenience. I am free after five
> o'clock every day and all day Saturdays. My
> home telephone number is Fairfield 0172.

Of course the best way to obtain an interview is to write the kind of letter that will make the employer eager to arrange a personal meeting. But even in the best of letters it is wise to ask for an interview unless distance makes one impracticable.

5. The Data Sheet. Many applications are written without a data sheet, in which event the most significant information is worked into the body of the letter. The advantages of the data sheet, however, are obvious, since it presents in the shortest possible space a complete outline of the candidate's qualifications and permits convenient reference if the employer wishes to re-check particular items.

Analysis of Failing Letters

The sample letter on page 371 is a most effective application. It is attractively arranged, logically organized, detailed in its treatment of education and experience, free from immodest judgments about the writer's qualifications, and clearly and correctly written. Such a letter is sure to make a good impression.

The following are examples of unsuccessful letters. To save space, the headings and signatures have been omitted:

> Dear Personal Manager:
>
> It was my ambition to be associate with a progressive firm like yours where my talents are appreciated.
>
> I am graduating from college in June. The major pursued here is industrial management.
>
> I would like a job as soon as possible.
>
>   Yours Respectively;

The natural response of an employer receiving such a letter would be to forward it to the college from which the writer claims to be graduating with a note asking if this boy was a typical product of the college. The letter is not only stylistically impossible; it fails completely to present any information (other than the questionable statement that the writer is about to graduate with a major in industrial management) which would be useful to a prospective employer. The only picture it presents is that of a person with no qualifications whatsoever, not even a sense of tact.

The next letter is only slightly better:

> Dear Sir:
>
> You have a vacancy in your accounting department according to my adviser, Mr. O. R. Strabe of Branch College. I am prepared to fill it. My qualifications are of the best.
>
> Your prompt reply will gratify me. I am so anxious to work for you.
>
>   Yours sincerely,

If this writer really wants serious consideration, he should present the evidence which makes him feel that he is well qualified. Judgments about one's own qualifications are always open to question, but unsupported judgments are flatly objectionable. The chief purpose of an application letter is to show why the applicant merits serious consideration. The way to do that is to present the *facts* of education and experience. This applicant has done Mr. Strabe and himself a disservice by his naïve assumption that he need not take the time to present a detailed picture of his qualifications. The letter says almost nothing.

The following paragraph illustrates an error that was discussed on pages 114–115 — the error of overreaching oneself in an attempt to achieve a dignified literary style:

> It is understandable that your highly re-
> spected firm is exceedingly anxious to
> secure the valuable services of competent
> young men who have undergone specialized and
> detailed training in the outstanding educa-
> tional institutions of our day -- and let
> me say in a patriotic aside, our noteworthy
> institutions are indeed comparable in
> prowess and achievement and dignity to the
> most heralded universities and colleges of
> any nation, bar none! -- and thus it is my
> earnest conviction that, when you go far
> afield in search of promising prospects for
> your dominant organization, you will pro-
> ceed eventually to the hallowed college from
> which I send forth this missive.

This kind of writing is more likely to be amusing than annoying, but the purpose of an application is not to amuse; it is to get a job. An applicant cannot afford to make himself ridiculous; yet that is what this applicant does. What he has to say need not be said at all. Certainly it should not be said in such a wordy and preposterous way.

The next letter deserves special attention, since it is more representative than any already given of the kind of inadequate letter which competent college students are inclined to write:

> Gentlemen:
>
> Will one of your research laboratories
> need an assistant next year?
>
> Education: I am a graduate of Nelson High
> School and will graduate from
> Midwest College this June with
> a B.S. degree and a major in
> chemistry.
>
> Experience: During my summer vacations I
> have worked in the labora-
> tories of A. N. Weir and Com-
> pany. During the fall of 1949
> I worked in the plating de-

                    partment of the Maddox Hard-
                    ware Company where I had some
                    experience with metallurgy.

References: The following people have
              kindly allowed me to use their
              names as references:
                  Professor William Linbeck
                  Department of Chemistry
                  Midwest College

                  Mr. Thomas Norton
                  Weir Laboratories
                  Dunsan, Iowa

I should appreciate the opportunity of an interview any Saturday that is convenient to you.

                          Yours sincerely,

At first glance this may seem a satisfactory letter. But if it is compared with the sample letter given earlier, its inadequacies will be obvious. Assuming that most of the candidates for this position are college graduates with majors in chemistry, what has this letter to recommend it? It is little more than an outline. The applicant should at least have shown what kind of work he did in the Weir laboratories and what kind of metallurgical experience he has had. By failing to give details, he keeps his letter from offering a convincing picture of his qualifications. None of the other qualified applicants could do less than he has done, and the chances are that most of them will do more.

We can sum up this analysis of unsatisfactory letters by saying that the errors to avoid in a letter of application are:

1. Stylistic and grammatical imperfections.
2. Inadequate development of one's qualifications.
3. Unsupported judgments of one's abilities.
4. Statements which are arrogant, naïve, or in bad taste.
5. Unattractive appearance of the letter.

For the kind of position which requires a good letter of application, the employer is probably going to require an interview. If there are twenty or thirty candidates for the position, probably only three or four will be invited for interviews. The immediate purpose of the letter, then, is to get an interview. The best way to do that is to present the facts of one's qualifications clearly and fully. This can best be done in a well-organized data sheet and an accompanying letter which is clear, concise, and in good taste. The importance that will be attached to the application justifies the time and effort required to make it a good one.

The Letter Declining a Job

In one sense, a letter declining a job is an easy one to write. If all that the writer wants to do is to say "No," any courteous refusal will do. Thus he may merely say, "Thank you for offering me the position. It is in many ways an attractive one; but I have accepted an appointment with the W. F. Brenning Company and am therefore no longer available." Such a reply will meet the writer's minimum obligations to the company that offered him a position.

There are three considerations, however, that suggest something more than a minimum reply. First, if an employer has paid an applicant's expenses for an interview and has spent valuable time showing him around the plant and discussing with him the position and its possibilities, a minimum reply is an ungracious return for this hospitality. It is true that the employer has been acting in his own interests, but he has probably made a greater expenditure of time and money to fill the position than most applicants realize, and an abrupt refusal, even though politely expressed, is a disappointing return for his efforts.

Second, an offer of a position is the best kind of evidence that an employer thinks well of an applicant. That good will is a business asset and should, if possible, be preserved. There may later be more attractive opportunities in the company, or the employer may sometime be in a position to be helpful. The applicant therefore owes it to his own future to consider these possibilities before writing his letter of refusal.

Third, it often happens that for one of several reasons a position that looked most promising when it was accepted becomes less attractive later. A man may change his mind about the kind of work he wants to do; he may decide that a smaller company in a smaller town offers satisfactions that he had not previously appreciated; or he may find that the climate or the social environment to which his job commits him is not to his liking. In short, he may want to reconsider an offer which he had previously declined.

For these reasons, it is often wise to consider the letter declining a position as one which preserves a favorable business contact. How this should be done will depend on circumstances. There can be no one pattern to fit all conditions, but the following suggestions may be modified to suit particular situations.

1. Do not, even by the faintest suggestion, belittle the offer. It may be inferior to other offers you have received, but do not say or imply so.

2. Suggest that your refusal is not a hasty one but is carefully and reluctantly made.

3. Express appreciation of the offer in more than general or perfunctory terms. If possible, mention details that you found especially attractive.

4. If any one officer of the company spent considerable time with you during your interview, express your appreciation of his efforts, with specific

reference to any actions of his that showed more thoughtfulness than mere duty required of him.

5. There is no objection to describing briefly an alternative offer which you have accepted, if your experience suggests that the person you are writing to is genuinely interested in what you are going to do. But keep such description short and allow nothing in its tone to suggest bragging or gloating.

6. Keep the letter short but not abrupt.

The following letter illustrates the content and tone of a letter of refusal. To save space the heading and close have been omitted.

Dear Mr. Root:

I have spent several days thinking over and talking over with my wife your letter of May 27. The position you offer me is most attractive, and what I saw of Ruston and the plant makes me feel that Mary and I would have a congenial and satisfying future with the company and in the community.

But I feel that for my own professional training I need the experience of working in a large company in a metropolitan area. I have therefore decided to accept a position with Bowen-Revelson in Chicago. I will be working on public relations techniques in large industrial areas. I think it likely that Mary and I will finally want to settle and bring up our family in a smaller town, and that consideration made Ruston most attractive. But at this stage of my professional development I think the Chicago position offers me the experience I most need.

I want to thank you for all your many kindnesses to me during my visit to Ruston and for the very helpful overview you gave me of the public relations problems which new industry in the South is posing. I will be grateful for a copy of any article you write on that subject.

Exercises

A. Study each of the following student letters carefully. Then write a report in the form of a business letter to your instructor telling him how you would grade these letters and why. Since your report will itself be graded, be sure to detail the evidence for your judgments. To save space all headings have been omitted.

(*1*)

Dear Sir:

Your newspaper ad about wanting an experienced, capable man to fill position of
office manager in your company interests
me. Provided the job pays enough, of
course.

Rest assured I can handle your office staff.
Write me at once so an interview can be
arranged.

Confidently yours,

(*2*)

Dear Sir:

In two weeks I will receive my Bachelors
Degree in Architectural Engineering, and I
am very anxious to enter the Construction
field. I believe I am amply qualified to
begin my career in your field, and I am looking forward to working for your concern.

During my four years at the University of
Illinois I have maintained a numerical
average of 3.86. I have been subjected to
Construction business all my life, and during semester breaks I have built up my experience with actual field estimating. I
have taken every University estimating
course available. In view of this, I believe
I am capable of fulfilling an estimators
position. I consider $350.00 per month an
ordinary salary for this position.

During the period from June 23 to June 30, I
will be at the Mammoth Hotel in downtown
Indianapolis. I can be contacted at any

hour of the day, and I would appreciate an interview at your convenience. I will have my letters of recommendation and I will provide you with any information I may have neglected in the enclosed data sheet.

(3)

Dear Sir:

HONESTY	EFFICIENCY
RESOURCEFULNESS	ADAPTABILITY
LEADERSHIP	COURAGE
RESPONSIBILITY	INITIATIVE
NEATNESS AND CLEANLINESS	INTELLIGENCE

Would you employ a person if he possessed the above qualities? You would, no doubt.

But unfortunately, the perfect is seldom obtained. Then the next best thing is the object of your search. I can offer you the services of a person who is, altho far from perfect, far above average in all of the above fields and excels in many.

I will promise you one thing-----that you will realize that you selected the right man for the job. I will serve you faithfully and efficiently.

I can come to Chicago any week-end you may desire for an interview. I will be glad to serve you.

(4)

Dear Sir:

This is an application for a position.

For months I have been investigating different firms interested in hiring college

graduates that have majored in foreign economics and export trade. In the course of
my investigation I have found there is a
place in your organization for a man of my
talents and education.

Your firm is interested in men who have
majored in economics, with particular
stress on foreign trade. I have studied
every phase of economics and am well prepared.

I have not yet had any job -- I'm still
young -- but I am confident I can meet your
requirements.

The college officials will recommend me, if
you will write them.

I shall be glad to have an interview with
you. Any time will do.

(5)

Dear Mr. Jones:

In Tuesday's Sun I noticed your advertisement for a private secretary and correspondent. May I be considered an applicant for this position?

It is my understanding that you want a
young man with a working knowledge of
office methods. He must also be able to
take dictation rapidly and accurately, and
he must have a background of general business training.

I am a graduate of Larchmont High School,
Springfield, Illinois, class of 1953.
Here I took the four-year commercial
course. During the past four years since
graduation I have been private secretary to
Mr. James A. Parker, executive director of
the Illinois State Commerce Commission.

383

My work with Mr. Parker has been widely
varied. I have taken much dictation,
both by transcription from notes, and also
direct to the typewriter. I have handled
on my own responsibility much of the
routine correspondence and have found this
experience highly valuable in broadening my
general business and secretarial ability.
I have become thoroughly familiar with commercial and legal forms.

I believe I have developed the ability to
handle your position. My training and
experience have been of the type necessary
to the consistent handling of the duties
you require. I enjoy this kind of work. My
reason for making a change is to improve my
position. Mr. Parker now tells me I have
reached the maximum salary permitted by the
commission, and he fully understands and
approves my wishes for further advancement.

Mr. Parker has kindly permitted me to use his
name as a reference. On the enclosed data
sheet you will find further references and
data in regard to my general qualifications.

May I have a personal interview? My telephone is Grandview 4177, Springfield, if
you wish to make an appointment. My mailing
address is 36 North Avenue, Springfield,
Illinois.

B. Assume that you are about to graduate from college and have had
no more experience than you might reasonably obtain during your summer
vacations. Clip from a newspaper or magazine an advertisement of a position for which you might reasonably expect to compete. Write your letter
of application and hand it in to your instructor with the advertisement
attached.

C. Suppose that, having written letters of application and having been
interviewed, you have received two offers of positions and have accepted
one of them. Write a letter refusing the other position.

A Point of View Toward Grammar

Sentence Structure

Word Order

HANDBOOK

OF GRAMMAR

AND USAGE

Forms of Words

Punctuation

Mechanics

Glossary of Terms and Usage

A Point of View Toward Grammar

English, like all languages, has developed a great many conventions popularly and generally known as "the rules of grammar." The nature of these rules is widely misunderstood, and because of this misunderstanding, the study of the conventions of educated usage is often less profitable than it might be. The first step toward using your native language with confidence is to acquire a sensible attitude toward these rules. We shall attempt to foster such an attitude by showing you what we mean when we talk about rules of grammar, how these rules have grown up and are still growing, and how you can use this knowledge to solve your own language problems. A point of view from which you can see particular questions of usage in perspective will help you to judge for yourself which usages are acceptable, and when.

The Evolution of English

The language that Americans speak and write is descended from the language spoken by the English, Scottish, and Irish immigrants who founded the British colonies in America. Their language, in turn, was descended from the dialects of Germanic tribes which, during the fifth and sixth centuries, invaded Britain and settled there. One of these tribes, the Angles, later became known as the Englisc (English) and thus gave their name to a country and a language, both of which they shared with other peoples — the Saxons, the Jutes, and, later, the Danes and the Normans.

All these racial groups were the Founding Fathers of the English language, but other peoples, too, have made their contribution to its development. As England grew in political, economic, and cultural importance, the language borrowed from various sources the words it needed to name the things and ideas that Englishmen were acquiring. Today the vocabulary of the English language is international in origin, and to talk, as some people do, of "pure" English is to use an adjective that is as inappropriate as it is misleading.

Needless to say, the language which has come down to us through some fifteen centuries has undergone great changes. A modern college student would find the English that Chaucer wrote something of a puzzle to him. And before Chaucer's time — well, judge for yourself. Here are the opening lines of the Lord's Prayer in the English of nearly a thousand years ago:

> Fæder ūre,
> þu þe eart on heofonum,
> sī þīn nama gehālgod.
> Tōbecume þīn rīce.
> Gewurþe ðīn willa on eorðan swā swā on heofonum.

A contrast of this version of the Lord's Prayer with the modern version offers a brief but revealing impression of the changes that have occurred in the language during its development from an insignificant Germanic dialect to one of the most widely spoken languages the world has known. It is important to recognize that these changes were the product of evolution rather than of revolution. True enough, there were times when so many basic changes occurred so rapidly that they seem revolutionary in retrospect. But by and large, the language changed slowly as it reflected gradual and unprompted shifts in the speech habits of those who spoke English. Often the old and new forms persisted together in competition for centuries, and sometimes an older form which was threatened with extinction enjoyed a renewal of popularity and survived at the expense of its rival. But the process of evolution always put a premium on survival value. The test of competing usages was not which was the more logical, the more beautiful, or the more "correct," but which was the more *used*. Usage has always been, and is still, the ultimate maker of rules.

It is important also to recognize that the changes which have occurred in the English language were not always made painlessly. Whenever two usages compete for popularity, speakers tend to be confused about which one to accept. And the closer the competition, the greater the confusion. There must have been a time, for example, when our ancestors were perplexed whether to call a certain garment a *shirt* or a *skirt,* since both forms of the word were applied to the same garment and both were popular. That particular difficulty was resolved by using one form for a man's garment and the other for a woman's. This solution was not a deliberate one. It was not laid down by any authority, and it was not reached overnight. It simply happened that people gradually drifted into the habit of using the two forms in different ways and thus established a new usage.

Finally, it is important to recognize that this evolutionary process is still going on. Any one of us can notice hundreds of examples of it in our own experience. We can hear the older pronunciations of *penalize* (*pee*nalize), *status* (*stay*tus) and *detour* (de*toor*) being challenged by pronunciations which were at first labeled "uneducated" but which have gradually become more common, even in the speech of highly educated people. We can observe words acquiring new meanings. And we can watch grammatical distinctions which once were generally observed falling more and more into disuse as substitutes take over their work. Like our ancestors puzzling over *shirt* and *skirt,* we will fluctuate between the old usage and the new until one or the other triumphs. Then all the uncertainty will be forgotten, and we will use the new form with confidence.

The Rules of Grammar

Contrary to popular belief, the rules of grammar do not determine how the language should be spoken and written. Grammar is a science, and it follows the general scientific method of reporting not what *ought to be* but what *is*. Except for differences of subject matter, the rules of grammar are much like the laws of physics and chemistry: they are scientific generalizations about the facts. In grammar, as in physics, these generalizations must be verifiable. If the rule does not fit the facts, or if it ceases to fit them, it must be revised or discarded.

Ideally, the grammar of a language is a description of the speaking and writing habits of the people who use it. Since there are some 300,000,000 users of English, widely separated geographically, politically, economically, and socially, the task of drawing a picture of their common linguistic habits is not easy. The grammarian simplifies his task by confining himself to the basic patterns of speech intonation (pitch, pause, and stress), morphology (the forms of words), and syntax (the relations of words within a sentence). He collects samples, analyzes them, finds patterns in them, and generalizes the patterns into a system. By these means he describes the very elaborate set of signals by which English conveys grammatical meaning. But he is describing how the language works, not how he thinks it ought to work. The only "rules of grammar" he recognizes are those statements which most accurately describe the system.

What most people mean by "rules of grammar" are statements about preferred usage. In addition to studies of grammar, we have studies of how educated people speak and write English. Since the schools are committed to preparing their students to become members of the educated class, they have accepted the usage of educated people as their standard and they do what they can to help students observe that standard in their speech and writing. For this reason teachers insist that, in spelling, punctuation, sentence structure, grammatical agreements, and diction, students follow the conventions of standard usage. Some of these conventions include grammatical details, but others are not part of grammar as we described it above.

Decisions about usage are sometimes difficult for two reasons. First, in an ever-changing language, usage is not constant. Spellings, pronunciations, styles of punctuation, meanings, and grammatical constructions which were not recognized by one generation may be accepted by another, and there is likely to be a "usage gap" between what people think educated usage is and what it has in fact become. Second, many people have strong opinions about usage and approve or condemn certain uses no matter what the facts are. These two conditions make it difficult in particular constructions to get an authoritative description of usage which is acceptable to everyone. Fortunately, such constructions are relatively few. For the most part, the conventions of educated usage are clearly established and can be accurately described. If we want to call these descriptive statements "rules of grammar," we may do so, but it would be wise to remember in what sense we are using "rules" and "grammar."

The rules of grammar, then, are not "Thou shalt not's"; they say, "This is how it is done." They are explanations of conventions that have grown up between writers and readers. Learning to use one's language is learning to use these conventions. A writer who ignores them will find his work rejected or discredited. The penalty he pays for his ignorance is not just a failing grade in an English course. The real penalty is that he cuts himself off from economic, social, and intellectual opportunities that he will later value. The testimony of business and professional leaders on the importance of effective writing and speaking in an industrial society is almost unanimous.

On Being Your Own Authority

Socially, a sophisticated person is one who is familiar with social conventions and observes them naturally and comfortably. Linguistically, a sophisticated person is one who observes language conventions naturally and comfortably. One aim of the composition course is to encourage the student to develop linguistic sophistication, to make him aware how things are done in English, and to help him do them habitually without having to stop and puzzle over them.

There are two reasons why this aim cannot be met by viewing grammar as a set of arbitrary rules which must be learned and practiced. First, this view distorts the relationship between purpose and technique. Just as the Sabbath was made for man, not man for the Sabbath, so the conventions of usage should serve, not be served by, the writer's purpose. A student whose main thought is to get his spelling, punctuation, and grammatical forms "correct" is in no condition to communicate. For him, writing will be a frustrating exercise, to be done only under compulsion and to be avoided whenever the compulsion is removed. This is why some students believe that all their linguistic worries will be over as soon as they "pass" the composition course.

Second, memorizing the conventions of usage is at best a poor substitute for working with them. All we know about learning tells us that memorized facts are soon forgotten unless they are clearly related to life goals and put to use outside the classroom. A student who conscientiously learns the rules of spelling or punctuation *in order to please or pacify his instructor* will soon forget them, and the progress that he and his instructor worked so hard to achieve will largely be lost. This is one reason why student writing so often deteriorates after completion of the composition course.

To accomplish the purpose of the course, at least with respect to the conventions of usage, a student must realize two things: he must recognize that following the conventions of language may help him communicate better and so make him a more powerful person; and he must understand that, while dictionaries and handbooks are helpful reference works, he must often make his own decisions about usage when these books are not available or are not decisive.

This second requirement may seem like a tall order, since, in effect, it asks the student to become his own authority on language. But there is no alternative. To use a language well, one must use it confidently. No one can speak or write with confidence if he continually depends on the crutch of a handbook. It is only a temporary aid, useful for those linguistic questions which cannot yet be answered from experience, but to be dispensed with as soon as possible.

How is this confidence to be won? In the long run, it is gained, as are so many things, by observation. That is how the grammarian learns grammar and how the editors of dictionaries learn the meanings of words — by observing how educated people use their language. An intelligent curiosity about language is therefore the first requirement for using it effectively. A student who has or develops that curiosity will seldom be seriously bothered by the "rules," because he has discovered them through his own observation of language practices.

The handbook that follows is a temporary substitute for your own experience. It presumes to tell you what the conventions are. If you know what they are, you do not need the advice. If you do not know, the advice will provide you with information to solve some of your immediate writing problems. It is assumed that your instructor will decide from your writing which conventions you need to study and will refer you to the section or sections dealing with them. It is hoped that you yourself will care enough about your own writing to make a special point of mastering, by observation as well as by handbook exercises, whatever conventions are now conspicuously ignored in your writing.

The material of the handbook is organized under six main headings, the first four of which are marked by an identifying letter: *sentence structure* (**S**), *word order* (**WO**), *forms of words* (**F**), *punctuation* (**P**), *mechanics* (spelling, capitalization, italics, etc.), and a *glossary* of grammatical terms and usage. Under each lettered heading, the numbered sections deal with specific parts of the subject. Thus, **S1–S3** review the basic grammar of sentences and so provide the apparatus for analyzing sentence structure; **S4–S7** deal with the distinction between sentences and non-sentences; **S8–S11** deal with inconsistencies in sentence patterns. If you have occasion to use the handbook, it might be wise to familiarize yourself with at least its over-all organization.

S · Sentence Structure

S1 *Sentence Elements*

The elements of English sentences can be analyzed from two points of view, their forms and their functions. Many words change in form as they change in use, and the study of these changes is called "morphology." The classes into which such words are placed may be called *form units*. These are five: nouns, pronouns, verbs, adjectives, and adverbs. The study of the functions of sentence elements is called "syntax," and the elements may be called *function units*. These are: subjects, verbs, objects, complements, modifiers, connectives, and absolutes.

Form Units

Of the traditional eight parts of speech, three — prepositions, conjunctions, interjections — have no inflected forms and are therefore not form units.

NOUNS

Words such as *boy, girl, man, woman, child, dog, car, garage, house, flower, tree, kindness, faith,* and thousands of others belong to a class which usually has different forms for singular and plural and for the possessive case. The great majority of English nouns form the plural by adding *-s* or *-es* to the singular. About five per cent are irregular and form their plurals in one of the following ways:

a. **-en Plurals** (*children, oxen*).

b. **Vowel-Changing Plurals** (*foot-feet, goose-geese, louse-lice, man-men, mouse-mice, tooth-teeth, woman-women*).

c. **Unchanged Plurals** (*deer, sheep, swine*).

These irregular plurals are relics of Old English plural inflections which once were common but which, during the evolution of the language, have been generally superseded by the *-s* plural.

d. **Foreign Plurals** (*agenda, alumnae, bacilli, data, synopses*).

Words borrowed from foreign languages bring with them their foreign methods of forming the plural. If these words pass into popular speech there is a strong tendency to ignore their foreign plurals and to treat them like the great majority of English nouns. However, until that change has become accepted, it is conventional to use the foreign plural.

When used in a sentence, nouns serve as subjects, objects, complements, modifiers, or objects of prepositions, as in the following examples:

That *man* was here again. (Noun as subject.)
Our *neighbors* bought a new *car*. (Nouns as subject and object.)
Her *uncle* is a *physicist*. (Nouns as subject and complement.)
His *mother's* health is bad. (Nouns used as modifiers usually have the possessive case form shown here. Otherwise, nouns are not inflected for case.)
At the *door*, behind the *desk*, on the *table*, for *dinner*, with *cream*. (In these phrases the first word is a preposition, the last a noun.)

PRONOUNS

Personal Pronouns. Words such as *he, she, we, them, you, it,* etc., belong to a class called **personal pronouns,** which are inflected for gender, number, case, and person. The complete inflection of the personal pronouns follows.

NUMBER	CASE	1ST PERSON	2ND PERSON	3RD PERSON		
				mas.	*fem.*	*neut.*
	Subjective	I	you	he	she	it
Singular	*Possessive*	my (mine)	your(s)	his	her(s)	its
	Objective	me	you	him	her	it
	Subjective	we	you	they	all	
Plural	*Possessive*	our(s)	your(s)	their(s)	genders	
	Objective	us	you	them		

The case forms are used to indicate the function of the pronoun in its clause, whether subject, modifier, or object. The forms for person indicate the person speaking (first), the person spoken to (second), and the person spoken about (third). The word "pronoun" means "for a noun," and pronouns can be substituted for nouns in a sentence. That is, they serve as subjects, objects, complements, modifiers, or objects of prepositions, thus:

He was here again. (Subject.)
I saw *him* yesterday. (Subject and object)
Who put the dent in *your* fender? (Subject and modifier.)
The black hat is *mine*. (Complement.)
For *him*, to *me*, with *her*, behind *them*. (Objects of prepositions.)

Relative Pronouns. The pronouns *who, which, that, what,* with their compounds, *whoever, whosoever, whichever, whatever,* and *whatsoever,* are often used to relate a subordinate clause to its main clause. When so used, they are called **relative pronouns.** The only relative fully inflected for case is *who,* which has the forms: *who* (subjective), *whose* (possessive), *whom* (objective). This pronoun is not inflected for number or gender. The compounds *whoever* and *whosoever* have no distinct forms for the possessive, but become *whomever* and *whomsoever* respectively in the objective case — thus:

> *Whoever* did this should be horsewhipped.
> I'll take *whomever* I can get.
> *Whosoever* believeth in me shall not perish.
> To *whomsoever* it may concern.

Demonstrative Pronouns. When *this* and *that* are used as pointing words they are called **demonstrative pronouns.** When so used, they are inflected for number. Their plural forms are *these* and *those* respectively — thus:

> *This* is mine; *these* are yours.
> *That* was the seventeenth; *those* records were lost.

Reflexive Pronouns. In such sentences as *He corrected himself, You will hurt yourself, They are deceiving themselves,* we call *himself, yourself,* and *themselves* **reflexive pronouns** because the object refers to the same individual or group as the subject. Reflexive pronouns are inflected as follows:

	Singular	*Plural*
1st person	myself	ourselves
2nd person	yourself	yourselves
3rd person	himself, herself, itself	themselves

VERBS

Such words as *be, do, walked, told, have been, was, wrote, said, will try, shouting, scolded, to expect* belong to a class of words which are inflected to show number, person, voice mood, and tense. These words are **verbs.**

Principal Parts. All tenses are made from certain forms of the verb used either alone or in combination with other verbs. Thus, all tenses of the verb *to talk* are made from the forms: *talk, talking, talked* (I *talk,* I am *talking,* I do *talk,* I *talked,* I have *talked,* I have been *talking,* I will *talk,* etc.). Similarly, all tenses of the verb *to speak* are made from the forms: *speak, speaking, spoke, spoken.* These forms are called the **principal parts.**

As these examples show, some English verbs have three principal parts, others have four. The vast majority, known as **regular** verbs, are of the former type and form both the past tense and the past participle by adding *-ed* or *-d* to the first principal part (*talk, talked, talked; blame, blamed, blamed*). Such verbs have two characteristics: the vowel remains unchanged in all principal parts; and the forms for the past tense and the past participle are identical.

Verbs which do not have both these characteristics are said to be **irregular.**[1] Such verbs have four principal parts, the present and past tense forms, and the present and past participles:

[1] For a selected list of principal parts, see pages 433–434.

Present Tense	Present Participle	Past Tense	Past Participle
come	coming	came	come
see	seeing	saw	seen
conquer	conquering	conquered	conquered

Tense. Although it is possible to recognize some thirty different tenses, not counting idioms which do the work of tenses, six tenses are considered basic. These are

Simple present: They object
Simple past: They objected
Simple future: They will object

Present perfect: They have objected
Past perfect: They had objected
Future perfect: They will have objected

The uses of these tenses and their full conjugations are shown on pages 437–439.

Mood. Of the three moods of English verbs — the **indicative, imperative,** and **subjunctive** — the indicative is by far the most common. A verb is in the indicative mood unless:

1. It expresses a command or entreaty (*Sit down! Please listen to me!*), in which case it is in the imperative mood.

2. It is used in one of the following ways, in which case it is in the subjunctive mood:

   a. To express a condition contrary to fact (If I *were* you, I would go).

   b. To grant a concession (*Be* it as you say).

   c. To state an improbability (If this *were* the end of the matter, I'd be happy).

   d. To conduct certain parliamentary proceedings (I move that the committee *go* on record; it is moved and seconded that this measure *be* adopted).

The form used for the imperative mood is always the same as the first principal part. The subjunctive, once fully inflected, is so little used in modern English that we need consider only the forms for the simple present and past tenses of the verb *to be.* These are *be* for all persons in the singular and plural of the simple present and *were* for all persons in the singular and plural of the simple past.

Voice. English verbs have two voices: **active** and **passive.**

> *Active.* A girl *opened* the door.
> *Passive.* The door *was opened* by a girl.

When a verb is changed from active to passive, the object of the active verb becomes the subject of the passive verb. The passive voice is formed by adding the past participle to the appropriate tense form of the verb *to be* (The door *is opened, was opened, will be opened,* etc.).[2]

ADJECTIVES AND ADVERBS

Adjectives and adverbs cannot always be distinguished from each other by their form. Most adverbs end in *-ly,* but so do some adjectives (*silly* and *manly,* for example). Some adverbs (*clean, far, fast, straight,* etc.) do not have *-ly,* and some have two forms, one with and one without that ending (*late-lately, loud-loudly, slow-slowly,* etc.). For these reasons, adjectives and adverbs are best recognized by their function in a sentence: adjectives modify nouns or pronouns; adverbs modify verbs, adjectives, or other adverbs.

When an adjective precedes the noun or pronoun it modifies (a *blue* gown), it is called an **attributive adjective.** When it both completes a verb and modifies its subject (The man is *lazy*), it is called a **predicate adjective.**

Adverbs do not serve as complements, but in addition to their chief function of modifying verbs, adjectives, and adverbs, they are frequently used in the following ways:

1. As interrogative adverbs to introduce a question (*Where* were you? *When* did he go? *Why* did you say that?).

2. As sentence modifiers to modify a whole sentence rather than a single element (*Maybe* he is ill. *Incidentally,* that answer is wrong).

3. As conjunctive adverbs (or transitional connectives) to join two sentences and modify the second one (The men did not complain; they were, *however,* rather sullen for the rest of the evening. His wife was not hostile; *on the contrary,* she seemed most friendly).

Comparison. Modern English adjectives and adverbs have lost the inflectional endings they had in Old English except those which show **degree of comparison.** There are three such degrees: positive, comparative, and superlative.

There are three methods of indicating comparison in adjectives and adverbs: (1) by adding *-er* for the comparative and *-est* for the superlative; (2) by prefixing *more* for the comparative and *most* for the superlative; (3) by using different words for each degree:

	Positive	*Comparative*	*Superlative*
(1)	strong	stronger	strongest
(2)	beautiful	more beautiful	most beautiful
(3)	good	better	best

Of the three methods, the first two are considered regular. In general, words of one syllable take the *-er -est* endings, and words of more than two syllables use *more* and *most.* The usage in two-syllable words is divided, though words common in popular speech tend to retain *-er -est.*

[2] For the use of the passive voice, see page 120.

The third method is called irregular comparison. Several words that are irregularly compared have the same form for adjective and adverb. Here are the most common irregular comparisons:

Positive	*Comparative*	*Superlative*
bad, ill	worse	worst
far	farther, further	farthest, furthest
good, well	better	best
little	less, lesser	least
much, many	more	most

Function Units

If we use the letters *S* (Subject), *V* (Verb), *O* (Object), *M* (Modifier), and *K* (Connective) to label the function units of the following sentence, we can readily see the nature of their relationships:

S   K   S   V   O   M
Dad and Mother liked Alice at once.

The words in this sentence are related chiefly through word order or position. We saw in Chapter 5 (pages 102–107) that two of the basic patterns of English sentences were Subject-Verb (S-V) and Subject-Verb-Object (S-V-O). We also saw that these patterns are so dominant in English sentences that if we are given meaningless sentences, such as *The X's elled,* and *The X's elled the Y's,* we want to interpret the first as a S-V and the second as a S-V-O pattern. This illustration suggests that the relative positions of the function units in a sentence largely define the subject-verb-object relations. The other units are defined by their positions with respect to the subjects, verbs, and objects.

SUBJECT-VERB-OBJECT

The S-V-O sentence pattern, a favorite in English, is called the **actor-action sequence.** In such a sentence the subject identifies the actor, the verb identifies the action, and the object identifies the recipient of the action. If all English sentences followed this sequence, we could define our chief function units by saying that the subject tells us who or what performed the action suggested by the verb, and the object tells us who or what was acted upon. But this method of explaining subject-verb relationships works only with actor-action sequences. It does not work in the following sentences, which also follow established English patterns.

1. *She* was accepted by Dad and Mother at once. (Passive)
2. Our English *instructor* is Mr. Wesley. (Subject-verb-complement)
3. *He* seems older. (Subject-verb-modifier)
4. There is a *hole* in my sock. (Expletive)
5. Where have *you* been? (Question)

Because of such exceptions as these, the subject cannot be defined as the performer of the action, except in an actor-action sequence. It can better be defined in terms of word order or position, if the special order of the expletive and question patterns is kept in mind. It is still better not to define it at all, but to recognize it through experience. After all, this is how you recognize all language patterns. As we saw in Chapter 5 (pages 102–103), a subject may be a single word, a compound of two words connected by a conjunction, a series of words, a phrase, or a subordinate clause.

It is traditional to use the term "verb" as both a form and a function unit. It is a form unit by virtue of its various forms for tense, mood, number, etc. It is a function unit by virtue of its relation to subjects, objects, and complements. Confusion between the form and function of verbs often leads students to mistake infinitives, participles, and gerunds for finite verbs. If you have this trouble, see *Verbs and Verbals,* page 406.

Verbs are usually classified as **transitive, intransitive,** or **linking.** A **transitive verb** is followed by an object, which completes the predicate[3]:

> She *asked* an embarrassing *question.*
> He *wants sympathy.*
> I *wrote* a *letter.*

An **intransitive verb** is not followed by an object but makes a complete predicate by itself:

> The girls *have left.*
> Tomorrow our vacation *begins.*

A **linking verb,** also called a **copula,** connects the subject to a complement, a noun or an adjective:

> Smith *is* a sophomore.
> They *were* ill.
> He *felt* sick.
> The audience *became* restless.

The most common linking verb is the verb *to be.*

The objects we have considered so far are called **direct objects.** In the actor-action sequence they designate the receiver of the action. In sentences such as —

> I gave *him* the book. I gave the pen *to her.* I bought it *for her.*
> We asked the *teacher* a difficult question. —

the italicized words are called **indirect objects.** Single-word indirect objects usually come between the verb and the direct object; indirect object phrases (usually with *to* or *for*) generally follow the direct object.

🖒 Identify subjects, verbs, direct and indirect objects in the following sentences.

[3] For *predicate,* see page 103.

1. Somebody took my hat.
2. I called, but nobody answered.
3. The girls are giving a party; we have been invited.
4. The family bought Dad a new radio. We gave it to him yesterday.
5. Nothing has been done. The material has not arrived.
6. Give the boy another chance. He deserves it.
7. Try this one. It may fit you better.
8. We have not received your application; it may come in today's mail.
9. The test contained five questions. I finished early and gave my paper to the instructor.

Complements. Verbs such as *be, become, get, feel, look, seem, smell, taste,* and others often serve as "linking verbs" — that is, they link a completing construction to the subject, as in *Bill is a junior.* The unit that follows and completes a linking verb is called its **complement.** When the complement is a noun it looks exactly like a direct object. For example, in

> He consulted a doctor.
> He became a doctor.

we call the first "doctor" an object and the second a complement. The only difference between them is that the first follows a transitive verb, and the second follows a linking verb.

In some sentences, the complement of a linking verb is an adjective:

> We felt sleepy.   She seems happy.
> He looked sick.   This tastes good.

✔ Identify complements in the following sentences.

1. These nails look rusty. Throw them away.
2. Your watch is slow. You will be late.
3. Who is that girl? Isn't she Ted Norton's daughter?
4. This is my raincoat. Which one is yours?
5. His story was a strange one, but it sounded true.
6. The child remains stubborn. Perhaps he is scared of us.
7. The man they want must have a college degree and some practical experience in industry.

MODIFIERS

In general, a **modifier** describes a subject, object, complement, or another modifier, or tells how, where, when, why, or under what conditions the action of a verb took place. The italicized modifiers in the following sentences illustrate these uses:

> We took a *second* look. (Modifies object.)
> *Old* soldiers never die. (Modifies subject.)
> Honesty is the *best* policy. (Modifies complement.)

It was a *most* unlikely story. (Modifies the modifier *unlikely*.)
He arrived *later*. (Modifies the verb — tells when.)
He arrived *at the party*. (Modifies the verb — tells where.)
He went *for my sake*. (Modifies the verb — tells why.)
I will go, *if you pay my way*. (Modifies the verb — tells under what conditions.)
I will go, *even if I'm not invited*. (Modifies the verb — tells despite what conditions.)

The word being modified is called the **headword.** If the headword is a noun, the modifier consists of one or more adjectives preceding the noun, as in our first three examples, or of a phrase following the noun, as in *A man from the office called you*, or of a subordinate clause following the noun, as in *A man who works in your office called you*. If the headword is a verb, the modifier may be a single adverb, a phrase, or a subordinate clause, and may come either before or after the verb. For example, the italicized clauses in the last two items of the list above could be placed at the beginning of the sentence. If the headword is another modifier, the new modifier is usually an adverb preceding the headword, as in the fourth item on our list.

✔ Identify the modifiers in the following sentences.

1. My bicycle is a black one with white trim.
2. It was an oppressively hot day.
3. There is something strangely familiar about his face.
4. She lives in the brick house at the end of the block.
5. The new car was damaged beyond repair.
6. Go sit under that tree while I change the tire.
7. I'll go if you will wait till I get back.
8. Worried by his failure to write, his mother telephoned him.
9. Unless we get there by noon we won't have time for shopping.
10. Having studied the map at the last gas station, I knew we were on the wrong road.

CONNECTIVES

Connectives join other units in a sentence and usually come between these units. The three most common types are **coordinating, subordinating,** and **transitional** connectives.

A **coordinating connective** joins two similar, or coordinate, elements:

Tom *and* I will go. (Connects two subjects.)
Bill grumbled *and* sulked for days. (Connects two verbs.)
He fought cleverly *and* courageously. (Connects two modifiers.)
I'll do it *but* I won't like it. (Connects two main clauses.)
Either Bert *or* I will do it. (*Either* — *or* connects two subjects.)
We have *neither* the money *nor* the time. (Connects two objects.)

You pretend to be her friend, *yet* you gossip about her. (Connects two main clauses.)

A **subordinating connective** does two things: it joins two clauses and subordinates one to the other. If we take two main clauses

He is cross. He is tired.

and join them with *because — He is cross because he is tired —* we not only connect the two clauses but we subordinate the second to the first. In this example *because* is a subordinating connective. In the following examples the subordinate clauses are in parentheses and the connectives in italics:

I don't know (*why* he did it).
He did not say (*when* he would return).
I won't do it (*if* you seriously object).
You may go (*whenever* you please).

In these examples the subordinating connective comes between the clauses it joins. But a subordinate clause may precede the main one, and the connective may come at the beginning of the sentence:

(*If* you seriously object), I won't do it.
(*Because* I flatter him), he likes me.
(*Since* you are in a hurry), I won't bother you about it.

A **transitional connective** joins two sentences by providing a transition between them. See "Transitional Markers," pages 85–86.

✔ In the following sentences, identify coordinating and subordinating connectives.

1. Smile when you say that.
2. I have no idea what he wants.
3. When the right time comes, I will tell you.
4. I would do it if I could, but I cannot.
5. His only faults are that he has neither looks nor money.
6. She has had nothing to eat or drink since she came home.
7. Although he is taller, he weighs less.
8. While I want to be pleasant and agreeable, I cannot do what you ask.
9. Neither Helen nor Jean has the book you want.
10. Although he brings me nothing but trouble, I must do what I can for him.

Prepositions as Connectives. Such words as *after, around, at, behind, beside, for, in, into, of, on, to, with* are called **prepositions** when they precede a noun or pronoun and show its relation to some other word in the sentence, usually a verb, adjective, noun, or pronoun:

He is good *at* tennis. (Relates the noun *tennis* to the adjective *good*.)
They live *in* Detroit. (Relates the noun *Detroit* to the verb *live*.)
I am the head *of* the house. (Relates the nouns *head* and *house*.)

ABSOLUTES

Occasionally a unit in a sentence has no clear grammatical relationship to any other unit, yet clearly belongs. We call it an **absolute construction.** Consider the following sentences:

Nonsense, it is all a hoax!
Good heavens, is it that late?
Mr. Hughes, may I talk to you for a moment?
No, I won't do it!
I wish, *madam,* you would make up your mind.
She said — *as if I cared* — that she was through with me.

The italicized expressions serve useful purposes, but they are not grammatically related to other sentence elements. They are absolute constructions.

Summary of Sentence Elements

Sentences can be studied in terms of two kinds of units: *form* units, which show inflectional changes in a word, and *function* units, which show how words are related in a sentence, chiefly through word order.

FORM UNITS

Nouns. The largest class of words in English. These words are inflected for number and possessive case. The prevalent pattern for forming plurals is the addition of *-s* or *-es* to the singular, but some verbs, like *children, mice, sheep,* and foreign plurals (*bacteria, vertebrae, alumni, parentheses*) are irregular. Chief uses: subjects, objects, complements, modifiers (in possessive case), and objects of prepositions.

Pronouns. A class of words inflected for number, case, person, and gender. Personal pronouns are the most highly inflected class in English. Other pronouns (relative, demonstrative, reflexive) show only partial inflection. Chief uses: the same as nouns.

Verbs. A class of words inflected chiefly for tense, but also for number, person, mood, and voice. Verbs are the key words in sentences. They form the predicate, with or without object or complement.

Adjectives, Adverbs. Two classes of words inflected to show comparative and superlative degree. Chief uses: adjectives modify nouns; adverbs modify verbs, adjectives, and other adverbs.

FUNCTION UNITS

Subjects. The starting point in the subject-verb-object relationship. In the actor-action sequence, the subject identifies the performer of the action, but its relationship with the verb is predominantly one of position or word order. Any construction which can fill the subject position may act as the subject of a sentence, but most subjects are nouns or pronouns.

Verbs. Three classes: transitive (with object), intransitive (without object), linking (with complement). Verbs are both form and function units. As function units they should not be confused with verbals (infinitives, participles, gerunds).

Objects. Used to complete the predicate when the verb is transitive. Two types: direct and indirect. Complements perform a similar function by completing linking verbs.

Modifiers. Single words, phrases, or clauses which make the meaning of a headword more specific by describing or limiting it. Single-word modifiers are adjectives or adverbs and usually precede their headword. Phrase or clause modifiers usually follow their headwords, but the position of modifiers of verbs is quite variable.

Connectives. Also called *conjunctions.* Three types: coordinating, subordinating, transitional. Coordinating connectives join similar functions — two subjects, two verbs, two modifiers, etc. Subordinating connectives join subordinate clauses to main clauses; transitional connectives tie sentences together by providing a transition between them.

Prepositions, which relate nouns or pronouns to other words, also serve a kind of connecting function, although they are not usually classified as connectives.

Absolutes. Any unit which does not serve as subject, verb, object, complement, connective, preposition, or modifier in a sentence. It may at times be a mild modifier of the whole sentence, but it is usually grammatically independent of the rest of the sentence.

Review Exercise

Using the symbols, *S* — Subject, *V* — Verb, *O* — Object, *C* — Complement, *M* — Modifier, *K* — Connective, and *A* — Absolute, identify the underlined elements in the following sentences. For your convenience, subordinate clauses have been placed in parentheses. Occasionally an element and its modifier have been underlined as a single element.

1. The woman offered no explanation.
2. Henry, you are impossible!
3. Bill's father will retire next year.
4. My parents are moving tomorrow.
5. Mother wore a blue skirt and a white blouse.

6. She is irritable (when she is tired).
7. (When she feels well) she is a pleasant person.
8. He likes to wrestle and he wrestles well.
9. The governor was re-elected by a narrow margin.
10. The defeated candidate resumed his law practice.
11. Because of the wind, the mountain climbers abandoned the attempt.
12. He will try to speak (whenever he gets a chance).
13. Everyone hopes (that the worst is past).
14. The answer to that question is unknown.
15. The doctor will see you now, Mr. Brown.

S2 *Phrases and Clauses*

a. A phrase is a group of two or more words acting as a single element in a sentence but not having a subject and verb of its own.

In the following sentences the phrases are italicized.

She stood *by the door.* (Phrase modifies verb.)
He *has been calling* you. (Phrase is verb.)
Hunting big game is expensive. (Phrase is subject.)
A page *near the end* is missing. (Phrase modifies subject.)
Her brother is *a medical student.* (Phrase is complement of verb.)
My dear woman, I never said that! (Phrase is absolute.)

b. A subordinate clause is a group of words acting as subject, object, complement, or modifier, but having a subject and verb of its own.

In the following sentences the subordinate clauses are italicized.

Whoever did that is foolish. (Clause is subject of verb *is.*)
You may ask *whatever you want.* (Clause is object of verb *may ask.*)
The people *who lived there* have moved. (Clause modifies subject.)
I will go *wherever you send me.* (Clause modifies verb.)
This is the book *that I want.* (Clause modifies complement.)

In each of these sentences the subordinate clause is introduced by a subordinating connective. This connective may sometimes be omitted without changing the subordinate nature of the clause:

This is the book *I want.*
The plumber *you sent for* is here.

c. A main clause has a subject and verb but does not act as a subject, complement, or modifier.

It may be a complete sentence in itself; it may be part of a compound sentence; or it may be an absolute in a larger sentence.

I cut the lawn. (Main clause in a simple sentence.)

I cut the lawn, and *Joe raked it.* (Two main clauses forming a compound sentence.)

He said — *wasn't it mean of him?* — that I was an irresponsible adolescent. (Italicized main clause is an absolute in a complex sentence.)

✔ Distinguish between main and subordinate clauses in the following sentences by underlining main clauses once and subordinate clauses twice.

1. I will do whatever you say.
2. What he said is nobody's business.
3. The book that I bought cost a dollar.
4. The dress I bought is too tight.
5. If that is how you feel, you go your way and I'll go mine.
6. The man who is wearing the plaid shirt is his brother-in-law.
7. We don't want your advice; we just ask to be left alone.
8. Get a good night's sleep. That is the best preparation I know for the examination.
9. He said that he was terribly embarrassed. If I had been he, I would have been sick.
10. He said there was nothing he could do.

Review Exercise

In the following passages certain constructions have been underlined and numbered. Copy the numbers and opposite each write *Main Clause, Subordinate Clause,* or *Phrase,* whichever is appropriate.

A (1) It was a bright sunny day (2) when we left Columbus (3) in a tightly packed car (4) for Sparrow Lake, Canada. (5) Along the way (6) we stopped at Niagara Falls (7) to see one of nature's beautiful creations, and then (8) continued to drive (9) what seemed to be an endless distance. (10) At last (11) we arrived in Orillia, Canada, (12) bought a few necessary supplies, and (13) drove down a typical washboard road (14) till we arrived (15) at our destination.

B The relationship (1) between a writer and a reader may be illustrated (2) by an analogy with dancing. Anybody (3) who has danced knows (4) that both partners move (5) in accordance with patterns (6) which both understand and take for granted. The man, (7) by his leading, indicates which pattern (8) he wishes to set; (9) the girl follows. (10) If the man leads his partner (11) to expect one kind of movement and then switches to another, (12) the girl will have difficulty following.

(13) The relationship between the writer and reader is similar. Each assumes (14) that the other is familiar with the basic patterns of sentence structure. The reader, (15) like the girl in the dance, must follow the writer's lead, and (16) as long as the writer follows an accepted pattern (17) the reader has no trouble. But (18) if the writer sets one pattern in the first half of a sentence and (19) then shifts to another, (20) the reader is likely to be confused.

C (1) One day a girl brought me a composition (2) that had been corrected and returned. (3) On the two pages (4) that it occupied there was (5) a total of 127 corrections. (6) I could not get any coherent picture from (7) such a complete mess, (8) so I tabulated the errors (9) according to type. (10) Out of the 127 mistakes, (11) 92 came from wrong punctuation. There were no errors (12) of capitalization or grammar. (13) Two sentences were incomplete, (14) 19 were far too long and involved, (15) 8 contained wrong references, and (16) 6 lacked parallelism. The girl had another composition (17) to write at once. (18) I told her (19) to go to work on it, but (20) to concentrate on the avoidance of a single error — the long, loosejointed sentences. In fact, (21) I was so sure from the analysis (22) that her key mistake was mere length (23) that I instructed her (24) to use not over fifteen words per sentence. (25) She promised to keep within this limit. . . . (26) The total length of this second composition was (27) about twenty words more than the first, but (28) when it came back there were only eight errors — one incomplete sentence, three errors in spelling, and four unnecessary commas. All of the mistakes (29) the girl had made earlier had been pyramided upon the single error of (30) trying to write sentences that were too long.[4]

S3   *Verbs and Verbals*

Most trouble with verbs comes from failure to distinguish verbs from verbals. A **verbal** is derived from a verb but does not act as a verb in a sentence. For example, in the sentences

> *Wrestling* IS a body-building sport.
> *To wait* IS not easy.
> He SPOKE in *threatening* terms.

the verbs are in small capital letters. The words *wrestling, to wait,* and *threatening* may look like verbs but they do not act as verbs. *Wrestling* and *To wait* are the subjects of their sentences; *threatening* modifies *terms.* These words are verbals, not verbs.

Verbals are of three types: **infinitives, participles,** and **gerunds.**

a. Such verbals as *to do, to choose, to be seeking, to have said,* and *to have been invited* are called infinitives.

Usually, but not always, they have the infinitive marker *to.* They often serve as subjects (*To do* that is not easy; *to be excused* from class is a rare treat) or as complements (They asked *to go;* we expected *to be called*),

[4] From *The Backgrounds for College Teaching* by Luella Cole. Copyright, 1940, by Farrar & Rinehart, Inc. Reprinted by permission of Rinehart & Company, Inc.

but they occasionally act as modifiers (I bought it *to read;* we have no time *to spare*).

✔ Identify the infinitives in the following sentences.

1. Nobody wants to tell him.
2. He is said to have refused an offer to settle out of court.
3. I'd like to do good work and have fun, too.
4. We tried to call them and explain the difficulty.
5. To play as well as he does takes more time than I can afford to give.
6. You should be able to analyze and evaluate the information and reach sound conclusions from it.
7. She seems to be looking for an excuse to pick a quarrel with him.
8. He is said to have done the same thing in several states and to be wanted by the police in Texas.
9. Not to have invited her would have caused trouble.
10. He is thought to be willing to sell at a low price in order to settle the estate quickly.

b. A participle is a word or phrase which is derived from a verb but acts as a modifier.

The present participle ends in *-ing* (*crying, smiling, sulking*). The past participle most frequently ends in *-ed* (*disgusted, excused, inspired*), but many are irregular (*chosen, grown, kept, slung*). The following sentences illustrate forms and uses of participles.

His *fighting* days are over. (Present participle modifies subject.)
He is a *fighting* fool. (Present participle modifies complement.)
Having fought all challengers, he retired. (Past participle modifies subject *he.*)
Goldsmith wrote a poem about a *deserted* village. (Past participle modifies the object of *about.*)
Having been deserted by her husband, she supported the family. (Passive form of past participle modifies subject *she.*)

✔ Identify the participles in the following sentences.

1. She is a clinging vine.
2. A broken watch is of little use.
3. The metal is now near the breaking point.
4. This is a thrilling story.
5. Thrilled by the movie, we stayed up too late.
6. A drunken man is usually a bore.
7. Disappointed by the results, he gave up the experiment.
8. With screeching brakes the car came to a jarring stop.
9. They have forgotten that they called him the forgotten man.
10. The play having been called back, it was now third down and seven.

c. Gerunds, or verbal nouns, have the same form as the present participle but are used as subjects and objects in a sentence, not as modifiers.

The only difference between a gerund and a present participle is one of function.

> *Thinking* is hard work. (Gerund is subject of verb *is*.)
> That will take some *thinking*. (Gerund is object of verb *will take*.)
> *Looking* innocent won't help you. (Gerund is subject of *won't help*.)
> She can't stop *crying*. (Gerund is object of *can't stop*.)

✔ Distinguish between the participles and gerunds in the following sentences by identifying each verbal and explaining its function in the sentence.

1. Bacon said that reading makes a wise man.
2. During the semester his reading speed increased significantly.
3. This course requires too much reading.
4. They were looking for an abandoned mine.
5. Abandoned by her allies, Czechoslovakia was forced to yield.
6. Tired by the long hike, we took a nap before dinner.
7. Looking for trouble is the quickest way to find it.
8. Becoming angry will not help; try smiling for a change.

Review Exercises

Copy and turn in to your instructor the following sentences. Distinguish between verbs and verbals by underlining all verbs once and all verbals twice.

1. Swimming is fun. I would like to swim well. I was swimming yesterday. My brother has been swimming since he was four.

2. They say that a rolling stone gathers no moss; they could just as truthfully say that a stone that is rolling isn't gathering anything but momentum.

3. It is easier to win a letter in college than to receive a Phi Beta Kappa key. That is a point worth remembering when we are tempted to make fun of serious students.

4. The statement that a watched kettle never boils is not true. Water in a kettle boils just as quickly watched or unwatched. But you are more conscious of time when you are watching the kettle and therefore the time seems to be longer.

5. I am tired of having to be told what I may and may not do. My parents seem to have forgotten how they resented too much supervision when they were my age.

6. Discouraged by his grades, he was thinking of quitting school. But the dean persuaded him to revise his habits of studying and finish the semester before making a decision.

7. Leave him alone! Let him do it his own way. He has to learn some day to discover his own mistakes and correct them, and he might as well make a beginning now.

8. Having tried everything to get good grades without studying, we reluctantly decided to give that method a try.

9. Weakened by hunger and exposure, the old couple were in serious condition.

10. He said nothing would interfere with his ambitions, but he has found that it is easier to profess ambitions than to achieve them.

S 4   *Fragmentary Sentence and Period Fault*

a. A full sentence is grammatically complete.

In its simplest form the full sentence consists of only a main clause (see page 102) but it may contain more than one main clause and one or more subordinate clauses.

b. A fragmentary sentence is not grammatically complete, although in context it may make as complete a statement as is needed.

It may simply be an exclamation: *Oh! Nonsense! Wonderful! Good Heavens!* It may serve as a question: *Cigarette? Lemon or sugar? Anything else?* It may be a phrase or clause uttered in response to a question: *Maybe. Not at all. If you wish. Whenever it is convenient.* Or it may be a stereotyped expression, such as: *The more, the merrier. First come, first served. Like father, like son. Easy come, easy go.* When it is used in these ways, the fragmentary sentence is sometimes called a **minor sentence.**

The use of such fragmentary sentences is conventional in conversation and in writing which imitates the patterns of speech, such as dialogue in narration. As we saw in Chapter 6, sentence fragments are not uncommon in colloquial expository writing, and are sometimes, though not often, used in informal expository writing. There is, however, a strong objection to their use in most college expository papers. The objection is not to the fragment as a sentence pattern as much as it is to the uncritical use of fragments in contexts in which they are not appropriate.

c. Most unwarranted fragments in student essays result from confusion of main and subordinate clauses or confusion of verbs and verbals.

The writer thinks that two parts of a sentence are different sentences, and so separates them with a period. This use of the period is usually called a **period fault.** In the first three of the following examples a subordinate clause has been confused with an independent statement and separated from its main clause by a period. In the next three a verbal phrase has been cut off from its main clause by a period.

Fragmentary Sentence Structure	*Explanation*	*Full Sentence Structure*
He made a point of entering each misspelled word in a notebook. *Which he kept for that purpose.*	*Italicized subordinate clause modifies notebook and is not an independent statement.*	He made a point of entering each misspelled word in a notebook which he kept for that purpose.
I refused to go to the show. *Because I had been up late last night and needed sleep.*	*The italicized clause explains the refusal and is therefore a modifier of* refused.	Because I had been up late last night and needed sleep, I refused to go to the show.
He is always complaining about his grades. *Although he does nothing to improve them.*	*The italicized clause is a modifier, not an independent statement.*	He is always complaining about his grades, although he does nothing to improve them.
The Tigers made two runs in the ninth. *Thus tying* the score.	Tying *is not a verb, but a present participle modifying the main clause.*	The Tigers made two runs in the ninth, thus tying the score.
It was difficult to decide which choice to make. *To return* to school or *to accept* the job.	*The italicized infinitives modify* choice; *therefore they do not act as verbs.*	It was difficult to decide whether to return to school or to accept the job.
It was a wonderful week. *Fishing* and *swimming* every day and *dancing* every night.	*The italicized words are gerunds. They should either be made into verbs or should serve as complements of another verb.*	. . . We fished and swam every day and danced every night. (or) We went fishing and swimming every day and dancing every night.

As the revisions at the right indicate, period faults may be corrected either by changing the faulty period to a comma, thus incorporating the separated phrase or subordinate clause within the sentence to which it belongs, or by expanding the fragment into a main clause so that it can stand as an independent sentence.

✔ In the following sentences correct the period faults.

1. He refused to answer the question. Despite the fact that he knew his silence would be interpreted as guilt.

2. The author of such books or magazine articles writes to appeal to the general public. Not just to a few.

3. The judge said that the court was not inclined to show mercy. This being the third time the defendant had been convicted of that offense.

4. I refused the job. Although I could have used the money.

5. I think I would do as I did then. Conditions remaining the same.

6. The same procedure is used in the running of wind sprints as was used in the long runs. Twenty minutes of exercises. Two warm-up turns around a quarter-mile track. Followed by several fast sprints of 220 yards.

7. The technique of the Communists was to publicize every act of oppression and intolerance and at the same time to assure minority groups that the Communists were concerned about their plight. Thus exaggerating the failures of Democracy and implying that Communism was a philosophy of brotherly love.

8. He died alone and in poverty. Deserted by those who had once sung his praise and borrowed his money.

9. This has been one of those days that we all have once in a while. When, no matter how careful we are, everything seems to go wrong.

10. He said that all this talk about security puzzled him. That he knew no way of guaranteeing that his investments would turn out as he had planned them. Or even of being sure that he would live to know how they did turn out.

11. What he wants to know is. Will you date him?

12. After filling out the necessary papers and making a deposit. I was assigned to my room.

13. I am answering your advertisement expressing need of experienced draftsmen. Which appeared in a recent issue of the *Toledo Blade*. I should like to apply for one of those positions. And submit the following credentials.

14. The student of English grammar should recognize that there is likely to be some shuttling about between regular and irregular principal parts. That principal parts which were unacceptable a generation ago may have become established usage. While forms which were previously acceptable have passed out of fashion.

15. This spring my father had to make a very difficult decision. Whether to sell his business and move to California. Or to remain here where all his friends are. He finally decided to go to California. Which pleases me very much.

16. Two of the most unforgettable characters in my life are my parents. Unforgettable not only because of our common bond but also because of the striking differences in their personalities.

17. You should take into consideration whether such a marriage would force John into a type of work he dislikes. Instead of giving him the opportunity to look around for the kind of work he really likes.

18. The greatest struggle in the world today is caused by two opposing ways of life. The Communistic way being characterized by government control. And the American way which is characterized by liberty, freedom, and Christian principles.

19. The possible solution to the problem of juvenile delinquency could be more and better recreational facilities. Facilities that would fill the spare time of the teen-ager and keep him occupied.

20. It is an important question, Jane. One which cannot be answered without much thought.

S 5   *Fused Sentences*

When two sentences are run together without any separating punctuation or without an intervening connective, they are said to be fused.

Unless such sentences are separated they will create difficulty for a reader or will, at least, irritate him because they do not observe convention.

Fused Sentences	*Separated Sentences*
I want that boy how I want it.	I want that. Boy, how I want it!
I knocked on the door when the lady came I gave her my most ingratiating smile.	I knocked on the door. When the lady came I gave her my most ingratiating smile.
Why should I apologize when he insulted me he did not apologize.	Why should I apologize? When he insulted me he did not apologize.
It is difficult to believe that he said that what could he have been thinking of?	It is difficult to believe that he said that. What could he have been thinking of?
Why do you ask what concern is it of yours?	Why do you ask? What concern is it of yours?

✔ Separate the following fused sentences.

1. I will not object on the other hand don't expect me to contribute.

2. It could have been anyone I know of no way of finding out who did it.

3. The first couple of years will be difficult after that much of the work will be routine.

4. The northern pike is the gamest fish in these waters pound for pound he will outfight a walleye every time.

5. The sheriff's office is not willing to carry out the ruling of the court even though the evictions are legal they are afraid of public sympathy with the tenants.

6. Because of its involved forms for case and gender German is a difficult language for most students it is the most difficult language in college.

7. I wrote to Mother when she answered I knew that the story had been exaggerated since then I have learned that the newspaper printed a retraction.

8. Informative lectures bore me when information is available in books I would rather read it than listen to it.

9. In situations such as this one there is no way of reaching a compromise unless both sides are willing to make concessions the dispute will become a stalemate.

10. At Roosevelt's death Truman succeeded to the Presidency without any real executive experience, without previous training, and without a unified party to direct him, he was called on to fill the most exacting job in the world.

S 6 *Run-on Sentence*

When ideas are not shaped into a sentence but are merely hooked on to each other by the excessive use of *and* or *so,* the resulting collection of material is called a run-on sentence.

The best way to remove the run-on effect is to subordinate part of the material to the rest. See *Subordination,* page 105.

Run-on Sentence	*Revision*
I did not know how Mother would feel about my accepting the invitation, *so* I called her on the phone *and* she said it was all right, *so* I accepted.	Because I did not know how Mother would feel about the invitation, I called her on the phone. When she said it was all right, I accepted.

✔ Remove the run-on effect in the following examples.

1. The game went into extra innings and we had to go home and get dressed or we would be late for the party, so we had to leave at the end of the ninth.

2. I was standing by the window and looking into the street and two cars suddenly crashed together. So I ran down the stairs and joined the crowd that was beginning to collect.

3. He said that thousands of draftees could not pass the army physical tests and were rejected and that most of their deficiencies could have been cured by proper medical attention and that this proved that the health of the nation was bad and something should be done about it.

4. Final examinations are not a good way to find out what a student knows about his courses and they cause students to stay up most of the night before an exam and drink too much coffee and smoke too many cigarettes, and this causes eyestrain and headaches, so it is not good for their health, so I would think that somebody around this university could think up a better system.

5. I believe the most valuable quality a woman can have is the ability to be a good cook. Meals are a very important part of everyday life, and a man's whole day may depend on the kind of breakfast he has and the way it is served. So every girl should be taught to cook a good meal and serve it

attractively and her chances of making a successful marriage will be increased.

S7   *Comma Splice*

The use of a comma, instead of a period or semicolon, between two main clauses not joined by a connective is called a comma splice or comma fault.

For example:

It's a beautiful day, the park will be crowded.

A comma splice will trouble a reader most when a modifying phrase or clause comes between the two main clauses, since he may not be able to tell to which main clause the modifier relates. The following illustrates this difficulty:

He has never before been suspected of theft, *to the best of my knowledge,* he has been employed by his present firm since he graduated from high school.

To which main clause does the italicized modifier belong? Which statement is the writer qualifying: that the man has never before been suspected of theft, or that he has always worked for the same company? The reader is free to guess, but he will get no help from the sentence. This comma splice brings about a real failure of communication, the worst kind of sentence error.

Because the comma splice sometimes causes this kind of confusion, many teachers strongly condemn all comma splices, even though some cause no real break in communication, and even though comma splices are not rare in the writings of some competent professional writers. It would better accord with the facts to say that, at its best, the comma splice is unconventional and, at its worst, it makes communication impossible. The sometimes indiscriminate condemnation of comma splices by college instructors is a result of painful experience with the latter type.

Comma splices may be corrected by one of three methods.

1. The simplest way is to change the faulty comma to a period or a semicolon, whichever is more appropriate:

Comma Splice	*Revision*
His chances of election are not good, because the independents do not like him, it would be safer to nominate another candidate.	His chances of election are not good, because the independents do not like him. It would be safer to nominate another candidate.
This is the best book I have ever read, it kept me up all night.	This is the best book I have ever read; it kept me up all night.

2. A second method of revision is to provide a coordinating connective between the two main clauses, thus making the comma conventional punctuation:

She says she does not like football, I doubt that she has seen two games in her whole life.	She says that she does not like football, but I doubt that she has seen two games in her whole life.
It will cost a great deal of money, there is no guarantee that the plan will succeed.	It will cost a great deal of money, and there is no guarantee that the plan will succeed.

3. The third method is to subordinate one main clause to the other:

It is a beautiful day, the park will be crowded.	Because it is a beautiful day the park will be crowded.
He is discouraged about flunking, I think he will quit school.	He is so discouraged about flunking that I think he will quit school.

When two main clauses are joined by a transitional connective — *consequently, however, moreover, nevertheless, therefore* — the conventional punctuation between them is a semicolon, though a period is not unusual:

I admit that he is honest and conscientious; nevertheless, I will not vote for him.

When two short main clauses are felt to be closely related, informal usage sometimes prefers a comma to a semicolon:

> I passed, Mary doubled.
> The women like him, the men don't.

✔ Using whatever method seems best, revise the comma splices in the following sentences.

1. The two days preceding the Spring Carnival are filled with much excitement, all the houses and organizations try to create interest in their floats.
2. There is still plenty of opportunity in this country, if a young man really cares about building a career, his chances of success are as good today as ever.
3. There are two wires sticking out from two small holes in the center of the dash, they have to be crossed to turn on the ignition.
4. The school had an attendance of 1500 students, this number included night school enrollment.
5. Do you believe that children should never be spanked, or do you believe that moderate spanking helps them to develop self-discipline, this is a question on which many parents disagree.

6. The difficulties are great, but not insuperable, although the answer is not in sight, it can be obtained by patient and persistent work.

7. It has been observed that the average youth in America reads at least one of the many different types of comics, the most popular kinds are the comics that are based on sensationalism and fantasy.

8. There are too many students for each teacher, no one receives any direct help or attention.

9. There is a great amount of detrimental reading material on the magazine shelves, most of this cannot be defended, even by the most liberal-minded person.

10. When in high school a week-end meant two days of nothing to do, in college it means two days in which you have to work to catch up.

11. In all three of these bills there is free choice of doctors, dentists, and hospitals, the only requirement is that they must be participants in the plan.

12. I remember how I used to spend hours living in a dream world as I sat in my room and followed the adventures of men who had superhuman powers, some of them stopped bullets which bounced off their bodies, others jumped over buildings and flew through space under their own power.

13. Their vocabularies seem to be made up of twenty-letter words, their sense of humor, if they have one, is very dry.

14. I had to fight temptations which led me away from my music, much to my dismay, the temptations quite often won.

15. The wages are low and the work is monotonous, moreover, the job offers little chance of promotion.

S8 *Faulty Parallelism*

The convention of parallelism is that elements of equal importance should, as far as possible, be expressed in similar grammatical form.

Thus two or more sentence elements arranged in a series or joined by a coordinating connective should have the same form: a phrase should be followed by a phrase, a clause by a clause, a noun by a noun, and a verb by a verb. The following sentence contains a series which enumerates the powers of a commission:

> The Commission has the power *to investigate, to conciliate, to hold* hearings, *to subpoena* witnesses, *to issue* cease-and-desist commands, *to order* reinstatement of a discharged employee, and *to direct* the hiring of a qualified applicant.

Notice that, grammatically, most of the sentence is a series of infinitive phrases, each identifying one of the powers of the commission and therefore modifying the noun *power*. Since each element in the series has the same modifying function, it is given the same infinitive form. It would have been possible to use a form other than the infinitive, as long as the same form was used throughout — (The Commission has the power *of investigating, of conciliating, of holding,* etc.). What is not acceptable is to mix forms. Notice how the following student sentence shifts from nouns to verbs and thus disrupts the parallel structure which the series demands.

> The Commission has the power of investigation, conciliation, holding hearings, subpoena witnesses, issue cease-and-desist commands, order the reinstatement of a discharged employee, and direct the hiring of a qualified applicant.

Faulty Parallelism	Explanation	Acceptable Structures
Few people understood the full extent of his disappointment or *how angry* he really was.	*Compound object of* understood. *The first object is a phrase, the second a subordinate clause. The two should be in parallel form.*	Few people understood the full extent of his disappointment or *the degree of his anger.*
Because he has always been wealthy *and with indulgent parents,* he has never been forced to accept responsibility.	*Compound modifier consists of a subordinate clause and a phrase. Should be two clauses or two phrases.*	Because he has always been wealthy and *has been protected by indulgent parents, . . .* (or) Because of *his wealth* and *his indulgent parents, . . .*

✔ Rewrite the following sentences to revise faulty parallelism.

1. Many of our laws are descended from old Roman laws, but being changed to fit our modern needs.

2. A decision must be made as to whether the acres of grass surrounding the university buildings are more important from a standpoint of landscaping or to be converted into practical parking lots open to all personnel, staff, and students.

3. For a settlement I will accept either twelve new blinds or having the old ones perfectly repaired.

4. She is inclined to be giggly and always embarrassing her escort.

5. My two ambitions are to have my own business, thus being my own boss, and having enough money to provide my children with a good home and education.

6. There is no happy ending such as occurs in most novels, but rather how people that sin usually do not have a happy life as they grow older.

7. These discoveries may have been thought of back in the seventeenth century and being used now.

8. A recent shipment consisting of Venetian blinds was found damaged and for which some adjustment should be made.

9. He continued his work, without hope, without pleasure, and having no assurance that people would understand the significance of what he was trying to do.

10. For the sake of your parents, your friends, and in the interests of your future, I hope you will reject the offer.

11. The closeness of a family relationship is brought out and how typical family problems can be worked out.

12. Each of my courses has contributed in several ways to my being a more intelligent person to talk with, and to help me read efficiently.

13. Your main aims in life are to settle down and having a home and children.

14. Uncle John taught me such things as honesty, faith in God, to be considerate, and making progress but never at the expense of others.

15. My requirements for an ideal wife are honesty, intelligence, pleasantness, being able to cook and do housework, and to have confidence in me.

S 9   *Dangling Modifiers*

A dangling modifier is one which has nothing in the main clause to modify and is thus left dangling.

For example, in the sentence

By going to the various sorority houses on campus and meeting hundreds of new girls, my conversation, manners, and poise became more polished.

there is nothing in the main clause for the italicized modifying phrase to modify. When the author began to write that sentence, she was unquestionably thinking of herself as the subject of the main clause — she was going to make a statement about herself. Had she finished with "I polished my conversation, manners, and poise," she would have had a satisfactory sentence, because the introductory phrase would then have modified the subject "I." But by inadvertently making "conversation" the subject of the main clause she spoiled what she started to do and invited the ludicrous interpretation that it was her conversation that visited the sorority houses.

The dangling modifiers most frequent in student essays begin, like the one above, with a **verbal phrase** — participle, gerund, or infinitive — and are left hanging because the originally-intended subject is not retained in the main clause. The best precaution against this kind of error is to make sure that the opening verbal clearly modifies the subject of the main clause. A sentence written with a dangling verbal phrase may be revised either by rewording the main clause or by expanding the opening phrase into a subordinate clause. Notice how the italicized dangling modifiers in the left column are revised at the right.

Dangling Modifier	Explanation	Revised Version
Walking downtown, a streetcar jumped the tracks.	*In the absence of anything else to modify,* walking *seems to modify* streetcar. *The revised version contains a subject which the participle can logically modify.*	Walking downtown, I saw a streetcar jump the tracks.
After recording the information required of me, my adviser checked my card to see that I had followed instructions.	*It was the student, not the instructor, who did the recording, yet the gerund* recording *seems to modify* adviser. *If the opening phrase is changed to a clause, this possible misinterpretation will be avoided.*	When I had recorded the information required of me, my adviser checked my card to see that I had followed instructions.
To qualify for the position, a rigorous examination must be passed.	*While there is no ambiguity in this example, the dangling infinitive phrase creates an unnecessary shift in the sentence pattern. This shift can be avoided by keeping the whole sentence in the active voice.*	To qualify for the position you must pass a rigorous examination.
Impressed by the newspaper stories, war seemed inevitable.	*Who was impressed? The opening phrase needs something to modify. The revised version gets rid of this difficulty by making* we *the subject of the main clause.*	Impressed by the newspaper stories, we felt that war was inevitable.

Other revisions of these dangling modifiers are possible:

While I was walking downtown, I saw a streetcar jump the tracks. (This revision combines both methods suggested earlier.)

I recorded the information required of me; then my adviser checked my card to see that I had followed instructions. (This revision avoids the dangling modifier by changing the opening phrase to a main clause.)

You may qualify for the position by passing a rigorous examination. (This revision changes the phrase to a main clause and reduces the original main clause to a phrase. Since the final phrase modifies the verb, it does not dangle.)

Because we were impressed by the newspaper stories we felt that war was inevitable.

(or)

We were so impressed by the newspaper stories that we felt war was inevitable.

419

Sometimes a dangling modifier begins with an **elliptical clause** — a subordinate clause, some elements of which are not expressed. The simplest revision of a dangling elliptical clause is to supply the necessary elements and complete the clause.

Dangling Modifier	*Revised Version*
When only five years old, my mother died.	When I was only five years old, my mother died.
While still of preschool age, my father began daily batting practice with me.	While I was still of preschool age, my father began daily batting practice with me.
Although working full time on an outside job, my grades remained good.	Although I was working full time on an outside job, my grades remained good.

As all these examples suggest, the most troublesome dangling modifiers are those beginning with an introductory verbal phrase or an elliptical clause. A dangling modifier at the end of a sentence is more likely to be awkward or unemphatic than ambiguous.

Dangling Modifier	*Explanation*	*Revised Version*
He took a full program of studies during each summer session, *thus graduating in three years.*	*The main idea in this sentence is that the student graduated in three years. Since a main clause is grammatically more important than a phrase, the main idea should go in the main clause.*	By taking a full program of studies during each summer session he was able to graduate in three years.

✔ Improve the following sentences by revising the dangling modifiers.

1. Upon hearing a sharp click the suds subsided and the dial on the top of the washing machine read "drain."
2. Working in a drugstore, several professors chat with me every day.
3. After signing for all your classes, the next place to go is the finance office.
4. When in high school, classes were dull and monotonous.
5. When placing these men under arrest, comic books were usually found in their possession.
6. By getting your purpose clearly in mind at the beginning, the actual writing will be easier.
7. Without expecting a reply, a letter was written to the President.
8. Being very tired, the walk home took much too long.
9. By improving the English Department a student would not only be prepared for college English but for any subject.
10. After rushing to get to the station on time the information clerk said that the train would be more than an hour late.

11. Completely unaware that the landing gear had been damaged and that a crash landing at the end of the flight was inevitable, the plane, with its carefree passengers, sailed confidently through the night.

12. After having made all these plans and preparations and having such high expectations, the party was pretty much of a dud.

13. The car failed to observe the curve sign, thus losing control and going over the embankment.

14. Oddly enough, school was no more a drudgery, resulting in better grades.

15. I believe that, by delaying marriage until after your college graduation, the chances of happiness are much better.

S10 *Shifts in Subjects and Verbs*

Unintentionally shifting a sentence from one pattern to another results in awkward, inconsistent structures. The following kinds of inconsistencies arise from awkward shifts in the form of the subject or verb.

a. Awkward shifts in subject usually take one of two forms: unnecessary shift of subject within a paragraph, and shifts between personal and impersonal pronoun subjects within a sentence.

In the examples below, the grammatical subjects are italicized.

Shifted Subjects	*Explanation*	*Revised Version*
When *one* gets through with a three-hour examination *you* are exhausted.	*The subject shifts from the impersonal pronoun* one *to the second personal pronoun* you. *A shift from* one *to* he *is conventional but the shift to* you *is not. Any of the three revisions at the right would be an improvement.*	When *one* gets through . . . *one* is exhausted. When one gets through . . . *he* is exhausted. When *you* get through . . . *you* are exhausted.
The *worries* about entrance examinations leave the minds of the students before *they* leave for the campus. The last *days* are spent shopping for clothes during the day and	*Although these three sentences all deal with the same logical subject (the students' activities before leaving for college), the paragraph has five grammatical subjects. This unnecessary shifting of the subject weakens the unity of the paragraph. The revision at the right*	During the last week before leaving for campus, *students* spend their days shopping for clothes and their nights attending farewell parties with their friends. *They* have

Shifted Subjects	Explanation	Revised Version
gallivanting with friends at night. Their *families* receive little attention, and entrance *examinations* are no longer thought of.	*reduces the subjects to two forms: the noun* students *and the pronoun* they.	little time to spend with their families and no longer worry about entrance examinations.
I did not like to refuse his invitation, but a *person* can't spend all their time going to shows.	*Although the writer is the logical subject of both clauses, the grammatical subject shifts from* I *to* person, *and the pronoun* their *shifts in the second clause from singular to plural. The author would have been wiser to use the first personal pronoun throughout.*	*I* did not like to refuse his invitation, but *I* can't spend all my time going to shows.

b. Avoid unnecessary shifts in the forms of the verbs. Keep the tenses consistent and especially avoid shifting from active to passive voice.

In the following examples the verb forms are in italics.

Shifted Verb Forms	Explanation	Consistent Verb Forms
The older girls *had* a coke party to get us acquainted and it *was* deeply *appreciated* by me.	*The shift from active voice in the first clause to passive in the second is unnecessary and awkward. The revision subordinates the second clause and keeps both verbs in the active voice.*	I *appreciated* the coke party which the older girls *gave* to get us acquainted.
As centuries *passed,* the dress patterns *become* more and more complicated.	*The tense changes from past to present. Since the changes in dress were taking place while the centuries were passing, the verbs in both clauses should be in the same tense.*	As centuries *passed,* the dress patterns *became* more and more complicated.
He *said* he *will call* for me at eight.	*The author is confusing the tenses for direct and indirect discourse. Either form at the right will serve.*	He *said* he *would call* for me at eight. He *said,* "I will call for you at eight."

✔ Revise the following student sentences to remove the awkward shifts in subjects or verbs.

1. It often makes one shudder at the sights you see.

2. You know it's really very odd how a person can have so many different feelings about something they plan to do.

3. I have experienced the strange sensation of losing one's wallet. When something like this happens you do not know what to do.

4. Upon completion of my program I'm informed that all the sections I wanted have been closed.

5. I was told to hurry over to Civil Engineering Hall or I may not get what I wanted.

6. My high school days taught me the value of learning to get along with others. As you worked with others you learned to accept responsibilities and to be a good follower. We were supposed to learn to be both followers and leaders.

7. There I was with a stack of papers, cards, envelopes, a time table, and a catalog, and he wants me to stop and sign my name.

8. I asked Dad if I may borrow the car for the evening.

9. They had known hardship at first hand, for the dangers and misery of war had been experienced by them.

10. To do the author justice, a good job of exposing the foolishness of the English aristocracy was done in several instances in the book.

11. Faith means to have complete confidence in someone, even if they are under suspicion.

12. He said that we would be late anyway, so let's go ahead and not worry.

13. We talked over the problem for an hour but no decision was reached.

14. One way of judging the maturity of a person is to find out how well they are able to govern themselves.

15. I have been making these medallions since I was a junior in high school and I found it a satisfying hobby.

16. In choosing a mate for the rest of one's life certain qualities are searched for according to your individual preferences and standards.

17. There are a great many socially timid students on the campus. The University tries to help them. They are urged to join a group with similar interests. With the variety of possibilities offered, success is inevitable. An adjustment of this kind is every bit as important as academic success.

18. After paying my tuition and having my picture taken, an invitation to subscribe to the *Daily* was extended to me.

19. After an hour we came up with what my roommate called the perfect program. It looked awfully difficult to me, but if she said it was good what can a new freshman do but accept it?

20. To me dependability means simply what the word itself says — being able to depend on a person, whether it be simply to remember to pick up a loaf of bread at the grocery store, or whether it is depending on them to provide a home and love for your children.

S11 *Incomplete Constructions*

The omission of words necessary for a clear understanding of the thought often results in a difficult or unidiomatic sentence.

Careless omissions often occur in making a clean copy of a paper, since copying is a mechanical task which takes little attention to meaning. For this reason, the final copy should be carefully reread before it is turned in.

Other omissions are the result of confusion about the structure of a sentence. The constructions most likely to be incompletely written are illustrated below.

Incomplete	*Explanation*	*Complete*
We searched through all our pockets, but no money.	*Incomplete main clause. The conjunction* but *requires a main clause to balance the sentence. The verb* found *cannot be omitted.*	We searched through all our pockets, but *found* no money.
I don't like the crowd which he associates.	*Omitted preposition. With a choice of two forms of the subordinate clause —* with which he associates *or* he associates with — *the writer has failed to supply* with *in either position.*	I don't like the crowd *with* which he associates. (or) I don't like the crowd he associates *with*.
Statistics show that college men like their studies better than women.	*Omitted verb resulting in a possible ambiguity. What is being compared is* not *studies* and *women, but* men *and* women. *To avoid ambiguous comparison, the clause having* women *as the subject must be given a verb.*	Statistics show that college men like their studies better than women *do*.
Their hope is the child has wandered off with some older companions who will take care of him.	*Omitted subordinating connective. While such connectives may often be omitted without causing difficulty, an omission which allows the subject of the subordinate clause to be misread as the complement or object of the verb in the main clause should be avoided.*	Their hope is *that* the child has wandered off with some older companions who will take care of him.

Incomplete	*Explanation*	*Complete*
Today is as hot, if not hotter, than any day this summer.	*Confused comparison. This construction confuses two idioms — as hot as and hotter than. Since these idioms take different prepositions, than will not serve for both. Possibly the best way to express this comparison is to avoid this construction entirely by using one of the substitutes shown at the right.*	Today is one of the hottest days of the summer. (or) Today is at least as hot as any day we have had this summer. (or) Today may be the hottest day we have had this summer.

✔ Revise the following sentences to complete the incomplete constructions.

1. He is as old, if not older, than I.
2. He understands German better than his brother.
3. She is as proud of the choir as the students.
4. I advertised my car in the papers, but no response.
5. I have and always will say that he is innocent.
6. The state he wants to live in his old age is California.
7. The trouble was the fuel pipe was clogged.
8. He was patient and tolerant of the children's bickering.
9. It made her mother from a girl to a wrinkled old woman in twelve short years.
10. Nowadays glasses often add rather than detract from a girl's looks.
11. He is as good, if not better, than any guard in the conference.
12. Having eaten and my schedule once again altered, I went back to finish registration.
13. She would rather live in a large city than the country.
14. When at a party a man should show respect and attention to his wife.
15. Azaleas are easier to grow in the South than the Midwest.

WO · Word Order

WO1 *Normal Order and Accepted Inversions*

For word order in the normal English sentence, see Chapter 5, pages 105–106. For word order in the principal English sentence patterns, see section **S1** of this handbook, pages 397–399.

NORMAL ORDER

The normal order of words in English sentences may be summarized as follows:

1. Except in questions and expletive-type sentences (*There is a ray of hope*), the standard order of the main function units is subject-verb-object or complement.

2. Single adjectives precede, and adjective phrases follow, their headwords (a *trusted* man *of the people*).

3. Adverbs usually follow verbs, but may come elsewhere. Adverbs modifying adjectives or other adverbs precede the headword (He is *very* old. They dance *remarkably* well).

4. Main clauses usually precede subordinate clauses, but the following exceptions are common:

   a. Adjective clauses follow their headwords immediately (The man *who did it* should be punished).

   b. Adverbial clauses, especially conditional clauses, often precede the main clause (*If you do that,* you'll be sorry).

   c. Noun clauses acting as subjects or objects occupy the subject or object position (*That he will accept* is taken for granted. He says *that you are afraid*).

5. Closely related elements are kept as close together as possible. Thus a preposition immediately precedes the object and its modifiers (the top *of the highest mountain*); modifiers remain close to their headwords; and subject-verb, verb-object, and pronoun-antecedent combinations are not separated unless the special needs of the sentence require. In short, the order of the elements in a sentence should reveal their relationship.

ACCEPTED INVERSIONS

Any inversion of normal word order tends to attract attention and to emphasize the inverted expression. If this emphasis is desirable and if the departure from normal order is not outlandish or unidiomatic, a writer may gain interesting variety in sentence structure by moderate use of inversion. The commonest inversions for emphasis are as follows:

a. If it does not create misinterpretation or awkwardness, an element may be transposed from its normal order for emphasis.

Normal Order	*Emphatic Inversion*
The skies cleared *slowly*.	*Slowly* the skies cleared.
No leaf stirred *in all the forest*.	*In all the forest* no leaf stirred.
He threw *out* the runner.	He threw the runner *out*.
That is a good country *from* which to come.	That is a good country to come *from*.
There is no excuse *for him*.	*For him* there is no excuse.

b. For stylistic reasons, a normal sentence may be inverted into a periodic sentence.

Normal	*Periodic*
Think only this of me *if I should die*.	*If I should die*, think only this of me.
I broke the window *in order to unlock the car door*.	*In order to unlock the car door*, I broke the window.

For a more detailed discussion of the periodic sentence see page 109.

c. If no vagueness or awkwardness results, related elements, which normally would not be separated, may be interrupted by absolute or modifying constructions.

Interruption	*Explanation*
These, *I am told*, were his last words.	*Absolute between subject and verb.*
Their conduct *in this situation* was heroic.	*Modifying phrase between subject and verb.*
Related elements, *which normally would not be separated*, may be interrupted.	*Nonrestrictive modifying clause between subject and verb. This particular interruption is normal order.*
He answered, *with obvious annoyance*, that the story was false.	*Modifying phrase between verb and complement.*
Don't *under any conditions* make such a promise.	*Modifying phrase between parts of a verb.*

WO 2 *Ambiguous Order*

The relationship between a modifying word, phrase, or clause and the element it modifies must be clear.

If a modifier is so placed that it could modify either of two elements, its reference will be ambiguous. If the ambiguity is complete, the reader will be unable to tell which meaning was intended. More frequently he will be able to make the correct interpretation but will be conscious of the writer's ineptitude.

Ambiguous Order	*Explanation*	*Revised Order*
They talked about going on a second honeymoon *frequently,* but they never did.	Frequently *is closer to* going *than to* talked *and could modify either. It thus looks both ways, or "squints." Placing it immediately before or after* talked *removes the ambiguity.*	They talked *frequently* about going on a second honeymoon, but they never did.
The car is in the garage *which he smashed.*	*Since conventional order places adjective clauses after the nouns they modify, a reader is tempted to take* garage *as the antecedent of* which. *Putting the modifying clause immediately after* car *removes this possibility.*	The car *which he smashed* is in the garage.
There is a lecture tonight about juvenile delinquency *in the student lounge.*	*The italicized phrase was intended to modify the main clause but its position suggests that it locates the scene of the delinquency rather than of the lecture.*	Tonight there is a lecture *in the student lounge* about juvenile delinquency.

✔ Remove possible ambiguities in the following sentences by changing the position of faulty modifiers.

1. Fortunately, the fire was put out before any serious damage was done by the volunteer firemen.
2. A car came down the street decked with ribbons.
3. I listened while he talked attentively.
4. Everyone stared at the girl who was dancing with the dean in the low cut gown.
5. There was a noisy disturbance when the speaker said that at the back of the hall.
6. Humphrey Bogart played the part of the man who was corrupted by gold superbly.
7. He looked at the boy with sad eyes.
8. My roommate brought me the book from the library that I wanted.
9. At one time his neighbors said he had been in jail.
10. No one would treat his father like that unless he was irresponsible.

WO 3   *Awkward Separation of Elements*

Although related elements in a sentence may be separated (see page 427), there should usually be no unnecessary separation of subject and verb, verb and object or complement, modifier and its headword, or preposition and its object.

Unnecessary separation of such closely related elements distorts the sentence pattern and interferes with ease of reading.

Awkward Separation	Explanation	Revised Order
My *father*, after considering what the trip would cost and how long it would take, *refused* to go.	*Awkward separation of subject and verb. The unnecessary interruption of the main clause by a phrase and two subordinate clauses distorts the structure of the main clause.*	After considering what the trip would cost and how long it would take, my father refused to go.
The evidence *shows*, if you examine it carefully and impartially, *that the best baseball is played in the National League.*	*Awkward separation of noun and its object. The reader has to leap over the if-clause to find the object of shows.*	A careful and impartial examination of the evidence shows that the best baseball is played in the National League.
He gave the *sweater* to his girl *that he had won in track*.	*Awkward separation of verb and its modifying clause. This kind of separation resembles the ambiguous modifiers discussed on page 427.*	He gave the sweater that he had won in track to his girl. (or) He gave his girl the sweater that he had won in track.
We *have* since then *had* no more trouble.	*Awkward separation of two parts of verb by modifying phrase.*	Since then, we have had no more trouble.
I am neither in support *of* nor opposed to *the bill*.	*Awkward separation of preposition of and its object. The revision at the right is the best way of expressing the idea.*	I neither support nor oppose the bill.

The **split infinitive** often provokes criticism in college writing. An infinitive phrase is "split" when an adverb separates its parts (*to* almost *laugh, to have* never *tried*). In some sentences (I decided *to* almost *quit*) the split infinitive gives a wrong emphasis and is awkward. In others (The prosecution failed *to* completely *demolish* the alibi), the intervening modifier gives a more precise emphasis or is more idiomatic than if the position of the modifier were changed. Although neither the facts of usage nor the judgment of grammarians justifies blanket condemnation of split infinitives, the safest practice for a college student is to place the modifier before or after the infinitive, whichever position gives the emphasis he wishes. For example:

Split Infinitive	*Revision*
He tried *to* quickly *retreat*.	Quickly he tried *to retreat*.
	(or)
	He tried *to retreat* quickly.

✔ Revise the following sentences to eliminate any unnecessary separation.

1. Her father, even, admits that she is extravagant.
2. Dad promised that he would in plenty of time get the tickets.
3. I was until yesterday of that opinion.
4. Herself more than others she will hurt by her conduct.
5. He is reported to recently have denied the story.
6. He had no desire to or expectation of getting married.
7. Every one of my instructors, I am firmly of the opinion, acts as though his course was the only one I am taking.
8. Although some kinds of extracurricular activities are overrated for some students, those are often socially valuable that give a shy girl experience in working with both men and women.
9. I was so surprised that I forgot what I intended to say to her when she smiled.
10. He said while he did not object to our going that he would like to stay home.

WO 4   *Unemphatic Order*

Since the emphasis on any sentence element often depends on its position, a writer must be careful not to give too much or too little emphasis by placing an element in a wrong position. The following precautions should help you to avoid the most frequent faults of emphasis in student writing. See also the discussion of *Emphasis* on pages 117–121, and of the periodic sentence in Chapter 5, pages 109–112.

a. Do not place minor ideas at the ends of sentences.

The most emphatic position in an English sentence is the end; the next most emphatic position is the beginning; the least emphatic is the middle. Unimportant ideas coming at the end of a sentence will be made unduly conspicuous by their position, and the sentence will seem to run down hill. Notice the contrast in effectiveness in the following sentences.

Unemphatic Order	*Emphatic Order*
Last night someone stole our car while we were in the theater.	Last night, while we were in the theater, someone stole our car.
She is innocent in my opinion.	In my opinion she is innocent.
Nothing can be done, however.	Nothing, however, can be done.
He is going to propose, I think.	I think he is going to propose.

b. Do not weaken the force of an important concluding statement by reducing it to a participial phrase.

Many a good sentence ends with a participial phrase, but to use such a phrase for an idea which is important enough to deserve a main clause often creates a lame ending. For example, in

> He fell from the roof, *thus breaking his neck.*

the italicized phrase is at least as important as the main clause, yet it is grammatically subordinate and trails off weakly. The idea in the phrase is important enough to come at the end of the sentence, but it deserves the dignity of a stronger grammatical form:

> He fell from the roof and *broke his neck.*

c. Do not place a conjunctive adverb at the beginning of a sentence unless you deliberately wish to emphasize it.

Conjunctive adverbs — *however, moreover, nevertheless, therefore,* etc. — serve in a double capacity. As conjunctions they connect; as adverbs they modify. But they are relatively weak modifiers referring to the whole sentence rather than any element of it, and consistently placing them at the start of the sentence may give them too much emphasis. If they deserve emphasis, as the third example below may do, they may be used to start the sentence; but they are usually better near, not at, the beginning.

> I am willing to advise you. I will not, *however,* accept responsibility for what you do.
> He thinks she deceived him deliberately; he is *therefore* in no mood for a reconciliation.
> We have repeatedly tried to make friends with them and have been consistently repulsed; *nevertheless,* I shall try again.

d. Do not misrepresent meaning by putting a modifier in the wrong position.

Since a modifier usually seems to refer to the nearest referent, be careful that the position of modifiers gives the meaning you want to convey. The following sentence can mean quite different things depending on the position of the adverb.

They *secretly* intend to be married.	They intend to be married *secretly.*

In the first sentence the position of the modifier emphasizes the intention; in the second, it emphasizes the nature of the ceremony. Either meaning is possible, but the one expressed depends on the position of the modifier.

The following contrasts also show how much the position of a modifier can affect meaning.

John *just* made it.	*Just* John made it.
Mary knows *only* the date.	*Only* Mary knows the date.
Until today they promised to stay.	They promised to stay *until today*.
Even Mother is annoyed with him.	Mother is *even* annoyed with him.

e. Do not overindulge in inversion as a short cut to a "literary" style.

Inexperienced but ambitious writers sometimes try to create a literary style by using a great many self-conscious inversions. While unusual word order is arresting, strained or distorted inversion that does little but call attention to itself is more a vice than a virtue. Inverted order is exceptional order. It should be used deliberately and with restraint.

Affected	*Natural*
Pleasant were those days.	Those were pleasant days.
Little cared I what my parents said.	I cared little what my parents said.
Learn he must to appreciate his own deficiencies.	He must learn to appreciate his own deficiencies.

✔ Revise the following sentences to avoid misplaced emphasis.

1. The chairman said that the committee would continue in session until all business had been dispensed with, if there was no objection.
2. He scored through center after two unsuccessful plunges, thus tying the game.
3. I would have liked to take her to a movie but I did not even have a dollar; moreover, my only decent suit was at the cleaners'.
4. I almost read the whole novel last night. I could have finished it had I started an hour earlier, I believe.
5. Time for my assignments I never seem to find, thus being always behind.
6. Neither of the candidates intends to speak here, as far as I know.
7. He said that I could come over and listen to his records tonight, if I had time.
8. She graduated in three years with highest honors from the University.

F · Forms of Words

F1   *Wrong Principal Part*

a. Use the accepted principal part.

The use of the wrong principal part (*blowed* for *blew* or *seen* for *saw*) is often an advertisement of nonstandard speech habits. As we pointed out on page 394, the great majority of English verbs form the past tense and past participle by adding *-ed* to the first principal part. All exceptions are specifically listed in a good dictionary (see page 171). The following list contains the principal parts of irregular verbs which cause most trouble in college writing.

Present	*Past*	*Past Participle*
am, is, are	was, were	been
bear	bore	borne
beat	beat	beaten
begin	began	begun
bite	bit	bitten
blow	blew	blown
break	broke	broken
bring	brought	brought
burst	burst	burst
cast	cast	cast
choose	chose	chosen
come	came	come
deal	dealt	dealt
do	did	done
draw	drew	drawn
drink	drank	drunk
eat	ate	eaten
fall	fell	fallen
fly	flew	flown
forsake	forsook	forsaken
freeze	froze	frozen
give	gave	given
go	went	gone
grow	grew	grown
hang[1]	hung	hung

[1] Notice that the verb *to hang*, meaning execute, is regular: *hang, hanged, hanged.*

433

Present	Past	Past Participle
have	had	had
know	knew	known
lay	laid	laid
lie	lay	lain
ride	rode	ridden
ring	rang (rung)	rung
rise	rose	risen
run	ran	run
see	saw	seen
shake	shook	shaken
shoe	shod	shod
shrink	shrank (shrunk)	shrunk
sing	sang (sung)	sung
sink	sank (sunk)	sunk
slay	slew	slain
slink	slunk	slunk
speak	spoke	spoken
spin	spun	spun
spring	sprang (sprung)	sprung
steal	stole	stolen
strive	strove	striven
swear	swore	sworn
swim	swam	swum
take	took	taken
teach	taught	taught
tear	tore	torn
throw	threw	thrown
wear	wore	worn
weave	wove	woven
win	won	won
write	wrote	written

b. Distinguish between the forms for the past tense and the past participle.

In verb phrases the past participle, not the past tense form, should follow an auxiliary verb (is *done,* has *been*). Except when the verb is acting as an auxiliary (*had* gone, *was* crying), its past tense form is not used in combination with another verb.

Confusion of Forms	*Conventional Forms*
It is *broke.*	It is *broken.*
These tires are *wore* out.	These tires are *worn* out.
He has *began* all over again.	He has *begun* all over again.
I *seen* him do it.	I *saw* him do it.
The river is *froze* solid.	The river is *frozen* solid.
Everybody has *went* home.	Everybody has *gone* home.
Have you *wrote* to him?	Have you *written* to him?
They *come* back yesterday.	They *came* back yesterday.

✔ Write out and hand in to your instructor the conventional verb form in each of the following sentences:

1. They said they had (went, gone) home.
2. I was told that you had (come, came) to an agreement.
3. Prices have (fell, fallen) considerably.
4. As soon as I had (wrote, written) the letter I mailed it.
5. They must have (chosen, chose) their own way.
6. I (seen, saw) him yesterday.
7. Beatty has (run, ran) the mile several times under four minutes.
8. One of the prisoners was (hung, hanged).
9. That is the best horse I have ever (rode, ridden).
10. She is reported to have (drunk, drank) poison.
11. The wind (blew, blowed) all night.
12. I would have (swore, sworn) that he was innocent.
13. This is the third time he has (broken, broke) that arm.
14. All the tomato plants were badly (froze, frozen).
15. I would have called if I had (knew, known) you were sick.
16. I have never (saw, seen) anything so vicious.
17. After a while we (begun, began) to get tired.
18. It was a good fight. He was (beaten, beat) fairly.
19. He was (bit, bitten) by the dog.
20. The plane has (flew, flown) out of sight.

c. Distinguish between the uses and forms of *lie, lay, rise, raise, sit, set.*

The principal parts of these verbs are:

Present	Present Participle	Past	Past Participle
lie	lying	lay	lain
lay	laying	laid	laid
rise	rising	rose	risen
raise	raising	raised	raised
sit	sitting	sat	sat
set	setting	set	set

As grouped above, these verbs can be seen to be three pairs, each pair having principal parts which are similar, though not the same, in form and general meaning. The chief difference in each pair is that the first verb is intransitive, the second transitive; that is, the first needs no object to complete the action of the verb; the second does need an object. Thus, whether we *lay* a rug, *raise* an alarm, or *set* a bone, we always *lay, raise,* or *set something.*[2] But we never *lie, rise,* or *sit* anything. Determining the accepted form, therefore, depends on the answers to two questions: (1) Does the sentence require the transitive or the intransitive verb? (2) What are the principal parts of the required verb?

[2] Notice, however, that *The sun sets early now* is an exception to this generalization. In this sentence *sets* is used intransitively.

In the examples that follow, the unacceptable forms at the left are revised at the right.

Unacceptable	*Explanation*	*Accepted*
We *laid* breathless with suspense.	*The sentence contains no object; therefore the intransitive verb is wanted. The past form of* lie *is* lay.	We *lay* breathless with suspense.
It was *setting* on the table.	*No object; therefore intransitive form* sitting *is required.*	It was *sitting* on the table.
They have *lain* the carpet.	Carpet *is an object; therefore transitive* laid *is required.*	They have *laid* the carpet.
It has been *laying* there all night.	*No object; therefore intransitive* lying *is required.*	It has been *lying* there all night.
After a while he *raised* up and walked to the bench.	*No object. Intransitive* rose *is required.*	After a while he *rose* and walked to the bench.

✔ Write out and hand in to your instructor the conventional verb form in each of the following sentences:

1. They were (sitting, setting) the chairs in a circle.
2. The hat was (lying, laying) in the corner.
3. We (lay, laid) the money on the counter and left.
4. We (lay, laid) on the pier and dozed.
5. I have (laid, lain) out your new suit.
6. I would like you to (rise, raise) my wages.
7. Go out and (rise, raise) the flag.
8. Finally, the curtain (raised, rose).
9. They (raised, rose) the curtain promptly.
10. I could (sit, set) here all day.
11. It was (sitting, setting) there a minute ago.
12. (Sit, set) down and rest for a while.
13. (Sit, set) the book on the table.
14. These tools have been left (lying, laying) in the rain.
15. They were (laying, lying) in wait for us.
16. He (raised, rose) himself on his elbow.
17. (Sit, set) up and take this.
18. She has (laid, lain) down for a rest.
19. Clothes were (lying, laying) all over the room.
20. He is out (rising, raising) the money.

F2 *Tense Forms*

USE OF TENSES

In theory, verbs are inflected to show the time at which an action occurs. In practice, the tense of an English verb sometimes has little relation to the time of the action. The present tense may refer to past, present, or future actions, or to actions that run through past, present, and future, as the following sentences show:

> While Sharkey *is claiming* a foul, Dempsey *knocks* him out. (Tense, present; time, 1927.)
> This fall Liston finally *gets* a chance at the title. (Tense, present; time, future.)
> At the moment he *objects*. (Tense, present; time, present.)
> History always *repeats* itself. (Tense, present; time, past, present, and future.)

Moreover, English has ways of indicating time by idiom rather than by tense. For example, in the following sentences the events have not yet occurred, yet not once is a future tense used. The "progressive" present, various uses of the infinitive, and adverbs of time are used instead.

I am going to do it tomorrow.
We are to see them next week.
They are to be married this summer.
I expect to hear from him in a day or two.
Be sure to call me when you come to town.

The uses of the six basic tenses are as follows:

Simple Present. The chief uses of the simple present tense are to indicate present action, action which occurs at all times (the timeless present), and past action which, for dramatic purposes, is described as occurring in the present (historical present).

Present time:

Bill *is* absent; his father *is* ill.

Timeless present:

The rain *falls* alike on the just and the unjust.
Nature *abhors* a vacuum.
The sum of the angles in a triangle *equals* 180 degrees.

Historical present:

> Finally, Caesar *makes* his decision. He *gives* the order, and his troops *begin* the fateful march to the Rubicon.

Present Perfect. The present perfect tense indicates that the action has recently been completed.

> She *has broken* her engagement.
> They *have built* a new house.
> He *has moved* to New York.

Simple Past. The simple past tense is used to indicate an action which may have occurred at any time in the past. It therefore is not so close to the present as the present perfect.

> She *broke* her engagement.
> They *built* a new house.
> He *moved* to New York.

Notice that the use of an adverb of time along with the simple past tense achieves the same effect as the use of the present perfect:

> She broke her engagement yesterday.
> They recently built a new house.

Past Perfect. The past perfect is used to indicate that, of two past actions, one took place before the other.

> He *had been* sick only a few days when he died.
> I *had left* before she arrived.
> We *had expected* little, but we received nothing.

Simple Future. The simple future is used to indicate an action still to occur.

> He *will sail* tomorrow.
> They *will try* to persuade you.

Future Perfect. The future perfect is used to indicate that, of two future actions, one will occur before the other.

> By the time you get there they *will have gone*.
> He *will have spent* all his allowance by the end of the week.

The inflection (conjugation) of the indicative mood of typical regular and irregular verbs is given below:

	Regular verb, *to talk*		Irregular verb, *to write*	
	Singular	*Plural*	*Singular*	*Plural*
Simple	1. I talk	1. we talk	1. I write	1. we write
Present	2. you talk	2. you talk	2. you write	2. you write
	3. he talks	3. they talk	3. he writes	3. they write

Method of forming: Use first principal part unchanged for all forms except to add *s* in third person singular.

Present	1. have talked	1. have talked	1. have written	1. have written
Perfect	2. have talked	2. have talked	2. have written	2. have written
	3. *has* talked	3. have talked	3. *has* written	3. have written

Method of forming: Add past participle to simple present tense of verb *to have*. Except for third person singular, forms are the same throughout.

Simple	1. talked	1. talked	1. wrote	1. wrote
Past	2. talked	2. talked	2. wrote	2. wrote
	3. talked	3. talked	3. wrote	3. wrote

Method of forming: Third principal part unchanged throughout.

Past	1. had talked	1. had talked	1. had written	1. had written
Perfect	2. had talked	2. had talked	2. had written	2. had written
	3. had talked	3. had talked	3. had written	3. had written

Method of forming: Add past participle to simple past tense of *to have*.

Simple	1. will talk	1. will talk	1. will write	1. will write
Future	2. will talk	2. will talk	2. will write	2. will write
	3. will talk	3. will talk	3. will write	3. will write

Method of forming: Add first principal part to *will*. In formal usage *shall* is sometimes used instead of *will* in the first person singular and plural.[3]

Future	will have talked (same form in all persons and numbers)
Perfect	will have written (same form in all persons and numbers)

Method of forming: Add past participle to *will have*. In formal usage *shall* is sometimes used instead of *will* in the first person singular and plural.

a. Avoid illogical or unconventional sequence of tenses.

1. Keep the tenses of main clauses consistent.

Do not shift needlessly from present to past or from historical present to simple past.

Inconsistent	*Explanation*	*Consistent*
She laughed, and I asked her what she knew about him. She *laughs* again, this time much louder.	*In the first sentence all verbs are in the past tense; but in the second sentence* laughs *is present. There is no reason for the shift.*	She laughed, and I asked her what she knew about him. She *laughed* again, this time much louder.

[3] For comment on the *shall-will* distinction, see page 443.

Inconsistent	*Explanation*	*Consistent*
For five rounds the young challenger danced and ducked and jabbed and piled up points. Then the champion found an opening – and Bam! The fight *is* over.	*All the verbs except the last are in the past tense. The last sentence shifts to historical present tense. Either that tense or the simple past should have been used throughout.*	For five rounds the young challenger danced and ducked and jabbed and piled up points. Then the champion found an opening – and Bam! The fight *was* over.

2. Keep the tense of a subordinate clause in logical sequence with that of the main clause.

Illogical Sequence	*Explanation*	*Logical Sequence*
They *have made* so much money last year that they bought a second store.	*The present perfect* (have made) *suggests a more recent action than the simple past* (bought); *it is illogical to use the present perfect for the earlier action.*	They *made* so much money last year that they *have bought* a second store.
Before I was introduced to her I *heard* rumors of her unsavory reputation.	*Since the rumors came before the introduction, the past perfect tense should be used in the main clause.*	Before I was introduced to her I *had heard* rumors of her unsavory reputation.

3. In converting direct discourse to indirect discourse observe the conventional change in tense.

Direct discourse reports the actual words of the speaker, and quoted verbs should be in the tense the speaker used. When direct discourse is converted to indirect discourse, the tenses of the original quotation are, whenever possible, pushed one stage further into the past. Thus an original present tense form becomes past and an original past becomes past perfect. Since there is no tense more past than past perfect, an original verb in that tense does not change.

Direct Discourse	*Explanation*	*Indirect Discourse*
He said, "I *want* to read that novel."	*Change simple present to simple past.*	He said that he *wanted* to read that novel.
He said, "I *wanted* to read that novel yesterday."	*Change simple past to past perfect.*	He said that he *had wanted* to read that novel yesterday.

Direct Discourse	Explanation	Indirect Discourse
He said, "I *had wanted* to read that novel until I *saw* the movie."	*Leave the verbs as they are. There is no way to make* had wanted *more past than it is, and to change* saw *to* had seen *would destroy the sequence of tenses.*	He said that he *had wanted* to read that novel until he *saw* the movie.

The following examples contrast faulty and accepted conversion from direct to indirect discourse.

Direct Discourse	Faulty Conversion	Accepted Conversion
I said, "He *is* a good financial risk."	I said he *is* a good financial risk.	I said he *was* a good financial risk.
I asked, "*Have* you *consulted* your physician?"	I asked if he *consulted* his physician.	I asked if he *had consulted* his physician.

4. Observe the conventional tense relationships between verbs and verbals.

The tense of a verbal is not determined by the tense of the verb in the main clause. Regardless of the tense of the verb, a present participle is used to express an action occurring at the same time as that of the verb. A perfect participle expresses time before that of the verb. A present infinitive indicates the same time or a time later than that of the verb. A perfect infinitive suggests time before that of the verb.

Rounding the last turn he *was* ahead by two yards.	The present participle (*rounding*) and the past tense verb refer to simultaneous actions.
Having finished housecleaning she *washed* her hair.	The perfect participle (*having finished*) refers to an action before that of the verb (*washed*).
I *tried to telephone* you.	The verb (*tried*) and the present infinitive (*to telephone*) refer to actions occurring at the same time.
I *expect to hear* from him tomorrow.	The expectation is now; the hearing has yet to occur. Therefore the present infinitive refers to a time later than that of the verb.
They *are reported to have adopted* a child.	The perfect infinitive points to a time before the reporting.

Unconventional Sequence	Explanation	Conventional Sequence
Asking the blessing, we began to eat.	*Since the blessing was asked before the eating began, the perfect participle is required.*	*Having asked* the blessing, we began to eat.

Unconventional Sequence	*Explanation*	*Conventional Sequence*
Having faced the spectators, the referee signaled a holding penalty.	*Since both actions took place at the same time, the present participle is required.*	*Facing* the spectators, the referee signaled a holding penalty.
We meant to *have told* you earlier.	*The perfect infinitive suggests that the telling occurred before the intention. The present infinitive is the required form.*	We meant *to tell* you earlier.
I am sorry *to overlook* that fact.	*Since the overlooking occurred before the regret, the perfect infinitive should be used.*	I am sorry *to have overlooked* that fact.

✔ Revise the following sentences to correct any illogical sequence of tenses.

1. There is little chance of promotion in that job unless you had a college degree.
2. While the outlook wasn't hopeless, it is discouraging.
3. We wanted to have reported the robbery earlier, but we thought we had better wait until we are sure.
4. Before I arrived they had a serious quarrel.
5. I asked if she has seen him recently.
6. She answered, "I had not seen him for more than a year."
7. We wondered what they are thinking now.
8. Finishing the job, he put away his tools.
9. For years now they had been good friends but they disagree more and more frequently.
10. He asked if I consider him a good teacher.
11. I said that I thought he is better than average.
12. Meeting Bill's wife, I have asked her when he would be home.
13. She said that he had been coming next Saturday.
14. I intended to have ignored the gossip, but I could not.
15. They sat up all night studying, having hoped to get at least a B on the final examination.
16. I would have liked to have seen that movie.

b. In the future tense indicate either by context or by the appropriate auxiliary whether you imply simple futurity or determination.

1. Shall — Will

Whether to use *shall* or *will* in the future tense is a vexed question, partly because usage is divided, and partly because many people have an allegiance to the *shall-will* distinction that transcends the evidence of usage. Hence teachers and textbooks (including this one) often devote more attention to this question than it warrants.

The distinction is generally stated as follows: when the verb is intended to express only the idea that an action will occur in the future (simple futurity), *shall* is used in the first person, singular and plural, and *will* in the other two persons (I *shall* write tomorrow; they *will* probably be home next week). When the verb is intended to express determination, resolve, or compulsion, as well as futurity, *will* is used in the first person and *shall* in the other two (We *will* go regardless of the consequences; they *shall* pay for their negligence).

Although many careful users of English observe this distinction, many equally careful ones do not. For example, Winston Churchill, speaking on a most formal occasion (an address in the House of Commons after the evacuation of Dunkirk in World War II) consistently used *shall* in the first person to express determination:

> . . . we shall not flag or fail. We shall go on to the end, we shall fight in France, we shall fight in the seas and oceans, we shall fight with growing confidence and growing strength in the air, we shall defend our island, whatever the cost may be, we shall fight on the beaches, we shall fight on the landing-grounds, we shall fight in the fields and in the streets, we shall fight in the hills; we shall never surrender . . .[4]

The distinction between *shall* and *will* is further obscured by the following facts:

1. In the United States, *will* alone is the preferred form in all areas except northeast New England.[5]
2. The context is often a better clue to the writer's purpose than is the form of the auxiliary. In speech the distinction between simple and emphatic future is indicated more by the speaker's stress on the auxiliary verb than by its form.
3. Both simple and emphatic futurity are often expressed by idiomatic constructions rather than by a future tense (see page 437).
4. *Shall* is predominantly used in statements of laws (Congress *shall* have the power . . .), in military commands (The regiment *shall* proceed as directed), and in formal directives (All branch offices *shall* report weekly to the home office).
5. In questions, *shall* is often used in the third person as well as in the first ("Where *shall* he be tomorrow?" But also, "Where *will* he be tomorrow?").

[4] From *Their Finest Hour,* by Winston S. Churchill. Copyright, 1949, by Houghton Mifflin Company.
[5] See Margaret M. Bryant, *Current American Usage* (New York, 1962), p. 183.

6. The popularity of the contracted forms (*I'll, she'll,* etc.) in the conversation of educated speakers tends to weaken, or even nullify, any distinction between *shall* and *will* in speech, and these colloquial contractions are often carried over into informal writing.

In view of this diversity of usage, any concise statement is bound to oversimplify, but the following summary for declarative statements should fit most of the needs of American college students:

1. To express simple futurity only, *will* is used in the second and third persons and either *will* or *shall* in the first person, *shall* being the more formal. *Shall* in the second and third person is not conventional when the sentence implies futurity only.
2. To express determination, resolve, or compulsion, *shall* is used in the second and third persons and either *shall* or *will* in the first person. But if the context clearly implies determination rather than futurity only, *will* may be used for all persons.

2. Should — Would

These words are used as the past forms of *shall* and *will* respectively and follow the same pattern (I *would* [*should*] be glad to see him tomorrow; he *would* welcome your ideas on the subject; we *would* [*should*] never consent to such an arrangement). They are also used to convert a *shall* or *will* in direct discourse into indirect discourse.

Direct Discourse	*Indirect Discourse*
"Shall I try to arrange it?" he asked.	He asked if he *should* try to arrange it.
I said, "They *will* need the money."	I said that they *would* need the money.

In addition, *should* and *would* have specialized uses:

Should is used:

1. To express obligation, necessity, or duty (I really *should* go to her tea; the two sides of the equation *should* balance).
2. To express probability (She *should* be home by then; these tires *should* be good for another 5000 miles).
3. In a subordinate clause, to express a supposition (If I *should* be late, will you hold dinner for me?).

Would is used:

1. To express a customary action in the past (During those years he *would* write once or twice a year and send a card at Christmas).

2. As a synonym for "were willing" in conditional clauses (He could do it, if he *would*).

3. As a polite form in requests or commands (*Would* you mind making three copies of this letter?).

Avoid the overuse of the auxiliary *would*. Repeating *would* in a compound sentence is often awkward or wordy.

Awkward	*Revised*
If they *would have done* that earlier, there *would have been* no trouble.	If they *had done* or (*Had* they *done*) that earlier, there *would have been* no trouble.
We *would want* some assurance that they *would accept* before we *would make* such a proposal.	We *would want* some assurance of their acceptance before we *made* such a proposal.
If I *would be* in your place, I *would apologize*.	If I *were* in your place, I *would apologize*.

c. Use the subjunctive form of *to be* in conditional clauses contrary to fact.

This use of the subjunctive is discussed on page 395. The last revised example above illustrates the construction. Other examples:

If she *were* my daughter, I would spank her. (She is not the speaker's daughter.) *Were* I ten years younger, I'd propose to her. (He is not ten years younger.) What would Lincoln say about that if he *were* alive today? (He is not alive.)

✔ Some of the following sentences are quite acceptable; others contain faulty or undesirable verb forms. On a sheet of paper write down the number of each sentence. Opposite that number place a check mark if the verb forms need no revision. If they do need revision, write the appropriate forms. Then hand in the sheet to your instructor.

1. I am sure you shall be very happy together.
2. He said he shall be home late for dinner.
3. They shall probably get here right after you leave.
4. It shall be the duty of the treasurer to collect dues, to keep an accurate record of all monies received and spent, and to submit a monthly report of the club's finances.
5. If I would miss that bus I'll come on the next one.
6. Every night when I left the office she would be waiting for me.
7. If they would have come, the family reunion would have been complete.
8. If I would have difficulty, may I call you?
9. Was there any alternative, I should refuse.

10. I think that you should know within a week.

11. It should be awkward, would they refuse.

12. Was I the judge, I'd be lenient in a case like that.

13. If I would have known you were coming I would have baked a cake.

14. It is a safe prediction that they shall feel ashamed of themselves tomorrow.

15. The law reads that no one shall be placed in jeopardy twice for the same offense.

16. She said that she will be busy for the rest of this week.

17. When they were children they should be at our house most of the time.

18. If you should do it, I should be grateful.

19. There should still be some money in the account.

20. It would be a relief, would they be pleasant for a change.

F3 *Case*

Case is a system of inflection to show the relation of nouns and pronouns to other words in the sentence. English has three cases: **subjective, possessive,** and **objective.** In general, a word is in the subjective case when it acts as a subject, in the objective case when it acts as an object, and in the possessive case when it modifies a noun (*his* bicycle).

English nouns, pronouns, and adjectives were once fully inflected to show case, but word order and idiomatic constructions have largely replaced case endings in modern English. Adjectives are no longer inflected; nouns are inflected only in the possessive case (the boy*'s* cap); only pronouns (and chiefly the personal pronouns) still make any considerable use of case forms. The study of case in modern English, therefore, is pretty much restricted to the case of pronouns.

a. The case of a pronoun is determined by its function in its own clause.

If a pronoun is the subject of its clause, it takes the subjective case; if it is an object, it takes the objective case; if it is a modifier, it takes the possessive case. There are two modifications of this practice: (1) a pronoun subject of an infinitive takes the objective case (I want *him to see* it); and (2) the complement of the verb *to be* takes the subjective case in formal usage (It was not *I* who said that).

The general convention stated above may be broken down as follows:

Pronouns take the subjective case when:
1. They are subjects of verbs (*I think* that *he missed*).

2. They are in apposition with subjects (Three men — Fred, Roy, and *I* — were elected delegates).

3. They are complements of the verb *to be* (I am sure it *was he*).

Pronouns take the objective case when:

1. They are objects of verbs (Mother *likes her*).

2. They are objects of prepositions (They pointed *at me*).

3. They are in apposition with objects (They gave *us* — Dave and *me* — the money).

4. They are subjects or objects (or complements) of infinitives (I want *her to go.* We didn't expect *to see him.* Wouldn't you like *to be me?*).

Pronouns take the possessive case when:

1. They modify a noun or a pronoun (Those are *my* six *children;* this is *his one*).

2. They precede and modify a gerund (What's wrong with *his swimming? His winning* was a surprise).

The following sentences illustrate the general convention that the case of a pronoun is determined by its function in its own clause:

> Please don't misunderstand *me.* (Objective case, object of *don't misunderstand.*)
> Try to be nice to *her.* (Objective case, object of preposition *to.*)
> I asked *him* to write. (Objective case, subject of infinitive *to write.*)
> Find out *who* did it. (Subjective case, subject of *did.*)
> *Whoever* wrote that was a genius. (Subjective case, subject of *wrote.*)
> Tell *whoever* will listen. (Subjective case, subject of *will listen.*)
> I wish it were *he.* (Subjective case, complement of *were.*)
> I like *his* dancing. (Possessive case, modifier of gerund *dancing.*)
> We can't stop *his* drinking. (Possessive case, modifier of gerund *drinking.*)
> The terrible thing is *his* having lost all that money. (Possessive case, modifier of gerund *having lost.*)
> *His* hopes are shattered. (Possessive case, modifier of noun *hopes.*)
> *He whom I* love is dead. (*He,* subjective case, subject of *is dead; I,* subjective case, subject of *love; whom,* objective case, object of *love.*)

b. Most errors in case occur in a few constructions.

In general, errors in case occur for two reasons: (1) because the construction is such that the student does not readily see the function of a pronoun; and (2) because the case which is inappropriate in writing is so often used in speech that the colloquial form seems more natural than the more formal one. Often these two reasons merge. That is, the construction requires more deliberate analysis than speakers have time to give it and so begets a colloquial usage which competes with the formal one.

The following constructions create most of the "case" troubles in college composition:

1. Parenthetical constructions. Any construction which interrupts the normal pattern of a clause is likely to obscure the function of a pronoun in the clause. In the following sentence it is quite clear that *who* is the subject of *won* and takes the subjective case:

447

That is the man *who* won the prize.

But if we introduce a parenthetical clause — *they say* — into the original sentence, the function of *who* becomes less clear:

That is the man who they say won the prize.

There is now a tendency to assume that *who* is the object of *say* and to put it in the objective case. But grammatically its function has not changed. The parenthetical clause is an absolute and has no grammatical relationship to any element in the sentence. Yet the faulty analysis suggested by the interrupting construction often leads to the selection of the wrong case.

Wrong Case	*Explanation*	*Correct Case*
The man *whom* they think did it has been arrested.	*Pronoun is subject of* did *and should be subjective.*	The man *who* they think did it has been arrested.
A girl *whom* I hear is her sister is being sought.	*Pronoun is subject of* is *and should be subjective.*	A girl *who* I hear is her sister is being sought.
She introduced me to a man *whom* she said was her employer.	*Pronoun is subject of* was *and should be subjective.*	She introduced me to a man *who* she said was her employer.
He is the general *whom* the reporters agree was most popular with the troops.	*Pronoun is subject of* was *and should be subjective.*	He is the general *who* the reporters agree was most popular with the troops.

2. **Complement of "to be."** In formal usage the complement of the verb *to be* takes the subjective case (It is *I*. Was it *she?*). In colloquial usage the objective is more common in the first person (It's *me*). The choice, therefore, between *It is I* and *It's me* is not a choice between standard and nonstandard usage but between formal and colloquial styles. This choice seldom has to be made in college writing, since the expression, in whatever form it is used, is essentially a spoken rather than a written sentence. Its use in writing occurs chiefly in dialogue, and then the form chosen should be appropriate to the speaker.

The use of the objective case in the third person (That was *her*) is less common even in colloquial usage and should probably be avoided in college writing except when dialogue requires it. The use of the objective case in a clause containing a subjunctive form of *to be* is especially to be avoided, because the subjunctive is a fairly formal construction, and the contrast between formal and colloquial usage points up the inappropriateness of the pronoun form:

Inappropriate	*Appropriate*
If I were *him,* I should resign.	If I were *he,* I should resign.
Would you do it, if you were *her?*	Would you do it, if you were *she?*

But notice that when the infinitive form of *to be* is used, its subject and complement both take the objective case:

She wants *me* to be there. (Pronoun is subject of infinitive.)
I wouldn't want to be *her.* (Pronoun is complement of infinitive.)

3. **"Whoever" and "whomever."** These two pronouns follow the rule that the case of a pronoun is determined by its function in its own clause, but because they often follow a transitive verb or the preposition *to,* they are often mistaken as objects when they are not.

Confused	*Explanation*	*Revised*
Give it to *whom-ever* wants it.	*Pronoun is subject of* wants; *its whole clause is the object of* to.	Give it to *who-ever* wants it.
Invite *whomever* will come.	*Pronoun is subject of* will come; *whole clause is object of* invite.	Invite *whoever* will come.
Send it to *whom-ever* you think would like it.	*Pronoun is subject of* would like. *The preposition* to *and the absolute* you think *do not affect its case.*	Send it to *who-ever* you think would like it.

4. **Comparative with "than" or "as."** The case of a pronoun following *than* or *as* in a comparison often causes difficulty. Such comparisons as

He is at least as old as *she.*
I am about twenty pounds lighter than *he.*
The judge liked us better than *them.*

are considered as contracted statements which in full would be

He is at least as old as *she is.*
I am about twenty pounds lighter than *he is.*
The judge liked us better than *he liked them.*

In the expanded form *than* and *as* are connectives joining two clauses, and the pronouns are the subjects of the italicized clauses. The convention is that the pronoun in the contracted comparison takes the case it would have if the comparison were fully expanded. That is, it takes the subjective case if it is the subject of the unexpressed verb, and the objective case if it is the object of that verb.

There is often a difference between colloquial and formal usage in such constructions. In colloquial usage, *than* and *as* tend to be interpreted as prepositions, and the pronouns are often in the objective case even when they are actually subjects. The more formal usage is expected in college writing.

5. **Possessive with a gerund.** We have seen (page 447) that a pronoun preceding and modifying a gerund takes the possessive case (I am opposed to *his going*). In a formal style, a noun modifying a gerund also takes the possessive case (Imagine *John's saying* that!). Colloquial usage, which usually ignores this convention and puts the modifier in the objective case (Imagine *John* saying that!), has influenced both speech and informal writing.

The following sentences further illustrate the use of the possessive case when a noun or a pronoun modifies a gerund:

> There is really no excuse for *his failing* the course.
> I resent *David's trying* to influence her.
> We are embarrassed by *their* continual *begging*.
> They object to *my having dated* you.
> *Mary's interrupting* annoys him.
> *Their believing* that doesn't surprise me.

In observing this convention it is necessary to distinguish between a verbal used as a gerund and one used as a modifier. For example, in *Can you imagine him kissing a girl?* the event to be imagined is *him* in the act of *kissing* a girl. *Him* is considered the object of the verb, and *kissing* a modifier of the object. This distinction, it must be admitted, is often subtle. The following contrast may illustrate it:

Verbal as a Modifier	*Verbal as a Gerund*
It was painful to see *him weeping*.	*Her weeping* is a triumph of art over nature.
We found *him sleeping*.	He gave up Sunday-morning golf because it interfered with *his sleeping*.
I want to see *him killing* the hog.	*His killing* that hog was a slick job of butchering.
You will see *them working* till all hours of the night.	We must put a stop to *their working* till all hours of the night.

Exercises

A. In the following sentences some of the italicized case forms are conventionally acceptable in college writing and some are not. Write out and turn in to your instructor a report on the acceptability of each form. If the acceptable case has been used, merely write the word "Acceptable" opposite the number of the sentence. If the wrong form has been used, write the acceptable form opposite the number of the sentence and justify your revision.

1. Between you and *I*, she is asking for trouble.
2. I think I am a little older than *him*.
3. Was it really for my mother and *I*?
4. She wants you and *I* to get married.
5. I am as much to blame as *her*.
6. All the men went fishing, *him* along with the others.
7. A group of *we* girls are planning a party.
8. I want *him* to be notified.
9. Can you imitate *his* singing?
10. I would like to catch *him* doing that.
11. The instructor was disappointed by *us* doing so badly.
12. Helen, *who* I dislike, is coming with her.
13. *Whom* can you imagine did such a thing?
14. He was the kind of man *whom* everybody said would have made a wonderful father.
15. There is a girl *whom* I admire.
16. *Whoever* you are, come out.
17. Tell it to *whomever* will listen.
18. I shall marry *whoever* I please.
19. We can play as well as *them*.
20. *His* refusing our offer was a serious disappointment.
21. We were all relieved by *him* leaving early.
22. They asked the Johnsons as well as *we* to come.
23. He means *us* two, you and *I*.
24. Communism does not appeal to *we* Americans.
25. The prize should go to *whoever* has the highest score.
26. That is the man *who* they say used to be married to her.
27. There are few men more capable than *he*.
28. That was the last of *me* running for office.
29. If you were *me*, would you take this job?
30. Select *whomever* you wish.
31. She does not care *who* she gets the money from.
32. I don't know whether I can do it as well as *him*.
33. We had trouble finding out *whom* the thief was.
34. Let's keep this a secret between *we* two.
35. He said he liked us both, but *me* better than *her*.

B. Rewrite the following selection to revise any case forms unacceptable in college writing:

When Dude Nissen turned down the nomination there was nothing for we sophomores to do but find someone who we could count on to represent our interests and who the sorority girls would vote for. Ted Newsome seemed to be our best bet. He was a good speaker, and we had no doubts about him attending meetings regularly or about his following our advice. It was generally agreed that it was him who was most responsible for the success of the freshman formal last year, and the fact of him dating June Hallison would win sorority votes, both for him and for whomever served as his running mate. His grades were so low that there was some risk of him not being eligible next semester, but he was the only man who we could win with; so we agreed to nominate him.

F4   *Agreement (Subject — Verb)*

In grammar the term **agreement** is used to describe the relationship between the inflectional forms of different elements within a sentence. When two related elements (subject and verb, pronoun and antecedent) show the same kind of inflection, they are said to agree. Thus a verb agrees with its subject if its form shows the same number and person as the subject. A pronoun agrees with its antecedent if both show the same gender, number, and person.

The fundamental convention of agreement is that the inflectional endings of two related elements should agree as far as possible. Since different parts of speech are inflected for different purposes (verbs for person, number, and tense, not for gender or case; nouns for number and possessive case, not for person or tense), related elements can agree only in those qualities which they have in common. If they agree in these, complete agreement is taken for granted. Therefore, the general rule might be more usefully stated in the negative: *There should be no grammatical disagreement between the inflectional endings of related elements within a sentence.*

Verbs agree with their subjects in number and person.

A singular subject requires a singular form of the verb, a plural subject a plural form. If the subject is a personal pronoun, inflected for person, the verb agrees in person. If the subject is a noun it is always considered to be in the third person, and takes the third person form of the verb. The following sentences illustrate this agreement:

> *I am* late. (Subject first person singular; verb first person singular.)
> *He is* sorry. (Subject third person singular; verb third person singular.)
> The *man works* slowly. (*Works* is third person singular to agree with *man.*)

Most troubles in agreement arise in the constructions that follow.

1. When two or more singular subjects are connected by *and*, a plural form of the verb is required.

He and his brother *are* identical twins.
Tom, Joe, Graff, and I *make* a good foursome.
Both the bull and the calf *have won* prizes.
A fool and his money *are* soon *parted*.

There are three modifications of this convention. First, when each of the singular subjects is considered individually, the singular form of the verb is used. This usage is most frequent after *each* or *every:*

Here, every man and woman *works* for the good of the organization.
Each boy and girl *makes* a separate report.

Second, when the two singular subjects refer to the same person or thing, the singular verb is used.

My wife and boss *has* something to say about that.
Grape juice and ginger ale *is* a good drink.

Third, mathematical computations may take either a singular or a plural verb.

Five and five *is* ten.   Two times three *is* six.
Five and five *are* ten.   Two times three *are* six.

2. When two or more singular subjects are connected by *or, nor,* or *but,* a singular form of the verb is required.

Mason or Dixon *is* to be elected.
Neither Bill nor Hugh *has* a chance.
Not Sue but Betty *was invited*.
Neither the Giants nor the Dodgers *is* the team to win.
Not only his wife but even his mother *finds* him selfish.

3. When one of two subjects connected by *or, nor,* or *but* is singular and the other is plural, the verb agrees in number with the nearer one.

Neither Lewis nor his lawyers *were* there.
Not only the boys but also their father *encourages* it.

4. When two subjects connected by *or* or *nor* differ in person, the verb agrees with the nearer.

Jean or you *are* to go.
Either Red or I *have won*.

When conforming to this rule creates an awkward sentence, we usually restate the idea in a form which is both correct and natural. For example, rather than write

Neither Mary nor I am to blame.
You or he is the leading contender.

we would restate these sentences as follows:

453

Mary is not to blame; neither am I.
You and he are the leading contenders.

5. A singular subject followed immediately by *as well as, in addition to, including, no less than, with, together with,* or a similar construction, requires a singular verb.

The husband as well as the wife *needs* advice.
The coach together with his assistants *was praised.*
The president no less than the secretary *is* responsible.
The store in addition to the farm *was sold.*

Because this convention sometimes seems illogical (since more than one person or thing is included in the subject phrase), there is a tendency to avoid the construction altogether and to write:

Both the husband and the wife *need* advice.
The coach and his assistants *were praised.*
The president *is* just as responsible as the secretary.
The store and the farm *were sold.*

6. A singular subject followed by a plural modifier requires a singular verb.

The *attitude* of these men *is* definitely hostile.
The *leader* of the rebel forces *has* been captured.
One of the women in the back row *looks* sick.
A *list* of the names of all survivors *is* available.

In speech, a plural modifier immediately before a verb often leads to a plural verb. This is particularly true in a sentence like the fourth above, in which the subject is followed by a long modifier containing two plural nouns. This colloquial usage has less justification in writing, since the more deliberate nature of writing and revision makes it easier to use the conventional form.

7. Such indefinite pronouns as *anybody, anyone, each, either, everybody, neither, nobody, no one,* and *somebody* generally require a singular verb.

Anybody who does that *is* just reckless.
Does anyone want to split this with me?
Each of them *makes* fifty dollars a week.
Somebody has been using my shaving soap.
Nobody in town *admits* seeing him.
Everybody does as he pleases.

8. The pronouns *any* and *none* take either singular or plural verbs.

Are any of you *going* to the show?
Any of these times *is* satisfactory.
None works so faithfully as he.
None are expected from that district.

In general, the preference is for the singular verb after these pronouns in a formal style, and for the plural verb in an informal one. Either form, however, is generally acceptable in college writing.

9. When the subject is a relative pronoun, the verb agrees with the antecedent of that pronoun.

> He is one of the *men who act* as advisers.
> This is one of those *problems which have* two solutions.
> *One* of the *girls who sing* in the choir *is being married.*

The last example is rather tricky. Its construction may be better seen if we enclose the modifier in parentheses:

> *One* (of the *girls who sing* in the choir) *is being married.*

10. When a sentence is introduced by the expletive *There* or the adverb *Here*, the verb agrees with the following subject, not with the introductory word.

> Here *is* your *money.*
> Here *are* the *receipts.*
> There *are* no second *chances.*
> There *are* a *man* and a *boy* in that boat.
> *Is* there a *chance* of his winning?
> *Were* there many *people* present?

This convention is not strictly observed in spoken usage, because we often begin a sentence with an expletive followed by a single subject and then add more subjects before we finish the sentence. For example:

> Did you see anyone there that I know?
> Well, there was Joe Botts, and Ray Carroll, and Dan Snader.

In speech, we cannot conveniently revise the verb to take care of these additional subjects. But we do have such an opportunity in writing, and hence a plural verb is more common in such sentences.

11. When a sentence is introduced by the expletive *It*, the verb is always singular, regardless of the number of the subject.

> It *is* the *Johnsons.*
> It *is we* whom they want.

12. The complement of the verb *to be* does not affect the number of the verb.

> *Books are* her chief source of enjoyment.
> The one *thing* you must be ready for *is* their attempts to disguise the play.
> *What annoys me* about them *is* their constant complaints.
> Her chief *source* of enjoyment *is* books.

If the demands of this convention result in an awkward sentence, the wisest thing to do is to recast it.

Conventional but Awkward	*Revised*
The amusing *thing* about campaign speeches *is* the attempts that both sides make to represent themselves as the only friends of the people.	In campaign speeches, it is amusing to see how both sides attempt to represent themselves as the only friends of the people.

13. A collective noun takes a singular verb when the class it names is considered as a unit, a plural verb when the members of the class are considered individually.

Singular	*Plural*
The jury *is* finally complete.	The jury *were* divided in their opinions.
The family *holds* an annual reunion.	My family *have* never been able to agree.
The clergy *is* wretchedly underpaid.	The clergy *are* supporting this proposal from their pulpits.

This convention also applies to such nouns as *number, part,* and *rest.*

A large number *is* expected.	A number of errors *have* been found.
Only part of the order *was* delivered.	A great part of the people *have* no opinion on the question.
The rest of the page *is* illegible.	The rest of the votes *are* about equally divided among the three candidates.

14. Titles of books, magazines, movies, newspapers, plays, and the like take a singular verb.

> *The Good Companions* is a fine novel.
> *The Outcasts* was not a success at the box office.
> *The New York Times* is his bible.

15. Plural numbers take a singular verb when they are used in a phrase to indicate a sum or a unit.

> A million dollars *is* a great deal of money.
> Ten years *is* too long to wait.
> Five per cent *is* good interest.
> A thousand yards *is* more than a half-mile.
> Forty hours *is* the regular work week.

16. Certain nouns which are plural in form but singular in meaning generally take a singular verb. The most common of these are *dynamics, economics, electronics, ethics, mathematics, news, physics, semantics, statics, whereabouts.*

> Economics *has* been called the dismal science.
> No news *is* good news.
> Semantics *is* the study of meanings.

Exercises

A. Write out and turn in to your instructor the form in parentheses which would be preferred in college writing:

1. All hope of finding the victims alive (has, have) been abandoned.
2. One of the two girls (is, are) going.
3. Neither of my uncles (have, has) any children.
4. There (is, are) plenty to go around.
5. There (is, are) two mistakes in your work.
6. There (is, are) an apple and an orange for each child.
7. Five hundred dollars (is, are) more than I can afford.
8. Either Mary or Jean (was, were) here.
9. Neither Roy nor his dad (have, has) seen it.
10. The gangster, with all his henchmen, (were, was) arrested.
11. The father no less than the children (is, are) to blame.
12. The parents no less than the children (is, are) to blame.
13. Every one of the group (are, is) here.
14. Here (is, are) a piece of cake and a glass of milk.
15. (Is, are) there two pictures like that?
16. Two hundred pounds (were, was) his best weight.
17. The engine in addition to the body (was, were) in bad shape.
18. Bacon and eggs (are, is) the favorite breakfast.
19. It (is, are) the Thompsons.
20. There (is, are) one for each couple.

B. Revise the following sentences to remove any subject-verb disagreements or any awkward constructions caused by following the conventions too closely. Some sentences may be satisfactory as written.

1. Neither of the applicants are fully qualified.
2. The cost of food, clothing, and household goods have risen considerably.
3. He is one of those men who votes against any measure that costs money.
4. Don't tell me that; it don't make sense.
5. There is two or three things that you ought to know about him.
6. What they are looking for is girls who can swim.
7. Not only his clothes but even his appearance were shabby.

8. The money, including the day's receipts, were stolen.

9. The extent of his injuries have not yet been determined.

10. The Twins led the league at the beginning of the season and is now in fourth place.

11. Either Helen or I am going to the convention.

12. One of the girls who work in the office is wearing a ring.

13. That he will be elected by a large plurality is almost certain.

14. The works of such a poet contains something for each of us.

15. Investment in government bonds is a secure way of saving.

16. One of the things I like best about summer is the attractive dresses the girls wear.

17. What I would like to know is the costs of the program.

18. There has never been any reports made public.

19. This is one of those questions that has two answers.

20. Languages are difficult for me; so are economics.

F5   *Agreement (Pronoun — Antecedent)*

Pronouns agree with their antecedents in gender, number, and person.

If the antecedent is a masculine singular noun, the pronoun should be the masculine singular third person pronoun (*he, his,* or *him*). A pronoun does not necessarily agree with its antecedent in case, since its case is determined by its function in its own clause (see page 446).

Examples	*Explanation*
The *men* got *their* wages.	*Their* is third person plural to agree with *men.* The plural form of the pronoun is the same for all genders.
The *girl* found *her* watch.	*Her* is third person feminine singular to agree with *girl.*
The *boy* misses *his* dog.	*His* is third person masculine singular to agree with *boy.*
The *ship* changed *its* course.	*Its* is third person neuter singular to agree with *ship.*

TROUBLESOME CONSTRUCTIONS

Most troubles with agreement of pronouns occur in a half-dozen constructions, and arise because of conflict between formal and colloquial usage. In general, formal usage insists that the *form* of the antecedent, not its *meaning,* determines the number of the pronoun, whereas colloquial usage tends to be governed by *meaning.* For example, *everybody* is singular in form but plural in meaning, since it refers to more than one person. Formally, *everybody* requires the singular form *his;* colloquially, it often is followed by the plural form *their.* In general, this colloquial usage is discouraged in college writing, so that *his* rather than *their* is the safer form.

1. When two or more antecedents are connected by *and,* a pronoun referring to them is plural.

> *Bill* and *Ted* are looking for *their* girls.
> *Helen* and *I* are buying *our* tickets today.
> That *man* and his *partner* have ruined *themselves.*

2. When the antecedent is *each, either,* or *neither,* followed by a plural modifier, a singular pronoun is preferred.

> *Each* of the girls is sure *she* is going to win.
> *Neither* of the men would admit *his* mistake.
> *Either* of these women may lose *her* temper at any time.

3. When the antecedent is *everybody, each, either, everyone, neither, nobody,* or *a person,* a singular pronoun is preferred.

> *Each* has *his* own group of supporters.
> *Everybody* had *his* work in good shape.
> *Nobody* had *his* speech ready today.
> *Everyone* was keeping *his* fingers crossed.
> *A person* finds *himself* in trouble if he begins to cut classes.

Notice that the masculine form of the pronoun is generally used when the sex of the antecedent is unknown or when the antecedent refers to both sexes, thus:

> *Everyone* should vote for the candidate of *his* choice.
> The boys and girls have been told that *everybody* must do *his* share of the work.

But if the context clearly shows that the antecedent is feminine, the feminine pronoun is used:

> When we girls have a picnic *everyone* brings *her* own utensils.

4. When the antecedent is the impersonal *one,* the third person pronoun is generally used, unless the style is very formal.

> *One* must watch *his* step with that girl.
> *One* can't really blame *himself* for that.
> If *one* had a second chance, how much wiser *he* might be.

In a very formal style the impersonal pronoun is sometimes used throughout.

> Under such conditions *one* laments *one's* utter incapacity to be of any genuine service.
> *One* finds *oneself* wishing that the evidence were more convincing.

5. When the antecedent is a collective noun, the pronoun may be either singular or plural, depending on whether the group is considered as a unit or as a number of individuals.

Singular	*Plural*
The *family* keeps pretty much to *itself.*	The *family* may have *their* private quarrels but *they* always agree in public.
The judge reprimanded the *jury* for *its* disregard of the evidence.	At the request of the defense attorney, the *jury* were polled and *their* individual verdicts recorded.
The *team* had *its* back to the wall.	The *team* are electing *their* captain.

6. The relative pronoun *who* is used when the antecedent is a person; *which* is used when the antecedent is a thing; *that* is used to refer to persons, animals, or things.

> This is the *man who* drove the car.
> The *girl who* found it is here.
> The *woman that* I mean had brown hair.
> Here is the *parcel which* (or *that*) she left.
> This is the *cow that* jumped the fence.

The possessive form *whose* is theoretically confined to persons, but in practice is often used when the more formal *of which* seems awkward.

> The *nation whose* conscience is clear on that score is exceptional.
> The newspaper *whose* reporters are most alert gets the most scoops.

✔ Write out and turn in to your instructor the form in parentheses which would be preferred in college writing:

1. A person has to decide for (himself, themselves).
2. Neither of them will promise (their, his) support.
3. Everyone must bring (his, their) own food.
4. A person must do (one's, his) best.
5. Each of the boys tried as hard as (they, he) could.
6. One must do (one's, their) utmost.
7. The team was cheered for (its, their) courage.
8. Nobody in the room (were, was) willing to give up (their, his) (seat, seats).
9. He would just as soon insult a person as look at (them, him).
10. One must work twenty years to be eligible for (their, one's, your) pension.
11. There is the man (which, that) lost the money.
12. Each girl must contribute (their, her) share of the expenses.
13. Every boy and girl in the class (were, was) awarded a certificate for (their, his, her) work.
14. The car (with the broken fender, whose fender is broken) is mine.
15. Give this to the lady (which, who) lost it.

16. The committee (has, have) always voted according to (its, their) consciences.

17. Has everyone got (his, their) own coat?

18. After Ohio State won the title (they, it) went on to play in the Rose Bowl.

19. He is the instructor (which, who) told me my English was weak.

20. The nation to (whom, which) I am referring is not Russia.

F6 *Vague Pronoun Reference*

In speech, a pronoun often refers to an unspecified or implied antecedent, but in college writing it is desirable to make pronoun references as specific as possible.

A pronoun which refers to a whole clause rather than to an explicit antecedent sometimes puts an additional strain on the reader by requiring him to do something which is really the writer's responsibility. The following examples illustrate pronoun references which, because they are unnecessarily vague, make the writing less precise than it should be.

Vague Reference	*Explanation*	*Revision*
They have agreed to have a formal church wedding, *which* pleases their parents.	*The pronoun* which *has no explicit antecedent but refers to the whole idea expressed in the main clause. The vague reference may be improved by supplying an antecedent as in the first revision or, better, by recasting the sentence as in the second revision.*	They have agreed to have a formal church wedding, *a decision* which pleases their parents. (or better) Their decision to have a formal church wedding pleases their parents.
The bigger car will be expensive to operate. Not only will its repairs cost more but its gasoline consumption will be greater. You should take *this* into account.	*The demonstrative pronoun* this *has no explicit antecedent, is singular in form, and refers to two different costs. In the revised version, the phrase* these added costs *removes the difficulties.*	The bigger car will be expensive to operate. Not only will its repairs cost more but its gasoline consumption will be greater. You should take *these added costs* into account.
The crash is being investigated. At present *they* think that the planes must have collided.	*The antecedent of* they *is not identified. The writer, of course, is thinking of the investigators. The statement would be improved by dropping the pronoun entirely.*	At present the investigators think that the planes must have collided.

Vague Reference	*Explanation*	*Revision*
If he does not get to work on his research assignment pretty soon *it* is going to be difficult for him to get it finished on time.	*The first* it *is impersonal but looks at first glance as if it should refer to* research assignment — *particularly unfortunate because the second* it *does have this reference. The sentence would be improved by keeping* he *the subject of both clauses.*	If he does not get to work on his research assignment pretty soon he may not get it finished on time.

✔ Revise the following sentences if necessary to make the pronoun references clear.

1. When you advance to the upper grades — fifth, sixth, seventh, and eighth — there are two grades in each room, which allows you to become acquainted with more pupils.

2. She hasn't a good word to say for anybody. Her parents are old-fashioned, her girl friends are catty, her boy friends are conceited, and her instructors are sarcastic. This makes me discount anything she tells me about a person.

3. I expect to receive a D in History and, at best, another D in Accounting, which means that I will be on probation next semester.

4. In high school they always told us exactly what we were to do and how we were to do it.

5. In the book it says that the meanings of words are determined by the ways people use them, which surprised me.

6. In college I like the way they treat you as an adult and call you Mister and Miss. This is a pleasant change from the way it was in high school.

F7 *Faulty Complement*

a. Avoid an illogical or awkward construction as the complement of the verb *to be.*

The verb *to be* is most frequently used either as an auxiliary verb (I *am* learning) or as a linking verb (Honesty *is* the best policy). When used as a linking verb, it links its complement to its subject and thus acts as a kind of equals sign (Honesty = best policy). A reader who is familiar with the conventions of English sentence structure expects two things of this linking verb: (1) that it will be followed by a complement, (2) that the complement will be such that it can be logically equated with the subject. If either of these expectations is denied him, he will be bothered. Thus, if he encounters the sentence, "Honesty is in the little details of everyday life," he will feel that the promised linking relationship has not been provided. He will want to revise the sentence to read, "Honesty is best expressed in the little details of everyday life," thus changing *is* from a linking to an auxiliary verb (*is* expressed).

Similarly, a reader who meets the sentence, "Honesty is what you do in such a situation," will feel that the complement throws the equation out of balance, since it equates the abstract noun "Honesty" with a statement of action. He will want to revise the sentence to read, "What to do in such a situation is to tell the truth," so that both sides of the equation refer to an action (*to do* and *to tell*).

In order to avoid such annoying constructions, a writer should make sure that the complement of *to be* can be logically equated with the subject. If it cannot, or if the equation results in a wordy or awkward sentence, the writer should either revise the form of the complement or rewrite the sentence to get rid of the misleading linking verb.

Illogical or Awkward Complement	*Explanation*	*Revised Sentence*
Before I built the house all I had learned about carpentry was *watching my dad.*	*The equation requires some statement of knowledge, not a statement of how the knowledge was obtained. Of the various possible revisions, perhaps the best is to substitute a more active verb which does not promise an equation.*	Before I built the house all that I knew about carpentry I had learned from watching my dad.
The chief disadvantage of weeping willows is the branches are brittle and break easily.	*The sentence has two faults. Logically, it is the brittleness that constitutes the disadvantage, not the branches; grammatically, the plural noun* branches *following* is *sounds like a subject-verb disagreement. The sentence may be saved very simply, by providing a subordinate conjunction so that the final clause is revealed as a complement.*	The chief disadvantage of weeping willows is that the branches are brittle and break easily.
The most unusual food I ever had was when I ate a serving of boiled snails.	*The reader expects the food to be identified immediately after the linking verb. The adverbial clause stresses time, instead, and is wordy.*	The most unusual food I ever ate was a serving of boiled snails.

b. Avoid the use of *is when*, *is where*, and *is if* when the complement of *to be* is intended to describe or define the subject.

This advice is a special application of the more general statement given in **a.** The use of an adverbial clause instead of a noun or noun phrase is one kind of illogical complement which occurs frequently in student definitions. This error and its revision are illustrated by the following examples.

Faulty Complement	*Explanation*	*Revision*
Plagiarism is *when you represent another person's writing as your own.*	*The reader expects to find what plagiarism is, not when it is. The construction calls for a noun phrase similar to the italicized phrase at the right.*	Plagiarism is *the representation of another's writing as one's own.*
Manslaughter is *where a person is killed deliberately but without premeditation.*	*Again, the construction requires a statement of what manslaughter is, not where it is.*	Manslaughter is *the deliberate but unpremeditated killing of a person.*
A comma splice is *if a comma is used to separate two independent sentences which are not connected by a coordinating conjunction.*	*The complement should tell what a comma splice is, not how a comma splice is made. Use a noun such as* use *at the right.*	A comma splice is *the use of a comma to separate two independent sentences which are not connected by a coordinating conjunction.*

c. Use the appropriate case for a personal pronoun acting as the complement of *to be.* (See F3.)

d. Use the adjective form for the complements of sensory verbs.

A **sensory verb** is one which identifies some action of the senses — seeing, hearing, feeling, etc. Since the complements of these verbs usually describe the subject rather than the action of the verb, they are adjectives, not adverbs. Their adjectival function can be illustrated by expressing the complement as an attributive adjective, as in the parenthetical phrases at the ends of the following sentences:

> Your hands feel rough. (rough-feeling hands)
> This tire looks good. (good-looking tire)
> That dog smells awful. (awful-smelling dog)
> This water tastes bitter. (bitter-tasting water)

To use an adverb after these verbs would suggest that the writer was describing the manner in which the feeling, looking, smelling, and tasting were performed. Unless the modifier completing a sensory verb is clearly intended to describe the action suggested by the verb, an adjective is the correct form.

✔ Revise the following sentences to remove the faulty complements.

1. The source of his fortune was from real estate.
2. The reason I failed the course was I missed a third of the lectures.

3. A hybrid is when you cross two different types of plants.

4. Whatever is in the oven smells deliciously.

5. The chief merit of the play was in its humor.

6. I read in this morning's paper where there has been another airplane crash.

7. Technically, a sophomore is having 26 hours of credit.

8. What annoys me about him is he plays practical jokes.

9. Conduct unbecoming a student is if you do something you shouldn't and get caught.

10. Half an hour after dinner he became quite sickly.

11. One of his greatest assets is how well he can tell a story.

12. The thing I most regret about working my way through college was the dates I never had time for.

13. After that kind of experience I can't help feeling bitterly about her.

14. The most embarrassing thing that can happen to you on a trip is when you run short of money and try to cash a personal check at a gas station.

15. The reason they were divorced was not supporting his family.

16. The thing that troubled me most was cats all over the place.

17. An Act of God is when something happens, like a flood, which nobody is really to blame for.

18. The difference between an amateur and a professional is when an athlete is paid for playing a sport.

19. An honor student is if you have a straight B average.

20. The only money he has is his grandfather left him a small inheritance.

F8 *Confusion of Adjective – Adverb*

Faulty modifiers which are a result of word order are discussed in **WO2.** This section is limited to errors in the form of the modifier.

a. Do not use an adjective to modify a verb.

Adjective Misused for Adverb	*Correct Form*
The old car still runs *good*.	The old car still runs *well*.
Do it as *careful* as you can.	Do it as *carefully* as you can.
Listen *close* to what I tell you.	Listen *closely* to what I tell you.

b. Do not use an adjective to modify an adverb or another adjective.

Adjective Misused for Adverb	*Correct Form*
He is *considerable* better today.	He is *considerably* better today.
It was a *real* difficult decision.	It was a *really* difficult decision.

c. Do not use an adverb as the complement of a sensory verb unless you clearly intend to modify the verb, not the subject. (See F7)

d. When a modifier could modify either a noun or a verb, indicate by the form which you intend.

Adverb	*Adjective*
Tie the knot *tightly* and *securely*.	Tie the boat *tight* to the dock.
Her husband held her *firmly*.	He kept his resolutions *firm*.
John spoke out *forthrightly*.	His answers seemed *forthright*.

✔ Rewrite the following sentences to revise or delete faulty modifiers.

1. He plays every shot so easy that it looks simple.
2. The way you put it, it sounds pretty well.
3. She near fainted when he told her.
4. We ought to treat everybody fair and square.
5. It was obviously a cheap made dress.
6. Let's divide the work equal among the three of us.
7. The nightwatchman had been gagged and tied tight in a chair.
8. After I had explained the problem as good as I could, she was real nice to me.
9. The work had been done so sloppy that I spoke real sharp to him.
10. We were considerable wiser after that experience.

P · Punctuation

P1   Uses of the Comma

In English there are about a dozen common marks of punctuation: *period* [.], *comma* [,], *semicolon* [;], *colon* [:], *question mark* [?], *exclamation mark* [!], *quotation marks* [" " or ' '], *apostrophe* ['], *dash* [—], *parentheses* [( )], and *brackets* [ ]. Most of these marks have highly specialized functions, and once these are understood, it is easy enough to use them conventionally. The chief exception, perhaps, is the comma, which is at once the most common mark of punctuation and the one with the most complex uses.

The comma is used to make the internal structure of the sentence clear. It does so in three general ways: (1) by separating elements which might otherwise be confused, (2) by setting off interrupting constructions, and (3) by marking words out of normal order. This section will specify and illustrate these three uses.

a. Use commas to separate elements which might otherwise seem to run together.

1. To prevent a confused, ambiguous, or awkward reading.

We saw on pages 409–415 that a major cause of confused sentence structure is inadequate punctuation. The most important use of the comma is to prevent a confused, ambiguous, or awkward reading. All other uses are subordinate to this one. Notice how the confused sentences at the left are made clear at the right by the use of commas.

Confused	Explanation	Clear
Mr. Smith our milkman has been hurt.	*Is this a statement to or about Mr. Smith?*	Mr. Smith, our milkman has been hurt. (or) Mr. Smith, our milkman, has been hurt.
I do not care for money isn't everything.	*Lest money seem to complete care for, a comma should be inserted after care.*	I do not care, for money isn't everything.

467

Confused	*Explanation*	*Clear*
A hundred yards below the bridge was flooded.	*Comma necessary to avoid misreading of* bridge *as the object of* below.	A hundred yards below, the bridge was flooded.
When we had finished eating the cigarettes were passed around.	*Comma necessary to show that* cigarettes *is not the object of* eating.	When we had finished eating, the cigarettes were passed around.

2. To separate two main clauses joined by a coordinating conjunction (and, or, nor, but).

The real purpose of this convention is to prevent possible misinterpretation on first reading, specifically to keep the subject of the second main clause from being misread as a second object in the first clause. Consider the following sentences:

> He sprained his ankle and his temper was ruined.
> He traded his car and his wife was angry.

In both these sentences the noun following the conjunction appears, at first reading, to be part of a compound object of the first verb. The comma before the conjunction shows clearly that the two nouns are in different clauses:

> He sprained his ankle, and his temper was ruined.
> He traded his car, and his wife was angry.

When there is no possibility of a confused reading, the comma becomes less necessary and is often omitted. But even when it is not functionally necessary, careful writers insert a comma between two connected main clauses if the subject of the second differs from that of the first, as in the following examples:

> I tried to sleep, but my neighbor's radio made that impossible.
> The huge elm had been cut down, and a garage now covered the spot where it once stood.

But notice that a comma is not used when the subject of the first clause is understood as the subject of the second:

> I discussed the question with the family and then made my decision.

3. To separate elements in a series.

> He promised them only *blood, sweat, toil,* and *tears.*
> *Reading, swimming,* and *dancing* are my favorite recreations.
> It was said of Washington that he was *first in war, first in peace,* and *first in the hearts of his countrymen.*

North passed, East bid two spades, South bid three hearts, and *West doubled.*

We were *tired, hungry,* and *disconsolate.*

As these illustrations show, the series may consist of single words, phrases, or clauses. The items in the series may be nouns, pronouns, verbs, verbals, adverbs, or adjectives, though within a single series they must not shift from one part of speech to another. The comma before the conjunction joining the last two items is optional. Its use is largely a matter of personal preference, though it is more likely to be omitted in an informal style than in a formal one.

> She is small, dark, and vivacious.
> (or)
> She is small, dark and vivacious.

4. To separate contrasted elements in a *this, not that,* construction.

> He is sick, not drunk.
> We are disgusted, not angry.
> The German schools became institutes of propaganda, not of education.
> This is a problem which must be handled with sympathy, not harshness.

5. To separate direct quotation from such constructions as *He said, She answered, We replied,* etc.

> He said, "You are only half right."
> "This," I said, "is the last straw."
> "Nobody asked you, sir," she said.
> "But," he asked, "what if they refuse?"

Since the quotation marks themselves set off the quoted material, no confusion would result if the comma were omitted; but convention requires the comma. Whether the punctuation should come *inside* or *outside* the quotation marks is discussed in **P9.**

6. To separate elements in dates, addresses, and place names.

> January 1, 1960; Dec. 25, 1910. (Comma between day and year.)
> 875 Main Street, Galesburg, Illinois. (Comma between street and city and between city and state.)
> Chicago, Illinois, is the second-largest city in the country. (Notice the comma before and after the state.)
> He was born in London, England. (Comma between city and country.)

7. In the following miscellaneous constructions:

> In figures — 22,745; 1,000,000; 150,743,290.
> In names followed by titles — R. W. Leeds, M.D.
> At the end of the salutation in informal letters — Dear Joe,
> After an introductory *Yes* or *No* — Yes, I'll do it.

✔ In the following sentences insert commas where they are needed for ease of reading or are conventionally required. Some of the sentences may be satisfactory as they are.

1. This summer our family tried a split vacation. Dad went fishing in Minnesota with Bill and me and Mother took my sister to New York.

2. Below the town glittered with a million lights.

3. My roommate learned about the deal and wrote a story about it for the *Daily*.

4. The correct quotation is "And malt does more than Milton can to justify God's ways to man."

5. The author was Housman not Pope. He was born on March 26 1859.

6. Will you please forward my mail to 1620 Third Avenue Anoka Minnesota?

7. I expect to be there as long as the fishing is good.

8. The correct sum is 14530 not 14350.

9. I'll take orange juice ham and eggs and coffee.

10. He praised the food and the waitress seemed pleased.

11. He married Helen and her sister served as bridesmaid.

12. "I wonder" he said "if she still lives in Geneva Illinois."

13. "I think not" I answered. "She was living in Kansas City Missouri when I last heard of her."

14. Throughout the ceremony was inspiringly conducted.

15. The room was a clutter of discarded clothing strewn books and newspapers overflowing ash trays and dirty dishes.

16. After all their hopes were too ambitious.

17. We tried to look in the cellar windows but someone had placed cardboard rectangles against them on the inside.

18. I cannot stay longer for Susan will be expecting me to meet her at the station.

19. The students sat tensely while the test papers were being distributed and then began to write feverishly.

20. The letter should be addressed to A. D. Jones M.D. Christie Clinic Champaign Illinois.

b. Use commas to set off an interrupting construction.

Any construction which comes between subject and verb, verb and object or complement, or any two elements not normally separated, may be called an interrupting construction. If the interruption is awkward, it should be avoided; but many interrupters are necessary and conventional. They should, however, be set off by commas so that a reader can recognize them and still see the basic pattern of the sentence.

We must distinguish, however, between constructions which actually interrupt and those which come between related elements without interrupting them. For example, in

The girl, *you say*, has gone.

the italicized clause comes between subject (*girl*) and verb (*has gone*). The interrupter need not occupy this position. The sentence could have been written:

> You say that the girl has gone.
> The girl has gone, you say.

But in the sentence

> The girl *you want* has gone.

the italicized clause identifies the particular girl and cannot be moved without weakening the sentence. Although the clause modifies the subject, it so closely identifies it that we consider *The girl you want* as the "whole subject" of *has gone*. A modifying phrase or clause which is so closely related to another element that it is felt to be a part of that element should not be set off with commas, since the commas would distort the relationship, not clarify it. The italicized modifiers in the following sentences are so necessary that they are not considered interrupting constructions:

> The man *with him* is his brother.
> The girl *at the piano* is his wife.
> The leader *of the revolt* has been captured.

As you study the following uses of commas to set off interrupting constructions, notice this about all of them: *an interrupting construction between subject and verb or verb and complement requires two commas to enclose it.* These commas act like mild parentheses and are always used in pairs.

1. To set off an appositive.

An **appositive** is an identifying word or phrase (a noun or pronoun and its modifiers) which is considered grammatically equivalent to the noun or pronoun it identifies:

> Patterson, *the champion*, will defend his title this summer.
> His father, *the president of the company*, will be responsible.
> They want us, *you and me*, to go.
> I want to see Dr. Roberts, *the English professor*.

The first three examples show that the appositive is often a particular kind of interrupter. The fourth appositive does not interrupt the main clause, but is conventionally separated from the rest of the sentence by a comma.

2. To set off nouns of address.

A **noun of address** is a proper or common noun used to name the listener when we are speaking to him directly (I wish, *Dad*, you would reconsider your decision. I understand, *Mrs. Ellison*, that you are now a

471

grandmother). Such nouns may occupy the beginning, middle, or end of a sentence, so that strictly speaking they are not always interrupters. But they are always set off from the rest of the sentence by commas.

> I would like to ask you, *Mr. Jones,* for your opinion.
> I think, *madam,* that you had better leave.
> *Sir,* I'd like to ask a question.
> Listen, *chum,* I've had enough of you!
> I wish I were going with you, *Ted.*

3. To set off conjunctive adverbs and other transitional markers.

Conjunctive adverbs (*however, moreover, therefore,* etc.) are adverbs which double as connectives between sentences. Usually they provide a transition between two sentences and usually they come *near,* and occasionally *at,* the beginning of the second sentence.

> We thought, moreover, that we could get away with it.
> There was a chance, on the other hand, that prices would go up.
> You must try, first of all, to consider it objectively.

In informal usage the commas around common conjunctive adverbs are omitted if the writer feels that they would provide more separation than he desires (I am therefore canceling the order).

4. To set off a nonrestrictive modifier.

A modifier is said to be **restrictive** when it specifies a particular member or members of a group. Thus in "The President *who succeeded Eisenhower* came from Massachusetts," the italicized modifier selects from the whole class of Presidents a particular one. When a modifier does not limit a class to a particular group or individual but modifies the whole class, it is said to be **nonrestrictive.** Thus in "The President of the United States, *who is both the chief of state and the leader of the majority party,* holds one of the most powerful offices in the world," the italicized modifier refers to all Presidents of the United States and does not restrict the statement to any particular one. It is a nonrestrictive modifier.

The following examples include restrictive and nonrestrictive modifiers. We should recognize that context often determines how a modifier is to be interpreted and that it might be possible to place the sentences at the right in contexts which would make the modifiers restrictive.

Restrictive	*Nonrestrictive*
All students *who were absent* will be required to do an additional assignment.	College students, *who represent a superior intellectual group,* must be asked to accept the responsibility of leadership.
Soldiers *who have flat feet* had better stay out of the infantry.	Soldiers, *who are selected by physical fitness tests,* should show a lower sickness rate than that of the total population.

Restrictive modifiers are so much a part of the whole subject that they cannot be omitted without changing the basic meaning of the sentence. Nonrestrictive modifiers, on the other hand, can be omitted without significant change in basic meaning. Compare the following revisions with the originals which we just read.

All students . . . will be required to do an additional assignment. (This is not what the original statement meant.)

College students . . . must be asked to accept the responsibility of leadership. (This is substantially what the original statement meant.)

Soldiers . . . had better stay out of the infantry. (Not the original meaning.)

Soldiers . . . should show a lower sickness rate than that of the total population. (The original meaning has not been substantially changed.)

Restrictive modifiers are not set off by commas, because they are felt to be an essential part of the element they modify. Nonrestrictive modifiers are felt to be similar to the interrupting constructions shown earlier and are therefore enclosed by commas. The examples already given illustrate this difference in punctuation.

✔ In the following sentences, provide commas to set off appositives, nouns of address, conjunctive adverbs, and nonrestrictive modifiers. Some sentences may require no additional punctuation.

1. Mr. Ludovic the new German instructor was born in Berlin.
2. The man wearing the Stetson is his uncle.
3. The tall man who happened to be wearing a Stetson said he had never been west of Chicago in his life.
4. Do you think Bill that we could play a round after work?
5. Are these your gloves Mrs. Davidson?
6. The suit that he bought two years ago fits him better than the one he bought last winter.
7. The doctor looking very grave came towards us.
8. I thought however that things would be different this time.
9. The girl evidently on the edge of tears could hardly finish her story.
10. Sir may I trouble you for a light?
11. My girl's mother who used to be an English teacher helps me with my themes.
12. The dog which had evidently been trained sat beside the table and begged charmingly for food.
13. First turn on the gas and oil; second set the choke; third pull the rope.
14. I had a talk with her father who is not so crotchety as you led me to believe.
15. I had a talk with the man who witnessed the accident.
16. The elm tree disease is killing off most of the old elms; consequently the people in our neighborhood are planting maples.
17. No, I mean the Mr. Brown who lives over on Florida Avenue.

18. I hear that Abelson the fire marshal was badly hurt last night.

19. A scientist called Fermi was chiefly responsible for the success of the Chicago experiment.

20. Mr. Welch our next door neighbor has a daughter who placed second in a national beauty contest. There is some talk that she will be given a movie contract. That however may be merely rumor.

c. Use commas to mark an inversion.

1. To emphasize an inverted element.

Any word, phrase, or clause transposed from its normal position is said to be inverted.

Myself, I will vote in favor of it.
Except for physics, my courses are not difficult.

But if the inversion is so common as to seem normal, the comma is usually omitted. No commas would be used in the following inversions:

Yesterday I had a bad time of it.
In 1913 the concept of total war was unknown.
In the following sentences the verbs are underlined.

2. To cut off a long introductory phrase or an adverbial clause preceding the main clause.

When a sentence opens with a long phrase or adverbial clause, it is conventional to use a comma between this element and the main clause:

Pulling over to the curb at the first opportunity, I waited for the fire engines to pass.
If there is going to be any difficulty about this request, I would rather withdraw it.
Being ignorant of the facts of the situation, I could say nothing.
If I go, you'll be sorry.
To be sure of getting up in time to catch the train, I left a call with the switchboard operator.
When you say that, smile.

This convention is not universal, for writers sometimes feel that a particular introductory construction is so closely related in meaning to the main clause that the separating comma is undesirable. The comma is generally used when, as in the last example, the introductory construction is clearly an inversion, when an introductory phrase contains a verbal (examples 1, 3, 5), and when the subordinate and main clauses have different subjects (example 4). The comma should always be used if it makes the sentence pattern clearer and the reader's job easier.

✔ In the following sentences insert commas to set off inversions and introductory constructions where desirable.

1. Dissatisfied with our blocking the coach announced an extra session on defense.
2. In a last desperate effort to score the team went into a spread formation.
3. If you want it take it.
4. On learning that his wife had never formally renounced her share of the property and could still block its sale we told the real estate agent that we were no longer interested.
5. As far as I know that is the answer.
6. Just the other day I saw his mother.
7. Whoever he is he should be punished.
8. If he objects tell him to talk with me.
9. Knowing that he had a tendency to make a ten-minute speech in five minutes Hugh timed his delivery with a stop watch.
10. Angry my roommate threw the tickets in the fireplace.

P2 *Misuse of the Comma*

Too many commas are often more annoying than too few. The following "don't's" should be carefully observed.

a. Do not use a comma instead of a period between independent sentences.

The use of a comma instead of a period between independent sentences may cause serious misinterpretation. (See "Comma Splice," **S7;** see also **P3a.**)

Comma Splice	*Conventional Punctuation*
He spoke very quietly, as I listened, I had the impression that he was speaking to himself.	He spoke very quietly. As I listened, I had the impression that he was speaking to himself.
There was nothing more to be said, when they took that attitude, further negotiation was impossible.	There was nothing more to be said. When they took that attitude, further negotiation was impossible.

b. Do not use a comma between closely related elements except to mark an interrupting construction.

The comma should reveal the structure of a sentence, not disguise it. Closely related elements (subject-verb, verb-object, verb or noun and

475

modifier) are unnecessarily separated if a single comma is placed between them. If, however, these elements are interrupted, a pair of commas to enclose the interrupting construction helps to bridge the interruption.

Misuse of Comma Between Related Elements	*Correct Use of Comma Between Related Elements*
My car, is at the service station.	My car, which is at the service station, needs a thorough overhauling.
He said, that he would try.	He said, when I asked him, that he would try.
The student who lost this money, may need it badly.	The student, who had lost money on other occasions, was reprimanded for his carelessness.

The last illustration contrasts a restrictive with a nonrestrictive clause (see page 472). The comma is misused in the version at the left because the subordinate clause is not an interruption but a necessary part of the whole subject. It is a restrictive modifier.

c. Do not use commas excessively.

The modern tendency, especially in informal writing, is to keep punctuation to a minimum. Hence it is usual to avoid commas which serve no recognizable purpose. Moreover, it should not be assumed that a comma *must* be used in a particular sentence because convention recommends its use in sentences of that type. The conventions are statements about general practice. There are times when slavishly following the rules will chop a sentence to pieces by commas. In such cases, either revise the sentence or ignore the strict letter of the convention. The following examples illustrate excessive and adequate punctuation:

Excessive	*Adequate*
However, it is not, in my opinion, desirable.	However, it is not in my opinion desirable.
Yesterday, a little, old lady, in a dilapidated, old Ford, picked me up, and brought me home.	Yesterday a little old lady in a dilapidated old Ford picked me up and brought me home.
Sometimes, she would appear in an elaborate beach outfit, sometimes, she wore a simple, white suit, and, occasionally, she put on a red, white, and blue bathing suit, with a detachable skirt.	Sometimes she would appear in an elaborate beach outfit, sometimes she wore a simple white suit, and occasionally she put on a red white and blue bathing suit with a detachable skirt.

P3 *Uses of the Semicolon*

a. Use a semicolon to separate closely related independent clauses not connected by a conjunction.

> Try this one; it seems to be your color.
> His mother won't let him; she is afraid he might get hurt.
> Your car is new; mine is eight years old.

In each of these sentences a period could be used instead of the semicolon. But the clauses, even though grammatically independent, are felt to be so closely related that a period makes too sharp a separation.

The semicolon provides a more emphatic separation than the comma; it affords an easier transition between statements than the period; it is therefore the most appropriate punctuation to balance two contrasted ideas parallel in form:

> Take care of the children; the adults can take care of themselves.
> It was not the hours or the wages that discouraged me; it was the constant monotony of the work.

b. Use a semicolon before a transitional connective (conjunctive adverb) between two main clauses.

The most common transitional connectives are *also, besides, consequently, furthermore, hence, however, likewise, moreover, nevertheless, in addition, so, then, therefore, yet.*

> It won't work; *therefore* there is no sense in buying it.
> His argument has some merit; *however,* he goes too far.
> His eyes went bad; *consequently,* he had to resign his position as a proofreader.

c. Use a semicolon to separate elements in a series when they contain internal punctuation.

> Among those present were Dr. Holmes, pastor of the First Methodist Church; A. C. Levitt, superintendent of schools; B. L. Rainey, manager of the Benson Hotel; and M. T. Cord, vice-president of Miller and Sons.

Had commas been used between the elements in this series they might be confused with the commas which set off the appositives.

P4 *Misuse of the Semicolon*

a. Do not use a semicolon as the equivalent of a colon.

Although their names suggest a close relationship, semicolons and colons have quite different uses and are not interchangeable. The colon (see **P7**) is used chiefly to indicate that something is to follow, usually a series of items; the semicolon is never used between an independent clause and a subordinate construction. In the following examples the faulty semicolon is followed by the correct colon in parentheses.

> My records show that the following students have not handed in the assignment; (:) Mr. Andrews, Mr. Richardson, Mr. Smith, and Miss Wallace.
> Dear Sir; (:) May I call your attention to an error. . . .

b. Do not use a semicolon as the equivalent of a comma.

A comma is internal punctuation and is used only *within* a sentence; a semicolon is a stronger mark and, as we have seen, is used between grammatically independent statements. A semicolon may be substituted for a comma between main clauses joined by a conjunction when more emphatic punctuation is desired (*My old job paid higher wages; but the new one offers a brighter future*); but a semicolon cannot be substituted for a comma between a main clause and a subordinate construction. In the following examples the faulty semicolon is followed by the correct comma in parentheses.

> Although I seldom have trouble with grammar or spelling; (,) I never seem to use the right punctuation.
> We stayed up until two o'clock in the morning; (,) hoping that they would arrive.
> We could come to only one conclusion; (,) that his mother had changed his mind.

c. Avoid indiscriminate substitution of semicolons for periods.

Using a semicolon for a period will do less harm than using a semicolon for a colon or a comma. Yet the semicolon and the period have different functions and should not be used interchangeably. The normal punctuation between independent statements is the period. Between sentences this is the conventional mark to use; but if a writer wishes to relate the two sentences more closely than a period would permit, he may use a semicolon. This specialized substitution, however, does not abolish the distinction between the two marks. In the following passage the parenthetical periods are preferable to semicolons. The first word following the period would, of course, be capitalized.

> Today it is easy to smile at such superstitions and to assume that they are the products of an uncivilized age, but the close association of words and things which is the basis of word magic is a subtle association which persists even in the thinking of highly civilized societies; (.) some of the opposition to daylight-saving time illustrates this confusion of word and thing; (.) people uneasily suspect that if they turn the hands of the clock ahead, they have dropped an hour out of their lives; (.) often the best argument for such people is not to deny that they will have "lost" an hour, but to promise that

they will get it back in the fall; (.) the common practice of skipping thirteen in numbering the floors and rooms of a hotel is another illustration of the lingering belief in word magic.

P 5 *The Period*

a. A period is used to mark the end of a declarative sentence.

Unless a sentence is intended as a question, a command, or an exclamation, it is declarative and is closed by a period:

> Today is Tuesday.
> We have three days to go.

Even when a sentence is mildly imperative or exclamatory, modern usage often prefers a period to an exclamation mark:

> Be careful of the step.
> Let's forget the whole matter.
> How pleasant it would be to be there now.

b. A period is used to mark an accepted abbreviation.

> *Titles:* Col., Dr., Hon., Mrs., Rev.
> *Degrees:* B.A., B.S., M.D., Ph.D.
> *Names:* John A. Jones; Chas. W. Brown
> *Months:* Jan., Feb., Aug., Nov.
> *States:* Ala., Ga., Me., Ill., Wash.
> *Miscellaneous:* Ave., St., vol., p., U.S.A., B.C., A.D.

Notice, however, that when usage has sanctioned the dropping of the period, it is no longer required — *exam, gym, prom, per cent, 1st, 2nd, 3rd.* Periods are usually omitted in abbreviations of government agencies — *USNR, TVA, AEC, FBI.*

c. A period is used before a decimal and between dollars and cents.

> The error is less than .01 inch.
> The correct answer is 57.39.
> The price tag read $11.98.

P 6 *Question and Exclamation Marks*

a. The question mark is used almost entirely to indicate that a sentence is to be understood as a question.

Whose is this?
You mean he's ill?

It is sometimes used in parentheses to question the accuracy of the preceding word:

These amateurs (?) make a comfortable living out of sports.
His funny (?) remarks were more than I could bear.

As a device for irony, however, it is generally weak.

b. The exclamation mark is used to show that a statement is imperative or that it is spoken with strong emotion.

Be quiet!
Attention!
Leave the room at once!
Oh, you fool!
God help us!

P7   *The Colon*

The main uses of the colon are:

a. To indicate that something is to follow, especially a formal series.

Here are the facts: The money was there five minutes before he entered the room; it was missing immediately after he left; the next day he bought a new suit, although he had previously spent all of this month's allowance.

The slogan goes like this: Look sharp! Feel sharp! Be sharp!

b. In place of a comma before long or formal direct quotations.

In that speech Bryan said: "You shall not press down upon the brow of labor a crown of thorns; you shall not crucify mankind upon a cross of gold."

This is his statement as reported in the papers: "I have never advocated such ideas; I do not advocate them now; I do not approve of them; and I have no reason for believing that I ever will approve of them."

c. Before a clause which is intended to restate in different form the idea of the preceding clause.

Henry V is one of the great experiences in the history of motion pictures. It is not, to be sure, the greatest: the creation of new dramatic poetry is more important than the re-creation of the old.

Except for differences of subject matter, the rules of grammar are exactly like the laws of physics and chemistry: they are scientific generalizations about the facts.

In each of these examples the clause following the colon says, in another way, what was already said in the clause preceding the colon. The restatement, however, is not needless repetition: it serves to illustrate or amplify the content of the preceding clause.

P 8   *Quotation Marks*

This section is limited to the use of quotation marks. The troublesome question of the position of other punctuation with respect to quotation marks is treated separately in the next section.

Quotation marks may be double (" ") or single (' ').

DOUBLE QUOTATION MARKS

Double quotation marks have the following uses:

a. To enclose the actual words of a speaker (direct discourse).

I said, "That's your worry."
"Bob," he said, "you can't do that!"
"What is the matter?" she asked.

Notice that since all the words of a speaker are enclosed in quotation marks an interrupting *he said, she replied,* etc., requires two sets of quotation marks in the sentence. Notice also that when direct discourse is reported as indirect discourse the quotation marks are not used.

She asked what was the matter.

b. To identify words which are being discussed as words.

The word "garage" comes from the French; the word "piano" comes from the Italian.
"Buxom" originally came from the Old English verb meaning "to bend."
"To be" is the trickiest verb in the language.

This use is sometimes extended to include technical terms (*A "field" in mathematics is not what it is in agriculture*) and slang terms (*Her brother "socked" her in the eye and "beaned" her with a ruler*). Though occasionally acceptable, this usage is often overdone in student writing. Quotation marks do not make a term appropriate. If a word is appropriate in context, it can usually stand without quotation marks; if it is not appropriate, it should not be used.

c. To enclose the titles of short stories, poems, songs, etc. (but not books).

> I think Kipling's best short story is "Without Benefit of Clergy."
> Have you read Emerson's "Self-Reliance"?
> It was Cole Porter who wrote "Begin the Beguine."
> Tennyson asked to have "Crossing the Bar" placed at the end of every edition of his poems.
> He says that Da Vinci's "Mona Lisa" is a portrait of an Italian noble-woman.

d. In bibliography, to distinguish the title of a selection from that of the whole book in which the selection is printed.

> Faulkner, William. "Two Soldiers," *Collected Stories of William Faulkner.*
> New York: Random House, 1950.

For additional examples of this use, see pages 249–251. Notice that · titles of books are set in italics rather than in quotation marks.

SINGLE QUOTATION MARKS

Single quotation marks are used:

a. To mark quotations within quotations.

When it is necessary to include one set of quotation marks within another, the internal quotation is placed in single quotation marks, the longer quotation in double quotation marks:

> Here is an excerpt from my brother's letter: "Today in class Mr. Blair quoted Wordsworth's line 'A three-months darling of a pigmy size,' and said it appeared in one edition as 'A three-months darling of a pig my size.' "

> When the director said, "Let's try that passage again, beginning with 'Once more into the breach,' and remember that this is a battle, not a declamation contest," there was an audible bronx cheer from one of the soldiers.

b. In print, as a substitute for double quotation marks to improve the appearance of the page.

When in a printed work it is necessary to place quotation marks around a great many single words, an editor will sometimes attempt to improve the appearance of the page by substituting single marks for double marks. The need for this substitution almost never exists in college writing.

P9 *Punctuation with Quotation Marks*

Whether punctuation should be placed *inside* or *outside* quotation marks is often a problem. Practice is not uniform, but the following excerpt from

The MLA Style Sheet — a respected authority among English instructors — states the prevailing procedure succinctly:

> For the sake of appearance put all commas or periods *inside* quotation marks. . . . Other punctuation goes inside quotation marks only when it is actually part of the quoted matter.[1]

This convention may be stated in detail as follows:

a. When the quoted words are followed by a comma, put the comma inside the quotation marks.

"If you insist," I said, "I'll do it."

The word "skirt," for example, has both standard and slang meanings.

"But," Bill objected, " 'Knabe,' in German, doesn't mean 'knave'; it means 'boy.' "

Notice that this convention applies only to quoted material. It does not mean that a comma after *he said, she replied,* etc., should be placed inside the quotation marks.

b. The period, like the comma, always goes inside the quotation marks.

That is not the way to spell "eclectic."

He said, "You can always count on Tom to muddle the issue."

c. If the quotation is a question, the question mark goes inside the quotation marks; otherwise, it goes outside.

Somebody yelled, "Why don't you go home?" (What was yelled was a question.)

Did he actually say, "Let Williams do it"? (The quotation is not a question, but the whole sentence is; therefore the question mark goes outside the quotation marks, and no other punctuation is used at the end of the sentence.)

Well, how *do* you spell "eclectic"? The whole sentence is a question, not the word "eclectic.")

d. The exclamation mark, like the question mark, goes inside if the quoted part is an exclamation; otherwise it goes outside.

"Get out of my sight!" he yelled. (The quoted part is an exclamation.)

[1] From *The MLA Style Sheet*, Revised Edition, p. 9. Compiled by W. R. Parker, for the Modern Language Association of America, 1947–56. By permission. The omitted material indicated by the ellipsis refers to exceptions which almost never occur in freshman writing.

I did, too, say "Friday"! (The whole sentence is an exclamation; "Friday" is not.)

His only answer was "Nonsense!" (Only the quoted word is an exclamation.)

e. Since the semicolon and the colon almost never occur as part of quoted material in terminal position, the practice is always to place them outside the quotation marks.

He said, "You can be confident that I'll do it"; but I was by no means confident.

If the sentence ended with the quotation, there would be a period inside the quotation marks. The semicolon is used to provide contrast between the two main clauses, not to end the first one.

"There are three parts," she said; "we have two of them."

Although the semicolon would be included in the quotation if it were written — She said, "There are three parts; we have two of them." — the semicolon is always placed after *she* (*he,* etc.) *said* when it interrupts such quotations.

f. When the dash is used to stand for an omitted part of a quotation, it is included within the quotation marks.

Occasionally a speaker is interrupted or for some reason fails to finish what he has begun to say. When this happens, a dash is used to show that the quotation is not finished.

"But Mary said — " she began, then stopped suddenly.
Nicholson said loudly, "In my opinion, our instructor is — " Just then the instructor walked into the room.

Notice that a concluding period is not used after the dash.

P10   *The Apostrophe*

The apostrophe (') has three general uses:

a. Use an apostrophe to indicate the possessive case of a noun.

An apostrophe followed by *s* is added to the common case of the following types of nouns:

Both singular and plural nouns, neither of which ends in s:

boy's, girl's, ox's, mouse's, tooth's, antenna's
men's, women's, oxen's, mice's, teeth's, antennae's

Singular nouns ending in s:

James's, Charles's, Keats's, Burns's, Dickens's

Usage for the latter group varies. Some writers omit the final *s* (James', Charles', etc.). When a noun already contains two *s* sounds, there is a greater reluctance to add a third one (Massachusetts', mistress', Jesus'), but since most written communications are not read aloud the repetition of *s* sounds is usually not so objectionable as it might seem to be. With such nouns, follow your own preference. Notice that an apostrophe without an *s* is added to plural nouns ending in *s* — *babies' clothing.*

Indefinite pronouns:

anybody's, anyone's, everybody's, one's, nobody's, someone's

b. Use an apostrophe to indicate the omission of letters or figures.

I've, can't, hasn't, isn't, '48 (1948), the class of '39

c. Use an apostrophe to indicate the plural of letters or figures.

Let's begin with the A's; look under the K's; the S's look like 8's.

P 11 *Ellipsis and Dash*

Ellipsis (. . .)

The basic use of the ellipsis (three periods) is to mark an incomplete construction.

Usually the ellipsis indicates that one or more words have been omitted from a quotation. It is also used to indicate that a progression of numbers continues beyond the last figure given (1,4,7,10,13,16 . . .). If an ellipsis occurs at the end of a sentence, a fourth period is usually added:

Original Quotation	*Elliptical Quotation*
Death is at all times solemn, but never so much as at sea. A man dies on shore, his body remains with his friends, and "the mourners go about the streets," but when a man falls overboard at sea and is lost, there is a sadness in the event, and a difficulty in realizing it, which gives it an air of awful mystery.	Death is at all times solemn, but never so much as at sea. A man dies on shore, his body remains with his friends, . . . but when a man falls overboard at sea and is lost, there is a sadness in the event, and a difficulty in realizing it. . . .

Dash

The dash should not be used as a general utility mark to substitute for a comma, period, semicolon, or colon. It is a specialized punctuation mark which serves the following purposes:

a. To stress a word or phrase at the end of a sentence.

In the whole world there is only one person he really admires — himself.

And now it is my pleasure to present a man whom we all know and admire and to whom we are all deeply indebted — the Reverend Dr. Mason.

Absence makes the heart grow fonder — of somebody else.

b. To sum up or complete an involved sentence.

To live as free men in a free country; to enjoy, even to abuse, the right to think and speak as we like; to feel that the state is the servant of its people; to be, even in a literal sense, a trustee and a partner in the conduct of a nation — all this is what democracy means to us.

c. To mark an interrupted or unfinished quotation.

"I'd like to," he said, "but I'm — "
"You're what?" I asked.
"Well, I'm — I — you see, I've never done anything like that before."

d. When used in pairs, to set off a pronounced interruption.

There will never again be — you may be sure of this — so glorious an opportunity.

This answer — if we can call it an answer — is completely meaningless.

P12 *Parentheses and Brackets*

Parentheses

The three most common uses of parentheses are:

a. To enclose an explanation, qualification, or example:

His wife (he married about a year ago) is a member of a very fine New England family.

Nice (in the old sense of discriminating) has almost fallen out of use.

Foreign words (*data,* for example) slowly become naturalized and lose their foreign characteristics.

b. To enclose cross-references:

(*See* Appendix A), (See page 271), (Consult *Webster's Biographical Dictionary*).

c. In formal business transactions, to repeat a sum previously stated in words:

I enclose three hundred dollars ($300.00) to cover my share of the costs.

Brackets

Brackets are used chiefly to enclose an editorial explanation or comment within a passage being edited or reported. The words within the brackets are supplied by the editor; the rest is the work of the author.

According to the Associated Press, Mrs. Henry Thall [the former June Wexler of this city] was a passenger on the missing plane.

I have written to [name of correspondent illegible] that I will not be a party to that transaction.

Brackets are occasionally used to enclose symbols which cannot conventionally be left without some enclosing device. The identification of the various punctuation marks on page 467 is an example of this use.

Review Exercises

A. Rewrite and hand in to your instructor the following sentences, inserting as you write any punctuation clearly required by the conventions. If no punctuation is necessary, do not copy the sentence. To make your insertions obvious, use red ink or red pencil for punctuation which you add.

1. He said I propose to transfer at the end of the semester.
2. He said he would transfer at the end of the semester.
3. I expect he said to transfer at the end of the semester.
4. Dr J A Frazer was born on March 18 1901.
5. Dr Koch a German scientist discovered the tuberculosis bacillus.
6. The lecturer was the Rev Nelson Laird D D
7. Have you read his latest book
8. The cars in that series were as follows Aerosedan Fleetline Fleetmaster and Stylemaster.
9. The manuscript was dirty blotched and unevenly typed.
10. I have not seen him since his wife left he has been keeping to himself.

11. Mr. Reynolds the insurance man called.

12. She is quite inexperienced and has never worked in an office before.

13. See the new revolutionary car of the year the Ford.

14. She said, When I asked his opinion, he answered, I don't give advice on such questions.

15. I am enclosing eighty-five dollars $85.00 for the semiannual premium.

16. This meaning See *The American College Dictionary* is now established usage.

17. He looked at it enviously. Its a beauty he exclaimed

18. However I still have five payments to make.

19. That she wont like it may be taken for granted.

20. Do you think he will accept she asked

B. Distinguish between restrictive and nonrestrictive modifiers by inserting commas around the nonrestrictive modifiers in the following sentences. Use red ink or red pencil for inserted commas.

1. Girls who hate cooking are poor matrimonial risks.

2. Girls who are physically less rugged than boys should not be subjected to strenuous athletic programs.

3. The man driving the Maxwell is Jack Benny.

4. Benny driving a Maxwell was charged with obstructing traffic.

5. Salesmen who don't argue with customers make more money.

6. Salesmen most of whom are young men lead an unsettled life.

7. The pilot realizing his plight radioed for instructions.

8. The pilot who radioed for instructions does not answer.

9. His wife satisfied with these concessions wisely kept quiet.

10. His wife resentful of his extravagance asked for an increased allowance.

11. They questioned the man who reported the robbery.

12. The man who reported the robbery cannot be found.

13. The man at the back of the room was told to leave.

14. The man evidently seriously hurt was taken to the hospital.

15. The fighters who were quite obviously stalling were disqualified.

16. Their wives who needed the money were indignant.

C. The best way to develop a confident knowledge of the conventions of punctuation is to observe how punctuation marks are actually used in modern writing. In the following selection, which is fairly formal, particular punctuation marks have been numbered. Write down each number and describe the purpose for which the punctuation is being used.

Turning to the more modern theories,[1] which agree at least that language is of human rather than divine origin,[1] we encounter first what is best known by its nickname,[2] the "bow-wow" theory. This asserts that primitive language was exclusively *"echoic"; that is,*[3] that its words were directly imitative of the sounds of nature or of animals. All the wordstock is thought to have originated in a way parallel to the child's calling a dog "bow-wow"[4] or a duck "quack-quack."[4] The great objection to this theory is that it has not been demonstrated that early or primitive languages are composed exclusively or in great part of onomatopoetic words; on the contrary,[5] it is clear that the primitive languages of savage tribes are largely made up of words that are quite as conventional as those of civilized peoples. At best,[6] the "bow-wow" theory can explain the origin of but a part,[7] and not the largest part,[7] of language. Yet it seems fair to add that the theory has in the past been somewhat unjustly derided. Words that are imitative or at least partly so —[8] for there are many gradations between the purely imitative and the purely conventional —[8] do form an appreciable part of the vocabulary of most languages. There are many words that we instinctively feel to be symbolic, or semi-echoic. Thus,[9] such English words as *battle*,[10] *roar*,[10] and *thunder* have not perhaps a completely imitative quality, certainly not as compared with *hiss*,[11] *whistle*,[11] *bang*,[11] and *crash;* yet they approach echoism in a way that the conventional words of language do not. If,[12] then,[12] the "bow-wow" theory does not solve the riddle of the origin of language,[13] it does at least help to account for the sounds of many words.*

D. In the following selection all punctuation has been omitted, except the periods at the ends of the sentences. Copy the selection, adding all necessary punctuation in red.

The Bible is written in very poor English isnt it remarked a grade school child to his father as they walked home from church.

What makes you say that inquired the astonished parent for whose ears the musical dignity of the King James Version approached the perfection of English prose.

Well our teacher said it was bad English to begin sentences with and. But almost every sentence the minister read this morning began with and replied the child.

The father smiled as he recognized the accuracy of the childs observation. The reading had been from the eighth chapter of the Gospel according to St Matthew it was true enough that almost every sentence began with and. He thought a moment longer before he spoke. Your teacher has made a natural mistake he began. In trying to give good advice to boys and girls just learning to write she has made a rule about and. The rule is too big. People who know how to write well use and correctly and effectively at the beginning of sentences. On the other hand boys and girls in schools use and too much. Your teachers purpose in trying to help you was good but the rule she stated is untrue.

In this trifling episode may be found the epitome of the problem of correctness in English. It lies in the recurrent conflict between rule and practice. Rules of usage are usually made to cover specific situations to govern the use of language at a certain time for a certain purpose. Gradually as the rule is taught and applied the specific purpose for which it was created is forgotten and the rule is applied universally often in defiance of a language custom centuries old. Take for example the much taught but erroneous rule that a sentence must not end with a preposition. Or as one grammar is supposed to

* From *The Development of Modern English,* Second Edition, by Stuart Robertson and Frederic G. Cassidy. © 1954 by Prentice-Hall, Inc. Reprinted by permission.

have stated it A preposition is a bad thing to end a sentence with. In certain types of formal literary English the terminal preposition is considered undesirable because of the rhetorical looseness it gives to the style. Because certain formalists disliked the construction the rule was created. It was repeated copied placed in school books. Teachers unaware of the reason behind the origin of the rule taught that a sentence must never end with a preposition. Teachers are still teaching this rule. Yet English for centuries has been idiomatically and correctly expressed in such sentences as Where are you from I didnt know whom to give it to. John will go but I dont expect to. What city has he lived in To apply the rule to such sentences as these which are characteristic of informal or colloquial English is to make an absurdity of a caution. Many such absurdities have been created and are being perpetuated through honest but misguided zeal.*

* From *Teaching English Usage,* by Robert C. Pooley. Copyright, 1946, by the National Council of Teachers of English. Reprinted by permission of Appleton-Century-Crofts, Inc.

Mechanics

sp _Spelling_

One requirement of standard English is that words be spelled as they are spelled by educated writers and recorded in dictionaries. Colleges and universities are held responsible by society for ensuring that their graduates have a reasonable mastery of standard English. It is for this reason that college instructors insist that all college writing — even the most informal — show a decent regard for accepted spelling. The real purpose of this insistence is to protect the student; for conspicuously bad spelling is generally considered a clear sign of illiteracy. Socially and professionally, a student who cannot spell is at a disadvantage. It is easier to judge a man's spelling than most other things about him; and, whether rightly or not, people do jump to conclusions about a person's education and intelligence on the evidence of his spelling. A student who refuses to make a serious and sustained effort to cure major spelling deficiencies penalizes himself in college and out of it.

Students who spell poorly usually act on one of three assumptions: (_a_) that spelling is not important, (_b_) that nothing much can be done to improve one's spelling, or (_c_) that the only way to learn is to spend hours memorizing spelling lists. None of these assumptions is sound. Spelling _is_ important. Provided that misspelling is not a result of an organic or psychological disorder, there is no reason why any student cannot train himself to be a reasonably good speller within a single semester. And an uncritical memorizing of spelling lists is not conspicuously effective.

HOW TO IMPROVE YOUR SPELLING

The first step in improving your spelling is to take an inventory of your errors. Keep a record of those words _which you actually misspell in your writing._ The best way to begin such an inventory is to take a standard spelling list, such as the one on pages 497–501, and check those words which cause you difficulty, ignoring those you seldom use or never misspell. The checked words then become your basic, private spelling list. You should copy their correct spellings in alphabetical order into a special notebook, leaving space for later additions. Your basic list probably will not exceed fifty words. Even an unusually poor speller could probably correct ninety per cent of his spelling errors by concentrating on a carefully selected list of 100 words.

You should keep your basic list up to date by scoring out words you have mastered and adding new words you have misspelled. This step is most important. Your original list was merely an estimate of your spelling weaknesses, but actual misspellings are a record of errors. Remember, it is the errors you have made that you are really interested in correcting, and the more accurately your list records them, the more useful it will be. Also, because the frequency with which you misspell a word is part of your spelling record, you should indicate repeated misspellings of the same word by adding a check mark each time you misspell it.

Keeping such a list will of itself help a great deal, but the list should be reviewed regularly. Any normal student who conscientiously studies such a list for ten minutes a day should be able to eliminate all his common spelling errors within a single semester. If you think this statement is an exaggeration, put it to the test. The experiment may give you a lasting sense of confidence in your spelling ability that will more than justify the time spent.

In studying your list, concentrate on the *part* of the word which you misspell. Generally we do not misspell words but syllables. For example, most students who misspell *secretary* interchange the second and third vowels; most misspellings of *tragedy* are a result of placing an extra *d* before the *g;* and misspellings of such words as *receive, belief,* and *friend* come from reversing the *i* and *e*. Identifying your specific errors allows you to concentrate on the syllable in which the error occurs.

For words which prove unusually troublesome it is often helpful to learn or invent some memorizing device: a rule, a slogan, a jingle — anything, no matter how absurd, which will remind you of the correct spelling of a particular syllable. The rule of *i* before *e* except after *c,* which is stated as a jingle on page 495, and the rules for prefixes and suffixes, are generally useful memorizing devices. Unfortunately some rules have so many exceptions that they are hardly worth learning. It is therefore often wise to invent your own memorizing device. Some students find it extremely helpful to remember statements like *A good secretary keeps a secret, Remember the gum in argument,* and *Every cemetery has a "meter" in the middle.* Other students are helped by capitalizing the danger spots during spelling practice — tRAGedy, mainTENance, desPERate. If these devices help you, use them; if not, invent your own.

Finally, a concern with spelling during composition should, so far as is practicable, be postponed until revision. If you break off the writing of a paragraph to consult a dictionary, you may lose a thought you cannot recapture. If you keep a record of your misspellings, you will be conscious of troublesome words, so that when you are uncertain of a spelling, you can place a check in the margin and go on. Then, when the first draft is finished, look up the correct spelling of all checked words. Indeed, a student with severe spelling troubles will be wise to proofread his whole paper at least once for spelling alone.

In short, then: (1) Keep a spelling record, (2) study it at regular periods, (3) identify the trouble spot in the word, (4) devise a means of remembering the correct spelling, and (5) check your spelling when proofreading. If this procedure is followed conscientiously, spelling will soon cease to be a problem.

THE MOST COMMON TRAPS IN SPELLING

Although any word which is not spelled phonetically (as it sounds) may give trouble, six types of words are especially likely to cause errors. These are:

1. Words containing a "colorless" vowel. Vowels in unstressed positions (*a*go, *a*gent, awkw*a*rd, maint*e*nance, incred*i*ble, bachel*o*r) are likely to be pronounced as a very weak *uh*. This sound is called the colorless or neutral vowel.[1] Because it is quite common in English and because its sound gives no indication of its spelling, the colorless vowel is responsible for many spelling errors. There is nothing to guide one in spelling this sound. The only solution is to memorize the vowel in any word which repeatedly causes trouble. The best help is a memorizing device, such as magnifying the syllable in question — *baLANCE, independENT, eligIBLE, sponSOR, foREIGN, chauffEUR.*

2. Words with ie or ei. Words like *niece, receive,* and *friend* are frequently misspelled through the interchanging of the *e* and the *i*. Most of these errors may be easily removed by following Rule 4 on page 495 and memorizing the eleven exceptions.

3. Words with similar sounds but different meanings. Such words as *altar, alter; peace, piece; weak, week; weather, whether* are easily confused. A list of troublesome contrasted pairs is given on pages 501–502. You should study that list and copy into your personal spelling record any pairs which you tend to confuse.

4. Words with irregular plural forms. Since most English nouns take *s* plurals, all plurals formed in any other way may be considered irregular. The most troublesome plurals to spell are those of nouns ending in *o* or *y*. Such nouns have regular *s* plurals when the *o* or *y* immediately follows a vowel (*cameo, cameos; key, keys; studio, studios*), but are generally irregular when the *o* or *y* follows a consonant (*cargo, veto, lady, torpedo*). See Rules 6 and 7 on pages 495–496.

5. Words which double the final consonant before a suffix beginning with a vowel. Some words double a final consonant before adding a suffix beginning with a vowel (*refer, referred*), while others (*benefit, benefited*) do not. This lack of consistency causes many spelling errors, and the "rule" is so cumbersome and has so many exceptions that students often

---

[1] Students using *The American College Dictionary* or Webster's *New World Dictionary* should notice that in these dictionaries the colorless vowel is represented by the phonetic symbol called the *schwa,* and written ə, like an inverted *e*.

prefer to study the individual words which cause them trouble. The more useful part of the rule concerning doubled consonants is given as Rule 9 on page 496.

6. Common exceptions to general rules. Any exceptional spelling is likely to be difficult because of the tendency to make it conform to the regular pattern. For example, a student who is not sure how to spell *seize* is likely to interchange the *e* and *i* because of the *i*-before-*e* rule. Similarly the rule that a silent *e* at the end of a word is retained in adding a suffix beginning with a consonant leads many students to misspell *argument*. Words like these are exceptions to general rules and cause many spelling errors. The only safe procedure is to *memorize the exceptions along with the rule.* Whenever a rule is given in the following pages the common exceptions are noted. Study these as carefully as you study the rule itself.

RULES OF SPELLING

The rules given here are those which are most generally useful.

1. The prefixes un-, dis-, mis- do not affect the spelling of the root.

Thus, *unafraid* but *unnecessary; disappoint* but *dissatisfy; misrepresent* but *misspell.*

unable	disable	misbehave
unknown	disorder	misconduct
unopened	disregard	misguided
but	*but*	*but*
unnatural	disservice	misshapen
unnerved	dissimilar	misspent
unnoticed	dissolve	misstatement

2. When a suffix beginning with a consonant is added to a word ending in silent e, the e is retained.

Examples: *absolutely, achievement, extremely, indefinitely, sincerely.*

Exceptions: *argument, awful, duly, ninth, probably, truly, wholly.*

Three common words have alternative spellings:

abridgment, abridgement; acknowledgment, acknowledgement; judgment, judgement.

3. When a suffix beginning with a vowel is added to a word ending in silent e, the e is dropped unless it is required to indicate pronunciation or to avoid confusion with a similar word.

Examples: *accumulating, achieving, boring, coming, grievance, icy.*

Exceptions:

To Keep *a c or g Soft*	*To Prevent* *Mispronunciation*
advantageous	canoeist
changeable	eyeing
courageous	hoeing
manageable	mileage
noticeable	shoeing
outrageous	
peaceable	*To Prevent Confusion*
serviceable	*with Other Words*
singeing	
tingeing	dyeing
vengeance	

4. The order of the vowels in the *ie* combination (c*ei*ling, n*ie*ce) is explained in the jingle:

> Write *i* before *e*
> Except after *c*
> Or when sounded like *ay*
> As in *neighbor* and *weigh*.

Exceptions: *counterfeit, either, foreign, forfeit, height, leisure, neither, seize, seizure, sovereign, weird.*

5. Words ending with the sound *seed* are usually spelled -*cede*.

Examples: *accede, concede, intercede, precede, recede, secede.*

Exceptions: There are only four exceptions. Three of them end in -*ceed* (*exceed, proceed, succeed*); the fourth is the only word that ends in -*sede* (*supersede*).

6. Singular nouns ending in a consonant plus *y* form their plurals by changing the *y* to *i* before adding -*es*.

This rule also applies to the third person singular of verbs.

Examples: *ally, allies; baby, babies; city, cities; cry, cries; try, tries.*

Exceptions: The plurals of proper names often add *s* immediately after the *y: the Kellys, the Marys, the Sallys.*

Notice that singular nouns ending in a vowel plus *y* are regular and simply add -*s* to form the plural:

> *attorneys, donkeys, valleys.*

7. Singular nouns ending in a consonant plus *o* generally form their plurals by adding -*es*.

There are, however, so many exceptions that it may be safer to dispense with the rule and learn troublesome words individually.

Examples: *buffaloes, cargoes, echoes, heroes, potatoes, torpedoes, vetoes.*

Exceptions: The chief exceptions are musical terms: *altos, bassos, oratorios, pianos, solos, sopranos.* Others are *autos, cantos, dynamos, Eskimos, halos, mementos, provisos, quartos.*

Notice that singular nouns ending in a vowel plus *o* are regular and simply add *-s* to form the plural:

cameos, folios, radios, studios.

8. Most singular nouns ending in *-s, -ss, -sh, -ch, -x,* or *-z,* form their plurals by adding *-es.*

Examples: *Jameses, Joneses, ashes, bushes, matches, pitches, foxes, taxes, buzzes.*

Exceptions: *bass, fish, perch, six's, Swiss,* and borrowed Greek nouns ending in *-is (ellipsis — ellipses, thesis — theses,* etc.).

9. Words of one syllable double the final consonant before adding a suffix beginning with a vowel if (1) they end in a single consonant, and (2) they contain a single vowel.

Notice that the rule holds only if both conditions are satisfied. Thus a word of one syllable ending in two consonants does not double the final consonant before a suffix beginning with a vowel (ac*t*ing, as*k*ed, par*t*ing, sif*t*ed, etc.). And a one-syllable word containing two vowels does not double the final consonant (bea*r*ing, cree*p*ing, dea*l*ing, ree*l*ing, soa*r*ing, etc.).

This rule is extended to words of more than one syllable, provided that the accent falls on the last syllable (thus prefér — preferred, but bénefit — benefited; confér — conferring, but cónference). This part of the rule, however, has so many exceptions that students sometimes find the rule more confusing than helpful.

Review Exercises

A. Following is a list of words frequently misspelled by college students. When two spellings are given for the same word, both are correct and the first is preferred.

As you read through the list underline those words which you recognize as being part of your writing vocabulary and which you have had trouble spelling. Then copy the correct spelling of the underlined words into a special notebook so that you will have a preliminary record of your spelling difficulties. Revise this list periodically by adding the correct spelling of any word which you misspell in subsequent papers and scoring out words which you no longer misspell. Check, also, the list given in Exercise B.

abbreviate	antecedent	boundaries
absence	anxiety	breathe
absolutely	apartment	brilliant
absurd	apparatus	Britain
accelerate	apparent	Britannica
accidentally	appearance	Briton
accommodate	appropriate	bulletin
accomplish	arctic	buoyant
according	argument	bureau
accumulate	arising	buried
accustom	arithmetic	burying
achievement	arouse	business
acoustics	arranging	busy
acquaintance	article	cafeteria
acquitted	artillery	calendar
across	ascend	candidate
address	association	can't
adoption	athlete	carburetor
advice (noun)	athletics	carrying
advise (verb)	attempt	casualties
adviser, advisor	attractive	causal
aggravate	audible	ceiling
aggression	audience	celebrity
airplane	authorities	cemetery
alleviate	automobile	certain
alley	auxiliary	changeable
allotted	awkward	changing
allowed	bachelor	characteristic
all right	balance	chauffeur
ally	balloon	chief
already	barbarous	choose
although	barring	choosing
altogether	battalion	chose
always	bearing	chosen
amateur	because	clause
ambiguous	becoming	climbed
ammunition	before	clothes
among	beggar	colloquial
amount	beginning	colonel
analogous	believe	column
analysis	beneficial	coming
analyze	benefited	commission
annual	biscuit	commitment

committed
committee
companies
comparatively
compel
compelled
competent
competition
complaint
completely
compulsory
concede
conceivable
conceive
condemn
condescend
condition
conjunction
connoisseur
conqueror
conscience
conscientious
considered
consistent
contemptible
continuous
control
controlled
convenient
co-operate, coöperate
copies
corner
coroner
corps
corpse
costume
countries
courteous
courtesy
cozy
cries
criticism
criticize
cruelty
cruise
curiosity
curriculum
custom
cylinder

dealt
debater
deceitful
deceive
decide
decision
defendant
deferred
deficient
definite
definition
democracy
dependent
descendant
describe
description
desirable
despair
desperate
destruction
develop, develope
developed
development
device (noun)
devise (verb)
diaphragm
diary
dictionary
dietitian
difference
digging
diphtheria
disappearance
disappoint
disastrous
discipline
discussion
disease
dissatisfied
dissipate
distribute
divine
doctor
doesn't
dominant
don't
dormitories
dropped
drunkenness

echoes
ecstasy
efficiency
eighth
eligible
eliminate
embarrass
eminent
emphasize
employee
encouraging
encyclopedia
enthusiastic
equipment
equipped
equivalent
erroneous
especially
eventually
exaggerate
exceed
excel
excellent
exceptional
excitement
exercise
exhaust
exhilaration
existence
experience
explanation
extensive
extracurricular
extremely
exuberance
fallacious
fallacy
familiar
fascinate
February
fiery
finally
financial
financier
forehead
foreign
foremost
forfeit
forty

frantically
fraternities
freshman
friend
fulfill, fulfil
furniture
gaiety
generally
genius
genuine
glorious
government
grammar
grandeur
grievous
guarantee
guard
guardian
guerrilla, guerilla
guess
guidance
handicapped
handkerchief
harass
hearse
height
heinous
heroes
hesitancy
hindrance
hoarse
hoping
horde
human
humane
humorous
hundredths
hurries
hygiene
hypocrisy
hysterical
illiterate
illogical
imaginary
imagination
imitative
immediately
implement
impromptu

inadequate
incidentally
incredible
indefinitely
independent
indicted
indispensable
inevitable
influential
innocent
inoculate
intellectual
intelligence
intentionally
intercede
interested
interpret
interrupt
irrelevant
irreligious
irresistible
irreverent
itself
judgment, judgement
judicial
khaki
kindergarten
knowledge
laboratory
laid
later
latter
legitimate
leisure
library
lightning
likable, likeable
likely
literature
loneliness
losing
magazine
magnificent
maintain
maintenance
maneuver
manual
manufacture
mathematics

mattress
meant
medicine
medieval
messenger
millionaire
miniature
minute
mischievous
misspelled
modifies
modifying
momentous
mortgage
mosquitoes
mottoes
mountainous
murmur
muscle
mysterious
naïve, naive
naturally
necessary
necessity
Negroes
neither
nervous
nevertheless
nickel
niece
ninety
ninth
noticeable
notorious
nowadays
obedience
obliged
obstacle
occasionally
occur
occurred
occurrence
o'clock
official
officious
omission
omit
omitted
oneself

opinion
opportunity
optimistic
organization
original
orthodox
ought
outrageous
overrun
paid
pamphlet
parallel
parliament
participle
particularly
partner
pastime
peaceable
perceive
perform
perhaps
permissible
perseverance
persuade
Philippines
phrase
physical
physician
picnicked
piece
planed
planned
playwright
pleasant
politics
possess
possessive
possible
potatoes
practice
prairie
precedence
precedents
preceding
predominant
prefer
preference
preferred
prejudice

preparation
prevalent
primitive
privilege
probably
professor
prominent
pronounce
pronunciation
propaganda
propeller
protein
psychology
pursue
pursuing
putting
quantity
quarantine
quarter
questionnaire
quizzes
realize
really
recede
receipt
receive
receiving
recognize
recommend
refer
reference
referred
referring
regard
regional
relevant
religion
religious
remembrance
reminiscence
rendezvous
repetition
replies
representative
reservoir
resistance
restaurant
reverent
rhetoric

rheumatism
rhythmical
ridiculous
sacrifice
sacrilegious
safety
salary
sanctuary
sandwich
scarcely
scene
scenic
schedule
scrape
secretarial
secretary
seized
sense
sensible
sentence
sentinel
separate
sergeant
severely
shining
shriek
siege
sieve
similar
sincerely
sincerity
skeptical
slight
soliloquy
sophomore
source
specifically
specimen
sponsor
spontaneous
statement
statue
stature
statute
stomach
stopped
strength
strenuously
stretched

struggle	therefore	valuable
studying	they're	vengeance
subordinate	thorough	victorious
subtle	though	view
succeed	thought	vigilant
success	till	vigorous
successful	tired	village
suffrage	together	villain
superintendent	tournament	volume
supersede	toward, towards	warrant
suppress	traffic	warring
surely	tragedy	weird
surprise	transferred	welfare
suspense	tremendous	where
swimming	tries	which
syllable	truly	whole
symmetry	Tuesday	wholly
synonym	twelfth	whom
synonymous	typical	wiry
taboo, tabu	tyranny	woman
tangible	unanimous	women
tariff	undoubtedly	won't
tasting	unnecessary	worried
technical	until	worrying
technique	usage	writing
temperament	useful	written
tenant	using	yacht
tendency	usually	your
than	vacancy	you're (you are)
therefor	vacuum	zoology

B. Errors in the following words may be classified as errors in spelling or errors in diction, since both meaning and spelling are involved in the correct usage. Study these words carefully. Check those which you have confused in the past or of which you are uncertain and look them up in your dictionary.

accept, except	censor, censure
access, excess	cite, sight, site
adapt, adopt	coarse, course
adaptation, adoption	complement, compliment
affect, effect	conscience, conscious
all together, altogether	council, counsel
altar, alter	dairy, diary
angel, angle	decent, descend, descent
berth, birth	desert, dessert
born, borne	dining, dinning
canvas, canvass	dying, dyeing
capital, capitol	elicit, illicit

emigrant, immigrant
euphemism, euphuism
fare, fair
formally, formerly
forth, fourth
hear, here
holy, wholly
instance, instants
irrelevant, irreverent
its, it's
knew, new
know, no
later, latter
lead, led
loath, loathe
loose, lose
luxuriant, luxurious
moral, morale
past, passed
peace, piece
plain, plane

precede, proceed
presence, presents
principal, principle
prophecy, prophesy
quiet, quite
respectively, respectfully
right, rite
shone, shown
sleight, slight
speak, speech
staid, stayed
stationary, stationery
straight, strait
suit, suite
threw, through
to, too, two
troop, troupe
vain, vein, vane
weak, week
weather, whether
who's, whose

C. Some of the following words form their plurals by adding -*s* to the singular form, some by adding -*es*. Write out the plurals which take -*es:*

alto, analysis, auto, ditch, dynamo, echo, Eskimo, fox, hero, piano, radio, solo, synopsis, tobacco, tomato, veto.

D. Write the plural forms of the following nouns:

alley, alumna, alumnus, attorney, axis, baby, basis, belief, category, crisis, half, key, lady, loaf, major general, mother-in-law, ox, quantity, study, tax, taxi, try, 5, 7, A.

E. Write the simple past tense form of the following verbs:

act, annul, benefit, confer, crop, defer, develop, drip, drop, equip, excel, gas, kidnap, occur, propel, quiz, reap, rebel, refer, regret, rip, rob, scar, slip, stop, strap, worship, wrap.

abr *Abbreviations*

In general, abbreviations should be used in college writing only if they satisfy two conditions: they must be standard abbreviations recognized by dictionaries, and they must be appropriate to the context. The first condition rules out such slang abbreviations as *b. f.* (boy friend) and *n. g.* (no good). The second requires students to recognize that many standard abbreviations (*advt., Ave., Feb., Xmas*) are inappropriate in a formal style and that abbreviations of certain titles (*Col., Dr., Mr., Rev.*) are used only when followed by the name of the person to whom the title applies.

The following is a summary of the most common standard abbreviations. For the correct form of abbreviations not included in this list, consult your dictionary.

Bibliographical terms: *cf., op. cit., vol., pp.* (For these and others, see pages 266–269.)

Names of days: *Sun., Mon., Tues., Wed., Thurs., Fri., Sat.* (Used only in dates.)

Names of months: *Jan., Feb., Aug., Sept., Oct., Nov., Dec.* (Used only in dates.)

Names of organizations: *A.F.L., C.I.O., D.A.R., U.S. Steel, W.C.T.U.*

Names of government agencies: *AAA, CIA, FBI, SEC, TVA.* (Notice that abbreviations of government agencies generally do not require periods.)

Names of states: *Calif., Del., Mass., N.Y., Ill.* (Used chiefly in addresses.)

Signs: When the context permits, the following signs are used as abbreviations: & (ampersand: see Glossary), $ (dollar), £ (British pound sterling), % (per cent), " " (ditto marks, used in tabulations to repeat the item immediately above the marks).

caps *Use of Capital Letters*

a. Capitalize the first word of each sentence and of each line of regular poetry.

Ask for Mr. Lane. He is in charge of service.
Too bad! Better luck next time.

> Earth has not anything to show more fair;
> Dull would he be of soul who could pass by
> A sight so touching in its majesty: . . .
> — Wordsworth, "Composed Upon Westminster Bridge"

b. Capitalize the first word of a direct quotation.

The President's answer was, "No comment."
"If you will give me a receipt," I said, "you can have the money now."

c. Capitalize proper nouns.

Sergeant York was one of the great heroes of World War I.
She works for the National Broadcasting Company.

Laurence Olivier was knighted after his production of *Henry V*.
I find French easier than German.
The *Saratoga* was sunk at Bikini.
The Amazon is longer than the Mississippi.

Note: Words which were originally proper nouns but have taken on more general meanings are regarded as common nouns and are not capitalized: *boycott, calico, china, port* (wine), *tweed*.

d. Capitalize adjectives formed from proper nouns.

They seem to be ignorant of the *American* point of view.
There is a *Miltonic* quality in this verse.
The *Renaissance* period was Italy's second hour of glory.
The inductive method has been called the *Baconian* method.
He is studying the *Pauline* doctrines.

Note: Words originally derived from proper nouns cease to be capitalized when they are used as allusions rather than as direct references to the original noun. For example, *colossus, gargantuan, herculean, meandering,* and *panic* do not take capitals. *Philippic* is capitalized when it refers directly to the orations made by Demosthenes, but not when it is used to describe some other denunciatory speech.

e. Capitalize nouns or pronouns referring to the deity:

God, Lord, our Father, Saviour, Messiah, Trinity, Holy Ghost, He, His, Him.

f. Capitalize names of offices only when they are used as titles:[1]

Capitalized	*Not Capitalized*
District Attorney Johnson	Tell it to the district attorney.
Prime Minister Macmillan.	Eden is a former prime minister.
Dr. A. L. Street, Chairman of the Civic Betterment Committee.	He was made chairman of the committee.

Note: President, Presidential, and *Presidency* are capitalized when they refer to the office of President of the United States: *One of these men will be our next President; the Presidency is at stake.*

g. Capitalize *north, south, east,* and *west* and their derivatives only when they refer to geographical areas.

[1] The convention stated here is a simplification of actual practice. The usage of newspapers varies: some capitalize important offices when they are not used as titles; others omit capitals even in titles.

Capitalized	*Not Capitalized*
We found the South charming.	Next year we are going south.
Her parents live in the East.	New York is east of Chicago.
They live on the West Side.	The west side of the field is wet.
The Southern armies fought gallantly.	The house has a fine southern exposure.

h. Capitalize titles of books, magazines, plays and the headings of chapters or sections of a work.

The preferred practice is to capitalize all significant words in a title, including the first word:

A Child's History of the United States
The Return of the Native
Mourning Becomes Electra

Some publishers, however, capitalize every word in the title:

A Child's History Of The United States

Either form is acceptable in college writing, but be consistent.

i. Capitalize the names of days, months, and holidays.

New Year's Day will fall on Thursday.
Next Sunday is Mother's Day.
The favorite vacation months are July and August.

j. Avoid unnecessary capitalization.

In general, do not use capitals unless they are required by one of the conventions stated above. The modern tendency is to use a small letter whenever the conventions permit. Especially avoid unnecessary capitalization of the names of the seasons, of family relationships (*father, mother, sister, uncle*), and of such words as *army, college, freshman, navy, sophomore, university,* unless they are being considered as proper nouns.

Capitalized	*Not Capitalized*
He is a captain in the Army of the United States.	In foreign affairs an army is a political instrument.
Whom do you pick in the Army-Navy game?	The senator said we must have an army and a navy second to none.
Uncle Bill and Aunt Martha are here.	All the uncles and aunts were present.
Where is Sanford Junior College?	He wants a college education.

Capitalized	*Not Capitalized*
The University will have a strong team next year.	He is a university professor.
Are you going to the Freshman Hop?	Are you a freshman or a sophomore?
The Summer Festival starts next week.	I like summer best and winter least.
He belonged to The Society for the Prevention of Cruelty to Animals.	He belonged to a society for the prevention of cruelty to animals.

hyph   *Hyphenation*

Hyphens are used for two purposes: to divide a word at the end of a line, and to join two or more words of a compound which is not written solid.

a. Use a hyphen to break a word at the end of a line.

The use of a hyphen to break a word at the end of a line is less frequently necessary in manuscript copy than it is in print. In student writing, words should be broken at the ends of lines only when failure to hyphenate would result in obviously awkward spacing. If hyphenation seems necessary, the following conditions should be observed:

1. Do not break words of one syllable.

If there is not room at the end of a line for such words as *burst, change, drink, through,* carry the whole word over to the next line.

2. Do not separate a suffix of less than three letters from the rest of the word, or break on a one-letter prefix.

An *-ing* may be separated, but single letters or *-al, -le, -ly,* and *-ed* endings should not. Words like *about, against,* and *open* should not be broken.

3. Break words only between syllables.

When in doubt about syllables, consult your dictionary.

4. Break compound words between the elements of the compound.

Compound Word	*Hyphenation*
armchair	arm-chair
blackbird	black-bird
sailboat	sail-boat

5. Subject to the limitations stated in (2), hyphenate between prefix and root or between root and suffix.

Between Prefix and Root	*Between Root and Suffix*
ante-cedent	adapt-able
be-loved	back-ward
com-mit	depend-ent
con-tagious	ego-ism
dis-appear	kitchen-ette
inter-rupt	lemon-ade
intro-duce	mile-age
per-suade	racket-eer
trans-late	trouble-some

b. Use a hyphen between elements of a compound when usage calls for it.

Hyphenation of compounds varies so much that college students should keep two points in mind: (1) for any particular word, the only safe authority is a reliable, up-to-date dictionary; (2) whenever usage is uncertain, a writer is allowed a choice between competing usages.

Some compounds (*applesauce, blackboard, steamship*) are written solid; others (*dirt cheap, place kick, wedding ring*) are nearly always written as separate words; still others (*father-in-law, ready-made, up-to-date*) are usually hyphenated. There is an increasing tendency to write compounds solid, especially in an informal style, but in general a hyphen is preferred in the following types.

1. Hyphenate a compound modifier preceding a noun.

A self-made man	An off-the-cuff judgment
A well-dressed woman	A tear-jerking movie
A pay-as-you-go tax	A Sunday-morning golf game
A round-by-round report	A dog-in-the-manger attitude

Notice that compound numerical modifiers fall into this class: *Twenty-seven dollars, one hundred and twenty-five pounds, a two-thirds majority.* However, whole numbers below twenty-one are not hyphenated: *Their nineteenth anniversary; the sixteenth of May.* Notice also that a compound modifier following a noun is usually not hyphenated: *The woman was well dressed; the machine is worn out.*

2. Hyphenate a compound consisting of a prefix and a proper noun.

Pro-Russian, un-American (also unAmerican), anti-Hitler.

3. Hyphenate compounds of *ex* ("former") and a noun.

ex-wife, ex-sweetheart, ex-President.

4. Hyphenate most compounds beginning with *self.*

self-satisfied, self-government, self-conceit. (But *selfless* and *selfsame* are written solid.)

ital *Use of Italics*

Words in print are made to stand out by using a special kind of slanting type called *italic;* they are similarly set off in manuscript by underlining. Italics or underlining is used for the following purposes:

a. To indicate that a word is still considered a foreign element in the language.

en rapport, in absentia.

(See "Foreign Words," page 172.)

b. To mark titles of publications, movie and stage productions, songs, etc., and the names of airplanes, ships, and trains.

Mencken's *The American Language*
the *Saturday Review*
Beethoven's *Eroica*
Berlin's *White Christmas*
Da Vinci's *Last Supper*
the New York Central's *Twentieth Century Limited*
Lindbergh's *Spirit of Saint Louis*
the *Queen Elizabeth*

Except for book titles, this use of italics is an alternative for the use of quotation marks. See page 482.

c. To call attention to a word being named.

The word *judgment* has two spellings.
What does *discriminate* mean?
A good example is the phrase *to go scot free.*

In handwritten work or typescript, quotation marks are more common than italics (see page 481). Both, however, are standard.

d. To emphasize a word.

Not *Angles* but *angels.*
That is *precisely* the point.

This last device should be used sparingly. Overused, it becomes a poor substitute for emphatic diction.

no *Forms of Numbers*

Whether numbers should be written in words or figures depends partly on the nature of the writing. Scientific, statistical, and technical writing uses figures whenever possible. In essays and literary publications numbers are more frequently written out, and the more formal the style, the less figures are used. The following advice holds for the kind of writing you will do in a composition class.

a. Figures are used in writing dates, hours, and street numbers.

January 22, 1949	5:00 A.M.	17 Main Street
January 1	6:15 P.M.	417 Fifth Avenue
the year 1860	0430 (military style)	1021 Third Street

Notice that figures are used for street numbers but that street names, even when they are numbers, are usually written out to avoid confusion.

b. Figures are used in recording sums of money other than round sums.

$2.75; 98 cents; *but* a hundred dollars; thirty cents

If the style is informal, even round sums may be expressed as figures.

$40 million; 100 dollars; 30 cents; 40,000 spectators

c. Use figures for large numbers that would be awkward to write out.

365 days; 1760 yards; 14,320 students

d. Use figures in citing volume, chapter, and page references.

This whole question is discussed in Volume 2 of Brand's work.
Our topic is discussed in Chapter 5; turn to page 37.

e. Do not use figures at the beginning of a sentence.

Sixty per cent is a passing grade.
The minimum passing grade is 60%.
Not: 60% is a passing grade.

f. Generally avoid figures when a number can be conveniently expressed in one word.

one, five, third, quarter, twelve

But in an informal style, numbers over ten are frequently expressed in figures.

g. Do not use figures in a formal invitation or reply.

on Saturday the twenty-third of June
at seven-thirty o'clock in the evening

This most formal usage is an exception to the practice recommended in **a** above.

h. Roman numerals are used chiefly as volume and chapter numbers in some books and as page numbers in the front matter of books.

Because Roman numerals are so little used, they are often confusing to students. Most of this confusion can be eliminated by first recognizing the key numerals and then understanding the principle by which these are combined.

The key numerals are i (1), v (5), x (10), 1 (50), c (100), d (500), m (1000), which may be written in capitals: I, V, X, L, C, D, M. The basic principle is that higher numbers are created by adding another unit to a lower number — i, ii, iii, vi, xi — or by subtracting a unit from a higher number — iv, ix, xl, xc.

	Units	*Tens*	*Hundreds*
1	i	x	c
2	ii	xx	cc
3	iii	xxx	ccc
4	iv	xl	cd
5	v	l	d
6	vi	lx	dc
7	vii	lxx	dcc
8	viii	lxxx	dccc
9	ix	xc	cm

Mechanics: Review Exercises

A. Rewrite the following sentences to substitute abbreviations and figures where permissible in college composition:

1. Have you seen the new professor? He has a Doctor of Philosophy degree from Cornell.
2. Mister Thompson is not here, but you can telephone him at Main five-seven-five-two.
3. My sister graduated from the University of Illinois with a Bachelor of Arts degree in February nineteen hundred and forty-eight.
4. She was married on the twenty-first of October, nineteen hundred and forty-nine.
5. Her husband is Doctor William Reid, a research economist with the American Federation of Labor.
6. Look on page one thousand four hundred and seventy.
7. He was born on January thirty-one at five minutes after eleven post meridian.
8. The date of the battle of Hastings is anno Domini 1066.
9. Send this letter to Colonel Donald Andrews, care of the Thirty-third Division at Fort Sam Houston.

10. Fifty-four people were hurt in the wreck, including the three top executives of the Columbia Broadcasting System.

B. Rewrite the following sentences to remove any abbreviations or figures which would be undesirable in college composition:

1. The speaker was a prof. from the U. of Indiana.
2. I saw her downtown this A.M.
3. 10 days later, the man died.
4. The candidate spoke as often as 8 times in a single day.
5. Somebody said to me, "Mr., this man needs a Dr."
6. The party consisted of Brig. Gen. T. A. Smith, a Col., and two Lt. Cols.
7. The math exam will be held in Rm. 511 at 2:00 P.M.
8. He paid $20; he could have bought a good second-hand one for $5.

C. In the following sentences, change lower case letters to capitals wherever the conventions require such a change:

1. She asked, "what makes it spin?"
2. it is one of the best of the english movies.
3. Some of his activities are alleged to be unamerican.
4. The words are, "our father which art in heaven, hallowed be thy name."
5. The greeks called their chief god *zeus;* the romans called him *jupiter.*
6. The king James bible is called the authorized version. It was translated by a committee of biblical scholars.
7. The title is *20,000 leagues under the sea.*
8. F. D. Roosevelt is the only president who won the presidency four times.
9. What did you get your mother for mother's day?
10. The bowl games are played chiefly in the west and south. The winter weather in the north and east is not suitable for post-season football.

D. In the following sentences remove unnecessary capitalization:

1. He is a Four Star General in the U.S. Army.
2. Our Navy is twice as large as that of the British.
3. This course is required for all Freshmen. Sophomores who are transfers from another University may also be required to take it.
4. My Father wants me to be a University Professor, but I prefer a better-paying Profession.
5. Spring may be the most beautiful Season, but I prefer Fall.
6. Go East for three blocks and then turn North.
7. It will soon be time for the birds to start their Southern migrations.
8. Her Uncle is a Rear-Admiral in the Navy and an authority on Naval strategy.
9. He studied for the Ministry before going to Law School.
10. "I will do it," She said, "If you will help me."

E. Rewrite the following letter to revise any unconventional use of abbreviations, capitals, hyphens, or numbers.

```
                                   Twenty-five Main Street
                                   Ridgeville, Minnesota
                                   Aug. 17, 1962
Doctor L. P. Wright
English Dept.
U.of M.

Dear Dr. Wright:

    When I entered the University in Feb. I was
notified that because of a one-Unit deficiency in
High School english I would have to take a non
credit course called remedial english.  I took the
course, but because I was ill most of the Semester
I missed the Final Examination and received a Final
Grade of f.  My instructor, Mister Larsen, told me
it would be possible to remove my failure by peti-
tioning for a Make Up Examination.

    If possible I would like to take the Exam before
School starts in Sept. so that I can begin the reg-
ular comp. course this coming Semester.  Would that
be possible?  I must complete 15 credit-hours next
term to be eligible to join a Fraternity and there-
fore cannot afford to take a 3 hour non credit
course.  I could take the Make Up anytime before the
15th of Sept., preferably between the 5th and 10th.

                                   Yrs. Sincerely,
```

F. Write the following figures as Arabic numerals:

ix	xcv	cml
xiv	cxv	cmxc
xl	cccix	mclx
xlvi	cd	md
lxxi	dcx	mcml

Write the following figures as Roman numerals:

3	10	50	400
4	14	80	550
5	19	90	1776
9	30	154	1962

Glossary

This is a reference section. Its main purpose is to list those words and constructions which frequently cause trouble in composition and to advise you whether particular usages are acceptable in college writing and, if they are, under what conditions. A secondary purpose is to explain some grammatical and rhetorical terms not discussed elsewhere in the text. Since this book has a separate index giving page references for all subjects discussed in the text, the Glossary usually does not duplicate these references.

The judgments about usage recorded here are based chiefly on five sources: *The American College Dictionary, The Oxford English Dictionary, Webster's Third New International Dictionary, Webster's New World Dictionary,* and Margaret M. Bryant's *Current American Usage.* Since dictionaries do not distinguish between formal and informal standard usage, except by the label "Colloquial,"[1] it has seemed wise to indicate whether particular usages would be more appropriate to a formal than to an informal style, and whether certain colloquialisms would be generally acceptable in college writing. The usefulness of this advice, however, depends on your understanding its limitations. In any choice of usage, the decision depends less on what dictionaries or textbooks say than on what is consistent with the purpose and style of the writing. The student and his instructor are the best judges of that question. All that this Glossary can do is report what is generally acceptable. You yourself must decide whether a specific usage is appropriate in the particular paper which you are writing. The general assumption in the Glossary is that college writing is informal rather than either colloquial or formal.

accept — except Words frequently confused because of similar sound. *Accept* is roughly synonymous with *take* [I will accept your thanks, but not your money]. *Except,* as a verb, means roughly *to leave out* or *exempt* [Present company is excepted].

access — excess The second syllable of both words comes from a Latin root meaning "to go." Etymologically, *access* means "a going toward," hence "approach" or "admission" [The auditor has access to the records]. *Excess* originally meant "going out or beyond," hence its present meaning of "beyond what is necessary or desirable" [He worries to excess; a tax on excess profits].

Accusative case In modern English, the objective case.

ad Clipped form of *advertisement*. Colloquial. Generally inappropriate in

[1] *Webster's Third International Dictionary* has dropped the "Colloquial" label used in previous editions of *Webster's New International Dictionary* and no longer identifies usages which are more appropriate in conversation than in writing.

college writing or business correspondence — especially in letters applying for a position — in which the word should be written in full.

A.D. Abbreviation for Latin *Anno Domini* (in the year of our Lord). Opposite of B.C. (before Christ). Used to distinguish dates before and after the beginning of the Christian era [He lived from 31 B.C. to A.D. 12; from 100 B.C. to A.D. 100 is 200 years]. A.D. is properly written before the figure; B.C., after it.

adapt — adept — adopt *Adapt* means "adjust to meet requirements" [The play was adapted for the movies; the human body can adapt itself to all sorts of environments]. *Adept* means "skilled" or "proficient" [He is adept at various sports]. *Adopt* means "to take as one's own" [We are going to adopt a child; he immediately adopted the idea] or — in parliamentary procedure — "to accept as a law" [The motion was adopted].

adaptation — adoption *Adaptation* is the act of adapting. See **adapt** [This play is an adaptation of a popular novel]. *Adoption* is the act of adopting [The adoption will not be legal until all the papers have been signed].

affect — effect Words often confused because of similarity of sound. Both may be used as nouns, but *effect,* meaning "result," is almost invariably the word wanted [His speech had an unfortunate effect; the treatments had no effect on me]. The noun *affect* is a technical term in psychology. Though both words may be used as verbs, *affect* is the more common. As a verb, *affect* means "impress," "influence," or "disturb" [His advice affected my decision; does music affect you that way?]. As a verb, *effect* is rarely required in student writing, but may be used to mean "carry out" or "accomplish" [The aviator effected his mission; the lawyer effected a settlement]. For students who have chronic difficulty with these words, a useful rule is to use *affect* only as a verb, and *effect* only as a noun.

affective — effective See **affect — effect**. The common adjective is *effective* [an effective argument], meaning "having an effect." The use of *affective* is largely confined to technical discussions of psychology and semantics, in which it is roughly equivalent to "emotional."

ain't Nonstandard contraction for "is not" and "are not." Some grammarians would accept it as colloquial in the form of "ain't I" on the grounds that it is historically and logically a suitable contraction of "am I not." But unless a student is attempting to record nonstandard speech, the use of *ain't* is not acceptable in college speech or writing.

alibi In formal English the word is a legal term used to indicate that a defendant was *elsewhere* when the crime was committed. Colloquially *alibi* is used to mean excuse [I'm not worried about being late, I have a good alibi]. This usage is becoming increasingly common in informal writing.

all the farther, further, quicker Colloquial in some areas but generally unacceptable in college writing. Use "as far as," "as quick as."

all together — altogether Distinguish between the phrase [They were all together at last] and the adverb [He is altogether — i. e. entirely — to blame].

All together means "all in one place"; *altogether* means "entirely" or "wholly."

Alliteration Repetition of the same consonant, especially an initial consonant, in several words within the same sentence or line of poetry [The *mur*muring of *imme*morial el*m*s; *T*ippecanoe and *T*yler *t*oo]. Alliteration is a common device in poetry and in slogans, but it should be used with restraint in ordinary prose since its overuse or inappropriate use may seem affected.

allow When used to mean "permit" [No smoking allowed on the premises] *allow* is acceptable. Its use to mean "think" [He allowed it could be done] is nonstandard and is not acceptable in college writing.

allusion — illusion Words sometimes confused because of similarity of sound. An *allusion* is a reference [The poem contains several allusions to Greek mythology]. An *illusion* is an erroneous mental image [Rouge on pallid skin gives an illusion of health].

alright An established variant spelling of *all right,* but there is still considerable objection to it. *All right* is the preferred spelling.

altar — alter The first word is a noun [They stood before the altar]; the second is a verb [We will alter the coat without charge]. If you confuse the two spellings, try associating the *a* in *sacred* with the alt*a*r of a church.

altho Now accepted as a variant spelling of *although,* but the longer form is preferred in English classes.

A.M., P.M.; a.m., p.m. Abbreviations for the Latin phrases *ante meridiem* (before noon), *post meridiem* (after noon). A.M. is used to indicate the period from midnight to noon; P.M., from noon to midnight. These abbreviations are used only when a specific hour is named [The first watch on a ship is from 12 P.M. to 4 A.M.]. The use of these abbreviations to stand for *morning* and *afternoon* when no hour is named [He gets up late in the a.m. and goes back to bed early in the p.m.] is a slang use not acceptable in college writing. Notice that either capital or small letters may be used in these abbreviations.

amount — number The occasional confusion of these words in college writing creates awkwardness. *Amount* is roughly synonymous with "deal" or "quantity" [He has a great amount of money; we collected a considerable amount of scrap iron]. *Number* is used for groups, the individual members of which may be counted [He has a large number of friends; there is a number of letters to be answered].

Ampersand The sign &, an abbreviation for *and,* is used in some company names [G. & C. Merriam Co.] and in various types of notations. Except in statistical tabulation it is not acceptable in college writing.

an Variant of indefinite article *a.* Used instead of *a* when the following word begins with a vowel sound [an apple, an easy victory, an honest opinion, an hour]. When the following word begins with a consonant sound, including *y,* the article should be *a* [a yell, a unit, a history, a house]. Such constructions as *a apple, a hour* are nonstandard usage. The use of *an* before *historical* and *humble* is an older usage which is dying out.

and etc.   *Etc.* is an abbreviation of the Latin phrase *et cetera* (and so forth). *And etc.* is therefore redundant. Use either *and so forth* or *etc.* in an informal style but only *and so forth* in a formal style.

angle   The use of *angle* to mean "point of view" [Let's look at it from a new angle] is acceptable, but the word is so overused in college writing — and so often used inaccurately — that many instructors object to it. Use it sparingly, and do not confuse its spelling with that of *angel*.

Antonym   A word opposite in meaning to a given word. Thus, *love* is the antonym for *hate*.

anybody's else   An old form of *anybody else's*. It is no longer conventional.

anywheres   A nonstandard variant of *anywhere*.

Apposition   In grammar, two constructions are in apposition when the second follows and identifies the first, as in "Mr. Botts, *the chemistry instructor,* has resigned." Most frequently the appositive is treated as a nonrestrictive modifier (see pages 471–473) and is therefore set off by commas, as above. When, however, the appositive word or phrase is felt to be so closely related to the construction with which it is in apposition that the two cannot be separated, it is treated as a restrictive modifier and written without commas [*Secretary of State* Rusk, *Commander-in-Chief* John F. Kennedy].

apt   See **liable.**

Arabic numerals   The numbers 1, 2, 3, etc., as contrasted with Roman numerals [I, II, III; i, ii, iii].

around   The uses of *around* to mean "about" [He arrived around four o'clock], "near" [That is how they pronounce it around Brooklyn], and "throughout" [We traveled around the country] are colloquial. They are generally acceptable in college writing.

as . . . as   The use of *as . . . as* in a negative statement [I am not as old as she is] is sometimes censured on the assumption that this construction should be used only for affirmative statements and that the correct negative form is "not *so* old as." In a very formal style the "not so . . . as" form may be preferable; but both forms are educated usage, and either is appropriate in college writing. In an affirmative statement, use *as . . . as.*

as = because   Although it is accepted standard English, *as* is weaker than *because* to show causal relation between main and subordinate clauses. Since *as* has other meanings, it may in certain contexts be confusing [As I was going home, I decided to telephone]. Here *as* may mean *when* or *because.* If there is any possibility of confusion, it is wise to use *because* or *while* — whichever is appropriate to the meaning.

as if = as though   Synonymous constructions. The first is slightly less formal, but either is appropriate in college writing.

as = that The use of *as* to introduce a noun clause [I don't know as I would agree to that] is colloquial. This usage would be hopelessly inappropriate at a formal level and would be rejected by most college instructors at an informal level. Unless you are deliberately aiming at a colloquial style, use *that*.

as to = with respect to Although *as to* is unquestionably standard usage, many instructors object to it on the ground that it is jargon (see page 528). Certainly its overuse should be avoided, and in an informal style *about* would be more appropriate than either *as to* or *with respect to*. For example, "I am not concerned as to your father's reaction" sounds stilted. It would be more natural to say, "I am not concerned [or I do not care] about your father's reaction."

Assonance The similarity of vowel sounds in words which do not rhyme [we — weep, fine — white].

Asterisk The sign *. A single asterisk is sometimes used as a footnote marker or to indicate items in a list which deserve special attention. A row of asterisks is sometimes used to indicate that the action of a story has been broken off or to suggest an interval of time.

at Avoid the use of the redundant *at* in such sentences as "Where were you at?" "Where do you live at?"

auto A clipped form of *automobile*. Inappropriate in formal writing, but appropriate in an informal or colloquial style.

Auxiliary verb A "helping" verb which combines with another to form a verb phrase [I *am* going; he *has been* talking]. The most common auxiliaries are *be, can, do, may, must, ought, shall, will*.

awful, awfully The real objection to *awful* is not that it is colloquial but that it is worked to death. It is inappropriate in a formal style unless used to mean "awe-inspiring." As a utility word it has become almost indispensable in informal speech, but the more deliberate nature of writing and the opportunities it allows for revision make the overuse of this word objectionable.

back of = behind The latter is the more formal usage, but both are generally acceptable in college writing.

bad The ordinary uses of *bad* as an adjective cause no difficulty. As a predicate adjective [An hour after dinner I began to feel bad] it is sometimes confused with the adverb *badly*. After the verbs *look, feel, seem*, the adjective is preferred. Say, "It looks bad for our team," "I feel bad about that quarrel," "She seemed bad this morning." But do not use *bad* when an adverb is required, as in "He played badly," "A badly torn suit."

badly = very much *Badly* is used in informal and colloquial writing as an intensifying word [I wanted badly to be asked; he was badly in need of a shave]. When it is used in this way, care should be taken to avoid misleading word order. In "I wanted to play very badly" the adverb may be interpreted as a modifier of *to play*, which the writer did not intend. In college writing it would be safer to avoid this use of *badly* and to use one of various possible synonyms. For example, "He was obviously in need of a shave," "I was eager to play."

balance = rest of, remainder Now accepted as established usage in all dictionaries, though *rest of* or *remainder* would be preferred in a formal style.

bank on = rely on In college writing the more formal *rely on* is generally preferred.

because See **reason is because.**

being as The use of *being as* for "because" or "since" in such sentences as "Being as I am an American, I believe in democracy," is nonstandard and is not acceptable in college speech or writing. Say, "Because I am an American, I believe in democracy."

berth — birth Do not confuse the spelling of *berth* [The man in the lower berth was ill; the tugs pushed the liner into its berth] and that of *birth* [The birth of the prince was celebrated for days].

between, among In general, *between* is used of two people or objects and *among* for more than two [We had less than a dollar between the two of us; *but* We had only a dollar among the three of us].

The general distinction, however, should be modified when insistence on it would be unidiomatic. For example, *between* is the accepted form in the following examples:

He is in the difficult position of having to choose between three equally attractive girls.
A settlement was arranged between the four partners.
Just between us girls . . . (Any number of girls)

Bible When used to refer to the Scriptures, "Bible" is always capitalized, but not italicized. When used metaphorically [*Das Kapital* is the bible of the Communists], the word is not capitalized.

blame on This usage [He blamed it on his brother] is accepted without reservation by some dictionaries but labeled colloquial by others. The more formal usage would be "He blamed his brother for it," but either would be generally acceptable in college writing.

born — borne Although both words come from the verb *to bear,* the form without the *e* (*born*) refers only to birth and is used in the passive voice [He was born lame]. The form with the final *e* (*borne*) is used in the active voice to mean "given birth to" [She has borne four children], but also has the more general meaning of "supported" or "carried" [The ship was borne on the waves; the troops were airborne; he has borne his troubles with quiet courage].

broke When used as an adjective, *broke* is a slang synonym for "bankrupt" or "out of funds." This usage is common in informal, educated speech, but in college writing it should be restricted to papers clearly colloquial in style. The use of such circumlocutions as "financially embarrassed" is generally more objectionable than the slang itself. Simply say, "I had no money."

When used as a verb, *broke* is the simple past tense of *break* (past participle, *broken*). Do not confuse the past tense with the past participle. Say, "He has broken his leg," not "He has broke his leg."

bunch Avoid the overuse of *bunch* as a general utility word. In formal English it is used to refer to a cluster of objects [bunch of grapes, a bunch of carrots]. Colloquially, it is used as a synonym for *group,* as in "A fine bunch of friends you have." This colloquial use is overworked in college writing. The following contrasted synonyms illustrate more discriminating choices:

A bunch of material	A collection of material
A bunch of money	A quantity of money
A bunch of enemies	Many enemies
A bunch of examples	Several examples
A bunch of radicals	A clique of radicals
A bunch of lumber	A supply of lumber
A bunch of errors	A number of errors

bunk A slang synonym for *nonsense.* Seldom appropriate in college writing in this sense.

bust At a formal level *bust* is used as a synonym for *bosom* and to represent the sculptured head and shoulders of a person. The use of *bust* to mean "failure" [The party was a complete bust] is classified as slang by some dictionaries and as standard usage by others. Bryant's evidence shows that it is standard in the phrase "boom and bust." But there is still objection to *bust* as a synonym in college writing for "failure." The use of *bust* to mean "burst" [The pipes have bust again] is nonstandard and not acceptable in college writing.

can = may The distinction that *can* is used to indicate ability and *may* is used to indicate permission [If I can do the work, may I have the job?] is a stylistic distinction. It is not generally observed in informal usage but is still observed in a formal style. Either form is acceptable in college writing.

can but A formal variant of *can only* [I can but hope you are mistaken].

cannot but A formal variant of *cannot help* or *must* [We cannot but accept the verdict]. In most college writing "We must accept the verdict" would be preferred.

cannot (can't) help but While this construction is accepted in informal usage, it represents a confusion between the formal *cannot but* and the informal *can't help.* In college writing, the form without *but* is preferred.

can't hardly A confusion between *cannot* and *can hardly.* The construction is unacceptable in college writing. Use *cannot, can't,* or *can hardly.*

can't seem A colloquial short cut for "I seem to be unable." Acceptable at informal levels.

canvas — canvass The form with one *s* is a heavy cloth [a canvas tent, a canvas bag]; the form with two *s's* means generally "to solicit" [I am canvassing for the Red Cross; he canvassed every voter in the precinct].

capital — capitol The form *Capitol,* used only to designate the building which houses the seat of government, takes a capital letter when it refers to the building in which the U.S. Congress meets. When it refers to the building in which a state legislature meets it is sometimes spelled with a small letter [The

Capitol and the White House are the most famous buildings in Washington, D.C.; our state capitols are not always models of the best architecture; he has an office in the Capitol in Columbus].

The form *capital* has a variety of meanings, the nucleus of which is "chief" or "first-rate" [The capital city, capital punishment, a capital letter, a capital idea]. Unless you are referring to a building, the form you want is *capital*.

Caret The symbol ($\wedge$) used to identify the place in a printed, typed, or written line at which something is to be inserted.

case = instance, example There is no question that this usage [In the case of John Jones . . .] is established, but a widely read essay labeling it jargon has created some objection to it. Like most utility words, *case* (meaning *instance*) may be overused, but its restrained use in college writing should be acceptable.

censor — censure Both words come from a Latin verb meaning to "set a value on" or "tax." *Censor* is used to mean "appraise" in the sense of appraising a book or a letter to see if it may be made public [All outgoing mail had to be censored] and is often used as a synonym for "delete" or "cut out" [That part of the message was censored].

Censure means "to evaluate adversely," "to find fault with" or "rebuke" [The editorial writers censured the speech; such an attitude will invoke public censure].

Circumlocution Literally, "round-about speech." An attempt to avoid a direct statement by a circuitous reference.

cite — sight — site *Cite* means "to refer to" [He cited chapter and verse]. *Sight* means spectacle or view [The garden was a beautiful sight]. *Site* means "location" [This is the site of the new plant].

claim = assert *or* maintain All dictionaries accept this usage [I claim that the assignment was never announced] as established. There would seem to be no valid objection to the construction in most college writing.

Cliché A synonym for "trite expression": an overused or threadbare expression, or an observation which lacks originality.

Clipped words Shortened forms [auto, exam, gym, plane] which are considered whole words rather than abbreviations of the longer form. Clipped words do not require a period to mark abbreviation and are more appropriate to informal than to formal styles.

Coherence The quality of being logically integrated. In composition, chiefly used to refer to the integration of sentences within a paragraph. See page 82.

combine = combination This use of *combine* [Several fraternities have formed a combine which will present its own slate of candidates] is colloquial. It is acceptable at informal levels of college writing. The more formal statement would be "Several fraternities have combined to present a common slate of candidates."

compare, contrast *Contrast* always implies differences; *compare* may imply either differences or similarities. When they are followed by a preposition, both verbs usually take *with* [Contrast the part of the lawn that has been fertilized with the part that has not; the handwriting on the lease compares with this signature; if you compare the old leaves with the new you will see that the old leaves are darker]. However, the past participial form, *compared,* usually takes *to* as its preposition [Compared to her mother, she's a beauty].

complected Nonstandard form of *complexioned.* Not acceptable in college writing.

Complement Literally, a completing construction. Used in grammar chiefly to refer to the construction which completes a linking verb. See pages 398–399.

complement — compliment The confusion of these two words lies entirely in the middle vowel. If you remember that *complement* means "to complete" you may associate the *e* of *complement* with the *e* of *complete* [a complement of troops, complementary angles].

   A *compliment* is a word or gesture of praise [My compliments to the cook; the line between compliment and flattery is often a faint one].

Complex, compound sentences Sentences are usually classified as follows:
simple: containing only one clause, and that a main clause.
compound: containing two or more main clauses but no subordinate clauses.
complex: containing a main clause and one or more subordinate clauses.
compound-complex: containing two or more main clauses and at least one subordinate clause.

conscience — conscious *Conscience* is a noun indicating a sense of right conduct [Let your conscience be your guide]. *Conscious* is an adjective meaning "to be capable of sensations" or "to be aware of" [It will be some time before he is conscious; I am conscious of having done wrong].

considerable The use of *considerable* as a noun [I have spent considerable on this enterprise] is acceptable at a colloquial level. In a formal style, the preferred usage would require a noun after *considerable* [I have spent considerable money on this enterprise].

Contractions The use of contractions [I'll, can't, couldn't, didn't, he's, shouldn't] is appropriate in informal and colloquial styles but not in a formal style.

could of = could have Although these two constructions have almost the same sound in informal speech, *of* for *have* is not acceptable in college writing. In writing, *could of, should of, would of* are nonstandard.

council — counsel A *council* is an advisory group [He was elected to the council]. *Counsel* means "advice." In law, a *counsel* is one who gives legal advice [My friend counseled me to take this course; he refuses to testify without advice of counsel].

couple The use of *couple* to mean "two" [The tickets will cost a couple of dollars] or even more than two [I would like to tell him a couple of things] is acceptable at informal levels. Its use to mean a man and his wife is acceptable at all levels.

cute A utility word used colloquially to indicate the general notion of "attractive" or "pleasing." Its overuse in writing shows haste or lack of discrimination. A more specific term will generally improve communication.

> His girl is cute. [lovely? petite? pleasant? charming?]
> That is a cute trick. [clever? surprising?]
> She has a cute accent. [pleasant? refreshingly unusual?]
> She is a little too cute for me. [affected? juvenile? demonstrative? clever?]

dairy — diary Pronunciation offers the best clue to the spelling of these words. The *a* comes first in the *ay*-sound, as in *maid*. *Diary* comes from the same root as *dial* and means a record of daily activities.

data Since *data* is the Latin plural of *datum* (given or admitted as a fact) it has long taken a plural verb or pronoun [These data have been double-checked]. This requirement is beginning to be ignored so that in informal English "This data has been double-checked" is acceptable. *Data* is thus losing its foreign characteristics and being made to fit the general pattern of English nouns. The requirement of a plural verb is still observed, however, in scientific writing and in a formal style. For alternative pronunciations, see dictionary.

Dative case In Old English, generally the case of the indirect object.

decent — descent Most students who misspell *descent* (downslope) have no trouble with the verb *descend*. Associate the *s* in descend with that in *descent*.

> *Decent* — without the *s* — means "fitting" or "proper" [the decent thing to do].

Demonstrative *This, that, these, those* are called demonstratives when they are used as pointing words [This is the man; that coat is mine].

desert — dessert The word used for the final course of a meal has two *s*'s. The word with one *s* designates a wasteland [the Sahara Desert] or the action of running away from something [He deserted his wife; they deserted from the Army].

Dialect A pattern of speech habits shared by members of the same geographic area or social level.

didn't ought Nonstandard for "ought not" [You didn't ought to have told her] and not acceptable in college writing or speech. Say, "You ought not to have told her" or "You should not have told her."

different than The preferred idiom is *different from,* although all dictionaries recognize *different than* as established usage. *Different to* is British usage.

Digraph Two letters pronounced as a single sound, as in bl*ee*d, b*ea*t, *th*in, sti*ck*, *p*sychology, gra*ph*.

dining — dinning In general, a double consonant shortens the vowel preceding it. That is why the *i* in *dine* is long and the *i* in *dinner* short. Compare *filing–filling, pining–pinning, writing–written.*

Diphthong A combination of two vowel sounds run together to sound like a single vowel. Examples are the *ah-ee* sounds combining to form the vowel of *hide, ride, wide* and the *aw-ee* sounds combining in *boy, joy, toy.*

don't As a contraction for "do not" it is appropriate in informal and colloquial styles, but not acceptable in college speech or writing as a contraction for "does not."

Double negative The use of two negative words or particles within the same construction. In certain forms [I am not unwilling to go] the double negative is educated usage for an affirmative statement; in other forms [I ain't got no money] the double negative is uneducated (nonstandard) usage for a negative statement. The fact that the latter usage is an obvious violation of the conventions of standard English justifies its censure in high school and college speech and writing, but the objection that "two negatives make an affirmative" in English usage is a half-truth based on a false analogy with mathematics.

dove = dived Both forms are established usage. *Dived* would be preferred in a formal style.

due to The use of *due to* to mean "because of" in an introductory adverbial phrase [Due to the icy roads, we were unable to proceed] is an established usage to which some people object. The objection reflects personal preference rather than the facts of usage.

dying — dyeing When dye is used to color clothes the process is called *dyeing.* Normally the *e* would be dropped before *ing,* but it has been retained in *dyeing* to avoid confusion with the common *dying —* about to die.

economic — economical *Economic* refers to the science of economics or to business in general [This is an economic law; economic conditions are improving]. *Economical* means "inexpensive" or "thrifty" [That is the economical thing to do; he is economical to the point of miserliness].

effect See **affect.**

either Used to designate one of two things [Both hats are lovely; I would be perfectly contented with either]. The use of *either* when more than two things are involved [There are three ways of working the problem; either way will give the right answer] is not generally accepted. When more than two things are involved, use *any* or *any one* instead of *either* [There are three ways of working the problem, any one of which will give the right answer].

elicit — illicit The first word means to "draw out" [We could elicit no further information from them]; the second means "not permitted" [an illicit love affair].

Elliptical constructions A construction which is literally incomplete but in which the missing terms are understood [*I am taller than he* (is tall); Who told him? (It was) *Not I* (who told him)].

emigrant — immigrant An emigrant is a person who moves *out* of a country;

an immigrant one who moves *into* a country. Thus, refugees from Europe who settled in the United States were emigrants from their native countries and immigrants here. A similar distinction holds for the verbs *emigrate* and *immigrate*.

enthuse Colloquial for "to be (become) enthusiastic." The more formal phrase is preferred in college writing.

equally as In such sentences as "He was equally as good as his brother," the *equally as* is a confusion of *equally* and *as good as*. Write, "He was his brother's equal," "He was as good as his brother," or "Both brothers were equally good."

etc. An abbreviation for *et cetera* (and so forth). Should be used only when the style justifies abbreviations and then only after several items in a series have been identified [The data sheet required the usual personal information: age, height, weight, religion, etc.]. Avoid the redundant *and* before *etc.* **See and etc.**

Etymology The study of the derivations of words.

euphemism — euphuism A *euphemism* is a word or phrase used as a substitute for an expression which is felt to be crude, improper, or vulgar. Examples are "a lady dog" for "a bitch," "pass away" for "die." *Euphuism* is a name given to an ornate and affected literary style which was popular in England at the end of the sixteenth century and to any modern style which shows similar characteristics.

exam A clipped form of *examination*. Although classified as colloquial by some dictionaries, it is accepted at all but the most formal levels of college writing.

expect = suppose *or* suspect This is a colloquial usage. In college writing, use *suppose* or *suspect* [I suppose you have written to him? I suspect that we have made a mistake].

Expletive In such sentences as "There are two answers to the question" and "It seems to me that you are mistaken," the words *There* and *It* are called *expletives*. In such sentences the order is expletive, verb, and real subject, the expletive occupying the normal position of the subject.

famous, notorious *Famous* is a complimentary and *notorious* an uncomplimentary adjective. Well-known people of good repute are famous; those of bad repute are notorious (or infamous).

fare — fair *Fare* comes from the OE verb *faran* (to travel) and is related to the expression *fare you well*. It is most commonly used today to indicate the cost of transportation [The fare to Chicago is $10.40]. *Fair* has a variety of meanings [a fair decision, a fair copy, a fair skin, just fair, fair weather, a fair profit, a county fair].

farther, further The distinction that *farther* indicates distance and *further* degree is now less widely observed than it used to be. All dictionaries consulted recognize the two words as interchangeable. But to mean "in addition," only *further* is used [Further assistance will be required; we need further information on that point].

feature (verb) The use of *feature* to mean "give prominence to" [This issue of the magazine features an article on juvenile delinquency] is established standard usage and is appropriate in college writing. But this acceptance does not justify the slang use of *feature* in such expressions as "Can you feature that?" "Feature me in a dress suit," "I can't feature her as a nurse."

fellow As a noun, *fellow* for "man" or "person" is appropriate only in colloquial and informal styles. As an adjective [fellow students, a fellow traveler] *fellow* is acceptable at all levels.

Figures of speech Metaphors, similes, personifications, allusions, and similar devices are grouped under the general name *figures of speech*. See page 152.

Fine writing In college, often used as an uncomplimentary term for writing which, because of its attempts to be "literary," is artificial, pretentious, or wordy.

fix As a noun, *fix* is colloquial for "predicament" [Now we *are* in a fix!]. As a verb, it is colloquial for "repair" or "adjust" [My pen is broken and I can't fix it; will you help me fix this desk?]. Both uses are appropriate in an informal style. The verb *fix,* meaning "to make fast," is acceptable at all levels.

flunk = fail Colloquial. Not suited to a formal style, but so commonly used in college that there would seldom be objection to its use in an informal paper.

folks = people (especially relatives) Generally acceptable in college writing.

formally — formerly *Formally* means "in a formal manner" [They dressed formally]. *Formerly* means "previously" [He was formerly with A. C. Smith and Company].

forth — fourth The common word is *fourth* [I was *fourth* in line]. Associate *fourth* with *four* to remember the *ou*. *Forth* generally means "forward" [They went forth to battle].

funny The use of *funny* as a utility word [She gave me a funny look; it was a funny observation to make] is greatly overdone in college writing. Although appropriate at informal and colloquial levels, its constant use makes for vague diction. Select a more exact synonym:

> She gave me a funny look. [hostile? alarmed? annoyed? scathing? perplexed? baffled?]
> It was a funny observation to make. [comical? humorous? astounding? puzzling? unusual?]

gentleman, lady These are good words, but avoid their use as synonyms for "man" or "woman" in expressions in which the latter terms are normal [manservant, man of the house, women's building, woman's point of view]. Also avoid their euphemistic use to designate the sex of animals [bull, tomcat, mare, ewe].

get The use of *get,* either as a single verb or in combination with infinitives, adjectives, or adverbs, is extremely popular and varied in colloquial and informal styles. It should be used discreetly in a formal style, but the student should also guard against overuse of more formal and pretentious synonyms such as *acquire* or *obtain.*

good The use of *good* as an adverb [He talks good; he played pretty good] is not acceptable in college writing. Even though it is recognized as established by *Webster's Third International,* this usage is discouraged in college speech. In both writing and speaking, the accepted adverbial form is *well.*

This discussion does not apply to the use of *good* as an adjective after verbs of hearing, feeling, seeing, smelling, tasting, etc. See **bad.**

good and Used colloquially as an intensive in such expressions as "good and late," "good and sleepy," "good and ready," "good and tired." The more formal the style, the less appropriate these intensives are.

got See **get.**

gotten Leading dictionaries now accept *gotten* without comment as one of two past participles of *get.* The other one is *got.*

guess The use of *guess* to mean "believe," "suppose," "think" [I guess I can be there on time] is accepted by all dictionaries on which this glossary is based. There is still objection to its use in formal college writing, but it should be acceptable in an informal style.

Hackneyed diction See **Cliché.**

had have, had of Neither form is appropriate in college writing. Use *had.*

had (hadn't) ought Nonstandard for *ought (ought not).* Not acceptable in college writing or speech.

hanged, hung Alternative past participles of *hang.* When referring to an execution, *hanged* is preferred; in other senses, *hung* is preferred.

hardly See **can't hardly.**

heap In formal usage the noun *heap* means a "pile" or "accumulation" of things [a heap of stones, a heap of junk]. Colloquially, the noun is used to mean "a great deal," "a considerable amount" [He made a heap of money; it takes a heap of living to make a house a home]. This colloquial usage is usually acceptable in an informal style, but is not appropriate in a formal style.

height — heighth The form *heighth* is nonstandard and probably reflects a confusion with the final *th* in *breadth* and *width.*

Historical present Also called *dramatic present.* The use of the present tense in narrative style to record action in the past [His friends try to persuade him to escape, but Socrates reasons with them and shows them he must die].

holy — wholly *Holy* means "sacred" [The Holy Bible, the holy city of Jerusalem]. *Wholly* comes from the same root as *whole* and means "completely" [He is wholly well again; it is wholly my fault].

home   Used colloquially and informally for "at home" [We have been home all afternoon; if you arrive too late, we will not be home]. In a formal style "at home" would be preferred.

Homonyms   Words which are pronounced alike [air, heir; blew, blue; plain, plane; sail, sale].

idea   In addition to its formal meaning of "conception," *idea* has acquired so many supplementary meanings that it must be recognized as a utility word. Some of its meanings are illustrated in the following sentences:

The idea [thesis] of the book is simple.
The idea [proposal] he suggested is a radical one.
I got the idea [impression] that she is unhappy.
It is my idea [belief, opinion] that they are both wrong.
My idea [intention] is to leave early.

The overuse of *idea,* like the overuse of any utility word, makes for vagueness. Whenever possible, prefer a more precise synonym.

in back of   See **back of.**

individual   Although the use of *individual* to mean *person* [He is a fascinating individual] is accepted by the dictionaries, college instructors frequently disapprove of this use, probably because it is overdone in college writing. In its formal uses *individual* signifies "single" or "separate" [We are all Americans but we are also individuals; the instructor tries to give us individual attention].

inferior than   Possibly a confusion between *inferior to* and *worse than.* Say "inferior to" [Today's workmanship is inferior to that of a few years ago].

in regards to   The only acceptable form is *in regard to.* The *-s* ending is not uncommon in speech but it is not acceptable in college writing.

inside of   The use of *inside of* to mean "in less than" [I'll be there inside of an hour] is accepted as established usage. There should be no objection to it in college writing.

instance — instants   An *instance* is an example, illustration, or case in point [That is just one instance of his attitude]. *Instants* is the plural of instant, meaning "moment."

Intensives   Such modifiers as *much, so, too, very* merely add emphasis to the words they modify [much obliged, so tired, too bad, very good], but the overuse of intensives (especially *very*) is more likely to result in wordiness than in emphasis. The pronouns *myself, yourself, himself, herself, themselves* may also be used as intensives [You yourself are the best judge; he built the cabin himself].

irrelevant — irreverent   *Irrelevant* means "having no relation to" or "lacking pertinence" [That may be true, but it is quite irrelevant]. *Irreverent* means "without reverence" [Such conduct in a church is irreverent].

its — it's   The confusion of these two forms causes frequent misspelling in college writing. *It's* always means "it is" or "it has." The apostrophe is a sign of contraction, not of possession [The dog wagged its tail; it's (it is) too difficult a problem; it's (it has) been raining all night].

it's me   This construction is essentially a spoken one. Except in dialogue, it rarely occurs in writing. Its use in educated speech is thoroughly established. The formal expression is *It is I.*

Jargon   A name applied to diction which is wordy and unnecessarily abstract. The name is also applied to the technical vocabulary and usages of special groups — the jargon of the medical profession, legal jargon.

kind of, sort of   Use a singular modifier and a singular verb with these phrases [That kind of person is always troublesome; this sort of attitude will get us nowhere]. The use of *a* or *an* after *of,* in this construction, is colloquial and is avoided by most careful writers.

kind (sort) of = somewhat   This usage [I feel kind of tired; he looked sort of foolish] is colloquial. It would be inappropriate in a formal style and should be used sparingly in an informal style.

knew — new   The misspelling arising out of a confusion of these two common words is usually a result of carelessness. *Knew* comes from OE *cunnan* and is related to *ken* and *cunning;* hence the *k*, which remains in the written form although it is not pronounced. *New* [a new hat, a new leaf] has historically no reason for being spelled with a *k*.

lady   See **gentleman.**

later — latter   The confusion of these two words in college writing is probably a spelling error. *Later* is the comparative of *late* [It is later than you think]. *Latter* is the opposite of *former* and is used to refer to the second of two things previously mentioned [The latter choice seemed the better; World War I and World War II were both global wars, but the latter involved civilians to a much greater extent than the former].

lead — led   The principal parts of *lead* are *lead, led, led*. Do not confuse the spelling of the past tense, *led,* with the spelling of the name of the metal, *lead*.

learn = teach   The use of *learn* to mean "teach" [He learned us arithmetic] is nonstandard and is not acceptable in college speech or writing. Say, "He taught us arithmetic."

leave = let   The use of *leave* for *let* [Leave us face it] is slang and is not acceptable in college speech or writing. Say, "Let us face it," "Let (*not* leave) us be friends."

let's   A contraction of *let us*. The expression *let's us* is redundant and not acceptable in college writing.

liable, likely, apt   *Liable* to mean "likely" or "apt" [It is liable to rain; he is liable to hit you] is a colloquial usage to which instructors sometimes object. *Liable* means "subject to" or "exposed to" or "answerable for" [He is liable to arrest; you will be liable for damages]. In formal usage *apt* means "has an aptitude for" [He is an apt pupil; she is apt at that kind of thing]. The use of *apt* to mean "likely" is accepted colloquially [She is apt to leave you; he is apt to resent it].

like = as, as though   The use of *like* as a conjunction [He talks like you do; it looks like it will be my turn next] is colloquial. It is not appropriate in a formal style and many people object to it in an informal style. The safest procedure is to avoid using *like* as a conjunction in college writing.

likely   See **liable.**

line   The use of *line* to indicate a type of activity or business [What's your line? His line is dry goods] is accepted as established usage; its use to indicate a course of action or thought [He follows the party line] is also accepted. However, the overuse of *line* in these senses often provokes objection to the word.

loan, lend   Both forms of the verb are accepted in educated American usage.

loath — loathe   The form without *-e* is an adjective meaning "reluctant," "unwilling" [I am loath to do that; he is loath to risk so great an investment] and is pronounced to rhyme with "both." The form with *-e* is a verb meaning "dislike strongly" [I loathe teas; she loathes an unkempt man], and is pronounced to rhyme with "clothe."

locate = find   This usage [I cannot locate that quotation] is established, but its extension to mean *remember* [Your name sounds familiar, but I cannot locate your face] is not acceptable.

locate = settle   This usage [He and his family have located in San Francisco] is colloquial. In college writing *settled* would be preferred.

loose, lose   The confusion of these words causes frequent misspelling. *Loose* is most common as an adjective [a loose button, a loose nut, a dog that has broken loose]. *Lose* is always used as a verb [You are going to lose your money; don't lose your head].

Loose sentence   A technical term used to describe a sentence in which the main thought is completed before the end. The opposite of a *periodic sentence.* Loose sentences are normal sentences and should not be thought of as implying a fault.

lot(s) of   The use of *lot(s)* to mean a considerable amount or number [I have lots of friends; they gave us a lot of excuses] is colloquial. This usage is common in informal writing.

Lower case (l. c.)   Printer's terminology for small letters as contrasted with capitals. Frequently used by college instructors in marking student papers.

luxuriant — luxurious   These words come from the same root but have quite different connotations. *Luxuriant* means "abundant" and is used principally of growing things [luxuriant vegetation, a luxuriant head of hair]. *Luxurious* means "luxury-loving" or "catering to luxury" [He finds it difficult to support so luxurious a wife on so modest an income; the appointments of the clubhouse were luxurious].

mad = angry or annoyed This is colloquial [My girl is mad at me; his insinuations make me mad]. In formal and informal styles, use *angry, annoyed, irritated, provoked,* or *vexed,* which are more precise.

Malapropism A humorous, though unintentional, confusion of words similar in form and sound [Henry VIII died of an *abbess* on his knee; one of the most momentous events in early English history was the invasion of the *Dames*]. The error is named for Mrs. Malaprop, a character in Sheridan's play *The Rivals,* whose speech often illustrated this kind of confusion.

math A clipped form of *mathematics.* Appropriate in a colloquial or informal style but not in formal writing.

may See **can.**

maybe = perhaps Both usages are established; *perhaps* is the more formal.

mean = unkind, disagreeable, bad-tempered These uses of *mean* [It was mean of me to do that; please don't be mean to me; that dog looks mean] are colloquial. They are appropriate in most college writing, but their overuse sometimes results in vagueness. Consider using one of the suggested alternatives to provide a sharper statement.

might of See **could of.**

mighty = very This usage [I'm mighty fond of her; that's a mighty big house] is colloquial. It could be used discreetly in informal college writing, but it is often an unnecessary intensive.

moral — morale Roughly, *moral* refers to conduct and *morale* refers to state of mind. A *moral* man is one who conducts himself according to the conventions of society or religion. People are said to have good *morale* when they are cheerful, cooperative, and not too much concerned with their own worries.

most = almost This usage [I am most always hungry an hour before mealtime] is colloquial. In college writing *almost* would be preferred in such a sentence.

movie Although "movie" is the predominant usage in newspapers and magazines, some dictionaries still record this word as colloquial. If it is good enough for the *Saturday Review,* it should be good enough for a composition course. The formal term is "motion picture."

muchly There is no such word. Say *much* [I am much pleased by the news].

must (adjective and noun) The use of *must* as an adjective [This book is must reading for anyone who wants to understand Russia] and as a noun [It is reported that the President will classify this proposal as a must] is accepted as established usage by the dictionaries.

must of See **could of.**

myself = I This usage [John and myself will go] is not generally acceptable. Say, "John and I will go." *Myself* is acceptably used:
(1) as an intensifier [I saw it myself; I myself will go with you];

(2) as a reflexive object [I hate myself; I can't convince myself that he is right].

myself = me This usage [He divided it between John and myself] is not recognized by the dictionaries, though Professor Marckwardt considers it "fully established in literature and current English" (*Scribner Handbook,* p. 241). The preferred usage would be "He divided it between John and me."

naive, naïve Both spellings are now accepted.

neither See **either.**

nice A utility word much overused in college writing. Avoid excessive use of it and, whenever possible, choose a more precise synonym.

It was a nice dance. [enjoyable? exciting? genteel? well-organized?]
That's a nice dress. [attractive? becoming? fashionable? well-made?]
She's a nice girl. [agreeable? beautiful? charming? virtuous? friendly? well-mannered?]

nice and See **good and.**

nickel Unlike *fickle, sickle, trickle,* and other similar-sounding words ending with the syllable pronounced *ul, nickel* ends in *el.* This exception often causes misspelling.

Nominative absolute An introductory participial phrase which is grammatically independent of the rest of the sentence [*All things being considered,* the decision is a fair one; *the interview having been ended,* the reporters rushed to the phones]. This construction is common in Latin but should be used sparingly in college writing, partly because it is sometimes unidiomatic, and partly because it may result in a dangling modifier. The first example given above is idiomatic English; the second would normally be written, "When the interview was ended, the reporters rushed to the phones."

Nominative case Another name for the subjective case.

not . . . as, not . . . so See **as . . . as.**

nowhere near = not nearly Established usage, but *not nearly* is often preferred.

nowheres Nonstandard variant of *nowhere.*

Object An object is a noun or pronoun which completes the action of a transitive verb [We bought the *car;* I asked *her*] or completes a preposition [She smiled at *me;* it is lying on the *table*]. An *indirect object* identifies the recipient of the action indicated by a verb-object combination [We bought *Dad* a car; the children gave *her* a party].

off of In such sentences as "Keep off of the grass," "He took it off of the table," the *of* is unnecessary and undesirable. Omit it in college speech and writing.

OK, O.K. Its use in business to mean "endorse" is generally accepted [The manager OK'd the request]. Otherwise, it is colloquial. It is a utility word and is subject to the general precaution concerning all such words: do not overuse it, especially in contexts in which a more specific term would give more efficient communication. For example, contrast the vagueness of OK at the left with the discriminated meanings at the right.

| The garagemen said the tires were OK. | The garagemen said the tread on the tires was still good. |
| | The garagemen said the pressure in the tires was satisfactory. |

one . . . he, his   The feeling that the repetition of *one . . . one's* [One must do what one can to ensure one's family a decent standard of living] makes for a stilted style has led to the permissible shift from *one, one's* to *he, his* [One must do what he can to ensure his family a decent standard of living]. In general a shift in the number or nature of pronouns is undesirable, but this particular shift is established usage.

only   The position of *only* in such sentences as "I only need three dollars" and "If only Mother would write!" is sometimes condemned on the grounds of possible ambiguity. In practice, the context usually rules out ambiguous interpretation, but a change in the word order would often result in more appropriate emphasis [I need only three dollars; if Mother would only write].

out loud = aloud   Generally acceptable in college writing. In a formal style, prefer *aloud*.

outside of = aside from, except   This usage [Outside of his family, no one respects him; outside of that, I have no objection] is colloquial. It would be inappropriate in a formal style, but not objectionable in an informal one.

over with = completed, ended   This usage [Let's get this job over with; she is all over with that romance] is informal. It should be generally acceptable in college writing unless the style is quite formal.

part, on the part of   This usage [There will be some objection on the part of the students; on the part of businessmen, there will be some concern about taxes] often makes for a wordy and flabby style. Simply say, "The students will object," "Businessmen will be concerned about taxes."

party = person   Colloquial, and generally to be avoided in college writing. In telephone usage, however, party is the accepted word [Your party does not answer].

past — passed   Although both forms may be used as past participles of the verb *to pass, past* is primarily used as an adjective or a noun [in days past, the past tense, she is a woman with a past]. *Passed* is a past tense or past participle form [They have passed the half-way mark; he passed all his examinations].

peace — piece   Associate *peace* with *calm* as a reminder that *peace* is spelled with an *a* [a peaceful sleep, an hour of peace]. Associate *piece* with *bit* as a reminder that *piece* is spelled with an *i* [a piece of chalk, a piece of news, in small pieces].

per = a   This usage [You will be remunerated at the rate of five dollars per diem; this material costs $1.50 per yard] is established. As the second illustration shows, the *per* need not be followed by a Latin noun. This use of *per* is most common in legal and business phraseology. For most purposes, "five dollars a day" and "$1.50 a yard" would be more natural expressions.

per = according to, concerning   This usage [The order will be delivered as per your instructions; per your inquiry of the 17th, we wish to report] is business slang which is unacceptable in both college and business writing. Use "according to" or "concerning."

per cent, percent   Originally an abbreviation of the Latin *per centum*, this term has been Anglicized and is no longer considered a foreign word. It may be written as one or two words and no longer requires a period to indicate abbreviation [There is a ten percent markup; interest is at three per cent].

Periodic sentence   A sentence in which the main thought is not completed until the end. The opposite of a *loose* sentence. See page 109.

Personification   A figure of speech in which animals, inanimate objects, and qualities are given human characteristics [Death cometh like a thief in the night; the breeze caressed her hair].

phone   Clipped form of *telephone*. Appropriate at informal and colloquial levels. In a formal style use the full form.

Phonetics   The science dealing with the sounds of language. These sounds are represented by phonetic symbols which ignore the appearance of a word and record only its pronunciation [Phonetically, *schism* is transcribed sɪzəm]. When words are spelled as they are pronounced, the spelling is said to be phonetic.

photo   Colloquial clipped form of *photograph*. In a formal style, use the full form.

Plagiarism   The offense of representing as one's own writing the work of another. The use of unacknowledged quotations.

plain — plane   As an adjective, *plain* means "simple," "unadorned," "easily seen" [a plain dress, the plain truth, as plain as the nose on your face]; as a noun, meaning an open expanse of land, it occurs most commonly in the plural in North American usage [The covered wagons crossed the plains]. *Plane* as adjective, noun, and verb means "level" [a plane surface, all on the same plane, he planed the board]. The short form of *airplane* is *plane*.

plan on   When *plan* is used in the sense of "arrange" [I plan to be in Columbus on the seventh], the accepted idiom is *plan to*. When, however, *plan* means "intend" or "hope" [I plan to see that picture whenever it comes to town; they are planning on saving enough money to buy a new car], either *plan to* or *plan on* is acceptable. The safer usage is *plan to*.

plenty   The use of *plenty* as a noun [There is plenty of room] is acceptable at all levels. Its use as an adverb [It was plenty good] is colloquial and would not be appropriate in college writing.

precede — proceed   The basic distinction in the use of these words is that *precede* means to "go before" and *proceed* means to "go forward." Thus ladies precede gentlemen in entering a vehicle. But a car proceeds along a road, and one proceeds with one's plans.

Précis A summary which preserves the organization and principal content of the original.

Predicate That part of a sentence which states the action performed by or upon the subject. The predicate may consist of an intransitive verb, with or without modifiers, or of a transitive verb and its object, with or without modifiers.

Predicate adjective An adjective completing a linking verb [His mother is *sick;* oh, it is *beautiful!*].

Predicate noun Same function as *predicate adjective* above [His mother is a *writer;* her brother became a successful *lawyer*].

Prefix A word or syllable placed before the root of another word to form a new word [*anti*bodies, *mono*syllabic, *un*natural].

presence — presents *Presence* is the opposite of *absence* and ends in *-ce* [Your presence is requested]. *Presents,* when used as a noun, is the plural of *present,* meaning "gift" [He bought presents for everyone]. *Present* (accent on the second syllable) may also be used as a verb [Present arms; present your credentials].

principal — principle The confusion of these words is a common source of misspelling. For the purpose of college writing it might be useful to over-simplify the distinction between their uses and say that *principal* is always an adjective unless it means "the principal (officer) of a school" and that *principle* is always a noun.

> *Principal:* The principal point is this . . .
> He is one of the principal offenders.
> He is a principal stockholder.
> One school has a new principal.
> *Principle:* He is a man without principles.
> I object to the principle of the thing.
> Principles are nice; but profits are necessary.

prof A clipped form of *professor.* In college writing use it only at a colloquial level.

prophecy — prophesy *Prophecy* is always used as a noun [The prophecy came true; the prophecies of the Bible]. *Prophesy* is always a verb [He prophesied another war; don't be too eager to prophesy].

proposition The use of *proposition* as a verb [They propositioned us to buy the car] is slang and is not acceptable at any level of college writing. Its use as a noun, meaning "proposal" [I have a proposition I'd like to make to you] is a colloquialism much overused in college writing. Say, "They proposed that we buy the car," "I have a proposal I'd like to make to you."

proven Alternative past participle of *prove.* The preferred form is *proved,* but *proven* is permissible.

providing = provided This usage [I will go, providing you accompany me] is established. Either form is acceptable in college writing, though *provided* is more common and more widely accepted.

quiet — quite Although pronunciation is often a doubtful guide to English spelling, the careful pronunciation of *qui-et* as a two-syllabled word would help eliminate the confusion of the spelling of these two words [The orchestra played quietly; quiet please! I am quite tired; that is quite proper].

quite In formal English *quite* is used to mean "entirely" or "wholly" [The statement is quite in accordance with the facts]. The use of *quite* as an intensive [The news was quite a shock to us] is colloquial but generally acceptable in college writing.

raise — rear The use of *raise* meaning to *bring up* [She raised a large family] is recognized by the dictionaries, though *rear* would be preferred in a formal style.

real = really (very) At formal and informal levels of college writing use *really* [It was a really (*not* real) difficult assignment; she can be really (*not* real) annoying when she talks that way].

reason is because Although Bryant offers impressive evidence (*Current American Usage,* pp. 170–171) to show that this is an established idiom, there is still some objection to it. In a formal style, "The reason is that" would be preferred.

Redundancy Repetitious wording. For an example, see the next entry.

refer back A confusion between *look back* and *refer.* This usage is objected to in college writing on the ground that since the *re* of refer means "back," *refer back* is redundant. *Refer back* is acceptable when it means "refer again" [The bill was referred back to the committee]; otherwise, say *refer* [Let me refer you to page 17; from time to time he referred to his notes].

Referent The *thing* as contrasted with the symbol which refers to it. The person, object, event, or idea to which a word refers.

respectfully — respectively *Respectfully* means "with respect" [He spoke respectfully; Respectfully submitted]. *Respectively* means roughly "each in turn" [These three papers were graded respectively A, C, and B].

Reverend *Reverend* is used before the name of a clergyman and in formal usage is preceded by *the* [I met the Reverend Alexander White]. It is not used immediately preceding the surname [the Reverend White], but must be followed by Dr., Mr., or a Christian name or initials [Rev. Dr. White, Rev. Mr. White, Rev. A. L. White]. In informal usage, the *the* is often omitted and the word *Reverend* abbreviated.

Formal	*Informal*
The Reverend Alexander L. White	Rev. A. L. White
2472 Bancroft Street	2472 Bancroft Street
Toledo, Ohio	Toledo, Ohio

right — rite A *rite* is a ceremony or ritual. This word should not be confused with the various uses of *right*.

right (adv.)   The use of *right* as an adverb is established in such sentences as "He went right home," "It served him right," "Please try to act right," "I will go right away." Its use to mean *very* [I was right glad to meet him; that's a right pretty girl] is colloquial and should be used in college writing only when the style is colloquial.

role, rôle   The preferred spelling is now *role*, without the circumflex.

Run-on sentence   A sentence which consists of a number of main clauses loosely joined together by *and*'s and *so*'s. The ideas in the sentence lack organization. See page 413.

said (adj.)   The use of *said* as an adjective [said documents, said offense] is restricted to legal phraseology. Do not use it in college writing.

same as = just as   The preferred idiom is *just as* [He acted just as I thought he would].

same, such   Avoid the use of *same* or *such* as a substitute for *it, this, that, them* [I am returning the book, since I do not care for same; most people are fond of athletics of all sorts, but I have no use for such]. Say, "I am returning the book because I do not care for it," "Unlike most people, I am not fond of athletics."

scarcely   In such sentences as "There wasn't scarcely enough," "We haven't scarcely time," the use of *scarcely* plus a negative creates an unacceptable double negative. Say, "There was scarcely enough," "We scarcely have time."

scarcely than   The use of *scarcely than* [I had scarcely met her than she began to denounce her husband] is a confusion between *no sooner . . . than* and *scarcely . . . when.* Say, "I had no sooner met her than she began to denounce her husband," or "I had scarcely met her when she began to denounce her husband."

seldom ever   The *ever* is redundant. Instead of saying, "He is seldom ever late," "She is seldom ever angry," say, "He is seldom late," "She is seldom angry."

self, selves   The plural of *self* is *selves.* Such usages as "They hurt themselfs," "They hate theirselfs," are nonstandard and are not acceptable in college speech or writing.

Semantics   The science of the meanings of words as contrasted with phonetics (pronunciation) and morphology (form).

sensual — sensuous   Avoid confusion of these words. *Sensual* has unfavorable connotations and means "catering to the gratification of the senses" [He leads a sensual existence]. *Sensuous* has generally favorable connotations and refers to pleasures experienced through the senses [The sensuous peace of a warm bath; the sensuous imagery of the poem].

Series   Parallel constructions arranged in succession [He was *tall, tanned,* and *lean*]. The elements of a series may be single words, phrases, subordinate clauses, or main clauses, but all elements must be in the same grammatical form. See page 416.

shape = condition This usage [Both fighters are in good shape; the house has been neglected for years and is now in wretched shape] is colloquial but generally acceptable in college writing.

sharp = attractive, stylish Slang, generally unacceptable in college writing.

shone — shown *Shone* is the past tense and the past participle of *shine* [The sun shone; her eyes shone with happiness]. *Shown* is the past participle of *show* [You have shown it to me before]. The form *showed* is an alternative past participle for *shown*.

should of See **could of.**

show = chance This usage [Give him a fair show] would be appropriate only in a colloquial style. In formal and informal style use *chance* or *opportunity*.

show = play, motion picture Generally acceptable in college writing, but the other terms may be more precise.

show up The uses of *show up* to mean "expose" or "appear" [This test will show up any weaknesses in the machine; I waited for an hour, but he didn't show up] are established. The use of *show up* to mean "prove much superior to" [The girls showed up the boys in the spelling bee] is colloquial but would not be objectionable in college writing.

sic The Latin word *sic,* pronounced *sick,* is used in brackets to indicate that an error in a quotation appeared in the original source and was not made by the person copying the quotation. Example: "The significant words in the paragraph are these: 'No person will be allowed on the premises unless he is duely [*sic*] authorized.' "

sick = disgusted This usage [All these pious platitudes make me sick] is now recognized by the dictionaries. It should be acceptable in most college writing, but not in formal style.

sleight — slight *Sleight* comes from the same root as *sly* and is usually associated with a clever trick [sleight of hand]. The more common word *slight* means "slender," "flimsy" [a slight girl, slight hope, a slight protection]. It is also used as a verb to mean "treat disdainfully" [They consistently slighted their opponents; he was quite obviously slighting his wife].

so (conj.) The use of *so* as a connective [She refused to exchange the merchandise, so we went to the manager] is thoroughly respectable, but its overuse in college writing is objectionable. There are other good transitional connectives — *accordingly, for that reason, on that account, therefore, for example* — which could be used to relieve the monotony of a series of *so's.* Occasional use of subordination [When she refused to exchange the merchandise we went to the manager] would lend variety to the style.

some The use of *some* as an adjective of indeterminate number [Some friends of yours were here; there are some questions I'd like to ask] is acceptable in all levels of writing. Its use as an intensive [That was some meal] or as an adverb [She cried some after you left] is slang and should be avoided in college writing.

somebody's else   Say, "somebody else's." See **anybody's else.**

somewheres   Nonstandard variant of *somewhere*. Not acceptable in college speech or writing.

sort (of)   See **kind (of).**

speak — speech   The difference in vowels between the verb *speak* and the noun or adjective *speech* causes frequent misspellings. The only solution is to memorize the spelling and uses of these words [a long speech; a speech impediment; speak honestly; the ability to speak effectively].

staid — stayed   *Staid* means "sedate" or "decorous" [a staid old woman]. The more common word *stayed* is the past tense form and the past participle of *stay* [We stayed a week; he has stayed there].

stationary — stationery   *Stationary* means "fixed," "unchanging" [The front was stationary; his opinions are so stationary they have taken root]. *Stationery* means "writing materials" [a box of stationery; stationery and other supplies].

straight — strait   The more frequent word is *straight* [a straight line, straight talk, straight from the heart]. *Strait* is a common name for a narrow water passage [the Strait of Gibraltar] and is extended to mean any difficult condition [in financial straits, straitened circumstances, in desperate straits].

Strong verb   A verb which uses a change in the vowel rather than inflectional endings to distinguish between present and past tenses [sing, sang, sung]. Weak verbs [walk, walked, walked] are regular, strong verbs irregular.

suit — suite   The common word is *suit* [a suit of clothes, follow suit (in cards), suit yourself, this doesn't suit me]. *Suite* means "retinue" [The President and his suite arrived late], "set" or "collection" [a dining room suite, a suite of rooms]. Check the pronunciation of these words in your dictionary.

sure = certainly   This usage [I sure am annoyed; sure, I will go with you] is colloquial. Unless the style justifies colloquial usage, say *certainly* or *surely*.

swell = good, fine   This usage [It was a swell show; we had a swell time] is slang. It is generally unacceptable in college writing.

Symbol   A word, signal, or sign. The word as contrasted with what it stands for. See **Referent.**

Synonym   A word having the same meaning as a given word. Thus, *patio* is often a synonym for *courtyard*.

Syntax   The relationships of words within a sentence. The chief units of syntax are the subject, verb, object, and modifiers.

take and   This usage [In a fit of anger he took and smashed the bowl] is not acceptable in college writing. Simply say *smashed* [In a fit of anger he smashed the bowl].

take sick This usage [He took sick and died] is disputed. Authorities differ in classifying it as established, dialectal, or regional. It would generally be safer to avoid it in college writing.

taxi Used either as a noun [We took a taxi to the station] or as a verb [The big plane taxied to a stop] the word is now acceptable at all levels of style.

terrible, terribly An overused colloquialism for *very* [She was terribly nice about it]. Its restrained use in informal papers is not objectionable.

terrific Used at a formal level to mean "terrifying" and at a colloquial level as an intensive. The overuse of the colloquialism has rendered the word almost useless in formal writing. For most students the best thing to do with this word is to forget it.

Theme Used in two ways in college composition courses: (1) the dominant idea of an essay [The theme of this essay is that self-deception is the commonest of vices]; (2) a general name for a composition assignment [Write a 500-word theme for Monday]. The first meaning is synonymous with *thesis* as it is used in this book.

there — their The confusion of these words causes one of the commonest errors in spelling. *Their* is the possessive form of the pronoun *they* [They have their money; where are their things?]. *There* is the adverbial form contrasted with *here* [Put it there; it fell over there]. *There* is also used as an expletive to begin a sentence [There used to be a man . . . ; there were once three bears . . .].

Thesis As used in this book, the dominant idea or purpose of an essay. The most restricted form of the purpose statement.

tho A variant spelling of *though*. The longer form is preferred in formal usage.

threw — through Distinguish between the verb *threw* [He threw quickly to first base; he threw away his money] and the preposition *through* [through the woods, through the window, down through the years].

through = finished This usage [Aren't you through with that story yet?] is now accepted by all dictionaries consulted. "Finished" would be preferable in a formal style [Haven't you finished (*not* finished with) that story?].

to — too — two Distinguish the preposition *to* [Give it to me] from the adverb *too* [That is too bad] and the number *two* [Two chickens in every pot].

tough The uses of *tough* to mean "difficult" [a tough assignment], "hard fought" [It was a tough game], "hard to bear" [It was a tough blow for all of us] are accepted without qualification by reputable dictionaries.

toward, towards Both forms are acceptable. *Toward* is more common in America, *towards* in Britain.

troop — troupe Both words come from the same root and share the original meaning, "herd." In modern usage *troop* is used of soldiers and *troupe* of actors [a troop of cavalry, a troop of scouts; a troupe of circus performers, a troupe of entertainers].

try and *Try to* is the preferred idiom. *Try and* would generally be acceptable in informal and colloquial styles.

Understatement The opposite of exaggeration. The device of deliberately saying less than one means, as in Winston Churchill's comment, "My life so far has not been entirely uneventful." Understatement is often used for ironic or humorous effect.

unique The formal meaning of *unique* is "sole" or "only" [Adam had the unique distinction of being the only man who never had a mother]. The use of *unique* to mean "rare" or "unusual" [Spinal anesthetics allow the patient the unique experience of being a witness to his own appendectomy] has long been popular and is now accepted. But *unique* in the loose sense of uncommon [a very unique sweater] is generally frowned upon, especially when modified by an intensive adverb.

up The adverb *up* is idiomatically used in many verb-adverb combinations which act as a single verb [break up, clean up, fill up, get up, tear up]. Often *up* adds a note of thoroughness to the action of the verb. Compare "They ate everything on their plates" with "They ate up everything on their plates." Avoid unnecessary or awkward separation of *up* from the verb with which it is combined, since this will have the effect of making *up* seem to be a single adverb modifying the verb rather than combining with it. For example, "They held the cashier up" is subject to misinterpretation; "She made her face up" is simply awkward. Say, "They held up the cashier," "She made up her face," "They filled up the front rows first."

used to Notice the final *d* in *used.* We do not pronounce it in informal speech because it is elided before the *t* of *to.* But the phrase is written *used to,* not *use to.*

used to could Nonstandard for *used to be able.* Not acceptable in college speech or writing.

vain — vane — vein *Vain* means "useless" [a vain hope] or conceited [a vain woman]; a *vane* is a marker which is moved by wind or water [a weather vane]; a *vein* is a blood vessel [the jugular vein] or a seam of ore [a rich vein of gold].

very A common and useful intensive, but avoid its overuse in any one paper.

vice — vise Distinguish between these nouns. A *vice* (compare *vicious*) is an evil [Virtues when carried to excess may become vices]. A *vise* is a tool [I put the board in a vise and sawed it].

Vulgate Synonymous with *nonstandard.* Any usage characteristic of uneducated speech.

wait on *Wait on* means "serve" [A clerk will be here in a moment to wait on you]. The use of *wait on* to mean "wait for" [I'll wait on you if you won't be long] is a colloquialism to which there is some objection. Say *wait for* [I'll wait for you if you won't be long].

want for   The use of *for* or *should* after *want* in such sentences as "I want for you to come," "I want you should come," is not acceptable in college speech or writing. After *want* in this sense use the objective case plus an infinitive [I want you to come; I want them to go at once]. When the sentence does not require an object, the infinitive is used immediately after *want* [I want to go home; he wants to return next week].

want in, out, off   This usage [The dog wants in; I want out of there; I want off now] is colloquial. In college writing it would be safer to supply an infinitive after *wants:* "The dog wants to come in," etc.

want = ought   This usage [You want to save something every month; they want to be careful or they will be in trouble] is colloquial. *Ought* is the preferred idiom in college writing.

ways   Colloquial for *way* in such sentences as "You must have come a long ways from home," "They walked a long ways this morning." Except in a colloquial style the accepted form in college writing is *way* [You must have come a long way; they walked a long way].

when (in definitions)   In college writing avoid the use of a *when*-clause in defining a term [A comma splice is when you put a comma between two separate sentences]. Instead of *when* use a noun phrase or clause [A comma splice is the use of a comma between two separate sentences].

where (in definitions)   Same comment as for **when** above.

where . . . at, to   The use of *at* or *to* after *where* [Where was he at? Where are you going to?] is redundant. Simply say, "Where was he?" "Where are you going?"

where = that   The use of *where* in such sentences as "I heard on the radio where there was a violent storm in Chicago," "I see in the paper where that bandit was caught," may be occasionally acceptable in a colloquial style, but it is inappropriate in formal or informal writing. Use *that* [I heard on the radio that there was a violent storm in Chicago; I see in the paper that the bandit was caught].

which   *Which* is not used to refer to persons. It is used to refer to things [The house which he built]. When referring to persons use *who, whom,* or *that* [The man who is talking, the girl whom I love, the doctor that I called].

who — whom   In informal and colloquial writing *who* is often used instead of *whom* when the pronoun is in subject territory — that is, when it comes at the beginning of the sentence [Who is she marrying? Who are you looking for?]. This is the colloquial and informal usage of educated people, but in a formal style *whom* would be required [Whom is she marrying? For whom are you looking?].

who's — whose   *Who's* is a colloquial and informal contraction for *who is* [Who's there? See who's at the door]. *Whose* is the possessive case of *who* [The man whose car he took; whose is this?].

whose In informal and colloquial writing *whose* is a popular substitute for the formal and awkward *of which* [The nation whose army is occupying the territory will exert the greatest influence]. No good writer would be so concerned about the demands of formal grammar as to revise this sentence to read, "The nation the army of which is occupying the territory. . . ." Instead he would dodge the *of which* construction by saying, "The nation which occupies the territory . . ." or "The army which occupies the territory will exert the greatest influence."

wire The use of *wire* as a noun to mean "telegram" [Your wire arrived this morning] and as a verb to mean "telegraph" [Wire me when you arrive] is colloquial. It is appropriate in informal writing but *telegram* and *telegraph* would be preferred in a formal style.

would have The use of *would have* for "had" [If he would have told me I would have helped him] is generally unacceptable in college writing. Say, "Had he told me . . ." or "If he had told me . . ." See page 445.

would of See **could of.**

you = one The use of *you* as an indefinite pronoun instead of the formal *one* is characteristic of an informal style, but be sure that this impersonal use will be recognized by the reader; otherwise he is likely to interpret a general statement as a personal remark addressed to him. Generally avoid shifting from "one" to "you" within a sentence.

Index

CORRECTION SYMBOLS

adj	Use adjective instead of adverb (p. 464)
adv	Use adverb instead of adjective (p. 465)
agr	Make circled words agree (subject-verb, pp. 452-457; pronoun-antecedent, pp. 458-460; tenses, pp. 439-442)
apos	Use apostrophe (pp. 484-485)
bib	Check form of bibliography (pp. 246-252)
cap	Use capital letter(s) (pp. 503-505)
case	Use correct case form (pp. 446-450)
cs	Remove comma splice (pp. 414-415)
det	Provide details (pp. 16-18)
det?	Details not pertinent (pp. 74-75)
d	Indicated diction needs revision (See Reference Chart)
gen	Diction or statement too general (pp. 147-150)
?	Illegible word
lev	Confusion of stylistic levels (pp. 145-147)
lc	No capital. Use small letter(s) (pp. 503-505)
no ¶	No paragraph
no p	No punctuation needed
ns	Nonstandard usage (p. 135)
no	Use numbers (pp. 509-510)
∧	Something omitted
¶	Begin new paragraph
p	Punctuation needed
ref	Clarify reference of pronoun (pp. 461-462) or modifier (pp. 427-428)
rep	Undesirable repetition
sp	Consult dictionary for correct spelling
t	Use correct tense form (pp. 439-445)
wo	Revise word order (See Reference Chart)
wordy	Reduce wordiness (pp. 113-117)
wr	Write out. Do not abbreviate or use numbers
ww	Wrong word
/	Remove word, letter, or punctuation so slashed
x	Careless error
,/;/	Provide punctuation indicated